The Budapest Operation (October 1944-13 February 1945): An Operational-Strategic Study examines in detail the Red Army's operations on the approaches to Budapest and the city's ultimate capture following a long siege. The first part of the study deals with the Red Army's arrival in central Hungary, following the successful conduct of the Iasi—Kishinev operation in late August 1944 and the subsequent development of the offensive through Romania, Bulgaria and eastern Yugoslavia. By mid-October the Soviets were poised to continue the offensive into Hungary and its capital of Budapest, the capture of which would clear the path for a subsequent advance into Austria and southern Germany. This study examines the rapid advance to the outskirts of Budapest, where stubborn German-Hungarian resistance forced them to halt, after which the Soviets sought to surround the city, finally closing the ring at the end of December.

Also examined are the Germans' repeated attempts to break the siege by launching several counter-offensives to the west and south of the city. However, these were all beaten back in heavy fighting and the enemy garrison was forced to capitulate on 13 February. This study also devotes considerable attention to the combat arms (artillery, tank and mechanized forces, aviation, and engineering troops) during the operation.

The other study is an internal General Staff Academy document dealing with the activities of the Third Ukrainian Front during the Budapest operation. Throughout the greater part of the operation the Third Ukrainian Front played a decidedly secondary role, charged with protecting the flank of the Soviet advance through Yugoslavia and Hungary, with the Second Ukrainian Front slated to receive the accolades for taking Budapest. However, the bitter enemy resistance along the approaches to Budapest gradually forced the Soviet high command to increasingly shift its efforts to the right bank of the Danube River, first to help in isolating the Budapest garrison inside the city, and then to fend off repeated German counter-offensives to relieve the city. It was the Third Ukrainian Front's successful repulse of these efforts that enabled the Soviets to finally bring about the garrison's capitulation and the end of the operation.

Richard W. Harrison earned his undergraduate and master's degrees from Georgetown University, where he specialized in Russian area studies. In 1994 he earned his doctorate in War Studies from King's College London. He also was an exchange student in the former Soviet Union and spent several years living and working in post-communist Russia.

Dr Harrison has worked for the US Department of Defense as an investigator in Russia, dealing with cases involving POWs and MIAs. He has also taught Russian history and military history at college and university level, most recently at the US Military Academy at West Point.

Harrison is the author of two books dealing with the Red Army's theoretical development during the interwar period: *The Russian Way of War: Operational Art, 1904–1940* (2001), and *Architect of Soviet Victory in World War II: The Life and Theories of G.S. Isserson* (2010). He has also authored a number of articles on topics in Soviet military history. He is currently working on a history of the Red Army's high commands during the Second World War and afterwards.

Dr Harrison currently lives with his family near Carlisle, Pennsylvania.

THE BUDAPEST OPERATION
(28 OCTOBER 1944-13 FEBRUARY 1945)

AN OPERATIONAL STRATEGIC STUDY

THE BUDAPEST OPERATION (28 OCTOBER 1944-13 FEBRUARY 1945)

An Operational Strategic Study

Soviet General Staff

Edited and Translated by Richard W. Harrison

Helion & Company

Published in cooperation with the Association of the United States Army

Helion & Company Limited
Unit 8 Amherst Business Centre
Budbrooke Road
Warwick
CV34 5WE
England
Tel. 01926 499619
Email: info@helion.co.uk
Website: www.helion.co.uk
Twitter: @helionbooks
Visit our blog at http://blog.helion.co.uk/

Published by Helion & Company 2017, in cooperation with the Association of the United States Army. Reprinted in paperback 2022

Designed and typeset by Mach 3 Solutions Ltd (www.mach3solutions.co.uk)
Cover designed by Paul Hewitt, Battlefield Design (www.battlefield-design.co.uk)

ISBN 978-1-80451-045-2

British Library Cataloguing-in-Publication Data.
A catalogue record for this book is available from the British Library.

For details of other military history titles published by Helion & Company Limited contact the above address, or visit our website: http://www.helion.co.uk.

We always welcome receiving book proposals from prospective authors.

Contents

List of Maps

List of Tables

Preface to the English-Language Edition

Unlike other works in this series, which are translations of a single major work, this study is a composite one, consisting of several parts, each drawn from a different source and separated by several years. Unfortunately, such a study of the Budapest operation, and it must surely exist, has not yet been released for public consumption, leaving us with the expedient at hand.

The material for this study has been taken from two sources. The first is from the *Sbornik Materialov po Izucheniyu Opyta Voiny* (no. 21, 1945), an internal publication by the Red Army General Staff's Directorate for Employing the Experience of the War. Over the years the directorate released a number of studies for the purpose of conveying the recent war's experience in conducting operations to high-ranking commanders and staffs.

The second is another internal publication issued by the General Staff Academy in 1957, entitled *The Third Ukrainian Front's Operation in the Budapest Operation*, by Major General S.P.Tarasov. The Third Ukrainian Front was on the left flank of the Soviet advance in the Balkans and played a key role in covering the Second Ukrainian Front's advance on Budapest and in repelling repeated German counteroffensives in the area west and south of Budapest.

The book contains a number of terms that may not be readily understandable to the casual reader in military history. Therefore, I have adopted a number of conventions designed to ease this task. For example, a *front* is a Soviet wartime military organization roughly corresponding to an American army group. Throughout the narrative the reader will encounter such names as the Second and Third Ukrainian fronts. To avoid confusion with the more commonly understood meaning of the term front (i.e., the front line); italics will be used to denote an unnamed *front*. Similar German formations (i.e., Army Group South) are also spelled out in full.

I have chosen to designate Soviet armies using the shortened form (i.e., 46th Army). Axis armies, on the other hand, are spelled out in full (i.e., German Sixth Army, Hungarian Third Army). In the same vein, Soviet corps are designated by Arabic numerals (75th Rifle Corps), while German units are denoted by Roman numerals (e.g., IX SS Army Corps). Smaller units (divisions, brigades, etc.) on both sides are denoted by Arabic numerals only (110th Guards Rifle Division, 76th Infantry Division, etc.).

Given the large number of units involved in the operation, I have adopted certain other conventions in order to better distinguish them. For example, Soviet armored units are called tank corps, brigades, etc., while the corresponding Axis units are denoted by the popular term *panzer*. Likewise, Soviet infantry units are designated by the term rifle, while the corresponding Axis units are simply referred to as infantry. Hungarian units are designated the same way.

The work subscribes to no particular transliteration scheme, because no entirely satisfactory one exists. I have adopted a mixed system that uses the Latin letters ya and yu to denote their Cyrillic counterparts, as opposed to the ia and iu employed by the Library of Congress, which tends to distort proper pronunciation. Conversely, I have retained the Library of Congress's ii ending (i.e., Malinovskii), as opposed to the commonly-used y ending. I have also retained the apostrophe to denote the Cyrillic soft sign.

Unfortunately, the difficulties of translating place names from the Cyrillic to the Latin alphabet, which always present a problem, have been greatly magnified in this instance by the spelling vagaries of the Hungarian language. I have made a conscientious effort throughout to discover the proper spelling of the various towns, rivers and individuals listed in the book, although I was not always successful. In those cases where I was unable to find the place or individual and determine the proper spelling, I was forced to rely on my best judgment, an approach, which I admit, is fraught with danger. However, since these instances chiefly involve very small towns or villages, I hope the damage to the reader's understanding of the overall course of the fighting will not be too serious.

Part 1

Introduction & Narrative of the Budapest operation

1

Introduction

The Budapest operation, which was conducted by the forces of the Second and Third Ukrainian fronts from 28 October 1944 through 13 February 1945, was carried out under the direct control of the *Stavka* of the Supreme High Command.[1] This two-*front* operation resolved a task of major strategic significance, as a result of which fascist Germany's last satellite—Hungary—was taken out of the war and the conditions were created for the development of the Red Army's subsequent offensive into the confines of Austria.

The combat operations for defeating the enemy's Budapest group of forces, which unfolded at the end of October 1944, from the line of the Tisza River, were carried out by the forces of the Second Ukrainian Front's left wing.

By the time of our forces' arrival immediately at the southeastern approaches to Budapest, the enemy had managed to transfer significant forces from the reserve to the threatened axis and to halt the offensive along this axis.

Subsequently, the *front's* forces, through a series of consecutive and concentrated attacks, cut off the enemy's path of retreat to the northeast and north as far as the Danube, inclusively, and reached the immediate approaches to the outer ring of the eastern part of Budapest.

At the end of November 1944, upon the instructions of the *Stavka* of the Supreme High Command, the main forces of the Third Ukrainian Front are rapidly castled from Yugoslavia and Bulgaria to the left flank of the Second Ukrainian Front's forces.

On 22 November 1944 the Third Ukrainian Front's forces launched a decisive offensive by forcing the major water barrier of the Danube River and by 10 December 1944 reached the enemy's powerful defensive line—the "Margarita" line—along the southwestern approaches to Budapest. This created a favorable operational situation for the forces of the Second and Third Ukrainian fronts for the encirclement and destruction of the enemy's Budapest group of forces.

From 20 December 1944 both *fronts* went over to a decisive offensive to encircle and destroy the enemy's Budapest group of forces. On 26 December, with the arrival of the Second and Third Ukrainian front's units at the Danube in the Esztergom area, the encirclement was completed. On 13 February 1945 our forces took the capital of Hungary—Budapest—and by 16 February eliminated the last remnants of the enemy's encircled group of forces.

The Budapest is an operation on the strategic scale.

Its significance is determined by the following:

- the simultaneous conduct of military operations along an enormous area, exceeding 115,600 square kilometers;
- the swallowing up of a significant portion of the strategic and operational reserves of the high command of the German army;

1 Editor's note. The *Stavka* of the Supreme High Command was the Soviet Union's highest military organ during the Second World War. This body was also known as the *Stavka* of the VGK (*Verkhovnogo Glavnokomandovaniya*)

- the elimination of an industrial center in the Budapest area, to where the German command had evacuated a significant part of its air and other industrial enterprises;
- depriving Germany of its last source of fuel in the Nagykanizsa area;
- opening access to Austria and threatening a breakthrough by our forces into the southern part of Germany through the Viennese gates.

The significance of the Budapest operation is also great because it, having swallowed up the greater part of the German command's operational reserves along the Soviet-German front, made easier the German forces' defeat along other sectors.

A characteristic feature of the Budapest operation is that during its first stage only the forces of the Second Ukrainian Front took part, which through consecutive and concentrated attacks cut off the enemy's Budapest group of forces from his Miskolc group. These forces subsequently encircled the eastern part of Budapest (Pest), with their flank anchored on the Danube. The Third Ukrainian Front's forces routed the enemy's Danube group of forces in a vigorous offensive and reached the heavily fortified "Margarita" line along the southwestern approaches to Budapest. And, finally, among the features of the Budapest operation is also the concentration of the simultaneous efforts of both *fronts* to encircle and destroy the enemy's Budapest group of forces.

The principle of the growing strength of attacks at the operational level was most brilliantly realized in this operation.

Besides this, the Budapest operation has great significance in studying questions at the operational level.

Among these questions are:

1. The organization and conduct of a series of consecutive and concentrated attacks on the *front* scale, with small operational pauses.
2. The forcing of major water barriers (the Danube and Tisza rivers) by troop and tank formations along a broad front.
3. The organization and conduct of offensive engagements and the employment of the combat arms while capturing a major city (Budapest).
4. Fighting the enemy's counteroffensive by major tank formations.

The rout of the German-Hungarian forces in the Budapest operation is a model of our generals' high level of military art, our officers' combat mastery and the stubbornness of the troops in carrying out their assigned tasks.

A Short Military-Geographical Description of the Operational Area

The Budapest operation by the forces of the Second and Third Ukrainian fronts unfolded chiefly within the confines of Hungary, although it also embraced some areas of Romania, Yugoslavia and Czechoslovakia.

The borders and size of the operational area. The operational area is bordered by the following imaginary lines: from the north, Roznava—Nitra; from the west, Nitra—Nagykanizsa, and then along the Drava River; from the east, Timisoara—Arad—Miskolc—Roznava. From north to south, the length of the area (from Zvolen to the mouth of the Drava River) is 340 kilometers, and from east to west (from Arad to Nagykanizsa) is also 340 kilometers. The overall size of the area is 115,600 square kilometers.

Thus in its development, the Budapest operation embraced an extensive territory.

The general nature of the surface terrain. The greater part of the operational area was part of the Middle-Danube (Hungarian) lowland. This lowland has its highest heights (90-100 meters) in the center; to the north and east, toward the foothills of the Carpathian Mountains, it rises gently, ending in heights of 200-250 meters. The western (Danubian) part of the lowland (within the operation's confines) rises to 200-300 meters and is cut by low-lying ridges and the plateau of the western part of the Central Hungarian hills (the Bakony Forest, Vertes Hegyseg). The plains along the Hungarian right bank are divided into two parts: the Danubian plain south of the hills (the Bakony Forest), with the small Hungarian lowland to the north.

The slopes of the Alps and the Carpathians go down directly to the Danube in places, and these narrow sectors of the Danube valley are called gates (the Visegrad gates are located north of Budapest).

The Middle-Danube lowland is a generally flat plain, accessible to the conduct of offensive military operations by major troop formations.

The single natural obstacle is the rivers. Loose black earth and loess soils predominate throughout the plain.

The entire area between the Danube and Tisza rivers, as well as the left-bank area of the Tisza River are completely flat plain areas.

The Danubian plain stretches south and east of the Bakony Forest and Lake Balaton, occupying the area between the Danube and Drava rivers.

The Central Hungarian Hills and the southern slopes of the Slovakian Rudohorie Mountains.

The Central Hungarian Hills represent a broken chain of separate plateaus and low-lying ridges, stretching from the northeast to the southwest.

Along the northern shore of Lake Balaton is a mountain ridge bearing the name of the Bakony Forest. It is 70 kilometers long and consists of sloping plateaus with a height of 400-500 meters. The slopes in these uplands are mostly gently sloping. Individual peaks in the Bakony Forest reach a height of 700 meters.

To the northeast of Lake Balaton and the Bakony Forest lies the Vertes Hegyseg range. This range represents several ridges of flat and cupola-shaped limestone hills, rising to 630 meters at the highest and up to 300 meters over the surrounding countryside. The slopes are sharply cut by deep and narrow gorges into steep slopes. The western part of the ridge west of the Visegrad Gorge commands over the Danube.

East of the Vertes Hegyseg are the Pilis (Visegrad) Mountains, which represent a group of parallel low-lying ridges, reaching more than 750 meters at their greatest height. The Pilis Mountains comprise the right (southern) side of the Vertes Hegyseg Gorge of the Danube, towering 250-300 meters over the river. These ridges are made up of volcanic rocks, steep and deeply cut. The eastern ledges of all the ridges tower over the Danube, while the slopes of the two southern ridges also tower over Budapest. The ridges are divided by longitudinal valleys and lined with each other by low cofferdams.

The Budapest—Esztergom paved road and railroad runs along one of these valleys (the second from the south). The Borzsony Mountains, the highest peaks of which reach 650 meters, comprises the left (northern) side of the Visegrad Gorge.

On the whole, the overall nature of the terrain favored the development of military operations by large troop formations and broad-ranging maneuver by both our and the enemy's motor-mechanized forces.

The area's hydrography. The area's rivers comprise part of the broad Danubian basin, which flows in its middle course within the confines of the area of operations.

The Danube's channel and that of its branches are quite winding and has abundant sandbanks, islands and spits. Below the town of Komarno the Danube flows along a single channel, while between the towns of Esztergom and Vac it breaks through the mountains in a narrow and deep valley known as the Visegrad Gates. Near Budapest the Danube goes out into the Middle Danube lowland and overflows, branching out among low-lying and marshy banks into numerous tributaries. The width of the Danube's valley here reaches 22 kilometers in places and 300-640 meters near Komarno, 450-520 meters near Esztergom, and 970 meters near Budapest. The Danube's depth varies from 7.5-12 meters. The average speed of the current is one meter per second. The Danube serves as Central Europe's major shipping artery.

The width, depth and large amount of water and the abundance of channels and tributaries make the Danube a natural line of operational significance.

The Tisza River (with an overall length of 966 kilometers) is the Danube's largest tributary. Within the confines of the area of operations the Tisza flows along the lower Hungarian lowland, where its length is 240 kilometers. It flows along flat terrain with sparse sandy hills. The flood plain is swampy and overgrown with bushes and trees and covered along significant sectors by glades. Its channel is quite winding and forms a large number of branches, old river beds, islands, and sandbanks. The right bank is precipitous and the left gently sloping. On the average, the height of the banks reaches 4.5-7.5 meters. The river's width within this area is up to 150 meters, with a depth of 2-3 meters. The speed of the current varies from 0.3 to 1.5 meters per second.

The Tisza is a major natural line.

Of the area's rivers that played a role in the Budapest operation, one should also note the Hron and Ipel. Each of these has an average width of up to 80 meters and up to 0.9 meters deep. The soil on the bottom of these rivers along their upper course is rocky and sandy along the lower course, with a shallow shingle. In places the Hron and Ipel rivers are fordable.

Of the area's lakes, one should note above all Lake Balaton, which is located along the right bank of the Danube. It is the largest lake in Central Europe. The lake's northern shore rises to the mountains of the Bakony Forest along a steep and mountainous shelf. The southern and western shores are flat, low-lying and swampy. The eastern shore is bounded by a narrow strip of flood plain and terraces, with steep shelves in the south and north. The overall size of the lake is 700 square kilometers, with a length of 80 kilometers and width of 6-10 kilometers. The average depth is eight meters, with a maximum depth of 13.5 meters. The water in the lake is salty. The lake freezes in winter, but the resulting ice is very unstable, due to the warms springs at the bottom of the lake.

Lake Velence, which is located 36 kilometers to the northeast of Lake Balaton, is of some significance. Lake Velence is ten kilometers long, with a maximum width of three kilometers; the lake is shallow, overgrown with reeds, but was impassable for troops.

The Danube and Tisza rivers constricted the operations of large combined-arms and motor-mechanized formations and special technical equipment was required to force them. The Danube divided our forces operating to the east and west of it.

Communications routes. Budapest, a major rail junction, is the center of the area's railroad network. Eight main routes linked with each other by secondary lines, radiate from it in all directions.

The main routes are: Budapest—Gyor—Vienna; Budapest—Vacs—Lucenec; Budapest—Miskolc; Budapest—Szolnok—Gyula; Budapest—Szeged; Budapest—Subotica, and; Budapest—Nagykanizsa. Aside from Budapest, Miskolc, Hatvan, Szolnok, and Szeged are major railroad junctions in the area of operations.

During the Budapest operation the railroads were put out of commission by our air raids and could not be employed for military purposes.

The paved and dirt road network was highly developed (up to 100 kilometers of roads for every 100 kilometers of territory). There was a through dirt road in any direction per five kilometers of front. During the dry part of the year almost all of the dirt roads were passable for auto transport. Movement could only be slowed by unstable wooden bridges and the sands, encountered in the area between the Tisza and Danube rivers. In wet weather the majority of the natural dirt roads become impassable, particularly for auto transport. Sticky mud forms on the roads and deep ruts appear during heavy traffic.

The most important paved roads in the area of operations were: Timisoara—Szeged—Kecskemet—Budapest and Zvolen—Sahy—Budapest—Kalocsa—Baia to the east of the Danube, and Osijek—Szekszard—Budapest and Budapest—Gyor—Vienna.

On the whole, the widely developed network of paved and dirt roads allowed for maneuver by large combined-arms, motor-mechanized and tank formations for us and the enemy.

The population and inhabited locales. As has already been noted above, the area of operations embraced a significant part of Hungary and some areas of Czechoslovakia, Romania and Yugoslavia.

One should note that a significant part of the pro-Fascist elements that had been serving the Germans ran away along with the retreating German-Hungarian forces. At the same time, during the withdrawal the Fascists left behind a significant element of spies, saboteurs among the local population, with the mission of fighting against the Red Army. This circumstance forced our forces to be particularly vigilant and careful as regards the local population. In the Hungarian capital of Budapest (with a population of 1,488,000 as of 1 January 1938), a large element of Fascists and pro-Fascist residents had been left behind. These elements played a direct role in the fighting inside Budapest alongside the German and Hungarian field forces. Of course, this circumstance significantly complicated the fighting in the city and laid a special imprint of intensity on its course. There are a large number of inhabited locales in the area of operations and a significant part of them had been prepared by the enemy command for defense, both along the outskirts and within them.

The forces of the Second and Third Ukrainian fronts had to take nearly every inhabited locale in fighting, which naturally stretched out the operation's development and lowered the pace of our forces' advance.

Hungary, along the territory of which the Budapest operation chiefly developed, is an agrarian-industrial country, although the basis of its economy is agriculture. There were aircraft construction, tank production and gun factories, and factories preparing artillery shells and rifles in Hungary.

Bauxite and oil occupy the most important place among raw materials. The chief deposits of bauxite are in the Vertes Hegyseg Mountains near the town of Gant , 50 kilometers west of Budapest. At the time of the development of the Budapest operation, Germany shipped 700,000-800,000 tons of bauxite from Hungary, which accounted for approximately 35-40 percent of all raw materials exported to Germany. Four new aluminum plans were built in Hungary during the Second World War. In 1943 15,000 tons of aluminum were produced in Hungary.

There are oil deposits near the town of Nagykanizsa, not far from the Yugoslav border.

In 1943 a total of 1,400,000 tons of oil was extracted in the country, of which up to 1,000,000 tons was sent to Germany. There were seven oil-refining factories in Hungary, with a productive capacity of 400,000 tons of oil.

Hungary's chief industrial areas were located in its northern part: Budapest, Gyor, Miskolc, Esztergom, Szekesfehervar, and Nagykanizsa.

Budapest was the chief center of all Hungarian industry. In the city itself and in its environs there were more than 1,900 enterprises, including very large ones, which comprise nearly half of all the industrial enterprises in Hungary.

In the city itself there were more than 30 machinery-construction and casting factories; that is, about 80 percent of all the machinery-construction factories in Hungary.

Thus the Red Army's forces had to conduct combat operations amidst a significant stratum of hostile elements. The Budapest area was very important for Hitlerite Germany. This circumstance spoke to the fact that the enemy command would try to take all measures to hold this area.

An operational-tactical description of the area of operations. The relief and overall nature of the terrain, as well as the presence of communications routes within the confines of the Budapest operation's area of development allowed for the employment of large combined-arms, motor-mechanized and tank formations. The Danube divided our forces operating to the east of the river from those operating in the trans-Danube area. Reaching a width of nearly 1,000 meters near Budapest, it created significant difficulties for forcing a crossing. The terrain conditions to the west of the Danube gave the enemy the opportunity to create a powerful fortified line along the south-western approaches to Budapest along the line Erd—Lake Velence—Lake Balaton. The enemy had previously created a deeply echeloned defense around Budapest and within the city, which naturally had a direct influence on the intensity of the fighting in the city and on its duration.

The area of the Vertes Hegyseg Mountains to the west and northwest of Budapest was very difficult for combat activities and required not only persistence in achieving assigned objectives and endurance on the part of the troops, but also great skill in waging the engagement in mountainous and wooded conditions. The forces of the Third Ukrainian Front had to fight in extremely difficult conditions during the January fighting against the enemy who had gone over to a counteroffensive. Despite this, the enemy's two powerful counteroffensives were beaten back, which created conditions for the complete rout of the enemy's Budapest group of forces and the occupation of Budapest.

The forces of the Second Ukrainian Front had to operate in the very difficult conditions of mountainous and wooded terrain upon their arrival in the area of the eastern part of the Middle Hungarian Mountains. Despite these difficulties, all of the tasks assigned to the Second Ukrainian Front, both in fighting in Budapest and in forcing the Danube, and in fighting in the area of the Middle Hungarian Mountains, were brilliantly accomplished by the troops.

The Overall Situation

1944 was the year of the Red Army's decisive victories over the German-Fascist aggressors. In ten crushing blows by our forces the entire German defensive front was broken and his main forces located on the Soviet-German front were destroyed to a significant degree, or captured. The prerequisites were created for the Red Army's grandiose decisive operations of 1945. The Budapest operation was an operation by our forces' ninth blow. It began on 28 October 1944. By this time the overall situation on the Soviet-German front was as follows.

In the far north of Finland the forces of the Karelian Front had defeated the Germans' northern group of forces, liberated the Pechenga (Petsamo) district and entered the territory of our Norwegian ally.

As a result of the rout of the German Eighteenth Army around Leningrad, Novgorod and in the Baltic States the Estonian Soviet Republic and a large part of the Latvian Soviet Republic had been liberated.

Germany's Finnish ally had been removed from the war and had declared war on Germany. More than 30 German divisions had been cut off from Prussia and had been pressed into the area between Tukums and Libava.

In Belorussia the Red Army had utterly defeated the German forces around Vitebsk, Bobruisk and Mogilev, concluding its attack with the encirclement of 30 German divisions near Minsk.

The Belorussian SSR had been completely liberated, as well as a significant part of our Polish ally and a large part of the Latvian Soviet republic. Upon forcing the Neman River, our forces reached the borders of Germany and arrived at the Vistula River.

In Western Ukraine the Red Army routed the German forces around L'vov and had thrown them beyond the San and Vistula rivers. Our forces forced the Vistula and carved out a mighty bridgehead beyond the river west of Sandomierz.

In Bessarabia, in the Iasi and Kishinev area, the forces of the Second and Third Ukrainian fronts utterly defeated the German-Romanian armies, concluding their attack with the encirclement of

22 German divisions around Kishinev. The Moldavian Soviet Republic had been liberated, while Germany's Romanian ally was taken out of the war and declared war on Germany and Hungary, as well as Bulgaria, which also declared war on Germany. The way for our forces into Hungary, Germany's last ally in Europe, was opened. The opportunity appeared to extend the hand of assistance to our Yugoslav ally against the German aggressors. The forces of the Second and Third Ukrainian fronts set about carrying out these tasks in October 1944.

In September 1944 the Second Ukrainian Front's forces were engaged in heavy offensive battles on Hungarian territory. At the end of October the *front's* forces defeated the Germans' major Oradea—Mare group of forces, which tried to launch a counterblow against our forces operating north and northwest of Arad. In order to delay the Red Army's successfully developing offensive, in the second half of October the enemy undertook a new counteroffensive from the Szolnok area in the direction of Karcag, Puspokladany and Laba. However, this counteroffensive was also beaten off by the *front's* forces. As a result of successful activities of the *front's* mobile formations, the enemy's bridgehead along the eastern bank of the Tisza was eliminated in the area east of Szolnok.

By the close of October 1944 the forces of the Second Ukrainian Front's right flank had reached the line of the Tisza, while the center had arrived at the eastern bank of this river along a broad front and the left wing (46th Army) had forced the Tisza and reached the area between the Tisza and Danube rivers along the important Budapest operational-strategic direction.

During the second half of October 1944 the Third Ukrainian Front's forces, as a result of their successfully conducted offensive operation, had liberated the capital of our Yugoslav ally—Belgrade—from the German aggressors. Following this operation, the Third Ukrainian Front's main forces were castled to the north into Hungarian territory and to the forces of the Second Ukrainian Front's left flank, which were conducting a broad offensive along the Budapest direction.

As early as 18 October the *Stavka* of the Supreme High Command, in its directive no. 220244, ordered the commander of the Third Ukrainian Front to pull a three-division rifle corps to the northern bank of the Danube and by 25-27 October occupy defensive positions along the Danube along the Sombor—Novi Sad sector, in order to cover the Second Ukrainian Front's left flank and to subsequently concentrate the *front's* main forces along this sector.

By 28 October units of the 57th Army's (Third Ukrainian Front) 75th Rifle Corps, having relieved units of the Second Ukrainian Front's 46th Army, occupied the sector along the Danube indicated by the *Stavka* of the Supreme High Command.

The Third Ukrainian Front's main forces continued to concentrate to the northern bank of the Danube under cover of the 75th Rifle Corps.

In the middle of October the 4th Guards Army, which was also concentrating along this axis, was attached to the Third Ukrainian Front from the *Stavka* of the High Command reserve. Thus by the end of October 1944 the shock groups of two *fronts* were concentrating in the area to the south and southeast of Budapest, for the purpose of launching a decisive offensive to defeat the enemy's Budapest group of forces.

2

The Rout of the German-Hungarian Forces in the Area Between the Tisza and Danube Rivers by the Forces of the Second Ukrainian Front. The Forcing of the Danube by the Forces of the Third Ukrainian Front along the Batina—Apatin Sector and the Seizure of an Operational Bridgehead Along the Western Bank of the Danube (The Operation's First Stage, 28 October-30 November 1944)

During the period 28 October-30 November 1944 the forces of the Second Ukrainian Front's left wing—53rd, 7th Guards and 46th armies, 2nd and 4th guards mechanized corps and General Pliev's[1] cavalry-mechanized group—were mostly involved in the operation to defeat the enemy's Budapest group of forces.

The main task of the Second Ukrainian Front's left-wing forces at this stage of the operation was to consecutively defeat the German-Hungarian forces, which were grouping along the left bank of the Danube to the south and southeast of Budapest, and to reach the outer ring of the city's fortifications along these axes.

This task was resolved by two consecutive attacks: an attack by the 46th Army and the 2nd and 4th guards mechanized corps in the area between the Tisza and Danube and our forces' arrival at the outer ring of the city's fortifications from the south (28 October-4 November) and an attack by the 7th Guards Army, General Pliev's cavalry-mechanized group and the 2nd and 4th guards mechanized corps from the Szolnok area in the general direction Gyongyos and Hatvan, with our forces arriving at the outer ring of the city's fortifications from the southeast and east. The 53rd Army's forces played an important role at this stage of the operation by securing the *front's* main group of forces.

The forces of the Third Ukrainian Front's right wing became involved in the Budapest operation only from 22 November; that is, when the Second Ukrainian Front's forces were completing the

1 Editor's note. Issa Aleksandrovich Pliev (1903-79) joined the Red Army in 1922. During the Great Patriotic War he commanded a cavalry division and corps and later a cavalry-mechanized group in Europe and the Far East. Following the Great Patriotic War he commanded armies and a military district and was the commander of Soviet forces in Cuba during the Missile Crisis.

Map 1 The Soviet Forces' Offensive in the Carpathians, Hungary and Yugoslavia (October 1944-February 1945.

defeat of the German-Hungarian forces in the area between the Tisza and the Danube and were nearing the immediate approaches to Budapest.

The main task of the Third Ukrainian Front's forces during the 28 October-30 November period was to regroup their main forces from Yugoslavia to the left flank of the Second Ukrainian Front to the Baja—Sombor—Subotica area, to force the Danube near Batina and Apatin, to fight to create an operational bridgehead along the right bank of the Danube to the southeast of Lake Balaton, and to capture this bridgehead.

The Second Ukrainian Front's Combat Operations (28 October-26 November 1944)

On 28 October 1944 a directive by the *Stavka* of the Supreme High Command (no. 220251) to the commander of the Second Ukrainian Front, Marshal of the Soviet Union Malinovskii,[2] assigned the mission of launching an offensive with the forces of the 46th Army and the 2nd Guards Mechanized Corps between the Tisza and Danube rivers for the purpose of rolling up the enemy's forces along the western bank of the Tisza and transferring the 7th Guards Army to its right bank. Subsequently, with the arrival of the 4th Guards Mechanized Corps, it was to launch a decisive attack against the enemy group of forces defending Budapest.

The defeat of the German-Hungarian forces in the area between the Tisza and Danube. The arrival of the 46th Army at the outer ring of Budapest's fortifications (28 October – 4 November). In carrying out the directive of the *Stavka* of the Supreme High Command, the commander of the Second Ukrainian Front assigned his forces the following missions: the 46th Army, with the attached 2nd Guards Mechanized Corps, was to attack at 1400 on 29 October in the general direction of Kecskemet and Budapest, launching its main attack with two rifle corps and the 2nd Guards Mechanized Corps along the army's right flank, and with its left flank deploy a front along the Danube. By the close of 30 October the army was to reach the front Nagykoros—Lajosmizse—Solt and then along the Danube. The army's boundary on the right ran along the line from Nagykoros was extended as far as Albertirsa, inclusively. The 2nd Guards Mechanized Corps received orders from the commander of the 46th Army that upon the arrival of the infantry at the line Cirko—Jozsef—Szappanos-Elek, to enter the breach along the Kiskunfelegyhaza, Kecskemet and Kiskunmajsa and Kecskemet axes and by the close of 30 October reach the line Albertirsa—Orkeny. The corps was to subsequently be ready to develop the success in the direction of Budapest.

The 7th Guards Army was to be ready to attack on the morning of 30 October with the forces of four rifle divisions and the Romanian army[3] along the left flank with the task of reaching the line Toszeg—Nagykoros.

The 40th, 27th and 53rd armies and the General Pliev's cavalry-mechanized group were to continue the offensive, carrying out their previously assigned tasks.

The 5th Air Army received orders to support the 46th Army's offensive with all their forces and on 30 October the 7th Guards Army's offensive with part of their forces. Besides this, the 5th Air Army was supposed to cover General Pliev's group in the Nagykallo—Ujfeherto—Balkany area.

2 Editor's note. Rodion Yakovlevich Malinovskii (1898-1967) joined the imperial Russian army in 1914 and the Red Army in 1919. During World War II he commanded a corps, armies and various *fronts*, including the Trans-Baikal Front in the brief war with Japan in 1945. He remained in the area as a military district commander for a number of years. Malinovskii later served as commander-in-chief of the Ground Forces and defense minister from 1957 to his death.

3 By the close of 28 October the Romanian army was stationed as follows: the 2nd Infantry Division along the eastern bank of the Tisza, along the sector excluding Tisza—Nagy—Rev, Tiszakurt, the 9th Cavalry division along the western bank of the Tisza in the area north of Tiszaug, and the 19th Cavalry Division in the Alpar area.

The combat strength of the Second Ukrainian Front's left-wing forces that took place in the Budapest operation is shown in table 1.

Table 1 Combat Strength of the Second Ukrainian Front's Left-Wing Forces in the Budapest Operation

53rd Army
49th Rifle Corps—110th Guards, 6th, 243rd and 375th rifle divisions; 1st Guards Airborne Division.
57th Rifle Corps—203rd and 228th rifle divisions; 6th Guards Airborne Division.
Units subordinated to the army—17th and 152nd cannon-artillery brigades; 18th Guards, 67th and 95th howitzer artillery brigades; 71st Light Army Mortar Brigade; 12th, 22nd and 31st anti-tank artillery brigades; 1316th Anti-Tank Artillery Regiment, 27th Mechanized Brigade, 461st Motorized Regiment, 27th Anti-Aircraft Artillery Division; 54th Engineer-Sapper Brigade.

7th Guards Army
24th Guards Rifle Corps—72nd and 81st guards rifle divisions.
25th Guards Rifle Corps—36th Guards, 53rd and 297th rifle divisions.
27th Guards Rifle Corps—227th and 303rd rifle divisions.
Units subordinated to the army—409th Rifle Division; 27th Guards Tank Brigade; 41st Guards and 61st cannon-artillery brigades; 90th Heavy Howitzer Artillery Brigade; 52nd and 109th howitzer brigades; 49th Light Artillery Brigade; 2nd and 11th anti-tank artillery brigades; 114th and 115th anti-tank artillery regiments; 14th Mechanized Brigade; 263rd, 290th and 493rd motorized regiments; 5th Anti-Aircraft Artillery Division; 60th Engineer-Sapper Brigade.

46th Army
10th Guards Rifle Corps—49th, 86th and 109th guards rifle divisions.
31st Guards Rifle Corps—34th and 40th guards rifle divisions.
37th Rifle Corps—59th and 108th guards and 320th rifle divisions.
Units subordinated to the army—4th Guards Rifle Division; 991st, 1505th and 1897th self-propelled artillery regiments; 7th Artillery Division; 9th and 45th Guards and 17th cannon-artillery brigades; 92nd Corps Artillery Regiment; 25th Howitzer Artillery Brigade; 11th and 105th light artillery brigades; 437th Anti-Tank Artillery Brigade; 3rd Mechanized Brigade; 462nd Motorized Regiment; 38th Anti-Aircraft Artillery Division; 51st Engineer-Sapper Brigade.

6th Guards Tank Army
5th Guards Tank Corps—20th, 21st and 22nd guards tank brigades; 6th Guards Mechanized Brigade; 454th Motorized Regiment; 375th Heavy Self-Propelled Artillery Regiment; 390th Guards Self-Propelled Artillery Regiment; 392nd Guards Anti-Aircraft Artillery Regiment; 391st Guards Anti-Tank Artillery Regiment, 127th Independent Guards Mortar Battalion; 80th Motorcycle Battalion.
9th Guards Mechanized Corps—30th, 31st, 18th, and 46th Guards mechanized brigades; 458th Guards Motorized Regiment; 388th and 389th self-propelled artillery regiments; 35th Independent Guards Mortar Battalion; 14th Guards Motorcycle Battalion.
Units subordinated to the army—51st Guards Self-Propelled Artillery Brigade; 367th Heavy Self-Propelled Artillery Regiment; 49th Guards Tank Regiment; 301st Light Artillery Regiment; 202nd Light Artillery Brigade; 22nd Engineer-Sapper Brigade.

Formations and Units Subordinated to the *Front*
23rd Rifle Corps—68th Guards, 99th and 316th rifle divisions.
2nd Guards Mechanized Corps—4th, 5th and 6th guards mechanized brigades; 37th Guards Tank Brigade; 30th Guards Independent Heavy Tank Regiment; 251st Guards and 1509th self-propelled artillery regiments; 99th Guards Motorcycle Battalion; 524th Motorized Regiment; 408th Guards Mortar Battalion; 159th Anti-Aircraft Regiment; 4th Guards Mechanized Corps--13th, 14th and 15th guards mechanized brigades; 36th Guards Tank Brigade; 352nd Guards Heavy Self-Propelled Artillery Regiment; 129th Guards Mortar Battalion, 1512nd Anti-Tank Artillery Regiment; 292nd Guards Self-Propelled Artillery Regiment, 740th Anti-Aircraft Artillery Regiment; 527th Motorized Regiment; 62nd Motorcycle Battalion.

General Pliev's Cavalry-Mechanized Group
4th, 5th and 6th guards cavalry corps, 7th Mechanized Corps, and 23rd Tank Corps.

Air Force Units
5th Air Army

By the close of 28 October the *front's* forces directly taking part in the Budapest operation occupied the following positions: the 53rd Army was fighting along the front excluding Balmazujvar—Tisza-Be. The army had the assignment of capturing the Polgar area, and therefore its main forces were concentrated along the right flank. The 7th Guards Army, upon encountering stubborn resistance by the enemy occupying a previously prepared defensive line along the western bank of the Tisza, was delayed along the eastern bank of this river along the Fegyvernek—Tiszaug sector, with a bridgehead on the right bank in the areas of Toszeg and Tiszaug. The 46th Army had forced the Tisza in the preceding fighting and, while developing the offensive in the general direction of Budapest, by the close of 28 October was fighting along the line Alpar—Baja. The eastern bank of the Danube to the south of Baja was being observed by individual detachments. The army's main forces were concentrated along its right flank along the Kecskemet and Kiskeres axes. To the right of the 53rd Army were the units of the 4th Romanian Army, while to the left of the 46th Army units of the Third Ukrainian Front's right wing were approaching. By the close of 28 October the 6th Guards Tank Army was located in the Kaba—Karcag—Bihar Udvari area, was repairing its equipment after the preceding intensive fighting and preparing for forthcoming operations along the Budapest direction.

Part of General Pliev's cavalry-mechanized group was fighting along the line Nagykallo—Ujfeherto, while its main forces were grouped in the Balkany—Bokony—Sakoli area. By the close of 28 October the 2nd Guards Mechanized Corps had concentrated in the Kiskundorozsma area, while units of the 4th Guards Mechanized Corps continued concentrating in the Szereg area.

The 23rd Rifle Corps (316th, 99th and 68th rifle divisions) was in the Totkomlos—Pitvaros—Mezohegyes area.

Formations and units of the German Sixth and Hungarian Third armies were grouped opposite the forces of the Second Ukrainian Front's left wing. See table 2.

Table 2 Enemy Forces Facing the Second Ukrainian Front's Left-Wing, End of October 1944

Facing the 27th and 53rd armies—units of the German Sixth Army—23rd Panzer Division, 76th and 46th infantry divisions, *Feldherrnhalle* Motorized Division, 13th Panzer Division, 2nd Panzer Division (Hungarian), 4th Reserve Infantry Division (Hungarian), 12th Light Infantry Division (Hungarian), 6th Reserve Infantry Division (Hungarian), 25th Infantry Division (Hungarian), 27th Light Infantry Division (Hungarian), 8th SS Cavalry Division, 8th Light Infantry Division.

Facing the 7th Guards Army—units of the German Sixth Army—4th SS *Polizei* Motorized Division, the "Rhodes" Assault Division, a combat group from the 153rd Reserve Infantry Division, 1st Light Infantry Division (Hungarian), 16th Infantry Division (Hungarian), 20th Infantry Division (Hungarian).

Facing the 46th Army—units of the Hungarian Third Army—31st SS Infantry Division, 24th Panzer Division, 5th Reserve Infantry Division (Hungarian), 8th Reserve Infantry Division (Hungarian), an infantry regiment from the 2nd Infantry Division (Hungarian), 1st Panzer Division (Hungarian), 1st Cavalry Division (Hungarian), 23rd Reserve Infantry Division (Hungarian), 10th Infantry Division (Hungarian). Units of the 13th SS Infantry Division were operating along the right bank of the Danube against units of the 46th Army.

Both armies were extremely varied in their composition (a significant number of regiments and independent special designation battalions, construction units, security battalions, and others). Besides this, some enemy units and formations had been exhausted and thus were small in numbers (for example, the 24th Panzer Division, which was operating along the Budapest direction, had only 30 tanks). On the whole, the forces of the Second Ukrainian Front's left wing, which were operating along the Budapest direction, enjoyed a small numerical superiority over the enemy, namely 1.4:1 in men, 2.8:1 in artillery (all calibers, including mortars) and 2.6:1 in tanks.

Thus our forces' chief superiority over the enemy was in artillery and tanks.

In carrying out the orders issued, the forces of the Second Ukrainian Front's left wing attacked on 29 October. The enemy put up stubborn resistance and intensive fighting broke out along the entire front. The 53rd Army, which was directing its main efforts to capture Polgar, advanced up to 13 kilometers along this axis and its right-flank units reached the immediate approaches to Polgar; the army's left-flank units did not advance and, while remaining along the eastern bank of the Tisza River, were preparing to force it. The 7th Guards Army, having concentrated its efforts along its left flank, advanced from 8-13 kilometers and reached the front Tosz—Vacmai. The army failed to advance along the remainder of the front and was preparing to force the Tisza here.

At 1400 on 29 October the 46th Army made an energetic attack along the sector from Alpar to Rem (a front length of up to 95 kilometers). The army launched its main attack along the Kecskemet axis along the front Alpar—Jassentlaslo (32 kilometers), where more than 40 percent of the army's and the 2nd Guards Mechanized Corps' entire forces were concentrated. By the close of the day the army had advanced 8-15 kilometers, while repulsing the enemy's numerous counterattacks.

The fighting continued into the night. The 2nd Guards Mechanized Corps was committed into the breach at 1730 and, upon deploying its combat formations, pushed forward its vanguard units, which on this day entered into fighting with the enemy's tanks along the approaches to Kecskemet. In order to increase the efforts along the 46th Army's main operational axis, the *front* commander on that day made the decision to bring up to the front line units of the 23rd Rifle and 4th Guards Mechanized corps.

During the subsequent days the 46th Army's offensive developed successfully along the entire front, and by the close of 31 October the army's forces had reached the front excluding Vacmai—southern outskirts of Kecskemet—Lajosmizse—Izsak—Kecel—Kalocsa, having captured a large number of major inhabited locales; by the close of 31 October the 2nd Guards Corps' forward units captured Lajosmizse, while its main forces had concentrated southeast and southwest of Kecskemet, getting ready from the morning of 1 November to continue carrying out the assigned task. During 29-31 October the 5th Air Army carried out 950 sorties, concentrating its efforts on supporting the activities of the 46th Army and the 2nd Guards Mechanized Corps.

Thus by the close of 31 October the 46th Army along the Budapest direction had achieved a significant success, having advanced 24-40 kilometers. The resulting situation along the Second Ukrainian Front's left flank demanded the rapid advance by our forces toward Budapest, or otherwise the enemy might shift forces against the 46th Army and delay its offensive.

In accordance with instructions from the *Stavka* of the Supreme High Command on concentrating forces along the left flank, the commander of the Second Ukrainian Front issued the following tasks to the armies:

By the morning of 4 November the commander of the 27th Army was to relieve units of the 53rd Army along the front Polgar—Tiszafured.

The commander of the 53rd Army, following a regrouping, was to be ready from the morning of 7 November to force the Tisza and, while attacking along its right flank, to take the line Fuzesabony—Jaszapati. The armies were issued new boundary lines: on the right, with the 27th Army Puspokladany—Tiszafured—Eger (all locales, except for Eger, exclusively for the 53rd Army), and on the left, with the 7th Guards Army, Tiszabe—Jaskiszer—Jaszapati (all locales, except for Turkeve exclusively for the 53rd Army).

The commander of the 7th Guards Army was ordered to continue a decisive offensive and, while rolling up the enemy's defense opposite the army's right flank, to capture by the morning of 2 November the line Szolnok—Abony—Hartany and by the close of 3 November reach the front Bessenszeg—Uiszasz—Tapiobicske.

The 46th Army was reinforced with the 4th Guards Mechanized Corps. The army commander received orders to capture Budapest by the close of 3 November and reach the line Pand (43 kilometers southeast of Budapest)—Ujpest—Budakeszi—Erd, and then south along the Danube.

In carrying out the assigned task, the 4th Guards Mechanized Corps, along with the 23rd Rifle Corps' 68th Rifle Division, which had been loaded onto motor vehicles, was to attack on the night of 1-2 November in the direction of Izsak, Solt, Domsod, and Budapest, reaching by the morning of 2 November the Ocsa—Rakocziliget—Szigetcsep. The 23rd Rifle Corps' remaining two divisions received orders to follow by forced march behind the 4th Guards Mechanized Corps. By the morning of 2 November the army's right-flank forces were to capture the line Cegled—Erken—Kunszentmiklos, while one corps was supposed to cover the army's left flank along the Danube. By the close of 2 November the 2nd Guards Mechanized Corps was to reach the Monor—Ullo—Inarcs area. The army's right boundary would remain the same as far as Nagykoros, and was then extended to Cegled and Pand (both locales inclusively for the 46th Army).

Thus by this order the *front's* three left-flank armies (53rd, 7th Guards and 46th) and two mechanized corps (2nd and 4th guards) were directed to the northwest against the enemy's Budapest group of forces. The 53rd Army's neighbor on the right (27th Army) was to attack in the general direction of Miskolc, while the *front's* right-flank army (40th Army) was to go over to a solid defense along the line of the Tisza River.

The greatest successes at this stage of the operation proved to be along the 46th Army's sector. By the morning of 1 November the 4th Guards Mechanized Corps had concentrated in the Kiskunfelegyhaza—Monostorfalva area. In accordance with orders, the corps commander decided to launch his main attack in the direction of Izsak, Kunszentmiklos and Rakocziliget area, covering its left flank from the direction of the Danube with one mechanized brigade and a rifle regiment from the 68th Division (23rd Rifle Corps), which received orders to operate in the direction of Izsak, Solt, Domsod, and Taksony.

The corps set about carrying out its mission and from 1800 on 2 November its advance was vigorous from the first day.

The enemy, while attempting at any cost to eliminate the breakthrough and delay the 4th Guards Mechanized Corps' advance, hurriedly transferred the III Panzer Corps, consisting of the 1st, 13th and 23rd panzer divisions, and the *Feldherrnhalle* Motorized Division, from the Miskolc axis to the Budapest axis.

The corps, while destroying the enemy's counterattacking units, bypassing the enemy's strong points in the villages and pushing aside his covering forces, was approaching Budapest and as early as the close of 2 November was fighting in the Rakocziliget—Ocsa area; the 68th Guards Division (23rd Rifle Corps), which was following behind the mechanized brigades, passed through Kunszentmiklos (south of Budapest) on motor vehicles at 1600 on this day. On 3 November the 15th Mechanized Brigade broke into Kussuthfalva (south of Budapest), having broken away from the corps' main body, which be this time were fighting enemy tanks in the Rakocziliget area. The brigade, which was not supported in time by the infantry, was unable to hold on to its occupied area and, under pressure from the enemy's numerically superior forces (tanks, artillery and infantry), was forced to fall back on the corps' main forces in the area five kilometers south of Rakocziliget. The corps' attempt to break through to Budapest was unsuccessful.

By the close of 1 November the 2nd Guards Mechanized Corps was fighting enemy tanks in the following areas: three kilometers south of Albertirsa and southwest, south and southeast of Cegled. The corps, through its energetic actions, threw back the enemy's tank units and by the close of 2 November was fighting in the area Vasad—excluding Ullo. The corps' subsequent progress was halted and by the close of 4 November it was engaged in intensive fighting against the enemy's counterattacking infantry and tanks in the same area.

During 1-4 November the 23rd Guards Corps operated jointly with units of the 4th Guards Mechanized Corps and by the close of 4 November was fighting five kilometers west of the line Ullo—Rakocziliget.

The 46th Army's combined-arms formations, while repelling the enemy's numerous infantry and tank counterattacks, was advancing successfully behind the units of the 4th Guards Mechanized Corps and by the close of 4 November was fighting along the front Ullo—Rakocziliget—Taksony—Domsod and further along the Danube. On this day the army received orders to temporarily take up the defensive along the line reached.

The 7th Guards Army's forces, in accordance with their orders, continued to develop the offensive, although the troops did not advance as rapidly as the *front* commander demanded. The fighting was quite bitter and the enemy put up stubborn resistance, while often counterattacking.

On 4 November the army's forces stormed the city and major railroad junction of Szolnok—an important enemy strong point along the Tisza River.

The 53rd Army, which had been drawn into the fighting for Polgar, was unable to carry out in time the transfer of a sector of the front along the right flank to the 27th Army's units. On 1 November it was still fighting along the entire front. On the following day, 2 November, the army captured Polgar. Simultaneously, the army's forces carried out a relief of units and regrouped their own forces to a new zone, and also prepared to force the Tisza within its new boundary lines. The army did not advance along the left flank.

During 1-4 November the 5th Air Army (in three flying days, as the weather on 3 November prevented flying) carried out 1,296 combat sorties, of which 544 were to carry out assault-air and bomber strikes.

On 2 November General Pliev's cavalry-mechanized group was ordered to concentrate in the Karcag—Kisujszallas—Turkeve area.

The 6th Guards Tank Army, while being reinforced, remained in its previous concentration area.

The German-Hungarian command, which had been seriously concerned by the possibility of the imminent seizure of Budapest by our forces, and desiring to hold the city at any cost, continued to transfer units of the III Panzer Corps to the Budapest axis, having concentrated here a powerful tank group numbering about 200 tanks. This tank group, which was supported by a large amount of artillery and, acting in conjunction with infantry, attempted to hold off both the 46th Army and the 2nd and 4th guards mechanized corps through uninterrupted counterattacks. The enemy organized a solid defense along the Monor—Ullo—Rakocziliget line, strongly suffused with anti-tank and fire weapons, as well as anti-tank and anti-personnel obstacles. The approaches to the forward edge of this defensive line were mined along extensive sectors. These were the defensive structures of the outer ring of the city's fortifications.

The 46th Army's formations were halted by the enemy along this line. The enemy was simultaneously putting up stubborn resistance to the advance by the 7th Guards and 53rd armies' forces.

Thus during 1- 4 November the 46th Army's forces, while throwing back the opposing enemy and his arriving tank and combined-arms reserves, successfully advanced to the north and reached the outer defensive line of the Budapest fortifications from the south. The army was unable to capture Budapest, because the enemy was able to transfer the III Panzer Corps and several infantry divisions to the Budapest axis, was able to strengthen the Budapest garrison itself, and was able to occupy the southern approaches to the defensive line of the outer ring of the city's fortifications with troops and halt the 46th Army's offensive. However, this energetic attack by the forces of the Second Ukrainian Front along the Budapest axis played a significant operational and political role. In order to hold off the offensive by our forces, the enemy was forced to transfer forces here, removing them from other sectors of the front, particularly from the sectors facing the Second Ukrainian Front's right flank, from the Fourth Ukrainian, and even from the First

Ukrainian fronts. The reserves being transferred by the enemy came under attack by our aviation, tank and mechanized forces, and our artillery and infantry. The enemy suffered heavy losses and was exhausted. The arrival of our forces at the immediate approaches to the Hungarian capital undoubtedly had major political significance, because it united the Hungarian people's democratic forces, which were operating within the country and inspired them to fight the Hitlerite and Szalasist[4] bosses.

With the arrival of the 46th Army's and 2nd and 4th guards mechanized corps' forces at the powerful outer ring of the Budapest defensive structures, further attempts to take Budapest by an attack from the south did not promise success, because the enemy here had concentrated significant forces and had managed to occupy powerful and deeply echeloned lines in an organized manner.

Due to the operational situation that had arisen here, the *Stavka* of the Supreme High Command, in its directive no. 220256 of 4 November, pointed out to the *front* commander that an attack on Budapest along a narrow front with the forces of only two mechanized corps and an insignificant amount of infantry might lead to unjustified losses and place the forces operating along this axis in danger of an enemy flank attack from the northeast.

The *Stavka* of the Supreme High Command ordered the *front* to move its right flank as quickly as possible to the western bank of the Tisza, in order to carry out an offensive along a broad front and to defeat the enemy's Budapest group of forces by a turning maneuver and an attack from the north and northeast, in conjunction with an attack by the 46th Army and the 2nd and 4th guards mechanized corps from the south. In order to support the plan, the *Stavka* ordered the *front* commander to launch an attack with the forces of General Pliev's cavalry-mechanized group from the Szolnok to the north, no later than 7 November, for the purpose of rolling up the enemy's defense along the western bank of the Tisza and to bring the *front's* right wing up to the river.

In order to carry out the directive by the *Stavka* of the Supreme High Command, the *front* commander decided on the following:

The 46th Army was to temporarily take up defense along the front Ullo—Rakocziliget—Taksony—Rackeve, and then along the Danube, improving only its tactical situation along this sector; by the morning of 5 November the 2nd and 4th guards mechanized corps were to be moved to the areas of Inarcs and Ocsa, where they were to be put in order; the army's right-flank rifle corps were to continue the offensive, with the task of reaching the line Tapiosuly—Ullo by the close of 5 November.

The 7th Guards Army was to continue a decisive offensive and by the morning of 6 November reach the line Jaszapati—Jaszbereny—(excluding) Tapiosuly, while General Pliev's cavalry-mechanized group was to be crossed over the Tisza River near Szolnok and Somsicz and concentrated in the Abony—Cegled—Nagykoros area, with the idea of employing it within the next few days for an attack in the direction of Jaszapati. The *front's* right wing (40th, 27th, 4th, and 53rd armies) was to launch a decisive offensive on the morning of 7 November.

After midday on 5 November, a group of 30-40 enemy tanks, reinforced with infantry on armored transports, attacking from the areas northeast and southeast of Pilis, broke through the 46th Army's front, which was occupied in insufficient strength along this sector. While pushing back our units, the enemy, upon receiving reinforcements in tanks and infantry, reached the areas of Gyori and Orkeny, thus cutting the mechanized corps' communications and those of the 46th Army's rifle formations. Units of the 2nd and 4th guards mechanized corps, which had been

4 Editor's note. This is a reference to Ferenc Szalasi (1897-1946), the leader of the Iron Cross Party in Hungary, whom the Germans placed in power in late 1944, following the overthrow of Admiral Miklos Horthy's government, which was trying to arrange a separate peace with the Allied powers. Salaszi's reign was brief, however, and following the war he was turned over to the new Hungarian authorities and executed.

relieved along the front by the army's combined-arms formations, were thrown in to eliminate the enemy's breakthrough units. Thus these corps did not have the opportunity to carry out the order to move into the areas indicated for them by *front* directive no. 00701/op of 4 November. The fighting to eliminate the enemy's breakthrough forces lasted until 6 November, after which the 4th Guards Mechanized Corps concentrated in the Tararszentgyorgy—Lake Madarasito area, while on November 8 the 2nd Guards Mechanized Corps reached the area Gyori—Orkeny—Ujhartyan. In these areas the corps set about restoring their equipment and taking on munitions and fuels and lubricants.

During 4-8 November the 46th Army, while carrying out its assigned task, was securely defending its occupied lines along the southern approaches to Budapest, while the advance by the 7th Guards and 53rd armies during these days was very insignificant. As a result, as early as 8 November the *front* commander made the decision, upon concentrating a shock fist along the 7th Guards Army's left flank, to launch a powerful attack against the enemy from the Szolnok—Cegled area to the north. This was already the second attack directed at defeating the German-Hungarian forces grouped to the southeast of Budapest.

The chief result of the combat operations by the Second Ukrainian Front's left-wing forces during the period 28 October-8 November was the defeat of the German-Hungarian forces along the southern approaches to Budapest and the arrival of the 46th Army's units at the Budapest external defensive line from the south. However, the enemy continued to put up stubborn resistance along the southeastern approaches to Budapest and efforts were still required from the *front's* left-wing forces, in order to defeat the enemy opposite them.

The defeat of the German-Hungarian forces along the southeastern approaches to Budapest. The 7th Guards Army's arrival at Budapest's outer ring from the east (11-26 November). As has been noted earlier, on 8 November the *front* commander made the decision to shift the main attack to the 7th Guards Army's zone. In accordance with this decision contained in directive no. 00714/op, the *front's* formations were assigned the following tasks: on the morning of 10 November, the commander of the 7th Guards Army, having concentrated no less than 1,600 artillery tubes along his left flank, was to break through the enemy's defensive front and secure the commitment of General Pliev's cavalry-mechanized group[5] and the 2nd and 4th guards mechanized corps into the breach. By the close of 11 November the army was to reach the line Aszod—Dany. Due to the new assignment, the army boundary lines were refined, namely as far as Jaszapati on the right, as before, and then to Karacsond (inclusively for the 7th Guards Army), and on the left, as far as Pand, as before, and then including Aszod. General Pliev, the commander of the cavalry-mechanized group, received orders to enter the breach on the morning of 10 November along the 7th Guards Army's sector, with the 23rd Tank Corps in the first echelon and, while developing the offensive in the direction of Jaszapati, to capture the line Karacsond—Vamosgyork, with one cavalry division apiece in the Kapolna—Kal area and in the Gyongyos area. By the morning of 9 November (*front* directive no. 00712/op) the 4th Guards Mechanized Corps was to concentrate by night marches to the area south of Cegled and on the morning of 10 November enter the breach along the 7th Guards Army's sector, with a tank group in its first echelon and, while developing the offensive in the direction of Jaszbereny, by the morning of 11 November capture the Hatvan area. The 2nd Guards Mechanized Corps received orders to (directive no. 00712/op) to concentrate by a night march in the area southwest of Cegled by the morning of 9 November and to enter the breach on the morning of 10 November along the 7th Guards Army's sector, with a tank group in the first echelon and, while developing the offensive in the direction of Nagykata, by the close of 11 November capture the Szamok—Szentmartonkata area.

5 The group included the 4th and 6th guards cavalry and 23rd tank corps.

The commander of the 53rd Army was ordered to continue the offensive and by the close of 11 November reach the front Maklar—Erk.

The 46th Army was also to continue to attack along its right flank and by the close of 11 November reach the front excluding Dany—Isaszeg—Rakoscsaba—Vecses and, along the left flank, while securely holding its line, reach the Csepeli Dunaag and Danube rivers, having eliminated all the enemy's bridgeheads along the eastern bank of these rivers, particularly in the Solt area.

In order to make it possible to more carefully and in a more well-rounded manner prepare for the forthcoming operations, the deadline for the beginning of the offensive was shifted from 10 (as was planned earlier) to 11 November.

By the close of 10 November the *front's* formations, without halting the fighting, occupied the following front: 53rd Army excluding Mezokovesd—excluding Tiszasul; 7th Guards Army excluding Tiszasul—Cegled; 46th Army Alberti—Ullo—Taksony—Solt—Baja. General Pliev's cavalry-mechanized group had concentrated in the Szolnok—Abony—Toroszentmiklos—Turkeve area. The 2nd Guards Mechanized Corps had concentrated southwest of Cegled and the 4th Guards Mechanized Corps was in the area to the south of Cegled. The 6th Guards Tank Army remained in the *front* commander's reserve and was located in the Kisujszallas—Toroszentmiklos—Turkeve area.

Combat operations by the Second Ukrainian Front's left-wing forces during 11-26 November developed generally in the following manner.

The 53rd Army did not cease attacking and from the morning of 11 November its forces continued to wage stubborn fighting along the entire front, beating off the enemy's numerous and persistent counterattacks. On this day the forward units of the army's right-flank corps became involved in bitter fighting along the southern outskirts of Fuzesabony. In subsequent days, the enemy, having come under flanking attacks by our forces from the area south of Fuzesabony and under pressure from the army's left-wing corps, was forced to fall back to the north. During 13-14 November our forces advanced 10-12 kilometers along various sectors. On 15 November, following prolonged and bitter fighting, Fuzesabony fell. On 16 November the commander of the 53rd Army received orders from the *front* commander to continue to energetically develop the offensive, launching its main attack along its right flank in the general direction of Verpelet; on 17 November it was to capture the Verpelet area and Gyongyos area; by the close of 19 November it was to reach the line Petervasara—Kisterenye—Paszto.

Due to the new assignment, the boundary line on the left was refined and was to run through Gyongyos—Balassagyarmat (both locales inclusive for the 53rd Army). The army set about carrying out this new task, without halting its offensive.

On 18 November the army captured Tofalu and Kapolna, major Hungarian inhabited locales. Due to the threat hanging over Gyongyos, on 19 November the enemy undertook several consecutive and powerful counterattacks in the general direction of Gyongyos. On 20 November the army's right-flank forces began fighting along the southern outskirts of Eger. Upon reaching the Eger and Gyongyos areas, the 53rd Army's forces found themselves directly at the southeastern slopes of the Central Hungarian Mountains, where the enemy was able to organize a powerful defense. Subsequently, all the way up to 26 November, the army did not advance significantly and was involved in local fighting to improve its position..

At 0850 on 11 November the 7th Guards Army, following a 20-minute powerful artillery preparation, launched a decisive offensive. Following stubborn fighting, the army's forces broke through the enemy defense and, having advanced up to ten kilometers, captured Jaszladany, along with units of the 23rd Tank Corps.

General Pliev's cavalry-mechanized group, which was operating along the 7th Guards Army's sector, had taken up by 0700 on 11 November its jumping-off positions for the attack, having concentrated in the Ujszasz, to the east, and north of Szolnok. The 4th Guards Mechanized Corps deployed south and southwest of Kissiresi, while the 2nd Guards Mechanized Corps was south and southwest of Cegled.

General Pliev's cavalry-mechanized group attacked simultaneously with the combined-arms formations. Its 23rd Tank Corps attacked at 0830 on 11 November just like the infantry, and from the beginning of the attack operated ahead of the infantry and played a significant role in breaking through the enemy's defensive front. By 1300 the tank corps' units captured Jaszladany. The corps' subsequent advance was halted by the enemy's powerful fire resistance. Somewhat less successful on this day were the 2nd Guards Mechanized Corps' units, which had advanced only 2-6 kilometers in the day's fighting. The tank and mechanized troops' operations on this day unfolded in extremely difficult conditions, because the very swampy and waterlogged terrain considerably restricted their freedom of maneuver. On the operation's second day, 12 November, the mobile troops' (General Pliev's cavalry-mechanized group and the 2nd and 4th guards mechanized corps) advance was also generally insignificant, amounting to only 10-16 kilometers, and by the close of the day they had reached the Jaszkiser—Jaszbereny—Nagykata and had begun fighting for these locales. On 13 November General Pliev's group, while moving ahead, saw its 23rd Tank Corps' units get involved in fighting for Jaszdozsa, and its cavalry for Jaszapati and Jaszjakohalma. The 4th Guards Mechanized Corps was drawn into extended fighting for Jaszbereny, while the 2nd Guards Mechanized Corps captured Nagykata and, having advanced to the northwest, was fighting for Szentmartonkata. On 14 November the cavalry-mechanized group advanced very little. The 4th Guards Mechanized Corps remained along its previous line, while the 2nd Guards Mechanized Corps, upon advancing eight kilometers, reached the Toalmas area. The 7th Guards Army's combined-arms formations, which were fighting along with the tank and mechanized forces, also advanced to the north with them. By the close of 14 November the 7th Guards Army's forces were fighting along the following line: Erk—Jaszdozsa—Jaszjakohalma—Jaszbereny—Szentmartonkata—Tapiosuly. At this time the 46th Army's right-flank units were still mainly along their former lines.

Thus the advance by the shock group of the *front's* left-wing forces (7th Guards Army, General Pliev's cavalry-mechanized group, 2nd and 4th guards mechanized corps) was quite slow. The mobile forces had been unable to break out into the operational depth and carry out a deep turning movement for enveloping the enemy's Budapest group of forces from the east and northeast. One must consider the main reasons for this to be the difficulties of local conditions and the reinforcement of the enemy's troops. From 11 November the enemy transferred the Hungarian 2nd Panzer Division, units of the German 15th Infantry Division, the 662nd Assault Gun Battalion, and an assault battalion from the Eighth Army to the Budapest axis. The Second Ukrainian Front's left-wing forces were already faced by the German 23rd and 24th panzer divisions, 18th SS Panzer Division, 2nd SS *Polizei* Motorized Division, *Feldherrnhalle* SA Motorized Division, 8th Light Infantry Division, and the 46th and 76th infantry divisions, and the Hungarian 1st and 2nd panzer, 20th, 25th and 27th infantry divisions, 5th Reserve Infantry Division, 26th Border Battalion, 9th Border Division, and the 16th Reconnaissance Detachment. The offensive by the shock group of the *front's* left-wing forces continued to develop, slowly but uninterruptedly. Characteristic of its development was the fact that the tank and mechanized units operated almost without pause in the combined-arms formations' combat formations and, if they did push forward 5-8 kilometers, then the infantry, which was supported by the artillery following directly behind it, quickly caught up with them. By 26 November the shock group of the Second Ukrainian Front's left-wing forces were fighting along the following line: 7th Guards Army excluding Aszod—Tapiosuly; General Pliev's cavalry-mechanized group was fighting east and southeast of Lorinci; on the previous evening; that is, 25 November, the 4th Guards Mechanized Corps captured Hatvan and was fighting for the crossings over the Zagyva River and to the northwest of Hatvan; the 2nd Guards Mechanized Corps was fighting south and west of Hereg.

The 46th Army, in accordance with its assigned tasks, attacked at 0850 on 11 November with its right-flank corps, although the offensive failed to achieve significant successes on the first day. On the offensive's second day, 12 November, the army's right-flank units advanced 5-10 kilometers along some axes and captured a number of powerful enemy strong points. On 13 November the army's right flank did not advance, although on this day its left-flank formations captured the important road junctions and enemy defensive strong points of Solt and Dunaenyhaza. While developing its success here, the army's forces on the following day, 14 November, completely cleared the eastern bank of the Danube of the enemy, eliminating enemy bridgeheads in the area of Solt and Dunaenyhaza. The army was subsequently unable to achieve more or less significant results, and by the close of 26 November its forces, without ceasing to fight, were located along the line excluding Tapiosuly—excluding Vecses—excluding Rakocziliget—Szigetszentmiklos and then along the eastern bank of the Danube as far as Baja.

Due to the situation that had come about on 25 November, the *front* commander on the afternoon of that day, in a special report (no. 00736/op of 25 November 1944, 1630 hrs) presented for confirmation to the *Stavka* of the Supreme High Command a plan for the *front's* subsequent operations.

The *front* commander requested that he be allowed the following:

1. To temporarily halt the offensive by the 53rd, 7th Guards and 46th armies.
2. To launch an offensive with the forces of the 27th Army's right flank and the 40th Army's left flank for the purpose of capturing the Miskolc area.
3. To launch an offensive on the morning of 4-5 December with the forces of the 7th Guards Army's left flank, General Pliev's group and the 6th Guards Tank Army in the general direction of Sahy, in order to capture the Balassagyarmat—Sahy—Sob—Felsogod area, with a simultaneous attack by two of the 46th Army's rifle corps, and by the 2nd and 4th guards mechanized corps in the direction of Becske, with the task of capturing the area Esztergom—Becske—Budapest, while the 46th Army's right flank would tie down the enemy with a frontal attack on Budapest from the southeast.

The *Stavka* of the Supreme High Command, in its directive no. 220273 of 26 November, confirmed the plan presented by the *front* commander, pointing out the necessity of the following measures:

1. To concentrate no less than two artillery breakthrough divisions along the 7th Guards Army's sector, to guarantee the success of the planned operation.
2. To bring Colonel General of Tank Troops Kravchenko's[6] 6th Guards Tank Army into the offensive along the 7th Guards Army's sector.
3. To employ General Pliev's group for developing the offensive behind the 6th Guards Tank Army.
4. To broaden the 53rd Army's offensive sector to the southwest, in order to strengthen the 7th Guards Army's combat formations, thus enabling the 53rd Army to bypass from the west the wooded and mountain area north of Gyongyos.
5. The offensive was to begin no later than 2-3 December.

6 Editor's note. Andrei Grigor'evich Kravchenko (1899-1963) joined the Red Army in 1918 and fought in the civil war and the Soviet-Finnish War. During the Great Patriotic War he commanded a tank brigade and a tank corps, and then a tank army in Europe and the Far East. Following the war, Kravchenko commanded an army and retired in 1955.

Thus the Second Ukrainian Front's left-wing forces for the first days of December, which was meant to encircle the enemy's Budapest group of forces and Budapest.

This comprised a new stage in the Budapest operation, the description of which will be given below.

During 11-26 November the Second Ukrainian Front's left-wing forces inflicted a serious defeat on the German-Fascist troops grouped to the southeast of Budapest, threw back their remnants to the wooded Central Hungarian Mountains and reached the external ring of Budapest's defensive structures from the southeast and east. This created real conditions for launching a subsequent attack from the Hatvan area to the northwest in order to isolate the enemy's Budapest group of forces from his Miskolc group of forces, to cut the communications running from Budapest to the northeast, and to encircle Budapest from the north, northeast, east, southeast, and south. A simultaneous attack by the 46th Army's forces from the area south of Budapest, with a forcing of the Danube to the north, would create an opportunity for encircling Budapest from the west.

Combat Activities by the Third Ukrainian Front's Forces (28 October-30 November 1944)

As was noted earlier, as early as 18 October the *Stavka* of the Supreme High Command, in its directive no. 220244, ordered the commander of the Third Ukrainian Front to pull one three-division rifle corps to the north bank of the Danube, for the purpose of covering the Second Ukrainian Front's left flank[7] and by 25-27 October occupy defensive positions along the Danube along the Sombor—Novi Sad sector.

In carrying out the instructions of the *Stavka* of the Supreme High Command and the order by the commander of the Third Ukrainian Front, on 28 October units of the 57th Army's 75th Rifle Corps, having relieved units of the Second Ukrainian Front's 46th Army, occupied the defensive lines indicated by the decision by the *Stavka* of the Supreme High Command. According to a decision by the *Stavka* of the Supreme High Command, on 31 October the entire 57th Army was shifted to the northern bank of the Danube.[8]

The regrouping of the Third Ukrainian Front's forces to the right flank at the end of October and beginning of November 1944 marked the beginning of the Second and Third Ukrainian fronts' joint combat activities in the Budapest operation, which concluded in the middle of February 1945 with the complete encirclement and destruction of a major enemy group of forces and the capture of the capital of the Germans' Hungarian satellite—the city of Budapest.

The forcing of the Danube and the creation of an operational bridgehead on the western bank of the Danube. On 9 November the Third Ukrainian Front's 57th Army forced the Danube with part of its forces in the Batina—Apatin area and carried out successful fighting to expand the bridgeheads west of these locales, where by this time the forward elements of the 75th Rifle Corps, which had crossed during the night of 7-8 November, were fighting. On this day the *front* command, in its directive to the commander of the 57th Army, instructed him that "in the next few days the army will have to attack." The army command was ordered to immediately set about thoroughly preparing an offensive operation and secretly reconnoitering possible areas for forcing the Danube along the sector Baja—mouth of the Drava River.

During the first half of November the units of the 57th Army, supported by the 17th Air Army and the Danube Flotilla, successfully repulsed numerous counterattacks by the enemy attempting to throw our crossed units from the western bank of the Danube, expanded their bridgeheads

7 By 28 October the Second Ukrainian Front's left flank was located in Baja.

8 The sector of the front previously occupied by the 57th Army was turned over to units of the Yugoslav People's Liberation Army.

west of Batina and Apatin and simultaneously crossed their main forces for an offensive from the bridgeheads.

On 14 November the *Stavka* of the Supreme High Command, in its directive no. 220265, ordered the commander of the Third Ukrainian Front to continuing forcing the Danube, with the task of reaching the line Bataszek—Pecs—Harkany, thus securing behind itself operational space along the western bank of the Danube.

In anticipation of the offensive operation, the *Stavka* of the Supreme High Command continuously reinforced the Third Ukrainian Front. In the middle of October the 4th Guards Army was transferred from the *Stavka* reserve to the *front*. On 31 October the 18th Tank Corps was subordinated to the *front*. On 14 November General Gorshkov's[9] cavalry-mechanized group (5th Guards Cavalry and 7th Mechanized corps) was transferred to the *front*, and on 18 November the 31st Guards Rifle Corps arrived from the Second Ukrainian Front. Reinforcement units also arrived to the *front* during this time.

On the morning of 22 November the 57th Army, having gone over to a decisive offensive, crushed the enemy's resistance with a concentric attack from the north and south and by the close of 23 November the Batina and Apatin bridgeheads had been linked up an formed a single bridgehead, 35 kilometers in width and 14 kilometers in depth. On this day units of the 4th Guards Army took over the combat sector of the 57th Army's units along the left bank of the Danube along the line Baja—Mohacs, and on 24 November began the combat forcing of the Danube northeast of this locale.

By the close of 29 November our forces had expanded the bridgehead to more than 180 kilometers along the front and up to 50 kilometers in depth, having seized a major road and railroad junction and important economic center of Hungary—the city of Pecs, as well as the major inhabited locales of Bataszek, Mohacs and others.

The task assigned by the *Stavka* of the Supreme High Command to the Third Ukrainian Front's forces for creating an operational bridgehead along the western bank of the Danube had been fulfilled. The attacking units of the 57th, and later of the 4th Guards Army, fought off uninterrupted counterattacks by enemy infantry, supported by tanks and assault guns, aviation and massed artillery fire. The German command, while striving to prevent during the first period of fighting the expansion of our bridgeheads, and later to prevent the breakthrough of its defense in the direction of Lake Balaton, which would place the entire southern flank of its Budapest German-Hungarian group of forces under threat of attack, hurriedly threw in new units from other sectors of the front and reserve to the breakthrough sector.

During 9-29 November the enemy transferred five German and Hungarian units, plus reinforcements, from southern Serbia, northern Italy and from Hungary.

As a result of 20 days of fighting our forces completely defeated the German 31st SS Infantry Division and inflicted a heavy defeat on the German 44th, 32nd and 71st infantry divisions, five regiments, one motorized brigade, and other units.[10]

The enemy lost more than 32,000 soldiers and officers killed and captured. The losses in equipment, destroyed and captured by our forces were 95 tanks, assault guns and armored transports,

9 Editor's note. Sergei Il'ich Gorshkov (1902-93) joined the Red Army in 1920 and fought in the civil war. During the Second World War he commanded a rifle and cavalry divisions. He later commanded a cavalry corps and a cavalry-mechanized group. Following the war, Gorshkov continued in commanded of a cavalry corps until his retirement in 1946.

10 Among the units that suffered heavy losses were the 99th Mountain Rifle Regiment/ 1st Mountain Rifle Division; 749th Infantry Regiment/ 117th Light Infantry Division, and; the 750th Infantry Regiment/118th Light Infantry Division; the 28th Infantry Regiment/13th Muslim SS Infantry Division; 8th Infantry Regiment/Hungarian 4th Infantry Division, and the 92nd Motorized Brigade.

410 guns of various calibers, 320 mortars, 1,500 heavy and light machine guns, 56 planes, and a large number of other military equipment and property.

The German-Hungarian forces, having suffered heavy losses, were forced to fall back to the northwest and west.

Thus during the first stage of the Budapest operation the Second Ukrainian Front's forces created the prerequisites for launching a decisive attack for the purpose of splitting the Budapest group of forces from the Miskolc group and for the purpose of cutting the enemy's communications running from Budapest to the northeast and north. The Third Ukrainian Front's forces captured a significant operational bridgehead along the western bank of the Danube, enabling them to cross over the Danube and concentrate to the northeast of Lake Balaton the necessary men and materiel for developing the subsequent offensive.

Characteristic of the activities by the forces of the Second Ukrainian Front during the first stage of the operation was the rapid advance by the 2nd and 4th guards mechanized corps and the 46th Army toward Budapest and the rapidity with which the operational maneuver by the 2nd and 4th guards mechanized corps was carried out to the 7th Guards Army's sector, where a second attack was planned and carried out by the forces of the Second Ukrainian Front's left wing.

The attack by the 7th Guards Army from Szolnok to Hatvan was actually prepared and carried out without any kind of operational pause and without a preparatory period. The concentration of men and materiel for the breakthrough of the enemy's front was actually carried out in three days (the order to carry out the operation was issued by the *front* command on 8 November and on 11 November the units had already begun the attack). In these conditions the necessity of "attaching" the recently arrived artillery batteries to the firing positions of the batteries already in place was revealed. As experience showed, this method in this specific situation proved to be the most expedient.

Worthy of note in the actions of the 7th Guards Army and the mobile formations (2nd and 4th guards mechanized corps, 23rd Tank Corps, and Pliev's cavalry) are their slowness. One must search for the reason for this exclusively in the very difficult local conditions, in the washed-out roads and in the enemy's considerable strengthening of the enemy's tank forces along the axis of the army shock group's operations. It was precisely this that prevented the mobile forces from rapidly gaining operational freedom for developing the success into the depth. The mechanized and tank units operated here throughout the entire period of the offensive (11-26 November) in close tactical interaction with the combined-arms formations. The mobile forces' maneuver was restricted and they had to operate exclusively along the roads, because off the roads, due to the washed-out roads, the movement of auto transportation and even tanks, not to mention artillery, was made extremely difficult.

Worthy of note in the actions of the Third Ukrainian Front's forces was the mobility and precision with which they carried out the regroupings of significant forces and equipment from the Belgrade to the Budapest axis, the precision and rapidity in forcing such an impressive river barrier as the Danube with two armies (57th and 4th Guards), and the tenacity by our forces in achieving their assigned objectives in capturing a bridgehead of operational importance.

In the enemy's actions one may notice the extreme stubbornness of the resistance and the broad employment of defensive works for fortifying the external defensive rings of Budapest itself. The enemy put all his efforts into holding Budapest. However, under the attacks by the Second and Third Ukrainian fronts, he was forced to give up one defensive position after another to the Red Army.

3

The Defeat of the Enemy's Hatvan Group of Forces by the Second Ukrainian Front and the Defeat of the Enemy's Danube Group of Forces by the Third Ukrainian Front (The Operation's Second Stage, 1-9 December 1944)

The first stage of the Budapest operation concluded with the arrival of the Second Ukrainian Front's left-wing forces at the outer ring of the Budapest defensive structures from the south, southeast and east on 26 November. In accordance with the directive by the *Stavka* of the Supreme High Command and the plans of the *front* commander, the troops faced the new task of encircling the enemy's Budapest group of forces in Budapest.

The Third Ukrainian Front's forces, without halting combat operations, continued to develop their success to the northwest toward Szekesfehervar, and to the west toward Nagykanizsa. As was shown above, the *Stavka* of the Supreme High Command set the beginning of the offensive by the Second Ukrainian Front's left-wing forces for carrying out its new tasks for 2-3 December, although by this deadline the *front's* forces were not completely ready for operations and thus the deadline for the offensive was moved back to 5 December.

The Second Ukrainian Front's Combat Operations (5-9 December)

In accordance with the *Stavka* of the Supreme High Command's instructions, the *front* commander issued the following directives to his troops.

Directive no. 00744/op of 26 November ordered:

a) the commander of the 7th Guards Army is to turn over to the 53rd Army by 1800 on 28 November, together with its combat sector, the headquarters of the 24th Guards Rifle Corps, consisting of the 81st and 72nd guards rifle divisions;

b) by 1800 on 28 November the commander of the 53rd Army is to receive the headquarters of the 24th Guards Rifle Corps, along with the 81st and 72nd guards rifle divisions' combat sector; he is to relieve the units of the 7th Guards Army within the confines of the new boundary line on the left;

c) to establish from 1800 on 28 November the following boundary line between the 53rd and 7th Guards armies: as far as Jaszapati as before, then Jaszarokszallas—Kekenies—Sirok—Balassagyarmat, with all locales inclusively for the 53rd Army.

On this day the *front* commander ordered (directive no. 00738/op):

1. The commander of the 7th Guards Army is to completely relieve during the night of 26-27 November units of General Pliev's cavalry-mechanized group.
2. Upon the relief of his group's units by the 7th Guards Army's forces, General Pliev, the commander of the cavalry-mechanized group, is to concentrate the group, consisting of the 4th and 6th guards cavalry corps and the 4th Guards Mechanized Corps, to the area Csani—Pusztamonostor—excluding Jaszdozsa. The 23rd Tank Corps is to be pulled back into the area seven kilometers southwest of Jaszbereny in to the *front* reserve.

On this same 26 November the commander of the 30th Rifle Corps[1] was ordered to depart during the night of 26-27 November along the route Mezokovesd—Fuzesabony—Heves—Jaszapati—Jaszbereny and by the morning of 29 November to concentrate in the Toalmas area and to the east, where it was to be subordinated to the commander of the 7th Guards Army.

On 27 November the *front* commander issued directive no. 00745/op, according to which the troops were assigned the following objectives:

The commander of the 53rd Army was to break through the enemy's front with the forces of four rifle divisions along the front excluding Gyongyospata—Lorinci and develop the offensive in the general direction of Szarvasgebe and Szecseny.

The commander of the 7th Guards Army was to break through the enemy's defense with the forces of eight divisions (with six divisions in the first echelon) along the front Hered—excluding Aszod and develop the offensive in the general direction of Verseg, Csovar and Nyotencs With the army's arrival at the line Kekenies—Verseg—Pusztamagylos, it was to secure the commitment into the breach of the 6th Guards Tank Army and General Pliev's cavalry-mechanized group. By the close of the third day it was to capture the line Ipolszeg—Nograd—Veroce and completely reach the Danube with its left flank.

The commander of the 46th Army was ordered to force the Danube with the forces of six rifle divisions and the 2nd Guards Mechanized Corps and to develop the offensive in the general direction of Bicske, outflanking Budapest from the west.

The army was to seize bridgeheads along the right bank of the Danube on 30 November and 1 December.

The 2nd Guards Mechanized Corps was to be committed into the fighting on the second day of the offensive, with the task of attacking in the general direction of Etyek and Esztergom and to cut off the path of retreat for the enemy's Budapest group of forces to the west and northwest. The army's right wing was to launch active operations for the purpose of tying down the enemy's forces in Budapest.

With the arrival of the 7th Guards Army's units at the line Kekenies—Verseg—Puspokmagyalos, the commander of the 6th Guards Tank Army was to be ready to enter the breach and to develop an energetic offensive in the general direction of Verseg and Borsosbereny.

Upon the arrival of the 7th Guards Army's units at the line Lorinci—Kekenies, General Pliev, the commander of the cavalry-mechanized group, was to be ready to enter the breach behind the 6th Guards Tank Army and to develop an energetic offensive in the general direction of Kekenies, Sirok and Balassagyarmat.

The commander of the 5th Air Army was ordered to concentrate the activities of all his assault and bomber aviation along the 7th Guards Army's breakthrough front and, besides this, to allot

1 The 30th Rifle Corps was transferred to the Second Ukrainian Front from the *Stavka* of the Supreme High Command reserve.

one assault air division apiece for cooperating with the cavalry-mechanized group and the 6th Guards Tank Army, to cover the 7th Guards Army's main group of forces and the 46th Army's crossing; to cover the cavalry-mechanized group and the 6th Guards Tank Army.

Thus the general idea of the *front* commander's operation lay in the simultaneous double attack by means of a flanking maneuver to the east and west of Budapest, with a concentration of forces east of the city.

The 7th Guards Army would launch the main attack along a 9-kilometer front, with six divisions in the first echelon and two in the second. The army had been reinforced with two artillery divisions (5th and 16th). A total of 2,012 tubes (including 82mm mortars, without which there were 1,700 tubes) was concentrated along the main attack sector. The 6th Guards Tank Army, with 331 tanks, would be committed into the breach accomplished by the 7th Guards Army. Behind it, from behind its right flank, General Pliev's cavalry-mechanized group, consisting of the 4th and 6th guards mechanized corps, would be committed. The group had 99 tanks. The 27th Independent Tank Brigade, consisting of 62 tanks, was detailed for direct infantry support. Thus along the main attack sector the artillery density was 224 tubes per kilometer of front and a tank group with 492 tanks overall.

The 53rd Army, which was operating to the right of the 7th Guards Army, was to launch its attack with the forces of four divisions along a 7-kilometer front, with an artillery density of up to 100 tubes per kilometer of front. The army had no tanks. The 46th Army, which was operating to the left of the 7th Guards Army, was to direct its main efforts at overcoming the Danube and outflanking Budapest from the west. The army had been reinforced with the 2nd Guards Mechanized Corps. Overall, there were 160 tanks in the army.

In order to support the forcing of the Danube with artillery, an artillery group was created with a strength of 1,300 tubes. The crossing was to be supported in the engineer sense with ferries (seven ferries with a capacity of 50 tons and 18 with a capacity of 30 tons). Besides this, a floating 60-ton bridge from captured Krupp materials was being prepared, as well as a 16-ton bridge with high-level viaducts, with a floating part from the wooden bridge park.

The attack by the Second Ukrainian Front's left-wing forces. Their arrival at the Danube north of Budapest (5-9 December). By the close of 4 December the preparations for the offensive had been completed and the Second Ukrainian Front's left-wing forces occupied the following positions: 53rd Army, Eger—Lorinci; 7th Guards Army, excluding Lorinci—Tapiosuly—Szigetszentmiklos, and then along the eastern bank of the Danube; 6th Guards Tank Army was concentrated in the Hatvan—Tura area; General Pliev's cavalry-mechanized group (4th and 6th guards cavalry and 4th Guards Mechanized corps) in the Csani—Pusztamonostor—excluding Jaszdozsa area; 23rd Tank Corps in the area of the woods seven kilometers southwest of Jaszbereny, and; 2nd Guards Mechanized Corps in the area five kilometers east of Rackeve.

Operating opposite the Second Ukrainian Front's left-wing forces were units of the German Sixth and Hungarian Third armies, which by 4 December numbered 19 divisions, of which seven were tank, three motorized, seven infantry, and two cavalry. These forces were grouped in the following manner: the enemy had five divisions (three tank and two infantry) opposite the 53rd Army; the 7th Guards Army was opposed by seven divisions (three tank, two infantry and two motorized), and the enemy had seven divisions (three infantry, one tank, one motorized, and two cavalry) opposite the 46th Army.

By the start of the operation the Second Ukrainian Front's left-wing forces had 32 rifle divisions (nine in the 53rd Army, ten in the 7th Guards Army, ten in the 46th Army, and three in the *front* reserve).

By the start of the operation; that is, by 5 December the correlation of forces along the Budapest direction was as follows (table 3).

Table 3 Correlation of Forces Along the Budapest Direction, Second Ukrainian Front, 5 December 1944

Men and Materiel	Enemy	Our Forces	Correlation of Forces
Men	84,050	276,173	3.2:1
Tanks	164	492	3.0:1
Anti-Tank Guns	301	740	2.4:1
Artillery (all calibers) and mortars	751	2,012	2.7:1

Thus our forces outnumbered the enemy on an average of three to one. However, one should bear in mind that opposite the 53rd and 7th Guards armies' forces the enemy was defending in the Central Hungarian Mountains and the mountainous conditions enabled the enemy to conduct a defense with comparatively few forces: part of his forces had been detached to the reserve, which the enemy had an opportunity to maneuver. Opposite the 46th Army's forces the German-Hungarian troops were defending along the previously prepared and deeply developed defensive lines of the Budapest fortifications.

At 1015 on 5 December, following a brief but powerful artillery preparation, the 53rd, 7th Guards and 46th armies' combined-arms formations attacked. The 7th Guards Army's forces broke through the enemy's defense along the sector Hered—excluding Aszod and advanced 4-8 kilometers into the depth, having expanded the breakthrough front up to 18 kilometers. By order of the *front* commander, at 1530 the 6th Guards Tank Army was committed into the breach, because by this time the breakthrough had not been carried out to the entire depth and in places the tank troops had to finish the breakthrough of the enemy's defense. By the close of 5 December the lead units of the 9th Guards Mechanized Corps had captured Kekenies, while units of the 5th Guards Tank Corps were fighting for Verseg. The cavalry-mechanized group was not committed on the first day of the offensive.

The 53rd Army, which was operating to the right of the 7th Guards Army, advanced 2-4 kilometers on the first day, having encountered the enemy's stubborn resistance in the mountains.

The 46th Army, which was operating directly opposite Budapest from the south and outflanking it from the west, as early as 2300 on 4 December began to force the Danube with the forces of four rifle divisions along the sector excluding Erd—excluding Lorev. As a result of the most intense fighting, the army's forces successfully forced the Danube and, having seized bridgeheads along the western bank, advanced to a depth of 2-4 kilometers along almost the entire forcing sector. Along the right flank the army's units were fighting in individual detachments and by the close of the day occupied their former positions.

The 2nd Guards Mechanized Corps was not committed into the operation on this day. On 5 December it crossed in full a branch of the Danube River and concentrated in the Rackeve—Lorev area.

Thus on the offensive's first day (5 December) the enemy's defensive front along the 7th Guards Army's main attack axis had been broken through and the 6th Guards Tank Army committed into the breach. On this day the 46th Army's left-flank units forced the Danube and seized bridgeheads along its western bank. The 5th Air Army, while supporting the offensive of the *front's* forces along the Budapest direction, carried out 803 combat sorties that day, of which 419 were directed at bombing and strafing the enemy's men and equipment. 15 enemy planes were shot down in 15 air battles. The enemy's air force bombed the 7th Guards and 46th armies' combat formations and the crossings over the branch of the Danube and the Danube. 350 enemy sorties were noted this day.

Throughout the entire night of 5-6 December the fighting did not cease along entire front. At dawn on 6 December the troops continued to develop the offensive. The 6th Guards Tank Army captured Gula with units of the 9th Guards Mechanized Corps, while units of the 5th Guards

Tank corps took Csovar On 7 December the 6th Guards Tank Army began fighting for Bank with units of the 9th Guards Mechanized Corps, while the 5th Guards Tank Corps was fighting along the approaches to Vac along the bank of the Danube.

On 8 December the 9th Guards Mechanized Corps captured Diosjeno and Nograd; two brigades of the 5th Guards Tank Corps were engaged in street fighting for Vac, while another two brigades were outflanking the town from the southeast. On this day the commander of the 6th Guards Tank Army received orders to launch an attack with one corps, in conjunction with units of the 7th Guards Army, from the Vac area to the south along the Danube, with the task of capturing the Dunakeszi area. The army's remaining forces were to take the Dregelypalank—Nograd area and hold it until the arrival of the 7th Guards Army's combined-arms formations. In carrying out the new order, on 9 December units of the 6th Guards Tank Army's 9th Guards Mechanized Corps began fighting for Dregelypalank and the 5th Guards Tank Corps completely captured Vac and occupied Felsogod.

By the morning of 5 December General Pliev's cavalry-mechanized group had reached the Hatvan—Zsambok area and had still not been committed into the operation on this day. It began to move up into the breach behind the 6th Guards Tank Army only at 1330 on 6 December; that is, on the offensive's second day, while on that same day its 4th Guards Mechanized Corps captured Sirok; at 1900 the 6th Guards Cavalry Corps passed through Kekenies and at 2100 the 4th Guards Cavalry Corps was located five kilometers north of Verseg. Thus the cavalry-mechanized group's forces were actually only fighting with units of the 4th Guards Mechanized Corps on the second day of the offensive. On the following day (7 December) the cavalry-mechanized group's units were fighting in the Becske area and to the south. On 8 December, while continuing to develop the successes achieved, the 4th Guards Mechanized Corps, together with units of the 6th Guards Cavalry Corps, captured Nandor and Szud and continued the offensive on Balassagyarmat. Following intensive fighting on 9 December, the group's units captured Balassagyarmat. On this day General Pliev, the group commander, received an order from the *front* commander: while firmly consolidating Balassagyarmat until the infantry's arrival, launch an attack with the group's main forces to the east, with the task of capturing the Salgotarjan area by the close of 10 December.

Thus the mobile group of forces; that is, the 6th Guards Tank Army and units of General Pliev's cavalry-mechanized group advanced 60 kilometers in five days of attacking; that is, at an average speed of 12 kilometers per day. One should view this speed as normal in the difficult mountainous conditions and powerful enemy defense.

From the first day of the offensive; that is, from 5 December to the complete encirclement of the enemy's Budapest group of forces from the east and north on 9 December, the 7th Guards Army's combined-arms formations operated in close contact with the forces of the *front's* mobile groups—the 6th Guards Tank Army and General Pliev's cavalry-mechanized group.

As was mentioned earlier, the 7th Guards Army attacked at 1015 on 5 December and, having broken through the enemy's defense along the sector Hered—Aszod, as early as the first day of the offensive advanced 4-8 kilometers, widening the breakthrough front to 18 kilometers. On the second day of the operation the combined-arms formations, attacking behind the units of the 6th Guards Tank Army, advanced up to 20 kilometers along individual axes, capturing major and important inhabited locales, which had been prepared by the enemy for defense. In the unfolding fighting the German-Hungarian troops suffered heavy losses and under the blows from our tank and mechanized forces and pressure from the combined-arms formations were forced to fall back, partially to the north and partially to the northwest, toward Budapest. On 7 December the 7th Guards Army's offensive continued to just as successfully develop and its units advanced up to 15 kilometers. On the operation's fourth day (8 December) the army advanced another 17 kilometers and units from one of the divisions (53rd Rifle Division) reached the left bank of the Danube along the sector Veroce—Vac, thus cutting all the enemy's routes of retreat from Budapest to the east, northeast and north.

On 9 December the army's forces continued to develop the successes achieved and advanced in some areas up to 15 kilometers and by the close of the day were fighting along the line Ipolszeg—Dregelypalank—Diosjeno—Veroce, and then along the Danube as far as Felsogod and then through Orszentimiklos to Tapiosuly. The 7th Guards Army's forces in this vigorous offensive displayed high examples of organizing capability, toughness and decisiveness of action and great striking power.

The 53rd Army, which was operating to the right of the 7th Guards Army, advanced only with its left-flank units. The extremely difficult mountainous conditions along the Eger and Gyongyos axes denied them the opportunity of developing the offensive here and the army's formations along the sector from Eger to Gyongyos remained along their previous lines. By the close of 9 December the 53rd Army's forces were locate along the line Eger—Gyongyos—excluding—Bujak—excluding Megyer.

As has already been shown, throughout 5 December the 46th Army's left-flank units forced the Danube along the sector excluding Erd—excluding Lorev and by the close of that day had seized bridgeheads along the western bank of the Danube. During 6-9 December the army's right-flank formations, which were operating directly against Budapest from the south, encountered as before the enemy's stubborn resistance along the external defensive line and did not advance, remaining along the lines they occupied up to 5 December.

Throughout this entire time the army's left-flank units were engaged in intensive fighting to widen the bridgeheads seized along the western bank of the Danube. While breaking the enemy's bitter resistance and repelling powerful counterattacks by enemy tanks and infantry, the army's units gradually broadened the bridgeheads, securely holding the captured space. By the close of 9 December the 46th Army's forces were located along the line excluding Tapiosuly—excluding Vecses—excluding Rakocziliget—Szigetszentmiklos—the southern part of Erd—Gardony.

On 3 December the *front's* right-wing forces (40th and 27th armies) captured the major communications center and the enemy's powerful strong point, the city and railroad junction of Miskolc, an important center of military-industrial production, by a skillful turning movement and storming. Before 9 December the troops continued to attack and by the close of the day their main forces were located approximately along the same line as the left-wing forces. By this time the Third Ukrainian Front's right-wing forces, having defeat the enemy's Danube group of forces, had reached the enemy's "Margarita" defensive line and were along the same line as the 46th Army's left-flank units.

Thus as a result of a powerful attack by the 7th Guards and the 6th Guards Tank armies and General Pliev's cavalry-mechanized group, the powerful German-Hungarian Hatvan group of forces had been routed, while the Budapest group of forces had been divided from the Miskolc group. The routes of the enemy forces, which had been pushed into Budapest, had been cut off to the north, northeast, east, and south.

However, the task of the 46th Army's left-flank forces to encircle Budapest from the west remained unresolved. This army's forces had been halted by the enemy along the powerful "Margarita" defensive line and were not able to advance to the north. Now our forces operating opposite the enemy's Budapest group of forces were faced with two tasks—it was necessary to create a secure external front to the north and northwest of Budapest, in order to deprive the enemy of the opportunity of providing aid to Budapest from along these axes, and it was necessary to simultaneously continue to carry out the still unresolved task of encircling Budapest from the west.

The Third Ukrainian Front's Combat Operations (1-9 December)

By seizing an operational bridgehead along the western bank of the Danube, the size of which reached 50 kilometers in depth and 180 kilometers in width by 30 November, prerequisites were created for the Third Ukrainian Front's forces that would secure the opportunity to both concentrate men and materiel and the opportunity to maneuver them to develop the subsequent offensive along the Budapest axis. This offensive developed without pause and in the first days of January actually grew into a pursuit of the enemy forces, which were falling back to the north, northwest and west.

The development of the offensive by the 4th Guards and 57th armies from the bridgehead. The rout of the enemy's Danube group of forces and the arrival of the *front's* forces at the Germans' "Margarita" defensive line. On 30 November the situation of the forces of the Third Ukrainian Front, which were conducting an offensive along Hungarian territory, was as follows: the 4th Guards Army's right-flank 31st Corps was defending along the left bank of the Danube along the line excluding Nagy-Vadas—Baja, and the 20th and 21st corps, which had crossed the Danube, continued to attack in the general direction of Szekesfehervar. On 30 November units of these corps reached the line Tolna—Harc—Kisvaszar.

The 57th Army, consisting of the 6th Guards, 64th and 75th rifle corps, while developing the offensive in the general direction of Nagykanizsa, reached the line Sasd—Pellerd—eastern outskirts of Szalanta—eastern outskirts of Turony—east of Harkany—six kilometers west of Torjanc, and then along the left bank of the Drava River as far as Bilje. Units of the 1st Guards Fortified Area occupied a line along the left bank of the Danube along the Dalj—Cseb sector.[2]

The enemy had three infantry divisions, one motorized brigade, nine infantry regiments from different divisions, seven battalions, and one border group (in all, about 7-8 divisions) opposite the 4th Guards and 57th armies.[3]

During the first days of December the *front's* forces, while carrying out the mission assigned by the *front* command (*front* directive no. 00817/op of 12 November 1944), upon reaching the line Szekesfehervar—Lake Balaton—Nagykanizsa, were to continue the offensive from the bridgehead to the north and northwest.

During the night of 30 November–1 December the 4th Guards Army, with units of its right-flank 31st Guards Rifle Corps, in conjunction with a brigade of armored cutters from the Danube Military Flotilla and a brigade of naval infantry, forced the Danube in the Madocsa area and, having seized a bridgehead, began to successfully develop the offensive into the enemy's flank and rear. On 3 December the corps' units captured the town of Dunapentele. The forcing of the Danube along the army's right flank by the 31st Corps and the simultaneous successful development of the offensive along the army's left flank put the enemy in danger of encirclement and forced him to hastily withdraw. The army's left-flank units took up the pursuit of the enemy in the direction of the southeastern shore of Lake Balaton, outflanking the enemy's group of forces facing it from the southwest. Covering up to 80 kilometers in four days, on 4 December they reached the southeastern shore of Lake Balaton, captured Siofok and occupied a very important crossing in the Szanto area.

The enemy's attempts to halt the offensive by the army's forces along the right flank and center through bitter counterattacks with infantry and heavy tanks, supported by powerful artillery and mortar fire, were unsuccessful.

2 To the south were units of the Yugoslav People's Liberation Army (NOAYu) and units of the 37th Army.

3 The enemy's group of forces consisted of the 31st, 44th and 13th Muslim infantry divisions, 92nd Motorized Brigade, 44th, 194th, 750th, 99th, 8th, 749th, 1st, and 2nd infantry regiments.

The right-flank formations, while rolling up the enemy's defense along the Danube, on 8 December reached the southwestern extremity of Lake Velence. Units of the 31st Guards Rifle Corps linked up with units of the 46th Army (Second Ukrainian Front) in the area 12 kilometers northwest of Adony.

By the close of 8 December the 4th Guards Army had reached along the entire front the enemy's previously prepared defensive position along the line Lake Velence—Lake Balaton. Attempts by the army's units to break through the Germans' defense from the march along this line and to capture Szekesfehervar did not result in success. Our units penetrated the enemy's defense in only a few sectors on the night of 8-9 December, but were unable to develop this tactical success due to powerful organized fire and counterattacks by infantry and tanks by the enemy, who was relying on powerful defensive structures. On 9 December, in accordance with the order by the army commander, the 4th Guards Army went over to the defensive and began to prepare to break through the enemy's defensive zone, the so-called "Margarita" defensive line.

The 57th Army, while successfully developing the offensive to the northwest and west, by 5 December had reached the southeastern shore of Lake Balaton in the Balatonboglar area. By this time the army's forces along the Nagykanizsa axis had captured Marcali, Szigetvar along the left flank.

On 6 December the *Stavka* of the Supreme High Command, in its directive no. 206190, ordered the commander of the Third Ukrainian Front to temporarily halt the offensive and consolidate upon the 57th Army's arrival at the line southeastern shore of Lake Balaton—Nagykanizsa—the mouth of the Mura River (18 kilometers southwest of Nagykanizsa).

Throughout the following days the army's forces, while encountering continually increasing enemy resistance, advanced somewhat to the west and south and on 9 December the army's units on the right flank and in the center were consolidating along the lines reached, while repelling enemy counterattacks: along the left flank they crossed over to the southern bank of the Drava River in the Barcs area and, while developing the offensive to the south, captured the town and major road and railroad junction of Virovitica and making contact along this line with units of the Yugoslav People's Liberation Army (NOAYu).

The offensive by the Third Ukrainian Front's forces was supported from the air by the 17th Air Army. During the most decisive fighting, units of this army launched bombing and assault air attacks against the enemy's combat formations and rear establishments, inflicted heavy losses on the enemy's personnel and put a large amount of his combat equipment out of service, thus rendering a great service to the ground forces. For example, during the period 20-23 November up to 1,750 sorties were carried out, with 600 sorties carried out in two days (25 and 27 November). In the beginning of December, when our units encountered stubborn resistance and frenzied counterattacks by the enemy, who was relying on the fortified line which ran along the line Lake Velence—Lake Balaton, the 17th Air Army's aviation carried out about 800 sorties in two days (11-12 December).

By 10 December the Third Ukrainian Front's main forces had reached the powerful and previously prepared enemy defensive line and, upon going over to the defensive, began to regroup their forces and to prepare an offensive to the north, for the purpose of encircling the enemy's Budapest group of forces. With their arrival at the line of Lake Velence—Lake Balaton—excluding Nagykanizsa, the second stage of the Budapest operation ended for the forces of the Third Ukrainian Front.

As a result of the November offensive of the Third Ukrainian Front's 57th and 4th Guards armies along the western bank of the Danube, which was carried out according to the instructions of the *Stavka* of the Supreme High Command, the powerful German-Hungarian Danube group of forces was defeated, as well as recently arrived major enemy reserves from Yugoslavia, Italy and Hungary.

With their arrival at the powerful defensive line, which covered the approaches to Budapest from the south and southwest, the forces of the Third Ukrainian Front created the opportunity for concluding the complete encirclement of the enemy's Budapest group of forces from the west, because by this same time the forces of the Second Ukrainian Front had reached the Danube in the Vac area north of Budapest, cutting the enemy's communications to the east and north.

After the operation's second stage, the common efforts of the Second and Third Ukrainian fronts' forces could be directed for a simultaneous and coordinated attack, for the purpose of completing the encirclement of Budapest and the enemy's Budapest group of forces from the west.

Characteristic of the Second Ukrainian Front's forces during the operation's second stage is the vigor of their advance and their tenacity in achieving their assigned objectives. The force of the initial attack was so great that the enemy's operational depth was overcome during the first two days. The enemy was deprived of the opportunity for maneuver, thanks to the fact that his main communications, which ran to the northeast, were cut and the remnants of the defeated German-Hungarian forces were thrown back into the mountains. At the same time the *front's* right-flank armies (40th and 27th) developed a successful offensive, while preventing the enemy from removing forces from these sectors, so as to throw them into the fighting along the Budapest direction.

A very important factor in the second stage of the Budapest operation was the arrival of the Second Ukrainian Front's forces at the Danube north of Budapest. Thus were created not only all the conditions for the successful conclusion of the attack for the purpose of completely encircling Budapest from the west, but a favorable situation was also created for developing the Red Army's offensive into Czechoslovakia, which was extremely important for the forces of the Second Ukrainian Front.

4

The Encirclement of the Enemy's Budapest Group of Forces in Budapest (The Operation's Third Stage, 10-31 December 1944)

On 10 December the third stage of the Budapest operation began.

Its chief content was the completion of the encirclement of Budapest and the enemy's Budapest group of forces, the creation of an external front and the beginning of intensive fighting in the city.

Before our forces launched the December offensive; that is, before 20 December, the Second and Third Ukrainian front's combat activities developed in the following manner.

The Second Ukrainian Front's Combat Activities

The combat activities of the Second Ukrainian Front's left-wing forces during 10-19 December mainly came down to creating a secure external front along the Ipel River and the complete isolation of enemy group of forces encircled in Budapest from the Miskolc group. As early as 10 December units of the 6th Guards Tank Army's 9th Mechanized Corps captured the important road junction and inhabited locale of Dregelypalank along the southern bank of the Ipel River (50 kilometers north of Budapest) and, on this same day units of the 7th Guards Army's combined-arms formations arrived behind the mobile units. the 6th Guards Tank Army's 5th Tank Corps began fighting for Dunakeszi. Units of General Plievs' cavalry-mechanized group were continuing the fight to hold Balassagyarmat and were fighting for Szecseny. The 53rd Army advanced very little and the 46th Army was consolidating along the lines reached. The 5th Air Army did not carry out combat activities on 10 December, because of the poor meteorological conditions. On 11 December fighting continued along the entire front, with insignificant advances by our forces along some axes. On this day the *front* commander ordered the commander of the 7th Guards Army to relieve units of the 5th Guards Tank Corps and to concentrate them along the Sahy axis in the area to the north of Borsosbereny.

On 12 December the *Stavka* of the Supreme High Command, in its directive no. 220280, ordered the commanders of the Second and Third Ukrainian fronts to defeat the enemy's Budapest group of forces with a joint attack and to capture Budapest. According to this directive, the 46th Army, consisting of nine rifle divisions, the 2nd Guards Mechanized Corps and the 7th Breakthrough Artillery Division, with all reinforcements (including the 9th Anti-Aircraft Artillery and 12th Anti-Tank divisions, 45th Guards Artillery Brigade, and the 47th Guards Mortar and 92nd Guards Corps artillery regiments) from the Second Ukrainian Front was to be transferred to the Third Ukrainian Front from 2400 on 13 December.

The commander of the Second Ukrainian Front received orders, while continuing the offensive along the *front's* left wing on Budapest, to launch an attack with the forces of 2-3 rifle corps, the 6th Guards Tank Army and General Pliev's group, following the latter's completion of its local task of rolling up the enemy's defense facing the 53rd Army, from the Sahy area in the general direction of Szoldiny, with the task of reaching the northern bank of the Danube along the sector Neszmely—Esztergom and to prevent the withdrawal of the enemy's Budapest group of forces to the northwest.

Simultaneously, the commander of the Third Ukrainian Front received orders to launch an attack with the forces of the 46th and 4th Guards armies, along with the 18th Tank, 2nd Guards and 7th mechanized and 5th Guards Cavalry corps, from the Lake Velence area in the direction of Bicske and to reach the southern bank of the Danube along the sector Esztergom—Neszmely sector, in order to cut off the enemy's Budapest group of forces' path of retreat to the west. With part of its forces, the Third Ukrainian Front was to attack toward Budapest from the west and, in conjunction with the Second Ukrainian Front's left wing, to capture it. The *Stavka* designated 19-20 December as the start of the offensive for both *fronts*. Thus the idea by the *Stavka* of the Supreme High Command to completely encircle and defeat the enemy's Budapest group of forces lay in the simultaneous double concentric attack from the northeast to the southwest by the Second Ukrainian Front's forces, and from the south to the north by the Third Ukrainian Front.

The attack by the Second Ukrainian Front's left wing on Esztergom and Neszmely. From 12 December, along with the unremitting fighting for the creation of an exterior front and an attack from the north, east and south on Budapest, the staffs and forces of the Second Ukrainian Front carried out a broad-ranging preparation for the forthcoming offensive. The commander of the 18th Guards Rifle Corps, which was located in the *front* reserve in the Verseg—Tura area from 9 December, was ordered to concentrate in the Mende—Ullo—Vasad area, for the purpose relieving the 46th Army's right-flank units by the morning of 14 December. On 14 December units of the 9th Guards Mechanized Corps captured the important road junction and enemy defensive strong point of Sahy. On this day General Pliev, the commander of the cavalry-mechanized group, was ordered, having covered himself from the Szecseny area, to launch an attack in the general direction of Kisterenye with the task of capturing this area in cooperation with the 53rd Army's left-flank units. The 53rd Army's forces were to launch a decisive attack in the direction of Paszto and Kisterenye, together with units of General Pliev's cavalry-mechanized group and to destroy the opposing enemy and capture the line Nagyfaly—Kisterenye—Megyer.

In carrying out directive no. 220280 by the *Stavka* of the Supreme High Command, on 15 December the *front* commander issued order no. 00768/op, which assigned his forces the following tasks: the commander of the 7th Guards Army, having gone over to a temporary defensive during 16-17 December and having regrouped his main forces to the army's right flank, was to attack on the morning of 20 December with one corps in the direction of Szoldiny and Sakalos and with one corps in the direction of Szokolya, Marianosztra and Muzla and, in conjunction with the 6th Guards Tank Army, reach the line Zeliezovce—Szoldiny—Mocsa and then to the east along the Danube. The commander of the 6th Guards Tank Army received orders to be ready from the morning of 20 December to attack from the Sahy area, together with the 7th Guard's Army's right-flank units, in the direction of Szanto, with the task of seizing the road junctions of Levice and Svaty Jur on the Hron River and Szanto, in order to secure the operation from the north. The army was to occupy before 20 December its jumping-off position for the offensive from the Sahy area.

General Pliev's cavalry-mechanized group, having been drawn into prolonged fighting for Szecseny, failed to carry out before 15 December the task assigned it as early as 9 December regarding an attack to the east. On 15 December the *front* commander was forced to point out in a special instruction (no. 00770/op) that the group's operations were unfolding in an unsatisfactory manner and that the group's forces were marking time and that their activities were marked by indecisiveness and a lack of desire to thrust forward. The *front* commander ordered him to widely take advantage of the night and carry out the task assigned on 14 December regarding the group's arrival in the Kisterenye area, exactly according to schedule; that is, by 17 December.

During 15-18 December the Second Ukrainian Front's left-flank formations were fighting for the purpose of occupying a convenient position for the forthcoming offensive and for creating a secure external front, although it did not advance more or less significantly. General Pliev's cavalry-mechanized group was not able to develop the attack in the direction of Kisterenye.

At 1700 on 18 December the *front* commander, in his order no. 00776/op, refined the tasks assigned to the armies on 15 December, for the forthcoming offensive from the morning of 20 December. The task for the 7th Guards Army's right-flank units remained as before, although its left-flank formations (30th Guards Rifle Corps and the Romanian 7th Army Corps), were to also attack on the morning of 20 December, with the task, along with units of the 18th Guards Rifle Corps, of taking Budapest. On the morning of 20 December the 18th Guards Rifle Corps was to attack and capture the southern part of Budapest. The 6th Guards Tank Army's task remained as before: in conjunction with the 7th Guards Army's right flank, it was to attack on the morning of 20 December in the direction of Szanto, for the purpose of capturing the road junctions of Levice and Svaty Jur on the Hron River, and Szanto. On that same day, 18 December, the commander of the 53rd Army was ordered to relieve the units of General Pliev's cavalry-mechanized group, which was to concentrate by the morning of 21 December in the Dregelypalank—Ipolszeg area, where it would receive a new assignment.

On 19 December the 53rd Army was given the task, with its main forces along the left flank, of continuing the offensive for the purpose of reaching the front Vel'ky Krtis—Nemce—Zeliezovce. The 40th and 27th armies were also to continue the offensive.

In accordance with the orders received and the operational plans adopted, the formations of the Second Ukrainian Front's left wing occupied the following positions by the close of 19 December.

The 53rd Army was fighting along the front excluding Bator (35 kilometers north of Gyongyos)—Balassagyarmat. Along the Megyer—Szecseny sector units of General Pliev's cavalry-mechanized group were operating with the combined-arms formations. The 7th Guards Army was located along the front excluding Balassagyarmat—excluding Pecel (15 kilometers east of Budapest); in the Sahy area units of the 6th Guards Army were operating jointly with the combined-arms formations. The 18th Guards Rifle Corps occupied the sector of front excluding Pecel—Dunaharaszti.

The *front* reserve: 23rd Tank Corps had concentrated in the Kartal—Aszod—Bag area; the 297th Rifle Division was in the Cegled area and the 93rd Guards Rifle Division was moving to the Gyongyos area.

To the right, by the close of 19 December the 27th Army was fighting along its left flank along the front Visni (55 kilometers northeast of Gyongyos)—excluding Bator (32 kilometers northeast of Gyongyos); to the left, the 46th Army, as before, was facing the enemy's defensive line and preparing to launch an attack on Bicske on the morning of 20 December, and then on Esztergom and Neszmely.

By 19 December formations from the Germans' Eighth and Sixth armies and the Hungarian Third Army faced the Second Ukrainian Front's left wing. A detailed disposition of the enemy's forces is shown in table 4.

Thus during 10-19 December the Second Ukrainian Front's left-wing forces were engaged in extremely intense fighting to create a secure external front. Our units did not advance significantly, but by the day of the decisive attack for the complete encirclement of the enemy's Budapest group of forces a secure external front had been created, from which our units could attack. Simultaneously with the fighting that did not cease for even a single day, the business-like preparation for the forthcoming offensive was going on within the headquarters and among the troops, in conjunction with the Third Ukrainian Front's right-flank units, which were to launch an attack from Lake Velence to the north, through Bicske to Esztergom and Neszmely.

Table 4 Combat Strength of the Enemy Facing the Second Ukrainian Front Left-Wing, 19 December 1944

Facing the 53rd Army and General Pliev's cavalry-mechanized group: Hungarian 9th Border Division; Hungarian 27th Division; Hungarian combat groups "Noske," Botton," "Kavocs," and "Botke"; Hungarian 25th Infantry Division; 76th and 46th infantry divisions, SS *Polizei* Motorized Division, and the 18th SS Panzer Division (from the German Eighth Army).

Facing the 7th Guards and 6th Guards Tank armies: Hungarian 357th Infantry Division and 24th Cavalry Regiment; 8th Light Infantry Division; Danube Flotilla; *Feldherrnhalle* Motorized Division; 109th Panzer Brigade, 13th Panzer Division; Hungarian 10th Infantry Division, Hungarian 12th Light Infantry Division; 8th SS Infantry Division, Hungarian 1st Panzer Division, 22nd SS Infantry Division, Hungarian 1st Cavalry Division, and the 10th Motorized Division (east of Lucenec).

Facing the 46th Army: Hungarian 271st Infantry Division, 24th Infantry Regiment/20th Infantry Division, 8th Panzer Division, 239th Assault Gun Brigade, Hungarian 1st Panzer Regiment, Hungarian 1st Panzer Division, and units of Hungarian 1st Cavalry Division and a screening detachment.

At 1000 on 20 December the Second Ukrainian Front's left-wing forces attacked. The most decisive successes on the first day of the offensive were achieved by the forces of the 6th Guards Tank Army. Its 9th Guards Mechanized Corps, while vigorously developing the offensive, captured Moravce by the close of the day and, without halting, continued to advance toward Nagysany. The 5th Guards Tank Corps captured Magyarovce, Szanto, Chankov, Varsani, Levice, and Mytne-Ludany with a vigorous attack and by the close of 20 December was already fighting for Kalnica along the bank of the Hron River.

Thus as early as the first day of the attack units of the 6th Guards Tank Army, having broken through the enemy's defense, advanced in a narrow wedge as much as 32 kilometers into the depth of the enemy's position and, having seized the main dirt and paved road junctions (Szanto, Levice, Moravce, and others), deprived the enemy of his freedom of maneuver from Levice to Sahy.

On the first day of the offensive the 53rd Army made only local advances. The 7th Guards Army enjoyed the greatest success on the first day of the offensive in the mountainous and wooded area south of Sahy. Here the important road junction and powerful strong point in the enemy's defense of Nagyboerzsoeny was taken, and the army's combined-arms formations reached the front excluding Bernece—Nagyboerzsoeny—Ipolytotoyes—Szob—Nagymaros, having thus overcome the mountainous and wooded area and entered the plain of the Ipel River.

On the army's right flank, to the west of Balassagyarmat, there was little progress and Koszeg and Inam and a number of other inhabited locales were occupied by our forces. The army's left-flank units, which were attacking directly on Budapest, did not advance very far. In accordance with the *front* commander's order, General Pliev's cavalry-mechanized group, having turned over its combat sectors to the 53rd Army's units by the close of 20 December, concentrated in the Dregelypalank—Vadkert—Ipolszeg area.

In the following days, from 21-26 December, very intense fighting unfolded to the southwest of Sahy, between the Hron and Ipel rivers. The enemy, having brought up units of the 6th and 8th panzer divisions and a motorized regiment from the 3rd Panzer Division, as early as the second half of the day attacked simultaneously from the Dolne Zemberovce area with the forces of up to two infantry divisions and a *panzer* division, attacking to the south and from the Sakalos area and attacking toward Sahy. At the same time the enemy made a number of powerful counterattacks against the right-flank forces from the Nekia area toward Inam. By launching attacks from the area of Dolne Zemberovce and Sakalos, the enemy tried to prevent our troops' advance to the west from the Ipel River and to simultaneously threaten the 6th Guards Tank Army's rear establishments.

Following the unsuccessful counterattacks of 20-21 December, the enemy continually increased the strength of his attacks and on 22 December up to 125 tanks and assault guns took part in his attacks.

Having been drawn into the fighting against the 7th Guards Army's infantry in the Sakalos area and to the north, the enemy exposed his left flank to an attack by the 6th Guards Tank Army. As early as 21 December, the *front* commander ordered the 6th Guards Tank Army, upon covering itself with part of its forces from the north, to launch an attack with its main forces to the south along the eastern bank of the Hron River, for the purpose of encircling and destroying the enemy, in conjunction with the 7th Guards Army's combined-arms formations, operating between the Hron and Ipel rivers.

In order to carry out the order, the commander of the 6th Guards Tank Army, having left two of the 9th Guards Mechanized Corps' brigades in the Dolne Zemberovce area, created a shock group from units of the 5th Guards Tank Corps, which as early as 0500 on 22 December reached the area Lekyrsky—Bielovce area with two brigades.

On the morning of 22 December the enemy once again launched a series of fierce attacks in the Viskovce—Novy—Ivanka area, for the purpose of cutting our troops' communications in the Tompa—Slatina area. By the close of 22 December the enemy managed to break through the 7th Guards Army's front and reach the Tompa—Grkovce area. In order to eliminate the breakthrough, two of the 9th Guards Mechanized Corps' brigades were quickly moved from the Bielovce area to the Lontov area, where on 22 December they got into a fight with the enemy's tanks. For this purpose, the *front* commander ordered General Pliev to roust the 4th Guards Mechanized Corps and move it to the Krinta—Tompa—Grkovce area, where it was to take up a perimeter defense with the task of preventing the enemy's further development of the breakthrough. The corps reached the designated area by the morning of 22 December and entered the fighting. From 23 December the 4th Guards Mechanized Corps was transferred to the 6th Guards Tank Army.

In order to free all this army's forces to carry out its main task of defeating the German-Hungarian forces in the area between the Hron and Tisza rivers, the *front* commander ordered General Pliev, the commander of the cavalry-mechanized group, to relieve units of the 6th Guards Tank Army, which were covering the operation from the north, and to take up defensive positions along the line Fedimes—Iskorn—Plastovce and to securely hold the line Nagysany—Dolne Zemberovce—Levice.

The fighting by the 6th Guards Tank Army and the 7th Guards Army to eliminate the enemy's breakthrough group and to encircle and defeat the German-Fascist troops between the Hron and Ipel, continued to 29 December. Throughout 23 December units of the 6th Guards Tank Army were fighting north of Zalaba, west of Sakalos and northwest of Setik.

On this day the 7th Guards Army forced the Ipel River with part of its forces in the Leleghidi area and was fighting for Leleg and Helemba.

On 24 December units of the 6th Guards Tank Army continued the intensive fighting to destroy the enemy's tank group in the areas of Trginja and to the west of Setik. Units of the 7th Guards Army were energetically beating off the enemy's attacks and themselves repeatedly counterattacked, but, upon encountering the enemy's resistance, did not advance very far.

Starting on 25 December a break in our favor was noted in the fighting between the Hron and Ipel. On this day units of the 6th Guards Tank Army captured Lontov and Pincek, broke into Sakalos and began street fighting. Units of the 7th Guards Army, having repelled several powerful enemy infantry attacks, supported by large groups of tanks from the areas of Viskovce, Pekocseny and Vamosmikola, captured Ivanka and Lontov by the close of the day.

26 December was the decisive day for the entire operation to encircle the enemy's Budapest group of forces and Budapest. On this day the 6th Guards Tank Army's forces captured Sakov, Darmotky, Pald, Sakalos, and Bielovce and were fighting north of Kicsind and along the approaches

to Pastovce. Units of the 7th Guards Army, having repelled enemy counterattacks, each launched with the forces of 1-2 battalions and 6-12 tanks and assault guns, captured Viskovce and Lelde by the close of the day and simultaneously were advancing along the northern bank of the Danube from Helemba to Haramkevesg. On 26 December the Third Ukrainian Front's right-wing forces, which were attacking from the area of Lake Velence and Lake Balaton through Bicske toward Esztergom and Neszmely, reached the southern bank of the Danube and captured Esztergom, linking up with the forces of the Second Ukrainian Front operating along the northern bank of the Danube. Thus on 26 December all of the routes of retreat for the enemy's Budapest group of forces to the west and northwest were cut. The encirclement ring around Budapest and around the troops grouped inside and outside the city was closed. The Budapest group of forces, consisting of the German 13th Panzer Division, the SA *Feldherrnhalle* Motorized Division, 271st Infantry Division, the 8th and 29th cavalry divisions, and 239th Assault Gun Brigade, and the Hungarian 1st Panzer, 10th, 12th and 13th infantry divisions, 1st Security Regiment, 3rd Police Regiment, and the 206th Reserve Regiment wound up in the latest "cauldron."

On 27 December the 6th Guards Tank Army, in conjunction with units of the 7th Guards Army, completed the encirclement of the enemy forces operating between the Hron and Ipel rivers and was fighting to destroy them. By the close of the day the 7th Guards Army's units were fighting to take Haramakevesg. On 29 December this locale was taken. On 28 December the 7th Guards Army completed the destruction of the encircled enemy group of forces between the rivers and reached the eastern bank of the Hron River along the sector from Svaty Jur to the river's mouth. The army forced the Hron River in the Kicsind—Haramkevesg area with part of its forces, having seized some small bridgeheads.

On 29 December the commander of the 6th Guards Tank Army received orders to pull the army's units back to the Dolne Semerovce—Bory—Gont Darmotky—Saedice area for refitting and to prepare to carry out subsequent combat tasks.

During 22-29 December, simultaneous with the fighting that had unfolded between the Hron and Ipel rivers, intense fighting was going on directly for Budapest. By 29 December the 53rd Army had reached the front Kutas—Szecseny—Balassagyarmat, and General Pliev's cavalry-mechanized group was fighting along the front excluding Balassagyarmat—Plastovce—excluding Moravce—Dolne Zemberovce—Levice—Svaty Jur. Thus the task assigned by the *Stavka* of the Supreme High Command to the Second Ukrainian Front to encircle, in conjunction with the forces of the Third Ukrainian Front, the enemy's Budapest group of forces, had been accomplished. However, the forces of the 6th Guards Tank and 7th Guards armies were not able to reach the Neszmely area. The encirclement ring had been closed in the Esztergom area. By the close of 29 December the Second Ukrainian Front's left-wing forces occupied the following line: the 53rd Army, Kutas—Szecseny—Balassagyarmat; The cavalry mechanized group, excluding Balassagyarmat—Plastovce—Dolne Zemberovce—Levice—excluding Svaty Jur on the Hron; the 7th Guards Army, along the Hron River from Svaty Jur to the mouth and then along the Danube to the northern outskirts of Budapest and then along Budapest. The 6th Guards Tank Army had concentrated in the area of Dolne Semerovce—Bory—Gont Darmotky—Saedice. The *front* reserve (23rd Tank Corps) was, as before, located in the Kartal—Aszod—Bag area, and the 93rd Rifle Division in the Krinta—Tompa—Sahy area.

Combat Activities of the Third Ukrainian Front's Forces (20-31 December 1944)

By the middle of December 1944 the situation of the Third Ukrainian Front's forces along the Budapest direction was characterized by the decisiveness of combat activities, which were being prepared for the purpose of completely finishing the encirclement of the Budapest group of forces. The German command was taking all measures in order to hold along the previously prepared and powerful defensive line that ran along the line Erd—Lake Velence—Lake Balaton, understanding that the fate of the city depended on the breakthrough of this defense covering Budapest from the southwest.

The defensive line of the German-Hungarian forces covering Budapest from the south and southwest had been prepared beforehand and was built along terrain naturally favorable to the defense. The left flank of the defense was covered by the powerful water barrier of the Danube, with the right flank by Lake Balaton. It was as if the entire defensive line was divided into two independent sectors by Lake Velence, which was located in the center of the defense. The open terrain in front of the forward edge of the defense, which offered good visibility and firing, did not offer the attackers covered approaches. Between lakes Velence and Balaton the approaches to the forward edge were made difficult along many sectors by swamps and a large number of reclamation canals. In the depth of the defense the terrain is rife with a large number of heights, which make it difficult for an attacker to espy the depth of the defense. The heights and hills were employed by the enemy for organizing strong points and observation posts on them.

The enemy's defensive line represented field-type fortifications, developed up to 15 kilometers in depth. The depth was created by the presence of second and third defensive lines, as well as by employing all of the inhabited locales in the defensive zone as strong points and centers of resistance. The approaches to the forward edge along the main axes were covered by anti-tank ditches and minefields along certain sectors.

A second defensive line was built in the tactical depth (3-6 kilometers), which represented a chain of resistance centers and strong points (Tarnok, Tordas, Kajaszoszentpeter, Pazmand, Janostanya, and Nadap).

The terrain along which ran the "Margarita" line, rising above the terrain occupied by our forces, enabled the enemy to create a good observation system and to control our tactical depth and immediate approaches with fire. Steep embankments and railway cuttings along the railroads and roads, which had been skillfully prepared in a number of places against tanks, were barriers that were hard to overcome.

The organization of the defense in the defile between lakes Velence and Balaton did not much differ in character from the defense along the sector Erd—Lake Velence. The enemy here had field-type defensive structures, with two prepared lines: the first ran along the line Borgond—Tac—south of Polgardi—Balatonfokajar, and the second along the line Kisfalud—Szekesfehervar—Varpalota—Fuzfo.

Along the axis of the 4th Guards Army's main attack, in the Lake Velence—Sarviz Canal zone, the enemy had a developed system of trenches, open in one, two and, in places, three lines, with attached foxholes for firing and machine gun nests. A small number of covered wood and earthen firing points had been built along the swampy sector west of Lake Velence. The most important roads along the main axes had been covered with anti-tank and anti-personnel explosive obstacles.

On the whole, the enemy facing the 4th Guards Army had a tactically favorable and engineering outfitted defensive line, located along the slopes of the commanding heights. In connection with the terrain naturally favorable to the defense, this was a powerful defensive line, which covered the approaches to the Germans' very important strong point of Szekesfehervar.

Having occupied the defensive line and having temporarily stabilized their front, the Germans began to urgently improve and strengthen their defense in the engineering sense.

The enemy, while striving to hold our offensive through stubborn defense and fierce counterattacks, was simultaneously preparing a major counteroffensive against the Third Ukrainian Front's forces for the purpose of throwing then against the left bank of the Danube and removing the danger of the Budapest group of forces being encircled.

As was stated earlier, the idea of the offensive operation and our forces' tasks along the Budapest direction had been determined by a *Stavka* of the Supreme High Command directive of 12 December 1944.

The Third Ukrainian Front's forces received orders to launch an attack from the Lake Velence area in the direction of Bicske, so as to arrive at the southern bank of the Danube along the Esztergom—Neszmely sector and to cut off the retreat route of the Budapest group of forces to the west.

Part of the *front's* forces was to attack Budapest from the west and, in conjunction with the Second Ukrainian Front's left flank, capture Budapest. As has already been mentioned, the beginning of both *fronts'* offensive was set for 19-20 December.

In carrying out the directive by the *Stavka* of the Supreme High Command, the commander of the Third Ukrainian Front, Marshal of the Soviet Union Tolbukhin,[1] decided to prepare the breakthrough simultaneously along two sectors with the forces of the 46th and 4th Guards armies.

The 46th Army received orders to prepare to break through the enemy's defense along the sector northwest of Baracska—Kapolnasnyek with the forces of two rifle corps (seven rifle divisions), plus reinforcements. It was ordered to launch the main attack toward Etyek and Bicske. In order to support the shock group, the army was to prepare an auxiliary attack with the forces of a single rifle division from the Baracska area in the direction of Tordas. Upon breaking through the enemy's defense, the army was to launch an attack with the forces of one rifle corps north of Lake Velence toward Lovasbereny to assist the 4th Guards Army in taking Szekesfehervar.

The 46th Army's immediate task was to defeat the enemy group of forces between the Vali River and Lake Velence and capture the line Tordas—Lovasbereny, where the 2nd Guards Mechanized Corps would be committed into the breach, with the immediate objective of reaching the Etyek—Zsambek—Bicske area, from where it was to be ready to capture the western part of Budapest, in conjunction with the infantry.

The 46th Army was to subsequently develop the offensive to the northeast and, in conjunction with the 18th Tank Corps, cut the retreat route of the enemy's Budapest group of forces to the west, encircle and destroy it and captured the western part of Budapest as far as the Danube.

The accomplishment of the assigned tasks by days was planned in the following manner.

No later than the offensive's second day, the 46th Army's units were to capture the line Ofalu—Lovasbereny. By the close of the fourth or fifth day, while developing the attack to the northeast, it was to reach the line Danube River—Erd—Soskut—Etyek—Zsambek, having at this time along the front Zsambek—Etyek no less than a rifle corps (three rifle divisions) ready to attack Budapest together with the 2nd Guards Mechanized Corps.

By the close of the eighth or ninth day of the operation, the 46th Army, together with units of the 4th Guards Army and the 18th Tank Corps, had the mission of completely defeating the enemy's encircled group of forces, capturing the western part of Budapest and reaching at the same time the Danube along the army's entire front.

The 4th Guards Army received orders to break through the enemy's defense with three rifle corps southwest of Lake Velence along the front height 130 (four kilometers southwest of Dinnyes)—height 124 (two kilometers east of Potolle). With three rifle corps (five rifle divisions) in the first echelon, the army was to launch its main attack in the general direction of Szekesfehervar and a supporting one—with the forces of a rifle division—toward Szabadbattyan.

1 Editor's note. Fedor Ivanovich Tolbukhin (1894-1949) joined the imperial Russian army in 1914 and the Red Army four years later. During World War II he served as a *front* chief of staff and as an army and *front* commander. Following the war, Tolbukhin commanded the southern group of forces in the Balkans and a military district.

The army's immediate objective was to defeat the enemy's group of forces between Lake Velence and the Sarviz Canal and capture the city of Szekesfehervar. The army was to subsequently develop the offensive with two rifle corps on Csakvar and Szar and reach the front Esztergom—Neszmely—Tata—Kornye. One rifle corps (two rifle divisions), together with the 7th Mechanized Corps, was to develop the attack in the direction of Mor and Varpalota. The 7th Mechanized Corps also had the task, together with the left-flank rifle corps, of roll up the enemy's combat formations between the Sarviz Canal and Lake Balaton. As a result, the 4th Guards Army was to reach the line Almasfuzito—Tata—Banhida—Mor—Varpalota—Osku—the northeastern shore of Lake Balaton and securely support from the west and southwest the encirclement and destruction of the enemy's Budapest group of forces and the capture of Budapest.

The missions by day were planned in the following manner: to capture Szekesfehervar by no later than the first or second day and reach the line Patka—Szekesfehervar—Osi—Polgardi. By the close of the third or fourth day, while developing the attack with mobile formations, to reach the line Szar—Verteskozma and create a stable security front along the line west of Mor—Varpalota—Osku—Fuzfo. It was planned to secure the base of the breakthrough most securely. The army was simultaneously instructed to keep one division in reserve in the Szekesfehervar area.

By the close of the fifth or sixth day of the operation, the 4th Guards Army, with one rifle corps in the Bajna—Tarjar area (both locales 18-26 kilometers southwest of Esztergom), ready to attack together with the 18th Tank Corps on Budapest, was to reach the security line indicated for the final task with its remaining forces.

The plan called for the commitment of the 7th Mechanized Corps into the breach following the capture of Szekesfehervar, with the task of capturing the Mor area and, the Varpalota area together with the army's infantry, in order to encircle and destroy the enemy group of forces southwest of Szekesfehervar. Upon the infantry's arrival at these lines, it was planned to pull the 7th Mechanized Corps into the army reserve.

It was planned to commit the *front's* mobile formations in the 4th Guards Army's sector.

The *front* commander, in his operational directive no. 00962/op of 18 December, assigned the commander of the 18th Tank Corps[2] that upon the capture of Szekesfehervar by the army's infantry, it was to enter the breach and develop the offensive in the general direction of Csakvar, Many and Esztergom.

By the close of the operation's second day, the 18th Tank Corps was to reach the Tokod—Nyergesujfalu—Bajna—Dorog area and cut the retreat of the enemy's Budapest group of forces to the west and northwest. The corps was ordered to capture with part of its forces by the close of the third day the pass west of Pilisvorosvar. Simultaneously, it was planned that in case the operation by the forces of the 4th Guards Army to capture Szekesfehervar and the success of the offensive east of Lake Velence should be delayed, the corps should be committed into the breakthrough in the 46th Army's sector, with the subsequent arrival at its own axis.

According to the plan, the 5th Guards Cavalry Corps, along with reinforcement units, was to be committed into the breakthrough for developing the 7th Mechanized and 18th Tank corps' success along the following axes: Csakvar—Szar—Tata and Csakbereny—Kornye. Before the arrival of the 4th Guards Army's infantry, the cavalry corps was to deploy with part of its forces along the line Neszmely—Tata—Banhida—Kornye—Pusztavam and conduct reconnaissance to the west. The beginning of the 46th and 4th Guards armies' offensive was planned for 20 December.

2 The 18th Tank Corps consisted of the 110th, 170th and 181st tank brigades, the 78th Independent Motorized Pontoon Battalion, 419th Independent Signals Battalion, the 32nd Motorized Rifle Brigade, and artillery. The corps was reinforced from the *front* reserve with two regiments from the 42nd Anti-Tank Artillery Brigade, two regiments from the 22nd Anti-Aircraft Division, one mortar and one guards mortar regiments.

Thus the plan of the commander of the Third Ukrainian Front came down to simultaneously breaking through the enemy's defense along two neighboring sectors of the front with the forces of the 46th and 4th Guards armies. Following the breakthrough of the enemy's defense, both shock groups, while vigorously developing the offensive to the north toward the Danube along the Esztergom—Neszmely toward the Second Ukrainian Front's formations, were to complete with them the complete encirclement of the enemy's Budapest group of forces. During this offensive the 46th Army's main forces and part of the 4th Guards Army's forces, in conjunction with the 18th Tank Corps, were to turn around to the northeast from the front Bicske—Zsambek and create an internal encirclement ring around the German-Hungarian forces located in the city itself. At the same time, the forces of the 4th Guards Army, in conjunction with the 5th Guards Cavalry Corps, would create an external front, reliably securing from the west and southwest the encirclement and elimination of the encircled enemy group of forces in Budapest.

The overall depth of the *front* operation was 65-85 kilometers.

A depth of 65-70 kilometers was planned for the 46th Army's operation and up to 85 kilometers for the 4th Guards Army. The length of the operation for accomplishing the complete encirclement of the enemy's Budapest group of forces was determined at 5-6 days. In the armies the pace of the offensive was planned at 8-13 kilometers per day while carrying out the immediate tasks and at 16-20 kilometers per day in carrying out their subsequent tasks.

The armies' combat formations were organized as follows.

The 46th Army had six rifle divisions along the main attack axis: there were four divisions (two divisions from each corps) in the first echelon and two divisions in the second. Besides this, the army commander had one rifle division, reinforced with a regiment of self-propelled artillery at his disposal along the main axis.

In the 4th Guards Army there were seven rifle divisions along the main axis, of which five were in the first echelon and two divisions in the second. There was one division in the army reserve.

The 46th and 4th Guards armies had a mechanized corps apiece for developing the success following the breakthrough and for pursuing the enemy.

33 artillery and mortar regiments (not counting guards mortars) had been brought in along the 46th Army's breakthrough sector. The average density per kilometer of front along the breakthrough sector reached 99 tubes (not counting 45mm guns). The length of the artillery preparation was set at 40 minutes.

In the 4th Guards Army a density of up to 183 tubes per kilometer of front was created along the axis of the main attack. The artillery preparation was planned to last 65 minutes. The offensive by the *front's* armies would be supported by the 17th Air Army.

Preparing the operation. The preparation for breaking through the enemy's defensive zone for the purpose of encircling and destroying the German-Hungarian Budapest group of forces unfolded in the armies from 10 December and continued up to 19 December, inclusively. During this period the concentration, regrouping and training of forces was underway, as well as the drawing up the plans for the offensive operation, the preparation of the bridgeheads for the offensive in the main attack sector and the all-round reconnaissance of the enemy.

Along the left flank of the 4th Guards Army's front during the preparatory period, operational masking was successfully carried out for the purpose of distracting the enemy's attention to the secondary axis. Alongside active measures to improve the jumping-off positions in the area south of Tac and the groves south of Kelestelek, false artillery position areas were built and 50 false guns set up. "Roving" guns fired to liven up the firing positions along the army's left flank. 65 false tanks were built along this same flank in the area of the northern outskirts of Ening. In order to liven up the concentration area, several tanks and self-propelled guns churned up the ground. The appearance of movement of supplies, tanks and motorcycles to the front was carried out along the sector of the southern shore of Lake Balaton, along roads running along the shore.

The enemy, who had been deceived by our measures, carried out intensified reconnaissance, particularly in the Ening area, where he "managed to unearth a concentration" of tanks and artillery batteries.

Throughout 18 December the enemy waged intensive artillery fire from long-range artillery and cutters from the Lake Balaton Flotilla was waged against the area of false artillery positions.

Besides the enumerated measures, according to the operational masking plan, the work of the army's radio stations in their former sector created the appearance that the disposition of the army's main forces along the left flank had not changed. Defensive work (digging trenches, setting up wire obstacles, false mining, etc.) was carried out on a large scale along the axis of the main attack during the operation's preparatory period.

The well thought-out and successfully conducted measures for operational masking along the entire front guaranteed that our offensive would be a surprise for the enemy, which facilitated the operation's success.

On 19 December the Third Ukrainian Front's forces fully completed their preparations for the operation. By the close of the day the sides' situation was as follows.

Opposite the *front's* left flank the enemy was defending with formations of the Germans' Sixth Army and the Hungarian Third Army, consisting of two infantry, one *panzer* and one cavalry divisions, as well as a brigade of assault guns, three infantry regiments from various divisions and seven battalions, as well as reinforcements. The forward edge of the German-Hungarian forces' defense ran along the line north of Szigetszentmiklos—Erd—Baracska—Velence.

Opposite the *front's* left wing was an enemy group of forces with an overall strength of up to six infantry divisions and two panzer divisions, with reinforcements. The forward edge of the enemy's defense ran along the line Pakozd—east of Borgond—Kulsobarand—north of Potolle—Tac—Besnye—north of Balatonfokajar—Balatonakarttya.

The Third Ukrainian Front's forces, which were operating along the Budapest direction, occupied the following position[3]: the 46th Army was located along a line 1.5 kilometers northeast of Szigetszentmiklos—excluding Erd and then to the southwest to the shore of Lake Velence. The overall length of the army's front reached 38 kilometers by the start of the offensive. The 23rd Rifle Corps, which occupied a front of 28 kilometers, was along the army's right flank along an auxiliary axis.

The 37th and 10th Guards corps, with an overall strength of six rifle divisions, were concentrated along the left flank along the axis of the main attack. These two corps occupied a 10-kilometer front from Baracska to Lake Velence (west of Kapolnasnyek). The 2nd Mechanized Corps was located within the left-flank rifle corps' zone, at a distance of 5-7 kilometers from the forward edge. One rifle division was concentrated in the Erigyesmajor area as the army commander's reserve.

The 4th Guards Army occupied a 44-kilometer line from the southwestern shore of Lake Velence to Lake Balaton. The army was to launch its main attack along its right flank between Lake Velence and the Sarviz Canal, along the sector excluding Borgond—Potolle. The 31st and 20th guards and 135th rifle corps were concentrated here. The 21st Guards Rifle Corps was located along the remainder of the front, from the Sarviz Canal to Lake Balaton, along the secondary axis, while the 7th Mechanized Corps was concentrated in the area to the south and southeast

3 By 20 December the Third Ukrainian Front had two armies (46th and 4th Guards) along the Budapest direction, while the 57th Army continued to operate southwest of Lake Balaton and did not take part in the Budapest operation of December 1944. The 37th Army, which was part of the Third Ukrainian Front, was removed from the *front* by a *Stavka* of the Supreme High Command order on 12 December and subordinated directly to the *Stavka*.

of Sarkeresztur, and the 18th Tank Corps in the Nagyperkata—Sarosd area, and the 5th Guards Cavalry Corps was to concentrate in the area west of Hercegfalva by the close of 19 December.

Such was the jumping-off situation of the Third Ukrainian Front's forces before the start of the offensive.

As a result of the concentration and regrouping of its forces, by 20 December the Third Ukrainian Front had achieved the following correlation of forces: 1:3.3 in men, 1:4.8 in guns, 1:3.5 in tanks and self-propelled guns, and 1:1.25 in planes.

Thus along the entire front and particularly along the axes of the main attacks, the Third Ukrainian Front's forces had achieved a superiority in men and materiel.

A detailed combat composition of the Third Ukrainian Front's forces and those of the enemy along the Budapest direction is shown in table 5.

Table 5 Correlation of Forces Along the Budapest Direction, Third Ukrainian Front, 20 December 1944

A. The Third Ukrainian Front's Forces Along the Budapest Direction by 20 December 1944

46th Army

10th Guards Rifle Corps—49th Guards, 180th and 109th Guards rifle divisions;

23rd Rifle Corps—83rd Naval Infantry Brigade, 99th and 316th rifle divisions;

37th Rifle Corps—59th Guards, 108th Guards and 320th rifle divisions.

Units subordinated to the army—86th Guards Rifle Division; 1897th, 991st and 1505th self-propelled artillery regiments.

7th Artillery Division—11th Light Artillery Brigade (210th and 525th light artillery regiments), 25th Howitzer Brigade (124th, 320th and 877th howitzer regiments), 17th Cannon-Artillery Brigade (213th and 1092nd cannon-artillery regiments), 9th Cannon-Artillery Brigade (215th and 216th cannon-artillery regiments), 3rd Mortar Brigade (101st, 103rd and 107th mortar regiments), 105th Heavy Howitzer Brigade, 12th Anti-Tank Artillery Brigade (417th, 1255th and 1658th anti-tank artillery regiments), 9th Anti-Aircraft Artillery Division (800th, 974th, 981st, and 993rd anti-aircraft artillery regiments), 45th Guards Cannon-Artillery Brigade, 437th Anti-Tank Artillery Regiment, 462nd Motorized Regiment, 92nd Guards Corps Artillery Regiment, and 47th Guards Mortar Regiment.

2nd Guards Mechanized Corps—4th, 5th and 6th guards mechanized brigades, 37th Guards Tank Brigade, 30th Guards Tank Regiment, 251st Guards and 1509th self-propelled artillery regiments, 524th Motorized Regiment, 408th Guards Mortar Battalion, 99th Guards Motorcycle Battalion, and 159th Anti-Aircraft Artillery Regiment.

51st Engineer-Sapper Brigade.

4th Guards Army

20th Guards Rifle Corps—5th and 7th guards airborne divisions, 80th Guards Rifle Division;
21st Guards Rifle Corps—41st, 62nd and 69th guards rifle divisions;
31st Guards Rifle Corps—4th, 34th and 40th guards rifle divisions;
135th Rifle Corps—84th and 252nd rifle divisions.
9th Artillery Division—26th Light Artillery Brigade (407th and 456th light artillery regiments), 23rd Howitzer Brigade (212th, 221st and 230th howitzer regiments), 30th Cannon-Artillery Regiment (222nd and 1232nd cannon-artillery regiments), 10th Mortar Brigade (188th, 200th and 205th mortar regiments), 42nd Anti-Tank Artillery Brigade, 123rd Cannon-Artillery Brigade, 438th, 521st and 1312th anti-tank artillery regiments, 466th Mortar Regiment, 5th Anti-Aircraft Artillery Division (1089th, 1114th and 1118th anti-aircraft artillery regiments), 22nd Anti-Aircraft Artillery Division (1335th, 1341st, 1347th, 1353rd, 257th, and 1384th anti-aircraft artillery regiments), 56th Engineer-Sapper Brigade, and 152nd Howitzer Regiment.
7th Mechanized Corps—41st Guards Tank Brigade, 16th, 63rd and 64th motorized brigades, 1440th and 1289th self-propelled artillery regiments, 78th Guards Heavy Tank Regiment, 614th Guards Mortar Regiment, 109th Anti-Tank Artillery Regiment, 1713th Anti-Aircraft Artillery Regiment, and 40th Independent Guards Mortar Battalion.

5th Guards Cavalry Corps (as of 1 January 1945)—11th, 12th Guards and 63rd cavalry divisions, 150th Guards Anti-Tank Artillery Regiment, 72nd Guards Mortar Battalion, 1896th Self-Propelled Artillery Regiment, 585th Anti-Aircraft Artillery Regiment, and 9th Guards Mortar Regiment.
18th Tank Corps—170th, 110th and 181st tank brigades, 32nd Motorized Rifle Brigade, 363rd Heavy Self-Propelled Artillery Regiment, 73rd Independent Motorcycle Battalion, 1438th Self-Propelled Artillery Regiment, 1000th, 1961st and 1962nd anti-tank artillery regiments, 1341st and 1335th anti-aircraft artillery regiments, 106th Independent Guards Mortar Battalion; the artillery group—1694th Anti-Aircraft Artillery Regiment, 200th Mortar Regiment, and the 58th Independent Guards Mortar Regiment; engineer units—115th Sapper Battalion and the 217th Motorized Engineer Battalion.
Air Force units—17th Air Army

B. The Enemy Opposite the 46th and 4th Guards Armies as of 20 December 1944

Facing the 46th Army: a Hungarian security detachment and parachute battalions; Hungarian 271st Infantry Division and the 24th Infantry Regiment/20th Infantry Division (Hungarian); 64th Construction Battalion and a machine gun battalion; 8th Panzer Division and the 17th Infantry Regiment/8th Infantry Division (Hungarian), and the 239th Assault Gun Brigade; units of the Hungarian 1st Panzer Division, units of the Hungarian 1st Cavalry Division; the 8th Police Regiment, 302nd Sapper Company, 159th Battalion (6-barreled mortars); the Hungarian 23rd Infantry Division and the Hungarian "Saint Laszlo" Infantry Division.

Facing the 4th Guards Army: General Kiss's group (Hungarian) (131st Composite Infantry Regiment, 3rd Cavalry Regiment, a composite regiment, 152nd artillery battalion, a panzer group); elements of the Hungarian 2nd and 23rd infantry divisions; 23rd Panzer Division and units of the 1st Panzer Division; 31st SS Infantry Division, units of the Hungarian 20th and 24th infantry divisions, and nine battalions of specialized units.

The breakthrough of the enemy's defense (20-23 December). On the morning of 20 December, following a powerful artillery preparation and massed strikes by the 17th Air Army, the Third Ukrainian Front's forces launched a decisive offensive.

Along the 46th Army's main attack axis the artillery preparation lasted 40 minutes and the rifle formations attacked at 1145.

Despite the enemy's stubborn defense, the 46th Army's left-flank corps broke into the first trench line as the result of an energetic attack and, following an hour's fight, occupied it. The army's units, supported by aviation and artillery, and while overcoming the enemy's fire resistance and counterattacks, occupied the second and third trench lines by the middle of the day and by the close of the day the enemy's defense along the sector Baracska—Kapolnasnyek had been penetrated to a depth of 4-6 kilometers.

The army along the right flank was engaged in active combat activities and, while tying down significant enemy forces along a broad front, thus facilitated the units' successful attack along the main axis.

Along the 4th Guards Army's sector the fighting unfolded no less successfully on the first day of the offensive. Here the army's main forces, following an hour's-long artillery preparation, which yielded good results, attacked at 1115. By the middle of the day the enemy had been thrown out of his first defensive zone along the sector between Lake Velence and the Sarviz Canal. Under the blows of our attacking forces, the enemy, while covering himself with individual groups of infantry and tanks, supported by artillery fire from the depth, was forced to begin falling back to the north. During the second half of the day the German-Hungarian units, having brought up tank, self-propelled guns and armored transports, increased their resistance. While approaching the Kisfalud—Szekesfehervar—Zagan line, our attacking units were met with powerful fire and counterattacks. The enemy counterattacked five times, supported by artillery and mortar fire. The enemy had tanks buried in the ground along some sectors, which he employed as firing points. The enemy put up especially heavy resistance along the approaches to Szekesfehervar.

By the close of the day, having beaten off all the enemy counterattacks, units of the 4th Guards Army broke through the enemy's defense along the main attack axis, 15 kilometers along the front and up to eight kilometers in depth.

As a result of the offensive's first day, the Third Ukrainian Front's forces, having broken through the enemy's first line of defense and having advanced from three to eight kilometers in depth, reached the line Baracska—Kenesseytanya—Velence—Pakozd—excluding Zagan. The enemy suffered heavy losses in men and materiel and, while striving to delay our offensive, was hurriedly bringing up new infantry and tank units to the breakthrough zone.

Throughout the night of 20-21 December the *front's* forces, without halting combat activities, brought up their artillery and rear establishments and in the morning resumed the offensive with their main forces along the previous axes. Particularly characteristic of the fighting on the offensive's second day, compared to the first day, was the enemy's continuously increasing resistance and an increase in the number of tanks committed by him while counterattacking.

The 46th Army's units, in conjunction with the artillery and assault and fighter aviation, while overcoming the enemy's increased fire resistance and successfully repulsing the frequent counterattacks by his infantry and tanks, continued to attack to the north, eliminated the enemy's strong points and centers of resistance. In the middle of the day, the divisions of the rifle corps' second echelons were committed into the fighting to augment the attack. By the morning of 21 December, when the success of the rifle units became clear along the sector east of Lake Velence, the commander of the 46th Army decided to commit the 2nd Guards Mechanized Corps into the fighting, with the task of breaking through the enemy's defense throughout the entire depth and to developing the offensive in the direction of Vereb.

Upon leaving its jumping-off position in the Adony area, the 2nd Guards Mechanized Corps' units bypassed the infantry at 1000 and entered into the fighting against the enemy. While overcoming the enemy's stubborn resistance and repelling his tank attacks, the corps' units slowly advanced and by the close of the day were fighting for Kajaszoszentpeter and Vereb. Especially heavy fighting unfolded along the 46th Army's left flank. It was here that by the close of the day and group of enemy tanks, with automatic riflemen on board, managed to break through the combat formations of the left-flank division's rifle regiment along the Lovasbereny—Nadap paved road and then on to Velence. There arose the threat that the enemy might get into the flank and rear of our units. However, this danger was eliminated by the measures taken.

In order to keep the enemy from spreading to the north and northwestern outskirts of Kapolnasnyek, a rifle regiment was dispatched from the reserve of the commander of the 10th Guards Rifle Corps. Throughout the day the 46th Army's units repelled 11 enemy counterattacks, each with a strength of up to two infantry battalions and 30-40 armored vehicles, with heavy losses for him.

As a result of the offensive's second day, the 46th Army's units advanced up to six kilometers and, having expanded the breakthrough front to 12 kilometers, reached the line excluding Martonvasar—Nadap—Sukoro. The 46th Army's attacking units killed may enemy soldiers and officers during the day's fighting and destroyed a great deal of military equipment. The enemy lost during the day's fighting 26 vehicles knocked out and burned from his armored forces.

On the offensive's second day the 4th Guards Army concentrated its main efforts on capturing the city of Szekesfehervar. As early as the close of 20 December the *front* commander issued an order to the army commander to break through the internal ring of the city's defense during the night and capture the eastern suburbs of Szekesfehervar, in order to secure the commitment of the 7th Mechanized Corps into the fighting along the western shore of Lake Velence. The army's main forces, according to this order, were to continue a decisive offensive from the morning of 21 December to the northeast and, in conjunction with the 7th Mechanized Corps, to capture Szekesfehervar. Particular attention was paid to the creation of powerful anti-tank areas along the flanks.

In carrying out the *front* commander's order, during the first half of the night the 46th Army's units advanced up to three kilometers to the northwest and captured the enemy's strong points along the approaches to Szekesfehervar. At 1100, following a short artillery preparation, the army's main forces renewed the attack. By 0900 the 7th Mechanized Corps had been concentrated in its waiting area, Dinnyes—Borgond—Seregelyes.

The enemy, striving to retain Szekesfehervar in his hands at all costs, carried out 15 counterattacks that day, in strength from two companies to four battalions of infantry, supported by 8-20 tanks and self-propelled guns in each instance. The enemy carried out powerful artillery-mortar fire against our attack forces from the areas north and northwest of Szekesfehervar, north of Szabadbattyan, and northwest of Polgardi. However, the 4th Guards Army's units, while overcoming the enemy's fire and frequent counterattacks, continued to advance, while attacking the enemy's defense along three axes: the right-flank 31st Rifle Corps on Csala and the eastern outskirts of Szekesfehervar; in the center, the 20th Corps was attacking in the general direction of the southern outskirts of Szekesfehervar; along the left flank of the main axis, units of the 135th Corps, having routed the enemy along an intermediate defensive line in the Zagan—Szabadbattyan area and having repelled an enemy infantry attack, supported by 20 tanks, began fighting for the southern outskirts of the suburbs of Szekesfehervar. On this day the corps' units captured 54 "Messerschmitt"[4] aircraft on the enemy's airfield. Following stubborn fighting, the right-flank division along the auxiliary axis captured the enemy's important strong point of Tac and Szabadbattyan.

During the middle of the day the 7th Mechanized Corps received orders to enter the breach along the sector Lake Velence—eastern outskirts of Szekesfehervar and to attack, with the immediate objective of capturing heights 183 and 165 (2-5 kilometers northeast of Szekesfehervar) no later than 1400, from where with part of its forces, including tanks foremost, it was to launch an attack to the southwest and, in conjunction with the rifle units, capture the city of Szekesfehervar. By the close of 21 December the corps' main units were to capture the line Zamoly—Bodajk—Csor. However, at the time of the corps' arrival at the breach, the enemy's defense had not yet been completely penetrated. The corps was to be committed along a 3-kilometer sector (between Kisfalud and the eastern suburbs of Szekesfehervar), which was occupied by the enemy, which extremely constricted and tied down the maneuver of the corps' units. Besides this, the corps had to attack along a single road. Throughout the day, the 7th Mechanized Corps was engaged in unrelenting fighting with the enemy's infantry and tanks and by the close of the day, having crushed the enemy's resistance and having advanced up to three kilometers, it captured Csala and the northeastern part of the city of Szekesfehervar.

In conclusion, on 21 December the 4th Guards Army advanced 3-5 kilometers and seized a number of important fortified inhabited locales along the approaches to Szekesfehervar; however, the tasks assigned to the army by the *front* command were not carried out in full. Although he had suffered heavy losses, the enemy never the less held on to Szekesfehervar. In striving to strengthen his units, the German command hurriedly shifted groups of tanks and infantry elements to the breakthrough area from the depth and other sectors of the front and committed them into the fighting from the march. The commander of the 4th Guards Army decided to capture the city of Szekesfehervar, without halting the offensive at night.

By the close of 21 December, when a larger success was becoming evident in the 46th Army's offensive sector east of Lake Velence, the commander of the Third Ukrainian Front decided to commit the 18th Tank Corps into the breach (according to the plan's second variation) and

4 Editor's note. This refers to any number of possible aircraft, including fighters and/or bombers, produced by Wilhelm Emil "Willy" Messerschmitt's design bureau.

issued orders to the corps commander to leave for the waiting area. By 2100 on 21 December the tank corps, having carried out a march, concentrated in the Kenesseytanya—Janostanya—Kapolnasnyek area.

During the night of 21-22 December and during the day the fighting along the entire front became even more bitter, particularly along the 46th Army's left flank, in the Nadap—Velence area and along the 4th Guards Army's front for Szekesfehervar. The enemy opposite the 46th Army committed fresh units of the 23rd Infantry Division into the fighting and the 6th Panzer Division, newly arrived from Germany and completed outfitted. The situation for the 46th Army's forces was becoming more difficult because the enemy's tanks with automatic riflemen on them and self-propelled guns, with an overall strength of up to 40 vehicles, began to spread from the Velence area in the direction of Kapolnasnyek. The enemy was counting on a powerful frontal infantry attack, supported by tanks and self-propelled guns, against the rear establishments and units of the 46th Army, to halt their further advance and throw them back to their starting points. The fighting to destroy the enemy's tanks and forces that had broken through continued throughout the entire day.

On the morning of 22 December the 46th Army's main forces, in conjunction with tank and mechanized units, continued to develop the offensive.

Due to the arrival of the 18th Tank Corps during the night for commitment into the breach in the direction of Bicske, the 2nd Guards Mechanized Corps was turned to the northeast, with the immediate task of capturing the inhabited locale of Val and to subsequently, while carrying out its previous task, capture the Etyek—Zsambek area. Without halting its nighttime activities, at 0930 the 2nd Guards Mechanized Corps, having left behind the 10th Guards and 37th rifle corps' infantry (46th Army), launched a decisive offensive toward Val. The enemy was overthrown by an unexpected attack. While destroying with fire and treads the Germans, who had begun to retreat in panic, the corps' units broke into the southern outskirts of Val and by 1100 had completely cleared this inhabited locale of the enemy. Continuing to develop the offensive to the northeast, the corps' units, having beaten off a series of enemy infantry and tank counterattacks, by the close of 22 December had reached the area excluding Gyuro—Farkasfa. By 1800 the 18th Tank Corps had occupied jumping-off positions in the area north and northwest of Pazmand and attacked at 1000 in the direction of Vereb, Vertesacsa and Bicske.

The enemy brought up to 40 tanks to the Vereb area and was putting up powerful resistance to the corps' attacking units. By this time the German tanks that had broken through to the Kapolnasnyek area were still counterattacking in order to cut the Kapolnasnyek road and reach the rear of our attacking units.

Despite the enemy's desperate resistance, units of the 18th Tank Corps, supported by the 46th Army's artillery and the 17th Air Army's aircraft, following a stubborn tank battle involving joint attacks by tanks, self-propelled artillery and motorized infantry from the south and southeast and a flanking maneuver from the southwest, captured Vereb by the close of the day. One tank brigade, operating in the second echelon, fought throughout the day in the area northwest of Kapolnasnyek with the enemy's tank breakthrough group.

The 46th Army's rifle corps attacked behind the mobile units. While overcoming powerful fire resistance and the enemy's infantry and tank counterattacks from the area of Val and Vereb, the army's formations made a fighting advance of 4-8 kilometers during the day.

On 22 December, simultaneously with the offensive along the main attack axis, on orders of the army commander, the 23rd Rifle Corps, which was located along an auxiliary axis, attacked along its left flank. In close cooperation with units of the 37th Rifle Corps, the enemy's resistance was crushed and our units stormed and captured the inhabited locale of Martonvasar and continued a successful attack to the north. Along with the main forces' offensive from the front, units of the 46th Army and the 18th Tank Corps' 181st Tank Brigade successfully coped with the task of eliminating the enemy's tank breakthrough group in the Kapolnasnyek area. In the fighting against the tanks on this day a major role was played by anti-tank artillery, which had been committed into the fighting from the reserve. As a result of fierce fighting by the infantry and artillery, part of the enemy's tanks were destroyed and the remainder managed to break through in the direction of Nadap.

By the close of the day the threat of the enemy's tanks getting into the flank and rear of our attacking units had been eliminated and the Kapolnasnyek—Pazmand had been cleared.

The offensive's third day was the decisive one in the fighting to break through the enemy's defense between the Danube and Lake Velence. Despite the German-Hungarian forces' stubborn resistance and the German command's commitment of fresh infantry and tank units, the 46th Army's forces, in conjunction with the 18th Tank and 2nd Guards Mechanized corps, supported in the air by units of the 17th Air Army, inflicted a heavy defeat on the enemy, who was forced to retreat.

Along the left wing the 4th Guards Army's forces, while continuing to carry out their assigned objective throughout the night of 21-22 December, were fighting to capture the city of Szekesfehervar.

At dawn, following fierce fighting, the army's units, by means of simultaneous attacks from the south, east and northeast, and having crushed the resistance of the enemy's infantry and tanks, completely captured the eastern suburbs of Szekesfehervar. Throughout the day the right-flank 31st Guards Rifle Corps was developing the offensive from the line north of Pakozd along with units of the 7th Mechanized Corps to the northeast and, while overcoming resistance and repelling enemy counterattacks, by the close of the day, having advanced 5-6 kilometers, reached the line Janosmajor—southern outskirts of Lovasbereny—Patka—Mariamajor. In the center, units of the 20th Guards Rifle and the 7th Mechanized corps were by the close of the day fighting, with their front facing westward, along the line 1.5 kilometers southwest of Mariamajor—west of height 165—the northeastern—eastern—and southeastern suburbs of Szekesfehervar. To the left, the 135th Rifle Corps, having crushed the stubborn resistance of the enemy, who was relying on a previously prepared defensive line from the southern outskirts of the Szekesfehervar suburbs to the Sarviz Canal, was developing the offensive to the northwest, bypassing the city from the west. By 1900 the corps' units, having advanced up to six kilometers, were fighting along the line southwestern outskirts of Szekesfehervar—excluding Gusztus. Along the auxiliary axis, the 21st Guards Rifle Corps' right-flank units, while continuing the offensive, captured the inhabited locales of Szabadbattyan and Urhida and by the close of the day were fighting along the line Urhida and then south as far as Alsosomlyo. The corps' remaining units occupied defensive positions along the line excluding Alsosomlyo—eastern outskirts of Polgardi and then two kilometers northwest of Balatonfokajar—southern outskirts of Balatonakarttya.

Thus during 22 December the 4th Guards Army's forces, while continuing to widen and deepen the breach in the German-Hungarian forces' defense between lakes Velence and Balaton, captured the major inhabited locales of Patka, Urhida and Szabadbattyan. In the Janosmajor area the army's right-flank units were linking up along the northern shore of Lake Velence with the 46th Army's left-flank units.

On 23 December the offensive by the Third Ukrainian Front's forces continued at an increasing pace. The 2nd Guards Mechanized Corps operated particularly successfully on this day along the 46th Army's right flank. Without halting the offensive at night, the corps' units, combining skillful maneuver with bold and vigorous attacks, reached the Laszlo Canal and, preventing the enemy from blowing up the bridge, crossed over to the eastern bank and captured the inhabited locale of Gyuro. Subsequently, the 2nd Guards Mechanized Corps, having crushed the enemy's stubborn resistance along the Etyek—Tabajd fortified line captured Etyek through a flanking movement from the west. By the middle of the day, having made a fighting advance of up to 15 kilometers, the mechanized corps reached the Budapest—Bicske railroad and, having occupied Herceghalom station, cut the path of retreat for the Budapest group of forces to the west and continued to pursue the enemy retreating in panic in the direction of Paty, and with part of its forces on Zsambek.

The 18th Tank Corps continued to develop the offensive in the general direction of Bicske. The corps' units threw the enemy out of the major inhabited locale of Vertesacsa with a bold night attack and by the morning of 23 December reached the Vali Canal southwest of Alcsutdoboz. Despite the fact that during his retreat the enemy managed to blow up the bridges over the canal, the corps units forced the canal under the cover of tank fire and began fighting for Alcsutdoboz.

In the middle of the day, when the tank corps's main forces had been crossed over the canal along crossings laid down, the enemy was thrown out of Alcsutdoboz.

By the close of the day the corps, having encountered stubborn resistance by the enemy, who threw major tanks forces into the counterattack, was engaged in heavy fighting with the enemy's tanks and infantry along the line northeast of Alcsutdoboz—Bodmer.

Throughout 23 December the 46th Army's units, while closely interacting with the mobile units, continued their successful offensive in the direction of Bicske, despite resistance by the enemy's bomber aviation and fierce counterattacks by his combat groups, destroying centers of resistance and strong points in the enemy's defense. Having advanced 6-12 kilometers into the depth of the enemy's defense, by the close of the day the 46th Army's formations reached the line Tarnok—Soskut—Etyek—Bot—Alcsutdoboz.

At 0150 on 23 December the 4th Guards Army received orders from the *front* commander to continue the further offensive, having as its chief task the capture by the left-flank rifle formations, together with the 7th Mechanized Corps, of the city of Szekesfehervar. The army was to attack with its right-flank formations behind the 18th Tank Corps and, while closely interacting with the 46th Army's left-flank units, reach the line Vertesboglar—Forna by the close of the day.

In carrying out the tasks set by the *front* commander, the 4th Guards Army, following stubborn and heavy fighting, crushed the enemy's fierce resistance and at 1100 on 23 December stormed and captured Szekesfehervar. The intensity of the fighting on this day is shown by the fact that the army's units had to beat off 23 infantry attacks, supported by tanks and self-propelled artillery, numbering up to 100 vehicles.

By the close of the day the 4th Guards Army's right-flank formations, having advanced as much as 15 kilometers, reached the line southwest of Felcsut—east of Vertesboglar—marker 226—Forna—marker 136—marker 149—Gyulamajor—one kilometer south of Moha. In the center and along the left flank the army's units advanced 4-6 kilometers and reached the line Gusztus—west of Urhida—northern outskirts of Polgardi—excluding Fule—southern outskirts of Balatonakarttya.

Thus on 23 December, following heavy fighting, the Third Ukrainian Front's forces broke through the powerfully fortified and multi-echeloned defense of the German-Hungarian forces southwest of Budapest throughout the entire depth.

Upon arriving at the *front's* right wing and at the enemy's major strong point of Bicske and having cut the railroad east of the town, and also having captured the German-Hungarian forces' major communications center and important strong point of Szekesfehervar along the left wing, the Third Ukrainian Front's forces cut all of the major withdrawal routes of the enemy's Budapest group of forces to the southwest. On 23 December the breakthrough of the enemy's defense had been widened to 100 kilometers along the front and to 27 kilometers in depth.

The attempts by the German command to delay our offensive and prevent the arrival of the Third Ukrainian Front's forces at the western communications of the Budapest group of forces' suffered a complete collapse. By this time the Second Ukrainian Front's forces had already broken through the enemy's defense and were successfully developing the offensive in the general direction of Levice, with a subsequent turn toward Esztergom.

The development of the offensive and the encirclement of the enemy's Budapest group of forces. After the German-Hungarian defense southwest of Budapest had been broken, the Third Ukrainian Front's forces were faced with the task of developing the offensive for the purpose of finally and completely finishing the encirclement of the enemy's Budapest group of forces.

During the subsequent three days (24-26 December) the Third Ukrainian Front's forces carried out this task. The offensive from the line reached on 23 December unfolded with all the *front's* forces and the forces of the 46th and 4th Guards armies and the 18th Tank Corps, while the 5th Guards Cavalry Corps was committed into the fighting on 25 December. The 18th Tank Corps and the 46th Army launched an attack to the north and northeast, while the 4th Guards Army and the 5th Guards Cavalry Corps attacked to the north and northwest. On the morning of 24 December the 2nd Guards Mechanized Corps began an attack from the area east of Herceghalom station and by the close of the day, having overcome the enemy's resistance, advanced as much as 22 kilometers and broke into the western outskirts of Budapest and became involved in street fighting.

On 24 December the 18th Tank Corps, while continuing the offensive to the north, as a result of a decisive concentric attack and street fighting along with units of the 46th Army, captured the important strong point and major railroad junction of Bicske.

Under the blows of the corps' units, the enemy fell back to the west and northwest, while attempting to delay our advance through frequent attacks by screens covering the retreat. However, as early as the close of 25 December the corps' units, following stubborn fighting with enemy tanks and artillery, captured the inhabited locales of Dorog and Tat and on December broken into Ezstergom on the Danube.

The enemy put up fierce resistance. However, following five hours of street fighting, units of the 18th Tank Corps, attacking from the south, southeast and east, crushed the enemy's resistance and by 1300 on 26 December captured Ezstergom, making contact with units of the Second Ukrainian Front operating along the northern bank of the Danube. With the arrival of the Second and Third Ukrainian fronts' units in the Ezstergom area, the encirclement of the German-Hungarian Budapest group of forces was complete. The 46th Army's combined-arms formations, attacking in close cooperation with the mobile forces and taking advantage of their success, attacked with one rifle corps in the direction of Pilisvorosvar and with two rifle corps on Budapest. On 25 December the 46th Army, following bitter fighting, broke through the enemy's defensive line along the approaches to Budapest and, having eliminated a number of powerful enemy strong points, including Pilisvorosvar, together with the 2nd Guards Mechanized Corps began street fighting along the western and southwestern outskirts of Budapest.

On 26 December, while continuing to develop the offensive north of Budapest, units of the 46th Army's 10th Rifle Corps captured the major inhabited locale of Budakalasz, and upon reaching the Danube, split the enemy forces operating northwest of the city from the forces defending the city and close the encirclement ring directly north of Budapest.

At the same time, when the 46th Army and the 18th Tank Corps were attacking along the *front's* right wing to the north and northeast and were successfully concluding the operation to encircle the enemy's Budapest group of forces and creating the internal encirclement ring, the 4th Guards Army and 5th Cavalry Corps were no less successfully continuing to carry out the task assigned by the *front* commander to create an external front.

Throughout 24-25 December the army's units in the center and along the left flank, while crushing the enemy's resistance and repelling his fierce counterattacks, which were supported by tanks, self-propelled guns and aviation, continued to attack to the north and northwest. Along the right flank units of the 4th Guards Army, taking advantage of the 18th Tank Corps' success and encountering insignificant enemy resistance were fighting in the general direction of Many, Zsambek and Piliscsaba. On the night of 24-25 December the 5th Guards Cavalry Corps was committed into the fighting along the Szar—Csakvar sector, with the mission of attacking to the northwest and reaching the area west of Tarjan, Tatabanya and Oroszlany.

While throwing the enemy back to the northwest and west, the 4th Guards Army made a fighting advance of 8-9 kilometers along the right flank and on 25 December, while cooperating with the 5th Guards Cavalry Corps, advanced 14 kilometers, capturing along with the 18th Tank Corps, the town of Bicske and the major inhabited locales of Piliscsaba, Uny, Kirva, Zsambek, Many, Szar, Felcsut, Vertesboglar, and others.

In the center and along the left flank the army continued to be engaged in stubborn fighting, without advancing significantly.

The 4th Guards Army's task for 26 December was defined by the *front* commander's directive, which ordered that the right-flank 31st Guards Rifle Corps to attack with one division behind the 18th Tank Corps and by the close of the day reach the line Csev—Kesztolc—the Ezstergom camp, with its front facing east. Two other divisions, taking advantage of the 5th Guards Cavalry Corps' success, was to attack to the northwest and reach the front Bajna—Hereg—Tarjan—Felsogala. In the center the 20th Guards Rifle[5] and the 7th Mechanized Corps, in cooperation with the 5th Guards Cavalry Corps' 63rd Division, were to attack to the west and by the close of the day capture Csakvar and reach the line Csakbereny—Fehervarcsurgo—Ujgut. On the left flank the 21st Rifle Corps, with the support of the 135th Rifle Corps' 252nd Rifle Division from the north, was to crush the enemy's resistance and reach the line Osi—Csajag.

Throughout 26 December units of the 4th Guards Army and the 5th Guards Cavalry Corps, while carrying out their assigned tasks, continued to attack. Along the right flank, units of the 4th Guards Army, while meeting insignificant enemy resistance and closely coordinating with units of the 18th Tank Corps, advanced up to 16 kilometers and reached the Danube along the sector Esztergom—Nyergesujfalu. Part of the forces having reached the line Csev—Kesztolc—Esztergom and consolidated here with its front facing east.

In the center the combined-arms formations, in close coordination with the 7th Mechanized and 5th Guards Cavalry corps' units, while repelling the enemy's infantry and tank counterattacks, also advanced to the northwest and west. Along the left flank the army's units were readying themselves for an attack and were engaged in a fire fight with the enemy.

By the close of 26 December the 4th Guards Army reached the line Esztergom—Tat—Nyergesujfalu—west of Tarjan—Banhida—Tatabanya—west of Szar—west of Gant—east of Zamoly—Moha—west of Urhida—Fule—Balatonakarttya.

By 26 December the enemy had been thrown up to 40 kilometers back from his group of forces encircled in Budapest and the 4th Guards Army's and the 5th Guards Cavalry Corps' forces had created an external front that secured from the west the successful elimination of the encircled enemy group of forces and the capture of Budapest. The 17th Air Army rendered a great deal of assistance during the offensive by the Third Ukrainian Front's forces. During 20-30 December the air army's units carried out up to 5,000 sorties, of which more than 4,500 were for the air assault and bombing of the enemy and accompanying the *front's* rifle and mobile formations. During this period the air army's units carried out 122 air battles and shot down 93 enemy planes.

Thus the task assigned to the Third Ukrainian Front's forces by the 12 December directive from the *Stavka* of the Supreme High Command to break through the defense southwest of Budapest and to encircle the enemy, had been fully carried out.

5 By order of the command of the 4th Guards Army, another division and the main body of the 135th Rifle Corps' artillery were also brought in to carry out this task.

During the course of the final days of December, the Third Ukrainian Front's forces were engaged in fierce street fighting involving the main forces of the 46th Army in the western part of Budapest. Overcoming the enemy's powerful fire resistance and furious counterattacks, blocking and destroying his strong points and centers of resistance, the 46th Army's units, while operating in storm groups and detachments, squeezed the encirclement ring and occupied more than 500 blocks in the western part of the city.

Part of the 46th Army's forces and a single division from the 4th Guards Army continued to destroy the encircled German-Hungarian group of forces in the woods northwest of Budapest and on 31 December completely eliminated it.

The Third Ukrainian Front's forces continued to attack to the west with the forces of the 4th Guards Army and the 18th Tank and 5th Guards Cavalry corps.

The enemy facing the 4th Guards Army put up stubborn resistance. Taking advantage of the mountainous and forested terrain favorable to the defense, the German-Hungarian units sought to delay the further advance of our forces to the west with fire and frequent tank and infantry counterattacks.

In the final days of December the activity of the enemy's tanks and self-propelled guns increased sharply. Every day from 100 to 150 tanks and self-propelled guns were operating opposite the 4th Guards Army's front. In becoming more active, the enemy was preparing for a counteroffensive for the purpose of breaking through the encirclement ring and linking up with its group of forces encircled in the city.

Despite the difficulties with which operations in the mountainous and wooded area were connected, as well as the enemy's stubborn resistance, the units of the 4th Guards Army and the 18th Tank and 5th Guards Cavalry corps during 27-31 December advanced 15-20 kilometers along the right flank and in the center and up to ten kilometers along individual sectors along the left flank.

On 31 December, according to the order by the commander of the Third Ukrainian Front, the 4th Guards Army took up the defensive along the entire front and was fighting off powerful enemy counterattacks, which were particularly strong along the army's left flank. By the close of 31 December the situation of the Third Ukrainian Front's forces was as follows.

The 46th Army's main forces were fighting in the northwestern, western and southwestern parts of Budapest. The 4th Guards Army's forces occupied 110-kilometer front along the southern bank of the Danube along the sector Nyergesujfalu—Neszmely and then south through height 294 west of Szomod—0.5 kilometers east of Lake Nagy—eastern outskirts of Vertesszollos—Banhida—east of Kornye—Oroszlany—east of Pusztavam—two kilometers east of Mor—eastern outskirts of Csokako—Borbalamajor—Moha—two kilometers east of Csor—Osi—Balatonfokajar—0.5 kilometers south of Balatonakarttya.

According to the *front* commander's directive, the 18th Tank Corps, having turned over its combat sectors to the 4th Guards Army's rifle units, by the close of the day had secretly concentrated to the *front* reserve in the areas of Bicske, Many and Zsambek.

The 5th Guards Cavalry Corps was located with one division in the area east of Kornye, with its remaining formations in the area northeast of Mor. The Third Ukrainian Front's 57th Army continued to defend south of Lake Balaton, between Lake Balaton and the Drava River, with its front facing west.

As a result of the offensive by the forces of the Third Ukrainian Front during 20-31 December 1944, a major German-Hungarian group of forces, which was defending southwest of Budapest, was defeated. The enemy lost more than 61,000 soldiers and officers in killed and captured alone. Our forces destroyed more than 700 tanks, self-propelled guns and armored transports, about 400 guns of various calibers, 120 planes, and much other military equipment.

Among the prizes taken by the Third Ukrainian Front's forces were 215 tanks and self-propelled guns, armored cars and armored transports, more than 200 guns of various calibers, 62 planes, and also an enormous amount of military apparel, ammunition and other military hardware located at captured depots and bases.

The result of joint offensive operations by the Second and Third Ukrainian fronts' forces, which led to the complete encirclement of a major enemy group of forces numbering about 180,000 soldiers and officers in the Hungarian capital of Budapest, had enormous significance.

Now the *front's* forces faced their next task—to completely defeat the encircled German-Hungarian group of forces and capture Budapest along with the Second Ukrainian Front.

Thus at the third stage of the development of the Budapest operation the Hungarian capital of Budapest had been surrounded by the jointly operating forces of the Second and Third Ukrainian fronts. The enemy's group of forces, which numbered up to 180,000 enemy soldiers and officers overall and which consisted of the German IX Army Corps (units of the 13th Panzer Division, the SA *Feldherrnhalle* Motorized Division, the 8th and 22nd SS cavalry divisions, units of the 271st Infantry Division, the 239th Assault Gun Brigade, the 959th Artillery Brigade, and the 13th Light Artillery Brigade) and the Hungarian I Army Corps (10th and 12th infantry divisions, units of the "Saint Lazslo" Infantry Division, units of the 9th, 19th and 20th infantry divisions, the 1st Panzer Division, and independent gendarme battalions and various training subunits) was locked up in the city. Its command refused to surrender and barbarously shot our parliamentarians who tried to present the surrender ultimatum. Fighting began in the city to destroy the German-Hungarian forces not wishing to lay down their arms.

At the same time, very fierce fighting broke out along the entire front of the Second and Third Ukrainian front's forces, because the enemy undertook a series of very powerful counteroffensives for the purpose of rendering assistance to his encircled forces from without.

5

The Repulse of the Germans' Counteroffensive. The Defeat of the Enemy's Budapest Group of Forces and the Capture of the Hungarian Capital of Budapest (The Operation's Fourth Stage, 1 January-13 February 1945)

Combat operations during the last, fourth stage of the operation developed in an extremely complex situation. At the same time the Second and Third Ukrainian fronts' forces were engaged in intensive street fighting in Budapest, the German command, while seeking to render aid to its group of forces encircled in Budapest, undertook several consecutive major and powerful offensive operations for the purpose of defeating and throwing our forces to the east of Budapest. Particularly intense fighting unfolded in January to the west of Budapest, along the Third Ukrainian Front's forces' sector, where the enemy launched three consecutive major offensive operations in the course of a single month. The situation along the Third Ukrainian Front's front was critical at times and required a great deal of military art from the generals, combat skill from the officers and tenacity and valor from our troops in order to crush the enemy's forces, eliminate the offensive operations undertaken by him and, through the joint efforts of the Second and Third Ukrainian fronts' forces, to defeat the German-Hungarian forces encircled in Budapest.

The Second and Third Ukrainian fronts' forces during this final stage of the operation interacted so closely that there is no possibility of describing the activities of each *front* separately. Not only would the historical correctness of the events suffer from this, but the value of the generalized experience would be lowered as well. This is why the description of the combat operations of the Second and Third Ukrainian fronts' forces will be related in their chronological order.

During the fierce fighting by the forces of the Third Ukrainian Front along the external front to repulse the enemy's offensive, intensive fighting to destroy the encircled enemy group of forces was being waged by the forces of the Second Ukrainian Front.

The Third Ukrainian Front's right-wing forces had the task of continuing to squeeze the encirclement ring with the 46th Army's main forces and, in conjunction with the forces of the Second Ukrainian Front, destroy the German-Hungarian group of forces and capture Budapest.

Having taken up the defensive, the 4th Guards Army had the task of securely covering the Budapest direction from the west; simultaneously, it was preparing offensive operations in the center and along the left flank for the purpose of capturing the town of Mor and the northern shore of Lake Balaton.

The *front* reserve—the 18th Tank Corps (minus a tank brigade)[1]—was concentrated behind the army's right flank, in the Bicske—Many—Zsambek, with the task of launching counterblows in case the enemy went over to the offensive from the west or east from the Budapest area. The 57th Army continued to be located in defensive positions along the line of the southwestern shore of Lake Balaton as far as the Drava River.

The repulse by the Third Ukrainian Front's forces of the German offensive on Budapest from the area southeast of Komarno (2-7 January). On the night of 1-2 January the enemy in the 31st Rifle Corps' defensive sector, following a short artillery preparation, attacked along the line Dunaalmas—Tavaros—Banhida. The enemy's reinforced forward battalions, which were supported by tanks, managed to penetrate the corps' defense under cover of night. At 2130 on 2 January the enemy's main forces attacked. At the same time, the Germans forced the Danube east of Neszmely along the Neszmely—Nyergesujfalu sector, in order to get into the flank and rear of our defending formations.

Because the defense of the right-flank 80th Guards Rifle Division (31st Guards Rifle Corps) had been insufficiently developed in the engineering and particularly the anti-tank regard, the Germans, who enjoyed a superiority of forces, managed to break through this divisions' defensive line from the west.

Simultaneously the enemy made a landing along the southern bank of the Danube in the Sutto area with units of his 96th Infantry Division.

Throughout 2 January 1945 the enemy launched uninterrupted fierce attacks with large forces of tanks and motorized infantry, supported by massed assault air strikes. By the close of the day he managed to advance to the east to a depth of six kilometers and occupy Neszmely, Szomod, Agostyan, and Baj.

Along the southern bank of the Danube our small garrisons were thrown out of the inhabited locales of Nyergesujfalu, Labatlan, Piske, and Sutto by the enemy's landing units.

All of the enemy's efforts were directed at employing his numerical superiority along the breakthrough sector to develop a vigorous offensive in the general direction of Bicske and Budapest and, while depriving our forces of time to bring up reserves and organize a defense, link up with his encircled group of forces. In trying to tie down our forces' activities, the enemy on 2 January increased his activities along the entire front of the 4th Guards Army. On this day the Germans, while evidently operating according to their command's overall plan, having concentrated a powerful shock group, consisting of the 13th Panzer, 8th Cavalry and the *Feldherrnhalle* Motorized divisions along the northwestern outskirts of Budapest, in the Obuda area, launched an attack to the northwest. However, the Germans, having only insignificantly pressed units of the 180th Rifle Division (46th Army) and having suffered heavy losses, were halted and did not advance further.

During 2-7 January the Third Ukrainian Front's right-flank formations were involved in heavy defensive fighting, while repulsing the enemy offensive. Despite the Germans' numerical superiority, they were unable to disorganize our defense during the first days of the counteroffensive.

As the result of a rapid and skillful regrouping of forces to the breakthrough sector, army reserves, formations from others sectors of the front and part of the *front* reserve were thrown in on the first day of the offensive. The 93rd, 62nd, 40th, and 41st guards rifle divisions and units of the 5th Guards Cavalry Corps, which covered the breakthrough sector from the southeast and south, were committed into the fighting along the 4th Guards Army's right flank. Simultaneously, according to an order by the *front* command, the 2nd Guards Mechanized Corps and the 86th Guards Rifle Division were dispatched from the 46th Army's sector to cover the breakthrough

1 The 170th Tank Brigade was located in Dunaalmas.

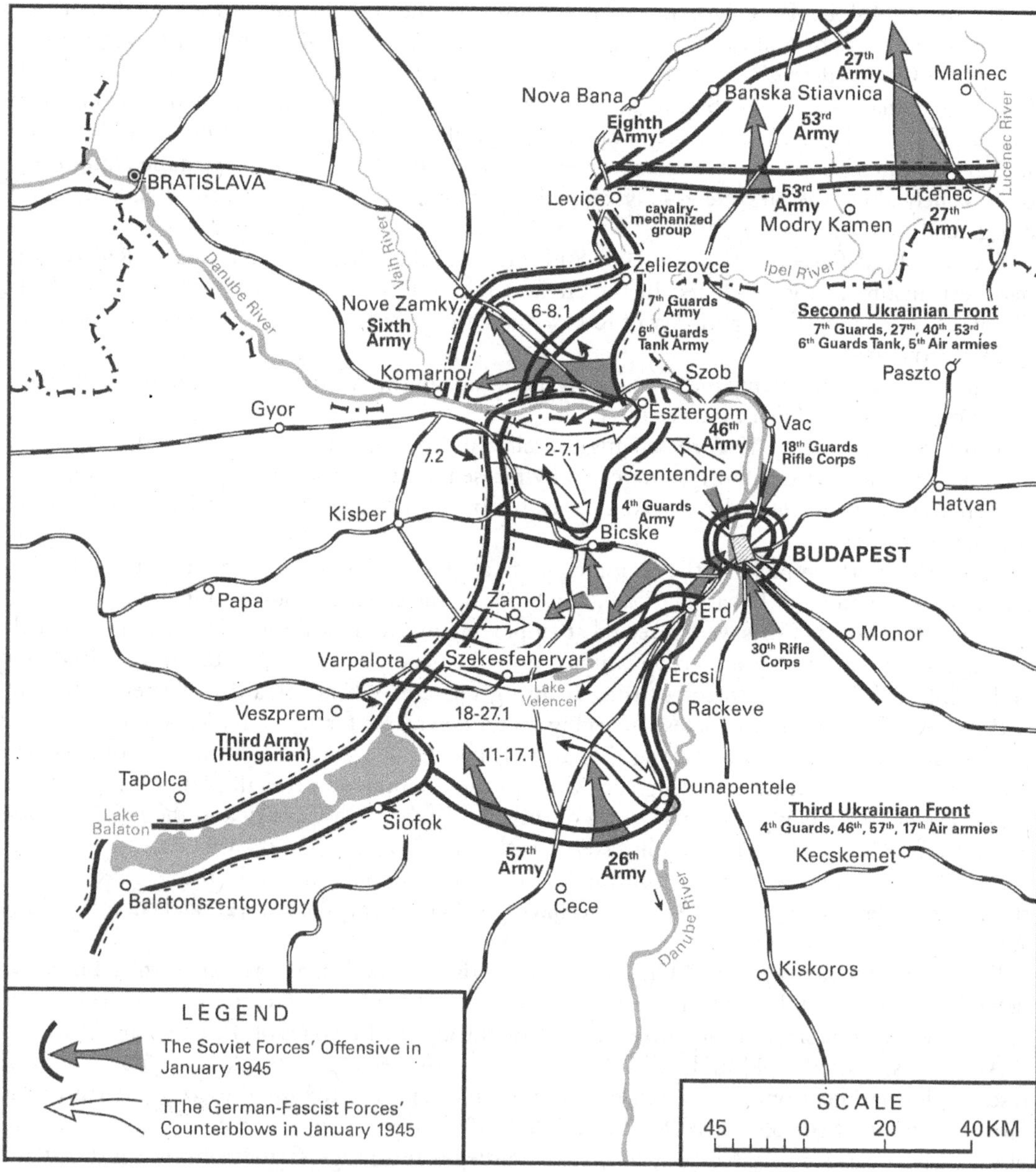

Map 2 The Completion of the Defeat of the Enemy's Forces in the Budapest Area.

from the northeast and east, and by the morning of 3 January the main forces of the 18th Tank Corps reached the line Tat—Sarisap—Bajna. The corps' 170th Tank Brigade, which had remained in Dunaalmas, along with the 1438th Self-Propelled Artillery Regiment, while skillfully taking advantage of the wooded area, made a fighting breakthrough out of the encirclement and by 0300 on 4 January reached the area north of Szomor.

Due to the developing situation facing the 4th Guards Army's right flank, the *front* commander ordered the commander of the 46th Army to halt offensive operations in the western part of the city on the morning of 3 January, in order to concentrate his forces, and to concentrate his chief attention on preventing the enemy's breakthrough to Bicske and Zsambek.

Throughout the first three days of the offensive the enemy advanced up to 30 kilometers to the southeast and reached the approaches to Bicske. However, the subsequent advance by the German shock group slowed down, thanks to the measures adopted by the *front* command.

The attack by the Second Ukrainian Front's forces on Komarno (6-10 January). Due to the developing situation, the *Stavka* of the Supreme High Command, in its directive no. 11002 of 4 January, ordered the commander of the Second Ukrainian Front to launch an attack with the forces of no less than two of the 7th Guards Army's rifle corps and the 6th Guards Tank Army from the area north of Esztergom along the northern bank of the Danube in the general direction of Komarno, to capture the crossings over the Danube near Komarno, to force the Danube and get into the rear of the enemy's Komarno group of forces to the south of Komarno with tank units and motorized infantry.

The Third Ukrainian Front's forces received orders to, having securely covered the axis to Budapest from the northwest, launch an attack with the forces of the 4th Guards Army, 5th Guards Cavalry Corps, and the 18th Tank and 1st Guards Mechanized corps from the area northwest of Bicske in the general direction of Neszmely and Komarno, with the task, in conjunction with the forces of the Second Ukrainian Front, of defeating the enemy group of forces attacking toward Budapest and capturing the line Komarno—Mor.

The main forces of the 17th and 5th air armies were supposed to support the ground forces' offensive. The start of the offensive was set for 6 January.

In carrying out the directive by the *Stavka* of the Supreme High Command, the commander of the Second Ukrainian Front issued the following orders to his forces on 4 January.

On the morning of 6 January the commander of the 7th Guards Army was to launch an offensive with the forces of two rifle corps, making the main attack with four rifle divisions and one tank brigade along the sector Kamendy—Parkany, in the general direction of Magyar Komarno; by the close of 8 January it was to capture the crossings over the Danube near Komarno and reach the line Tekov—Sarlugy—Senktgala—Komarno; it was to subsequently reach the line Velke Gindice—Vrable—Fedimes—Nitra River. The commander of the 6th Guards Tank Army was ordered to concentrate his army in the Salka—Haramkevesg—Leleg area on the night of 4-5 January and to be ready on the morning of 6 January to attack from the 7th Guards Army's main attack sector with the task of capturing the crossings over the Danube near Komarno by the close of 7 January and to get into the rear of the enemy's Komarno group of forces, which was operating from Komarno toward Budapest; part of its forces were to cover the operation from the direction of Nove Zamky until the arrival of the 7th Guards Army's infantry. The 5th Air Army received orders to support the operations of the 7th Guards and 6th Guards Tank armies, paying particular attention to covering the crossings over the Hron River and the 6th Guards Tank Army's combat formations.

From 30 December 1944 through 5 January 1945 there were no significant changes in the disposition of the 7th Guards and 6th Guards Tank armies, and these armies' units were basically operating along the Hron and Danube rivers along their previous lines.

Suddenly at 0300 on 6 January, without an artillery preparation, the 6th Guards Tank Army's formations attacked, in conjunction with units of the 7th Guards Army. Upon overcoming the minefields and having broken through the enemy's defense along the sector Kamendy—Danube River, together with the combined-arms formations, by the close of the day the 6th Guards Tank Army had advanced to a depth of 28 kilometers, having captured a number of major inhabited locales and important strong points in the enemy's defense. By the close of the day the 9th Guards Mechanized Corps was fighting west of Kebelkut, the 5th Tank Corps for Madar and Karva, and the 4th Motorcycle Regiment for Karva.

The 7th Guards Army's units attacked simultaneously with the 6th Tank Guards Army's units and, while energetically overcoming the enemy's resistance, by the close of 6 January had advanced as much as 18 kilometers along some axes and were fighting along the line: Kamendy—Diva—the southern outskirts of Bela—Kismuzsla—Katarinin—Csenke.

On the second day of the offensive (7 January) the 6th Guards Tank Army advanced to a depth of 25 kilometers and captured the major inhabited locales of Perbetsky, Svaty Peter and Chotin and by the close of the day were fighting along the following lines: the 9th Guards Mechanized Corps for Kebelkut, Batorove Kosihy and Nove Zamky; the 5th Guards Tank Corps was fighting for Komarno, repelling enemy infantry attacks with up to 30 tanks. In order to widen the breach and to augment the 6th Guards Tank Army's forces, the *front* commander subordinated to it the 4th Guards Mechanized Corps, which received orders to cross the Hron River near Haramkevesg and concentrate in the area Kebelkut—excluding Kismuzsla and at dawn on 8 January launch an attack in the direction of Szoldiny and Farnad, rolling up the enemy's defense along the Hron River.

Simultaneously with this, the commander of the 7th Guards Army received orders to launch a decisive offensive from the direction of Vozokany and Hronom in the direction of Farnad and from the direction of Kamendy toward Szoldiny On 7 January units of the 7th Guards Army continued their successful offensive, having advanced 10-15 kilometers along some axes. By the close of the day the army's attacking units were fighting along the line Kamendy—Diva—Kebelkut—Batorove Kosihy—Madar—Radvan.

Throughout 6-7 January the enemy put up stubborn resistance to our forces' offensive, while launching counterattacks along individual axes. On 8 January the enemy's counterattacks increased significantly.

The 6th Guards Tank Army's formations, despite the enemy's furious counterattacks on 8 January, continued to develop the offensive. On this day the 4th Guards Mechanized Corps captured Szoldiny and were attacking toward Velke Ludince; the 9th Guards Mechanized Corps was fighting for Nova Vieska with one brigade, while another brigade, having repulsed an enemy attack with more than two battalions of infantry and 15 tanks and self-propelled guns from the Nesvady area, continued to fight for Nove Zamky. Units of the 5th Guards Tank Corps and one brigade from the 9th Guards Mechanized Corps were fighting along the eastern outskirts of Komarno, repelling enemy counterattacks by more than an infantry regiment, supported by 25-30 tanks and self-propelled guns, of which eight were of the "Tiger"[2] type.

On this day the 7th Guards Army's attacking units along several axes beat off the Germans' numerous attacks. On 8 January the army's units captured Marcelova and Bokros and, in conjunction with units of the 4th Guards Mechanized Corps—Szoldiny, and by the close of the day were fighting along the line Kamendy—Szoldiny—the eastern slopes of height 214—Batorove Kosihy—the northwestern part of Madar—Marcelova—Bokros—Paty.

From 9 January the Germans' counterattacks increased significantly. In essence, the enemy had launched a broad counteroffensive with numerically superior forces. On this day the 6th Guards Tank Army was engaged in intense fighting with the Germans' counterattacking groups in the

2 Editor's note. The Panzer VI ("Tiger") was a German heavy tank which first appeared in 1943. One model weighed 54 tons and carried a crew of five. It was armed with an 88mm gun and two 7.92 machine guns.

areas of Velke Ludince, southeast of Nove Zamky and northeast of Komarno, where the enemy threw into a counterattack 45 tanks and self-propelled guns along a narrow front. By the close of the day the 4th Guards Mechanized Corps' forward units occupied Nasvady and were fighting for Nove Zamky and to completely clear the enemy out of Nova Ves; units of the 5th Guards Tank Corps and one brigade from the 9th Guards Mechanized Corps continued the fight for Komarno. On 10 January there was fighting along the entire front, but the enemy's counterblows continued to increase. By the close of this day the 6th Guards Tank Army's units were fighting along the following lines: the 4th Guards Mechanized Corps, as before, in the Velke Ludince area, the 9th Guards Mechanized Corps north of Bajcs and north of Pribeta, and the 5th Guards Tank Corps, as before, was fighting along the eastern outskirts of Komarno.

Due to the unrelenting attacks by major enemy tank and infantry forces, the forces of the Third Ukrainian Front during 2-7 January continued to wage defensive battles and, while holding the enemy along the main axes toward Budapest, were not able to organize an offensive in the direction of Komarno.

However, the attack by the forces of the Second Ukrainian Front on 6 January north of the Danube and the arrival of the 6th Guards Tank Army's units at Komarno had decisive significance for the development of military operations to the south of the Danube. Fearing that the Second Ukrainian Front's forces would seize crossings near Komarno and, upon forcing the Danube, would get astride the communications of the shock group, the enemy, having also encountered the stubborn resistance of the Third Ukrainian Front's forces, was forced to forego its offensive on Budapest from the northwest and to shift his efforts to another axis.

Thus the enemy's offensive, which was launched by him on 2 January from the area southeast of Komarno, was a failure.

The repulse by the Third Ukrainian Front's forces of the Germans' offensive on Budapest from the area northwest of Szekesfehervar (7-13 January). Having failed to carry out the assigned task of breaking through to Budapest from the northwest, by 7 January the German command prepared a new offensive, now in the center of the 4th Guards Army along the line Scokako—Csor. The attack had been prepared in the general direction of Zamoly in order, while developing the success to the northwest and southwest, to encircle our group of forces operating west of Bicske, to capture Szekesfehervar and to subsequently develop the offensive on Budapest.

The Germans, without breaking off their fierce attacks in the direction of Bicske and having thrown in two tank divisions from the north to the area northwest of Szekesfehervar and shifted the combat formations of one tank division from the line Osi—Balatonakarttya to the Moha area, attacked from the line Csokako—Moha at 0830 on 7 January, following an artillery fire onslaught.[3]

Throughout the entire day the units of the 20th Guards Rifle Corps defending along this sector, and units of the 7th Mechanized Corps, which was committed into the fighting from the 4th Guards Army commander's reserve, were engaged in fierce fighting with the attacking enemy. By the close of 7 January the Germans, having lost 45 tanks and self-propelled guns knocked out and burned, were able to advance as much as four kilometers, although they were not able to develop the success along this axis.

As a result of our rifle units' timely and skillfully organized defensive system and their precise interaction with the 5th Guards Cavalry Corps'[4] artillery, motorized infantry, tanks, and cavalry, the enemy, while suffering heavy losses, was only able to make slight progress on 8 January.

3 The composition of the Germans' group of forces was as follows: 3rd, 23rd and 1st panzer divisions, the 4th Cavalry Brigade and infantry units up to a division in strength.

4 On 7 January the 5th Guards Cavalry Corps was operationally subordinated to the commander of the 4th Guards Army.

In order to strengthen the center of the 4th Guards Army's front, the 93rd Rifle Division, which had been removed from the second defensive line south of Bicske, was moved up to the Zamoly—Patka defensive sector. Simultaneously, in order to prevent the Germans from further spreading along this axis, in accordance with a decision by the *front* commander, a joint counterblow was organized by the formations of the 20th Rifle Corps, the 7th Mechanized Corps and units of the 1st Guards Mechanized Corps, which had by this time just arrived at the *front*.

Having begun the offensive from the line Zamoly—Gyulamajor, at 0930 on 9 January, our units, while overcoming the enemy's stubborn fire resistance and numerous tank counterattacks, having advanced, consolidated along the lines reached. As a result of three days of bitter fighting, the enemy's offensive had been halted. Subsequently, our units successfully repulsed all the enemy's tank and infantry attacks from the line Sored—Zamoly—Gyulamajor—Moha with organized fire from artillery, tanks and infantry.

On 13 January the enemy was forced to halt his active offensive operations along the army's entire front.

The German group of forces that was attacking opposite the 46th Army's left-flank units along the line Esztergom—Many occupied the city of Esztergom and Esztergom camp on 6 January, at the cost of heavy losses, and Pilisszentkeraszt on 12 January. Along the Zsambek axis on 7 January the enemy occupied Felso; however, despite the commitment of the new 711th Infantry Division into the fighting, the Germans, having encountered our troops' stubborn resistance, were forced to call off the offensive and go over to the defensive on 13 January.

On 14 January the 46th Army's units themselves took up active operations. With a simultaneous attack from the north on Pilisszentelek from the north and on Pilisszentkeraszt from the south and southwest, units of the 5th Guards Cavalry Corps[5] and units of the 86th and 99th rifle divisions began to push the enemy breakthrough to the northwest. While operating in the difficult conditions of a mountainous and wooded terrain, they crushed the Germans' resistance and on 14 January captured Pilisszentkeraszt and on 17 January occupied the inhabited locale of Pilisszentelek.

Thus the German command's plan to break through from the west to Budapest to its encircled group of forces was a complete failure.

The forces of the Third Ukrainian Front and part of the forces of the 46th and 4th Guards armies and the forces of the 18th Tank, 1st and 2nd guards and 7th mechanized corps, and the 5th Guards Cavalry Corps, along with effective support from the air by the 17th and 5th air armies of the Second Ukrainian Front, inflicted enormous losses on the enemy's Komarno group of forces in fierce defensive battles during 2-13 January and forced the Germans to call off their attempts to break through to Budapest by the shortest route and to go over to the defense.

At the same time attempts by the enemy's encircled group of forces to break out from the western part of Budapest to the northwest were eliminated.

By the middle of January the situation of the Third Ukrainian Front's forces was as follows. The 46th Army, with units of the 37th and 75th rifle corps were continuing to fight to eliminate the encircled German-Hungarian group of forces in the western part of Budapest.

The 46th Army's main forces, consisting of the 10th Guards and 23rd rifle and the 2nd Guards Mechanized and 5th Guards Cavalry corps were strengthening their defensive lines and carrying out reconnaissance of the enemy. The front ran 4-5 kilometers east of Esztergom and then to the south west of Pilisszentelek, from where it turned to the west toward Satorke; the front then ran to the south, through Dorog, Sarisap, Dag, and Many.

5 The 5th Guards Cavalry Corps, minus the 63rd Cavalry Division, continued to operate with the 4th Guards Army and on 12 January was transferred to the 46th Army.

The 4th Guards Army was occupying defensive positions along the line Csabdi—Szarujtelep—Banhida—Oroszlany—east of Pustavam—east of Csokako—Csakbereny—excluding Zamoly—Gyula—height 153—height 113—Osi, from where the front turn to the south toward Lake Balaton.

Thus in 12 days the enemy managed to advance up to 30-35 kilometers along our forces' right flank and up to ten kilometers in the center.

However, the German command still had not renounced its decision to break through to its encircled troops in Budapest and began to forcibly prepare a new decisive offensive opposite the 4th Guards Army's left flank between lakes Balaton and Velence.

The enemy along the Komarno axis, having concentrated his forces during 10-11 January, counterattacked on 13 January against the Second Ukrainian Front's 6th Guards Tank and 7th Guards armies, forcing them to fall back from Komarno somewhat to the east. Intense fighting was going on in Budapest to eliminate the encircled German-Hungarian group of forces.

The repulse by the Third Ukrainian Front's forces of the Germans' offensive on Budapest from the area southwest of Szekesfehervar (18-27 January). From 11 January the Germans, having relieved their tank formations opposite the Third Ukrainian Front's right wing with German cavalry units and individual Hungarian units, carried out a regrouping of their forces from the north to the south, toward Lake Balaton. The preparation for this new offensive was conducted in extreme secrecy with the widespread employment of disinformation. For example, in order to fool our intelligence, the transfer of the main tank forces from the Esztergom—Bicske area to the Osi—Balatonakarttya area was not carried out by the Germans along the shortest routes along the front, but they were first pulled back deeply to the west to the Komarno area, and even to Gyor (50 kilometers west of Tata), from where the tanks then moved to the south and southeast to the Veszprem area (20 kilometers southwest of Varpalota). The regrouping was carried out at night, while observing all masking measures. As a result, by 18 January the enemy had managed to concentrate a powerful shock group in the area east and northeast of Veszprem.

The Germans, having concentrated in this area five panzer divisions[6] with an overall strength of 330 tanks and self-propelled guns, once more decided to break through our front and reach Budapest to link up with their encircled group of forces.

In an order to the IV SS Panzer Corps, which was seized by our units in the beginning of February the offensive's tasks were defined as follows:

> The IV SS Panzer Corps is to break through the position between Lake Balaton and Csor on 18 January and launch an attack to the northeast as far as the Danube River, with the task of establishing contact with the forces encircled in the city of Budapest.
>
> The subsequent task will be to destroy the enemy located in the area west and northwest of Budapest.
>
> The neighbor on the left is to support the corps' offensive by an attack on Szekesfehervar and then as far as Lake Velence.

By 17 January the disposition of the 4th Guards Army's forces remained the same as it had developed following the repulse of the enemy's offensive along the army's right flank and center. The army's main forces were in the area west of Bicske and north of the city of Szekesfehervar.

6 The shock group consisted of the 3rd and 1st panzer divisions, the 5th SS Panzer Division (*Wiking*), the 3rd SS Panzer Division *Totenkopf*, and the 23rd Panzer Division (in the area west of Sarkeresztes), the 509th Panzer Battalion of "King Tigers," the 325th Assault Gun Brigade, units of the 24th Panzer Division's 24th Panzer Regiment, as well as cavalry and infantry units, a powerful artillery group, and sapper units. Formations of the Fourth Air Fleet supported the shock group from the air.

Only the 135th Rifle Corps (252nd, 1st Guards Fortified Area and the 7th Mechanized Corps' 63rd Brigade)[7] was located directly along the 4th Guards Army's left flank.

Thus the Germans had an overwhelming superiority in forces, particularly in tanks, along the planned breakthrough sector.

At 0630 on 18 January the enemy, following a short but powerful artillery preparation, attacked from the line Osi—Balatonakarttya to the east and southeast.

Within three hours the Germans began an attack from the Sarkeresztes area toward Szekesfehervar. Simultaneously, small groups of infantry (100-200 men), supported by 10-15 tanks waged uninterrupted attacks against the 68th Rifle Corps' positions defending along the army's center northeast of Sarkeresztes.

The enemy's offensive along the main axis was supported from the air by assault air and bomber aviation.

During the first stage of the offensive the enemy committed up to 130 tanks and self-propelled guns and up to 60 armored transports into the fighting along the main axis.

Despite stubborn resistance by our defending units, the enemy, who enjoyed a numerical superiority, managed to break through the 135th Rifle Corps' defense along a 20-kilometer front. In order to halt the enemy's offensive until the arrival of the *front* reserves, the commander of the 4th Guards Army committed the 7th Mechanized Corps into the fighting with the task of leaving its occupied area at 1100 and, having taken up defensive positions along the line Nadasdladany—Fule, halt the enemy offensive.

However, the units of the 7th Mechanized Corps did not reach their areas in time, because the enemy had already occupied this line and were forced to begin fighting from the march against the enemy's tanks and infantry in the Falubattyan area and to the south. By the middle of the day the enemy's tank formations had reached the Sarviz Canal along a 6-kilometer line southwest of Szekesfehervar and Sarkeresztur and, having penetrated up to 15 kilometers into the defensive depth cut up the combat formations of the 135th Corps' units and disrupted the corps' command and control.

By the close of the day the 252nd Division, having suffered heavy losses, had been thrown back to the Sarviz Canal in the Szentvendel area. Elements of the 1st Guards Fortified Area fell back to the Lepseny area. The 7th Mechanized Corps was engaged in heavy fighting with two brigades against the enemy's tanks and infantry along the northwestern and western outskirts of Falubattyan, while one brigade was making a fighting withdrawal toward Polgardi. Part of the 1st Guards Fortified Area's and the 7th Mechanized Corps' forces were fighting in encirclement, while throughout the day the 68th Rifle Corps successfully repulsed up to ten enemy attacks from the Banhida—Bokod line and occupied its former line. In order to restore the situation, the commander of the Third Ukrainian Front decided to throw the 18th Tank and 133rd Rifle corps[8] into the breakthrough area. As early as the close of the day, the 133rd Rifle Corps had reached a position along the eastern bank of the Sarviz Canal along a 2-kilometer sector southeast of Falubattyan as far as Aba and was fighting with part of its forces against the enemy's forward units in Sarkeresztur. The 18th Tank Corps, having carried out a march from the Paty—Torbad area to the Aba—Sarkeresztur area, also entered the fighting on the morning of 19 January against the enemy's attacking units.

Simultaneously, measures were adopted to strengthen the defense of Szekesfehervar. On orders of the commander of the 4th Guards Army, the 21st Rifle Corps' 69th Guards Rifle Division occupied defensive positions south of Szekesfehervar, with its front facing south. The 68th Rifle Corps' 93rd Rifle Division was also thrown in here. The army's left-flank formations were reinforced with

7 The 21st Rifle Corps, which was defending north of Lake Balaton turned over its combat sector to the 135th Corps on 6 January and was transferred to the Vertesacsa area along the right flank.

8 By this time the 133rd Rifle Corps was being transferred from the 57th Army to the Seregelyes—Aba area.

anti-tank artillery. All the bridges over the Sarviz Canal were blown up by 0100 on 19 January and the crossings were under heavy bombardment by our artillery.

Throughout the night the enemy, under the cover of artillery and mortar fire, was hurriedly laying down crossings and in the morning began to force the Sarviz Canal.

Despite their heavy losses, the Germans stubbornly continued the offensive, trying to break through to Budapest as quickly as possible, for by this time the situation of their encircled group of forces had significantly worsened. On 18 January the forces of the Second Ukrainian Front completely captured the eastern part of the city (Pest) and all of the German-Hungarian forces had been pressed into a dense ring in the western part of the city (Buda).

The fierce fighting along the 4th Guards Army's left flank continued throughout the day of 19 January. Despite stubborn resistance by the army's formations, and that of the 7th Mechanized, 18th Tank and 133rd Rifle corps, the Germans managed to force the Sarviz Canal and break through to the Dunaujvaros area and reach the Danube by the morning of 20 January.

On 20 January the enemy, while continuing to develop the breakthrough, reached the line Siofok—Mezokomarom—north of Cece—Dunaujvaros—western outskirts of Sarkeresztur—Bergent—Szentvendel. Thus the enemy managed to cut the Third Ukrainian Front's forces into two parts. Besides this, the 18th Tank and 133rd Rifle corps were fighting in encirclement in the Sarkeresztur—Sarosd area. All of the enemy's attacks were beaten off along the Szekesfehervar axis and his units, having advanced little, were being held by units of the 252nd, 93rd and 69th Guards rifle divisions along the line Sarpentele—Szentvendel. By 20 January the breakthrough had reached 45 kilometers in width and more than 65 kilometers in depth. There was a real threat that the enemy would bypass Lake Velence from the east and reach Budapest from the south. Thus the *front* command and the commander of the 4th Guards Army took emergency measures to organize a defensive line between Lake Velence and the Danube.

Because the Second Ukrainian Front's forces had completely cleared the eastern part of Budapest (Pest) of the enemy, the *Stavka* of the Supreme High Command, in its directive no. 11009 to the commanders of the Second and Third Ukrainian fronts of 18 January, placed the control of operations to complete the destruction of the enemy group of forces in the western part of Budapest (Buda) on the commander of the Second Ukrainian Front.[9] The commander of the Third Ukrainian Front was ordered to restore the situation southwest of Szekesfehervar and prepare his forces to attack in order to rout the enemy group of forces operating between the Danube and Lake Balaton.

At the same time, in order to concentrate the main attention of the Third Ukrainian Front's commander on restoring the situation southwest of Szekesfehervar, the *Stavka* of the Supreme High Command ordered him to employ the headquarters of the 46th Army for controlling the forces along the *front's* right wing, having subordinated the 4th Guards Army's right-flank corps to it.

In carrying out the instructions of the *Stavka* of the Supreme High Command, by the close of 19 January the commander of the Third Ukrainian Front made the following decision.

The 4th Guards Army's right-flank 31st Guards and 68th rifle corps, together with all their reinforcements, were to be subordinated to the commander of the 46th Army, without removing them from their occupied areas.[10] From 2400 on 19 January the 133rd Rifle Corps was to be subordinated to the 4th Guards Army, as well as the 46th Army's 5th Guards

9 In accordance with these instructions, on 20 January the Third Ukrainian Front subordinated the 75th and 37th rifle corps and the 83rd Naval Infantry Brigade, along with all reinforcements that were fighting with the corps in the western part of Budapest to the commander of the Second Ukrainian Front.

10 Because of this, the boundary line was to be established along the line Baracska—Val—Vertesacsa—Csakvar—Csokako—Mor (all locales, except for Csakvar and Csokako were for the 4th Guards Army inclusively).

Cavalry Corps, the 1st Guards Mechanized Corps, the 113th Rifle Division, and four regiments of anti-tank and self-propelled artillery. The 5th Guards Cavalry Corps, to which was operationally subordinated the 113th Division, the 1st Guards Mechanized Corps and the reinforcement artillery, had the task of organizing a secure defense between Lake Velence and the Danube. By the close of 20 January the cavalry corps had occupied and outfitted a line facing south along the line Kisvelence—Groftanya and then to the east as far as the Danube River and covered the Budapest axis. The 4th Guards Army's overall mission consisted of securely holding the present defensive line and preventing the enemy's further advance to the north toward Budapest.

In order to construct a secure defense from the south, part of the 57th Army's forces were to be grouped to the northeast to the area southwest of Dunapentele. As early as 20 January the 32nd Motorized Brigade had been moved up to the line Simontornya—Siofok.

Simultaneously, the *Stavka* of the Supreme High Command ordered the commander of the Second Ukrainian Front to transfer the 30th Guards Rifle Corps (68th, 36th, 155th, and 74th rifle divisions) to the commander of the Third Ukrainian Front. On 21 January the corps crossed the Danube in the Dunapentele area, with the task of occupying defensive positions along the line northeast of Dunapentele—Cece. One of the 30th Guards Rifle Corps' divisions occupied defensive positions along the eastern bank of the Danube along the line Tokol—Solt. On 21 January, in accordance with the order by the commander of the Third Ukrainian Front, the 18th Tank and 133rd Rifle corps made a fighting breakout to the area northwest of Dunapentele through enemy-occupied territory and also took up defensive positions with their front facing north.

As a result of the regrouping of the Second and Third Ukrainian fronts' forces, the 4th Guards Army's defense was made denser and a new defense was created, which covered the breakthrough area from the south.

During 20-27 January the Third Ukrainian Front's formations were engaged in intense fighting against the attacking enemy opposite the 4th Guards Army's left flank. Particularly bitter fighting took place in the area of the city of Szekesfehervar and southeast and east of Lake Velence.

On 22 January, following three days of uninterrupted fighting, units of the 4th Guards Army's 21st Guards Corps were forced to fall back under pressure from superior forces and abandon Szekesfehervar and fall back to the line Patka—Kisfalud.

During the night of 23-24 January the Germans, following a powerful artillery preparation, once again attacked in the 5th Guards Cavalry and 1st Guards Mechanized corps' defensive sector between Lake Velence and the Danube, having up to 100 tanks and up to 70 armored transports[11] in their combat formations. Having begun the attack from the line Kisvelence—Felsobesnyo, the enemy, supported by powerful artillery and mortar fire, broke through our defense during the night of 23-24 January and on 25 January captured Pettend, from where he began to develop the attack to the northwest.

The 1st Guards Mechanized Corps and units of the 93rd Rifle Division, which were defending along this sector, having suffered heavy losses during the fighting, were unable to maintain a continuous front and by the close of 26 January had broken through with individual groups of tanks and armored transports to the Kajaszoszentpeter—Val—Vereb area.

However, the Germans were not able to develop this breakthrough. The units of the 104th Rifle and 23rd Tank corps, which had been subordinated to the *front* and which had been committed into the fighting, halted the enemy's further advance. Upon encountering the powerful resistance

11 The enemy attacked with the forces of the 1st Panzer Division, the SS *Totenkopf* Panzer Division, the *Wiking* SS Panzer Division, and the 503rd Army Battalion of "King Tigers."

of our tanks and infantry, the enemy on 27 January was forced to go over to the defensive along the front between Lake Velence and the Danube.

During 18-26 January the enemy opposite the 46th Army's front did not undertake a major attack and there was little change. However, the enemy carried out a local offensive operation in order to distract our reserves from the Lake Velence area. On 23 January the Germans began an attack from the area north of Bicske to the southeast with the forces of the 6th Panzer Division and the 3rd Cavalry Brigade, with the support of artillery and mortar fire. As a result, the enemy managed to penetrate our units' defense and capture the inhabited locale of Many and a number of heights southeast of this place. During 24-26 January the Germans tried to advance further to the east, however units of the 2nd Guards Mechanized Corps and the 59th Guards Rifle Division beat back all the enemy's attacks and forced him to go over to the defensive.

Due to the Germans' continuing offensive in the Szekesfehervar area and to the north and the threat here to the communications of the 46th Army's left-flank formations, during the night of 23-24 January they were pulled back from the line Banhida—Bokod—Csakbereny to a more favorable defensive line that ran through Kortvelyespuszta—Verteskozma—Gant.

During 20-26 January the enemy carried out continuous attacks along the southern sector, from a line north of Dunapentele, Cece and Siofok, for the purpose of securing the main forces' offensive along the Budapest direction. However, units of the 30th Guards Rifle, 18th Tank, and 133rd and 135th rifle corps[12] successfully beat off the Germans' attacks and by 26 January continued to fight essentially along the same line that they occupied on 20 January.

Thus the Germans' attempts to break through to Budapest from the southwest also ended in failure.

The task assigned to the troops by the *front's* military council to "stand to the death" and to prevent the German group of forces from reaching Budapest, despite the difficult fighting conditions and the enemy's numerical superiority, had been honorably accomplished. The enemy, having suffered enormous losses, had been halted along the approaches to Budapest.

However, the *front's* forces faced a subsequent task—to eliminate the enemy's breakthrough group of forces and restore the situation. They set about carrying out this task on 26-27 January.

The offensive by the Third Ukrainian Front's forces and the elimination of the enemy breakthrough. The end of the operation (27 January-16 February). With the enemy's breakthrough to the Danube south of Budapest, the situation became considerably more complicated for the troops of the Third and Second Ukrainian fronts. The real danger of the enemy's breakthrough to the encircled group of forces had arisen. The *Stavka* of the Supreme High Command adopted a number of organization measures directed at eliminating the threat.

The *Stavka* of the Supreme High Command, in a special directive no. 11013 of 22 January 1945, assigned the commanders of the Second and Third Ukrainian fronts new tasks.

In order to defeat the enemy group of forces that had broken through to the Danube, the commander of the Second Ukrainian Front was ordered, without halting operations to eliminate the encircled enemy group of forces in Buda and going over to a rigid defense along the Komarno axis, to concentrate the 23rd Tank Corps and no less than a rifle corps along the western bank of the Danube, in order to launch an attack no later than 25-26 January between Lake Velence and the Danube in the general direction of Sarosd, toward an attack by the Third Ukrainian Front's forces. The commander of the Third Ukrainian Front was ordered to reinforce the 18th Tank Corps with tanks and self-propelled guns and put the 133rd Rifle Corps in order and no later than 25-26 January launch an attack with the forces of the 18th Tank Corps and 4-5 rifle divisions between the Sarviz Canal and the Danube, also in the direction of Sarosd, to meet the

12 The headquarters of the 135th Rifle Corps was part of the 57th Army.

Second Ukrainian Front's attack. It was ordered to organize a defense along the eastern bank of the Danube, along the Adony—Dunapentele sector and along the sector from the Sarviz Canal to Lake Balaton and to prevent the enemy from breaking through to the east and south.

On 23 January, in order to unify the efforts to eliminate the enemy's breakthrough group, the *Stavka* of the Supreme High Command ordered the commander of the Second Ukrainian Front to transfer at 1200 on 24 January the 23rd Tank and 104th Rifle corps to the Third Ukrainian Front, upon crossing them to the western bank of the Danube.

On the basis of the *Stavka* of the Supreme High Command's instructions no. 11014 of 23 January, the commander of the Third Ukrainian Front decided to launch a simultaneous counterblow with part of the 4th Guards Army's forces and the 104th Rifle and 23rd Tank corps[13] from the north and the area northeast of Lake Velence in the direction of Sarosd, and with the forces of the 18th Tank Corps, 30th Guards and 133rd rifle corps and part of the 135th Rifle Corps's forces, also in the direction of Sarosd.

The commander of the 4th Guards Army was ordered to bring in for the offensive the 1st Guards Mechanized Corps, 2-3 rifle divisions and the greater part of the army's artillery. In planning the offensive, it was planned to have all of the army's forces attack in order to restore the former situation.

On 27 January the Third Ukrainian Front's forces were situated as follows: the 46th Army continued to occupy defensive positions along a front from the southern bank of the Danube (five kilometers east of Esztergom and then to the southwest and south through the inhabited locales west of Dorog—Sarisap—east of Szomor—west of Zsambek—southeast and south of Many—Csabdi—Gant.

The 4th Guards Army along the right flank occupied defensive positions along the line excluding Gant—two kilometers west of Patka—south of Kisfalud—Pakozd—Sukoro—Kapolnasnyek. In the center and along the left flank the 4th Guards Army's formations were waging defensive battles with the enemy's tanks and infantry that had broken through along a line northern part of Kapolnasnyek and then to the north through the southern outskirts of Pazmand—northern outskirts of Vereb—western outskirts of Val—Kajaszoszentpeter—Baracska and then to the southeast to the Danube (four kilometers south of Ercsi).

Between the Danube and Lake Balaton the 30th Guards, 133rd and 135th rifle corps and the 18th Tank Corps were engaged in defensive fighting, facing north.[14]

The enemy (as can be seen from the orders issued to the IV Panzer Corps of 27 January) had the task of temporarily taking up the defensive and to hold the occupied line at all costs.

On 27 January the *front's* forces, having completed their regrouping and preparations for the counterblow, began a counteroffensive with part of the 4th Guards Army's forces, together with the 23rd Tank and 5th Guards Cavalry Corps from the north, and the forces of the 18th Tank, 30th Guards and 133rd rifle corps and one division from the 135th Rifle Corps from the south, for the purpose of destroying the enemy's breakthrough to the Danube.

The offensive began at 1000 along the 4th Guards Army's front with the main forces of the 23rd Tank Corps and part of the 104th Rifle Corps' forces in the direction of Vereb and Pettend, for the purpose of eliminating the enemy's Pazmand salient. Despite stubborn resistance by the enemy, who sought to delay our offensive with powerful artillery and mortar fire and fire from cruising tanks, our units captured the greater part of Vereb and, following a fierce battle, the enemy's important communications center of Pettend.

13 The 104th Rifle Corps was subordinated to the 4th Guards Army on 25 January and the 23rd Tank Corps on 26 January.

14 On 28 January the 30th Guards Rifle, 133rd Rifle and the 18th Tank corps were unified by the 26th Army's newly-arrived field headquarters into the 26th Army.

Decisive attacks by the units of the 23rd Tank Corps on 27 January, although they did not end with the complete elimination of the enemy's group of forces which had broken through to the Vereb—Val area, nevertheless forced the enemy to begin a withdrawal under the threat of encirclement. By the close of the day the command of the German IV SS Panzer Corps issued an order to pull back the tank units from the Val—Vereb area and to occupy defensive positions along the line Baracska—Pettend—Kapolnasnyek.

On 27 January the offensive by the Third Ukrainian Front's forces developed more successfully between the Danube and Lake Velence. While overcoming the enemy's stubborn resistance and repelling counterattacks by tanks and infantry on armored transports, units of the 30th Guards and 133rd rifle corps, while attacking in close coordination with the 18th Tank Corps, advanced 3-9 kilometers in the day's fighting, capturing the major inhabited locales of Hercegfalva and Sarbogard.

By the close of the day, having thrown back the enemy to the north, units of the 30th Guards Corps were fighting along the line south of Dunapentele—Melykut—1.5 kilometers south of Nagyhantos. The 133rd Rifle Corps was fighting to the west, as far as the Sarviz Canal, along the line excluding Nagy—Bebic. The 57th Army's right-flank 233rd Rifle Division captured the inhabited locale of Saregres and was fighting for Igar. Attacking ahead of the infantry, units of the 18th Tank Corps reached Nagyperkata by the close of the day and began fighting for it.

During the night of 27-28 January fighting continued to eliminate the enemy's Pazmand salient, in order to secure a jumping-off line for an offensive by the main forces of the 4th Guards Army's shock group.

By the middle of the day on 28 January units of the 20th Guards Rifle Corps, along with tanks from the 23rd Tank Corps, completely captured Vereb after bitter fighting, while units of the 21st Guards Corps captured Pazmand, as a result of which the enemy's group of forces that had broken through northeast of Lake Velence was eliminated.

By this time the main forces of the 4th Guards Army's shock group—the 23rd Tank and 104th Rifle corps had occupied their jumping-off positions in the Pettend area along the Rajszentpeter—height 101 sector and, at 1300, following a short fire onslaught, launched a decisive attack to the south.

Throughout the following days the offensive by the Third Ukrainian Front's forces from the north and south continued with unabated force.

Despite the enemy's stubborn resistance, the 4th Guards and 26th armies' attacking formations persistently advanced, step by step, while clearing the enemy from territory seized by him during his offensive.

On 31 January, along with the development of the offensive along the main axis, the *front's* forces, while regrouping the 1st Guards Mechanized Corps and the 5th Guards Cavalry Corps to the area northeast of Szekesfehervar, the 4th Guards Army attacked with formations of the 20th and 21st guards rifle corps along the Zamoly—Pakozd sector in the general direction of Magyaralmas and the city of Szekesfehervar.

This attack forced the enemy to shift part of his forces to the Szekesfehervar area from the south, as well as the newly-arrived 356th Infantry Division.

Having broken through the enemy's defense, units of the 4th Guards Army captured the inhabited locale of Zamoly and occupied the eastern suburbs of Szekesfehervar and the city's northern outskirts and broke into the city with tanks.

With their attack in the direction of Szekesfehervar, the units of the 4th Guards Army pulled part of the Germans' forces from the front facing the shock group, which facilitated its success.

On 2 February the attacking units of the 104th Rifle and 23rd Tank corps reached the area southwest of Adony and Pusztaszabolcs. By this time the 26th Army's 30th Guards Rifle and 18th Tank corps had captured Dunapentele, Adony and Nagyperkata and reached the line northwest of Nagyperkata. As a result, the northern and southern groups of the 4th Guards and 26th armies linked up and formed a common front.

By the close of 2 February the Third Ukrainian Front's forces occupied the following position: the 46th Army continued to defend along a front along the southern bank of the Danube—Esztergom, as far as Gant; the 4th Guards Army was fighting along the line excluding Gant—west of Zamoly—Gyulamajor—the northern and eastern outskirts of Szekesfehervar—Kisfalud—Pakozd—southwest of Gardony—Ludovika. The 26th Army's formations reached the line four kilometers west of Nagyperkata—southeast and south of Nagyhantos—and then to the west as far as the Sarviz Canal. On the 57th Army's right flank, units of the 135th Rifle Corps were fighting three kilometers north of Saregres and Igar. Along the remainder of the front our units continued to defend along their previous line from Ozora to Siofok.

Thus the Third Ukrainian Front's forces crushed the enemy's resistance with a concentric attack from the north between Lake Velence and the Danube and from the south from the area west of Dunapentele and in six days of attacking completely cleared the western bank of the Danube of the enemy's group that had broken through.

After the 4th Guards and 26th armies' forced linked up, our units turned their attack front to the west and from 3 February continued to develop the offensive to the west. The 57th Army's formations attacked to the north.

While overcoming the Germans' stubborn resistance and numerous counterattacks, the Third Ukrainian Front's forces completely cleared by mid-February the territory east of lakes Velence and Balaton, which had been occupied by the enemy as a result of his offensive during the second half of January.

During the defensive fighting of 18-27 January and the offensive from 28 January to the middle of February, the *front's* forces inflicted heavy losses on the enemy in men and materiel.

The Germans' defeat in their counteroffensive against the Third Ukrainian Front from the area southwest of the city of Szekesfehervar deprived the encircled German-Hungarian group of forces of aid from without.

At the same time as the Third Ukrainian Front's forces, as a result of heavy defensive fighting, halted the enemy's group of forces that had broken through toward Budapest and then, having taken up the offensive, threw it back to its starting position, the Second Ukrainian Front's forces were successfully concluding the destruction of the encircled enemy in the western part of Budapest (Buda).

On 12 February, when the elimination of the encircled enemy group of forces in Buda was coming to an end, units of the encircled group of forces undertook a desperate attempt to break out of the encirclement. Individual enemy groups managed to break through the combat formations of the Second Ukrainian Front's units and they began to spread to the northwest into the rear of the Third Ukrainian Front's right-flank units.

However, a new defensive line was created by the rapid maneuver of reserves and units from other sectors of the front along the *front's* right wing west and northwest of Budapest, and as a result of joint actions units of the 46th Army, 11th Cavalry Division (5th Guards Cavalry Corps) and units of the Second Ukrainian Front, the enemy's breakthrough group was halted and then encircled, and was completely destroyed on 16 February in the woods southwest of Pilisvorosvar.

During the elimination of the remnants of the encircled enemy Budapest group of forces the Third Ukrainian Front's formations alone killed up to 9,600 enemy soldiers and officers and captured about 20,000, among which there were more than 9,000 German and more than 10,000 Hungarian soldiers and officers.

According to the command's orders, in the middle of February the Third Ukrainian Front's forces took up the defensive along the entire front. By this time the 46th Army's front line basically ran along the same line as was the case on 2 February, with the exception of the area north of Bicske, where the army's units occupied the inhabited locale of Many.

The 4th Guards Army was located along the line south of Gant—west of Zamoly—excluding Gyulamajor—eastern suburbs of Szekesfehervar—Kisfalud—east of Dinnyes—excluding Seregelyes. The 26th Army went over to the defensive along the line west of Seregelyes—Aba—northwest and west of Saponya—four kilometers west of Kaloz. Further to the west, the 135th Rifle Corps occupied defensive positions along the line Peterszallas—Balatonbozsok—Lake Balaton.

Thus during the very intensive fighting of January-February 1945, the forces of the Third Ukrainian Front repelled all of the Germans' major offensive operations, which had been undertaken by them for the purpose of defeating our forces grouped to the west of the Danube and relieving Budapest. This created the prerequisites and conditions for the complete elimination of the enemy group of forces encircled in Budapest. Characteristic of the Third Ukrainian Front's forces' activities at this final stage of the operation were the high degree of operational maneuverability, the unusually skillful and rapid creation of defensive lines in the operational depth of the troops' position, the powerful counterblows against the weakest parts of the enemy's formations, the skillful organization of anti-tank defense, and the skillful combat mastery of our tank troops. In this extremely intensive fighting the military art and combat mastery of our generals and officers, who were brought up and studied under our brilliant leader, Generalissimo comrade Stalin, enjoyed a total triumph. The enemy was forced give in to the Red Army's power and skill and to renounce his intentions to liberate his powerful group of forces encircled in Budapest.

The repulse of the enemy's offensive along the Komarno axis by the forces of the Second Ukrainian Front. The completion of the operation. Simultaneously with the unfolding fierce fighting by the Third Ukrainian Front's forces to repulse the Germans' major attacks in the area to the west of Budapest, no less intense fighting unfolded along the Second Ukrainian Front's sector along the Komarno axis. As has already been mentioned, the 7th Guards and 6th Guards Tank armies, which attacked on 6 January along the line of the Hron River, reached Nove Zamky and Komarno with their mobile units by 9-10 January, where they encountered the enemy's powerful tank counterblows. One could feel that the enemy had prepared a serious offensive operation along this line.

On 11 January the enemy, having concentrated more than 130 armored vehicles (50-60 tanks and self-propelled guns and 70 armored transports) in the Nove Zamky area, broke through from Nove Zamky toward Svaty Peter and Madar. Our units operating along this axis were forced to fall back.

As a result of the developing situation, the *front* commander issued the following order (no. 0021/op of 1300, 11 January).

The commander of the 6th Guards Army, in close cooperation with units of the 7th Guards Army, was to launch an attack and destroy the enemy in the Madar—Svaty Peter area, after which he was to concentrate the army in the Svaty Peter—Pribeta area and carry out reconnaissance toward Kolta, Dvory and Nove Zamky, in order to destroy the enemy along these axes. The 4th Guards Mechanized Corps was to remain for operations in the direction of Farnad.

Simultaneously, the commander of the 7th Guards Army was ordered to commit two anti-tank artillery brigades (2nd and 11th) into the fighting and, in close cooperation with the 6th Guards Tank Army, to destroy the enemy in the Svaty Peter—Madar area in order to secure capture the Zeliezovce—Farnad—Jasova—Bajcs—Imel' area and then to the south along the Nitra River to its mouth; the operation would be secured along the Danube River.

The commander of the 5th Air Army received orders to launch an attack on the enemy, in close coordination with the ground forces, in the Svaty Peter—Madar area, in order to completely destroy him.

As early as that same day units of the 6th Guards Tank and 7th Guards armies set about carrying out their assigned tasks. On 12 January the enemy continued to augment his forces and reinforced the attack against the 7th Guards Army's units, which were forced to fall back to the line of the southern outskirts of Svaty Dyala—Zeleny—Gai—excluding Dulov. Throughout the entire day units of the 6th Guards Tank Army were fighting to destroy the enemy's breakthrough tank group and by the close of the day were fighting along the following lines: 9th Guards Mechanized Corps, east of Nova Trstena and along the southern outskirts of Svaty Peter; 5th Guards Tank Corps, along the northern and southern outskirts of Madar; 4th Guards Mechanized Corps for Velke Ludince.

On the morning of 13 January the enemy's tank group, in strength of up to 150 vehicles (tanks, self-propelled artillery and armored transports) attacked from the Bajcs—Svaty Dyala area along the following directions: Svaty Dyala, Chotin and Bajcs, Pribeta, Nova Vieska. As a result of the fierce and stubborn fighting, the enemy managed to push units of the 7th Guards Army back to the line Kamendy—north of Szoldiny—two kilometers northwest of Nova Vieska—eastern outskirts of Madar—Marcelova—three kilometers west of Radvan.

In order to hold the bridgehead along the western bank of the Hron River, the *front* commander on 13 January issued order no. 0024/op, in which he ordered the commander of the 7th Guards Army to take up a solid defense by 1200 on 14 January along the line Bina—marker 273—Madar—Marcelova—three kilometers west of Radvan and then along the Danube River to the mouth of the Hron River. In order to secure the 7th Guards Army's units' occupation of this line, the 6th Guards Tank Army was ordered to counterattack the enemy with the forces of the 5th Guards Tank and 9th Guards Mechanized corps in the Madar area and to throw him back to the west. Following the counterattack, the army, except for the 4th Guards Mechanized Corps, was to be gathered in the Nova Vieska—Bucs area and the 4th Guards Mechanized Corps was to remain on the defensive in the Velke Ludince area until special orders.

The enemy, taking no notice of his great losses, tried to throw back our units from the bridgehead at any cost. Intensive fighting lasted continuously until 21 January, although the enemy enjoyed almost no success after 14 January. On 21 January the Germans' attacks weakened significantly and on the 23rd they stopped altogether.

Thus the bridgehead along the western bank of the Hron River along its southern course remained in the hands of the 7th Guards Army's units. Subsequently, all the way up to the defeat of the enemy's Budapest group of forces; that is, up until 13 February, our units securely held their previous positions and improved their defenses, and each time the enemy attempted to attack he was beaten off.

By the close of 13 February the forces that were taking a direct part in the offensive on Komarno occupied the following position: the 7th Guards Army was defending along the front Svaty Jur on the Hron—Kamendy—Szoldiny—Batorove Kosihy—Marcelova—three kilometers west of Radvan. The 6th Guards Tank Army had been pulled back for reinforcement and refitting its equipment to the Gogyollo area east of Budapest.

Simultaneously with the 7th Guards and 6th Guards Tank armies' combat activities in the area between the Hron and Nitra rivers, intensive fighting by the Second Ukrainian Front's forces was being conducted throughout January and the first half of February to eliminate the enemy's Budapest group of forces and to occupy Budapest. On 18 January the *front's* forces defeated the German-Hungarian forces fighting in Pest and completely occupied the eastern part of the city. On this day, 18 January, a decision by the *Stavka* of the Supreme High Command ordered that the defeat of the enemy forces in Buda, against which until this time the forces of the Third Ukrainian Front had been operating, was entrusted to the Second Ukrainian Front's forces. On 21 January this *front's* forces set about carrying out their new task and on 13 February had completely carried out the *Stavka's* task—the German-Hungarian forces encircled in Buda had been routed and the Hungarian capital of Budapest had been occupied by our forces.

On 13 February an order by the *Stavka* of the Supreme Commander-in-Chief, Marshal of the Soviet Union Stalin, followed to the commander of the Second Ukrainian Front, Marshal of the Soviet Union Malinovskii, the *front* chief of staff, Colonel General Zakharov[15], the commander of the Third Ukrainian Front, Marshal of the Soviet Union Tolbukhin, and the *front* chief of staff, Lieutenant General Ivanov.[16]

"The forces of the Second Ukrainian Front, assisted by the forces of the Third Ukrainian Front, following a month-and-a-half siege and stubborn fighting in the difficult conditions of a large city, today, 13 February, completed the rout of the encircled enemy group of forces in Budapest and thus completed took the Hungarian capital of Budapest, a strategically important German center of defense along the path to Vienna."

Conclusions

As a result of the Budapest operation, which was the concluding operation of the ninth blow, carried out by the Red Army in 1944, Hungary was removed from the war on Germany's side. The newly-created democratic government of Hungary broke all ties with fascist Germany and, upon adhering to the anti-Hitler coalition, declared war on Germany. With the defeat of the Hungarian army and the occupation of the Hungarian capital of Budapest, prerequisites were created for the development of the Red Army's subsequent offensive into the confines of Austria and to the Austrian capital of Vienna. Prerequisites were also created for the Red Army's' possible offensive into the confines of southern Germany.

The Budapest operation was conducted by the forces of the Second and Third Ukrainian fronts.

The cooperation of these *fronts* was achieved thanks to the direct control of the *Stavka* of the Supreme High Command.

Anticipating the necessity of joint efforts by the Second and Third Ukrainian fronts along the Budapest direction, the *Stavka* of the Supreme High Command ordered, as early as 18 October in its directive no. 220244, the commander of the Third Ukrainian Front to regroup his main forces to the Second Ukrainian Front's left flank. To a significant degree, this secured the close coordination of the *fronts* throughout the entire course of the fighting for in Hungary. *Stavka* directive no. 220270 of 12 December assigned the Second and Third Ukrainian fronts the task of organizing a simultaneous and organized attack for the purpose of completing the encirclement of a major enemy group of forces in Budapest.

Subsequently, on 18 January the *Stavka* of the Supreme High Command's directive no. 11099 placed the task of eliminating the encircled enemy group of forces in Budapest on the forces of the Second Ukrainian Front. This enabled the commander of the Third Ukrainian Front, Marshal of the Soviet Union Tolbukhin, to devote all of his attention to creating a stable situation along the outer front, while the commander of the Second Ukrainian Front, Marshal of the Soviet Union Malinovskii had the opportunity to concentrate sufficient forces for routing the enemy in Budapest.

15 Editor's note. Matvei Vasil'evich Zakharov (1898-1972) joined the Red Army in 1918 and fought in the civil war. During the Great Patriotic War he served as the chief of staff of a high command and of several fronts. Following the war he commanded Soviet forces in Germany and was twice chief of the General Staff.

16 Editor's note. Semyon Pavlovich Ivanov (1907-93) joined the Red Army in 1926 and studied at the Frunze Military Academy. During the Great Patriotic War he served as chief of staff of armies and *fronts*. Following the war, Ivanov served as chief of staff of a number of military districts and later commanded the General Staff Academy.

In the *Stavka* directive issued during the course of the operation to the commanders of the Second and Third Ukrainian fronts, a great deal of attention was devoted to problems of coordinating the *fronts*. The appointment of Marshal of the Soviet Union Timoshenko[17] by the *Stavka* of the Supreme High Command as its representative to coordinate the operations of the Second and Third Ukrainian fronts did much to facilitate the achievement of this coordination.

A study of the course of the operation's development ant the Second and Third Ukrainian front's combat activities enables us to make the following main operational-tactical conclusions.

In the Budapest operation, the period from 28 October 1944 through 13 February 1945; that is, 108 days, may be broken up into four main stages of its development, differing according to goals and the nature of the troops' combat activities.

The first stage, which lasted 33 days, embraces the time from 28 October through 30 November 1944. The chief task of the Second Ukrainian Front's forces during this period was the defeat of the German-Hungarian forces in the area between the Tisza and Danube rivers and the arrival of the *front's* left-wing forces at the outer ring of Budapest's urban fortifications. This task was carried out by the forces of the Second Ukrainian Front through two consecutive army operations—an attack by the 46th Army and the 2nd and 4th guards mechanized corps, and an attack by the 7th Guards Army, the 2nd and 4th guards mechanized corps, and General Pliev's cavalry-mechanized group.

The length of the 46th Army's operation was equal to six days (29 October-4 November), had a depth of 90 kilometers and an average daily rate of advance of 15 kilometers. The decision to capture Budapest by an attack from the south could not be carried out here. Our forces were delayed along the immediate approaches to the city. The chief reason behind this was due to the fact that the forces that could be set aside for capturing Budapest proved to be insufficient. By this time the Second Ukrainian Front had almost no reserves behind its left wing and the 23rd Rifle Corps (three divisions) had already been committed into the operation, while Colonel General of Tank Troops Kravchenko's 6th Guards Tank Army was not fully ready for operations. It was reinforcing and repairing its equipment following the preceding intensive fighting.

The Second Ukrainian Front's right-wing forces were engaged in heavy fighting along the approaches to the borders of Czechoslovakia and it was not possible to take from there even an insignificant part of its men and materiel.

The 46th Army, which had begun its offensive from along a 110-kilometer front, had by 4 November increased it to 220 kilometers; that is, by twice as much, and its striking power had been weakened to a significant degree. The 46th Army's right-flank neighbor, the 7th Guards Army, advanced very little and could not render realistic assistance to the 46th Army.

By 4 November the 2nd and 4th guards mechanized corps' combat possibilities had been weakened by the recent fighting.

In the developing situation, the Supreme Commander-in-Chief, Generalissimo of the Soviet Union comrade Stalin indicated to the commander of the Second Ukrainian Front the following:

> The *Stavka* of the Supreme High Command considers that an attack on Budapest along a narrow front with the forces of only two mechanized corps, with a significant amount of infantry, may lead to unjustified losses and place the troops operating along this axis in

17 Editor's note. Semyon Konstantinovich Timoshenko (1895-1970) was drafted into the imperial Russian army in 1914 and joined the Red Army in 1918. He commanded a cavalry division in the civil war and rose rapidly in the ranks during the interwar period, commanding military districts and various *fronts*. He was appointed defense commissar in 1940. During World War II he commanded several *fronts* and served as a *Stavka* representative with others, but was gradually pushed out of the limelight by younger and more talented commanders. Following the war, Timoshenko commanded military districts.

danger of the enemy's flank attack from the northeast. (*Stavka* directive no. 220256 of 4 November, addressed personally to the commander of the Second Ukrainian Front)

In this directive the *front* commander was ordered to organize and conduct an offensive along a broader front.

The arrival of the Second Ukrainian Front's forces at Budapest played a significant role in consolidating the democratic forces in Hungary and the activation of their activities against the pro-fascist government and sped up the creation of a democratic government of Hungary.

The second attack, launched by the forces of the 7th Guards Army and the 2nd and 4th guards mechanized corps and General Pliev's cavalry-mechanized group was quite lengthy in time—our forces' offensive continued uninterruptedly over the course of 16 days (11-26 November); during this time the army advanced to a depth of 60 kilometers, with an average daily rate of advance of 3.7 kilometers. Such a low rate of advance is explained by the extremely difficult local conditions (the onset of a thaw made the dirt roads impassable and movement off the roads was made difficult even for the infantry), the stubborn defense being put up by the enemy, and his significant reinforcement at the expense of reserves transferred from other fronts and from the depth. A characteristic feature of the activities of the Second Ukrainian Front's forces here was the fact that the *front* mobile groups did not get the opportunity of rapidly gaining operational freedom and throughout the entire 16 days operated in close tactical coordination with the combined-arms and cavalry formations and often fighting directly in the infantry's combat formations.

Characteristic for the Third Ukrainian Front's forces during the first stage of the Budapest operation was the rapidly accomplished regrouping of the 57th and 4th Guards armies along the Budapest direction, the combat forcing of the Danube and the capture of operational bridgeheads along the western bank of the Danube. During this period the *Stavka* of the Supreme High Command created all the conditions that subsequently secured the close cooperation between the *fronts* to the end of the operation.

The fighting by the forces of the Third Ukrainian Front to create a bridgehead was distinguished by unusual intensity and developed slowly. The forcing of the Danube by the 75th Rifle Corps' forward units was begun on the night of 6-7 November. During the first days our forces consolidated along the right bank of the Danube and, bringing up men and materiel, fought until 22 November to hold the tactical bridgeheads seized near Batina and Apatin. On 22 November units of the Third Ukrainian Front attacked from the bridgeheads and by 30 November had created a bridgehead of operational significance, having broadened its front to 180 kilometers and to a depth of up to 50 kilometers. Such sizes for the bridgehead enabled the command to concentrate along the western bank men and materiel necessary for developing the subsequent offensive. An operational bridgehead was actually created during the course of nine days (22-30 November) and our forces advanced at a daily rate of 5.5 kilometers. One must take into account that there were no mobile formations among the troops fighting to create a bridgehead, nor were there even a more or less significant number of troop tanks. Aviation activity was limited due to the poor weather. Anticipating all of the unfavorable consequences of the Third Ukrainian Front's advance along the western bank of the Danube, the enemy put up stubborn resistance and uninterruptedly reinforced his forces here, taking them from other fronts.

As a result, by the close of the operation's first stage the Second Ukrainian Front's forces had created the prerequisites for a vigorous flanking maneuver east of Budapest to the Danube, and the Third Ukrainian Front's forces' prerequisites for the successful development of a subsequent offensive to outflank Budapest from the west.

During the second and quite lengthy stage of the operation the attack by the Second Ukrainian Front's left-wing forces (7th Guards and 6th Guards Tank armies and General Pliev's cavalry-mechanized group) was launched along a narrow (9-kilometer) front and during the course of five days developed to a depth of up to 75 kilometers, with an average daily rate of advance of 15 kilometers. Such a pace in the difficult conditions of mountainous and wooded terrain and with the onset of the rainy season, should be recognized as high. Characteristic of the activities of the shock group's forces of the Second Ukrainian Front's left wing at this stage was the vigorous advance by the mobile groups subordinated to the *front*, which essentially guaranteed those significant operational results that were achieved by the Second Ukrainian Front's forces in this operation. General Kravchenko's 6th Guards Tank Army played the main and leading role here.

The Second Ukrainian Front's 46th Army during the second stage of the Budapest operation did not carry out the task entrusted to it by the *front* command. Having successfully forced the Danube, it was unable to develop its initial success to the north to outflank Budapest from the west. Here it encountered a numerically superior enemy who held the movement of the army's units through an active defense. The army's formations reached the "Margarita" defensive line only when units of the Third Ukrainian Front's 4th Guards Army's arrived at its left-flank units. As was the case with this *front's* forces, the 46th Army's forces required special training and additional men and materiel to overcome such a powerful defensive line.

During the second stage of the Budapest operation the Third Ukrainian Front's forces were basically completing the rout of the German-Hungarian Danube group of forces, while pursuing and destroying the enemy units falling back to the north and northwest. In eight days of attacking (1-8 December) the *front's* forces advanced 80 kilometers in depth, with an average daily rate of advance of ten kilometers. One should note that while withdrawing the enemy put up quite stubborn resistance, winning time necessary for occupying and deploying forces along the previously prepared "Margarita" defensive line. Among the Third Ukrainian Front's forces operating in this area (57th and 4th Guards armies) there were no mobile groups and, naturally, this rendered the combined-arms formations' fighting considerably more difficult. Besides this, the large-caliber artillery had not yet fully crossed the Danube, while aviation activities were limited by the inclement weather. Thus rates of advance by the Third Ukrainian Front's forces in this specific situation should be seen as justified in practice.

By the close of the operation's second stage, the forces of the Second and Third Ukrainian fronts were faced with the task of completing the encirclement of the Hungarian capital of Budapest and the major enemy group of forces that had been pushed into it.

The operation's third stage embraces the 10-31 December period; that is, it was equal to 22 days. Of this time, ten days were employed by the Second and Third Ukrainian fronts' forces to prepare the operation (10-19 December). Seven days (20-26 December) were required by the forces of the Second and Third Ukrainian fronts to resolve their main task; that is, to encircle the enemy from the west. The final five days were employed to squeeze the encirclement ring enough to create a continuous front and to organizing an uninterrupted and sufficiently strong external front.

Seven days (20-26 December) were required to complete the encirclement. During this time the Second Ukrainian Front's mobile forces (mostly the corps of Kravchenko's 6th Guards Tank Army) made a fighting advance of up to 80 kilometers, with an average daily rate of advance of 12 kilometers; the 7th Guards Army's combined-arms formations advanced 28 kilometers, with an average daily rate of advance of four kilometers.

In organizing the Second Ukrainian Front's December operation (20-26 December), when the 7th Guards Army was to launch the main attack to the southwest, the problem of securing this attack from the north and northwest became especially important. The *front* commander decided to capture the Levice—Santovka—Zemberovce area through a vigorous advance by the 6th Guards Tank Army's tank and mechanized formations to the northwest, thus depriving the enemy of the opportunity of undertaking a maneuver with large forces from this area toward Sahy or to the south. It was decided to cover the Zvolen axis with units from General Pliev's cavalry-mechanized group. Upon the arrival of the combined-arms formations and the transfer by the 6th

Guards Tank Army of the occupied area to them, it could be employed for augmenting the 7th Guards Army's efforts in the latter's offensive on Neszmely and Esztergom. The development of events forced us to make some changes to the operational plan. Due to the fact that the enemy was putting up very stubborn resistance to the forces of the 7th Guards Army and, having launched a counteroffensive along some sectors, he forced the 7th Guards Army's units to fall back somewhat to the east, the necessity arose of directing the 6th Guards Tank Army's attack to the south until our infantry's arrival to the Levice area and to entrust the support of the 7th Guards Army's operations and that of the entire shock group to the forces of General Pliev's cavalry-mechanized group. However, in this extremely complex situation, all the tasks before the *front* command were successfully resolved. Covering itself from the north, the 6th Guards Tank Army launched its main attack along the enemy's left flank and reached the Esztergom area to link up with the Third Ukrainian Front's forces.

The Third Ukrainian Front's forces during the operation's third stage broke through the powerfully fortified "Margarita" line and advanced 70 kilometers in seven days of offensive fighting, yielding an average daily rate of advance of ten kilometers. Such a pace in the conditions of the enemy's stubborn resistance and the continuous reinforcement of his forces should be considered normal. The entire depth of the enemy's defense was broken through by the *front's* forces over four days (20-23 December) to a depth of 20 kilometers, with an average daily rate of advance of five kilometers. Following the breakthrough of the defense and arrival of the mobile formations at the breach, the speed of the advance rose to 16 kilometers (50 kilometers were overcome over three days).

The fourth stage was more characteristic of the Budapest operation. Combat operations of decisive significance occurred simultaneously along the external front and in the city.

The duration of the fourth stage was 44 days (1 January-13 February). During this time the Third Ukrainian Front's forces repelled three powerful attacks by the enemy, who was striving to break through to his encircled forces. This task of decisive significance was completely resolved by the *front's* forces.

Characteristic of the *front's* activities at this stage of the operation was the broad employment of maneuver by artillery equipment, particularly anti-tank, which was able to stand like a shield against the enemy's powerful tank attacks. During the fighting along the external front the situation was sometimes critical. For example, the Germans' breakthrough to the Danube on 19 January and the attack from the captured area to the north created a very difficult situation. However, the Third Ukrainian Front command, while previously creating defensive lines in the depth and shock groups for counterattacks, found the correct decision in all cases and warded off the pending danger.

The Second Ukrainian Front's forces, while repelling the enemy's counterblows along the external front, fought throughout the entire stage to eliminate the German-Hungarian group of forces in Budapest.

The Red Army's successes around Budapest and the large losses inflicted by it on the enemy forces, forced the German command to dispatch reserves from various places to the Budapest area. For example, the 3rd Panzer Division from East Prussia, the 711th Infantry Division from the Netherlands, the 182nd Reserve Division from Denmark, the 6th Panzer Division from Germany, the 211th Infantry Division from the Second Belorussian Front, and the IV Panzer Corps (the *Wiking* and *Totenkopf* panzer divisions) from the Modlin area (East Prussia) were dispatched to Budapest. This speaks to the great significance which the German high command attached to the unfolding events in Hungary. Of course, it understood that the defeat of the Hungarian armed forces and the capture by the Red Army of the Hungarian capital of Budapest would bring about Hungary's exit from the war, and thus put all possible effort into holding our successfully developing offensive.

However, the German general staff found neither the means nor the methods for opposing the Red Army's victorious advance.

The Red Army's strength, the power of our combat equipment, the military art of our generals and officers and the heroism of our troops secured us a new victory.

The basis for this victory was the command genius of the Supreme Commander-in-Chief, Generalissimo of the Soviet Union comrade Stalin.

Part II

The Employment of the Combat Arms in the Budapest Operation

6

The Employment of Artillery in the Budapest Operation

The Budapest operation, which was conducted by the forces of the Second and Third Ukrainian fronts during the 28 October 1944-13 February 1945 time period, being a two-*front* operation, consisted of a number of individual army operations directed at carrying out the overall mission of encircling and destroying the enemy's Budapest group of forces and capturing Budapest.

In the following review the most characteristic features of the artillery's activities are examined, according to individual stages of the operation.

Artillery Support of the Enemy's Defeat along the Southern and Southeastern Approaches to Budapest

By the end of October 1944 the forces of the Second and Third Ukrainian fronts were attacking in southern Hungary.

On 29 October, having completed a partial regrouping of forces, the 46th Army, following a short artillery preparation, attacked and by the close of 4 November reached Budapest's outer defensive ring from the south.

On 30 October the 7th Guards Army attacked from the bridgeheads along the western bank of the Tisza River. While overcoming the enemy's stubborn resistance and inflicting heavy losses on him, by 26 November the army's forces reached Budapest's outer defensive ring from the east. Subsequently, while attacking from the Hatvan area in the general direction of Sahy and Vac, by 9 December the army's forces reached the Danube in the Sahy—Vac area, cutting off the enemy's path of retreat along the left bank of the Danube.

The artillery, which was supporting the 46th and 7th Guards armies' offensive operations, operated in conditions of washed-out roads, poor dirt roads and narrow paved roads that were often blown up by the enemy, which made not only the maneuver but the movement of artillery very difficult, especially during regroupings.

The Activities of the 46th Army's Artillery in Defeating the Enemy in the Area Between the Tisza and Danube (28 October-4 November)

The 46th Army (37th, 10th Guards and 31st Guards rifle corps) had the task, upon the attachment of the 2nd Guards Mechanized Corps, to attack at 1400 on 29 October in the general direction of Kecskemet and Budapest. While attacking along its right flank with two rifle corps (37th and 10th Guards) and the 2nd Guards Mechanized Corps along a 32-kilometer front, the army was to roll up the enemy's forces along the western bank of the Tisza River. Subsequently, upon the arrival of the 4th Guards Mechanized Corps, the army's forces were to launch a decisive attack against the enemy defending Budapest.

The distribution of the artillery by the start of the operation was as follows:

37th Rifle Corps—the 245th, 127th and 985th guards artillery regiments, 7th Breakthrough Artillery Division, minus the 11th Light Artillery Brigade and the 105th Heavy Howitzer Brigade, 48th Guards Mortar Regiment, and the 1405th Anti-Aircraft Artillery Regiment.

10th Guards Rifle Corps—the 100th Guards, 191st and 246th artillery regiments, 92nd Guards Corps Artillery Regiment, 45th Cannon-Artillery Brigade, 462nd Mortar Regiment, 437th Anti-Tank Artillery Regiment, and the 1409th Anti-Aircraft Artillery Regiment.

31st Guards Rifle Corps—only had its authorized artillery.

A DD (long-range) group was created in the army, consisting of the 9th, 17th and 45th cannon-artillery brigades, which, in turn, was divided into the subgroups of the 37th and 10th Guards corps.

The army planned to commit the 2nd Guards Mechanized Corps into the breakthrough, which had been reinforced by the 11th Cannon-Artillery Brigade, the 48th Guards Mortar Regiment and the 993rd and 991st anti-aircraft artillery regiments.

The 11th Light and 24th Anti-Tank artillery brigades were in the army's anti-tank reserve.

The overall density of artillery weapons for the 46th Army, which had an attack front of 120 kilometers, was 14.1 guns and mortars per kilometer of front, which reached up to 35 guns and mortars along the main attack axis.

The plan for the artillery preparation along the 46th Army's main attack axis called for a 20-minute artillery preparation and two 5-minute fire onslaughts against targets along the enemy's forward edge and in the immediate depth of his defense.

Frequent rains and fog, which limited observation to 100-200 meters, lowered the effectiveness of artillery fire from closed positions, and the artillery crews were forced to set aside up to 75 percent of divisional, regimental and battalion artillery for firing over open sights.

The expenditure of shells per day of fighting was established by gun calibers as follows (in combat loads): 0.5 for 76mm guns, 0.4 for 122mm howitzers, 0.2 for 122mm guns, and 0.25 for 152mm guns.

On 29 October, following a 30-minute artillery preparation, units of the 37th Rifle Corps attacked and, upon breaking through the enemy's defense, moved forward. The length of the artillery preparation for the 10th Guards Rifle Corps was reduced by five minutes, because the enemy had few engineering structures along the corps' sector.

Units of the 31st Guards Rifle Corps attacked without a preliminary artillery preparation and, while encountering insignificant enemy resistance, successfully moved forward.

The commitment of the 2nd Guards Mechanized Corps into the breakthrough was supported by the corps' own artillery, because the enemy's resistance was insignificant.

The lack of roads, due to the autumn rains, made the movement and maneuver of the artillery difficult and thus fighting with the enemy mainly broke out along the paved roads and for inhabited locales located along the roads. In these battles the suppression of personnel and firing points and the repulse of tank counterattacks were mainly carried out by accompaniment artillery from open positions.

Aside from the lack of roads, the artillery's forward movement was made more difficult by the fight against small groups of the enemy, which remained in the rear of our troops in woods and inhabited locales far from the roads. While trying to reach their forces, these groups would run into our artillery columns following behind the troops and delayed their advance.

The enemy put up stubborn resistance upon the arrival of our units to Kecskemet, throwing forces of up to two infantry battalions in strength and up to 60-70 armored vehicles into counterattacks. The enemy's attacks were repelled by artillery fire from the attacking units and anti-tank reserves, with significant losses for him.

By the close of 4 November the 46th Army's units, having arrived at Budapest's outer defensive ring and having encountered the enemy's stubborn resistance, advanced no further.

Thus great maneuverability and the widespread employment of guns of all calibers for firing over open sights were characteristic of the 46th Army's artillery operations at this stage of the operation.

The Actions of the 7th Guards Army's Artillery

During 24-29 October the 7th Guards Army's forces, having reached the Tisza River, forced this water barrier with part of its forces and, while holding a bridgehead along its right bank, carried out a troop regrouping. As a result, by the close of 29 October the 7th Guards Army's units on the bridgehead had 550 guns and mortars.

The artillery remaining on the left bank occupied firing positions predominantly near the river, ready to support the troops on the bridgeheads with fire.

The 7th Guards Army (24th, 25th and 27th guards rifle corps) had the task, upon attacking on the morning of 30 October and launching its main attack along the left flank, of reaching the line Toszeg—Nagykoros and to subsequently develop the offensive to the north and northwest toward the eastern outskirts of Budapest.

On 30 October units of the 25th Guards Rifle Corps, operating along the army's left flank, attacked toward Abony. The artillery support of the for the corps' attack was conducted through a 30-minute fire onslaught, which was divided into a 5-minute fire onslaught against targets throughout the entire depth of the enemy's defense, a 20-minute period for suppressing the enemy's targets with aimed fire and a 5-minute fire onslaught against targets along the forward edge and against the enemy's artillery and mortar batteries. According to the plan, the attack was to be accompanied by the sequential shifting of fire into the depth, according to sectors and individual targets, as well as guns firing over open sights against newly acquired targets. During the fighting in the depth the artillery had the task of destroying individual firing points, being ready to suppress the enemy's resistance in his strong points in the defensive depth with massed fire and to repelling his counterattacks. During this period it was planned to force the Tisza River with the artillery located along the eastern bank.

The enemy's resistance was suppressed by artillery fire. The enemy lost his command and control and the Hungarian soldiers began to surrender in groups.

The broadening of the bridgehead along the right bank of the Tisza River by the forces of the 25th Guards Rifle Corps enabled us to cross the artillery of the 27th Guards Rifle Corps, which was operating to the right of the 25th Guards Rifle Corps, to the western bank of the river and to prepare an offensive on Szolnok. Upon being reinforced with the 41st Guards Artillery Brigade, on 1 November the 27th Guards Rifle Corps attacked.

While successfully advancing, the corps' units arrived at Szolnok by the close of 3 November and began fighting along its outskirts. All of the regimental and divisional artillery was moved up for firing over open sights against the enemy's firing points in the city. As a result of the successful suppression of the firing points, the corps' units captured the city, while suffering insignificant losses.

Upon arriving at the line excluding Tiszasuly—Ujszasz—Cegled, the army's forces were halted by the growing enemy resistance and, in accordance with orders, began preparations for a subsequent offensive. The 7th Breakthrough Artillery Division and the 47th Guards Mortar Regiment arrived to reinforce the army.

Upon the adoption of the Second Ukrainian Front commander's decision to shift the main attack to the 7th Guards Army's sector, the commander of the 7th Guards Army received the following order: having concentrated no less than 1,600 artillery tubes along his left flank, break through the enemy's defensive front on 11 November and secure the commitment of General Pliev's cavalry-mechanized group into the breakthrough, as well as that of the 2nd and 4th guards mechanized corps. By the close of 11 November the army was to reach the front Jaszdozsa—Zsambok—Dany.

The army was to subsequently support the offensive in the general direction of Hatvan. The artillery was distributed among the corps for the forthcoming offensive in the following manner:

24th Guards Rifle Corps—34th Independent Anti-Tank Brigade, 263rd and 493rd army mortar regiments, which, together with the rifle divisions' artillery comprised 287 guns and mortars; that is, 20 guns and mortars per kilometer of front.

27th Guards Rifle Corps—41st Cannon-Artillery Brigade, 115th Guards Anti-Tank Regiment, 290th Army and 302nd Guards mortar regiments, which, together with the rifle divisions' artillery and that of General Pliev's cavalry-mechanized group comprised 643 guns and mortars, or 43 guns and mortars per kilometer of front; along the corps' 5-kilometer breakthrough sector the amount of artillery was raised to 511 guns and mortars, or 102 guns and mortars per kilometer of front.

25th Guards Rifle Corps—16th and 7th breakthrough artillery divisions, 2nd Independent Anti-Tank Brigade, and the 309th and 48th guards mortar regiments.

During the artillery preparation the artillery of the 2nd and 4th guards mechanized corps and the 6th Guards Airborne Division would be brought in. Such an artillery saturation, together with the rifle divisions' artillery, would yield a density of 128 guns and mortars per kilometer of front (in all, 1,285 guns and mortars along a 10-kilometer attack front).

As a result of the fact that the main mass of artillery supported the army's attacking forces even earlier and was in the breakthrough sector, it was not necessary to carry out large-scale regroupings. This shortened the deadline for preparing the artillery for the breakthrough. As a rule, movements were carried out at night, for masking purposes.

Because it was extremely difficult to concentrate this large amount of guns along a small sector of terrain and because there was a shortage of time, there was no opportunity to find firing positions for all the batteries and newly-arrived batteries were attached to the firing positions of the artillery that was already there. This measure proved to be quite expedient.

The plan for the artillery offensive called for a 20-minute artillery preparation in three fire onslaughts: a 5-minute fire onslaught against targets and target sectors along the forward edge and in the immediate defensive depth; salvos by guards mortars against sectors of the enemy defense; a 10-minute fire onslaught against targets and target sectors throughout the entire tactical depth of the enemy's defense, against artillery and mortar batteries and inhabited locales; a 5-minute fire onslaught against targets and target sectors along the forward edge of the enemy's defense, and; salvos by guards mortars against the strong points of the enemy's defense.

Support for the attack was planned at 45 minutes. During this period fire would be concentrated against target sectors and individual firing points hindering the infantry's passage. Guards mortars prepared to repel possible enemy counterattacks.

In supporting the enemy's fight in the depth of the enemy's defense, the plan called for the destruction of individual firing points hindering its passage and the suppression of newly acquired batteries and centers of resistance. At this stage of the fighting it was also planned to resubordinate the mechanized corps' and tank army's artillery units to their commanders.

The artillery support for the commitment of the mechanized and tank corps into the breakthrough was entrusted to the 41st and 61st cannon-artillery brigades and heavy artillery. This artillery during the artillery preparation and support for the attack, firing in accordance with the overall plan for the artillery offensive, was supposed to be ready to open fire when called by the tanks. It was planned to fire at maximum range. Two days before the attack the Second Ukrainian Front's artillery commander and the 7th Guards Army's artillery commander personally issued instructions for the preparation and conduct of the breakthrough to all the artillery commanders of the rifle corps and divisions, of General Pliev's cavalry-mechanized group and the commanders of the artillery reinforcement units, presenting them with a plan for the artillery offensive and a cooperation plan. Such a late issuance of missions was done for the purpose of disguising the axis of the planned breakthrough and the front sector along which it was being prepared.

For the artillery's cooperation with the tanks, a reconnaissance was carried out, the artillery's tasks were refined, and cooperation signals were established. Experienced artillery correctors were dispatched to radio tanks for defining calling in fire. Artillery command and control was centralized.

On 11 November the army's forces attacked.

As a result of the 20-minute artillery preparation conducted and with the infantry attack, the enemy suffered heavy losses and was forced to hurriedly fall back. Tanks and General Pliev's cavalry-mechanized group were committed into the breakthrough on the first day of the offensive.

The enemy sought to put up resistance against our tanks along the Jaszladan line and 20 kilometers to the west, having brought up his mobile reserves and ant-tank artillery. The tank elements had no opportunity to suppress the enemy fire with their own artillery. The enemy's anti-tank artillery was suppressed by the fire of the 61st Cannon-Artillery Brigade, which was corrected from a radio tank, and our tanks continued the offensive. Regimental artillery and the cannon batteries of divisional artillery accompanied the infantry during the offensive, moving in the latter's combat formations and firing over open sights. Division artillery's howitzer batteries supported the infantry's actions with fire from covered firing positions. As the troops moved forward, anti-tank artillery moved along the tank-sensitive axes in a timely manner and occupied lines in readiness to repel tank counterattacks. The chief means of communication in the artillery units and subunits in this fighting was telephone communications, which was duplicated by radio. During the subsequent offensive the enemy repeatedly sought to delay the army's forces, employing for this purpose strong points and centers of resistance, especially in major inhabited locales (Jaszbereny, Hatvan), which had been previously configured for defense. The army's units, while combining artillery fire with troop maneuver, continued their successful offensive and by 26 November reached the outer ring of the Budapest fortifications along the line Gyongyospata—Hered—Dany, where they encountered the enemy's stubborn resistance. Further offensive action was temporarily halted by order of the *front* commander and the troops set about preparing a new attack. During 26 November-5 December the army prepared a new breakthrough of the front along the sector Hered—excluding Aszod.

The first stage of the Budapest operation concluded with the arrival of the Second Ukrainian Front's left-wing forces at the outer ring of the Budapest defensive structures from the south, southeast and east on 26 November. The *front's* forces faced a new mission—to encircle the enemy's Budapest group of forces in Budapest. The 53rd, 7th Guards, 46th and 6th Guards Tank armies and General Pliev's cavalry-mechanized group were brought in to carry out this mission. The 7th Guards Army received orders to break through the enemy's defense on 5 December along the front Hatvan—excluding Aszod and to attack in the general direction of Verseg, Csovar and Notincs. After the breakthrough of the front, the army was to support the commitment of units of the 6th Guards Tank Army's and General Pliev's cavalry-mechanized group into the breakthrough.

The 5th Breakthrough Artillery Division arrived to reinforce the army. The artillery from General Pliev's cavalry-mechanized group and the 6th Guards Tank Army was to be brought in for the artillery preparation along the main attack axis.

The preparation of the breakthrough of the enemy's defense included:

- the regrouping of the artillery and its concentration in positional areas;
- the organization of reconnaissance of the enemy's fire system;
- drawing up a plan for the artillery offensive;
- transmitting fire tasks to the executors, refining them on the ground and organizing the artillery's interaction with the infantry and tanks.

The artillery's disposition for the breakthrough was as follows:

27th Guards Rifle Corps—the artillery of the 303rd and 227th rifle divisions, the 41st Cannon-Artillery Brigade and part of the artillery of General Pliev's cavalry-mechanized group. In all, 261 tubes; the average density was 209 tubes per kilometer of front.

25th Guards Rifle Corps—the artillery of the 6th Guards Airborne Division and the 53rd and 25th guards rifle divisions, the 5th Breakthrough Artillery Division, the 115th Guards Anti-Tank Artillery Regiment, 263rd and 493rd army and 302nd and 309th guards mortar regiments. During the artillery preparation, the artillery of the 9th and 4th guards mechanized corps and the 409th Rifle Division would be brought in, and part of the artillery of General Pliev's cavalry-mechanized group, the 290th Army Mortar Regiment and the 304th Independent Anti-Tank Artillery Brigade. In all, 1,066 tubes; the average density was 224 tubes per kilometer of front.

30th Guards Rifle Corps (instead of the 24th Guards Rifle Corps, which had been removed from the army)—the artillery of the 155th, 141st and 151st rifle divisions, the 16th Breakthrough Artillery Division, and the 66th Guards Mortar Regiment. During the artillery preparation, the artillery of the 5th Guards Tank Corps and the Romanian 7th Howitzer Regiment would be brought in. In all, 685 tubes; the average density was 228 tubes per kilometer of front.

Aside from this, a DD (long-range) artillery group was created in the army, consisting of the 41st, 17th and 61st cannon-artillery brigades, which were divided into subgroups according to the number of corps. The army commander's anti-tank reserve included the 2nd Independent Anti-Tank Artillery Brigade. This artillery grouping enabled us to concentrate 2,012 tubes along the 9-kilometer breakthrough sector, or 224 tubes per kilometer of front.

Just as when preparing for the preceding breakthrough, the newly arrived batteries were attached to the firing positions of the artillery which was already in place.

The artillery concentration proceeded in rainy weather; thus the capacity of the roads decreased sharply, which led to the formation of traffic jams near the bridges and corduroyed roads. The army artillery headquarters drew up a detailed plan for regrouping the artillery, showing the routes and the time for passing through lines and the time for occupying firing positions. The carrying out of this plan was controlled by special traffic posts, headed by staff officers. These officers had at their disposal traffic control commands and the necessary communications equipment. Positional area commandants were appointed to control the occupation of the firing positions. All of these measures allowed for the timely concentration of the artillery in the positional areas.

During the preparation for the breakthrough the artillery intelligence organs received orders to further refine the forward edge of the enemy's defense, his fire system and engineer structures, and to uncover the disposition of his artillery and mortars. This task was to be carried out through visual observation, the conduct of instrumental reconnaissance, through a reconnaissance in force by the infantry, and the attachment of artillery reconnaissance troops to the infantry's combat formations. Intelligence organized in such a fashion yielded positive results. The forward edge of the defense, the system of infantry and artillery fire and engineer structures were uncovered, which was confirmed by checking following the breakthrough of the defense.

The plan for the artillery offensive was drawn up on the basis of data from intelligence of all types and called for the following: a 50-minute artillery preparation, a 30-minute support for the attack and supporting the battle in the depth. The artillery preparation, in its turn, was divided into fire onslaughts and a 25-minute suppression of targets through deliberate fire. A final fire onslaught, lasting ten minutes, would begin five minutes before H hour and conclude five minutes after H hour. The working over of the forward edge of the enemy's defense, which would continue for five minutes after the attack signal, would enable the infantry to draw near the targets of the attack under the cover of their artillery fire. It was planned to accompany the attack by consecutive shifts of artillery and mortar fire along the lines of the enemy's resistance in leaps of 200-250 meters. The support of the fighting in the depth was planned as a continuous accompaniment of the infantry and tanks by fire and movement. During this period of the fighting the suppression of the firing points was called for, both by fire from covered firing positions and by fire over open sights.

In anticipation of possible enemy counterattacks from the areas of Verseg and Aszod, an anti-tank defense was chiefly organized for securing the army's left flank. It was planned to deploy the anti-tank reserve along lines and indicating their borders and strength. Besides this, it was planned to turn the 16th Breakthrough Artillery Division's front in the direction of assumed enemy counterblows. Three 152mm batteries, which were moving along with the infantry, were set aside from the 17th Cannon-Artillery Brigade for battling the enemy's heavy tanks.

Problems of the artillery's interaction with the infantry and tanks were coordinated during joint commanders' reconnaissance missions. Common cooperation signals were established, which were transmitted through widely employed communications equipment. The location of the combined-arms commanders' observation posts together with those of the artillery commanders also made it possible to quickly react to the enemy's actions during the fighting. Cooperation with the tanks was to be carried out through artillery fire spotters assigned to the radio tanks.

Upon completing the preparation for the breakthrough, the army's forces attacked at 1045 on 5 December, following an artillery preparation. The enemy's defense was penetrated and his firing points suppressed. The enemy sought to halt our forces' advance through frequent infantry and tank counterattacks, especially in inhabited locales that had been transformed into powerful strong points.

Crushing the enemy's resistance and repelling his frequent counterattacks, by the close of 9 December the army's forces reached the line Nandor—Borsosberenke—Giosjene—the left bank of the Danube in the Veroce—Vac—Aszod area, thus cutting off the path of retreat for the enemy's Budapest group of forces to the northeast and north, as well as along the left bank of the Danube.

Characteristic of the artillery's actions was its maneuverability and rapidity of concentration to a new axis and the rapidity of preparing the breakthrough. The method of attaching newly-arrived batteries and battalions to the firing positions of units that were already on the spot and which already possessed all the necessary firing data completely justified itself. The detachment of a large amount of artillery, including large-caliber, for firing over open sights also proved to be expedient.

Artillery Support for the Forcing of the Csepeli Dunaag and Danube Rivers by the Forces of the 46th Army (22 November-10 December)

In accordance with the order by the commander of the Second Ukrainian Front and the decision by the commander of the 46th Army, units of the 37th Rifle Corps, in conjunction with the 23rd Rifle Corps' 316th Rifle Division, forced the Csepeli Dunaag River on the night of 21-22 November, with the task of destroying the enemy between the Csepeli Dunaag and the Danube, to present a direct threat to Budapest from the south and to subsequently force the Danube and get into the flank of the enemy troops defending the city.

The forcing of the Csepeli Dunaag River was carried out at night, without an artillery preparation, along a front of about 25 kilometers. The artillery support for the forcing called for regimental and divisional artillery and reinforcement artillery from the eastern bank of the river. As bridgeheads were captured along the western bank of the Cselepi Dunaag River, the divisional artillery and reinforcement artillery were to be crossed over.

The unexpected landing of the first echelon on the western bank of the river captured a number of strong points in the enemy's defense from the march, including the major inhabited locales of Tokol, Szigetcsep and Rackeve. On the offensive's first day our forces reached the eastern bank of the Danube along a front of more than 20 kilometers.

In the fighting to take Csepel Island, the main role was played by the artillery, firing over open sights from the infantry's combat formations. A significant role was also played by regimental and battalion mortars, which had been crossed over the Csepeli Dunaag River together with the infantry. A major role was played by division artillery and reinforcement artillery, which fired from beyond the river on the enemy's centers of resistance and his artillery and mortar batteries.

The capture of Csepel Island enabled the army the begin preparations for forcing the Danube.

Having carried out a regrouping of forces, by the close of 4 December the 23rd and 37th rifle corps were ready for the forcing.

It was not planned to conduct an artillery preparation while forcing the Danube, but in the event of powerful enemy resistance an artillery support plan had been drawn up. According to the plan, a number of enemy defensive targets, in which he might put up resistance, would be subjected to artillery bombardment. The artillery support was prepared from the eastern bank of the river by suppressing and destroying the enemy's firing points, personnel and mortar and artillery batteries. The crossing of part of the 45mm guns was planned for directly accompanying the infantry with the first landing echelon.

Following the seizure of the bridgeheads on the western bank of the river, the divisional artillery immediately began crossing under the cover of artillery fire. With the expansion of the bridgeheads and the commitment of the divisional artillery into the fighting, the reinforcement artillery began to cross.

While the first echelon of troops was forcing the Danube, the command and control of the artillery, which was firing from the eastern bank of the river, was conducted from observation posts along the eastern bank, and as the troops advanced along the western bank command and control was shifted to the commanders within the troops' combat formations.

Having forced the Danube and broken through the enemy's defense along the western bank of the river, by 10 December the 46th Army's forces had made a fighting advance to the previously prepared "Margarita" defensive line, which ran along the line Erd—Martonvasar—Velence.

Thus the 46th Army's forces forced the Csepeli Dunaag and Danube rivers without a preliminary artillery preparation. This was done in order to hide from the enemy the time and crossing sectors. Such a forcing method in the situation that had arisen before the 46th Army was quite expedient. The artillery opened fire over open sights and from closed positions only on demand of the infantry. All of the artillery's firing data had been prepared. Guns firing over open sights rendered very effective assistance to the troops.

The Activities of the 4th Guards Army's Artillery in Forcing the Danube and Supporting the Arrival of the Third Ukrainian Front's Forces at the Line of Lakes Velence and Balaton (24 November-10 December)

By 24 November part of the 4th Guards Army's forces occupied defensive positions along the eastern bank of the Danube along the front Nagyvadasz—Mohacs, having received from the 46th Army the 31st Guards Rifle Corps, which was defending the Nagyvadasz—Baja sector.

During the night of 24-25 November units of the 41st Guards Rifle Division forced the Danube on improvised means southeast of Mohacs, captured a bridgehead along the western bank of the river and by 1800 on 26 November, having captured Mohacs along the left flank, linked up with the 57th Army's forces attacking to the south. While forcing the Danube, part of the 45mm guns and 82mm mortars were crossed over by the 41st Guards Rifle Division in the first echelon. Also crossed over were the battalions and battery divisional artillery commanders, who were entrusted with the task of supporting the first echelons' operations with fire from firing positions along the eastern bank. Horse-drawn regimental and divisional artillery guns were crossed with the second echelon. By the close of November 25 four divisional artillery guns, seven regimental artillery guns, nineteen 45mm guns, five 120mm mortars, and fifty 82mm mortars, for a total of 85 tubes, were located along the western bank. The remaining artillery was stationed along the eastern bank and fired across the river. While capturing Mohacs, a great amount of work was done by guns located among the infantry's combat formations. These guns, firing over open sights, destroyed the enemy's firing points in buildings that had been configured for defense, thus securing the rapid capture of heavily fortified strong points.

In order to broaden the bridgehead in the Mohacs area, on 26 November units of the 20th and 21st guards rifle corps began to cross over to the western bank. These units' crossing was carried out along the 57th Army's sector. Gradually augmenting its attack by committing new units into the fighting, by 30 November the 4th Guards Army had advanced up to 50 kilometers to the north and northwest, inflicting a serious defeat on the enemy.

Artillery support for the attacking troops was first carried out from the eastern bank of the river; as the troops advanced, the artillery units were also crossed over.

During the night of 30 November-1 December units of the 31st Guards Rifle Corps began to force the Danube in the Madocsa area. The enemy's personnel and fire system were suppressed by a short fire onslaught in conjunction with fire from a brigade of armored launches by the Danube Military Flotilla. The infantry's vigorous attack, in conjunction with the artillery attack, secured the crossing of the river and the enemy, having been placed under the threat of encirclement by the army's forces, began to hurriedly fall back, abandoning his equipment, killed and wounded soldiers and officers.

By the close of 8 December the army's forces along the entire front reached the defensive line previously prepared by the enemy along lakes Velence and Balaton, where, upon going over to the defensive, began preparing a breakthrough of the fortified defensive zone, followed by the subsequent arrival at the Danube (near Esztergom) to complete the encirclement of the enemy's Budapest group of forces.

Thus characteristic of the 4th Guards Army's artillery in forcing the Danube was the crossing of quite a significant portion of its artillery equipment immediately with the infantry's first echelon. Also characteristic is the fact that the artillery officers of those artillery units which remained on the eastern bank of the Danube and which were ready to open fire from their station area on the infantry's demand, crossed over with the first echelons.

Artillery Support for the Breakthrough of the "Margarita" Line by the Forces of the Third Ukrainian Front's 46th Army (20-26 December)

In accordance with the instructions of the *Stavka* of the Supreme High Command, the forces of the Second and Third Ukrainian fronts began to conclude from 20 December the complete encirclement of the enemy's Budapest group of forces. The Third Ukrainian Front's 46th Army received orders to break through the enemy's defense northeast of Lake Velence and, while developing the offensive to the northeast, to reach the Danube north of Budapest and to cut off the enemy's path of retreat to the west and to occupy the western part of Budapest.

In accordance with the adopted plan, the 46th Army's forces, consisting of two rifle corps of seven divisions, broke through the "Margarita" line along the line Baracska—Kapolnasnyek. One corps was to attack along a secondary axis. In order to develop the success along the main attack axis, it was planned to commit the 2nd Guards Mechanized Corps into the breakthrough. It was planned to create an artillery density of up to 150 tubes per kilometer of front to support the corps operating along the main axis.

The distribution of artillery equipment was as follows:

37th Rifle Corps: the artillery of the 108th and 59th guards and 320th rifle divisions, along with the 87th Guards Mortar Regiment and the 1505th Self-Propelled Artillery Regiment. The 25th

Howitzer and 11th Light Artillery and 9th and 17th cannon-artillery brigades were to support the corps.

10th Guards Rifle Corps: the artillery of the 49th and 109th guards and 180th rifle divisions, along with the 462nd Mortar, 437th Anti-Tank and 47th Guards Mortar, and 991st Self-Propelled Artillery regiments. The 3rd Mortar and 46th Cannon-Artillery brigades would support the corps.

23rd Rifle Corps: the artillery of the 99th and 316th rifle divisions and the 83rd Naval Infantry Brigade, along with the 12th Anti-Tank Artillery Brigade; upon the start of the 316th Rifle Division's attack, artillery from the Danube Military Flotilla would be employed in the attack zone. The commitment of the 2nd Guards Mechanized Corps would be supported by the artillery of the 37th and 10th Guards rifle corps in accordance with the plan of the army's artillery commander.

Given this artillery disposition, the artillery density along the main attack axis was to reach 99 tubes per kilometer of front (not counting 45mm guns).

Army long-range (DD) and destruction artillery (AR) groups were created from the army's artillery. Corps long-range groups and guards mortar groups (GMCh) were created in the corps operating along the main axis.

Infantry support (PP) groups were created from divisional artillery and reinforcements.

262 guns, of which 83 were 45mm, 83 76mm regimental artillery, 66 76mm divisional artillery, and 30 122mm howitzers, were allotted for firing over open sights during the artillery preparation.

Mortar fire from the rifle regiments and battalions during the artillery preparation was planned by the commanders of the infantry support groups.

The overall planning of the artillery offensive was carried out by the army artillery staff. As data about the enemy was refined, corrections were made in a timely manner to the plan. Further planning was carried out in the corps, divisions and infantry support groups.

The artillery preparation was planned for 40 minutes, during which the artillery was to carry out the following tasks: a) guns firing over open sights were to destroy individual firing points, to destroy overhead covers and wooden and earth pillboxes, to suppress newly discovered firing points along the forward edge and in the immediate depth of the enemy's defense; b)the rifle regiments' and battalions' mortars and infantry support groups were to destroy individual firing points, to suppress the enemy's personnel in his trenches and communications trenches along the forward edge and in the depth of the enemy's defense (individual batteries were set aside for taking part in the suppression of the enemy's batteries through short fire onslaughts) c) long-range groups were to fire to suppress the enemy's batteries; d) the destruction artillery group was to destroy particularly solid structures in the immediate depth of the enemy's defense, and; e) at the beginning of the artillery preparation groups of guards mortars were fire a salvo against the enemy's batteries, strong points and headquarters, and a salvo against the main center of the defense in the last five minutes.

With the beginning of the attack, all of the guns firing over open sights, mortars and infantry-support groups were to carry out a 5-minute fire onslaught along the entire tactical depth of the enemy's defense. The long-range groups were to carry out a 10-minute fire onslaught against the enemy's batteries. Part of the corps long-range groups' batteries was to be allotted for firing on trenches. From the beginning of the attack to H+90 minutes the guards mortar groups (M-13)[1] were to wage deliberate fire against roads junctions, headquarters and the enemy's immediate reserves. Subsequently, the guards mortars were given the task of being ready to repulse enemy counterattacks.

1 Editor's note. The M-13 was a Soviet-produced 132mm multiple rocket launcher, usually mounted on a truck. Various versions of this weapon were popularly known as "katyusha."

The expenditure of munitions was established according to the following norms: 0.3 combat loads for the artillery preparation; 0.2 combat loads for supporting the attack and the fighting in the depth, and; 0.4 combat loads per day for the second and third days of fighting.

During the preparation for the offensive the combined-arms officers and officers of specialized combat arms repeatedly carried out reconnaissance, as a result of which the artillery troops completely comprehended the tasks of the units and subunits they were to support and refined their combat tasks on site. The plan for the artillery offensive was relayed in a timely manner to the direct executors. Common cooperation signals were established for controlling the troops during the battle.

During the breakthrough of the defensive zone and the fighting in depth the artillery was basically entrusted with the tasks of destroying and suppressing the enemy's firing points and personnel hindering our troops' advance, the suppression of artillery and mortar batteries and the repulse of the enemy's infantry and tank counterattacks and preventing the arrival of his reserves. With the commitment of the 2nd Guards Mechanized Corps into the breakthrough, part of the artillery, while supporting its advance, was to destroy the enemy's anti-tank weapons.

The artillery carried out the above-enumerated tasks by firing over open sights and through massed and individual from covered firing positions.

On 22 December the enemy, having brought up fresh reserves, launched a counterattack by a large group of infantry and tanks against the 46th Army' left flank in the Lovasbereny area. Our forces' anti-tank artillery reserves and tanks, which had been brought up to the threatened axis, halted the enemy's breakthrough units and tanks and, having inflicted serious losses on him, threw him back.

Continuing the offensive, at the close of 24 December the 46th Army's 2nd Guards Mechanized Corps broke into Buda and began fighting along its western and southwestern outskirts. By the close of 26 December units of the 18th Tank Corps occupied the city of Esztergom, which concluded the complete encirclement of the enemy's Budapest group of forces. By the close of 26 December the forces of the 10th Guards Corps captured the large inhabited locale of Budakalasz, cutting up the encircled group of forces in Budapest and in the woods northwest of the city.

During the January fighting to repel the Germans' counteroffensive, the 46th Army's artillery was engaged in fierce fighting with the enemy's tanks in mountainous and wooded terrain, which, given the troops' insufficient artillery saturation, demanded of the anti-tank and reinforcement artillery a great deal of maneuverability. There were many instances of firing by large-caliber artillery (152mm gun-howitzers) over open sights during the fighting for repelling the enemy's infantry and tank attacks. As a rule, this firing was extremely effective.

Aside from firing over open sights, the artillery, while broadly maneuvering its trajectories, fired from covered positions, both by individual guns and batteries against individual firing points and using massed fire by battalions and groups against enemy troop concentrations, employing all methods of waging massed fire.

The artillery destroying the enemy's forces in Budapest was engaged in heavy street fighting.

Artillery Support of the Breakthrough of the "Margarita" Line by the Forces of the Third Ukrainian Front's 4th Guards Army (20-23 December)

In the operation to conclude the complete encirclement of the enemy's Budapest group of forces, the 4th Guards Army's forces had the task of breaking through the enemy's defense southwest of Lake Velence and, while developing the attack to the north and northwest, reach the line Esztergom—the southern bank of the Danube as far as Neszmely, and then south to the line of the northern shore of Lake Balaton. The army's forces were to create an external front along this line, securing from the west the operation to eliminate the enemy's encircled group of forces and to capture Budapest.

By the start of the breakthrough; that is, by 20 December, the army numbered up to 1,855 guns and mortars. Along the main attack axis (20th Guards Rifle Corps and the 31st Guards Rifle Corps' 40th Guards Rifle Division) the artillery density reached 183 tubes per kilometer of front.

All of the artillery was grouped into groups for firing over open sights and mortar, infantry-support, long-range, and guards mortar groups.

The artillery offensive was planned in the following manner.

65 minutes was allotted for the artillery preparation, in the beginning of which a 10-minute fire onslaught from all weapons (except for guns firing over open sights) was planned against the enemy's artillery batteries, his trenches and observation posts, individual guns, and immediate reserves. Following the fire onslaught, it was planned to conduct aimed fire for 50 minutes with guns firing over open sights, as well as deliberate and aimed fire by the mortar group and infantry-support and long-range artillery groups, while the guards mortar (M-13) group was to carry out a fire onslaught against the main strong point with a single brigade salvo. At the conclusion of the artillery preparation, a 5-minute fire onslaught was planned against targets along the forward edge and in the enemy's immediate depth.

During the infantry attack the consecutive shifting of fire along lines was planned, and during its fighting in the depth of the enemy's defense it was planned to uninterruptedly accompany the infantry through fire and movement.

The subsequent planning of the artillery offensive was carried out in the corps and division artillery headquarters and of the groups against specific targets of the enemy's defense. Each artillery subunit received specific orders to wage fire either against separate firing points or against target centers.

Aside from the plan for the artillery offensive, a counterpreparation plan was also drawn up, which called for foiling the enemy's offensive.

Simultaneously with the planning of the artillery offensive, planning the movement of the artillery's combat formations forward was carried out, as well as a cooperation plan with the 17th Air Army, reflecting the cooperation of the artillery's and aviation's work for supporting the infantry's attack.

Before the offensive, the commander of the army's artillery and the artillery staffs personally checked the units' readiness for the offensive and each battery's and gun's knowledge of their mission.

On 20 December, following the artillery preparation and massed air strikes, the army's forces attacked and, while breaking through the enemy's defense, penetrated up to nine kilometers into its depth during the first day.

While continuing to develop the offensive, the army's forces, while repelling the enemy's fierce infantry and tank counterattacks, stormed and captured the city of Szekesfehervar and a number of major inhabited locales on the morning of 23 December. By the close of the month the 4th Guards Army's units carried out their assigned task for creating an external defensive front.

The artillery played a major role during the fighting for the city of Szekesfehervar, firing over open sights. All of the divisional artillery and up to 50 percent of the reinforcement artillery, up to 152mm, was moved up to open firing positions for firing over open sights.

In all, while storming the city 58 45mm guns; 17 57mm guns; 30 76mm regimental guns, and 62 76mm divisional guns; 12 88mm guns, 12 122mm guns, and; 20 152mm guns were employed; in all, 211 guns.

During the storming of the city, aside from guns firing over open sights, artillery fired from covered positions, to suppress the enemy's centers of resistance with massed fire. The control of massed artillery fire was carried out from storm groups, where the battery and battalion commanders were located.

During the offensive a great deal of work was carried out by anti-tank artillery. In repelling enemy tank counterattacks, the anti-tank artillery subunits and units, in difficult conditions of a lack of roads, arrived in time to the threatened sectors and, entering the fighting from the march, inflicted significant losses on the enemy.

The Activities of the Third Ukrainian Front's 4th Guards Army's Artillery in the Defensive Fighting West and Southwest of Budapest (2 January-13 February)

On the night of 1-2 January the enemy, having concentrated up to five tank and three infantry divisions opposite the 4th Guards Army's right flank, attacked in the general direction of Bicske for the purpose of linking up with his Budapest group of forces. Having advanced up to 30 kilometers during the first three days, the enemy approached the town of Bicske. The army covered the breakthrough sector from the southeast and south through the commitment of four rifle divisions, units of the 5th Guards Cavalry Corps, and by maneuvering all types of artillery. Just as securely closed was the breakthrough sector from the east, to where the 2nd Guards Mechanized Corps, the 46th Army's 85th Division and the 18th Tank Corps were committed by order of the *front* commander. The enemy, while continuing his powerful attacks in the Bicske area, on the morning of 7 January attacked along the line Csakbereny—Sarkeresztes in the general direction of Zamoly. By the close of 8 January he had captured these locales, threatening to break through to Bicske and Szekesfehervar. However, the enemy's counteroffensive along this axis was halted as well.

Having concentrated in the area northwest of Lake Balaton a group of forces consisting of five tank divisions (up to 330 tanks and self-propelled guns), the enemy attacked on the morning of 18 January from the Osi—Balatonakarttya line, with the task of reaching Budapest, bypassing Lake Velence from the south. An attempt by the army's units to hold the enemy offensive through counterattacks was unsuccessful and by the close of 19 January the enemy reached the Danube in the Dunapatele area and Lake Velence in the Gardony area. On 21 January the enemy, having brought up major tank and infantry forces to the Gardony area, sought to break through to Budapest from the march, but failed. Simultaneously, the enemy attacked toward Szekesfehervar in order to distract our forces to a secondary axis and captured it after three days of fighting.

While continuing to hold the attacking enemy, the army's forces carried out a regrouping while inflicting significant losses on the enemy in heavy fighting, and on 28 January attacked from the Baracska area to the south, toward an attack by two rifle and one tank corps attacking from the south toward Sarosd.

Throughout January the 4th Guards Army's artillery had to engage in fierce defensive fighting against major enemy tank forces. In this fighting the main burden was on the artillery, which was operating within the infantry's combat formations and primarily firing over open sights.

The sectors' insufficient saturation with artillery, where the enemy broke through our defense, forced us to broadly maneuver artillery units and subunits, not only those being pulled back into the anti-tank reserve, by systems as well, up to an including 152mm guns. For example, on 2 January along the 31st Guards Rifle Corps's sector, when the corps' artillery had been suppressed by up to 70 percent during the enemy's breakthrough, the 127th and 222nd artillery regiments, consisting of six 152mm gun-howitzers, and a howitzer artillery regiment, consisting of 19 122mm howitzers, were shifted from the 20th Guards Rifle Corps' sector for fighting the enemy tanks.

Quickly reacting to the enemy's actions, the artillery gave us the opportunity to halt the enemy's offensive and to inflict heavy losses on him and to force him to go over to the defensive.

In the heavy fighting with the enemy tanks, the artillery units' rank and file were models of bravery and heroism. One may cite numerous examples, when individual gun crews perished but did not abandon their defensive sector; having lost their gun in the fighting, they took up infantry weapons and destroyed the enemy's forces.

Brief Conclusions

1. In the Budapest operation the artillery operated in conditions of the autumn's lack of roads, which greatly hindered its maneuver capabilities, particularly in mobile fighting and in defensive battles with the enemy's major tank formations. Despite this, the artillery was able to support the troops' activities, illustrating a high degree of maneuverability, the ability to overcome difficulties, precision and flexibility in their work, and selfless mass heroism.

2. The artillery support of offensive operations was planned, as a rule, by the armies' artillery staffs on the basis of the command's operational plan and broadly employed intelligence data about the enemy.

The plans called for additional intelligence of the enemy, the disposition of artillery for battle, the concentration of artillery into positional areas, the artillery support of the offensive throughout the entire depth of the operation, and the support of the artillery with ammunition.

Artillery reconnaissance of the enemy was carried out before the fighting and by all intelligence organs throughout the entire battle.

The most widespread type of intelligence was observation through a widely developed system of observation posts. The reconnaissance of artillery and mortar positions was carried out by means of instrumental intelligence and aviation. Intelligence data from other combat arms was employed widely.

3. The artillery's disposition in operations was subordinated to those tasks which were given to the troops. The largest grouping of guns, reaching up to 200 guns and mortars per kilometer of front, was concentrated along the axis of the main attack, which completely secured the troops' successful offensive.

4. The regrouping of forces was usually carried out at night, in order to deprive the enemy of the opportunity to uncover our command's plan. While concentrating large masses of artillery in small positional areas, serious attention was devoted to masking, headquarters commandant's service and traffic control.

5. At the start of the operation command and control of the artillery was, as a rule, centralized. Decentralization was allowed only in activities along a broad front and along heavily broken terrain. In fighting in the depth of the enemy's defense, the plans called for the resubordination of part of the combined-arms commanders' equipment. Radio, telephone and telegraph were employed for communications.

For the purpose of organizing better command and control, the artillery was broken up into groups: for firing over open sights, army infantry-support groups, army long-range groups, and groups of guards mortars. The latter two groups were, in turn, divided into subgroups according to the number of rifle corps operating along the main axis.

In distributing units and formations for supporting the infantry's and tanks' activities, the command sought to preserve their organizational structure, allowing the breakup of units only in extraordinary cases.

6. The artillery support for the offensive generally came down to a brief artillery preparation, the support of the attack and the artillery support of the engagement in the depth. The artillery preparation consisted of suppressing the enemy in his trenches and his reserves in their concentration areas, and the suppression of his artillery and mortar batteries. Support for the attack was carried out through a massed fire attack against the enemy's centers of resistance and defensive

strong points. Besides massed fire, guns firing over open sights were employed during this phase of the engagement.

7. While fighting in the depth and resubordinating part of the artillery to the combined-arms commanders, the artillery troops retained sufficient artillery weapons in their hands for influencing the outcome of the fighting in those places where the enemy was putting up the greatest resistance.

8. While forcing water obstacles, a large amount of artillery was shifted to firing over open sights, in order to support the landings with fire over the river. Guns and mortars were crossed together with the first echelon.

9. A great deal of attention was devoted to the troops' anti-tank defense. Powerful mobile anti-tank reserves were created, mechanized, as a rule, in both the offensive and the defense.

In the defensive fighting to the west of Budapest all gun systems took part in anti-tank defense, operating over open sights, or from covered firing positions.

The artillery and mortars of the *front's* attacking forces, due to the fact that supply was made more difficult, were forced to operate with a limited amount of ammunition. Thus in order to save ammunition, preference was given to firing over open sights. Understanding the entire importance of ammunition supply, the artillery troops always sought to reduce their expenditure to a minimum.

7

The Employment of Tank and Mechanized Forces in the Budapest Operation

The following tank and mechanized forces took part in the Budapest operation.

Second Ukrainian Front—the 2nd Guards Mechanized Nikolaev, 4th Guards Mechanized and 23rd Tank corps, 6th Guards Tank Army (5th Guards Tank and 9th Guards Mechanized corps), and the 27th Independent Guards Iasi Tank Brigade.

Third Ukrainian Front—the 1st Guards Order of Lenin Mechanized Corps, 7th Mechanized Novo-Ukrainskii Red Banner and Order of Suvorov Corps, the 18th Tank Znamenka Red Banner and Order of Suvorov Corps, 23rd Tank Corps (from 23 January), and the 2nd Guards Mechanized Nikolaev Corps (from 2 January 1945).[1]

Thus three tank and five mechanized corps took part in this operation; that is, eight formations, one tank brigade and independent tank and self-propelled artillery regiments.

The tank and mechanized forces' activities unfolded in the valley of the Danube, which was abundant in rivers and canals.

A description of the tank and mechanized forces' activities in the Budapest operation is related according to its four chief stages.

The Tank and Mechanized Forces' Activities During the First Stage of the Operation (28 October-30 November 1944)

Features of Employing Armored and Mechanized Forces

The situation before the start of the operation was laid out in the operational sketch of the Budapest operation, contained in the present collection.

During the first stage of the operation, the Second Ukrainian Front launched its first attack with its left-flank 46th Army in the direction of Kecskemet and Budapest. Thus the *front's* 2nd and 4th guards mechanized corps and the 991st, 1505th and 1897th self-propelled artillery regiments were attached to the 46th Army.

The 7th Guards Army, which was operating to the right of the 46th Army, was only reinforced with the 27th Guards Tank Brigade.

Following the capture of the bridgehead along the right bank of the Tisza River south of Szolnok, the 6th Guards Tank Army was pulled into the reserve to complete its replenishment and did not take part in the first stage. Nor did the 23rd Tank Corps take part in the first stage, but rather operated as part of the cavalry-mechanized group in the Nyiregyhaza area (145 kilometers northeast of Szolnok).

The First Attack Against the Enemy's Budapest Group of Forces. By the start of combat operations the 46th Army's tank and mechanized forces had the following: 2nd Guards Mechanized

1 These formations' names will be shortened in the future.

Corps—206 tanks and 42 self-propelled guns; 4th Guards Mechanized Corps—121 tanks and three self-propelled guns, and, finally; the tank breakthrough echelon (991st, 1505th and 1897th self-propelled artillery regiments—53 self-propelled guns. In all, 425 armored units.

The enemy had 161 tanks and self-propelled guns along the 46th Army's axis of operations. Thus the correlation of forces was 1:2.6 in our favor.

The course of combat operations. The commitment of the 2nd Guards Mechanized Corps into the breakthrough was planned for the first day of the 46th Army's operation, while the commitment was planned according to two variations, depending on the situation.

According to the first variation, along the boundary of the 37th and 10th Guards rifle corps in the Kiskunfelegyhaza area in the direction of Kecskemet and Uihartyon, with the task of reaching the Albertirsa—Orkeny area by the close of 30 October and to subsequently be ready to develop the success in the direction of Budapest.

According to the second variation, along the 10th Guards Rifle Corps' sector in the direction of Kiskunmajsa, Kecskemet and Uihartyon, with the same task.

Thus while operating along the main axis of the 46th Army's attack, the corps was supposed to reach 50-60 kilometers into the depth on the first day of the operation.

At 1400 on 29 October units of the 46th Army broke through the enemy's forward edge, having penetrated 5-6 kilometers into the depth of his defense. By this time the 2nd Guards Mechanized Corps had been concentrated at its jumping-off positions in the area of the eastern outskirts of Kiskunfelegyhaza, where it received the signal to enter the breakthrough. At 1730 the corps' formations overtook the infantry's combat formations and got into fighting with the enemy's 8th Infantry and 1st Cavalry divisions. By 0730 on 30 October the corps' forward units had begun fighting along the southern outskirts of Kecskemet, which they waged until the morning of 31 October.

In the first half of 31 October the corps bypassed Kecskemet from the west and, while advancing to the northwest, by the close of the day captured Lajosmizse. The enemy, while attempting to halt the further development of our troops' success, moved units of the 24th Panzer Division from the Szolnok area and, having concentrated them in the Nagykoros—Cegled area, attacked the 2nd Guards Mechanized Corps' right flank.

The threat of significant enemy tank forces to the corps' flank forced it, while remaining in the Lajosmizse area, to fight off enemy attacks throughout 1 November.

On 1 November the 4th Guards Mechanized Corps had concentrated in the area west of Kiskunfelegyhaza and here it received orders to, along with the 23rd Rifle Corps' 68th Rifle Division, which had been loaded on to motor vehicles, to attack in the direction of Izsak and Kunszentmiklos and by the morning of 2 November reach the area Alsonomedi—Szigetszentmiklos—Szigetcsep. It was to subsequently develop the success to the north and capture Budapest. At the same time, the 2nd Guards Mechanized Corps received orders to reach the Monor—Ullo area by the morning of 2 November and by the close of 3 November to capture Budapest.

Thus the 46th Army's mechanized formations were to attack in the direction of Budapest along converging axes.

At 1800 on 1 November the 4th Guards Mechanized Corps set out to carry out its assigned task. Along the Szabadszallas—Fulospszallas line the corps came into contract with the enemy. Covering itself with part of its forces, the corps outflanked this line from the east and continued a vigorous offensive to the north.

By 1000 on 2 November the corps lead brigade captured Bugyi and at 1300 captured Ocsa, having thus completed its mission for the day. The enemy put up powerful resistance to the 2nd Guards Mechanized Corps' advance and the corps was fighting in the Cegled—Orkeny area during the first part of 2 November.

The 4th Guards Mechanized Corps, having pushed far ahead and having no neighbors along its flanks, was forced to cover its flanks with part of its forces. For this purpose, the 14th Guards

Mechanized Brigade took up the defensive in Ocsa, thus securing the right flank, while the 36th Guards Tank Brigade occupied defensive positions in Bugyi, securing the corps' left flank and rear. The corps' remaining units continued attacking to the north.

The 4th Guards Mechanized Corps' arrival at this area and the advance behind it of the combined-arms formations, which were operating along the 46th Army's left flank, were creating a threat to Budapest from the south. The enemy, seeing the growing strength of our forces, sought to halt the further advance of the 46th Army's forces at any cost. For this purpose, he began to hurriedly transfer the III Panzer Corps, consisting of the 1st, 13th and 23rd panzer divisions and the *Feldherrnhalle* SA Motorized Division from the Miskolc axis and to commit these formations into the fighting against our troops operating along the Budapest direction.

The 27th Guards Tank Brigade, which was operating as part of the 7th Guards Army, attacked in the second half of 2 November from the Jaszkarajeno area in the direction of Abony and by 1900, together with units of the 25th Rifle Corps, had begun fighting three kilometers south of Abony.

While overcoming the enemy's stubborn resistance, on the morning of 3 November units of the 2nd Guards Mechanized Corps reached the Vasad area, thus easing the situation of the 4th Guards Mechanized Corps along its right flank.

On 4 November, as the result of stubborn fighting, one of the 4th Guards Mechanized Corps' brigades took Taksony, while the 2nd Guards Mechanized Corps was fighting three kilometers west of Vecses by the close of the day.

In the second half of 4 November the 27th Guards Tank Brigade, in conjunction with combined-arms formations, took Abony.

Further attempts by the 2nd and 4th guards mechanized corps to break through the enemy's defense were unsuccessful, because the enemy had organized a solid defense along the line Monor—Vecses—Szigetszentmiklos, which represented the outer ring of Budapest and defended by significant forces, as a result of which units of the two corps went over to the defensive along a line two kilometers north of Ullo and Taksony.

During the second half of 5 November the enemy himself began to launch counterattacks from the northeast. He managed to break through the 46th Army's combined-arms formations' positions in the area five kilometers northwest of Albertirsa with 30-40 tanks, reinforced by motorized infantry on armored transports. By the close of the day the enemy's breakthrough group had reached Alsodabas, cutting the communications of our forces operating to the north of that locale.

In order to eliminate the enemy breakthrough, the 4th Guards Mechanized Corps' 62nd Motorcycle Battalion, which had been reinforced by a tank battalion from the 36th Guards Tank Brigade was moved to the Alsodabas area. The 62nd Motorcycle Battalion, having taking up defensive positions, was involved in heavy fighting throughout the night of 5-6 November, while preventing the enemy's arrival at the Kecskemet—Budapest paved road.

In order to eliminate the enemy breakthrough, which was threatening the 46th Army's formations operating in the Vasad—Ullo—Taksony area, the army commander ordered the 2nd and 4th guards mechanized corps to turn over their combat sectors to the combined-arms formations and by the morning of November 6 the first was to concentrate in the Vasad area and the second in Orkeny.

As a result of a joint attack from the north, the enemy's breakthrough group from the south was routed and thrown back to the area north of Albertirsa. After this battle, the 4th Guards Mechanized Corps was concentrated by the morning of 7 November in an area 16-18 kilometers east of Kunszentmiklos, and the 2nd Guards Mechanized Corps in the Uihartyon area by the morning of 8 November.

As a result of the fighting from 28 October through 4 November, the 46th Army's formations threw back the enemy to the line Albertirsa—Monor—Taksony and then further to the south along the eastern bank of the Danube, with the exception of the Apostag—Solt area, where the enemy continued to occupy an insignificant bridgehead along the eastern bank of the Danube.

During this period the 7th Guards Army's units reached the line Kotelek—Ujszasz—Albertirsa.

The Second Attack Against the Enemy's Budapest Group of Forces. Following the adoption of the decision (8 November) by the commander of the Second Ukrainian Front on shifting the main attack to the 7th Guards Army's sector, involving a powerful attack against the enemy from the Szolnok—Cegled area in the general direction of Hatvan, General Pliev's cavalry-mechanized group (4th and 6th guards cavalry corps and the 23rd Tank Corps), as well as the 2nd and 4th guards mechanized corps began to concentrate to their new areas by night marches.

By the close of 10 November the above-named formations had concentrated in the following areas: the cavalry-mechanized group in the area Szolnok—Abony—excluding Toszeg; the 2nd Guards Mechanized Corps two kilometers southwest of Cegled, and the 4th Guards Mechanized Corps three kilometers south of Cegled.

By the start of the offensive (11 November) the tank and mechanized forces operating in the 7th Guards Army's sector consisted of the following: there were 107 tanks in the 23rd Tank Corps, 80 tanks and 19 self-propelled guns in the 4th Guards Mechanized Corps, 114 tanks and 23 self-propelled guns in the 2nd Guards Mechanized Corps, and 66 tanks and 71 self-propelled guns in the 27th Guards Tank Brigade, together with the 6th Cavalry Corps' tank and self-propelled gun regiments.

Thus 367 tanks and 113 self-propelled guns had been concentrated along the 7th Guards Army's sector. In all, this amounted to 480 vehicles.

The overall number of tanks and self-propelled guns in the enemy's mobile formations was as follows: 205 tanks and 120 self-propelled guns, or 325 vehicles, of which the enemy had one panzer division (24th), two motorized divisions (4th SS *Polizei* Motorized and 18th SS Motorized divisions) along the axis of the 7th Guards Army's attack, for a total of 65 tanks and 55 self-propelled guns. In all, this amounted to 120 vehicles, while the enemy had concentrated the 23rd, 1st and 13th panzer divisions immediately along the line south and southeast of Budapest opposite the 46th Army, with an overall number of 90 tanks and 63 self-propelled guns. In all, this amounted to 153 vehicles.

Thus we concentrated 367 tanks and 113 self-propelled guns along a 45-kilometer front along the 7th Guards Army's attack axis. In all, this amounted to 480 vehicles. The enemy along this axis had 65 tanks and 55 self-propelled guns. In all, this amounted to 120 vehicles. The enemy had a density of tanks per kilometer of front of 2-3 vehicles, while we had a density of 10-11 vehicles.

In accordance with the operational plan, the tank and mechanized formations were assigned the following missions: the 23rd Tank Corps, along with the 4th and 6th guards cavalry corps of General Pliev's cavalry-mechanized group, and in conjunction with the 7th Guards Army's formations, were to break through the enemy's defense on the morning of 11 November along the line east of Ujszasz and, while developing the offensive in the direction of Jaszladany, Jaszkiser, Jaszapati, and Karacsond, by the close of 11 November to capture the western part of Jaszapati, and by the close of 12 November Karacsond. To the right, the 4th Guards Cavalry Corps would attack, with the task of capturing the eastern part of Jaszapati by the close of the first day. To the left the 6th Guards Cavalry Corps would attack, with the task of capturing the Jaszdozsa—Jaszjakohalma area by the close of the first day.

The 4th Guards Mechanized Corps received orders to attack to the left of the 6th Guards Cavalry Corps, together with the 25th Rifle Corps' 53rd Rifle Division, and to break through the enemy's defense and subsequently develop the offensive in the direction of Tapiogyorgye, Jaszbereny and Pusztamonostor; by the morning of 12 November it was to capture Hatvan. One assault air and one fighter air divisions would support the corps' operations.

The 2nd Guards Mechanized Corps received orders to operate to the left of the 4th Guards Mechanized Corps, with its tank subunits in the first echelon; in conjunction with the Romanian 19th Infantry Division, it was to attack and break through the enemy's defense in the direction of Tapiobicske and by the close of 12 November reach the Zsambok—Koka—Szentmartonkata line. Thus the corps were to be employed as *front* means for developing the success, while cooperating with the 7th Guards Army's combined-arms formations.

The 27th Guards Independent Tank Brigade received orders to attack in conjunction with the 409th Rifle Division in the direction of Ujszasz and Jaszbereny. The 991st and 1897th self-propelled artillery regiments were to operate to the left of the 2nd Guards Mechanized Corps; the 991st Self-Propelled Artillery Regiment was to support the attack by the 59th Guards Rifle Division from the area two kilometers north of Albertirsa in the direction of Kava. The 1897th Self-Propelled Artillery Regiment was to support the 108th Rifle Division's attack in the direction of Pand.

In accordance with the assigned tasks, the tank and mechanized formations organized their combat formations for breaking through the enemy's defense.

The combat formation adopted enabled the corps to rapidly restructure itself for developing the success following the breakthrough of the enemy's defense. The tank brigade, which was operating in the center, was supported along the flanks by the mechanized brigades' tank regiments and motorized infantry, was able to rapidly plunge forward.

The combat formation was approximately the same in the 4th Guards Mechanized Corps.

The 23rd Tank Corps' combat formation was organized along a 6-kilometer front, with tank brigades allotted to the first echelon. An anti-tank artillery regiment was to support the right-flank brigade's operations. A motorized rifle brigade was to attack in the second echelon, reinforced by mortar and light artillery regiments. The corps commander's reserve, which consisted of a single tank battalion, a motorized battalion of automatic riflemen and an independent guards mortar battalion, was concentrated closer to the right flank.

The Course of Combat Activities. By 0700 on 11 November the tank and mechanized formations occupied the following jumping-off positions: the 23rd Tank Corps in the area ten kilometers east of Ujszasz, the 4th Guards Mechanized Corps in the area one kilometer south of Major, and the 2nd Guards Mechanized Corps in the area ten kilometers northeast of Cegled.

At 0850 on 11 November, following a 20-minute artillery preparation, the tank and mechanized troops attacked. The 23rd Tank Corps, while overcoming the enemy's stubborn resistance, captured Jaszladany by 1330 and, continuing the attack, by 1600 reached the area five kilometers southwest of Jaszkiser. The corps' further advance was halted by the enemy's powerful resistance. The corps' formations advanced 16 kilometers into the depth on the first day of fighting.

The 4th Guards Mechanized Corps, which was operating in the center of the 7th Guards Army, broke the enemy's defense along with the combined-arms formations and by 1500 captured the enemy defense's powerful strong point of Tapiogyorgye and by the close of the day, had advanced up to 13 kilometers into the depth.

The 2nd Guards Mechanized Corps, while encountering the enemy's fierce resistance and waging bitter battles with units of his 46th Infantry and 24th Panzer divisions, by the close of the day had advanced only 2-6 kilometers.

While continuing the offensive, the 23rd Tank Corps deployed its forward formations in a line for the purpose of capturing Jaszkiser. However, these activities led to undesirable results. In the 39th Tank Brigade, which was operating in the corps' vanguard, 19 tanks were put out of action during the attack, having gotten bogged down in the swamp. The corps was once again forced to attack in column formation.

On the offensive's second day the 4th Guards Mechanized Corps, together with the 27th Guards Independent Tank Brigade, while successfully developing a night attack, by 0900 on 12

November reached Jaszbereny and began fighting along its southern outskirts. It was not possible to take Jaszbereny from the march. The town was bounded on all sides by the Zagyva River, which represents a significant anti-tank obstacle. Besides this, the enemy, while taking into account the significance of Jaszbereny as an important strong point and road junction, reinforced its garrison with a significant amount of tanks, self-propelled guns and anti-tank artillery. The 4th Guards Mechanized Corps' fighting along the southern outskirts of Jaszbereny was also made more complicated by the fact that the corps operating along the flanks on 12 November had not yet arrived at the Jaszbereny line; the 23rd Tank Corps was fighting for Jaszkiser, while the 2nd Guards Mechanized Corps and the 991st and 1897th self-propelled artillery regiments were fighting along the line Farmos—Tapiobicske—Kava. Thus the 4th Guards Mechanized Corps' flanks were open and it was forced to fight in difficult conditions along this line throughout 12-14 November. All of the corps' attempts to bypass were not crowned with success, while its neighbors along the flanks did not advance.

The 23rd Tank Corps, having captured Jaszkiser, continued to attack toward Jaszapati and, following two hours of street fighting, captured the town at 1300 on 13 November. Continuing the offensive, the corps took Jaszdozsa at 1700 on 14 November, and at 1730 on the following day it completely threw the enemy out of Jaszarokszallas.

As a result of stubborn fighting, the 2nd Guards Mechanized Corps took Toalmas and Koka by 0900 on 15 November. On 15 November the enemy's Jaszbereny group of forces had been outflanked by the 23rd Tank Corps from the west, which created an immediate threat to the communications of the enemy garrison. The 4th Guards Mechanized Corps, while taking advantage of the developing situation, attacked and by 1300 on 15 November captured Jaszbereny in conjunction with the combined-arms formations.

Thus on the fourth day of the offensive the success development group had advanced 25-40 kilometers into the depth, captured the powerful strong points of Jaszarokszallas, Jaszbereny and Tapiobicske, while the further operations threatened the major communications center of Hatvan, which was located along the road leading from Budapest to the east.

In the Hatvan area our units were involved in ceaseless and stubborn fighting, as a result of which the 23rd Tank Corps captured Gyongyos and the 2nd Guards Mechanized Corps Tura. The 4th Guards Mechanized Corps' attempts to capture Hatvan from the east were not successful. Hatvan was captured on 26 November by an attack by the 23rd Tank Corps from the north, the 2nd Guards Mechanized Corps from the west, and the 4th Guards Mechanized Corps from the east. On 27 November the tank and mechanized formations turned over their combat sectors to the combined-arms formations and arrived at the area south and southeast of Hatvan, in order to put themselves in order.

The fighting during 11-26 November was extremely bitter. The enemy, taking advantage of the marshy terrain, the washed-out roads and the numerous canals, which were difficult for the tanks to traverse, based his defense on the main roads, along which our tank and mechanized formations could only operate. While defending, the enemy often launched counterattacks by powerful groups of infantry, supported by tanks. Tanks and self-propelled guns were employed for firing from behind shelters, which were located in places convenient for firing, usually along paved roads. Fire from tanks and self-propelled guns opened up at a distance of 800-1,000 meters. While withdrawing, the enemy created covering detachments numbering up to a battalion in size, supported by 6-10 tanks, 3-5 self-propelled guns, 3-5 light anti-tank guns, and groups of sappers. These groups, while covering the withdrawal of their units, waged stubborn fighting along lines favorable to the defense and, when approaching the next line, mined the roads and blew up bridges. The tank and mechanized formations, while fighting in these conditions, were forced, for the most part, to operate together with the combined-arms formations.

And only during the pursuit period from one line (stronghold) to another did the tanks break out 5-8 kilometers ahead. The fighting was chiefly waged by powerful forward detachments. Upon arriving at an enemy strong point, the tank and mechanized formations would bring up their artillery and mortars and, only after a powerful fire onslaught would the tanks and motorized infantry launch an attack. Thus our forces consecutively captured strong point after strong point.

As a result of the 11-26 November offensive, 60-80 kilometers were covered, for an average daily rate of advance of 4-5 kilometers.

The Tank and Mechanized Forces' Activities During the Second Stage of the Operation (1-9 December 1944)

The overall situation. The fighting during the second stage of the operation unfolded to the east, northeast and south of Budapest. The overcast and rainy weather and the thick clouds created unfavorable conditions for an offensive by tank and mechanized forces. The deep and thick mud and softened soil forced the formations to mainly operate along roads with a hard surface.

By the beginning of December 1944 the enemy's defensive line opposite the Second Ukrainian Front's forces rain along the line Felnemet—Gyongyospata—Aszod—Vecses—Szigetszentmiklos and then to the south along the eastern bank of the Danube.

Following the completion of the first stage of the operation, the Second Ukrainian Front's tank and mechanized forces regrouped for launching a new attack to outflank Budapest from the northeast and to reach the Danube north of the city.

The 23rd Tank Corps, having turned over its remaining equipment to the 4th Guards Mechanized Corps, did not take part in resolving combat tasks during the second stage of the operation and was pulled back into the *front* reserve and by 4 December had concentrated in the area of the woods seven kilometers southwest of Jaszbereny.

The 6th Guards Tank Army, which did not take part in the fighting during the first stage, had by the close of 3 December, in accordance with the regrouping plan, concentrated as follows: the 5th Guards Tank Corps in Tura and the 9th Guards Mechanized Corps in Hatvan.

By the start of combat operations, the 6th Guards Tank Army had 317 tanks in line and 14 self-propelled guns. Overall, this amounted to 331 armored vehicles.

The 4th Guards Mechanized Corps, which had been subordinated to General Pliev's cavalry-mechanized group and having put its equipment in order and stocked upon ammunition, fuel and lubricants, had concentrated by the morning of 5 December in the 6th Guards Tank Army's area, in the space between its corps. It disposed of 64 tanks and one self-propelled gun.

The 4th and 6th guards cavalry corps had 21 tanks and 13 self-propelled guns.

The 27th Guards Independent Tank Brigade, which had 43 tanks and 19 self-propelled guns, was concentrated on 2 December 1.5 kilometers north of the 4th Guards Mechanized Corps.

The 2nd Guards Mechanized Corps, having completed an 80-kilometer march, had concentrated by 0500 on 2 December in the Pereg—Domsod area and, according to the adopted plan, was to force the Danube along with the 46th Army's units and then attack to the north to outflank Budapest from the west.

Thus the tank and mechanized formations had been concentrated along the operational sector of the 7th Guards Army, which was to launch the main attack along the line of the Zagyva River and Kartal in the direction of Notincs There was a total of 439 tanks and 50 self-propelled guns along the 7th Guards Army's operational axis.

The 6th Guards Tank Army and the 4th Guards Mechanized Corps were *front* means and were designated for developing the success of the 7th Guards Army's forces.

By the start of the operation the enemy in the 6th Guards Army's operational area was defending along the line excluding Lorinci—Kartal—Aszod with units of the 357th Infantry Division, the 18th and 4th panzer divisions, and the 721st Anti-Tank Artillery Battalion. His operational reserves were grouped as follows: the 8th Infantry Division in the Balassagyarmat area and the Hungarian 20th Infantry Division in the Vac area. Thus the enemy had, including operational reserves, five divisions, of which three were infantry and two panzer, along the 6th Guards Army's operational axis.

The tank and mechanized troops' tasks. The start of the offensive by the *front's* forces was set for 5 December. The 6th Guards Tank Army received orders, following the breakthrough of the enemy's defense by the 7th Guards Army's forces and the infantry's (25th and 30th guards rifle corps) capture of the line Kekenies—Verseg, upon the personal signal of the *front* commander, to enter the breakthrough and with a vigorous attack develop the offensive in the general direction of Verseg, Acsa and Retsag. By the close of the first day it was to capture the Acsa—Csovar area; by the close of the second day, the Kekenies area. Thus by the close of the second day the tank army was to have penetrated 50-60 kilometers into the depth.

According to the decision of its commander, the 6th Guards Tank Army was to be committed into the breakthrough in a single echelon along two routes, with the greater part of its forces along the right flank. The corps were assigned the following tasks: the 9th Guards Mechanized Corps, along with the an anti-tank artillery brigade, the 3rd Artillery Regiment, and an engineer battalion, was to develop the 25th Rifle Corps' success in the direction of Kekenies and Varjarc and by the close of the first day capture the Gyula area. It was to subsequently be ready to operation in the direction of Nezsa and Nagyoroszi.

The 5th Guards Tank Corps was to develop the 30th Rifle Corps' success in the direction of Verseg and Acsa and by the close of the first day capture the Csovar—Acsa area. It was to subsequently be ready to operate in the direction of Csovar and Notincs. Thus the army was to attack along a 4-6 kilometer front. The corps' combat formations were organized into three combat echelons. A brigade, along with reinforcements, was located in each echelon. Operational groups of the corps' headquarters were with the first echelon, with the corps' headquarters with the second echelon.

The 4th Guards Mechanized Corps, located with General Pliev's cavalry-mechanized group, was to be committed into the breakthrough behind the tank army, with the task of developing the success from behind its right flank and by the close of the first day capture the Szirak—Varjarc area and by the close of the second day the Nandor area.

The 27th Guards Independent Tank Brigade was given the assignment of attacking in the direction of Mocsa in conjunction with the combined-arms formations.

Thus the tank army's flanks were covered on the right by General Pliev's cavalry-mechanized group and on the left by the combined-arms formations and the tank brigade.

The course of combat operations. At 0930 on 5 December the artillery preparation began and continued for about two hours. The tank army's artillery was brought in to take part in the 7th Guards Army's artillery preparation in the 25th and 30th rifle corps' sectors. Upon the completion of the artillery preparation, the tank army's artillery was to move in the corps' combat formations. At 1045, under the cover of a rolling barrage, the 25th and 30th rifle corps' formations attacked in the general direction of Kekenies and Verseg. The infantry threw the enemy out of his trenches in a vigorous leap, but afterwards ran into his stubborn resistance.

Before the breakthrough of the enemy's tactical defense was completed by the combined-arms formations, the 6th Guards Tank Army was committed into the fighting at 1530.

At 1700 the tank formations, without changing their planned combat formation, bypassed the infantry and their lead columns broke into Hered from the march, captured it and, without pausing, continued attacking toward Kekenies.

The 21st Guards Tank Brigade, which was operating in the 5th Guards Tank Corps' first echelon, encountered the enemy's stubborn resistance upon approaching Verseg. Without getting drawn into extended fighting, the brigade bypassed Verseg from the east and, upon arriving at the road northwest of Verseg, continued to develop the offensive on Kallo. By the close of the day the brigade had reached this inhabited locale and had begun fighting along its southern outskirts.

At 1900 the corps' second echelon (22nd Tank Brigade) reached Verseg and began fighting for it. By 0300 on 6 December Verseg had been completely cleared of the enemy, as the result of an 8-hour street battle.

Throughout 5 December General Pliev's cavalry-mechanized group was not committed and was located in its concentration area. The 6th Guards Tank Army's formations continued to attack at night as well. At 1100 on 6 December the 9th Guards Mechanized Corps's lead brigade captured Vamjarc through an attack by one tank battalion and motorized infantry from the southeast and its remaining forces from the south.

The 5th Tank Corps' lead brigade (21st Guards Tank Brigade) had fallen well behind. Only by the morning of 6 December did it throw the enemy out of Kallo. Continuing its further attack at night along a muddy and plowed-up road, the brigade lost its way and reached the 9th Guards Mechanized Corps' route, the corps' remaining forces followed behind it, and at 1230 on 6 December the corps reached the Vamjarc area. Having returned to its route and following a brief fight, the corps' units captured Csovar. Thus during the second half of the day the tank army reached the line Gyula—Csovar, having carried out its task for the day. Not lingering here, the army continued to attack in the direction of Nagyoroszi throughout the second half of the day and into the night of 6-7 December.

On the morning of 6 December the 4th Guards Mechanized Corps was in its jumping-off position. At 1230 it began to move along the 9th Guards Mechanized Corps' route. On 7 December the corps' lead brigade reached the area five kilometers north of Gyula and began to develop the offensive in the direction of Nandor.

At 0200 on 7 December the 5th Guards Tank Corps' 21st and 22nd guards rifle brigades reached the Notincs area. By this time the corps' remaining forces were 8-10 kilometers distant and were approaching Keszeg. At 0200 the corps received orders to halt the attack to the northwest and to develop the attack toward the town of Vac. Thus the corps was to turn more than 90 degrees and was to operate to the south. In carrying out the assigned task, the corps commander turned the 20th Guards Tank Brigade and the 6th Guards Motorized Rifle Brigade from the Keszeg area back toward Csovar, for the purpose of attacking Vac from the east with these two brigades, while he turned the 21st and 22nd guards tank brigades from the Retsag area to the south, intending to attack Vac from the north.

Insofar as the latter two brigades had been pulled away from the corps, we could not manage to rapidly turn them to the south, and they, while continuing to attack, captured Retsag at 1600 on 7 December. After the 9th Guards Mechanized Corps' formations arrived, these brigades turned over their combat sectors and began to move south. At 1400 on 8 December two of the 5th Guards Tank Corps' brigades were approaching the town of Vac from the north and two brigades from the east. The garrison of Vac consisted of infantry, a battalion of artillery, up to 13 tanks and self-propelled guns, and six armored transports. As a result of a simultaneous attack on Vac, by the close of 8 December the town had been taken by our forces.

In the fighting for Vac the enemy lost more than 500 soldiers and officers, 12 tanks, 7 self-propelled guns, and 12 150mm guns.

At the same time the 9th Guards Mechanized Corps, while attacking to the northwest, captured Nagyoroszi. The 27th Guards Independent Tank Brigade, while operating along the tank army's left flank, was fighting in the Mocsa area by the close of 8 December, while the 4th Guards Mechanized Corps captured Nandor; the 5th Guards Tank Corps continued to further attack to the south in the direction of Dunakeszi. The 9th Guards Mechanized Corps continued to carry out its previous assignment and, while operating to the north, captured Dregelypalank in an attack by a single brigade during the night of 8-9 December.

On the morning of 9 December the 5th Guards Tank Corps began to carry out its assignment. Pushing aside the enemy's insignificant screens along its route, at 1730 the corps reached the northern outskirts of Alsogod.

Here the 20th Guards Tank Brigade, which was operating in the corps' vanguard, encountered powerful enemy resistance by up to a battalion of artillery, two tanks and a company of infantry. The brigade was unable to bypass Alsogod, because it ran into an anti-tank ditch, which ran along the northeastern outskirts of Alsogod and then to the southeast. The ditch was up to eight meters wide and up to three meters deep and half-filled with water, with the approaches to it mined. All of the corps' attempts to overcome the anti-tank ditch during the night of 9-10 December were unsuccessful and the corps' formations took up defensive positions from the morning of 10 December, having simultaneously begun to clear the minefields and building passages through the ditch.

On 9 December the 9th Guards Mechanized Corps was fighting in the area north of Dregelypalank. The 4th Guards Mechanized Corps, while securing the tank army's right flank, captured Balassagyarmat and went over to the defensive, while beating off enemy counterattacks.

The 27th Guards Independent Tank Brigade, while operating along the left flank, captured Orszentmiklos during the night of 9-10 December.

In light of the developing situation, the commander of the tank army ordered the 5th Guards Tank Corps to reach the Nagyoroszi.

On 9 December the 4th Guards Mechanized Corps was turned from the Balassagyarmat area, together with the cavalry corps, to the east in the direction of Szecseny.

Thus on 9 December the 6th Guards Tank Army reached the Danube north of Budapest with part of its forces, thus securing the successful advance of the 7th Guards Army's forces. With the combined-arms formations' arrival at the Danube to the north of Budapest, all of the enemy's communications running to the northeast and north, had been cut and the enemy's Budapest group of forces found itself isolated from his Miskolc group of forces. Vigor and rapidity of maneuver were characteristic of the 6th Guards Army's activities.

The Tank and Mechanized Troops' Activities During the Third Stage of the Operation (10-31 December 1944)

During the 10-19 December period the Second Ukrainian Front's tank and mechanized formations, which were operating in the Budapest area, fought to create an external front along the line of the Ipel River and prepared for a new operation to complete the encirclement of the Budapest group of forces together with the forces of the Third Ukrainian Front. The Third Ukrainian Front's tank and mechanized formations during the 10-19 December period concentrated in the area of lakes Velence and Balaton and were also preparing an operation to complete the encirclement of the enemy's Budapest group of forces. This operation began for the Second and Third Ukrainian front's forces on 20 December. Its plan and the overall courser of its development is laid out in the operational sketch of the Budapest operation, which is located in this collection.

On 19 December the commander of the Second Ukrainian Front assigned the 6th Guards Tank Army the task of developing the offensive to the northwest and seizing Leivice and the crossings over the Hron River in the Kalnica area.

The course of combat operations. In carrying out its task, the 6th Guards Tank Army began its attack on the morning of 20 December. The 9th Guards Mechanized Corps was to attack in the direction of Dolne Semerovce, with the task of reaching by the close of the day the area 3-4 kilometers north of Santovka and to seize with a forward detachment a crossing over the Hron

River, ten kilometers north of Kalnica. The 5th Guards Tank Corps was to attack in the direction of Santovka and Levice, with the task of capturing the Levice—Kalnica area by the close of the day and seizing a crossing over the Hron River in this area.

Thus the army would be attacking along a 10-12 kilometer front and was to advance 25-30 kilometers in a day's fighting. In order to secure the army's right flank, the 4th Guards Motorcycle and 1426th Self-Propelled Artillery regiments were to be pushed forward, in order to take up defensive positions and to prevent the enemy's arrival at the army's flanks and rear.

On the morning of 20 December the army's formations began to carry out their assigned tasks. The corps had the following forces available: the 5th Guards Tank Corps had 89 tanks and the 9th Guards Mechanized Corps 107 tanks. The 27th Guards Independent Tank Brigade, along with the combined-arms formations, was operating in the Szokolya area on 19 December.

At 1700 on 20 December the 5th Guards Tank Corps seized Levice and Kalnica. The crossing over the Hron River was blown up by the Germans. The 9th Guards Mechanized Corps arrived a day later with two brigades at the line Batovce—Levice. Thus the army's assigned task had been carried out. The 7th Guards Army's combined-arms formations, which were attacking through Szoldiny to Esztergom, by the close of 20 December reached the line Slatina—Sazdice—Nagyboerzsoeny. The Germans' 8th Panzer Division, which was operating in the Sakalos area and to the south blocked the combined-arms formations' further advance. The division had 60 tanks and 20 self-propelled guns of the "Ferdinand"[2] type. Thus the Germans' panzer division hung over the left flank of the 7th Guards Army's combined-arms formations.

As a result of the developing situation, on 21 December the 6th Guards Tank Army was given a new mission, while holding the Dolne Semerovce—Levice area and securely covered itself from the north and northwest, to attack with its main forces along the Hron River to the south in the direction of Salov and then to the mouth of the Hron River, get into the rear of the Germans' 8th Panzer Division and, together with the 7th Guards Army's formations, cut off its routes from the crossings over the Hron River and to destroy it.

In carrying out this order, the commander of the 6th Guards Tank Army turned the 5th Guards Tank Corps, consisting of two brigades (21st and 22nd guards tank) and the 9th Guards Mechanized Corps, which also consisted of two brigades (46th Guards Tank and 30th Guards Motorized Rifle), at 1700 on 21 December for an attack to the south, while the corps' remaining forces remained in their previous areas with the task of defending Dolne Semerovce and Levice.

The Third Ukrainian Front's forces included the following: the 2nd Guards Mechanized, 18th Tank and 7th Mechanized corps, three tank and one self-propelled artillery regiments as part of the 5th Guards Cavalry Corps, 11 self-propelled artillery battalions and seven independent artillery regiments. As of 20 December, the Third Ukrainian Front's tank and mechanized forces numbered 413 tanks and 323 self-propelled guns, for a total of 736 vehicles. The tank and mechanized forces were distributed in the following manner: the self-propelled artillery regiments and individual battalions were subordinated to the combined-arms formations: the 2nd Guards Mechanized Corps to the 46th Army and the 7th Mechanized Corps to the 4th Guards Army, while the 18th Tank Corps was subordinated directly to the *front* commander.

As of 20 December, these forces were concentrated as follows:

- the 2nd Guards Mechanized Corps, consisting of 94 tanks and 14 self-propelled guns, in the Ivancsa area;

2 Editor's note. The Ferdinand, later known as the "Elefant," was a German heavy tank destroyer. A later model weighed 65 tons and carried a crew of six. It was armed with an 88mm gun and one 7.92 machine gun.

- the 7th Mechanized Corps, consisting of 80 tanks and 56 self-propelled guns, in the Sarkeresztur area;
- the 18th Tank Corps, consisting of 186 tanks and 41 self-propelled guns, in the Nagyperkata area.

During the third stage of the Budapest operation the Third Ukrainian Front's tank and mechanized forces were primarily employed for developing success.

The 2nd Guards Mechanized Corps was to develop the 46th Army's success. The corps was given the assignment, upon the infantry's reaching the line Tordas—Pazmand, of entering the breakthrough with the immediate task of reaching the area Zsambek—Bicske—Etyek and subsequently the western outskirts of Budapest. The corps was to be committed into the breakthrough along a 10-kilometer front and, while carrying out its immediate task, to reach a depth of 25-30 kilometers.

In accordance with the assigned task and taking into account the limited number of roads (during a period of many washed-out roads), the corps commander decided to commit the corps into the breakthrough in two echelons and along two routes, having in the first echelon two mechanized brigades, plus reinforcements, and a tank brigade in the second echelon behind the left-flank mechanized brigade, and upon the 4th Guards Army's combined-arms formations' capture of Szekesfehervar and their arrival at a line east and west of the city, to enter the breakthrough and launch an attack in the direction of Mor with the corps' main forces and with part of its forces in the direction of Varpalota. The corps' immediate objective was to capture Mor and Varpalota. The corps was to then firmly consolidate along the new line, holding it until the arrival of the rifle formations, reliably securing from the west (along the Mor—Varpalota line) the army's main group of forces, which was developing the offensive from the Szekesfehervar area to the north. Simultaneously with the commitment of the corps into the breakthrough, the 21st Guards Rifle Corps' formations were to develop the offensive to the left of the 7th Mechanized Corps for the purpose of capturing the line Varpalota—Vilonya and then to Lake Balaton. Thus the 7th Guards Mechanized Corps was to reach a depth of 25-30 kilometers and capture a line along a 20-kilometer front. The jumping-off area for the corps' commitment into the breakthrough was to be the northern and northwestern outskirts of Szekesfehervar.

In accordance with the assigned mission, the corps commander decided to attack in the direction of Mor with three brigades (two mechanized and one tank), organizing them into two echelons: a tank and one mechanized brigades in the first echelon, and a mechanized brigade in the second. A single mechanized brigade was to attack in the direction of Varpalota.

Directive no. 00962/op of 18 December, issued by the headquarters of the Third Ukrainian Front, ordered that the 18th Tank Corps,

> … upon the capture of the city of Szekesfehervar by the 4th Guards Army's infantry and following its arrival (together with units of the 46th Army) at the line Tordas—excluding Patka, is to enter the breakthrough in the general direction: Szekesfehervar, Csakvar, Many, Esztergom. By the close of the second day of the commitment into the breakthrough, it is to reach the Dorog—Nyergesujfalu—Bajna area and cut the path of retreat of the enemy's Budapest group of forces to the northwest and west. By the close of the third day of the commitment into the breakthrough, part of its forces is to capture the pass west of Pilisvorosvar.

In the case of a delay with the capture of Szekesfehervar and the event of success east of Lake Velence (along the 46th Army's sector), the corps was to be committed into the breakthrough along the 46th Army's sector, after which it would arrive at its own axis. The corps was to have the following jumping-off positions for the commitment into the breakthrough: a) along the 4th

Guards Army's sector—the eastern half of Szekesfehervar and then five kilometers to the east; b) along the 46th Army's sector—Pazmand—Lake Velence.

In the capacity of reinforcements, two regiments from the 42nd Anti-Tank Artillery Brigade, the 22nd Anti-Aircraft Division (two regiments), the 200th and the 53rd Guards Mortar regiments were attached to the corps from the *front* reserve.

Thus, in accordance with the overall operational plan, it was planned to employ the mobile forces in the following manner: the 2nd Guards Mechanized Corps, upon entering the breakthrough, would be directed to the north to a depth of 25-30 kilometers, after which it would turn sharply to the east on Budapest; the 7th Mechanized Corps would develop the success to the northwest to a depth of 25-30 kilometers, after which it would turn and face to the west; the 18th Tank Corps was to enter the breakthrough between the two mechanized corps and, while developing the success to the north to a depth of 60-70 kilometers, reach the Esztergom area.

Thus on 20 December the 18th Tank Corps, while operating as part of the Third Ukrainian Front, was to attack from south to north in the direction of Esztergom, while the 6th Guards Tank Army, operating as part of the Second Ukrainian Front, was to attack that same day from the north, from the Levice area, to the south, also in the direction of Esztergom.

These tank formations were separated from each other by more than 100 kilometers; their arrival at the Danube in the Esztergom area would signify the complete encirclement of the enemy's Budapest group of forces. By the beginning of combat operations the enemy had facing the 46th Army's forces the 8th Panzer Division (German) and the 1st Panzer Division (Hungarian), the 239th Assault Gun Brigade, the 20th and 271st infantry divisions, the 8th SS Police Regiment, and the Hungarian 1st Cavalry Division, while facing the 4th Guards Army he was defending with the following units: the German 271st and 153rd infantry divisions, the Hungarian 20th and 9th infantry divisions, reinforced by specialized units and subunits, and the 1st and 23rd panzer divisions. The 3rd Panzer Division, which had been transferred from East Prussia, was concentrating along the northern outskirts of Szekesfehervar, in the second echelon. The overall number of tanks and self-propelled guns available to the enemy along this axis was 200 vehicles.

The course of combat activities. On 20 December the Third Ukrainian Front's combined-arms formations attacked, and as a result of the fighting on 21 December success was achieved along the 46th Army's sector to the east of Lake Velence. The 2nd Guards Mechanized Corps was committed into the fighting to develop the success. At 1000, having overtaken the 10th Rifle Corps' combat formations, the 2nd Guards Mechanized Corps' formations got into a fight with the German 8th Panzer Division's tanks and moved slowly forward. By 1900 the corps reached the line Tordas—Vereb. The corps' left-flank brigade, having encountered the stubborn resistance of 20 tanks from the 8th Panzer Division and the newly arrived units of the 5th Panzer Division along the southern outskirts of Vereb, began to outflank this inhabited locale from the east.

The enemy put up stubborn resistance along the 4th Guards Army's sector and the infantry advanced slowly.

At 1300 on 21 December the 7th Mechanized Corps received orders to enter the breakthrough along the sector Lake Velence—eastern outskirts of the Szekesfehervar suburbs and, together with the 21st Guards Rifle Corps, capture the city of Szekesfehervar with an attack from north to south and by the close of the day reach the line Zamoly—Bodajk—Csor. Thus the corps was assigned a new mission to capture Szekesfehervar. The corps' activities were made more difficult by the fact that the terrain and the enemy's position prevented us from attacking the enemy with our entire force. The corridor for the commitment into the breakthrough was 1.5-2 kilometers wide and contained one road and was constricted on the right by the Sarviz Canal and on the left by the Szekesfehervar suburbs. Besides this, this corridor was being defended by units of the 23rd Panzer Division, which had up to 40-50 tanks and self-propelled guns, part of which were buried in the ground, while the 3rd Panzer Division, with up to 150 tanks, was concentrated in the depth.

At 1400 the corps' formations began carrying out their assignment and at 1600 had reached the area 2-3 kilometers east of Szekesfehervar, where the corps got into a heavy fight with the enemy's tanks. The 23rd and 3rd panzer divisions, which committed more than 150 tanks into the battle, put up stubborn resistance to the corps' advance. The corps' left flank was under heavy artillery flanking fire from the direction of the Szekesfehervar suburbs.

By the close of the day the 64th Mechanized Brigade reached the northern outskirts of the suburbs. Upon turning to the southeast from here, the brigade attacked the eastern outskirts of Szekesfehervar. The corps' remaining forces continued to advance to the north in the general direction of Zamoly.

On this same day at 1600, upon receiving a signal from the commander of the Third Ukrainian Front, the 18th Tank Corps began to move and reached the 46th Army's sector behind the 2nd Guards Mechanized Corps. By 2100 the corps had reached the Pazmand area.

Thus in the first two days of fighting the *front's* tank and mechanized forces were unable to reach the operational depth, because they were completing the breakthrough of the enemy defense and engaged in heavy tank battles.

Throughout the night of 21-22 December the corps continued to attack. The enemy threw fresh forces into the fighting and launched counterattacks. 40 tanks simultaneously counterattacked units of the 18th Tank Corps from Vereb and 20 enemy tanks against the corps' left flank. The enemy's 23rd Panzer Division was putting up resistance to the 7th Mechanized Corps' advance. As a result of the heavy fighting, the tank and mechanized formations advanced little throughout 22 December; namely, the 2nd Guards Mechanized and the 18th Tank corps advanced 4-6 kilometers and the 7th Mechanized Corps 3-5 kilometers. By 1600 the 2nd Guards Mechanized Corps captured Val and the 18th Tank Corps captured Vereb. One of the 7th Mechanized Corps's brigades was engaged in heavy fighting along the eastern outskirts of Szekesfehervar, while the corps' remaining forces were fighting along a line 4-6 kilometers northeast of the city.

Thus as a result of three days of fighting, the tactical depth of the enemy's defense had been broken and the corps received the opportunity to develop their success.

At this time the situation along the sector of Second Ukrainian Front's 7th Guards and 6th Guards Tank armies northwest of Budapest was as follows.

The enemy, seeing the growing threat to Budapest from the southwest and northwest, sought at any cost to halt our forces' offensive. From the morning of 22 December the enemy counterattacked units of the 5th Guards Tank Corps along the western bank of the Hron River in the Kalnica area, but was unsuccessful. Simultaneously, the enemy attacked with 60 tanks from the 8th Panzer Division and with up to a regiment of infantry and broke through the combat formations of the 7th Guards Army's combined-arms formations in the Viskovce area and by the close of the day had reached the area five kilometers northwest of Sahy. On this day the enemy counterattacked the 4th Guards Motorcycle Regiment, which was occupying defensive positions northeast of Slatina. The enemy was seeking to cut off the Second Ukrainian Front's group of forces to the northwest of Slatina. In light of the developing situation, the 6th Guards Tank Army's shock group, which was advancing to the south in the direction of Esztergom, was halted in the Salov area, in accordance with instructions from the *front* commander. From this area the 21st and 22nd guards tank brigades (5th Guards Tank Corps) were turned back to the north to the Sazdice area for an attack against the left flank of the tank group that had broken through. The 46th Guards Tank and the 30th Mechanized brigades (9th Guards Mechanized Corps) were turned toward Viskovce for launching an attack into the enemy's rear.

In order to deprive the enemy of the opportunity of spreading to the northeast, the commander of the Second Ukrainian Front ordered the 4th Guards Mechanized Corps to leave its occupied area and take up defensive positions in the Grkovce area. On 23 December the corps took up defensive positions in the indicated area and, on orders from the commander of the Second Ukrainian Front, was subordinated to the commander of the 6th Guards Tank Army. Simultaneously, the tank army's formations, which occupied defensive positions in the Batovce—Kalnica area and in the area northeast of Slatina, were to turn over their combat sectors to the combined-arms formations and concentrate in the Sazdice area and six kilometers to the west. The army finished concentrating on 24 December.

The army received orders to destroy the enemy breakthrough group in the Sakalos area and vigorously advance to the south to the Danube and seize crossings in the Esztergom area.

As a result of stubborn fighting on 25 December and the night of 25-26 December, the enemy in the Sakalos area was defeated and the tank army's formations began to successfully advance to the south.

The combat operations of the Third Ukrainian Front's tank and mechanized troops, beginning on 23 December, developed rapidly.

On the night of 22-23 December the 2nd Guards Mechanized Corps' formations, without halting their combat activities, advanced along their routes. Upon approaching the southern outskirts of Etyek, the 6th Guards Mechanized Brigade encountered powerful enemy resistance. The Germans in Etyek had concentrated 25-30 tanks and up to 2-3 battalions of artillery. The brigade, having left a screen along the southern outskirts of the town, began to outflank it from the west, followed by the 37th Guards Tank Brigade. These two brigades, arriving to the north, cut off the retreat from Etyek of the enemy garrison. The enemy, seeing the appearance of our forces in his rear, began to fall back in panic to the northeast, abandoning weapons and equipment. By 1600 the corps had passed through Etyek. On the night of 23-24 December the corps, according to orders by the 46th Army commander, was turned toward Budapest. While developing a vigorous attack, at 1100 the 6th Guards Tank Brigade, along with the 30th Guards Tank Regiment, defeated up to two battalions of infantry and 15 armored vehicles, which were defending Paty. The newly arrived 4th Guards Mechanized Brigade and the 37th Guards Tank Brigade took up the pursuit of the retreating enemy and the 37th Guards Tank Brigade, together with the 251st Self-Propelled Artillery Regiment, which had surged forward, broke into the western outskirts of Budakeszi at 1215. Failing to withstand the pressure of our tanks, the enemy began to fall back on Budapest, abandoning his equipment.

While continuing the offensive, at 2100 the corps broke into the western outskirts of Budapest and began intensive street fighting, as a result of which it defeated the enemy. Thus the corps advanced 30-35 kilometers in the day's fighting.

On the night of 22-23 December the 18th Tank Corps, while making a fighting advance along its assigned route, was pushing aside the enemy's screens. The 110th Tank Brigade reached the southwestern outskirts of Alcsutdoboz. In withdrawing, the enemy blew up the bridges over the canal that ran southwest of Alcsutdoboz, and the brigade's tanks were unable to cross the canal. The 32nd Motorized Rifle Brigade, which arrived before long, crossed the canal under cover of fire from the 110th Brigade's tanks and began fighting along the southern outskirts of Alcsutdoboz. By 1600 the sappers had restored the bridge, the tanks crossed it and the enemy was thrown out of Alcsutdoboz. At 1730 the enemy launched a tank counterattack, having up to 20 vehicles in each group. The 110th Tank Brigade entered the fighting along the eastern outskirts of Alcsutdoboz and the 170th Tank Brigade along the western outskirts. The enemy was forced to fall back, having lost 16 tanks.

On 26 December an order by the commander of the Third Ukrainian Front assigned the corps the task of defeating the enemy group of forces in the town of Bicske and to capture Tinnye by the close of the day. The corps attacked on the morning of 24 December.

The fighting for Bicske, which began at 0800, continued eight hours. At 1600 the town had been completely cleared of the enemy. The corps, without delaying in Bicske, began to pursue the enemy's retreating units in the direction of Zsambek and Many.

The 32nd Motorized Rifle Brigade took up the defensive in Telki and Perbal and Tinnye, with a battalion each, with the mission of preventing the enemy's retreat from Budapest to the west. The 170th Tank Brigade was attacking along the corps' left flank and by the close of 24 December had captured Szomor. The brigade subsequently advanced to the north and, pushing aside the enemy's screens, captured Tata at 2000 on 25 December.

The 181st Tank Brigade, which was moving along the 170th Brigade's route, was turned from the Kirva area toward Dorog and at 2000 on 25 December captured Dorog with an attack from the west and by the 32nd Motorized Rifle Brigade from the east. The 110th Tank Brigade was turned to the southeast in the direction of Pilisvorosvar, with the task of capturing the pass west of Pilisvorosvar and holding it. By 1200 on 25 December the brigade had carried out its assigned task and, operating from ambushes, routed an enemy column which was trying to break out of Budapest to the northwest.

Thus on 25 December the 18th Tank Corps was operating from the Szomor—Many area along three axes along a 20-25 kilometer front; one brigade seized Pilisorosvar, two brigades Dorog, and one brigade reached the Danube in the Tata area. Having seized these locales, the corps deprived the enemy of the opportunity of withdrawing from Budapest to the northwest and threatened Esztergom from the south. Developing the further offensive, on the night of 25-26 December the 181st Tank Brigade and the 32nd Motorized Rifle Brigade reached the southern outskirts of Esztergom at 0300 and, following a stubborn 5-hour battle, captured the town at 1300 on 26 December, having established communications with the Second Ukrainian Front's units operating along the northern bank of the Danube. Thus the path of retreat of the enemy's Budapest group of forces had been completely cut to the north and west. The corps' formations subsequently continued to advance along the southern bank of the Danube and on 27-28 December occupied the line Neszmely—Tata.

The 7th Guards Mechanized Corps, operating along the left wing of the 4th Guards Army, was engaged in very heavy fighting with the superior forces of the enemy's 3rd and 23rd panzer divisions during 23-26 December along the line Zamoly—Moha.

In the Second Ukrainian Front, the main forces of the 6th Guards Tank Army's formations reached the Danube north of Esztergom on 28 December.

In carrying out their tasks, the 6th Guards Tank Army's tank and mechanized formations were concentrated in the Santovka area by order of the commander of the Second Ukrainian Front, in order to put themselves in order. By order of the commander of the Third Ukrainian Front, the 18th Tank Corps concentrated in the Zsambek—Many area; from 31 December the 7th Mechanized Corps continued to fight along the line Csakbereny—excluding Moha; the 2nd Guards Mechanized Corps was defending northwest of Budapest along the line Pilisvorosvar—Pilisszanto—Pilisszentkeraszt.

Thus the Second and Third Ukrainian fronts' tank and mechanized forces played the leading role during the operation's third stage. Characteristic features of their activities are maneuverability and tenacity in carrying out their assigned missions. The combat activities of the operation's third stage are chiefly characterized by tank battles, because the enemy constantly threw tank groups into his counterattacks, often of an impressive size. The tanks constantly interacted with the infantry in the process of the unfolding battles. By breaking through into the depth of the enemy's position and destroying his arriving reserves, the tanks guaranteed a high rate of advance for the combined-arms formations of the Second and Third Ukrainian fronts' attacking armies.

The Tank and Mechanized Troops' Activities During the Fourth Stage of the Operation (1 January-13 February 1945)

As a result of combat activities during the third stage of the Budapest operation, the enemy had been thrown back behind the Hron River by the forces of the Second Ukrainian Front and a bridgehead seized near its mouth, from which our forces could further develop the offensive to the north and northwest.

Simultaneously, the Third Ukrainian Front's forces, while developing a vigorous offensive to the northwest, reached the line Neszmely—Szar—Csakbereny—Moha—Balatonfokajar. The linkup of the Second and Third Ukrainian fronts' forces along the Danube in the Esztergom area and their arrival at the indicated locales securely closed the encirclement ring around the enemy's Budapest group of forces.

In Budapest itself two panzer divisions (the Hungarian 1st Panzer Division and the German 13th Panzer Division), four infantry divisions (Hungarian 10th, 12th and 13th and the German 271st infantry divisions), one motorized division (*Feldherrnhalle*), one independent brigade (239th Assault Gun Brigade), six independent regiments, and 20 independent special designation battalions were encircled. The encirclement ring was gradually squeezed around this group of forces.

The German command, seeing the increasing threat to Budapest, attempted to bring its Budapest group of forces out of encirclement. For this purpose, by 1 January 1945 the enemy had concentrated a significant group of forces in the Komarno area for launching an offensive.

The enemy was simultaneously strengthening his defense along the western bank of the Hron River opposite the Second Ukrainian Front's forces and was bringing troops here from other axes so as to prevent our units' further offensive.

On 2 January the Germans had concentrated seven panzer divisions (1st, 3rd, 6th, 23rd, 3rd SS *Totenkopf*, and 5th SS *Wiking*) and the 130th Panzer Regiment from the high command reserve opposite the Third Ukrainian Front's forces in the area south of Komarno as far as Szekesfehervar. These formations had an overall strength of 435 tanks and 65 self-propelled guns.

The greater part of the tanks and self-propelled guns was concentrated along the line Tata and north to the Danube. The Germans had grouped along this line the 3rd SS Panzer Division *Totenkopf*, the 5th SS Panzer Division *Wiking*, the 6th and 3rd panzer divisions, part of the 23rd Panzer Division, and the 130th Panzer Regiment from the high command reserve. This group of forces had the mission of breaking through our defense with a powerful tank fist and, in a vigorous movement to the southeast, to break through to Budapest.

The Disposition of Tank and Mechanized Forces by Fronts, as of 1 January 1945

Third Ukrainian Front. The 2nd Guards Mechanized Corps was defending in the Pilisvorosvar—Pilliszanto area, with 38 tanks and 11 self-propelled guns in line. The 18th Tank Corps was in the Zsambek—Many area in the *front* reserve and was constructing a defensive line. The corps had 133 tanks and 13 self-propelled guns in line. The 170th Tank Brigade was in the Neszmely area and was strengthening the infantry's combat formations.

The 7th Mechanized Corps, which was defending along the line Sored—Sarkeresztes, had 80 tanks and 24 self-propelled guns.

On 3 January the 1st Guards Mechanized Corps arrived from the reserve of the *Stavka* of the Supreme High Command and had concentrated in the Nagyperkata—Nagyhantos, with 184 tanks and 62 self-propelled guns.

Thus by the start of the Germans' January offensive the Third Ukrainian Front's armored and mechanized forces had 545 tanks and self-propelled guns.

Second Ukrainian Front. On 4 January the Second Ukrainian Front comprised the following: 6th Guards Tank Army, 23rd Tank Corps, 4th Guards Mechanized Corps, 27th Guards Tank Brigade, seven tank regiments, and two regiments of self-propelled artillery. These units had a total of 383 tanks and 22 self-propelled guns.

The Course of Combat Activities

The enemy's offensive from the area south of Komarno. During the night of 1-2 January the German forces concentrated south of Komarno attacked along the sector west of Neszmely and Tata and simultaneously began to force with their 96th Infantry Division the Danube in the area to the east of Neszmely.

Having a numerical superiority in tanks and artillery along this sector, the enemy broke through our troops' defense with a night attack, advanced 3-5 kilometers into the depth and captured Agostyan. The Germans committed a tank group of up to 80 vehicles (primarily heavy tanks) into the breach.

The tanks began to rapidly advance to the east and southeast toward Esztergom and Bicske. The Germans committed behind the tanks armored transports with motorized infantry, to consolidate the tanks' success. The 18th Tank Corps' 170th Tank Brigade repulsed the enemy's attacks on Neszmely throughout the night and day of 2 January.

By the close of 2 January the enemy reached the Tardos area, while the landing east of Neszmely cut the road from Esztergom to Neszmely and began to spread to the south and east. Thus the danger of encirclement arose for the 170th Tank Brigade, which was located in the Neszmely area. The commander of the 18th Tank Corps issued an order to pull back the brigade to the Szomor area to link up with the corps. By 0300 on 4 January the brigade arrived in one piece north of Szomor, with 11 tanks and 11 self-propelled guns.

In the developing situation, on the night of 2-3 January the commander of the Third Ukrainian Front assigned the commander of the 18th Tank Corps the following task: to depart immediately for the Dag—Bajna area and be ready, in conjunction with units of the 86th Rifle Division and the 4th Guards Rifle Division, to launch an attack in the direction of Nyergesujfalu. The 170th Tank Brigade was temporarily subordinated to the commander of the 31st Rifle Corps.

In carrying out the assigned tasks, the corps' 181st Tank Brigade had passed through Sarisap by 0500 on 3 January. Not meeting strong enemy resistance, the brigade continued to attack to the north. The 110th Tank Brigade, with the 363rd Heavy Self-Propelled Artillery Regiment, entered Bajna at 0530 and began a tank battle in the center of town. Within three hours the 32nd Motorized Rifle Brigade arrived at Bajna and entered the fighting together with the 110th Tank Brigade's tanks. Throughout the day a difficult and stubborn tank battle raged in Bajna. All day the enemy's aviation hung over the brigade's combat formations in groups of 15-20 planes, and bombed and strafed the tanks with cannon fire.

By the close of the day the enemy had brought up to 80 tanks to Bajna and once again attacked. However, even this time he made no successful advance. The 110th Tank Brigade, along with the 363rd Heavy Self-Propelled Artillery Regiment, and the 32nd Motorized Rifle Brigade and the 292nd Mortar Regiment, prevented the enemy from passing through Bajna. By this time the 181st Tank Brigade was fighting two kilometers west of Sarisap.

During the night of 3-4 January the enemy carried out several powerful tank attacks on Bajna. Failing to achieve success, he began to outflank in groups of 10-20 tanks this locale from the west toward Tarjan and then to Szomor and Bicske. On the morning of 4 January the situation along the corps' front was as follows. The Germans' main tank group of forces had concentrated in the Bajna—Tarjan area.

According to aerial intelligence more than 160 armored vehicles had been spotted in this area and the tip of the tank wedge was aimed at Szomor and Zsambek. Thus the enemy was striving to crush the 18th Tank Corps in Bajna with a tank fist and reach Zsambek, from which lay the shortest route to Budapest.

Due to the developing situation, the *front* commander ordered the commander of the 18th Tank Corps to shift the 181st Tank Brigade from the corps' right flank to the area west of Szomor and to prevent the infiltration of the enemy's tanks. The brigade arrived at the indicated area at 0900 and took up defensive positions. Bitter tank battles took place south of Bajna throughout 4 January. Our tank units, operating from ambushes (4-5 tanks and 1-2 self-propelled guns each), repulsed more than ten enemy tank attacks; up to 30-40 tanks took part in each attack. The enemy, having lost 26 tanks burned, was unsuccessful. Seeing the lack of result in attacking along this axis, the Germans undertook a maneuver and the enemy tanks began to outflank the 110th Tank Brigade from the west toward Szomor and through Tarjan toward Many. Thus the main body of enemy tanks began moving toward Many and Szomor. By the close of the day the 49th Rifle Division arrived in the corps's combat area, and on orders from the *front* commander the corps turned over its combat sectors to the division. By 0600 on 5 January the 18th Tank Corps had concentrated in the Zsambek—Many area, where it went over to the defensive, with the task of preventing the enemy from getting to this area.

To the left of the 18th Tank Corps, the 7th Mechanized Corps' 16th Mechanized Brigade, which had been temporarily subordinated to the 18th Tank Corps, was defending in the Csabdi area.

Besides this, the 1st Guards Mechanized Corps' mobile anti-tank group arrived in the area occupied by the corps, consisting of the 182nd and 382nd self-propelled artillery regiments and the 24th Anti-Tank Artillery Brigade. This group was also subordinated to the commander of the 18th Tank Corps. It had the task of reinforcing the 49th Rifle Division's units.

On 5 January the 2nd Guards Mechanized Corps was shifted from the Pilisvorosvar area to the Dorog—Dag—Perbal area, where it took up the defense along a 15-kilometer front.

On this day the 1st Guards Mechanized Corps was shifted from the Nagyperkata—Nagyhantos area to the Paty—Bicske—Tabajd area and also took up the defense of strong points along a 20-25 kilometer front.

Thus on 5 January a one tank and two mechanized corps had been concentrated along the second defensive line of Dorog—Bicske—Tabajd.

Beginning from the second half of 5 January through 8 January inclusively, the enemy continuously attacked the formations of the 2nd Guards Mechanized and 18th Tank corps. The Germans attacked in large groups of tanks and motorized infantry on armored transports. The enemy's attack, as a rule, was accompanied by powerful artillery fire.

Our formations, in repelling the tank and motorized infantry attacks, securely held their positions and inflicted heavy losses on the enemy.

In three days of uninterrupted attacks along the 18th Tank Corps' defensive sector alone the enemy lost 66 tanks and 14 guns and was forced to go over to the defensive, shifting the main body of his tanks (3rd and 23rd panzer divisions) and infantry to the area northwest of Szekesfehervar. Simultaneously, the enemy began to maneuver groups of tanks and armored transports along the 2nd Guards Mechanized and 18th Tank corps' sector, trying to create an impression of a regrouping for launching new attacks.

The enemy's offensive from the area northwest of Szekesfehervar. On the morning of 7 January the enemy's tank group of forces, numbering up to 180 tanks and self-propelled guns, together with infantry, attacked from the area northwest of Szekesfehervar. Operating as a powerful tank fist, the Germans began waging stubborn fighting along the 7th Mechanized Corps' front. During a day of fighting the corps' formations beat off 23 attacks; the enemy, having lost 45 tanks and 12 armored transports, was forced to renounce further attempts to pass through the corps' combat formations.

At 0930 on 8 January, under the cover of a smoke screen and a powerful artillery onslaught, the Germans attacked for a second time the units of the 7th Mechanized Corps, but were also unsuccessful and, having lost up to 30 tanks, went over to the defense. Thus throughout 8 January the 7th Mechanized Corps prevented the enemy from breaking through to Szekesfehervar from the north. The enemy was not active along the Szekesfehervar axis before 18 January.

The offensive by the Second Ukrainian Front's forces. In order to render assistance to the Third Ukrainian Front's forces, the *Stavka* of the Supreme High Command ordered the commander of the Second Ukrainian Front to launch attacks along the northern bank of the Danube toward Komarno with the forces of the 6th Guards Tank and 7th Guards armies.

In order to carry out the *front* commander's order, on the night of 4-5 January the 6th Tank Army (5th Guards Tank and 9th Guards Mechanized corps and the 4th Guards Motorcycle Regiment) carried out a 55-60 kilometer march from the Santovka—Sazdice area and by the morning had concentrated in the Salka—Letkes area, having 170 tanks and eight self-propelled guns in line.

By the morning of 5 January the 27th Independent Tank Brigade, consisting of 16 tanks and eight self-propelled guns, had concentrated along the western bank of the Hron River, ten kilometers southwest of Salka.

The 4th Guards Mechanized Corps was located 4-5 kilometers east of Zeliezovce.

The 23rd Tank Corps was concentrated from the Aszod area to the Szokolya area and was in the *front* reserve.

The 6th Guards Tank Army received orders, together with the 7th Guards Army's forces, to attack at 0300 on 6 January, to break through the enemy's front along the Nana—Parkany sector (4-5 kilometers wide) and, attacking in the general direction of Muzla and Batorove Kosihy and Komarno, to capture a crossing over the Danube in the Komarno area by the close of 7 January and get into the rear of the enemy's group of forces attacking from the area south of Komarno toward Budapest. The army was to cover its combat formations with part of its forces from the north from the direction of Nove Zamky, until the arrival of the 7th Guards Army's infantry.

Thus the tank army was to destroy the opposing enemy with a vigorous attack, rout his reserves and seize crossings over the Danube in the Komarno area, thus depriving the enemy of the opportunity of maneuvering the breakthrough group's reserves along the Third Ukrainian Front's sector and along his retreat routes to the west and northwest.

In accordance with his assigned task, the commander of the 6th Guards Tank Army decided to attack in a single echelon, with his corps side by side.

The 9th Guards Mechanized and 5th Guards Tank corps were to attack in the general direction of Komarno, with the task of seizing crossings over the Danube near Komarno, while at the same time, with the 9th Guards Mechanized Corps' arrival in the Batorove Kosihy area it was to dispatch a brigade to the northwest with the task of capturing crossings over the Nitra River near Nove Zamky and to secure the operation from the north until the arrival of the 7th Guards Army.

The army was to attack along a 10-kilometer front, with the tank corps in the center of its combat formation, covered on the right by the mechanized corps and on the left by the motorcycle regiment. This organization of the combat formation was facilitated by the fact that the tank corps, located in the center, could develop the offensive at a high speed, without fearing for its flanks.

At 0300 on 6 January the 6th Guards Tank Army, in conjunction with the 7th Guards Army's infantry, attacked without an artillery preparation. The attack by the tank and mechanized formations was unexpected for the enemy and caught him regrouping. During the first half of the day the army advanced 8-12 kilometers into the depth. At 1200 the 9th Guards Mechanized Corps's lead brigade captured Kebelkut, while the 5th Guards Tank Corps occupied Muzla by 1400.

Having left part of its forces behind to defend along the northern and northwestern outskirts of Kebelkut, the 9th Guards Mechanized Corps' formations continued attacking and by the close of 6 January were fighting four kilometers west of Kebelkut. At 1700 the 5th Guards Tank Corps broke into the southeastern outskirts of Batorove Kosihy and captured it following a stubborn 5-hour battle.

The 4th Guards Motorcycle Regiment, attacking along the army's left flank, captured Karva and from 2000 continued attacking toward Mocsa.

Thus on the first day of fighting the units of the 6th Guards Tank Army advanced 20-25 kilometers into the depth.

On the night of 6-7 January the 5th Guards Tank Corps captured Madar by 0600 and continued to attack to the west.

The 9th Guards Mechanized Corps, while beating off powerful enemy counterattacks continued to develop the offensive to the northwest and by 1500 captured Pribeta and Svaty Peter.

In the Pribeta area the 31st Guards Mechanized Brigade went over to the defense, repelling powerful enemy tank and infantry attacks.

By 2000 the 5th Guards Tank Corps reached the line two kilometers northeast of Komarno. The corps got into intense fighting along this line and went over to the defensive, beating off repeated enemy counterattacks. The 4th Guards Motorcycle Regiment, having taking Mocsa, also went over to the defense, beating off enemy attacks.

The enemy, seeing the growing threat to Komarno and the crossings over the Danube in this area, threw all his available forces into the fighting against the tank army's formations and began to hurriedly shift the 20th Panzer Division from the Third Ukrainian Front to the Komarno—Naszvad line. Simultaneously, the Germans counterattacked from the area north of Batorove Kosihy and captured it.

On 7 January the situation for the 6th Guards Tank Army's units was tense. The 7th Guards Army's combined-arms formations had not yet arrived at the tank army's area of combat operations. The tank army was forced to wage a battle by itself, with its front facing north, along the line Batorove Kosihy—Kebelkut and its front facing south, along the line two kilometers northeast of Komarno—Mocsa.

In the developing situation, the 4th Guards Mechanized Corps was attached to the 6th Guards Tank Army. The corps was given the assignment of crossing the Hron River and concentrating in the Kebelkut area, and at dawn launching an attack in the direction of Szoldiny and Farnad, rolling up the enemy's front along the Hron River. At 0530 on 8 January the corps had been concentrated in the indicated area. Simultaneously, the 7th Guards Army was given the mission of launching a decisive offensive from the Zeliezovce—Salov area, also in the direction of Farnad. In this case, the attack by the 4th Guards Mechanized Corps and the 7th Guards Army's formations in the direction of Farnad would ease the 6th Guards Tank Army's operations along its right flank.

The 4th Guards Mechanized Corps, having launched its attack, captured Szoldiny, routing here a battalion of Germans and, developing the offensive further, by the close of 8 January, together with combined-arms formations, it threw the enemy back to the north of Bart, where it was involved in stubborn fighting throughout 9-10 January. During these days the 5th Guards Tank and 9th Guards Mechanized corps repelled fierce counterattacks from the Nove Zamky—Komarno axis. The fighting was fierce and the enemy launched counterattacks with large groups of tanks and infantry. On 9 January the enemy managed to break into Svaty Peter.

On 11 January the enemy along the tank army's operational sector had more than 70 tanks and self-propelled guns and up to 75 armored transports and armored vehicles. By this time the tank army numbered 23 tanks in the 5th Guards Tank Corps, 26 tanks in the 9th Guards Mechanized Corps and 23 tanks in the 4th Mechanized Corps. In all, 72 tanks remained in the army.

By the close of 11 January the enemy, at the cost of heavy losses, managed to occupy the line Madar—Svaty Peter and securely hold Pribeta.

On the night of 11-12 January the 5th Guards Tank Corps, in accordance with orders received, turned over its combat sectors to the 53rd Rifle Division and received orders to take Svaty Peter on the morning of 12 January, together with the 9th Guards Mechanized Corps. The offensive undertaken on Svaty Peter on 12 January was not crowned with success.

By order of the *front* commander of 13 January, the 7th Guards Army was assigned the task of taking up the defensive along the line Csata (north of Szoldiny)—Kert—Madar—Radvan and then along the northern bank of the Danube. This same order assigned the 6th Guards Tank Army the task of throwing the enemy out of the Madar area, having secured the arrival of the 7th Guards Army's infantry and its occupation of defensive positions along its indicated line. Upon completing the assigned task, the tank army was to concentrate in the Kebelkut—Bucs area and go over to the defense here. In carrying out its assigned task, the 6th Guards Tank Army's formations reached their appointed areas by the close of 14 January and went over to the defensive.

The enemy's offensive from the area southwest of Szekesfehervar. During 10-18 January the enemy was not active along the Third Ukrainian Front's sector, while carrying out a regrouping of his tank forces. The 5th SS Panzer Division *Wiking* and the 3rd SS Panzer Division *Totenkopf*, had been shifted from the Bicske area to the Varpalota area. the 6th Panzer Division had gone over to the defensive on a broad front along the sector north and northwest of Bicske. Units of the 3rd Panzer Division, which were defending southeast of Mor, were relieved by the remnants of the Hungarian 2nd Panzer Division and the 23rd Panzer Division by formations of the 4th Cavalry Division.

Thus as of 15 January the German command had concentrated a powerful tank group southwest of Szekesfehervar, consisting of the 5th SS Panzer Division *Wiking* and the 3rd SS Panzer Division *Totenkopf*, the 1st, 3rd and 23rd panzer divisions, the 509th Panzer Battalion of "King Tigers,"[3] and the 325th Assault Gun Brigade. This enemy tank group had up to 230 tanks and up to 100 self-propelled guns.

Aside from the tank group, two infantry divisions were concentrated in this area.

On 18 January the German tank formations were concentrated in the Berhida area and to the south, from where, following a powerful artillery preparation, they attacked along a 15-18 kilometer front. Their main attack was aimed between Battyan and Lepseny. The enemy simultaneously threw up to 130 tanks into the battle. The superiority in tanks and artillery enabled the enemy to break through the 135th Rifle Corps' defense and rapidly reach the areas of our forces' artillery positions. In order to prevent the enemy from further spreading, the 7th Mechanized Corps, minus its tank regiments (the latter had been left behind in the 41st Rifle Division's combat formations 12-14 kilometers north of Szekesfehervar) was moved to the Battyan—Polgardi line.

At the same time, the 18th Tank Corps was ordered to turn over the Zsambek—Many defensive line to units of the 3rd Guards Mechanized Brigade (1st Guards Mechanized Corps) and concentrate by 0800 on 19 January in the Seregelyes—Sarkeresztur area, with the task of occupying defensive positions in this area and preventing a further enemy advance to the east and southeast. The 7th Mechanized Corps' formations in the Battyan area got into a tank battle with the enemy; its 63rd Mechanized Brigade, operating along the left flank, arrived in the Fule area, where, together with the combined-arms formations, it repelled enemy attacks. The Germans, having a numerical superiority in forces, began to press the 7th Mechanized Corps and the latter fell back to the southwestern outskirts of Szekesfehervar, occupied defensive positions and, in

3 Editor's note. This was the popular name of the German Tiger II, which was first produced in 1943. This model weighed 68.5 tons and carried a crew of five. It was armed with an 88mm gun and two 7.92mm machine guns.

conjunction with the 93rd Rifle Division, continued to repel the German attacks. The enemy, while advancing in the direction of Aba, cut off the 63rd Mechanized Brigade from the corps' remaining forces; the brigade was forced to try to break out of the encirclement and by 21 January it reached the Kapolnasnyek area.

Thus the enemy reached the Aba—Soponya area on the first day of fighting (18 January), having penetrated our defense to a depth of 18-20 kilometers. Throughout the following day the enemy, at the cost of heavy losses, managed to take Szekesfehervar and the 7th Mechanized Corps was pulled back to the Kapolnasnyek area, where it occupied defensive positions. The 63rd Mechanized Brigade was subsequently removed from the corps and the corps' remaining forces were pulled back into the *front* reserve.

The 18th Tank Corps, upon arriving at its new defensive line, became involved in fierce fighting by 0900 on 19 January, together with units of the 133rd Rifle Corps. Despite his superiority of force, the enemy was unable to throw the corps' formations from the line Seregelyes—Sarosd. Employing maneuver, the enemy outflanked units of the 18th Tank Corps from the south and north and on 19 January reached the Danube along the Adony—Dunaujvaros sector, thus cutting the Third Ukrainian Front's southern group of forces off from the northern one and cut off formations of the 18th Tank and 133rd Rifle Corps. The commander of the 18th Tank Corps received orders from the *front* commander to break through to the south, along with the 133rd Rifle Corps, and reach the line Alap—Dunapentele, occupying defensive positions along this line facing north.

In order to break out of the encirclement, the 18th Tank and 133rd Rifle corps launched an attack on the night of 21-22 January to the southeast in the direction of Hercegfalva.

The 18th Tank Corps was operating along two axes. The right-hand column, which consisted of the 181st Tank Brigade, 21st Rifle Division, part of the 122nd Rifle Division's forces, and the 10th Anti-Tank Artillery Brigade moved on Sarkeresztur and Alap, while the left-hand column, which consisted of the 110th Tank Brigade, 104th Rifle Division, the 32nd Motorized Rifle and 170th Tank brigades and the 3rd Anti-Aircraft Division attacked toward Sarosd, Nagyhantos and Hercegfalva The joint attack by the two corps was completely successful. Having routed the opposing units of the German 3rd Panzer Division in the Hercegfalva area, the corps occupied defensive positions along the line Eloszallas—Alap, with their front facing north. Throughout 22-23 January the Germans repeatedly attempted to break through to the south through the 18th Tank and 133rd Rifle corps' defense and thus get into the rear of the 57th Army. Having suffered losses in men and materiel, by the close of 23 January the enemy halted his attacks along this axis, went over to the defensive and began to concentrate his main tank forces in the Adony area for the purpose of launching an attack to the north in the direction of Baracska.

In order to halt the offensive by the Germans' tank group of forces to the north, the 1st and 2nd mechanized brigades from the 1st Guards Mechanized Corps and units of the 5th Cavalry Corps were shifted to the Kapolnasnyek line and further to the east. The later formations were involved in unremitting fighting along this line, while preventing the enemy from spreading to the north. The Germans, while having a superiority in tanks, nevertheless managed to press our units and penetrate into our defense and by the close of 24 January reach the Kapolnasnyek—Baracska area and then to the southeast, four kilometers south of Ercsi, along the western bank of the Danube as far as Dunapentele and Hercegfalva. Thus an extremely intensive situation developed southwest of Budapest at the beginning of the last ten days of January. The enemy could reinforce his attacks to the north and northeast and link up with the encircled group of forces in Buda (the western part of Budapest).

In the developing situation, by order of the *Stavka* of the Supreme High Command, the 23rd Tank Corps, consisting of 156 tanks and 19 self-propelled guns, was transferred from the Second Ukrainian Front on 24 January to the Third Ukrainian Front and, which, having concentrated in the Paty—Torbad area, was subordinated to the commander of the 4th Guards Army.

Simultaneously, the Third Ukrainian Front's combat sector in Buda was transferred to the Second Ukrainian Front's forces. In order to prevent the enemy from forcing the Danube south of Budapest, our units took up defensive positions along the eastern bank of the Danube, from the southern outskirts of Budapest to the south.

A tank company apiece from the 5th Guards and 23rd tank corps was detached for joint operations with the infantry in storming the western part of Budapest (Buda).

By this time the situation along the 4th Guards Army's sector had become more complicated. The enemy, during the night of and from the morning of 25 January, continued to push to the north, toward Buda, with large groups of tanks, self-propelled guns and infantry, supported by artillery. Simultaneously, the Germans' 6th Panzer Division attacked from the Many—Csabdi area in the direction of Zsambek and Bicske, with the task of capturing these important strong points along the central axis.

The greater part of the enemy's tank forces (3rd and 5th SS panzer divisions), which had more than 100 armored vehicles, were concentrated in the Baracska—Kapolnasnyek area.

On 25 January the enemy launched a decisive offensive along all sectors. The 2nd Guards Mechanized Corps, on the defensive in the Zsambek area, had 23 tanks and 20 self-propelled guns on hand. Here the corps, along with the 23rd Rifle Corps, was securely holding its combat sectors, beating off attacks by the German 6th Panzer Division.

The 1st Guards Mechanized Corps, consisting of two brigades, was engaged in heavy defensive fighting along the line Kapolnasnyek—Baracska. At 1300 the enemy, following 90-minute artillery preparation, attacked. The result of the fighting was an insignificant success. At 2200 the Germans once again attacked, with up to 100 tanks and self-propelled guns in their combat formations.

This corps took upon itself the entire weight of the Germans' tank attack. Heavy fighting broke out, which lasted all of 26 January. During the night of 25-26 January the enemy continued to attack and he managed to break through to Vereb and to capture Val by the morning of 26 January. The formations of the 4th Guards Army and the 1st Guards Mechanized Corps fell back under heavy enemy pressure and occupied the line north of Vereb and also north and east of Val.

The elimination of the enemy breakthrough. The 23rd Tank Corps was committed into the fighting at 1000 on 26 January to defeat the enemy's tank group. An order by the commander of the 4th Guards Army of 1200 on 26 January assigned the corps the mission of taking the line Kapolnasnyek—Baracska. At the same time, the corps commander was instructed that this would be the jumping-off line for an offensive in the direction of Seregelyes.

On 25 January the commander of the Third Ukrainian Front ordered the 18th Tank Corps to attack in the general direction of Hercegfalva and Nagyperkata, with the task of, in close cooperation with the 30th Guards Rifle Corps, defeating the opposing enemy. The corps was to capture Nagyperkata on the first day of the offensive, and Adony on the second day; it was to subsequently be ready to turn its front west in the direction of Seregelyes.

Thus on 26 January the 18th and 23rd tank corps were to simultaneously attack and launch a concentric attack, as the corps were at a distance of 75-80 kilometers from each other.

Throughout 27 January the enemy continued to securely hold the Vereb area with the forces of the 3rd and 5th SS panzer divisions and the 1st Panzer Division and often launched counterattacks, attempting to throw the 23rd Tank Corps' formations back to the north. At 1930 on 27 January the corps commander received an order from the commander of the 4th Guards Army to leave one tank brigade and an anti-tank artillery regiment and a motorized rifle battalion in the Vereb area, while the corps' remaining forces, along with the combined-arms formations, were to launch an attack toward Kapolnasnyek. The attack would be launched to outflank the enemy's tank group from the east and was to put it in danger of encirclement. The offensive began on the evening of 27 January.

By 2000 on 28 January the corps reached the northern outskirts of Kapolnasnyek and four kilometers to the east, where it fought during the night. On the morning of 29 January the corps, along with units of the 104th Rifle Corps, continued to attack and, while engaged in stubborn fighting, by 1930 reached the area ten kilometers northwest of Adony.

Units of the 3rd and 1st panzer divisions, the 363rd Self-Propelled Artillery Brigade and individual units of the SS *Wiking* Panzer Division were operating against the 18th Tank Corps. At 1000 on 27 January the corps attacked in the direction of Hercegfalva and Nagyperkata.

Following an 8-hour battle, units of the 18th Tank Corps, in cooperation with units of the 30th Rifle Corps, captured Hercegfalva at 1800 on 27 January. Developing the offensive further, by the close of the day the corps had cut the road running from Dunapentele to Nagyperkata with one brigade, thus cutting off the German garrison in Nagyperkata. Throughout 28 January the Germans put up extremely stubborn resistance to the corps' advance.

By the morning of 29 January the situation opposite the corps' offensive front was as follows. The enemy continued to hold Nagyperkata. The 74th Rifle Division, which was attacking to the corps' right, was engaged in stubborn fighting along the southern outskirts of Dunaujvaros. The enemy, while attempting to break through to Dunaujvaros, threw 18 tanks and 20 armored transports from the Adony area to Nagyperkata. Upon reinforcing their group of forces in the Perkata area, the Germans attacked. All day on 29 January the corps' formations, interacting with the infantry, were engaged in difficult tank battles. By the close of the day the corps cut the Nagyperkata—Adony road, thus cutting off the enemy group of forces in Nagyperkata from the group of forces in Adony.

The corps subsequently outflanked Nagyperkata from the east with two tank brigades and a motorized rifle brigade and attacked toward Adony. Because the 74th Rifle Division, which was attacking toward Dunaujvaros from the south, was unsuccessful, the *front* commander ordered that the 181st Tank Brigade be turned to the south and attack toward Dunaujvaros from the north. The enemy garrison in Dunaujvaros was encircled.

During the night of 30-31 January an enemy column, consisting of more than 50 motor vehicles, with a group of infantry and tanks, attempted to break out of Dunaujvaros toward Nagyperkata. The column was met with heavy fire from our tanks. The enemy fell back to his jumping-off place, leaving 12 tanks and 20 motor vehicles on the battlefield. The enemy garrison was later routed by a simultaneous attack by the tank brigade from the north and the 74th Rifle Division's infantry from the south.

On the morning of 31 January the corps' main forces developed a decisive attack toward Adony. On 1 February the corps took Adony by storm and linked up with units of the 3rd Airborne Division, which was attacking from north to south. With this act the bank of the Danube along the Ercsi—Dunaujvaros sector was cleared of the enemy.

From 25 January the 7th Guards Mechanized Corps occupied defensive positions along the eastern bank of the Danube along the Apostag—Solt line.

By 30 January the situation south of Lake Velence had developed as follows. The enemy, while stubbornly resisting, was falling back slowly to the west under the attacks by our forces. Simultaneously, the enemy was hurriedly preparing a defense along the line between lakes Velence and Balaton, in order to cover the city of Szekesfehervar from the east and southeast. In order to bring about a sharp change in the situation, on orders from the commander of the Third Ukrainian Front, a mobile group was created, consisting of the 1st Guards Mechanized and 5th Guards Cavalry corps. On 31 January this group was concentrated northeast of Szekesfehervar in the Patka area and was subordinated to the commander of the 4th Guards Army. The 1st Guards Mechanized Corps was assigned the task of breaking through the enemy's defense northeast of Szekesfehervar through vigorous actions and, in conjunction with the formations of the 5th Guards Cavalry and 20th Guards Rifle corps, to capture the city of Szekesfehervar and subsequently, in conjunction with the forces attacking from the Adony—Kapolnasnyek area, defeat the enemy group of forces southeast of the city.

At 1400 on 31 January the corps attacked, having a two-echelon combat formation. The corps had to overcome the enemy's stubborn resistance, while the overcast weather and snowfall made it difficult to orient oneself and to observe the battlefield.

Despite this, the enemy's defense was pierced by the 1st Guards Mechanized Corps' powerful attack, and at 1700 the corps' units broke into the northeastern and northwestern outskirts of the city, where stubborn street fighting broke out. The 5th Guards Cavalry Corps' formations, operating to the right of the 1st Guards Mechanized Corps, had not managed to reach the city by this time and we were not able to capture the city of Szekesfehervar from the march.

Throughout 1-2 February the 1st Guards Mechanized Corps, together with the combined-arms formations, were defending along the northeastern outskirts of the city. At 1600 on 2 February the corps received orders from the commander of the 4th Guards Army to continue the offensive on the city. The fighting, which began during the second half of 2 February, continued to the morning of 4 February, but in light of the enemy's superior forces our units were unable to take the city.

At 1140 on 4 February the corps was ordered to take up the defense along the northern outskirts of the city and to prevent the enemy's breakthrough to the north. On the morning of the following day the enemy attacked with units of the 3rd SS Panzer Division and the 356th Infantry Division and the corps' formations became involved in tank battles. The fighting lasted until the onset of darkness and the corps suffered losses, but the enemy's attacks were beaten off.

The operations of the 18th and 23rd tank and 2nd Guards Mechanized corps developed in the following manner. The 18th Tank Corps, which was part of the 26th Army, continued to develop the offensive in the direction of Seregelyes; the corps, together with the 155th, 36th and 68th rifle divisions, was engaged in stubborn fighting throughout 6 February, repelling enemy attacks. On 6 February our group of forces, which was operating south of Lake Velence, reached a line five kilometers south of Dinnyes and Aba and by its actions threatened to seize the city of Szekesfehervar.

The 23rd Tank Corps, which was part of the 4th Guards Army, attacked south of Lake Velence in the direction of Dinnyes. As a result of stubborn fighting, the corps advanced slowly and by 1500 on 6 February captured Dinnyes.

The 2nd Guards Mechanized Corps had been concentrated in the Paty—Bicske—Tabajd area, where it was subordinated to the commander of the 46th Army and was preparing to carry out a new assignment.

The further offensive by our forces was halted by an order from the command. The units took up the defensive.

Thus in the January defensive fighting the Second and Third Ukrainian fronts' armored and mechanized forces, in conjunction with the combined-arms formations, exhausted and bled the enemy white in independent operations and at the end of January, following a regrouping and together with the combined-arms formations, launched a counteroffensive. Despite the enemy's powerful resistance, the Third Ukrainian Front's forces threw the enemy back and prevented the large and elite German tank divisions from reaching the enemy's group of forces encircled in Budapest.

Following the rout of the encircled group of forces and the occupation of Budapest on 13 February, the armored and mechanized forces were pulled back into the *front* reserve.

Brief Conclusions

In offensive operations the tank and mechanized formations were employed along the main axes and usually as *front* means for developing the success.

For example, the 23rd Tank and the 2nd and 4th guards mechanized corps operated as *front* success development groups during the first stage of the operation, in the sector of the Second Ukrainian Front's 7th Guards Army; the 6th Guards Tank Army and the 4th Guards Mechanized Corps during the second, third and fourth stages operated as *front* success development groups, also in the 7th Guards Army's sector, and, finally, the 18th Tank Corps during the third and fourth stages of the operation acted in the same capacity within the Third Ukrainian Front.

Thus the greater part of the tank and mechanized formations operated as *front* success development means. At the same time, characteristically, each corps resolved tasks, while operating along an independent axis. Such an employment of the corps was conditioned by the fact that the terrain and time of year did not allow us to consecutively commit several corps along a single axis for the purpose of augmenting the attack from the depth. At the same time, the requirements for offensive speed were planned the same as for operations in ordinary terrain conditions.

The overall depth of the advance into the enemy's defense during the first stage of the operation was 90-100 kilometers, 50-80 kilometers during the second stage and 150 kilometers during the third stage on the Second Ukrainian Front, and 25-70 kilometers on the Third Ukrainian Front.

The greatest average daily advance during the first stage was 18-20 kilometers for the 2nd Guards Mechanized Corps and 90-100 kilometers for the 4th Guards Mechanized Corps (while operating with the 46th Army during 28 October-4 November). The average daily rate of advance for all the corps at this stage, while operating with the 7th Guards Army (11-26 November) was the same (3-5 kilometers), at the same time the operational plan was calling for 16-50 kilometers. Such a rate of advance (3-5 kilometers) was conditioned by the difficulties of the terrain and the extremely heavy fighting, which did not cease over the course of 16 days. While operating in these conditions, the corps broke contact at a maximum of 5-8 kilometers with the combined-arms formations, retaining tactical cooperation with them.

During the second stage of the operation the average daily rates of advance were 12-14 kilometers, instead of the planned 20-23 kilometers.

Such a pace should be considered sufficient in actions in mountainous and wooded terrain. Subsequently, as a result of extended operations in these conditions and the frequent issuing of new orders, which required changing operational axes, the rate of advance fell.

During the third stage of the operation, instead of a planned daily rate of advance of 25-30 kilometers, the corps' pace of advance was 6-20 kilometers. The 7th Mechanized Corps advanced at a particularly low pace (3-4 kilometers). This is explained by the fact that the corps had to operate in the most complex conditions compared to all the tank and mechanized formations taking part in the fighting during the third stage of the operation. The 7th Mechanized Corps, operating along the 4th Guards Army's left wing, was engaged in extremely heavy fighting with two of the enemy's panzer divisions. Due to its actions, the corps prevented the enemy from reaching the 4th Guards Army's flank and thus secured the army's advance to the north.

On 19 December the 6th Guards Tank Army, having attacked in the direction of Levice, advanced 25-30 kilometers in the day's fighting. Half of the army's strength was subsequently turned from the Levice area to the south in the direction of Esztergom. In carrying out this task, the army's shock group was turned from the Salov area back to the north to the Sazdice area. Here the army was once again gathered into a fist and it defeated the enemy's powerful tank group. Following this, it began to rapidly advance to the south.

According to the terrain conditions and the weather, the tank and mechanized formations were forced to operate in columns and, in the majority of cases, only along the roads. Throughout the entire course of the operation, they were, for the most part, engaged in fighting the enemy's tank formations. During the offensive battles the corps could not but fight for inhabited locales and road junctions, because it was not possible to bypass them in view of the washed out roads, the swampy sectors of the terrain, a large number of rivers, and reclamation canals, which presented serious anti-tank obstacles.

Thus the tank and mechanized corps' remove from the combined-arms formations was only possible within the confines of 10-15 kilometers. Such a remove secured tactical cooperation during the operation. This cooperation was expressed in the fact that the tank and mechanized formations, while operating ahead of the infantry, seized the enemy's centers of resistance and held them until the arrival of the combined-arms formations, after which they would make their next leap. The combined-arms formations secured the tank troops' communications and lent immediate assistance, if needed.

In offensive operations the corps' combat formations were organized into three echelons, and thus each corps augmented its attack from the depth.

The organization of the success development groups was as follows. During the first stage of the operation, when the 46th Army was attacking Budapest, the 2nd and 4th guards mechanized corps were committed into the fighting at different times from the same area. At the same time, their operations developed along concentric axes; as a result of achieving their final task, their shock strength grew, because the front line narrowed and the depth of their combat formation increased.

At this stage of the operation in the 7th Guards Army's actions the success development group (2nd and 4th guards mechanized and 23rd Tank corps) was concentrated along a 30-35 kilometer front and, according to the operational plan, each corps was to operate along an independent axis, while it was planned that the corps' movement would be straight to the northwest. Thus in carrying out their final task, they were to also arrive along a 30-35 kilometer front. However, during the fighting, in view of the enemy's strong resistance, the necessity arose of turning toward the center the corps (23rd Tank and 2nd Guards Mechanized) that were operating along the flanks and thus launch a powerful attack with the forces of all three corps against the enemy in the Hatvan area.

During the fourth stage of the operation the tank and mechanized formations were employed in defense, located along the second defensive lines. They occupied defensive positions along a broad (10-20 kilometers) front, creating strong points along the likely avenues of the enemy's tank activities. In these battles the tank and mechanized corps were often shifted from one axis to others for the purpose of launching counterblows against the enemy's tank breakthrough formations.

Thus in the Budapest operation the tank and mechanized formations played the leading role in encircling the German-Hungarian forces in the Budapest area. In offensive operations they operated ahead of the combined-arms formations, capturing major enemy communications centers and thus deprived him of the opportunity of maneuvering his mobile forces. Through their actions, they tied down large enemy tank forces, thus easing the activities of the combined-arms formations along the other axes. The tank and mechanized forces subsequently took part in repelling attacks by large tank formations west of Budapest and, together with the infantry and anti-tank artillery, prevented the enemy from breaking through to his encircled group of forces.

The experience of the 6th Guards Tank Army's fighting confirmed the necessity of having 122mm and 152mm self-propelled artillery in the tank and mechanized formations, because its absence significantly complicated the army's actions. The German tanks operated very carefully where there was self-propelled artillery and were scared to openly join battle.

The experience of the fighting by the tank and mechanized formations that took part in the Budapest operation showed that in committing them into the breakthrough they had to complete the breakthrough of the enemy defense together with the infantry, after which they were able to develop the success. During the breakthrough of the front by the 7th Guards Army on 11 November, the tank and mechanized forces took part in the breakthrough of the enemy's defense from the beginning of the operation. Existing experience was confirmed, which spoke of the fact that while planning the operation to commit tank and mechanized formations into the breakthrough, we must take into account the possibility that they will have to complete the breakthrough of the enemy's defense together with the infantry. They should organize their combat formations in accordance with this; besides this, it is necessary to take into account that it may be necessary to develop the success in nighttime conditions.

These are the main conclusions which the experience of the tank and mechanized formations' combat operations offer us in the Budapest operation.

8

Features of Aviation Employment and Air Operations in the Budapest Operation

In the Budapest operation the ground forces of the Second and Third Ukrainian fronts closely cooperated with aviation, which supported them in the most varied conditions of combat activities.

The most instructive examples in aviation's combat activity in this operation are its activities in repelling the enemy's major counteroffensives in January 1945 and its participation in the fighting to eliminate the encircled enemy group of forces in Budapest in January-February 1945.

Aviation's Activities in Repelling the Enemy's Counteroffensives

The Overall and Air Situation Along the Third Ukrainian Front in January 1945

As a result of the December offensive operations, the forces of the Second and Third Ukrainian fronts, having surrounded the enemy group of forces in Budapest with a dense ring, reached the front already shown.

The enemy, while attempting throw our forces back beyond the Danube and save its encircled troops, had by the beginning of January concentrated major tank and infantry forces opposite the Third Ukrainian Front and conducted three major counteroffensives throughout January.

The first counteroffensive began on 2 January 1945 from the area southeast of Komarno. By 7 January 1945 the enemy, in employing his several-fold superiority in tanks, and ignoring his enormous losses had, as a result of five days of fierce battles, pushed back our units 20-25 kilometers and reached the line Esztergom—Csomor—Banhida. The Germans' further advance to the southeast toward Budapest was unsuccessful.

On 7 January the enemy once again attacked from the line Sored—Moha. As a result of four days of fighting, he pushed back our units a little and occupied the major inhabited locale of Zamoly. On 13 January the enemy offensive along this axis was halted.

The enemy began his third counteroffensive on 18 January from the area southwest of Szekesfehervar in the general direction of Nagyperkata.

As a result of the attack launched by major tank, self-propelled artillery and infantry forces, the enemy broke through our forces' defense, reached Lake Velence from the south and broke through to the Danube in the area north of Dunapentele. The enemy's subsequent attempts to break through to the north were unsuccessful and on 27 January his advance was halted by our forces' counterattacks.

On 27 January the Third Ukrainian Front's forces themselves launched a counterattack and through attacks from the north and south threw back to the west the German group of forces that had broken through to the Danube.

Such was the ground situation against the background of which the Third Ukrainian Front's 17th Air Army's combat activities unfolded, as well as the Second Ukrainian Front's 5th Air Army, which cooperated with it.

Taking into account the importance of the operations being conducted, the enemy sought to secure them against our aviation's pressure.

Not having the opportunity of quantitatively strengthening its aviation, operating against the Third Ukrainian Front, the German command sought to make its existing air power more active.

Changes in the enemy air force's quantitative strength, as well as its combat intensity throughout December 1944 and January 1945 are clear from the following:

- in December 1944 the enemy aviation operating against the Third Ukrainian Front numbered 820 planes, which carried out 1,544 sorties during December;
- in January 1945 the number of enemy planes fell to 775, although the number of sorties increased to 4,650; that is, by three times.

The threefold increase in the number of sorties confirms the tenet that in order to assist his attacking forces the enemy, without increasing the number of his sorties, demanded of his aviation a significant increase in the intensity of its operations.

The enemy's aviation was opposed by the 17th Air Army, which consisted of an assault air corps and five independent air divisions (bomber, night light bomber, and three fighter divisions).

In all, the 17th Air Army numbered 603 planes in working order, of which there were 214 fighters, 171 assault aircraft, 82 day bombers, and 42 reconnaissance and fire correction planes.

Aside from this, units of two assault air and one fighter corps were brought in, partially from the 5th Air Army, to assist the Third Ukrainian Front's forces; in the most difficult moments these air corps were fully redirected to supporting the Third Ukrainian Front's forces, which strengthened the 17th Air Army by 215 fighters and 135 assault aircraft.

Thus the 17th Air Army was somewhat inferior to the enemy air force, but when taking into account the reinforcements arriving from the 5th Air Army, the 17th Air Army had a superiority over the enemy, according to the chief types of aviation (fighter and assault air), while continuing to be somewhat inferior in bomber aviation.

One should bear in mind the fact that simultaneously with the fighting to repel the enemy's counteroffensives, a part of the 17th Air Army's forces was diverted to supporting the *front's* forces that were fighting the enemy's group of forces encircled in Budapest. The enemy, sensing that the fate of his encircled troops was to be decided by the success of his counteroffensive, concentrated the activities of the main body of his aviation along these sectors. Thus the 17th Air Army's main efforts were also concentrated along these sectors of the front.

Thus the sides' correlation of aviation forces and the decisive goals pursued by them, predetermined the intensity of the air situation and the inevitability of a stubborn struggle in the air.

Throughout January 1945 the enemy's aviation, while supporting its forces' counteroffensive, directed its chief efforts at covering the attacking forces and launching raids against the combat formations of our defending units. The enemy's bombers, in groups of up to 20 planes, operated on the battlefield and against our crossings over the Danube, while assault aircraft, in groups of up to 30 planes, attacked and bombed our troops on the battlefield and along the roads near the front. Large groups of fighters patrolled at various heights and covered their ground troops and important rear targets and secured their own combat aviation's operations. Individual planes such as the He-111[1]

1 Editor's note. The He-111 was a German-built medium bomber with a crew of five. One model had a range of 2,300 kilometers. The aircraft was armed with up to 7.92mm machine guns, some of which were replaced with other weapons in later models. This model could carry up to 2,000 kilograms of bombs in its bomb bay

and Ju-88[2] and small groups of fighters carried out reconnaissance of the battlefield and the army and *front* rear to a depth of 1,000 kilometers.

The meteorological situation in January was not favorable to air combat activities. Frequent snowfalls and fog, which only cleared up during the second half of the day, and the low cloud cover, greatly complicated air activity and sometimes excluded it altogether.

In all, there were seven flying days in January, 13 days of limited flying, and 11 days of non-flying weather.

Such was the general and air situation in the Third Ukrainian Front during January 1945, which conditioned the nature of the combat employment of the 17th Air Army and called forth certain features in air activities.

Air operations. Throughout January 1945 the forces of the Third Ukrainian Front had the following task: to repel all enemy attacks along the external front, to hold previous positions and to not let the Budapest group of forces out of the encirclement, thus creating the conditions for new attacks against the enemy.

Depending on these conditions, the main task of aviation, which was supporting our defending forces, was battling the enemy tanks and strikes against targets on the battlefield in direct tactical cooperation with the ground forces. Simultaneously with this, our aviation also had the task of battling the air enemy and thus securing our forces against strikes from the air.

This predetermined the predominant employment of assault air and fighter aviation as the types most corresponding to the resolution of those tasks that arose. For example, in January 1945 the 17th Air Army carried out 10,315 sorties, of which 5,207 sorties were carried out by assault aircraft and 4,103 by fighters.

Taking into account the intensity of the situation and the decisive significance of eliminating the enemy's counteroffensives, the command concentrated its chief efforts along the most important axes, facilitating our forces' repulse of the attacking enemy.

Thus our aviation avoided dispersing its strength and its actions were purposeful and directed at resolving the most important tasks.

Because the enemy operated with large forces, throwing them along narrow sectors of the front, as well as due to the fact that his aviation and anti-aircraft weapons were putting up powerful resistance, our aviation primarily operated in large groups (12-24 planes), sufficiently powerful to suppress resistance by the enemy's fighter aviation and anti-aircraft artillery and to launch powerful strikes against designated targets. Only given unfavorable meteorological conditions, which excluded the possibility of employing large groups, the assault aircraft and fighters operated in groups of 2-6 planes, without ceasing, however, to support the ground forces. The 17th Air Army ceased its combat operations only in absolutely non-flying weather (fog, thick snowfall, etc.).

Such are the chief features characteristic of our aviation's combat activities in repelling the enemy's counterattacks along the Budapest direction in January 1945.

During this period our aviation (17th Air Army) carried out the following missions:

- it scattered and destroyed the attacking enemy's groups of infantry and tanks through concentrated and echeloned strikes by assault aircraft and bombers, foiling the attacks and inflicting significant losses on them;
- it destroyed the enemy's men and materiel through bomber and assault air strikes in their concentration areas and along the routes of their arrival at the front;

and even more on its wings.

2 Editor's note. The Ju-88 was a German twin-engine medium bomber that was used in a variety of roles. One model carried a crew of four and had a range of 2,430 kilometers. This model was armed with five 7.92mm machine guns and 1,400 kilograms of bombs.

- it disrupted the command and control of forces through strikes against headquarters and communications centers;
- it covered our forces' combat formations and concentration areas through ceaseless patrolling by fighters;
- it secured assault air's and the bombers' combat activities through escort by fighters;
- it carried out the ceaseless reconnaissance of the enemy's forces through all kinds of aircraft.

Besides this, the 17th Air Army's aviation carried out a number of combat assignments to assist the ground forces in eliminating the garrison encircled in Budapest.

Despite the comparatively large number of tasks, the chief and main one was the task of battling the enemy's attacking tanks and the direct support of the defending troops on the battlefield. The 17th Air Army's main efforts were directed at achieving precisely these tasks.

Throughout January the command and control of the combat activities of the Third Ukrainian Front's aviation was concentrated in the hands of the commander of the 17th Air Army and was carried out by him from his command post, which was located with the command post of the commander of the Third Ukrainian Front.

Combat activities were conducted in conditions of a rapidly changing situation, and this required the very precise coordination of strikes in time and place with the activities of the ground forces. This circumstance required a great deal of efficiency on the part of the combined-arms and aviation commanders in all questions of organizing cooperation and its very scrupulous working out in detail.

To realize such command and control over our aviation's combat activities from the command post of the air army's commander was quite difficult. Due to this difficulty, during the operations to repel the enemy's counteroffensive, command posts were organized with the commander of the combined-arms formations for the commanders, which were supporting the aviation formations, at which the aviation commander and a small operational group were located, along with the necessary communications equipment: radio for communications with the air army commander's command post, with one's own headquarters and with subordinate aviation formations, telephone for communications with the commander of the formation being supported, and high frequency radio for communications with the army commander.

The command posts for the commanders of aviation formations among the troops were the primary links through which cooperation with the ground forces was exercised. The aviation commanders, while maintaining constant personal contact with the combined-arms chief, the troops of which were being supported by aviation, had the full opportunity to be constantly on top of things and to know all of the ground forces' requests, and thus employ every group of planes arriving at the battlefield precisely against those targets, the defeat of which most corresponded to the situation at the moment. In order to precisely guide the planes to their target, the aviation commander disposed of a special guidance radio set, with the help of which he guided his planes to the necessary targets, redirecting them in the event of a sudden change in the situation, informed them of the situation at the front, and issued instructions on the method for carrying out the combat assignment, etc.

During the defensive fighting the rapid summoning of aviation acquired particularly great significance. This summoning was carried out by radio from the air formation commanders' command posts, with the permission of the air army commander, or, given the absence of sufficient time, independently by the commander of the air formation. For example, during the operation to repel the enemy's counteroffensive, the air command post with the 18th Tank Corps summoned by radio and guided 74 groups of assault aircraft to their targets.

In a particularly difficult situation, when the air force's efforts were concentrated along a narrow sector of the front, the commanders of all the air formations who were with their command posts along a given sector, were subordinated to the senior officer among them, through whom the air army commander exercised control over all of the air force's combat activities.

For example, during the German's offensive on Esztergom, the commanders of the air formations, who were located with the 4th Guards Army and the 7th Mechanized, 18th Tank and 5th Guards Cavalry corps, were subordinated by order of the air army commander to the commander of the 288th Fighter Division. In this case, the command post of the commander of the 288th Assault Air Division became the center through which all requests for air activity along the Germans' offensive sector came together.

In certain, more intense moments of the fighting, assault aircraft and fighters from the 5th Air Army, which was part of the neighboring Second Ukrainian Front, were brought in to support the Third Ukrainian Front's forces.

The cooperation of the two air armies and the coordination of their activities required mutual information between their headquarters. This information was mainly carried out by radio and wire communications equipment through the headquarters of the Second and Third Ukrainian fronts.

The cooperation of the Second Ukrainian Front's 5th Air Army with the Third Ukrainian Front's ground forces, as well as the command and control of air operations over the battlefield was exercised by the commander of the assault air corps or the commander of one of the corps' assault air divisions from his command post, which was organized with the commander of the Third Ukrainian Front's army that was being supported. In this instance, the command post was outfitted completely by the forces of the 17th Air Army, which communicated its location to the headquarters of the 5th Air Army through coded radio messages, as it was ready. Thus the commander assigned by the 5th Air Army, would fly to the designated place and immediately set about exercising control over his aviation's combat activities. By maintaining personal contact with the combined-arms commander and communications with his own army's headquarters, he had the opportunity to systematically inform it of the situation along a given sector of the front. This circumstance enabled the headquarters of the 5th Air Army to refine its combat assignments, to coordinate them with the headquarters of the 17th Air Army, to determine the required amount of aviation, and to establish the intensity of its combat activities.

Thanks to this organization of command and control, complete coordination with the course of the ground forces' fighting was achieved in air operations, which enabled our aviation to render material and, in some cases, decisive support in repelling the enemy's tank attacks, through its strikes.

Assault air aviation carried the main burden in the fight with the attacking enemy. The enemy, in preparing for the offensive and foreseeing our aviation's high level of activity, also supported his actions with fighters, covered his force's combat formations and important rear targets with very dense fire from anti-aircraft artillery of all calibers. Aside from this, the enemy's tanks laid down heavy fire against assault aircraft flying at low altitudes. Assault air's combat activity was also made more difficult by the unfavorable meteorological conditions.

Assault aviation's fundamental and main tasks in repelling the enemy's counteroffensive were the fight against tanks and suppressing artillery in its firing positions. These tasks were carried out by groups of 9-24 and more planes, under fighter cover. In conditions of the enemy's resistance through fighter aviation and anti-aircraft artillery, the employment of smaller groups proved to be of little effect, because in this case it was impossible detach from the group a sufficient number of planes for suppressing anti-aircraft fire, and during a fighter attack a small group was unable to create a sufficiently dense fire and repel their attacks.

Actions by small groups (2-8 planes) were employed in poor weather, which protected to a certain degree against attack from the air enemy and secured assault air's surprise appearance over the target, which usually reduced the effectiveness of the enemy's anti-aircraft fire.

In counterattacking, the enemy usually operated in large groups of tanks along a narrow sector of the front. In accordance with this, strikes by assault air were directed at these sectors, along which, as was determined in the course of the battle, the enemy had concentrated his main tank forces. At the same time, assault air's actions usually took the form of echeloned strikes by large groups of aircraft. The uninterrupted attacks by assault aircraft against the enemy's attacking tanks and infantry rendered material aid to our forces. Often the enemy, upon suffering large losses from assault air fire, was forced to cease his attacks.

The most important tasks which our fighter aviation carried out were:

- covering concentration areas and our forces' combat formations against air strikes;
- supporting the operations of the other air arms;
- bombing and strafing the enemy's forces on the battlefield and in the immediate rear.

Besides this, our fighters destroyed enemy planes in the air during free flights and conducted reconnaissance of the enemy on the battlefield and in the immediate rear.

Cover of the ground forces was carried out by patrolling in groups of 8-12 planes, with a shift of patrols in the air, while patrolling in clear weather was carried out at heights of 2,000-8,000 meters and the planes were echeloned by altitude. If it was overcast, part of the fighters patrolled above the clouds and part under them.

All of the patrolling planes had internal radio communications, which enabled the patrol commander to control the activities of individual flights and planes. The group commander himself had communications with a guidance radio station, from which he received information about the air situation and all other necessary instructions as to the patrol's activities. The patrol area was usually pushed forward in the direction of the likely appearance of the enemy's aircraft, which enabled our fighters to still meet the enemy on the approaches to the battlefield and deny him the opportunity to aim his bombs.

During the repulse of the enemy's counteroffensives, our fighters covering our forces had to repeatedly repulse raids by enemy bombers and assault aircraft.

Escort of assault aircraft and bombers was carried out by 4-12 fighters, which depended on the situation and the size of the group being escorted. In poor meteorological conditions, escorting was conducted by a smaller number of fighters.

Tasks of assault operations were carried out by fighters along with their main tasks of covering the ground forces and escorting the other aviation arms. Strikes against ground targets were carried out by groups of 2-8 planes, with the main targets being artillery in firing positions and concentrations of infantry, motor vehicles, and supply vehicles, etc.

Bomber aviation destroyed day and night the enemy's personnel, tanks and other technical equipment in their concentration areas and on the battlefield. During the day bomber raids were launched by groups of 9-27 planes under fighter cover. In poor meteorological conditions and at night, strikes were launched by single crews, while each of them made 3-5 passes at the target. This enabled us to make lengthy attacks against the target and the effectiveness of the bombing was increased.

Reconnoitering the enemy's rear was carried out by Pe-2[3] aircraft from strafing height to 6,500 meters. Reconnaissance of the battlefield was carried out by single assault aircraft and fighters. The

3 The Pe-2 was a Soviet two-engine light bomber that entered service in 1941. One model carried a crew of

main task of battlefield reconnaissance in the interests of the Third Ukrainian Front's artillery was discovering the enemy's tanks and his artillery's firing positions.

Thus from an examination of the employment and combat operations of our aviation in repelling the enemy's counteroffensives, one can make the following conclusions:

- in repelling the enemy's counteroffensive, aviation represents a very powerful force, which is capable not only of rendering support to the ground forces in repelling enemy counterattacks, but in individual cases may also foil the counterblow being prepared by the enemy;
- because the enemy usually employs large infantry and tank forces along a narrow sector in a counteroffensive, the air force's actions must be concentrated precisely on this sector of the front and be characterized by unremitting strikes by large groups of aircraft, which enables us to keep the enemy under fire for extended periods; the dispersal of aviation forces in repelling enemy attacks is inadmissible; for this reason, the command and control of the air force in such a situation must be concentrated in the hands of the air army commander;
- in this situation, aviation's chief targets are the fight against the enemy's tanks and artillery on the battlefield, on the approaches to it, and in their concentration area;
- in repelling the enemy's counterattacks, assault air is most widely employed, the strikes of which should be exactly coordinated according to time and place with the ground forces' activities;
- the success of air activities in repelling enemy counterattacks depends on the precision of aviation command and control and its cooperation with the ground forces.

This is achieved by means of the aviation commanders organizing their command posts with the combined-arms chiefs being supported, the detailed working out of all questions of control of air activities (summoning aviation, guiding it to its target, rerouting, etc.) and its cooperation with the forces being supported.

Air Operations in the Fighting for Budapest

The Overall and Air Situation in the Budapest Area in January-February 1945

On 26 December 1944, as a result of the offensive by the forces of the Second and Third Ukrainian fronts, a large enemy group of forces was completely encircled in Budapest, numbering up to 180,000 soldiers and officers.

As has already been noted above, throughout January 1945 the enemy undertook three counteroffensives, having as their main goal breaking through the ring of our forces blockading Budapest and thus liberating the garrison in it.

While relying on a previously created defense system, and also hoping on aid from without, the encircled enemy met our troops' offensive with fierce resistance, employing for this purpose all existing means in the city and the civilian population.

By 18 January the enemy had been thrown out of the eastern part of Budapest (Pest) by the decisive actions of the Second Ukrainian Front's forces and the *front's* forces had reached the eastern bank of the Danube along the entire length of the city.

The enemy's defense in Buda was no less powerful than in Pest. It was strengthened by the fact that this part of Budapest was located on a high and hilly bank of the Danube, which made the already difficult street fighting even more difficult. However, the unrelenting and powerful attacks by our units inflicted heavy losses on the enemy and reduced his powers of resistance.

---

three and had a maximum speed of 580 kilometers per hour. This model was armed with four 7.62mm machine guns and could carry up to 1,600 kilograms of bombs.

During the night of 11-12 February the remnants of the encircled garrison, having undertaken an attack to the northwest with part of its forces, broke through into the area of the woods northwest of the city. On 13 February our forces completely occupied Budapest and by 16 February had completely finished clearing the wooded area northeast of the city of scattered groups of enemy forces, which were attempting to break through to their forces in the Esztergom area.

Throughout January 1945 the Second Ukrainian Front was faced by up to 525 enemy planes, of which 255 were bombers, 170 fighters and 100 reconnaissance planes and transport aircraft.

At the beginning of the operation the enemy air forces exhibited some activity, while attempting to operate against our attacking troops and to interfere with our combat aviation's operations.

The main enemy air arm operating during this period was fighter aviation, which was also brought in for assault operations against ground forces and airfields.

The enemy's fighters, while patrolling over the battlefield in groups of 6-8 Me-109[4] aircraft, covered their encircled forces and sought to combat our aviation's combat activities.

Upon encountering our fighters, the enemy usually declined to fight and, when attacked, would hide in the clouds. The enemy fighters would get into the fighting only given a significant superiority of forces.

The enemy's bomber aviation in the Budapest area was almost entirely absent during the day, limiting itself to night operations by single aircraft. His transport aviation worked sufficiently intensively, supplying the encircled troops with ammunition, weapons and food. Usually operating at night and in poor meteorological conditions, the enemy's transport planes landed at airfields in the suburb of Csepel (along the southern outskirts of Budapest), on the racetrack and on squares and avenues in the city park, which had been cleared for this purpose. Following our forces' capture of the left-bank part of the city and the squares located there, the enemy's transport aviation began to deliver cargoes by dropping them by parachute.

If during the first days of the operation the enemy's aviation attempted to put up resistance to our forces, then during the course of the operation it significantly reduced its activity and its operations began to take on a predominantly defensive character.

This is explained by the following reasons:

- our aviation, which had seized the air initiative during the preceding months, continued to hold it in its hands, putting up decisive resistance to the air enemy in his attempts to penetrate to the Budapest area;
- due to the enemy's unfolding counteroffensive along the Third Ukrainian Front's sector, he concentrated the main body of his aviation on supporting his forces that were attempting to break through from without the ring of our troops blockading Budapest;
- due to our troops' advance, the enemy was forced to rebase his aviation back to deeper airfields, which made its operations in the Budapest area more difficult.

The ground forces' operations to capture Budapest were supported by the Second Ukrainian Front's 5th Air Army, which as of 1 January 1945 numbered 655 planes.

The 17th Air Army rendered some support to the 5th Air Army in the first half of January through is bomber and assault air activities against the western part of Budapest (Buda). From the middle of January, due to the Germans' powerful counteroffensive in the Lake Balaton area, the

4 Editor's note. Me-109 was the popular term for the Bf-109; the most widely employed German fighter aircraft of the Second World War. One model had a top speed of 640 kilometers per hour and was armed with two 13mm machine guns and a 20mm cannon, or a 30mm and two 20mm cannons. This model could also carry rockets and 250 kilograms of bombs.

17th Air Army was completely shifted to operations against the attacking enemy, while the support of the ground forces' activities in the Budapest area was entrusted only to the 5th Air Army.

Because the combat operations of this army from the beginning of January were concentrated on supporting the troops engaged in eliminating the encircled enemy, its basing was moved closer to the area of operations, so that all of the air formations could carry out their combat tasks with the greatest effectiveness.

The basing of air units in immediate proximity to the forward edge of our troops, which were engaged in difficult street fighting, enabled us to increase the number of sorties by two, and on some days, by three times, which enabled us to render constant and timely assistance in the street battles in such meteorological conditions that would have excluded the possibility of our air activities given a more distant basing.

The meteorological situation throughout the fighting in Budapest was very complex: frequent fogs, low cloud cover and poor visibility significantly limited our aviation's combat activity and on certain days excluded it altogether.

During 1 January-13 February 1945 there were seven flying days, 18 days of limited flying, and 19 non-flying days.

Such was the overall and air situation, which characterized the combat activity of the 5th Air Army in the fighting to take Budapest in January-February 1945.

The 5th Air Army's combat operations. The 5th Air Army's combat operations in the operation to capture Budapest unfolded in a unique situation, which was conditioned chiefly by the fact that during the operation our aviation supported the activities of the ground forces, which were engaged in street fighting in a large inhabited locale, which had been configured for stubborn defense.

All of the city's major buildings had been prepared for extended defense: embrasures had been constructed in the walls of buildings for waging fire. Corner buildings, which came out on street intersections, contained prepared positions for artillery and mortars. Stone and earthen barricades stretched between structures, up to five meters wide and about three meters high, which together with rail tie obstacles and deep ditches, represented powerful anti-tank structures.

The enemy's artillery was sheltered predominantly behind barricades and could fire over open sights along the streets. Mortars were located in the foundation pits on broad streets and also in the attics of stone buildings. Machine guns were set up in many of the buildings stories, in attics and bell towers, and even factory smokestacks. Multi-story buildings with a large amount of stone and reinforced concrete covers could serve as good protection for the troops against our air strikes. Thus the enemy's personnel, his headquarters and communications centers were usually located in the basements and lower stories of such buildings.

In Budapest the Germans employed for anti-aircraft defense more than 20 batteries of anti-aircraft artillery, part of the field artillery (for shooting at assault aircraft) and their own fighters, when they were based at nearby airfields. However, our aviation, which held the initiative in its hands, was quite effective in supporting our forces in taking Budapest. At the same time, assault aircraft played a particularly large role in the infantry's and tanks' street fighting.

Assault air's combat activities against such a major inhabited locale were distinguished by features, of which the chief ones were as follows:

- the difficulties experienced by the crews in getting detailed orientation in the air and arriving at their targets in the thick smoke from fires;
- the constricted room for maneuver by assault aircraft in simultaneous actions by several groups against nearby targets or in strikes against small targets surrounded by our troops;
- the necessity of operating against targets located 100-150 meters from our troops, in order to support their advance;

- the difficulty of controlling the assault aircrafts' activities from the ground when they launched strikes against targets that could not be seen because of the tall buildings and other structures;
- the limited size of targets that did not admit of simultaneous actions against them by a large number of planes;
- the necessity of employing large bombs (250 and 500 kilograms) capable of destroying multi-story buildings.

These features predetermined a certain uniqueness in the employment and operations of our assault aircraft.

The basing of assault aircraft was moved as close as possible to the ground forces' operational area for the purpose of increasing their combat potential.

The 3rd Guards Assault Air Corps' assault planes, which took part in the street fighting, were located, for example, at airfields located 6-12 kilometers east of Budapest. Such a close basing of assault air units to the city enabled us to do the following:

- to increase the maximal employment of the assault aircraft, which in favorable meteorological conditions reached 5-7 combat sorties per day for one serviceable aircraft;
- to increase almost by twice the bomb load of the Il-2[5] aircraft by reducing the fuel supply;
- to carry out combat missions in complex weather conditions (ten degree cloud cover at heights of 150-200 meters and visibility of 1-1.5 kilometers);
- to reduce to a minimum the time needed for summoning assault aircraft to the battle area.

The basing of assault aircraft directly adjacent to the front line was secured by our aviation's complete air superiority and was possible only given the absence of the enemy's artillery fire against our airfields.

The close tactical cooperation with the ground forces in the street fighting was achieved only in those cases when the flight crew exactly knew of and could find the object of its attack, striking it namely at the time when it was needed by the ground forces. In order to achieve such a situation, each assault air strike was preceded by detailed planning and the careful preparation of the crews.

The control of assault aircraft, which were supporting the troops engaged in street fighting, required uninterrupted contact between the aviation and combined-arms commanders, as well as the organization of radio communications between the ground and the planes. This enabled us to coordinate all of the assault aircraft strikes with the requests of the ground troops and also gave the aviation command the opportunity, despite the difficulty of the situation, to direct the assault aircraft to their exact targets. In those cases when the assault aircrafts' targets could not be seen because of the tall buildings, an air guidance officer was dropped with a radio set either ahead or along the flanks, who observed all of the targets and guided the assault aircraft to them.

Thus the assault aircrafts' activities were corrected in two ways—by the air formation commander or air guidance officer. The latter method of controlling assault aircraft yielded particularly good results during the street fighting in the eastern part of the city (Pest), which was full of a large number of five and six-story buildings, and also in the fighting for the racetrack, the central railroad junction, the city park, and the military academy.

The length of and the unceasing nature of the assault aircrafts' activities against the enemy's forces had great significance in the street fighting. The enemy suffered heavy materiel losses, being

5 Editor's note. The Il-2 was a two-seat Soviet ground attack plane popularly known as the "Sturmovik." It had a maximum speed of 414 kilometers per hour and was armed with two 23mm cannon, two 7.62mm and one 12.7 machine-guns. It could also carry up to 600 kilograms of bombs and eight rockets.

under constant attack from the air, while he also became physically and morally exhausted. All of this considerably weakened his resistance.

The assault aircrafts' participation in the street fighting did not cease even in complex meteorological conditions. In this situation the assault aircraft, as a rule, operated in pairs or fours, without fighter cover.

The tactics of assault air activities while supporting the ground troops engaged in street fighting had certain features. The strength and combat formation of a group was chiefly determined by taking into account support for the assault aircrafts' freedom of maneuver, which was so necessary for operations over the city. Experience showed that in these conditions it was best of all to operate in small groups of 4-8 planes; in poor weather the number of planes in a group should be no more than four.

Assault aircraft snipers, which had a great deal of firing and bombing training, rendered a great deal of aid to the ground storm groups, and attacked targets of small size which were located in the immediate vicinity of our troops. During uninterrupted and echeloned strikes by assault aircraft against targets in the city, the assigned time and altitudes were very closely observed, because if not the groups of planes operating in the limited area could interfere with each other. Fire that the assault aircraft laid down against the front side of buildings was quite effective. This fire hit the enemy's personnel holed up in the building's lower stories.

In order to strike the enemy's personnel and fire means located in stone buildings and shelters, the assault aircraft usually employed 250-kilogram and 100-kilogram aerial bombs with delayed fuses.

In attacking the enemy's personnel and equipment on squares and in parks, ordinary bombs were used, which were also used on the battlefield (fragmentation, anti-tank, etc.), with instantaneous fuses.

In order to increase their bomb load, the assault aircraft would take on an incomplete supply of fuel, and in some cases carried out flights without gunners, while at the same time removing weaponry from the rear cabin.

Bomber aviation's combat activity while operating against the encircled group of forces was made considerably more difficult by the complexity of detailed orientation in urban conditions and by the poor state of the weather.

The difficulty in determining the front line while fighting in the city and the resulting danger of hitting our troops forced us to renounce bomber strikes against targets located directly in the area of the street fighting.

In this situation bomber strikes were directed against targets located in the enemy's depth, at a distance guaranteeing the safety of our troops.

On those days when poor meteorological conditions prevented flights in large groups, the bombers operated singly. On those days when weather conditions enabled us to more broadly employ the capabilities of bomber aviation, it was employed for launching concentrated strikes against particularly heavily fortified strong points and against concentration areas of enemy forces and his combat equipment.

In carrying out these tasks, the bombers operated in groups, reaching in certain cases, 50 planes. Strikes by such powerful groups caused the enemy significant materiel losses and great losses in personnel.

During the operation to capture Budapest our fighter aircraft waged an active battle with the air enemy through uninterrupted patrolling over the area of the besieged city, by free flights "to go hunting" and group duty flights over one's own airfields.

Groups of fighters patrolling over the city, aside from their main task of covering the ground forces and assault aircraft and bomber operations, struggled against the enemy's transport aviation, which sought to supply his encircled forces with ammunition and food.

Simultaneously with carrying out these tasks, La-5[6] fighters taking off to their combat assignment took along bombs and bombed previously noted targets or those indicated by radio guidance, and following this continued to cover the designated area.

Aerial reconnaissance had great significance in the street fighting, which was conducted nonstop by all types of aviation and did not cease even in poor weather. Assault aircraft carried out reconnaissance of the enemy's forces through special flights in conjunction with combat operations. The chief means of reconnaissance was photography. Among the tasks of reconnaissance were:

- determining the concentrations of the enemy's tanks, artillery, auto transport, and personnel on the city's streets and squares;
- photographing the city's fortified areas;
- uncovering the movements of the enemy's forces within the city and determining the likely axes of his counterblows;
- uncovering the enemy's anti-aircraft defensive system;
- determining the enemy air force's landing sites for transport aviation in the city.

Aerial reconnaissance was chiefly carried out on request from the combined-arms command; reconnaissance data was used by the ground forces and our aviation. Target reconnaissance preceded almost all assault air strikes, because target acquisition while operating within the city limits presented the greatest difficulty for the crews. This was conditioned by the uniqueness of the structures; particularly in the central part of the city and the extremely poor visibility of targets from the air as the result of artillery bombardment and the uninterrupted bombing from the air (dust and smoke often rose to an altitude of 400-600 meters and reduced horizontal visibility to 800-1,000 meters).

Brief Conclusions

1. The operation by the forces of the Second and Third Ukrainian fronts to capture Budapest showed how great a significance aviation operations have for street fighting by the ground forces. The chief role belongs to assault aircraft during actions in such a situation.

Assault aircraft's close tactical cooperation with the ground forces, when the latter are engaged in street fighting in a large inhabited locale, acquire decisive significance in the effectiveness of its strikes. The tactical effect from the assault aircrafts' operations may be achieved only as a result of their strikes against targets located in the immediate vicinity of the forward edge of our troops and those directly interfering with their advance. This is achieved by the precise coordination of the assault aircraft with the combined-arms formations and for resolving individual tasks even with a rifle regiment. In all cases, this cooperation is made easier primarily through the personal interaction of the combined-arms and aviation commander and their joint reconnaissance of the area of the forthcoming fighting.

2. The control of the assault aircraft, which support the troops engaged in street fighting, should be flexible and uninterrupted, while securing the guidance of the assault aircraft to small-size targets located in the immediate vicinity of the attacking forces. For this purpose, the command

6 Editor's note. The La-5 was a popular Soviet fighter of the Second World War, with a maximum speed of 648 kilometers per hour. One model was armed with two 20mm cannons and could carry up to 100 kilograms of bombs.

post of the commander controlling the assault aircrafts' combat operations should be moved as close as possible to the front line.

3. Uninterrupted and echeloned strikes by small groups of planes at low altitudes are the chief and most effective method of the assault aircrafts' operations in conditions of street fighting.

4. The conditions of street fighting (smoke from fires and dust from destroyed buildings) make it very difficult for assault aircraft to identify their targets. Thus target indication should be very precise, as in this regard much depends on the ground forces, which can render the assault aircraft material assistance in orienting them by designating their front line in a timely manner with rockets.

5. In street fighting the actions of bomber aviation are feasible only against targets located at a significant distance from the front line, because in carrying out bombing raids against battlefield targets in a city, due to the difficulties of detailed orientation in these conditions, the possibility of hitting one's own forces is not excluded.

6. In order to strike the enemy's defense throughout its entire depth and to more fully demoralize the encircled garrison, the bombers' actions against targets located in the depth of the encircled group of forces should be combined with assault aircrafts' operations launching their strikes along front-line targets within sight of the attacking infantry. So that the bombers' strikes against other targets were most effective, they should be launched by large forces and employ demolition bombs of 250 kilograms and more.

9

Engineer Support of the Budapest Operation

Engineer forces played an important role in the successes of the Second and Third Ukrainian fronts' forces in encircling and defeating the enemy's Budapest group of forces.

The most characteristic and instructive features of the engineer troops' actions are:

1. Engineer support for the forcing of the Danube.
2. Engineer support for the storming of Budapest.
3. The employment of engineer-sapper brigades in the fighting to repulse the Germans' counteroffensive in January 1945.

Engineer Support for the Forcing of the Danube

The overall situation. The Second Ukrainian Front's forces, while developing the offensive in the area between the Tisza and Danube, by December 1944 had arrived at the southern fortifications of Budapest's outer ring, while part of the 46th Army's forces reached the eastern bank of the Danube along the Taksony—Baja sector.

At the same time the forces of the Third Ukrainian Front, while regrouping from Yugoslavia to Hungarian territory, reached the left bank of the Danube with parts of the 57th Army along the front Mohacs—Batina—Novi Sad. The enemy, who by this time had fallen back to the right bank of the Danube, occupied defensive positions along its western bank and with part of its forces was defending Csepeli Island south of Budapest (between the Danube and the Csepeli Dunaag River).

The Danube was a broad water barrier of operational significance. Along its entire course it has a relatively straightened channel, with a large number of branches, tributaries, islands, and sandbanks. The western bank commands the eastern and has natural masks in the form of thickets of shrubbery, reeds and woods, particularly along the Ordas—Baja sector and then as far as the channel of the Drava River. Dikes stretch along both banks for protecting the river valley from flooding.

The width of the river along the Erd—Adony sector is 475-600 meters; 700 meters near Dunaujvaros; 350 meters near Dunapentele; 800 meters near Madocsa; 600 meters near Ordas; 650 meters near Baja; 400-800 meters near Mohacs, 450 meters near Batina, and; 400-500 meters near Apatin.

The speed of the current is 1.5-2 meters per second. The depth is 5-7 meters and 8-15 meters in places. The soil is sandy and gravelly.

All of the previously existing crossings over the river had been destroyed by the enemy and the bridges blown up.

The forcing was carried out in changeable weather. Rains and a thaw caused the ice to move and brought about a sharp fluctuation in the water level in the river. This circumstance required a lot of work to repair the moorings and docks and in preserving and maintaining bridges. At the same time, this required a significant intensification of work to maintain and repair the approaches to the crossings.

Thus the forcing of the Danube, this powerful water barrier, required significant engineer and pontoon forces and crossing equipment.

During the regrouping of the Third Ukrainian Front's forces and during the forcing of the Danube by the *front's* units, the engineer troops were assigned the following tasks:

- to secure the *front's* forces with crossings during their concentration along a new axis;
- to secure the crossing of the first echelon (75th Rifle Corps) and the main forces of the 57th Army across the Danube along the Batina—Apatin sector;
- to secure the 4th Guards Army with crossings along its forcing sector along the Danube;
- to assist the *front's* forces in seizing and widening a bridgehead along the western bank of the river;
- to repair roads and to strengthen the roadbed along the approaches to the crossings.

In the engineering regard, the following units supported the operation: the 65th Engineer-Sapper Brigade, 11th Assault Engineer-Sapper Brigade and units of the 5th Independent Motorized Pontoon Brigade supported the 57th Army; the 56th Engineer-Sapper Brigade, the 12th Assault Engineer-Sapper Brigade and units of the 5th Independent Motorized Pontoon Brigade supported the 4th Guards Army.

The *front* reserve contained the 44th Motorized Engineer Brigade, 6th Independent Motorized Pontoon-Bridge Regiment and the 64th and 72nd independent battalions of dog mine detectors.

The troops had the following for crossings over the Danube: 4.3 sets of bow half-pontoon parks, a PAP park, three UVSA-3 parks, a captured Krupp park, and locale crossing means found in various areas while preparing the crossings (up to 20 parks of various weight capacities and up to 100 fishing boats). 50 cubic meters of saw timber had been gathered and brought up during the preparatory period.

The Forcing of the Danube by the 57th Army's Forces. While preparing for the operation, the following crossing points were chosen in the army's sector—Mohacs, Batina and Apatin. The engineer and pontoon units as well as the crossing equipment were concentrated in the indicated areas.

Units of the 75th Rifle Corps, which by 7 November 1944 were located along the eastern bank of the Danube, occupied the following line: 233rd Rifle Division along the front Baja—Mohacs—Batina, and the 74th Rifle Division along the front excluding Batina—excluding Dalj.

On the night of 7-8 November four battalions of the 109th and 360th regiments of the 74th Rifle Division crossed on materials at hand in the area immediately west of Apatin and got into a fight for the bridgehead along the western bank of the river. During the night of 8-9 November another two companies of the 233rd Rifle Division's 703rd Rifle Regiment crossed to the right bank of the river near Batina and also got into an intense fight. Our units, having beaten off all of the enemy's counterattacks, securely consolidated along their new lines.

The bridgehead in the Apatin area represented very swampy terrain, overgrown with bushes and covered with water, in places up to a meter deep; there were absolutely no roads or paths. The soil was swampy and difficult of passage for all types of transportation.

The terrain conditions were more favorable in the Batina area—the bank was dry and had approach paths and roads.

By the close of 11 November the 703rd Rifle Regiment had been fully crossed and had captured Batina. At the same time the 74th Rifle Division's 209th and 360th rifle regiments had been crossed over near Apatin and had gotten into fighting west of Apatin.

Immediately following the seizure of the bridgeheads, the engineer units set about constructing ferry and bridge crossings for supporting the crossing of the 57th Army's forces to the western bank of the Danube.

The following crossings were created by the forces of the 5th Independent Motorized Pontoon-Bridge, the 65th Engineer-Sapper Brigade and the 6th Independent Pontoon-Bridge Regiment: four 16-ton and one 40-ton ferries from the bow half-pontoon park, a floating bridge with a capacity of 16 tons from the bow half-pontoon park, a barge with an overall length of 481.4 meters, and three ferries with a capacity of 60 and 30 tons from the SP-19 park, near Batina; two ferries with a 16-ton capacity from the bow half-pontoon park, a floating bridge from the bow half-pontoon park, a Krupp park, and a barge with a capacity of 16 tons, near Mohacs.

Near Apatin we had boats and ferries made of local materials.

The crossing of the first echelon's troops and equipment (consisting of five divisions and reinforcements) was carried out during 7-18 November.

The 57th Army's main body crossed during 19-30 November.

The Forcing of the Danube by the 4th Guards Army's Forces. The 4th Guards Army had the task of forcing the Danube followed by the development of the offensive to the northwest.

By 1800 on 24 November the army's forces occupied the following positions:

- the 31st Guards Rifle Corps (34th and 30th guards and 320th rifle divisions) was defending along the eastern bank of the Danube along the front Nagy-Vadas—excluding Baja;
- the 21st Guards Rifle Corps (41st, 62nd and 69th guards rifle divisions) reached the front Baja—Mohacs with units of the 41st Guards Rifle Division; the remaining two divisions were in the second echelon in an area 15-18 kilometers southeast of Baja;
- the 20th Guards Rifle Corps (80th Guards Rifle, 7th and 5th guards airborne, and 84th Rifle divisions) had concentrated in the area 5-15 kilometers east of Sombor.

The army's combat operations were supported by the following: the 56th Engineer-Sapper Brigade (consisting of four battalions), and from 7 December the 12th Assault Engineer-Sapper Brigade.

With the arrival of the army's units at the eastern bank of the Danube, preparatory work by the engineer units to secure the forcing began. For this, a reconnaissance group and the 18th Engineer-Sapper Battalion were sent out to the forcing area on November with the tasks of reconnoitering the river, local crossing and construction materials, the condition of the roads leading to the river, and uncovering the enemy's system of fortifications along the western bank of the Danube.

As a result of the reconnaissance, the qualities of the river and the nature of the enemy's defensive system were defined and places chosen for crossing the troops. From local crossing materials the forces of the 56th Engineer-Sapper Brigade found and put in working order 12 barges and 60 fishing boats; 50 cubic meters of saw timber were stocked and two launches were raised from the bottom of the river. Thus by the beginning of the forcing, the army disposed of, along with its authorized equipment: two UVSA-3 parks, 12 barges, 60 fishing boats, and two launches.

Crossing sites were noted in the area of Madocsa, Dunapataj, west of Ordas, Batya, and Mohacs.

Having reconnoitered the western bank of the river, at 1800 on 24 November units of the 41st Guards Rifle Division began crossing the Danube 2.5 kilometers southeast of Mohacs on fishing boats and A-3 boats and by 0900 on 25 November captured a bridgehead one kilometer wide and 250 meters deep. The enemy's attempts to throw the crossed elements into the river through counterattacks and fire were unsuccessful. The bridgehead was broadened throughout the day to two kilometers along the front and 1.5-2 kilometers in depth. By the close of 26 November units of the 41st Guards Rifle Division captured Mohacs and linked up with units of the 57th Army.

In order to secure the crossing of the 21st Guards Rifle Corps' remaining formations for the purpose of broadening the bridgehead in the Mohacs area, crossing materials for six 16-ton ferries were concentrated by the close of 27 November.

Two of the 20th Guards Rifle Corps' rifle divisions (80th Guards Rifle, 7th Guards Airborne) began to cross to the western bank of the Danube from the evening of 27 November in the Batina area (in the 57th Army's sector). This corps' remaining units were to cross behind the 21st Guards Rifle Corps near Mohacs.

Thus the crossing of the 4th Guards Army's formations and units occurred partially at the crossing near Mohacs and partially along the crossings in the Batina area, in the 57th Army's sector. Upon the arrival of the 20th Guards Rifle Corps' units at the line Tolna—Kisvaszar, on 30 November the commander of the 4th Guards Army ordered units of the 31st Guards Rifle Corps to set about crossing and seize a bridgehead in the Madocsa area.

By a decision of the commander of the 31st Guards Rifle Corps, the forcing was to be carried out along two sectors: the main crossing along the Madocsa—Ordas sector, and a second one in the area three kilometers northwest of Solt.

In order to mask the crossing of the corps' units along the Modocsa—Ordas sector, it was decided to organize a false crossing in the Dunapentele area, in order to distract the enemy, while smoke masking screens were set up in the areas of Dunaenyhaza, Solt and Ordas.

The following jumping-off positions for the forcing were planned: Dunapatai and five kilometers to the north for the 40th Guards Rifle Division; Dunavecse and Solt for the 34th Guards Rifle Division, while a reinforced battalion with a platoon of sappers was concentrated two kilometers northwest of Solt, ready to begin forcing along the sector of the false crossing. The 4th Guards Rifle Division was to cross behind the 40th Guards Rifle Division.

The corps's crossing was carried out in two echelons:

- the first echelon, consisting of the 40th Guards Rifle Division and the 466th Mortar Regiment, the 438th Anti-Tank Artillery and 23rd Artillery regiments, the 56th Engineer-Sapper Brigade with a UVSA-3 park, and a battalion from the 34th Guards Rifle Division's 105th Rifle Regiment, with a platoon of sappers, was to cross in a landing operation on A-3 boats and fishing boats;
- the second echelon (the reserve and rear establishments) were to cross on ferries and landing boats behind the first echelon.

The crossing of the first echelon's forward elements along the main axis and at the site of the false crossing was begun at 2145 on 30 November, without an artillery preparation and was carried out successfully. The enemy discovered our units only at the moment the landing party landed on the western bank of the Danube, after which he opened an intensive fire against the landing and the crossing. Four A-3 boats and 12 fishing boats were destroyed and damaged by enemy fire. On 1 December two regiments from the 40th Guards Rifle Division were crossed and by the close of the day units of the first echelon, having captured Madocsa, were fighting four kilometers northwest and west of the town.

Thus the following crossings were created and maintained by the engineer and pontoon units for the 4th Guards Army's units. See table 6.

Ferry crossings worked around the clock, in heavy rain and in a sharp rise in the water level. This made the work of the crossings significantly more difficult and we had to repair the moorings and piers several times a day, which, in its turn, increased the time needed for trips. 32 moorings were built on piles during the forcing.

Table 6 River Crossings Maintained by 4th Guards Army, December 1944

Engineer Units	Type of Crossing	Capacity (in tons)	Crossing Site	Crossing Equipment
56th Engineer-Sapper Brigade	Ferry-landing	6	Harta (15 km north of Dunapataj)	13 A-3 boats, 50 fishing boats
	Ferry-landing	6	Dunapataj	15 A-3 boats, 30 fishing boats
	Ferry-landing	6	Mohacs	11 ferries from the UVSA-3 park
50th Independent Motorized Pontoon-Bridge Brigade	Ferry	16	west of Ordas	2 bow half-pontoon park pontoons
	Ferry	16	Batya	" "
	Ferry	16	Mohacs	4 bow half-pontoon park pontoons
	Floating bridge	16	Mohacs	a bow half-pontoon park, a captured Krupp park, and barges
	Floating bridge	16	Batina	" "

The enemy employed floating mines to destroy the constructed crossings. In order to combat these mines, the engineer units on the upriver side of the crossings (particularly bridge crossings) constructed booms from logs across the entire river, while watch crews shot at the mines with rifle-automatic rifle and machine gun fire.

During the fighting to seize and widen the bridgeheads, the engineer units operating in the infantry's combat formations checked to see whether the march routes and inhabited locales were mined; built and restored bridges along the troop's routes of movement and repaired and improved roads in the crossing areas and on the bridgeheads.

The forcing of the Danube by the Second Ukrainian Front's forces. The forces of the Second Ukrainian Front's 46th Army, having attacked on 28 October in the area between the Tisza and the Danube, reached the approaches to Budapest from the south with their main forces by the close of 3 November and the eastern bank of the Csepeli Dunaag River, where they encountered stubborn enemy resistance along a powerfully fortified defensive line.

The army's forces, while continuing to push forth their right-flank formations to the outer ring of the enemy's fortified zone along the approaches to Budapest, were at the same time preparing to force two water obstacles—the Csepeli Dunaag River and the Danube.

The Csepeli Dunaag River has as its source in the main channel of the Danube near the southern outskirts of Budapest and flows into it again in the Tass area. The river's overall length is 50 kilometers, with a width of 50-150 meters and a depth of 3-4 meters, and a rate of flow of 0.3-0.5 meters per second. The river has floodgates, which allows for regulating the water regime.

Csepeli Island is 50 kilometers long and is 5-8 kilometers wide. The island's surface towers over the left bank. The soil is sandy, with a 10-15 centimeter layer of black earth. In rainy weather it is very difficult to move. There are a limited number of surfaced roads.

The enemy was defending the island with the forces of the Hungarian 1st Cavalry Division and had a number of inhabited locales configured for defense, which were outfitted with rifle trenches, machine gun emplacements and firing positions for artillery weapons.

Wire obstacles had been built along the forward edge with an overall length of up to 30 kilometers, through which ran a high-voltage electrical current.

The engineer troops were given the mission of securing the crossing of the 46th Army's forces, which were forcing the Csepeli Dunaag River and, while operating in the infantry's combat formations, and securing their passage through the enemy's barriers on the island and consolidating along its western bank.

In accordance with the decision of the commander of the 46th Army, the 37th Rifle Corps, consisting of the 108th, 59th and 4th guards rifle divisions and two regiments from the 316th Rifle Division (23rd Rifle Corps), with corresponding reinforcement equipment, was to cross the Csepeli Dunaag River. The Csepeli Dunaag River was first of all divided into four sectors: sector no. 1 was ran along the front Taksony—Majoshaza and was to be forced by the 316th Rifle Division (minus one rifle division); sector no. 2 was in the Aporka area to be forced by the 108th Guards Rifle Division; sector no. 3 was in the Kiskunlachaza area for forcing by the 59th Guards Rifle Division, and; sector no. 4 was in the Domsod are for forcing by the third regiment of the 316th Rifle Division.

The plan for the infantry support of the forcing called for the following distribution of equipment:

a) the 51st Engineer-Sapper Brigade was to support the crossing of landing parties and restore to a capacity of 60 tons the bridge blown up by the enemy in Rackeve;
b) the 2nd Independent Pontoon-Bridge Brigade was to support four landing-ferry sites in sectors 1 and 2 and the ferry crossings near Rackeve and Domsod, and to subsequently, in conjunction with units of the 1st Independent Pontoon-Bridge Brigade, to lay down a 16-ton bridge from the bow half-pontoon park west of Kiskunlachaza;
c) the 8th Independent Motorized Pontoon-Bridge Regiment was to maintain one 50-ton ferry for crossing tanks and self-propelled guns in the Rackeve—Domsod area;
d) the 7th Independent Electrical Obstacle Battalion was to reconnoiter render electric barriers harmless;
e) the 72nd Independent Battalion of dog mine searchers and a company from a detachment of operational obstacle removers was to check the mining of the roads and inhabited locales on Csepeli Island.

The following crossing equipment was set aside for crossing the troops: 4 1/6 of a set from bow half-pontoon parks, two ferries from heavy bridge train parks, one set of light pneumatic pontoon parks, 18 A-3 boats, 54 small pneumatic boats, 85 fishing boats, and 12 assault boats.

The concentration of crossing equipment at the river in the Kiskunlachaza—Domsod area and along the forcing sector was carried out during 16-21 November. The equipment was distributed in the following manner. See table 7.

The bridge crossing near Rackeve was supported by three pontoon battalions from the bow half-pontoon park's equipment.

By the close of 21 November units of the 37th Rifle Corps had occupied their jumping-off positions.

The 38th Anti-Aircraft Artillery Division secured the anti-aircraft defense of the crossing area. The crossing was also covered by smoke from the 670th Chemical Barrier Battalion.

In accordance with the decision by the commander of the 46th Army, the 37th Rifle Corps, along with reinforcements, had the task, in conjunction with the 316th Rifle Division (23rd Rifle Corps) of forcing the Csepeli Dunaag River along the Szigetcsep—Rackeve sector, and with one division force the Csepeli Dunaag River south of Szigetcsep and launch an attack in the direction of Tokol and Csepel, and a second division and a regiment from the 316th Rifle Division was to force the Csepeli Dunaag River in the area west of Aporka and, while attacking in the direction of Lorev and Makad and to reach the eastern bank of the Danube along the front excluding Szigetcsep—Makad. During the forcing it was ordered to hold the reinforcement artillery along the eastern bank, with the regimental artillery in the infantry's combat formations.

Table 7 Equipment Assembled for 46th Army's Crossing of the Csepeli Dunaag River, November 1944

Crossing Equipment	Name of Sector			
	No. 1, Taksony—Majoshaza	No. 2, Aporka	No. 3, Kiskunlachaza	No. 4, Domsod
Fishing boats	35	–	–	20
A-3 boats	3	5	10	–
Small pneumatic boats	10	20	24	–
Assault boats	7	–	–	5
Light pneumatic pontoons	–	14	11	–
Bow half-pontoon pontoons	2	1	2	1
16-ton bow half-pontoon ferries	1	1	1	1
Rafts	–	–	–	7
Reserve:				
Fishing boats	10	10	–	10
Bow half-pontoon pontoons	2	2	2	–
Bow half-pontoon ferries	1	–	–	4
Captured pontoons	–	–	–	4

The commander of the 23rd Rifle Corps received orders to force the Csepeli Dunaag River in the Szigetcsep area with the forces of the 316th Rifle Division (minus one regiment).

During the night of 21-22 November the 37th Rifle Corps, along with the 316th Rifle Division (23rd Rifle Corps) began to force the river simultaneously along all sectors, without an artillery preparation. The landing of the first echelon was completely unexpected for the enemy.

The bold and decisive actions along the western bank of the Csepeli Dunaag River, the troops' rapid securing of passages through the electrified barriers and the precisely organized crossing secured the success of the fighting on the island. By the morning of 23 November units of the 37th Rifle Corps, consisting of three divisions, had been crossed over to the island. As a result of a vigorous attack, the troops quickly captured the strong points of Tokol, Lorev, Makad, and Rackeve and reached the eastern bank of the Danube along a front of more than 20 kilometers. During the forcing the enemy made repeated air strikes against the area of the crossings, launching bombing strikes against our troops and crossing equipment.

The following were lost by our forces: eight fishing boats, 10 A-3 boats, 31 small pneumatic boats, three light pneumatic pontoons, and 71 bow half-pontoon semi-pontoons.

Having captured a bridgehead on Csepeli Island, our forces immediately began to prepare to force the Danube, having organized the careful reconnaissance of the river and the enemy's defense along its western bank along the sector from Tokol to Lorev. They were simultaneously carrying out defensive work to consolidate the captured bridgehead.

The engineer troops were assigned the following tasks by the *front's* military council: to support the 46th Army's crossing of the Danube; to render harmless the enemy's obstacles along the western bank of the river; to cover the troops with mines in consolidating their position on Csepeli Island and to repair roads and restore bridges along the main routes.

In a decision by the commander of the Second Ukrainian Front, the 46th Army commander was ordered to force the Danube along the Tokol—Lorev sector and, while developing the offensive in the general direction of Etyek, outflank Budapest from the west.

The army was to organize its combat formation in two echelons, with four divisions in the first echelon and two divisions and the 2nd Guards Mechanized Corps in the second.

The army's forces were to occupy a jumping-off position for the forcing on Csepeli Island and with part of its forces along the left bank of the Csepeli Dunaag River, while the 2nd Guards Mechanized Corps was to reach the Rackeve area.

The enemy had prepared the right bank of the Danube River for defense and had outfitted it in the engineering sense. A series of powerful strong points had been prepared, all structures carefully masked and configured to the terrain.

In accordance with the instructions of the *front* commander, it was decided to begin the forcing on the night of 4-5 December.

The troops were organized into two echelons for the forcing: in the first echelon were the 316th and 99th rifle divisions (23rd Rifle Corps) and the 108th and 59th guards rifle divisions (37th Rifle Corps; the second echelon contained the 320th Rifle Division and the 2nd Guards Mechanized Corps.

The army and *front* engineer units received the following orders during the forcing:

- the 51st Engineer-Sapper Brigade was to organize a crossing by a landing party on light crossing equipment with three battalions; one battalion was to remain in the reserve of the army's engineer chief;
- the 1st Independent Pontoon-Bridge Brigade was to secure the crossing of the 316th Rifle Division in the area west of Tokol, with one battalion, having five pontoons and 2 ferries with a capacity of 30 tons from the bow half-pontoon park and with motor speed launches, while one battalion was to support the crossing of the 99th Rifle Division in the area west of Szigetcsep, having five pontoons and two 30-ton ferries from the bow half-pontoon park and motor speed launches; the brigade's third battalion was designated for fire service and the fourth battalion comprised the reserve of the army's engineer troops;
- the 2nd Independent Pontoon-Bridge Brigade was to support the crossing of the 108th Guards Rifle Division three kilometers south of Ercsi with two battalions, having five pontoons and three bow half-pontoon ferries with a capacity of 30 tons and motor speed launches, and one battalion to support the crossing of the 59th Guards Rifle Division to the area west and southwest of Rackeve, having five pontoons and two ferries with launches; the brigade's remaining two battalions had been detailed for assembling parts for laying down a bridge from the captured Krupp park;
- the 8th Independent Motorized Pontoon-Bridge Regiment received orders to support the crossing of the 2nd Guards Mechanized Corps, having ten ferries with a capacity of 50 tons;
- the 5th Guards Engineer-Sapper Brigade was to outfit the approaches from Rackeve to the crossings south of Ercsi, so as to pass through units of the 2nd Guards Mechanized Corps, as was as to outfit the docks and moorings south of Ercsi;
- the 17th Military-Field Construction headquarters was to support the construction of a bridge with a capacity of 45 tons four kilometers south of Taksony and a bridge for ten tons near Rackeve;
- the 27th Independent Motorized Engineer Brigade received orders to organize reconnaissance of the obstacles and to clear the mine-explosive obstacles along the western bank of the Danube.

The concentration of troops, vehicles and floating equipment to the crossing areas was carried out only at night.

During the forcing the areas of the crossings were covered by the 8th and 39th anti-aircraft artillery divisions and by smoke.

For masking purposes, the first trip was carried out using oars, which took 2-3½ hours. The landing of the first-echelon landing party was carried out under the cover of powerful artillery fire. From 2300 on 4 December and throughout the night of 4-5 December up to two rifle regiments were crossed over to the western bank of the Danube from each rifle division that had seized bridgeheads along the western bank of the river, which by the close of 6 December had been expanded to 18 kilometers along the front and up to 3-4 kilometers in the depth. By 8 December these units, having crushed the enemy's resistance, reached the "Margarita" defensive line along the front Erd—Martonvasar—the northeastern shore of Lake Velence, where they linked up with the Third Ukrainian Front's right-flank units. Thus the forcing began with the crossing of landing groups on individual crossing equipment. Behind the landing of units, which were following in the first trip, the sappers and pontoon troops pitched into assembling of the ferry equipment from the bow half-pontoon park and from the morning of 5 December the troops and combat equipment were crossing by ferries and the existing landing equipment.

On the night of 8-9 December a bridge with a 16-ton capacity and a length of 623 meters was built by forces of the 1st Pontoon-Bridge Brigade and attached units in the area five kilometers south of Ercsi; from 1800 on 9 December the bridge began to work. During the forcing crossing over the bridge was twice interrupted. The first time the bridge was swung open during the daylight hours of 9 December in order to save it from air attacks, and the second time the crossing was disrupted from 1600 on 11 December to 1600 on 12 December, due to the fact that during an enemy bomber strike some anchor cables were smashed by bombs and three ferries broke away and were swept downstream. By 10 December the forcing and crossing of the army's forces over the Danube had been completely finished.

The precise planning and correct distribution of crossing equipment and the selfless work of the sapper and pontoon troops facilitated the successful forcing.

One can make the following conclusions from the experience of the Second and Third Ukrainian fronts' forces in forcing the Danube:

- landing-ferry crossings were the chief crossing methods;
- floating equipment (A-3 boats, small pneumatic boats, collapsible landing boats, and light pneumatic pontoons and bow half-pontoon pontoons) demonstrated good tactical-technical qualities;
- flooding conditions in the rivers should be carefully studied and taken into account; measures for supporting troop crossings should be planned in the event of flooding, for which purpose a reserve of floating equipment should be set aside;
- the construction of low-water bridges should be limited in anticipation of flooding;
- during flood periods there should always be back-up equipment in the form of ferries at the bridge crossing sites.

Engineer Support for the Assault on Budapest

In the storming of Budapest and in the fierce street fighting the assault sappers operated in close cooperation with the infantry, artillery and tanks. In the city the enemy had previously created a powerful defense. The enemy strengthened buildings occupied for defense, having made window embrasures with stone, bricks and earth in sacks and out of wood and other local materials. Overhead covers and walls between stories had been strengthened by additional overlapping.

Ports were made for firing and better maneuvering in the buildings' walls and embrasures were constructed.

The enemy had built trenches in the garden areas around buildings and in squares with attached and detachable firing trenches and machine gun emplacements. Individual areas within the city were outfitted with pillboxes in the form of sectional reinforced concrete and rock and concrete machine gun sites. A significant number of anti-tank and anti-personnel obstacles were created in the form of barricades, anti-tank ditches, stakes, wire obstacle tetrahedrons, and mine-explosive obstacles. Barricades 2-2½ meters thick and no less than 1.5 meters high were built every 300-400 meters along the streets. They were erected from stone, bricks, sandbags, wood, various factory equipment, railroad cars, furniture and rolls of paper.

The enemy, attaching great importance to Budapest, adopted all measures for creating powerful defensive lines along the approaches to the city and for configuring the city itself for static and stubborn defense. The city had been transformed into a fortress with powerful defensive lines along its approaches. The enemy's resistance in Budapest was extremely stubborn down to the last day. The Germans and Magyars who had fallen into the latest "cauldron" were ordered to resist to the last.

Our forces had to take each building by storm in both the eastern and western parts of the city.

Engineer units carried out the following tasks in storming Budapest: they carried out reconnaissance the enemy's engineer structures and obstacles, cleared mines and rendered harmless the enemy's mine-explosive and other obstacles; operated within storm groups in the fighting for strong points; supported our forces' combat formations with obstacles when consolidating along the lines reached and, finally, covered the troops against enemy counterblows with barriers. The engineer units were also entrusted with creating crossings over the Danube.

The 11th, 12th and 14th assault engineer-sapper brigades from the High Command Reserve, the 27th Motorized Engineer, 60th Army Engineer-Sapper and 1st Independent Pontoon-Bridge brigades, troop sapper units from the 18th, 30th, 37th, and 75th rifle corps, and the 61st and 70th independent battalions of dog mine searchers took part in the fighting for the city.

During the fighting for the city 1-2 engineer battalions were subordinated to the rifle divisions.

On the eve of the storming of the city exercises for operating in major inhabited locales were conducted in the engineer units together with the troops. During the exercises this attention was chiefly paid to the organization and training of the storm groups.

The engineer reconnaissance of the enemy's defense during the storming of the city was conducted uninterruptedly by infantry forces and elements of assault engineer-sapper brigades attached to them.

The chief tasks assigned to reconnaissance were uncovering the enemy's fortification structures, reconnoitering his obstacles and barriers and establishing approaches to the targets for assault.

Reconnaissance was conducted by means of observation and searches in close cooperation with combined-arms intelligence, or as part of its reconnaissance groups.

Reconnaissance through observation was organized from permanently operating observation posts, the number of which reached as high as 60. In places the upper stories of buildings were chosen for observation. With our troops' advance the posts' locations changed as well. Each observation post usually consisted of two sapper observers and one orderly; the observers were officers along the important axes.

Another and more effective kind of reconnaissance was the search. A search established not only the forward edge of the enemy's defense, but its depth as well. The storm brigades' search groups carried out more than 80 forays during the operation, of which 12 were as part of troop reconnaissance. A search group consisted of, on the average, 8-12 sapper-assault troops. The group's mission consisted of unearthing the enemy's engineer measures in the depth of his defense. For example, one of the groups was assigned the task of carrying out a reconnaissance of a sewage pipe running along one of the city's streets, in order to find an outlet into the enemy's rear. A group of three sappers got 1,130 meters into the rear inside the pipe, of which 700 meters was in territory occupied by the enemy. The scouts established that one could pass through the pipe, as its dimensions allowed for movement while hunched over (1-2 meters in height and 0.8-1.5 meters in width). The scouts also established that one could get into the enemy's rear through observation holes at the end of the pipe.

The soldiers of the engineer and sapper units were part of the assault groups being created and received orders for the engineer support of the assault. They made passages in obstacles, destroyed and burned the enemy's strong points, supported the infantry with mine-explosive obstacles when it consolidated on newly-won lines and in repulsing the enemy's counterattacks.

The composition of the storm groups was not uniform. In each separate case it was determined by the task assigned to the group and the size of the attack target, as well as by the enemy's fire system and the presence of natural and artificial obstacles. For example, according to the experience of the fighting by units of the 18th Guards Rifle Corps, a storm group consisted of 10-20 riflemen and automatic riflemen, 3-4 assault sappers, armed with 2- and 5-kilograms packs of explosives, wire cutters for cutting explosive obstacles and for making passages, and according to the experience of the 30th Guards Rifle Corps' fighting a storm group consisted of 20-25 riflemen and automatic riflemen, 3-5 assault sappers, 1-2 heavy machine guns, 3-4 light machine guns, 2-3 45mm guns, 2-3 battalion mortars, and sapper flamethrower operators with portable flamethrowers.

Reconnaissance sappers and artillery men, who reconnoitered the target of attack and its fire system, supported the actions of the storm groups. Groups for blocking and destroying enemy centers of resistance moved behind the storm groups. These groups consolidated the captured target. The group was supported by powerful fire from mortars and artillery of all calibers (artillery pieces from 45mm to 203mm), usually firing over open sights.

Each assault group received an independent assignment for capturing this or that enemy target. An assault usually began with a brief mortar preparation (most often from 120mm mortars). The attached artillery was usually hidden in shelters and would open fire over open sights on embrasures and windows, pinning down the enemy's observation and activities from the front; assault sappers would crawl up to the walls from the unobserved side, pile up charges of explosives and explode them, thus making breaks (passages). At the same time, the entire remaining part of the assault group, while operating against windows and firing ports with grenades, would hurl themselves against the target and destroy the surviving enemy soldiers, after which the group would immediately set about consolidating the captured site and prepared for subsequent activities.

As a rule, the assault groups did not operate along streets, which the enemy kept under particular fire, but through breaks in the walls of buildings, in fences, and throws cellars.

Thus the assault sappers rendered a great deal of support to the assault groups, clearing a path for the infantry, artillery and tanks under heavy fire. The sappers cleared the enemy's mines and mine-explosive obstacles, blew up barricades and stone fences and made breaches in the walls of buildings and cellars.

Simultaneously with the assault on fortified buildings, the assault sappers, while operating in small groups, laid out mine-explosive obstacles, barring with these the path for the enemy's infantry and tanks and repelling their counterattacks directed against our forces. In repelling enemy counterattacks and in consolidating blocks captured by us in the city, groups of mobile minelayers operated successfully, laying mines along a sector where the enemy's tanks and self-propelled guns appeared.

Particularly significant cover of our troops by mine-explosive obstacles was carried out by our units along the northern outskirts of the western part of Budapest (Buda), when the enemy undertook efforts to break through to his group of forces operating from the area south of Komarno. During this period the engineer units laid more than 9,000 anti-tank mines over several days along the western and northwestern outskirts of Buda, which significantly contributed to our forces' success. For this minefields and heavily-mined areas were cleared from previous areas and transferred to new areas for mining, which insured the economizing of mines and made up for their shortage along some axes.

Aside from mining, the engineer units erected barricades and laid down fire mines, employing captured explosives for this.

During the fighting in the city the engineer troops were also entrusted with clearing Budapest of mines.

During the work on clearing Budapest of mines it was established that the enemy had not carried out the preliminary mining of important industrial sites and buildings with delayed-reaction mines and bombs because of a shortage of mine-explosive equipment.

Mining was carried out by laying mines in separate groups on the streets and booby traps in buildings, and also bombs and aviation bombs in factories and bridges that had been prepared for demolition.

For setting up booby traps, the enemy employed Hungarian cumulative charges with a metal fixture with a guy detonator and grenades. The charges were placed on fences and sides of roads, in groups or pairs. Streets, lanes and crossroads were covered with mine groups (from 10-20 mines).

Bombs, booby traps and mine traps were most often laid in buildings. Domestic implements, stools, wardrobes, beds, chairs and even ovens and cookers were mined.

The subway was mined with 100 cumulative action charges and anti-personnel fragmentation mines.

Portable flamethrower battalions from the 12th and 14th engineer-sapper brigades took part in the assault on the town. Their operations boiled down to 2-3 sapper flamethrower operators, with flamethrowers, as part of the assault groups, carried out tasks of burning targets and burning out their garrisons with fire.

During the fighting for the western part of Budapest (Buda), the engineer troops successfully employed the method of lobbing captured shells for destroying targets in the enemy's defense, or "sapper artillery," the essence of which is that lobbing shells is carried out with the aid of high explosives, which yields a steep plunging trajectory that enables us to bombard the enemy's position in conditions of city streets with high buildings, when it is impossible to employ mortars. In all, 1,186 150mm, 105mm and 88mm shells were fired against the enemy over five days.

One may draw the following brief conclusions from the experience of our troops' engineer support during the fighting for Budapest:

- engineer reconnaissance of the assault target and the approaches to it should be carried out not only by specially detailed reconnaissance elements, but by assault sappers as well;
- the enemy constructed the defense of Budapest on a system of defensive lines, which ran along the main streets, with their flanks resting on the river, and along switch defensive positions, which ran along the radial streets; the basis of this system were the centers of resistance, which included several blocks, and strong points, consisting of one or several buildings;
- fences, walls, railings, and gratings were widely employed, barricades, spikes, tetrahedrons, ditches and roadblocks from barbed wire were set up, and streets, buildings and other urban structures were mined;
- the enemy stubbornly defended his strong points and the city, which required the employment of assault detachments and groups from our forces, consisting of infantrymen, assault sappers, sapper flamethrower personnel, and supporting artillery of all calibers;
- the success of the battle for the enemy's strong points in the city was resolved only by issuing a specific task to each soldier of the assault group and to the group as a whole;
- the group's actions should be coordinated according to time and lines;
- the destruction of buildings occupied by the enemy with explosive charges was a common phenomenon in the actions of the assault sappers;

- an important condition ensuring the success of the assault against objectives was the troops' ability to independently resolve the tasks that arose, to take advantage of surprise attack, and to employ decisiveness and boldness;
- it is necessary to supply sapper flamethrower operators with gas masks and inflammable protective clothing;
- dog mine detectors performed good work in clearing mines, especially where the sapper cannot operate with a probing rod and mine detector (metal rubble, asphalt, etc.).

The Employment of Engineer Troops in Repelling the Enemy's Counteroffensives

The forces of the Third Ukrainian Front's 46th and 4th Guards armies, having successfully concluded the encirclement of the enemy's Budapest group of forces in Budapest, fought with part of their forces to squeeze the ring and destroy the enemy garrison in Budapest, while the forces of the 4th Guards Army consolidated along the line Nyergesujfalu—Neszmely—Banhida—Pusztavam—Csokako—Sarkeresztes—Osi—Akarattya.

In January 1945 the *front's* forces were engaged in bitter fighting with major enemy forces that had launched a counteroffensive from the following areas: south of Komarno and northwest and southwest of Szekesfehervar. The enemy, having regrouped his forces and brought up forces from the depth, had by 2 January concentrated five panzer and two infantry divisions opposite the 4th Guards Army's right flank. On the night of 1-2 January the enemy's units attacked and throughout the first two days advanced up to 30 kilometers to the southeast, reaching the approaches to Bicske.

The army's forces closed the breakthrough sector from the southeast by committing additional forces into the fighting, maneuvering all types of artillery and by broadly employing mine-explosive obstacles.

While continuing powerful tank and infantry attacks near Bicske, on 7 January the enemy attacked with the forces of three tank divisions and one cavalry brigade along the sector Csakbereny—Sarkeresztes in the direction of Zampoly. Throughout the bitter fighting of 7-8 January he managed to capture the towns of Zampoly and Szrkeresztes.

The 4th Guards Army localized the enemy's offensive along this axis as well by the commitment into the fighting of reserves along his sector and by the 4th Guards Army's counterblows. On 18 January the enemy undertook a new offensive with major tank and infantry forces from the line Osi—Akarattya and, having broken through our defense, reached the Danube in the Dunaujvaros area and Lake Velence in the Gardony area.

The enemy, while augmenting his forces, penetrated our troops' position on the night of 25-26 January and reached the line Kajaszoszentpeter—Vereb. The further advance of the enemy's forces was halted.

In the defensive fighting by the Third Ukrainian Front's 46th and 4th Guards armies the engineer units, operating within the infantry's combat formations, carried out missions to repel the enemy's tank and infantry attacks with mine-explosive obstacles, to construct obstacles along tank axes in front of the forward edge of the defensive lines, and also to carry out reconnaissance of the enemy's engineer measures. Units of the 51st and 56th army engineer-sapper brigades and the 44th Motorized Engineer Brigade from the High Command Reserve operated to render engineer support to the *front's* forces in repelling the enemy's counteroffensive. Throughout January, a great deal of work to strengthen the defense was carried out by the army's and attached engineer troops. In supporting the troops' actions in their fight against the enemy's tanks and infantry, the engineer units broadly employed the tactics of minefields, bombs and booby traps; they mined bridges and road structures; they created obstacles in the forest and barriers from wire and wood.

During the fighting the engineer units were attached to reinforce the corps and also constituted the anti-tank reserve in the armies. Engineer units were employed as mobile obstacle detachments

(POZ) or carried out tasks of constructing anti-tank and anti-personnel explosive obstacles along selected defensive lines. Besides this, jumping-off areas and lines for our counterattacking forces were prepared by our sappers. Mobile obstacle detachments were organized in forces of a platoon to an engineer-sapper battalion in strength. The number of anti-tank and anti-personnel mines and explosives was determined by the transportation opportunities. For example, an army mobile obstacle detachment, which consisted of a battalion, had 1,500-2,000 anti-tank mines delivered by 5-7 motor vehicles. The engineer battalions, which were attached to the rifle corps, detached from themselves a mobile detachment apiece, consisting of a company, which had 750 anti-tank mines and 200 kilograms of explosives delivered on five motor vehicles.

A mobile obstacle detachment in a rifle division consisted of a sapper platoon, with 400 anti-tank mines and 100 kilograms of explosives, delivered by 2-3 motor vehicles; such a detachment in a rifle regiment usually consisted of one section of sappers with 100 anti-tank mines and 50 kilograms, delivered by two vehicles.

Minefields were laid in small groups (15-30 mines) in a scattered fashion and masked by materials at hand. This laying of mines secured the blocking of the road and at the same time made it possible to create obstacles in depth. Large wooden anti-tank mines were primarily laid in minefields, and they worked without fail, were easy to transport and safe to handle.

In all, during the period 1-31 January 1945 the engineer forces operating in the Third Ukrainian Front's 46th and 4th Guards armies' sector laid up to 100,000 anti-tank mines.

85 enemy tanks, 12 armored transports and two self-propelled guns were blown up on these minefields.

Simultaneous with the creation of minefields against tanks along their path of movement, all of the bridges and road structures were mined and destroyed. In all, during this time the engineer units prepared 124 bridges for detonation, of which 68 were blown up.

This brief description of the combat employment of the engineer troops during the repulse of the enemy's counteroffensives gives us the opportunity of drawing the following conclusions:

- in the defensive fighting the *front's* engineer units significantly assisted in the repulse of the enemy's counteroffensives;
- in this fighting the troops learned how to rapidly and massively mine under direct enemy fire;
- the engineer troops' actions as part of mobile obstacle detachments in the fight against the enemy's tanks demonstrated their vitality and necessity;
- the insufficient degree of coordination of the mobile obstacle detachments with the anti-tank artillery led to a situation in which the enemy tanks that blew up in our minefields were not completely destroyed;
- the insufficient cover of the minefields by fire from infantry weapons enabled the enemy to reconnoiter and clear them.

Part III

The Third Ukrainian Front's Activities in the Budapest Operation (An Operational–Tactical Sketch)

Major General S.P. Tarasov

10

The Strategic Situation Along the Soviet-German Front by the Start of the Budapest Operation (By 29 October 1944)

The Hitlerite general staff attached particular significance to the middle-Danube area of the theater of military activities as a likely strategic direction for an attack by Soviet forces against Hungary, Austria and southern Germany.

The importance of this direction was determined by the political, economic and geographical situation of these states.

A developed military industry and the presence of important strategic raw materials (oil, bauxite) in Hungary, Czechoslovakia and Austria by the end of 1944 had a decisive significance for strategic communications with one of the most important Danubian ports, representing a strategic gate opening a path to Austria and southern Germany. Besides this, Budapest was a powerful arsenal for the German-Fascist command and a major military base, numbering up to 1,900 factories, including many large industrial combines producing various munitions, equipment and ammunition for the army. From this it followed that the city of Budapest played an extremely important role, in the military-economic sense, for fascist Germany.

With the fall of the city of Budapest, the withdrawal of Hungary from the war and its turnabout against Hitlerite Germany would be secured, which would weaken the enemy's military power to a great degree.

It follows that the Budapest operation was a strategic offensive operation.

This operation pursued the following decisive goals: a) the defeat of Army Group South; b) the encirclement and destruction of the enemy's Budapest group of forces, and; c) the liberation of the city of Budapest from the German-Fascist occupiers and the creation of conditions for the development of an attack along the Vienna strategic direction.

On the whole, the Budapest operation, which was carried out in conditions of a complex and rapidly changing situation, led to a radical change in the military-political situation along the southern wing of the Soviet-German front.

The USSR's Military-Political Situation by the Start of the Budapest Operation

The political situation was characterized by the further strengthening of the Soviet Union's economic, moral-political and military situation.

The country's increased economic possibilities and the further growth of the Soviet army's military art were the basis for the Soviet army's successes in the Budapest operation.

The Budapest operation began at the end of October and the beginning of November 1944. By this time the strategic situation along the Soviet-German front was as follows. In the far north the operation to complete the defeat of the German-Fascist troops in northern Finland, which was a component part of the plan by the *Stavka* of the VGK for the 1944 campaign, had been basically completed.

This offensive operation, which was conducted by the Karelian Front's forces, in conjunction with the Northern Fleet, had important strategic significance. As a result of the tenth strategic blow[1], the main forces of the Twentieth Lapland Army were routed and heavy losses inflicted on the enemy's naval forces in the Barents Sea. Soviet forces, upon entering Norwegian territory, liberated part of the northern Norwegian areas from the fascist aggressors and captured the port and town of Kirkenes, the Germans' chief naval base on the Barents Sea.

With the loss of the Pechenga region and the northern part of Norway, the German-Fascist command was deprived of two important year-round ports—Petsamo[2] and Kirkenes, as well as very rich nickel mines, where before the war up to 70 percent of the nickel for the demands of Germany industry was mined.

Our forces' victory in the far north significantly improved the overall strategic situation.

During the second half of October 1944 the eighth strategic blow had basically concluded, as a result of which Army Group North and Group "Narva" were defeated. Simultaneously, the Estonian and a large part of the Latvian Soviet republics were liberated. As a result of the first, fourth and eighth blows, Germany's Finnish ally was put out of action and she declared war on Germany.

With the defeat of the German-Fascist forces' northern wing of the strategic front, the danger of a counterblow from the Baltic States into the flank and rear of the Soviet forces operating along the Berlin strategic direction was eliminated and a favorable situation for launching a crushing blow in East Prussia was created. For this blow, besides the Third Belorussian Front, a significant part of the three Baltic fronts could be employed.

By 8 October the Second Baltic Front had concluded the Riga offensive operation, as a result of which the *front's* forces, in conjunction with the Third Baltic Front, captured the city and port of Riga. Developing the subsequent offensive along the Kurland peninsula, in conjunction with the First Baltic Front, the *front's* forces captured the line excluding Tukums—Gardena station—Autse. Thus the entire enemy group of forces (up to 25 divisions), which was part of Army Group North, which remained on the Kurland peninsula, was cut off by land from Germany, with which remained only sea communications, which were subject to attack by our navy and air force. The front line ran as follows: Klapkalnciems (along the southern shore of the Gulf of Riga)—Smarde—Velluciems—Rizhskaya (all locales east and southeast of Tukums)—Gardena station—west of Dobele—Lake Zedres Ezers—Iles—west of Autse—Leckava, with the flank resting on the Venta River.

The First Baltic Front, having successfully completed the Siauliai—Memel operation, reached the front Leckava—south of Pikeliai—east of Priekule—Skuodas—Inci—along the shore of the Baltic Sea and the Kurisches Haff to the mouth of the Neman River—then along the northern bank of the Neman River to Sudargas.

The Third Belorussian Front's forces broke through the Germans' permanent and deeply echeloned defense, which was covering the borders of East Prussia. As a result of intense fighting, by the close of 27 October the *front's* forces had entered the confines of East Prussia to a depth of 30 kilometers along a 140-kilometer front and occupied up to 400 inhabited locales, including Stalluponen and Trakehnen.

By 28 October the front ran along the line Neman River—Sudargas—Shailen—Wilkallen—west of Stalluponen—west of Trakehnen—Goldap—Augustow.

The *front's* forces temporarily went over to the defensive along this line, while simultaneously continuing to prepare for the next offensive operation.

---

1 Editor's note. In 1944 the Soviet army carried out ten major strategic offensives, which were later termed the "ten Stalinist blows." Of these, the Soviet offensive in northern Finland was the last.

2 Editor's note. The town's name was changed to Pechenga under Soviet rule.

The Second Belorussian Front's forces had basically completed the local Rozan—Pultusk offensive operation, as a result of which they captured two bridgeheads over the Wieprz River.

The Second Belorussian Front, together with the Third Belorussian Front, was preparing for an offensive operation to defeat the enemy's East Prussian group of forces.

The First Belorussian Front's forces were also fighting to expand their bridgehead along the western bank of the Narew River.

In the area between the Western Bug and Vistula rivers the *front's* forces during the second ten-day period in October were waging offensive battles for the purpose of improving their positions and advanced 9-14 kilometers.

By the end of 1944 these forces had consolidated along the line east of Pultusk—Pokrzywnica—excluding Dembe—along the Narew River—Wieliszewo—Jablonna, then along the eastern bank of the Pilica River and the Vistula River, for an overall front of 268 kilometers in length.

Part of the First Ukrainian Front's forces was fighting to expand its bridgeheads and was preparing, in conjunction with the First Belorussian Front, to carry out an offensive operation from the Sandomierz bridgehead.

Its 38th Army, in conjunction with the Fourth Ukrainian Front, continued to attack along the First Ukrainian Front's left wing.

The Fourth, Second and Third Ukrainian Fronts' Situation

Along the southern sector of the Soviet-German front, the operational-strategic situation before the Budapest operation was determined by the results achieved by the Fourth, Second and Third Ukrainian fronts during the September-October offensive operations.

The Second Ukrainian Front's forces had successfully completed the Debrecen operation, inflicted a major defeat on Army Group South in the Debrecen—Oradea Mare—Salonta area, while its forces along the right wing and center had reached the Tisza River from Chop to Tiszafured. At the same time, the *front's* left-wing forces had forced the Tisza River along the sector from Tiszafured to the Danube River and had seized a major bridgehead along its right bank, thus creating favorable conditions for developing the offensive along the Budapest direction. Thus as a result of the October offensive the Second Ukrainian Front's forces broke the enemy's defense along the entire offensive front and advanced during 6-27 October 100-250 kilometers to the northwest. They cleared the entire northeastern part of Hungary of the enemy and all Yugoslav territory north of the Danube. Army Group South continued to defend opposite the Second Ukrainian Front.

The successful offensive by the Second Ukrainian Front's forces along the Debrecen axis had very great significance for the offensive operation conducted by the Fourth Ukrainian Front's forces, while it eased the crossing and then the preparations for forcing the Danube River by the Third Ukrainian Front's forces and the defeat of the enemy's Danube group of forces along the western bank of the Danube River.

Throughout the first half of October the Fourth Ukrainian Front's forces, in conjunction with the First Ukrainian Front's left-wing forces, were engaged in stubborn fighting with the enemy for the purpose of overcoming the main mountain ridge and by 18 October, having overcome it, occupied the town of Sighet.

By this time the Second Ukrainian Front's forces, having reached the line Sig Dej—Ordea-Mare and, developing the offensive on Satu-Mare and Debrecen, had created a direct threat to the rear of the First Army, which was operating in the Carpathians, and forced it to withdraw.

This had a decisive significance for the Fourth Ukrainian Front's subsequent offensive activities. By taking advantage of the favorable situation, the Fourth Ukrainian Front's forces, took up the pursuit along its center and left wing of the enemy, which was falling back along the Uzhgorod and Mukachevo axes, and by 28 October, having advanced 80-160 kilometers, had captured the towns of Uzhgorod, Mukachevo, Sighet, and Chop and had reached the Hungarian plain and the headwaters of the Tisza River.

During the offensive the *front's* forces inflicted significant casualties on the German First Panzer Army and routed, in conjunction with the Second Ukrainian Front, the main forces of the Hungarian First Army, liberated trans-Carpathian Ukraine and, having entered the territory of allied Czechoslovakia, rendered direct aid to its people in their struggle for liberation from the German-Fascist aggressors.

By the end of October the Third Ukrainian Front's forces had carried out the Belgrade offensive operation, as a result of which the German-Fascist troops in Yugoslavia were routed and the city of Belgrade liberated. While pursuing the enemy, the Third Ukrainian Front's forces crossed the Sava River and by the end of October reached the Ruma area.

By this time the 57th Army's left-flank formations had reached the line Gornji Milanovac—Kraljevo—Krusevac.

Bulgarian forces were operating along the line south of Krusevac as far as Petric.

The northern shore of the Aegean Sea along the front Serry—Kavala—Alexandroupolis was being covered by a single army corps (three infantry divisions) of Bulgarian troops.

The defeat of the enemy's Belgrade group of forces enabled the Third Ukrainian Front's forces to concentrate their efforts for developing the offensive in Hungary in close coordination with the Second Ukrainian Front's forces.

Thus the strategic situation along the Soviet-German front, which had arisen by the start of the Budapest operation, was, on the whole, quite favorable, particularly along the southern wing.

The Soviet forces' rapid pace of the offensive, which had unfolded along an enormous front, brought about the premature expenditure of the enemy's reserves and completely tied down the German-Fascist forces along all sectors.

The breakthrough by the Second Ukrainian Front's left wing beyond the Tisza and the concentration of the Third Ukrainian Front's main forces along the Danube were creating all the prerequisites for a successful offensive along the Budapest direction.

The Third Ukrainian Front's forces, having completed the clearing of the eastern and central part of Yugoslavia of the enemy, set about regrouping their troops to the Budapest direction.

All of the enemy's efforts during this period had been directed toward halting the Second Ukrainian Front's offensive on Budapest and on holding its lines along the Tisza and Danube rivers and in Yugoslavia in order to secure the withdrawal of the remnants of its forces, up to 15 divisions, from the southern part of Yugoslavia. Groups "Serbia" and "E," which were part of the enemy's Army Group F, were operating opposite the Third Ukrainian Front and the Yugoslav and Bulgarian forces.

The disposition of the enemy's forces by this time was as follows:

The entire front from the area of the Carpathian Mountains to the mouth of the Drava River was held by the German First Panzer Army, Group Woehler and the Sixth Army and the Hungarian First, Second and Third armies, which numbered overall 39 infantry, seven panzer and two mechanized divisions in the first line and in Army Group South's reserve, plus a cavalry division and two panzer brigades in Budapest.

Of these, 30 infantry and five panzer divisions, or 73 percent of all available forces, were operating opposite the right wing of the group of Soviet forces along a front from the Dukla Pass to Tiszafured. Up to two infantry divisions were defending along the right bank of the Danube, along the sector from Baja to the mouth of the Drava River, and only up to seven infantry, two cavalry, one motorized, and one panzer division (76th Infantry Division, 4th SS Motorized Police Division, 20th, 5th and 8th infantry divisions, 1st Panzer Division, 1st Cavalry Division, and the

23rd, 10th, 5th, and 22nd infantry divisions), or 20 percent of all available forces, were located along the Budapest direction along a 200-kilometer sector from Tiszafured to Baja.

On 20 October 1944 the Hungarian First Army was subordinated to the commander of Group Woehler. At the end of October the headquarters of the Hungarian Second Army was thrown into the area along the right bank of the Danube and, having assumed command of part of army group E's forces (up to two infantry divisions), was hurriedly organizing a defense along the sector Baja—mouth of the Drava River.

The German-Fascist forces' deep operational reserves basically continued to remain in Yugoslavia and a significant part of them (the German 181st, 118th, 369th, 264th, 237th, and 392nd infantry divisions) were along the shore of the Aegean Sea. Part of these forces were moving to the Budapest direction.

The overall operational density reached 25-30 kilometers per division.

In October the enemy's aviation (Fourth Air Fleet and the *Sudost* operational group) was concentrating its main forces against the forces of the Second Ukrainian Front (of 2,490 sorties, 2,000 were flown against the Second Ukrainian Front's forces). It was less active along the flanks (against the Fourth and Third Ukrainian fronts). The Fourth Air Fleet numbered 410 combat aircraft, and the *Sudost* group 150.

An enemy river flotilla was operating along the Danube, numbering up to 26 vessels of various classes.

The Overall Correlation of Forces		
Rifle Divisions	1.3:1	(48:37)
Tanks and Self-Propelled Guns	2:1	(811:398)
Cavalry Divisions	2:1	(6:3)
Aircraft	5.3:1	(2,920:550)
Military-River Craft	4.5:1	(118:26)

The Hitlerite command, taking into account the seriousness of the situation, was reinforcing Army Group South by transferring divisions from other directions (the concentration of the Hungarian Third Army and the German Second Panzer Army to the south). Besides this, it was improving and creating new defensive lines along the approaches to Budapest and transforming inhabited locales into centers of resistance.

Thus the troops' favorable operational situation, especially that of the Second and Third Ukrainian fronts, and the favorable correlation of forces, offered us the opportunity, following the necessary regroupings and the creation of a superiority of force along the decisive axes, to set about carrying out the second stage of the strategic operation without an operational pause.

Alongside its military successes, the moral-political unity of the Soviet people grew ever stronger.

Soviet patriotism is first of all the people's deep devotion and loyalty to its Soviet Motherland and the fraternal community of the peoples of the USSR, unified in a multi-national socialist state.

The party and government were carrying out enormous work to strengthen the Soviet Union's economic situation.

The Soviet economy, despite the enormous difficulties of wartime, was inexorably augmenting its productive capabilities each month and supplying the Red Army with all types of weapons and ammunition in ever increasing amounts.

In the international sphere, the authority and influence of the Soviet Union continued to grow. Diplomatic relations were renewed with Italy and an armistice agreement was signed in Moscow between the USSR, Great Britain and the USA, on one side, and Bulgaria, on the other.

Thus by the start of the Budapest operation the USSR's military-political situation had become even stronger.

The Fascist Bloc's Military-Political Situation

The sharp worsening of the fascist block's military-political situation was chiefly linked to the Soviet armed forces' brilliant victories.

Industrial production in Germany continued to fall and there was already nothing more to make up for the losses suffered in 1944, although a "super total" mobilization was being carried out. Prisoners confirmed this, and it is clear, for example, in the testimony of the former chief of the Hungarian General Staff, Janos Voros[3] and other captured generals from the Hungarian and German armies, that the Hitlerite command, due to its limited means (munitions, fuel and combat equipment) and the shortage of personnel, was not capable of carrying out major offensive operations and that, basically, it had decided to wage a drawn-out war, while hoping for disagreements in the Allied camp.

For example, in his testimony the former chief of the *Wehrmacht* staff of fascist Germany, Field Marshal Keitel[4], stated: "We waged the war in expectation of those events which were bound to happen, but did not take place."

Prisoner of war and colonel of the general staff Bernhard von der Chevallerie, confirmed this idea in replying to the question of the war's prospects:

> The Red Army's major successes along the southern sector of the Soviet-German front were unexpected for the German command and caught it off guard.
>
> Romania's and Bulgaria's exit from the war and their turn against Germany was also a complete surprise. The German command hoped that the Red Army's very rapid advance in the Balkans would create a source of sharp contradictions between Russia and its allies. In Hitler's opinion, these disagreements should lead to World War III and Germany could improve its situation, upon allying with the Anglo-Americans.

As a result of the successful accomplishment of the offensive operations in October, a large part of the territory of Poland and Czechoslovakia and a significant part of Hungary and Yugoslavia were liberated.

The German-Fascist command was faced with the real threat of the complete defeat of its southern wing and Hungary's exit from the war.

This was all the more so as the Hungarian dictator, Horthy,[5] having arrived at the conclusion that the situation was hopeless and that fascist Germany would suffer an inevitable defeat in the immediate future, began to sound the ground as to the possibility of concluding a peace favorable to Hungary. He sent a delegation to Moscow for this purpose and then on 15 October made a radio address expressing his desire to conclude an armistice.

3 Editor's note. General Janos Voros (1891-1968) fought in the Austro-Hungarian army during World War I on the Eastern and Italian fronts. He was appointed chief of the army general staff in 1944, when the Germans occupied Hungary, although he later went over to the Red Army. Voros was sentenced to life imprisonment in 1950, but was released in 1956.

4 Editor's note. Field Marshal Wilhelm Keitel (1882-1946) joined the German imperial army in 1901 and served in World War I. In 1939 he was appointed chief of the Wehrmacht High Command, becoming Hitler's prime military adviser. He was found guilty of war crimes and executed.

5 Editor's note. Admiral Miklos Horthy (1868-1957) joined the Austro-Hungarian navy in 1896 and fought in World War I. He was appointed commander-in-chief of the navy in 1918 and in 1919 he was named regent of Hungary, following the collapse of the Austro-Hungarian Empire. During the 1930s he allied Hungary with Germany and participated in the invasion of the Soviet Union. He concluded an armistice with the Soviets in October 1944, but his government was deposed and replaced by an overtly pro-German government under Ferenc Szalasti. Horthy was taken to Germany and arrested by US forces in 1945. Horthy later lived in exile in Germany and Portugal.

The behavior of Horthy and his circle obviously contradicted Hitler's plans for an extended war. For this reason, the Hitlerite command took emergency measures.

First of all, it removed Horthy and his circle and put into power the leader of the Hungarian fascist Arrow Cross party, the scoundrel and adventurist Szalasi.

From this moment Hungary lost any kind of appearance of self-sufficiency and independence. The Hungarian army and industry was put at the complete service of the German-Fascist command. The Gestapo was given unlimited powers.

The political situation in the country became extremely exacerbated. The dissatisfaction of the broad popular masses with Szalasi's openly pro-Hitler policy and his course of continuing the war rapidly increased.

The Situation in the Countries of Southeastern Europe

The Soviet Union not only protected the countries it liberated from Anglo-American intervention, but through its all-round support and assistance saved these countries from a new dependency on foreign, in this case Anglo-American, imperialists.

> This is a single case in history, when a country that was subjected to invasion and which repelled this invasion, is not subjugating other peoples to itself, but rather is helping them to rise, offering its friendship, while subjecting itself to harsh sacrifices, is helping to save themselves from poverty those who committed aggression against it. Only one state, only one people is capable of acting in this manner, the country of socialism, the great Soviet Union.[6]

The political situation in the countries liberated and being liberated by Soviet forces, such as Czechoslovakia, Hungary, Romania, Bulgaria, Greece, and Yugoslavia was as follows by the start of the conduct of the Budapest operation:

Czechoslovakia. Thanks to the enormous assistance and support of the Slovak uprising on the part of the Soviet government and Soviet army, the heroic struggle of the Slovak people continued throughout October.

The Soviet army, having overcome the Carpathians in October, set about liberating Czechoslovakia and thus foiled the plans of the Hitlerite command to defeat the Slovak people's uprising.

At the time when the Soviet government was rendering selfless assistance to the Slovak people, the Czechoslovak London government (Benes[7]) and his Anglo-American bosses were doing everything possible, up to attempts to undermine the Slovakian uprising from within, in order to prevent Soviet troops from entering Slovakia and to deprive the Czech lands and Slovakia from taking power into their own hands.

On 6 October 1944 the ambassador of the Czechoslovak government in Moscow, Zdenek Fierlinger, informed his government in London about the USSR's assistance to the Slovak uprising. He pointed out that the Soviet Union had done everything in its power for Slovakia and

6 Dolores Ibarruri, *Sovet i Nadezhda Narodov. Za Prochnyi Mir, za Narodnuyu Demokratiyu*, 21 December 1949.

7 Editor's note. Eduard Benes (1884-1948) was a leading figure in the Czechoslovak independence movement before and during World War I. Following independence in 1918, he served as the country's foreign minister and president, but resigned and left the country after the Munich agreements of October 1938, which awarded parts of the country to Germany. He organized the Czechoslovak government in exile in London and resumed his duties as president following his return in 1945. He resigned his office in 1948, following the communist coup.

recommended that the government approach the Slovak government to dispatch an experienced Soviet general to Slovakia to coordinate and guide the actions of the troops and people.

President Benes sharply rebuked Fierlinger, demanded that he refuse assistance and declared that Soviet forces not carry out an offensive over the Carpathians.

Relying on the bourgeois circles that had grouped around Benes, the US and English ruling clique once again attempted to employ Czechoslovakia to create a "*cordon sanitaire*" against the Soviet Union.

The Soviet army, despite the resistance of the Anglo-American imperialists and the London Czechoslovak émigré government, continued to carry out its liberation mission in regard to the Czechoslovak people. The entry of Soviet forces on to Czechoslovak territory raised the broad popular movement and the leading position of the communist party in the country even higher.

Hungary. As has already been mentioned, with the establishment in Hungary of the power of the Hitlerite protégé, Szalasi, the internal situation in the country became sharply antagonistic. After 15 October the Hungarian Committee of Liberation arose, this was a bloc of different party and military groupings, with a common platform, but was not unified organizationally.

As the Soviet forces advanced, the political activism of the Hungarian people increased. The necessity arose, along with local organs of self-government, of creating a temporary national government, which was created in Debrecen on 24 December 1944, during the offensive operation.

Insofar as incidents of entire subunits of Hungarian forces, dissatisfied with the continuation of the war, surrendering had become more frequent and the relations between Hungarians and the Germans had become noticeably more antagonistic, the German command more and more often resorted to repressions and fear.

From day to day the fascist press spread false information about imaginary "Russian atrocities in Hungary" and East Prussia, etc. Alongside this, they began to station Hungarian troops between German units and to station SS subunits in the rear. These measures enabled the Hitlerite command to temporarily strengthen discipline among the Hungarian troops and to force them to engage in combat operations against the Soviet forces.

Romania. The Soviet forces' vigorous offensive foiled the plans of the Romanian reactionaries, who were counting on stretching out the conclusion of an armistice with the USSR.

The Romanian communist party played a major role in unmasking the policy of the reactionary circles and in carrying out a state coup, which led to the overthrow of the Antonescu[8] dictatorship and the break with Hitlerite Germany.

However, the absence at this moment of the broad mobilization of the popular masses enabled the Romanian bourgeoisie, with the support of the US and British governments, to retain their power in the country. The subversive activity of the Anglo-American imperialists resulted in a political crisis in the country. The reactionary bourgeoisie, which was oriented toward England and the USA, seized power. Reactionary generals and representatives of the bourgeois-landlord-rich peasants and anti-popular parties—such as Maniu's[9] National Peasants' Party and Bratianu's[10] National Liberal Party—set the tone in the Romanian government.

8 Editor's note. Ion Victor Antonescu (1882-1946) joined the Romanian army in 1904 and served in the Second Balkan War and World War I. During the interwar period he rose rapidly through the ranks and became defense minister. He early on associated himself with the Iron Guard and came to power in a 1940 coup. He aligned Romania with Nazi Germany and took his country into war against the Soviet Union. Antonescu was deposed in August 1944 and arrested. He was later tried and executed.

9 Editor's note. Iuliu Maniu (1873-1953) was a Romanian political figure and leader of the National Peasants' Party. He served as prime minister in the 1930s. He was an opponent of both Antonescu and the Romanian communists. He was tried and sentenced to life imprisonment in 1947 and died in prison.

10 Editor's note. Constantin Bratianu (1866-1950) was a Romanian politician active in the National Liberal Party. He opposed the communists' postwar seizure of power and was imprisoned, where he died.

On instructions from the ruling circles in England and the USA, Maniu gathered around himself all of the country's reactionary forces, created a network of terroristic and espionage organizations, linked to English and American representatives in the Allied Control Commission[11] in Bucharest. Through sabotage, diversions, terror, and spies Maniu sought to create a panic that would favor the outbreak of a civil war in the country for the purpose of stifling the communist party and beheading the democratic movement.

King Michael[12] and the government sabotaged the carrying out of the armistice agreement. The Romanian divisions allotted by the armistice conditions and which were part of the Second Ukrainian Front, were poorly organized, clothed and armed; the officer corps was idle and almost did not command the troops. The king and the government sought to interfere with Romania's active participation in the anti-Hitler war, delayed the dispatch of Romanian forces to the front, slowed down the return of Soviet property stolen during the occupation and the payment of reparations, hid war criminals from punishment, and interfered with the establishment of a democratic regime.

Quite the opposite, they sought to reach an agreement with the American and English imperialists to restore a military-fascist dictatorship in Romania.

The Allied Control Commission was forced to present the Romanian government with a special memorandum, calling on it to carry out the conditions of the armistice.

Thus the political situation in Romania by the end of October 1944 was extremely tense and complex. It became less tense significantly later, when the ninth blow was already completed.

Bulgaria. In Bulgaria, the arrival of Soviet forces created the necessary conditions for the liberation of the Bulgarian people from fascist occupation and the overthrow of the fascist dictatorship and the establishment of the people's power in the shape of the Fatherland Front.

On 28 October 1944 an armistice agreement was signed in Moscow. According to this agreement, Bulgaria was obligated to actively participate in the war with Germany with its armed forces under the control of the Soviet command. Simultaneously, Bulgaria undertook obligations to supply with materiel resources the Soviet forces operating on Bulgarian territory, to extirpate the remnants of fascism, and to make up for materiel damage, etc.

As was the case with Romania, the conditions of the armistice with Bulgaria, presented by the Soviet government, were distinguished by their extraordinary generosity. Bulgaria was not deprived of her state autonomy and independence. No demands for reparations were presented, insofar as she had not participated in the occupation of Soviet territory, although her factual participation in the war against the Soviet Union on the side of Hitlerite Germany inflicted no small damage to our country.

In carrying out a policy of peaceful and friendly relations with Bulgaria, the Soviet government sought to establish a true Soviet-Bulgarian friendship and to help the Bulgarian people embark on the path of a people's democracy.

The Bulgarian government conscientiously carried out the armistice conditions. Its armed forces actively took part in the struggle against the German-Fascist forces.

11 Editor's note. The Allied Control Commission in Romania was one of several established in formerly German-allied countries following their occupation by Soviet forces. The commissions consisted of representatives from the US, USSR and Great Britain, although the Soviet Union, as the actual occupying power, had the upper hand.

12 Editor's note. King Michael (1921-) was king of Romania from 1927 to 1930, when he was deposed by his father, Carol II, who had temporarily renounced the throne some years before. Antonescu removed Carol in 1940 and reinstated Michael. In August 1944 he supported the coup that removed Antonescu. He continued to reign as a figurehead under increasing communist influence and was forced to abdicate in December 1947.

The Anglo-American reactionaries resisted this and, while not recognizing Bulgaria as an allied country, demanded the withdrawal of Bulgarian forces from the territory of Greece and Yugoslavia.

Marshal Tolbukhin, guided by the instructions of the Soviet government, rejected these demands, while comrade Molotov[13] transmitted declarations in which it was stated that the Bulgarian military units were located in Yugoslavia not as occupation forces, but as allied forces, fighting against the common enemy under the command of Marshal Tolbukhin.

Greece. The communist party organized and constantly controlled the struggle with the German-Fascist aggressors. As a result of the Soviet army's successful offensive in the Balkans, the people's liberation army of Greece, led by the communist party, was able to completely liberate the country from the Hitlerite occupiers.

The Greek patriots also had to battle not only the armed forces of the German-Fascist occupiers, but also against the Greek reactionaries.

The expulsion of the Hitlerites from Greece was a very powerful blow against the forces of internal reaction, particularly against its military organization, led by the traitor to the Greek people, Colonel Zervas.[14]

By the end of October almost all of Greece had been liberated and ELAS[15] maintained solid government control in the country.

Such a situation was contrary to the Anglo-Americans' imperialist plans in the Balkans.

Upon entering into a deal with the Greek émigré government of Papandreou[16], they went over to complete intervention directed against ELAS, for the purpose of restoring a monarchist regime in Greece. This intervention was disguised as an operation to drive the Germans out of Greece.

On 4 October the English made an airborne landing in the northern part of the Peloponnesian peninsula and occupied it.

During 22-23 October the English landed on individual islands in the Aegean Sea that had been abandoned by the Germans.

On 23 October, ten days after the withdrawal of the German forces, the English landed their expeditionary forces in Athens and at the same time the Greek émigré government of Papandreou and specially formed Greek combat units, formed from monarchists, in strength up to a division.

On 29 October English forces occupied the major road and railroad junction of Kozani in northern Greece, and on 1 November the major city and port of Thessalonica.

Papandreou, on instructions from the English, demanded the dissolution and disarmament of ELAS and established a police terror in the country, while openly preparing a monarchist coup.

During 50 days the English forces fought against the Greek People's Liberation Army. The result of this armed intervention was the enslavement of Greece by the English imperialists, its

---

13 Editor's note. Vyacheslav Mikhailovich Molotov (1890-1986) joined the Bolshevik faction of the Russian revolutionary movement in 1906 and quickly rose through the ranks. He allied himself with Stalin after the civil war and aided the latter in his rise to power. Molotov was elected to the ruling Politburo in 1930 and over the years served as chairman of the Council of People's Commissars, commissar of foreign affairs and member of the wartime State Defense Committee and the *Stavka*. He fell out of favor in Stalin's later years and was removed from his offices by Nikita Khrushchev in 1957.

14 Editor's note. Napoleon Zervas (1891-1957) joined the Greek army in 1910 and fought in the Balkan Wars of 1912-13, and in World War I. He later became involved in Greek politics and took part in a coup against the government in 1926. He headed the non-communist guerillas during the Axis occupation and worked to eliminate communist influence following the German withdrawal from the country.

15 Editor's note. The ELAS, or Greek People's Liberation Army was founded in 1942 as a pro-communist guerilla force to resist the Axis occupation of Greece. It also often fought the anti-communist guerillas, a struggle that grew into the Greek civil war of 1946-49, which ended with the communists' defeat.

16 Editor's note. Georgios Papandreou (1888-1968) became involved in Greek politics before World War I until his exile by monarchist forces in 1936. He served as the country's prime minister three times during the war and postwar years.

transformation into a colony and a bridgehead for the struggle against the people's democratic states in the Balkans.

Yugoslavia. The struggle of the Yugoslav people against the German-Fascist aggressors took place in a complex situation of the Anglo-Americans' political and military intrigues directed at the national liberation movement throughout all the Balkan countries and to foiling the offensive by Soviet forces into the depths of the Balkans.

The Anglo-Americans sought to occupy Yugoslavia under the guise of "aiding" the liberation of the Adriatic coast of Serbia and Belgrade from the Germans.

But with the liberation of Belgrade by the Soviet army, the plan of the reactionary ruling circles of England and the USA, which was directed at foiling the liberation of the Yugoslav peoples from fascist bondage by the Soviet army and the occupation of Yugoslavia by Anglo-American forces, completely collapsed.

The Soviet government and the Supreme High Command of the Soviet army, while striving to establish friendly and fraternal relations with the Yugoslav people and the People's Liberation Army, sought to meet the People's Liberation Army halfway in everything and rendered it enormous assistance.

Equipment for the formation of units and formations was allotted from our stocks.

50,000 tons of grain products were allotted to help the Yugoslav population.

Aside from this, the Third Ukrainian Front's forces allotted a significant part of its foodstuffs for the Yugoslav army from its own and captured stocks.

The outstanding successes of the Soviet forces aroused alarm and concern in the reactionary circles in the USA and England, which did everything possible to interfere with the Soviet army's liberating the countries of central and southeastern Europe, to deprive them of the opportunity to set out on the path of democracy and the creation of independent and democratic states and to transform these countries into colonies of American-English capital (Mikolajczyk[17], Benes, Antonescu, etc.).

By means of realizing the Balkan variant of the Churchill plan for an invasion through the Balkans and the creation of a "Balkan Federation," the Anglo-American imperialists sought to strengthen their position in the Balkans and to secure for themselves military-strategic positions leading to the direct approaches to the Soviet Union.

However, not disposing of their own armed forces in the Balkans, the US and English ruling clique sought to employ other means (political and economic pressure, dispatch of spies and the mobilization of reactionary forces in the countries liberated by the Soviet army, etc.) in order to put the brakes on the successful course of the Soviet forces' operations in the Balkans, to prevent the establishment of democratic freedoms and to undermine the faith of the peoples liberated by the Soviet army in the policy of the Soviet Union.

Given the overall favorable political situation, as was noted above, the Soviet government and the Supreme High Command, due to the machinations of the Anglo-American imperialist in the Balkans, had to reveal in a timely way not only the plans of the Hitlerite command, but also those of all the reactionary forces led by the reactionary Anglo-American circles and to render them harmless. This brought about additional difficulties and the expenditure of men and materiel.

17 Editor's note. Stanislaw Mikolajczyk (1901-66) joined the Polish army in 1920 and fought in the brief war with the Soviet Union. He later became active in the Polish People's Party and opposed the authoritarian interwar regime. Following the German invasion in 1939, he escaped to the West and became a high-ranking member of the Polish government in exile, based in London. Mikolajczyk participate in a postwar coalition government with the communists, but fled again after the falsified elections of 1947.

Thus the political and strategic situation preceding the Budapest operation was, on the whole, favorable and guaranteed the successful completion of the strategic operation to remove Hungary from the war on the side of fascist Germany.

Our forces, having defeated the northern strategic wing of the German-Fascist forces and one of the enemy's most important groups of forces in Belorussia and inflicted irreparable harm to it and reached the Vistula and the Neman, liberated a significant part of allied Poland and entered the confines of Germany itself through East Prussia.

In East Prussia and along the Vistula, our forces were preparing to carry out major strategic operations with the following forces: First Baltic, Third, Second and First Belorussian, and the First Ukrainian fronts.

Along the southern wing of the Soviet-German front the forces of the Fourth Ukrainian Front, having completed the Carpathian-Uzhgorod operation, the Second Ukrainian Front the Debrecen operation, and the Third Ukrainian Front the Belgrade operation, occupied a favorable operational position for defeating the enemy's Budapest group of forces and liberating the city of Budapest.

The Supreme High Command of the Soviet army, while taking into account features of the developing military-political situation along the southern wing of the Soviet-German front (signs of a political crisis in Hungary and the relatively weak covering of the Budapest direction) made the decision to set about, without an operational pause, conducting the Budapest operation.

The general plan of the *Stavka* of the Supreme High Command called for the launching of two enveloping attacks by the main forces of the Second and Third Ukrainian fronts to encircle and destroy the enemy's Budapest group of forces and to take Hungary out of the war on the side of fascist Germany.

It was planned to launch supporting attacks by part of the Second Ukrainian Front's forces on Miskolc and by the Third Ukrainian Front on Nagykanizsa.

Proceeding from this plan, the *fronts* were assigned the following tasks:

The Second Ukrainian Front was to defeat the enemy in the area between the Tisza and the Danube. The main attack was to be launched by the forces of the 46th Army and the 2nd Guards Mechanized Corps, with the object of rolling up the enemy's defense along the western bank of the Tisza River and assisting the arrival of the 7th Guards Army to its right bank. Subsequently, with the arrival of the 4th Guards Mechanized Corps, it was to attack the enemy group defending Budapest.

The Third Ukrainian Front was to force the Danube River and seize a bridgehead along its western bank. While developing the offensive from the bridgehead, it was to outflank Budapest from the west and, in conjunction with the Second Ukrainian Front's forces, encircle and destroy the enemy's Budapest group of forces.

During the first stage of the operation, measures had already been taken to strengthen the forces of the Second and Third Ukrainian fronts, which were operating along the Budapest direction and to create the Third Ukrainian Front's shock group in the Sombor area.

Upon completion of the Belgrade operation, the 4th Guards Mechanized Corps was transferred from the Third to the Second Ukrainian Front to reinforce the 46th Army.

The 4th Guards Army (eight rifle divisions), which had begun to concentrate in the Banat area of Yugoslavia, was transferred to the Third Ukrainian Front from the *Stavka* of the Supreme High Command reserve. The *front's* 57th Army was to be reinforced by the transfer of the 6th Rifle Corps from the 37th Army.

The favorable operational situation would enable us to carry out an offensive along the Budapest direction, without waiting for the complete concentration of major forces, rather to augment the force of the attack during the operation, thus achieving the assigned strategic goal.

The forces of the Second Ukrainian Front operating here were superior to the enemy facing them by 1½ in infantry and nearly twice in artillery and tanks.

However, a serious barrier for the development of the main forces' offensive along the Budapest direction was the Tisza River, relying on which the enemy counted on holding our forces and preventing their arrival at Budapest.

Such was the overall strategic situation which had developed before the conduct of the Budapest operation.

11

The Operational Situation in the Third Ukrainian Front's Sector Along the Budapest Direction by the end of October 1944

The forces of the Fourth, Second and Third Ukrainian fronts, as a result of the offensive operations conducted in September and October, had defeated the enemy's flank groups of forces in the areas of northern Transylvania and Belgrade and reached the middle Danube lowlands and created favorable conditions for a subsequent offensive along the Budapest—Vienna strategic direction.

The Third Ukrainian Front's forces, while pursuing the enemy, crossed the Sava River and by the end of October reached the Ruma area, 60 kilometers northwest of Belgrade.

Yugoslav forces, supported by Soviet troops, developed the offensive to the west of Belgrade and by the end of October had thrown the remnants of the German-Fascist troops to the line of the Drina River, 100 kilometers west of Belgrade.

Bulgarian forces, in carrying out the instructions of the Third Ukrainian Front's commander, continued to attack toward Mitrovica and Pristina.

The *Stavka* of the Supreme High Command, in its directive no. 82118 of 15 October 1944, assigned the Third Ukrainian Front's forces the following task: following the capture of Belgrade, to consolidate along the line west of Belgrade—Batocina—Paracin—Knjazevac and to advance no further into the depths of Yugoslavia.

These instructions flowed from the idea of the *Stavka* of the Supreme High Command, following the completion of the Belgrade offensive operation, to employ the Third Ukrainian Front's main forces along the left bank of the Danube—along the Budapest direction, in conjunction with the Second Ukrainian Front's forces.

Somewhat later (18 October 1944) the *Stavka* of the Supreme High Command demanded of the commander of the Third Ukrainian Front, following the completion of the Belgrade offensive operation, that he prepare a new offensive operation, also in conjunction with the Second Ukrainian Front's forces, to defeat the enemy's Budapest group of forces.

In order to carry out the new offensive operation, one combined-arms army (4th Guards Army, eight rifle divisions) was to be transferred from the *Stavka* reserve to the Third Ukrainian Front, and the 18th Tank Corps and a cavalry-mechanized group from the Second Ukrainian Front.

At first, this directive called for the movement of only one rifle corps to the northern bank of the Danube River to the Sombor—Novi Sad sector, for the purpose of covering the left flank of the Second Ukrainian Front's forces. The *front* commander later received additional instructions to regroup all of the 57th Army's forces and units subordinated to the *front* to the area Petrovgrad—Pancevo—Omaljica—Mramorak—Alibunar—Doblica. The *front* was ordered to keep individual battalions and artillery along the former line for covering the movement of troops in the Obrenovac, Lazarevac, Cacak, Kraljevo, and Krusevac areas.

The breakthrough by the Second Ukrainian Front's left-wing forces of the enemy's defensive line along the Tisza River and their arrival along the Danube created favorable prerequisites for a successful offensive along the Budapest direction and for castling the Third Ukrainian Front's main forces to the northern bank of the Danube.

The Third Ukrainian Front consisted of three combined-arms armies (57th, 37th and 4th Guards), one air army (17th), the Danube Military Flotilla, a fortified area (1st Guards Fortified Area), and three Bulgarian armies (1st, 2nd and 3rd) operationally subordinated along the following front: Blace—west of Kurshumli—east of Podujevo—Orljane—Hajkobilla—east of Bujanovci—Kumanovo—west of Kocana—northeast of Radoviste—along the Strumica River—east of Novo Selo.

The 37th Army remained deployed in Bulgaria in the Sliven—Stara Zagora—Burgas area.

The 4th Guards Army (eight rifle divisions) was to be moved by rail from the Slutska area and was to concentrate by the end of November in the Krajova area, which was later changed to the Timisoara area.

Thus by the end of October the Third Ukrainian Front actually disposed of only one combined-arms army (57th) for carrying out combat activities along the new axis. The *front* was reinforced with the following formations and units: a breakthrough artillery division, three anti-tank artillery brigades, one howitzer brigade, one mortar brigade, three anti-aircraft divisions, two independent anti-tank artillery regiments from the High Command Reserve, two howitzer regiments from the High Command Reserve, one artillery regiment from the High Command Reserve, an independent mechanized brigade, four self-propelled artillery regiments, a battalion of amphibious motor vehicles, a motorcycle regiment, a motorized engineer brigade from the High Command Reserve, a flamethrower battalion, and a chemical defense battalion. It was with these forces that the *front* initially set about conducting an operation to force the Danube River and defeat the enemy's Danube group of forces.

The forces of the Yugoslav People's Liberation Army were scattered over an enormous territory in their country in individual formations and units, while fighting with the German troops. Only a few individual brigades, which had the mission of reaching the line Ilok—Sid—Adasovci—Sremska Raca—Bielina—Studena—Loznica, were operating directly with the Third Ukrainian Front's forces. Up to six of the 57th Army's artillery regiments were supporting the operations of the Yugoslav forces.

The training and armament of the Yugoslav units was at a low level, and thus they were unable to offer any kind of material assistance to the Third Ukrainian Front's forces. Suffice it to say that of the Yugoslav army's 30 army corps, only three weak and poorly armed army corps, as well as a few brigades, were fighting in conjunction with the Third Ukrainian Front's forces. This circumstance forced the *Stavka* of the Supreme High Command to issue instructions to leave part of the 57th Army's forces (68th Rifle Corps and the 1st Guards Fortified Area) behind for securing the *front's* left wing.

By 29 October 1944 the Third Ukrainian Front's forces occupied a sector more than 300 kilometers wide with one army. Within this sector the overall amount of combat equipment reached 2,154 guns of various calibers, 99 tanks and self-propelled guns and 1,293 planes.

The operational density was 25-30 kilometers per division.

Upon receiving the directive from the *Stavka* of the Supreme High Command, the commander of the Third Ukrainian Front ordered the commander of the 57th Army to regroup one rifle corps (75th) to the Sombor area. Having begun the crossing over to the northern bank of the Danube on 19 October, as early as 24 October the corps had completed the crossing of three rifle divisions and reinforcement units, and on 26 October had taken up defensive positions along the Danube River along the front Sombor—Backa Palanka—Novi Sad, with the task of securing the Second Ukrainian Front's left wing and reliably covering the routes leading to the Danube from the west and south. By this time the neighbor on the right—the Second Ukrainian Front's 31st Guards Rifle Corps, had reached the Danube along the sector Mohacs—Baja.

A new boundary line was established between the Second and Third Ukrainian fronts: Vrsac—Novi Becej—Sombor, with these locales for the Third Ukrainian Front.

By the start of the Budapest operation the situation of the Third Ukrainian Front's forces was as follows (by 29 October 1944):

The *front's* headquarters was in Petrich (Bulgaria) and had the task of relocating to Vrsac by 5 November; the 57th Army's headquarters was in Belgrade, and the headquarters of the 17th Air Army was southwest of Sofia.

The 57th Army (75th, 64th and 68th rifle corps and the 1st Guards Fortified Area) continued to regroup and cross the Danube River into new area, while part of its forces were to remain along their previous lines. The army was to assist the Yugoslav and Bulgarian forces' offensive by artillery fire and air strikes.

As has been noted, the 75th Rifle Corps (74th, 299th and 233rd rifle divisions) occupied defensive positions with two divisions along the left bank of the Danube along the sector excluding Baja—Novi Sad; one division was in the second echelon in the Odzaci—Deronye—Parabuc area.

The 64th Rifle Corps (19th, 236th and 73rd Guards rifle divisions) was fighting along the line: Hrtkovci—Klenak—Kupinovo—Progar (73rd Guards Rifle Division); Obrenovac—then down the right bank of the Kolubara River—Lazarevac—Arandjelovac (19th Rifle Division). One of the corps' divisions (236th Rifle Division) had reached the Stara Pazova—Vojka—Nova Pazova area with its main forces. The corps had the task, upon leaving a covering force along its present lines, by 31 October to concentrate at the following crossings: Belgrade, Grocka, Dubrovica, and Surduk.

The 68th Rifle Corps (52nd, 93rd and 233rd rifle divisions) occupied the line west of Topola—Gornji Milanovac—Prielina (93rd Rifle Division); Ladevci—Vitkovac—Vrbas (223rd Rifle Division).

The corps' units were engaged in offensive fighting along the route to Cacak and Kraljevo, together with Yugoslav forces. One of the corps' divisions (52nd) was on the march in the Mladenovac area.

The 1st Guards Fortified Area had reached the line Ledinci—Vrdnik—Prnjavor—Sasinci—Jarak.

The army's anti-aircraft group (606th, 253rd, 1335th, 1341st, 1147th, 1118th, 1084th, 1114th, 1089th, and the 71st anti-aircraft regiments) was covering the troops' crossing near Grocka, Belgrade, Novi Becej, and Titel.

The army's artillery reserve (7th Independent Anti-Tank Artillery Brigade—417th, 418th and 419th anti-tank artillery regiments), (49th Anti-Tank Artillery Brigade—184th, 1008th and 1249th anti-tank artillery regiments), (42nd Anti-Tank Artillery Brigade—1961st, 1962nd and 1963rd anti-tank artillery regiments), (23rd Howitzer Brigade—1201st, 1202nd, 1891st, and 266th self-propelled artillery regiments), and the 58th Guards Mortar Regiment (20th Guards Mortar Brigade) received orders to concentrate in the Sombor, Bezdan and Apatin areas and was moving toward the crossings.

The following were located in the reserve of the commander of the 57th Army: one rifle division (113th), which was located by regiment in the Durinci, Vlaska and Mladenovac areas, the 5th Motorized Rifle Brigade (later the 32nd Motorized Rifle Brigade), with the 53rd Motorcycle Regiment, and a battalion of amphibious motor vehicles in the Belgrade area. The engineer troops (5th Pontoon Brigade and the 65th Engineer-Sapper Brigade) were working along the routes to and the crossings over the Danube.

Chemical troops: the 23rd Flamethrower Battalion was operationally subordinated to the commander of the 68th Rifle Corps in the area north of Cacak; the 5th Independent Flamethrower

Battalion was at the disposal of the commander of the 64th Rifle Corps guarding the bridge over the Sava River west of Belgrade; the 15th Independent Chemical Defense Battalion was along the southern outskirts of Belgrade.

The 17th Air Army consisted of the following units: 10th Assault Air Corps (30th and 136th assault air divisions and the 295th Fighter Division); two fighter divisions (288th and 194th), one assault air (189th), one bomber (244th Bomber Division) and one night bomber (262nd Night Bomber Division) divisions. Aside from this, the 17th Air Army also included an operational group consisting of the 10th Assault Air and 236th Fighter divisions.

In all, the air army numbered 1,293 planes, of which 421 were fighters, 382 assault aircraft, 130 night bombers, 116 day bombers, and 44 reconnaissance and artillery correction planes.

The 17th Air Army had the task of covering the regrouping of the *front's* forces from the air and supporting the offensive operations of the 57th Army and the Yugoslav and Bulgarian forces.

The 15th Bomber Division from Long-Range Aviation continued to operate in the interests of the Second and Third Ukrainian fronts' forces, mainly to interfere with the enemy's railroad shipments.

The American 15th Air Force continued to operate against the territory of Czechoslovakia, Hungary and Austria.

The Danube Flotilla (the Kerch' Brigade of river vessels, consisting of one battalion of monitors, four ships and two battalions of armored cutters, or 35 pennants); the Sulina Brigade of river ships, consisting of a battalion of monitors—three ships—and two battalions of armored cutters, or 32 pennants; a minesweeping brigade of 38 pennants, two high-speed landing barges and four landing boats facilitated the offensive operations of the *front's* forces through making tactical landings, with ship artillery fire and by carrying out operational deliveries, patrolled west of Novi Sad and continued to sweep the Danube's channel of mines.

Because of the increase of the number of combat vessels in the flotilla due to the capture of enemy vessels, the organizational structure of the flotilla was somewhat changed by 30 October 1944, while it also underwent qualitative and quantitative strengthening.

Thus the operational situation of the Third Ukrainian Front's forces following the completion of the Belgrade offensive operation was characterized by the 57th Army's significant lengthening and dispersal over an enormous area.

The complexity of the operational situation was exacerbated by the fact that alongside combat activities along the occupied lines, it was also necessary to prepare a new offensive operation involving a regrouping of the *front's* main forces, against a background of washed-out roads, a limited number of paved roads and the dirt roads' unfitness, to a new axis while crossing over powerful water obstacles, such as the Danube and Tisza, in conditions of a limited amount of crossing equipment. Simultaneously with the crossing, it was necessary to organize the command and rear organs along the new axis and to prepare a jumping-off position and concentration areas for the *front's* forces.

The 4th Guards Army, which was to be subordinated to the *front*, was to complete its concentration in the Timisoara area by 26-27 November, while the cavalry-mechanized group (5th Guards Cavalry and 7th Mechanized corps) was supposed to arrive by this time.

The 18th Tank Corps was supposed to arrive on 4-5 November, but it required significant refitting, both in personnel and in combat equipment. Thus combat operations along the Budapest direction in could at first only be undertaken in November by the forces of the 57th Army and *front* reinforcements.

In the present case, we see an example of how during the course of one offensive operation, at its concluding stage, the *Stavka* of the Supreme High Command rapidly created a powerful group of forces along a new axis, which achieved operational surprise and the development of a strategic offensive operation without an operational pause.

12

The Enemy's Plan: An Operational–Tactical Description of the Enemy's Group of Forces Along the Third Ukrainian Front's Operational Sector

As a result of the Belgrade operation, the remnants of the defeated enemy had been thrown back to the west and southwest of Belgrade and were attempting to consolidate along non-contiguous and hurriedly occupied lines along the Danube River along the line Cerevic-Mitrovica—then along the Drina River—Cacak—Kraljevo—then along the Ibar River—west of Kurshumli—east of Pristina—the Moravica River—Kumanovo—west of Kocan—Stip—the Strumica River—Novo Selo—Rodopolis—then along the Struma River.

The enemy's overall plan consisted of halting the offensive by the Second and Third Ukrainian fronts with a solid defense along the main axes, combined with powerful counterblows, and to prevent them front entering the depth of Hungary and Yugoslavia. The plan called for holding actions against the People's Liberation Army of Yugoslavia and the Bulgarian forces, for the purpose of removing Army Group E's forces from Greece and Yugoslavia to the northwest and the Budapest direction.

Formations and units of Army Group F, consisting of groups "Serbia" and "E" (Group E's main forces were marching to the northwest) continued to operate along the Third Ukrainian Front's sector and that of the People's Liberation Army of Yugoslavia and Bulgarian forces.

According to data by the Soviet army's intelligence directorate, by the start of the operation the overall group of German-Fascist forces numbered 200,000 men, 12,000 machine guns, 2,000 guns, 1,800 mortars, and 80 tanks.

In all, there were 17 divisions operating in the Third Ukrainian Front's sector, of which nine were infantry and three were mountain-infantry, which had been badly handled in the preceding fighting, one *Luftwaffe* field division, one fortress division, and three motorized divisions, three fortress brigades, two security regiments, and four independent fortress battalions.

Aside from these forces there were the following: a Russian security corps, consisting of four regiments and one cavalry division; up to 15 divisions of reactionary Yugoslav forces (Croatian and Ustase[1]) and several independent brigades.

As a result of the Belgrade operation, aside from the fact that three divisions and a number of independent units and subunits were destroyed, a defeat was also inflicted on the 7th SS Mountain Division "Prince Eugen," four independent regiments (a regiment from the "Brandenburg" Division, a Russian security regiment, a regiment from the 297th Infantry Division, and a police

1 Editor's note. The Ustase were members of the Croatian Revolutionary Movement, active since the early 1930s. They helped assassinate King Alexander I of Yugoslavia in 1934. Following the German invasion of Yugoslavia in 1941, they organized an independent Croatian state under German and Italian protection. The Ustase were notorious for their atrocities directed at Serbs, Jews and Gypsies.

regiment), and three independent battalions. The remaining forces operating in the first line also suffered heavy losses. As a result, the mobility and shock power of the enemy's first-line divisions dropped considerably.

In all, the enemy had up to ten divisions in the first line and in reserve in the operational depth—seven German divisions in the following areas: the 392nd Infantry Division in the Jezerane—Zuta-Lokva area; 373rd Infantry Division in Bihac; 264th Infantry Division in Drnis; 369th Infantry Division in Blagaj; 118th Light Infantry Division (minus one infantry regiment) in Ljubuski; 297th Infantry Division in Skoder, and; the 181st Infantry Division east of Skoder. The defense's operational density was 700:10, or 65-70 kilometers per division.

The defense was organized along individual axes according to the principle of creating strong points and centers of resistance in paved road, dirt road and railroad junctions, as well as in major inhabited locales and towns. Spaces between units were secured by fire or observation, and along the sector along the Drina River as far as Cacak, which was more than 120 kilometers, there were no enemy troops at all.

The enemy forces along the western bank of the Danube, with an overall strength of up to two divisions, occupied defensive positions along the sector from Baja to the Drava River, having only one position along the river's bank and inhabited locales in the depth that had been configured for defense.

The remnants of the German operational group *Sudost*, air force groups "Croatia," "Albania" and "Crete," with an overall strength of 130 combat aircraft, which were covering the German-Fascist troops' regrouping from Greece and Yugoslavia to the north, continued to move in the Balkans, in the eastern part of the Mediterranean Sea and in Yugoslavia.

The enemy aviation was based in the Sarajevo—Mitrovica—Pristina—Skopje area, usually at airfields near the main railroads and highways. The main types of planes, the Ju-87[2], Ju-88, He-111, and Hs-126[3], were out of date and only an insignificant part was represented by modernized types of fighter aircraft, such as the Me-109 and Fw-190.[4]

The Third Ukrainian Front only had a superiority of force in the air, infantry and artillery, while a superiority in tanks remained with the enemy.

The enemy's defense may be described as defense along a broad front, with powerful reserves in the depth (which were regrouping to new axes), which included well-outfitted and well-trained German cadre divisions.

The presence of large forces in the hands of the Hitlerite command and scattered over an enormous space, spoke to the fact that:

- first of all, the German command did not have a definite plan of operations during this period;
- second of all, a large number of non-German divisions were located in the rear, designated for fighting the Yugoslav partisans (the Yugoslav People's Liberation Army), including units of the Russian security corps;
- third, the fear of an Anglo-American landing forced the Germans to hold seven German, four Croatian and Ustase divisions near the shore of the Adriatic Sea and nearby.

2 Editor's note. The Ju-87, popularly known as the "Stuka" was a two-seat German dive bomber that played a major role in the early years of the Second World War. One model had a maximum speed of 390 kilometers per hour and was armed with three 7.92mm machine guns and could carry a bomb load of 450 kilograms.

3 Editor's note. The Hs-126 was a two-seat German reconnaissance aircraft. One model had a maximum speed of 356 kilometers per hour and was armed with two 7.92mm machine guns and could carry up to 150 kilograms of bombs.

4 Editor's note. The Fw-190 was a single-engine German fighter aircraft that entered service in 1941. One model carried a pilot and had a top speed of 656 kilometers per hour. It was armed with two 13mm machine guns and four 20mm cannons.

If in the present situation the *Stavka* of the VGK was boldly moving toward a justifiable risk—the regrouping of the Third Ukrainian Front's main forces (simultaneously reinforcing it with new formations for conducting a new strategic operation with a decisive goal), then at the same time the German command, while disposing of large forces, exhibited complete confusion and was late in creating a powerful defensive line along the Danube River and with withdrawing its forces from Yugoslavia to the Budapest direction. The enemy, having lost his most important communications for transferring his forces, which ran along the Morava River, was forced to attempt to transfer forces from the south partially along dirt roads through Skopje, Mitrovica, Kraljevo, Cacak, and Uzice and then to Sarajevo and to the northwest, under constant attack by Yugoslav forces, as a result of which, despite the hurried transfer of forces by all transportation means, all the way up to transport aviation, the withdrawal of the German-Fascist troops from Greece and the southern part of Yugoslavia became even more prolonged and by 28 October a significant part of army group E's forces nevertheless remained in the southeastern part of Yugoslavia. This explains why the Budapest direction was the most weakly covered and why a defense along a broad front along the Danube River was being hurriedly prepared by scratch subunits and units, primarily from the Third Hungarian Army.

It is necessary to note that the headquarters of the Third Ukrainian Front quite correctly evaluated the opposing enemy. All of the German first-line divisions, with a small exception, had been precisely established and the headquarters of the 57th Army and the *front* knew their strength with sufficient accuracy. The immediate and deeper operational reserves were also known to us.

Mistakes by the *front's* intelligence section mainly consisted of the fact that it mistook individual regiments from this or that division for the entire division. For example, according to the intelligence section's data, the 264th Infantry and 118th Light Infantry divisions were defending along the front Ilok—Mitrovica, while in reality these divisions' main forces were located along the shore of the Adriatic Sea. One can say the same thing about the 297th Infantry Division, which according to the *front* intelligence section's data, was fighting along the line Cacak—Kraljevo, when its main forces were actually concentrated in Skoder.

The presence of the 173rd Reserve Division, which is not mentioned in captured German documents, was also indicated.

13

An Operational–Tactical Description and Evaluation of the Terrain and the Enemy's Defense in the Sector of the Third Ukrainian Front's Forthcoming Offensive

The combat activities of the Third Ukrainian Front's forces, beginning from November 1944, unfolded along a broad territory, chiefly limited from the north by the Danube River and from the south by the Sava River, had a straight-line length of 260-270 kilometers from southeast to northwest.

This zone embraced the northern areas of Yugoslavia and the southern and central areas of Hungary, including the capital of Budapest and the following major cities: Esztergom, Bicske, Szekesfehervar, Dunafoldvar, Pecs, Szekszard, Mohacs, Kaposvar, Nagykanizsa, Vukovar, Osijek, and others.

The operational significance of this strip of terrain was determined by the fact that it was here that the shortest routes to the oil-extraction area of Hungary ran and that the forces of the Third Ukrainian Front, which were operating to the northwest, had cut the Budapest group of forces' main communications and had created conditions for its encirclement from the west.

This entire territory represented the so-called central Danubian lowlands, which, according to the nature of the terrain, may be divided into the trans-Danube plain, the central Hungarian mountains and the small Hungarian lowland.

The Nagykanizsa Operational Direction

The trans-Danube plain stretches south of Lake Balaton, occupying the area between the Danube and the Drava.

A low-lying and undulating plateau is the primary relief feature.

In the southern part of the plain there arise something akin to islands—the isolated, low-lying Mecsek and Harsan ridges, which are split by broad and deep gullies.

The plain is cut by an entire series of north-south running valleys, parallel to each other. The terrain is mostly without trees, while fields predominate. However, small oak groves are encountered along this territory, mostly on the tops of hills. The majority of roads are planted with trees. The majority of them run north to south.

The northeastern part of the trans-Danube plain represents a flat plain, accessible for all combat arms. The only obstacle is the numerous small rivers and canals.

Troop maneuver is made more difficult by Lake Balaton and the Drava River, as well as the Danube River.

The Szekesfehervar Operational Direction

The central Hungarian mountains represent a broken chain of separate plateaus and low-lying ridges, stretching from the northeast to the southwest. All of the ridges are easily overcome and may be even more easily bypassed along the low-lying areas and valleys separating them.

The Pilis (Visegrad) Mountains stretch in a group of parallel ridges, 20-30 kilometers in length, along the right bank of the Danube River in the Esztergom—Budapest area and form the Visegrad Gorge. These mountains are not high, with their highest peaks at 750 meters, but steep, sharply separated and formed by volcanic rocks.

The Vertes Hegyseg Mountains stretch from Szekesfehervar and Gyor to the Danube River and represent ridges of flat and dome-shaped lime hills up to 630 meters high, while their slopes are sharply divided by deep and narrow ravines. The mountains are easily traversed along the existing valleys.

The Bakony Forest Hills consist of sloping plateaus and low-lying ridges, with peaks of 400-500 meters, although individual heights reach 700 meters. Their slopes are usually gently sloping, although in places they are replaced by steep terraces.

The most defined terrace stretches along Lake Balaton. The mountains are easily traversed, while the broad valleys make for convenient passages in places.

The central Hungarian mountains are mostly covered in oak forests.

The small Hungarian lowland is cut by the Danube River and is separated from the trans-Danube plain by the central Hungarian mountains. The lowland stretches up to 150 kilometers from east to west and represents an undulating plain with its highest peaks 110-120 meters.

The Hungarian right bank is cut by a comparatively thick network of small rivers, creeks and canals. The majority of rivers in the small Hungarian lowland and the southern part of the trans-Danube plain flow through plains and have small and swampy flood plains.

In the northeastern part of the trans-Danube plain the rivers' flood plains are broader and quite swampy, while the majority of the rivers and canals are confined in their banks. Besides this, there are a large number of small land reclamation canals in this part of the plain, which represent an obstacle for tanks.

For the characteristics of the Danube and Drava rivers and lakes Balaton and Velence, see the physical-geographical description.

The Sarviz Canal was formed from a river of the same name, with a width of 15-35 meters, a depth of 2-4 meters and banks 1.5-2 meters high. The soil of the bottom is hard, sandy and made of clay.

The Jelusa Canal was formed from the Sio River. The banks have collapsed. The canal is 15-35 meters wide, with a depth of 2-5 meters, with the banks 2-6 meters high. The bottom is sandy and clayey.

The Val Canal runs through a well cultivated valley one kilometer wide cut by canals with a depth of 0.3-0.5 meters and up to one meter wide. The average width of the canal is 12 meters, with a depth of 2-3 meters, with a bank of 1-1.5 meters. There are bridge crossings near every inhabited locale.

The Laszlo Canal has an average width of ten meters and a depth of 2.5 meters. The height of the bank is one meter high. The bottom is sandy.

During heavy snowfall and also following frequent rains and rainstorms, the Val and Laszlo canals cannot handle the water entering them, as a result of which these canals' flood plains become so inundated that passage along the roads through the flood plain becomes difficult and, in places, impossible.

There was a well developed network of railroads in the Third Ukrainian Front's area of combat operations, which demanded the restoration of and increase of their capacity.

On the whole, the existing railroads secured the maneuver of the troops and their supply. The most important of these were:

Communications: Timisoara—Subotica—Baja—Kaposvar—Vrsac—Petrovgrad—Sombor—Pecs—Belgrade—Sid; lateral railroads: Arad—Vrsac—Szeged—Belgrade—Subotica—Novi Sad—Baja—Backa Palanka; Budapest—Szekszard—Donji-Miholjac; Budapest—Szekesfehervar—Kaposvar—Barc; Szekesfehervar—Nagykanizsa.

The network of paved and dirt roads is also widely developed, with up to 100 kilometers of roads per 100 square kilometers of territory. However, the usage of the thick network of dirt roads during the snowmelt and rains sharply is sharply limited by the complete dominance of loess soils, which form a sticky mud and deep ruts.

The most important and well-built dirt roads are:

a) Budapest—Sekesfehervar—Nagykanizsa, and then to Zagreb, in front of Lake Balaton. The road is branched. Both roads hugging the lake from the north and south are of equal quality.
b) Szkesfehervar—Veszprem, which is the second most important road after the Budapest—Vienna highway, which connects central Europe with the area of the middle Danube.

Thus in the majority of cases the terrain conditions in the Third Ukrainian Front's offensive sector, with the exception of certain areas, allowed for maneuver by major troop bodies and the conduct of operations at high speeds.

The German-Fascist command, while taking into account the developing situation and the importance of the operational directions toward Nagykanizsa, and in particular toward Szekesfehervar and Bicske, attached particular significance to the creation of firm defensive lines along these directions (along the western bank of the Danube River, the southwestern bank of the Danube River, southwest of Budapest in the direction of Lake Velence, in the area between lakes Velence and Balaton, and along the sector between Lake Balaton and the Drava River).

The most intensive defensive works began from the second half of October, when the Hungarian fascist Szalasi was placed in power by the Hitlerite command. The work was carried out by sapper units, the local population and special commands consisting of arrestees and prisoners of war.

The Enemy's Defense Along the Right Bank of the Danube River. Along the entire river an almost continuous trench had been dug, which had been configured for defense (for every 100 meters of trenches along the front there were 8-10 foxholes and 2-3 machine gun emplacements, while rifle trenches, 60-70 meters long, had been dug in places, with forward rifle foxholes of 6-7 apiece and 2-3 machine guns emplacements per trench). There was a small number of small wooden and earth pillboxes, with a covering of 2-3 boards and a flat wooden roofing of two rows of logs and a layer of dirt.

The defense of the bank of the Danube River mostly had an insignificant depth, with places and areas of likely crossings and major inhabited locales the most powerfully prepared for defense. The enemy's defense was as follows along the sectors most convenient for forcing the Danube River.

Along the Batina sector. The enemy's defense was of a field type—two fully-outfitted trenches. The first line of trenches was located along the steep slopes of the Danube River's right bank. A second trench ran 400 meters from it, which was connected with the first by a developed system of fully-outfitted communications trenches. The engineer structures were open rifle trenches, machine gun emplacements and foxholes for automatic riflemen. Individual buildings along the outskirts of inhabited locales had been carefully masked. Wine cellars, which were connected with each other by communications trenches, served as covers against artillery fire. The main roads and hidden approaches to the inhabited locales were mined by the enemy in small groups of anti-tank and anti-personnel mines. High-explosive landmines had been laid along narrow sectors of paved roads.

Along the Apatin sector. This also contained a field-type defense, involving the employment of favorable terrain features. There were three trench lines. The first line ran directly along the right bank of the Danube River and consisted of individual strong points, which controlled the river and were in fire liaison with one another. The second line ran along the first dike, running from marker 89—Kazuk, and then to the south. At a distance of 50-100 meters in front of the dike there was a canal, up to ten meters wide and two meters deep. There were minefields along separate sectors in the swampy terrain in front of the dike, at a depth of 1.5-2 meters. The dike was up to four meters high and guaranteed control over the entire adjacent terrain along both sides of the Danube River. The defense along the dike took the form of a system of trenches, foxholes, communications trenches, and shelters. The dead space behind the dike was employed by the enemy for maneuvering personnel and for the safe delivery of munitions.

The third enemy defense line ran along the Knezevi—Vinogradi—Osijek highway and represented a system of individual trenches, machine gun emplacements and firing trenches, connected by communications trenches.

All of the enemy's defense was organized according to the principle of platoon strong points and centers of resistance, located along the commanding heights and inhabited locales along the right bank of the Danube River; that is, according to the principle of defense along a broad front.

In the inhabited locales located in direct proximity of the Danube River, the enemy had small garrisons, supported by mobile weapons.

The Defensive Line Along the Sector Erd—Lake Velence—Lake Balaton—Nagybajom—Drava River

This line was prepared over 2-3 months by the forces of the local population, under the leadership of German and Hungarian engineer units.

Fully-outfitted trenches were dug in 2-3 lines along the entire sector, and in 5-6 lines along some axes. Some centers of resistance were developed to a depth of 6-8 kilometers and up to 15 kilometers along the Szekesfehervar.

Trenches throughout the entire depth were linked together by communications trenches, which served at the same time as switch positions. Overhead covers accommodating 10-12 men were prepared for covering the rank and file.

Positions for the artillery and heavy infantry guns were prepared. Anti-tank ditches were dug along axes favorable for tanks. The enemy subsequently was improving the line in the engineer sense: setting up wire obstacles and minefields, while inhabited locales were prepared for permanent defense. Strong points were created in the depth of the defensive zone.

The enemy's most solid and developed defensive system was created along the sector between lakes Velence and Balaton, covering the approaches to the important communications center and major strong point of Szekesfehervar. The first defensive line along this sector was supplemented by two rings of defensive lines along the approaches to the city.

The enemy did not have time to create permanent structures, although their construction had already begun.

The construction of a rear defensive line was going on in the depth of the enemy's defense along the line Budakeszi—Bicske—Vertes Mountains—Sarkeresztes—Berhida, but this line had not been completely prepared by the start of our forces' offensive.

Thus the third Ukrainian Front's forces had to force the powerful water barrier of the Danube River and, while developing the success, break through the enemy's previously prepared field-type defense from 5-8 kilometers deep, and up to 15 kilometers in the Szekesfehervar area.

Along the Nagykanizsa axis the enemy, taking advantage of the tactically favorable terrain, had prepared a line between Lake Balaton and the Drava River, along the line Lake Balaton—Gerde—Marcali—Nagybajom—Nagyatad—west of Babocsa—Drava River.

The enemy's defensive line chiefly consisted of individual rifle trenches, fully-outfitted trenches and open machine guns emplacements, not connected with each other by communications trenches. In the Kethely and Marcali areas the trenches were linked by communications trenches.

The major inhabited locale of Nagybajom had been configured for a perimeter defense and represented a center of resistance. Wire obstacles in 1-2 series of spirals had been set up along some sectors.

A second defensive line was being prepared for a long time along this axis by the local population along the line western shore of Lake Balaton—east of Kiskomarom—Iharosbereny—Csurgo—Gyekenyes station, and then along the northern bank of the Drava River.

This line's defensive structures consisted of trenches and foxholes, connected with each other by communications trenches. There were wire obstacles and anti-tank ditches along some sectors.

Of all of the defensive lines described here, only the right bank of the Danube River and the Budapest area had been occupied by the enemy's field troops.

As has been mentioned, major operational reserves were on their way from Italy, Albania and Yugoslavia.

This organization of the enemy's defense enabled our forces, following the successful forcing of the Danube River and the defeat of the defending enemy forces, to broaden the bridgehead and, having concentrated major forces there, to develop the attack in depth. Then, while successively defeating the enemy's arriving operational reserves and following a short preparation, to break through the prepared line and launch an attack on Budapest from the west.

In accordance with the *front's* assignment, the nature of the enemy's defense and the terrain conditions in the sector of the Third Ukrainian Front's forthcoming offensive, the following operational directions were noted:

The Szekesfehervar operational direction was the main direction up to the capture of the city of Szekesfehervar and Buda. The most intensive and decisive fighting unfolded along this direction.

This direction would lead the *front's* main group of forces along the shortest and best routes to the area west of Buda, for the purpose of encircling the enemy's Budapest group of forces. With our forces' arrival west of Buda, conditions would be created for the development of the attack along the Vienna strategic direction, as well as the opportunity for striking the enemy's forces covering Nagykanizsa in the flank and rear.

The length of the operational direction from southeast to northwest was 150 kilometers.

Our troops acting along this operational direction would have to force the Danube River and defeat the enemy's forces along its western bank and inflict a defeat on the arriving enemy reserves. They would then have to break through the prepared "Margarita Line," after which, while pursuing the enemy, reach the Danube River and encircle and destroy the Budapest group of forces.

The secondary Nagykanizsa dirction. The troops' operations along this direction were supposed to tie down significant enemy forces arriving from Yugoslavia, to prevent them from reaching the Budapest direction and thus create more favorable conditions for our forces active along the Szekesfehervar operational direction. The *front's* forces along this direction had to overcome the enemy's defense and, first of all, force the Danube River and defeat the enemy's Danube group of forces.

Thus by the time it received new orders, the Third Ukrainian Front's operational situation was complex and required a great deal of organizational work, particularly in creating a shock group of forces along a new operational direction.

The troops' regrouping was to take place in conditions of the fall rains and lack of roads, while crossing such major water barriers as the Tisza and Danube rivers. Simultaneously, it was necessary to fight along previous axes and transfer a significant number of formations over long distances.

This, on the whole, was the situation that had arisen by the close of October 1944.

14

The Third Ukrainian Front's Preparation for the Budapest Operation

The preparation for the operation actually began from the moment the directive by the *Stavka* of the Supreme High Command (no. 82798, of 18 October 1944) was received; that is, during the Belgrade offensive operation, at its concluding stage.

This directive, as has already been noted, required us to move one rifle corps to the northern bank of the Danube along the Sombor—Novi Sad sector, for the purpose of covering the left flank of the Second Ukrainian Front's forces.

This directive noted the reinforcement of the Third Ukrainian Front with the 4th Guards Army (eight rifle divisions), which was being moved up by rail to the Craiova area, although the Third Ukrainian Front's headquarters later shifted the detraining area to Timisoara. Transport by rail took up more than a month.

Such a long period is explained by the great length of the route from the loading station of Lutsk to Timisoara, as well as reloading the troops from trains using the USSR-gauge track into trains using the European gauge (eight divisions with their army reinforcements and rear establishments took up 135 trains).

The *front* staff drew up a timetable for the march to concentrate the 4th Guards Army, in accordance with which it was planned to deliver the eight divisions to the Timisoara area by 20 November and to the new concentration area of Stanisic—Svetozar—Miletic—Maly Idash—Subotica by no later than 28 November.

The average length of the overland routes was 200-300 kilometers; a day's march was 30-35 kilometers. The army artillery and an engineer-sapper brigade were to move together with the divisions. The army cannon artillery brigade and the munitions would be shifted by railroad to the Subotica area. The army's rear establishments were to complete their unloading in the Timisoara area on 25 November and arrive in the concentration area on 30 November. At the same time, up to 1-1.5 combat loads were to be moved along with the formations by the divisions' and army's means.

The *front* commander demanded that without waiting for the full concentration of all of the army's formations in the Timisoara area, by 26 November the main forces of two rifle corps (no less than six rifle divisions) were to concentrate in the indicated area.

The army headquarters was to be located in the Svetozar—Miletic area by no later than 22 November. The army's main routes of march were:

a) Arad—Nadlac—Mako—Szeged—Subotica—Sombor;
b) Timisoara—Velika Kikinda—Ada—Senta—Backa Topola.

The beginning of the march was set for 13 November, while at the same time the march was to be undertaken only at night. Movement during the day was authorized only during non-flying weather and no further than the line of the Tisza River, while careful masking was to be employed.

An operational group for the army's headquarters was ordered to remain behind for supervising the unloading in the Timisoara area.

Upon receiving the directive from the *Stavka* of the Supreme High Command, the *front* commander ordered the commander of the 57th Army to immediately set about regrouping the 75th Rifle Corps, along with its reinforcements, to the northern bank of the Danube. The commander of the 57th Army, in turn, issued orders to the commander of the 75th Rifle Corps to occupy defensive positions along the Danube River by 26 October along the front Sombor—Bac—Novo Selo—Backa Palanka—Novi Sad and to secure the Second Ukrainian Front's left flank.

The commander of the 75th Rifle Corps was ordered to establish communications with the headquarters of the 31st Guards Rifle Corps and with the Yugoslav forces in the Novi Sad area. By this time a brigade of the People's Liberation Army of Yugoslavia had occupied Titel and was moving on Novi Sad; another brigade was crossing the Danube River in the areas of Novi Futog and Backa Palanka.

The crossing by the 75th Rifle Corps' forces and their occupation of defensive positions along the Danube River took place during 19-26 October and on 30 October a supplementary order from the *Stavka* of the Supreme High Command followed on the regrouping of all the 57th Army's forces and *front* reinforcements to the north bank of the Danube River. The 17th Air Army was to rebase its planes from airfields south of the Danube River to airfields north of the river by 5 November.

The commander of the Danube Flotilla and the chief of the *front's* engineer troops received orders to support the crossing of the *front's* forces. The crossing would be supported by the 65th Engineer-Sapper Brigade and two battalions of armored cutters from the Kerch' Brigade (32 cutters). The main crossings were the crossing along the northern outskirts of Belgrade and in the Grocka area. An auxiliary crossing was in the Surduk—Dubrovica area.

By 24 October the 75th Rifle Corps had finished crossing and during 31 October-3 November the 236th, 73rd Guards and 19th rifle divisions, had crossed with reinforcements, with the task of concentrating in the Sambor—Stopar—Sivac—Svetozar—Miletic area by the morning of 9 November, in readiness to force the Danube River.

On the basis of orders by the *Stavka* of the Supreme High Command, the commander of the Third Ukrainian Front reinforced the 57th Army with a rifle corps (6th Guards Rifle Corps) and one artillery breakthrough division from the 37th Army. The 6th Guards Rifle Corps and the 9th Breakthrough Artillery Division, which were slated to be transferred to the 57th Army, were located in Bulgaria.

Simultaneously, the 9th Anti-Tank Artillery Brigade was to be removed from the 37th Army and transferred by its own means along the route Sofia—Pirot—Nis—Cuprija—Zabari—Velika Plana—Topola—Belgrade—Zemun and by the close of 19 November to concentrate in the Stara Pazova—Indija area.

The commander of the 17th Air Army had the task of covering from the air the concentration and unloading of the 6th Guards Rifle Corps' forces, as well as the crossing of the 75th Rifle Corps' forces over the Danube and its concentration in the Backi Monostor—Apatin—Sombor area. While carrying out the *front* commander's orders, during the 29 October-9 November period the 17th Air Army's planes, due to unfavorable meteorological conditions and rebasing to new airfields, conducted an average of 82 sorties per day, of which 50 percent were directed against enemy forces. The enemy's aviation during this period was not very active, limiting itself to reconnaissance, with a total of only 119 sorties noted by it in the Third Ukrainian Front's sector.

Taking into account the 57th Army's difficult situation with crossing equipment, on 31 October the *front* commander attached to it the 5th Pontoon-Bridge Brigade for supporting the crossing by the army's main forces.

On 31 October the *Stavka* of the Supreme High Command transferred to the Third Ukrainian Front the 18th Guards Tank Corps, which was supposed to concentrate in the

Zedani—Kovaci—Cerneteaz (all locales are 5-10 kilometers north of Timisoara) area by the morning of 4 November. The 18th Tank Corps was very much under strength: 2,786 men and 240 tanks and self-propelled guns, while it was 80 percent under strength in guns and 70 percent in motor vehicles. On 29 October the corps disposed of only 32 T-34[1] tanks and 53 self-propelled guns.

Somewhat later the *Stavka* of the Supreme High Command reinforced the Third Ukrainian Front with a cavalry-mechanized group consisting of the 5th Guards Cavalry and 7th Mechanized corps, which just as the 18th Tank Corps, was seriously under strength. The 5th Guards Cavalry Corps' shortages consisted of 39 guns and mortars, 118 machine guns, 905 rifles, and 3,871 horses. During 3-9 November the corps received reinforcements of 3,466 men. This group had the task of concentrating in the Szeged area by the close of 27 November.

In order to secure the *front's* southern wing following the forcing of the Danube, the *Stavka* of the Supreme High Command authorized the employment of Bulgarian troops for the offensive in Hungary. On the basis of this decision, the *front* commander on 17 November demanded that the commander-in-chief of the Bulgarian army allot one army headquarters and 5-6 divisions, along with reinforcements, and to concentrate them in the area west of Belgrade. The movement of five divisions of the Bulgarian 1st Army began on 25 November.

From 2400 on 19 November the following was established for the Third Ukrainian Front:

a) the *front's* distribution station was to be in Craiova, with separate distribution stations in Timisoara and Tirnovo;
b) a rear boundary: on the right (with the Second Ukrainian Front) Pitesti—Timisoara—Szeged—Dunapentele, followed by the operational boundary, with all locales except Szeged for the Third Ukrainian Front; from the rear, Pitesti—Rustchuk—Vara, for the Third Ukrainian Front.

The Third Ukrainian Front was allotted three trains a day along the sector Craiova—Turnu Severin—Lugoj—Timisoara—Szeged.

In order to improve troop control in the 57th Army and to concentrate all its efforts along the new axis, the *front* commander subordinated the 57th Army's 68th Rifle Corps (93rd, 223rd and 52nd rifle divisions) and the 1st Guards Fortified Area, along with reinforcements, including those supporting the Yugoslav People's Liberation Army's 12th Army Corps, directly to the *front*.

The preparation for the new operation also took place in a complex mine situation along the Danube. At the end of October several tugs and up to ten barges blew up on mines above Turnu-Severin, as a result of which unloading had to be carried out at a great distance from the troops (in Calafat and Turnu Severin). The King Peter I Ship Canal had also been mined. The enemy laid floating mines by plane and through agents.

Thus the powerful water artery of the Danube could not be fully employed in the interests of the forthcoming operation, particular as the sector from Sotin to the mouth of the Drava River remained in enemy hands, which excluded the possibility of employing the Danube Flotilla along the Danube north of the Drava River. There remained the possibility of the roundabout transfer of only cutters along the King Peter I Canal to the Danube.

By the start of the operation the Danube Flotilla had been reinforced and somewhat reorganized. A brigade of river vessels, consisting of four monitors and 35 armored cutters, had been created on the basis of the Kerch' Brigade. The Sulina Brigade of river vessels had three monitors

1 Editor's note. The T-34 was the Red Army's standard medium tank during the Great Patriotic War and afterwards. The 1941 model weighed 26.5 tons, carried a crew of our, was armed with a 76mm gun and two 7.62mm machine guns. A later model was fitted with an 85mm gun.

and 32 cutters. The minesweeping brigade had 36 sweepers and an independent detachment of landing craft, consisting of two high-speed barges and four landing boats.

Later on, on the basis of permission by the *Stavka* of the Supreme High Command, the *front* commander ordered the 83rd Independent Naval Infantry Brigade to concentrate from Burgas to the Novi Sad area by 25 November.

In these conditions, the *front* commander assigned the Danube Flotilla the following tasks: to continued clearing the mines from the Danube channel and in the King Peter I Canal; to support the success of those units of the *front* whose flanks rested on the Danube River, to prepare landing operations from the Batina area in the direction of Budapest and the mouth of the Drava River, and from the Novi Sad area in the direction of Vukovar, as far as the mouth of the Drava River; the vessels' artillery fire was to support the operations by the *front's* units.

Simultaneously, the *front* commander was orienting the commander of the 57th Army about the forthcoming offensive to the west and ordered the following: to initiate the covert reconnaissance of possible areas for forcing the Danube along the sector Baja—mouth of the Drava River, to account for all amphibious equipment along this sector and, upon taking measures to preserve them, to also prepare a plan for a local operation to seize and broaden a bridgehead along the right bank of the Danube.

Within the 57th Army's units located in the second echelon and the reserve during this time, work was conducted for the engineer outfitting of the positions, as well as combat training and gatherings of staff, brigade and division commanders.

Alongside this work continued on the combat organization of subunits and units, as well as reinforcing them with personnel and combat equipment.

Thus the Third Ukrainian Front's preparation for the new operation unfolded in complex conditions.

The forces designated for carrying out the operation were scattered over an enormous space (the *front's* forces from 200-300 kilometers and the rear establishments from 400-600 kilometers from the area of forthcoming operations, which is why their concentration to the areas for forcing the Danube would have to take a lot of time). Besides this, the mobile forces—18th Guards Tank and 7th Mechanized corps—arriving at the front—required considerable refitting and were in no position to take part in the *front's* combat operations before the first days of December.

Thus in November, of all the *front's* forces the only one capable of forcing the Danube was the 57th Army, which, in turn, would have to regroup its forces in conditions of the autumn rains, a lack of roads and a crossing over major water barriers, such as the Danube and Tisza, within a limited amount of time and with an insufficient amount of crossing equipment.

All of this required extremely flexible and precise work by the *front* command and staff and the 57th Army's headquarters.

15

The Forcing of the Danube River and the Defeat of the Enemy's Danube Group of Forces

The terrain for forcing the Danube River was extremely unfavorable. All of the shoreline along the left bank of the Danube River was lowland, cut by a thick network of channels, canals, lakes and boggy marshes.

The left bank of the river could be viewed at a great distance by the enemy.

The most favorable sectors for a crossing were the Mohacs and Batina areas.

In the Mohacs area the width of the river was 600-800 meters and 250-400 meters in the Batina area. In these areas the left bank was dry and there were paved roads leading to the crossings, as well as natural cover. Along the western bank of the Danube there were also paved roads leading into the depth of enemy-occupied territory.

The Apatin area was worse. The western bank was quite swampy and covered with small bushes. Roads and paths were absent. The Old Danube's channel was up to 100 meters wide and from 1-3 meters deep. The banks are silted, the soil viscous and difficult for passage by horses and impassible for all types of transport.

Favorable tactical targets were absent. The terrain had poor observation and fields of fire. There were no roundabout ways. Available chopped bushes were used for planking.

The uninterrupted rains raised the water level in low-lying areas and made the dirt roads completely impassible for horse-drawn and auto transport, which told negatively on the troops' forcing activities across the Danube, especially along the Apatin sector.

It was planned to begin the forcing operation across the Danube River on 15 November, but a combat reconnaissance was carried out on the initiative of the local commanders in the Batina area on the night of 6-7 November and the night of 7-8 November in the Apatin area, as a result of which we managed to seize two tactical bridgeheads from 1.5-3 kilometers in depth. The augmentation of forces along the right bank of the Danube River began from this moment.

The *front* commander, in his directive of 9 November, demanded that the commander of the 57th Army carry out an all-round preparation for the forcing and by 11 November report his plan for the offensive operation with a forcing of the Danube River:

- by employing only the forces of the 64th Rifle Corps and part of the 75th Rifle Corps; with the employment of the 6th Guards Rifle Corps, the 64th Rifle Corps and part of the 75th Rifle Corps.

It was then planned to covertly carry out work, under the guise of strengthening the army's defense along the sector Baja—mouth of the Drava River.

In order to speed up the regrouping and concentration of the 57th Army's main forces and the *front* reinforcement units, it was ordered to make an accounting of all the crossing equipment and bridges over the Tisza River and along all the water barriers between the Danube and Tisza rives in the army's sector. The construction of bridges over the Tisza River west of Petrovgrad was to be sped up, while work to strengthen the bridge near Stari Becej was to begin immediately.

Further on, the *front* commander ordered that the 4th Guards Army's 21st Guards Rifle Corps, which consisted of three divisions, was to be crossed over to the western bank of the Danube in the Batina area by 25 November and to be ready to attack to the northwest and west.

On the basis of the *front* commander's directive, the commander of the 57th Army made a decision that came down to the following: to complete the concentration of the army's forces in areas convenient for the forcing the Danube River by 18 November (within 10-12 days); the Bezdan—Kupusina—Sombor area for the 64th Rifle Corps; the Kula—Pivnica Srbobran area for the 32nd Motorized Rifle Brigade and the Backa-Topola area for the 53rd Motorcycle Regiment; the army's self-propelled artillery and the 9th Artillery Division's light artillery would concentrate in the Backa-Brestovac area. The remaining army reinforcements would concentrate in the Sombor—Telecka area.

The forcing sectors were Dunasekcse, Mohacs, Batina, and Apatin.

The forcing was to begin on 15 November with the following forces: along the Dunasekcse—Mohacs sector, one division from the 64th Rifle Corps, with crossings in the areas of Felse Kertik and Mohacs, with the task of seizing a bridgehead west of Felse Kertik and capturing Mohacs.

Along the Batina—Apatin sector two of the 75th Rifle Corps' divisions had the mission of seizing a bridgehead in the areas of Batina and Apatin along the western bank of the Danube River and connecting them into one tactical bridgehead and by 18 November expanding it to the line Topola—Podolje—Knezevi Vinogradi—Grabovac—Bilje, with a depth of up to five kilometers and up to 16 kilometers in width. By 23 November the unification of this bridgehead with the one in the Mohacs area would increase its depth to 20 kilometers and its width to 80 kilometers, with the arrival of the 64th and 75th rifle corps at the line Bataszek—Vemend—Nemetboly—Hercegtettes—Bolman, for the purpose of supporting the deployment of the army's main forces.

The boundary line between the 75th and 64th rifle corps was established along the line Zmaevac—Knezevo—Hercegtettes, with all locales for the 75th Rifle Corps.

It was planned to further develop the offensive with the forces of the 6th Guards Rifle Corps, 32nd Motorized Rifle Brigade, 53rd Motorcycle Regiment, and the 252nd Special Designation Battalion in the direction of Pecs and Oroszlo.

On the basis of this decision, the plan submitted for the offensive by the 57th Army and the forcing of the Danube River was confirmed by the *front* commander.

By the close of 9 November the 57th Army's operational situation continued to be characterized by the significant scattering of its forces along a great area in Yugoslavia and Hungary. The army's main forces were regrouping and crossing the Danube River and arriving in their new areas, while part of its forces remained along their previous lines. The army was supporting an offensive by units of the Yugoslav People's Liberation Army with artillery fire.

The 75th Rifle Corps (233rd, 74th and 299th rifle divisions), had three divisions in line occupying defensive positions along the left bank of the Danube River along a broad 130-kilometer front along the Baja—Novi Sad sector.

Two of the 64th Rifle Corps' (73rd, 19th and 113th rifle divisions) divisions had concentrated north and south of Sombor (the 73rd Guards Rifle Division in Gakovo, the 19th Rifle Division in Sveti Ivan, and the 113th Rifle Division, which was on the march, had reached Sivac.

The 6th Guards Rifle Corps (61st Guards, 10th and 20th Guards rifle divisions) had three divisions at the crossings over the Danube River in the areas of Grocka (61st Guards Rifle Division) and Belgrade (10th and 20th Guards rifle divisions).

The 68th Rifle Corps was regrouping and with part of its forces was fighting in conjunction with the forces of the Yugoslav People's Liberation Army along the line Trstenik—Krusevac. The 1st Guards Fortified Area occupied the line Petrovaradin—Ruma—Jarak.

The 236th Rifle Division and the 32nd Motorized Rifle Brigade constituted the reserve of the 57th Army's commander and was on the march (the 236th Rifle Division in the Zabalj area and the 32nd Motorized Rifle Brigade in the Petrovgrad area.

The average strength of the rifle divisions by the beginning of the forcing was 6,000 to 7,500 men. The strength of the rifle companies reached 50-90 men, while in the 6th Guards Rifle Corps this figure was 100-120 men in a company. The specialized subunits were close to authorized strength.

The armored forces were marching from the Belgrade area.

The artillery's situation by 9 November was as follows:

There were two reinforcement artillery regiments in the firing positions of two of the 75th Rifle Corps' divisions (74th and 233rd rifle divisions) and a guards mortar regiment in reserve.

The 64th Rifle Corps' artillery group was on the march, together with the corps' units.

The army's anti-aircraft group was covering the troops' crossing near Grocka, Belgrade, Novi Sad, Novi Becej, and Titel.

The remaining artillery was part of the army artillery group and during 1-14 November was marching to the Sombor—Bezdan—Apatin area.

Throughout 9-10 November the forcing of the Danube River was continuing by the 75th Rifle Corps' subunits. The commander of the 57th Army decided to reinforce the pace of the crossing and adopted measures to lay down pontoon crossings and reinforced the 75th Rifle Corps with artillery and mortars.

By the close of 10 November two reinforced battalions were operating along the Batina bridgehead, which were fighting along a line 1.5 kilometers northeast of Draz and Batina station.

Along the Apatin bridgehead one of the 74th Rifle Division's regiments reached the line of the dikes and the channel of the Old Danube.

The continuing rains over the last four days sharply worsened the condition of the roads.

The captured tactical bridgehead, despite the enemy's powerful resistance through artillery and mortar fire, already enabled us to organize a crossing on ferries, towed by cutters.

The enemy's attempt to throw our subunits off the bridgehead through counterattacks was not successful. Then the enemy began to commit into the fighting in detail the newly-arrived reserves (31st SS Infantry Division and the "Brandenburg" Division's 2nd Infantry Regiment.

Taking this into account, the commander of the 57th Army reinforced the troops operating on the bridgeheads and committed the 64th Rifle Corps, along with the subordinated 233rd Rifle Division into the fighting on the Batina bridgehead, with the following task: to widen the bridgehead by operating with two divisions (233rd and 73rd Guards rifle divisions) in the direction of Gaic and Zmaevac.

Two divisions (19th and 113th) remained in the second echelon in the Sombor area.

On 14 November the *Stavka* of the Supreme High Command ordered the commander of the Third Ukrainian Front to continue forcing the Danube, with the task of reaching the following line by 27 November: Bataszek—Pecs—Harkany, thus securing the operational bridgehead along the right bank of the Danube.

At 2400 on 18 November the three-division 31st Guards Rifle Corps was transferred from the Second Ukrainian Front and new boundary line was established with the Second Ukrainian Front along the line Timisoara—Szeged—Dunapentele—Szekesfehervar—Papa, with all locales, except for Szeged, for the Third Ukrainian Front.

On 15 November the commander of the Third Ukrainian Front made a decision, which came down to the following:

The 57th Army, with the forces of the 75th and 64th rifle corps, while taking advantage of the enemy's insufficient readiness and while firmly securing itself from the south along the northern bank of the Danube River, was to capture the line Mohacs—Magyarboly—Torjanc.

No later than 22 November the 6th Guards Rifle Corps was to be concentrated along the western bank of the Danube and was to develop the offensive and no later than 26 November capture the line Porboly station—Bataszek—Ofalu—Apatvarasd—Pecsvarad—Pecs—Kesu—Idsos Viszlo—Kemes, extending the security front along the Drava River.

The army was to subsequently attack to the west toward Nagykanizsa, while the 4th Guards Army was to attack from the area northwest and west of Mohacs to the north and northwest. As of 2400 on 23 November the boundary line with the 4th Guards Army was Vrsac—Novi Becej—Mohacs, with all locales, with the exception of Mohacs, for the 57th Army.

With the 4th Guards Army' arrival at the bridgehead, it was planned to subordinate the following reinforcement artillery to it: the 9th Breakthrough Artillery Division's 115th Cannon-Artillery Brigade, 23rd Howitzer Brigade, 10th Mortar Brigade, 9th Breakthrough Artillery Division, the 42nd and 49th anti-tank artillery brigades, the 28th Guards Mortar Brigade (minus one battalion), and the 12th and 366th guards self-propelled artillery regiments.

It was planned to complete the concentration of the army's reinforcement artillery at the areas of the bridgehead by no later than 16 November. The delivery of no less than 1.5 combat loads of ammunition of all types was to be carried out by this date.

The *front* commander also demanded that the captured sectors along the western bank of the Danube be securely consolidated, while paying particularly attention to the troops' anti-aircraft defense.

It was planned to present the plan for the offensive by no later than the morning of 16 November.

This decision by the *front* commander essentially made more concrete the previously issued instructions. The new elements were as follows: questions of the 57th Army's interaction while forcing the Danube and the chief axes for developing the offensive along the right bank of the Danube River—the 4th Guards Army on Szekesfehervar and the 57th Army on Nagykanizsa. At the same time, the significant reinforcement of the 4th Guards Army at the expense of the 57th Army indicated that the Szekesfehervar axis was the main one, and the Nagykanizsa was the secondary one. During the first stage the breakthrough of the defense and the seizure of an operational bridgehead were to be mainly entrusted to the 57th Army, which during this period was to resolve the main task.

The 57th Army's situation on 15 November at the moment of the *front* commander's decision was as follows: the 64th Rifle Corps (233rd, 113th and 73rd Guards rifle divisions) was fighting with two divisions to widen the bridgehead west and southwest of Batina and had arrived at the following line: the 233rd Rifle Division east of Draz, the 73rd Guards Rifle Division in Batina station, and the 113th Rifle Division had finished concentrating in the Sombor area.

The 73rd Rifle Corps' 74th Rifle Division was fighting to expand the bridgehead west of Apatin along the line two kilometers east of the water tower and the to the south, along the dike and along the left bank of the Old Danube's channel.

The 236th Rifle Division was at the crossings over the channels and the Danube's main channel in the area west of Kupusina.

The 299th Rifle Division was defending with three regiments along the left bank of the Danube along the sector excluding Apatin—Backa Palanka.

The 6th Guards Rifle Corps (10th, 20th and 61st guards rifle divisions) were moving to their concentration areas and were along the crossings over the Danube and Tisza rivers along the following routes:

a) Novi Sad—Novi Vrbas—Sombor, and
b) Belgrade—Petrovgrad—Novi Vrbas—Sombor.

The head of the column (10th Guards Rifle Division) reached Ruski Krstur by 16 November.

The 64th and 75th rifle corps' reinforcement artillery was located in the Batina, Bezdan and Apatin areas.

The army artillery group had not yet completed its concentration at the army's offensive front. The artillery regiments and brigades were still approaching Sombor and were along the crossings over the Danube River in the Novi Sad area and in the Novi Becej area over the Tisza River.

The 30th Artillery Brigade and the 47th Cannon-Artillery Regiment arrived in the Bezdan area.

The army anti-aircraft group was securing the crossings and march routes, with two regiments located in the Batina area and part of the anti-aircraft regiments on the march to Batina and Apatin.

The division and regimental artillery continued to cross over to the bridgeheads and by the close of 15 November there were 192 tubes on the Batina bridgehead and 111 on the Apatin bridgehead.

The provisioning of ammunition of all types was, on the average, 0.7-1.0 combat loads. The 57th Army had been reinforced with the 14th Assault Engineer-Sapper Brigade and a battalion from the 5th Pontoon Brigade. The 44th Assault Engineer Brigade, 5th Pontoon Brigade (minus one battalion), the 6th Pontoon Regiment, and other engineer units remained subordinated to the *front* for carrying out tasks for securing the troops' crossing over the Danube in the Belgrade and Novi Sad area and over the Tisza River in the Petrovgrad and Titel area.

The 12th Assault Engineer-Sapper Brigade, the 2nd Pontoon Regiment and the 36th Defense Construction Directorate continued to concentrate—the 12th Assault Engineer-Sapper Brigade completely arrived in the Sombor area only on 26 November.

The enemy took measures to move his reserves from the depth and castled his forces along the front and committed them into the fighting by battalion as they arrived, with the task of eliminating the bridgehead. For example, on 12 November the 1st Tatar Battalion, German 92nd Motorized Brigade, a battalion of Hungarian gendarmes, and units of the 44th Infantry Division, which had arrived from Italy, and units of the 13th SS Muslim Infantry Division were transferred to the Batina area.

The enemy air force continued to actively operate against the areas of the crossings and against our units in groups of 6-7 and up to 15 planes, with a large number of sorties.

The enemy carried out 4-5 counterattacks a day in strength of up to a battalion each, with the support of 2-5 tanks and self-propelled guns. Simultaneous with active operations along the front, the enemy continued to improve his defense, creating its depth. The enemy had consolidated on the commanding heights west of Batina.

The only paved road led directly to the enemy's defensive line and there were no detours for heavy combat equipment. The area adjacent to height 205 from the north was swampy terrain, visible from the height. The railroad bed leading to the southwest was employed by the enemy for defense. The only area for accumulating men and materiel was the strip along the bank, with the crest of the bank 20-25 meters high. The wine cellars in Batina could serve as shelters for the rank and file.

In these conditions, one could not count on success without reliable suppression by artillery and mortar fire and aviation.

During the period up to 18 November the 17th Air Army was rebasing to airfields north of the Danube and thus operated with very limited forces, carrying out an average of 85 sorties per day. Air strikes in the 57th Army's interests were directed at repulsing enemy counterattacks on the captured bridgeheads and at preventing the arrival of his reserves strikes at crossings over the Drava River in the Osijek area and against the Harkany and Villany railroad junctions.

On the Apatin bridgehead the enemy used two dikes with a height up to four meters for a defensive line.

If the northern part of the bridgehead, east of Aleksandrov Dvorac was not swampy and admitted the possibility of employing 76mm guns, then the southern part, between the main and old channels of the Danube, was very swampy and covered with water, the soil was viscous and there were was no road or path. The terrain was impassable for all types of transportation.

By 15 November the following crossing equipment was operating along the crossings: the 5th Pontoon Brigade's 30th Independent Pontoon Battalion, consisting of three cutters and five 16-ton ferries on the Batina bridgehead. Besides this, there were two captured cutters, seven motor boats, 25 small barges, 32 fishing boats, and four rubber boats;

- the 130th Independent Pontoon-Bridge Battalion, consisting of one cutter and two 16-ton ferries on the Apatin bridgehead; besides this, there was one civilian cutter, two large barges, one 3-ton ferry on boats, and 33 fishing boats.

On 19 November, on orders from the *Stavka* of the Supreme High Command, eight towboats and six 24-meter ferries from captured stocks were transferred from the Second Ukrainian Front for laying down a bridge near Novi Sad for before 5 December.

The limited supply of crossing equipment and the enemy's powerful fire resistance against the crossing areas made the timely crossing of major forces more difficult. Because of this, the accumulation of forces along the bridgeheads unfolded slowly and the crossed subunits were committed into the fighting in detail were engaged in prolonged fighting without results.

In was only by the morning of 20 November; that is, eight days after the start of the forcing was a floating bridge capable of bearing 16 tons completed by the forces of the 5th Pontoon Brigade in the area.

The new bridge immediately enabled us to sharply increase the pace of the crossing and during 20-21 November the 64th Rifle Corps' 113th Rifle Division and the corps' reinforcements (506th Cannon-Artillery Regiment, 274th and 152nd howitzer regiments, 49th Anti-Tank Artillery Brigade, 32nd Mortar Brigade, 523rd Mortar Regiment, and the 45th and 58th engineer-mine regiments.

On 14 November the commander of the 57th Army presented his decision to the *front* commander and a plan for the army's offensive operation and the forcing of the Danube.

The decision called for carrying out the immediate task of linking the Batina and Apatin bridgeheads into a single common one, with a sufficient depth for holding and committing the rifle corps' second echelons and reserves into the fighting.

The decision called for carrying out the subsequent task of widening the bridgehead along the front and in depth for housing the army's second echelon and mobile group (6th Guards Rifle Corps and the 32nd Mechanized Brigade) and through activities by part of the 64th and 75th rifle corps' forces to the north and south, to firmly secure the flank while committing the army's second echelon into the battle.

While carrying out the subsequent task, a part of the army's forces were to be freed up and reserves (233rd and 73rd Guards rifle divisions) created for developing the subsequent offensive.

The plan for the 57th Army's offensive operation foresaw three stages:

The operation's overall depth was to be 55-60 kilometers; the immediate task was to a depth of 6-10 kilometers; the breakthrough front along the Batina bridgehead was two kilometers, and two kilometers along the Apatin bridgehead.

A simultaneous attack along two sectors of the front, with the development of these attacks along converging axes: the one from the Batina and Apatin bridgeheads to Knezevi Vinogradi had the limited aim of broadening the bridgehead and was to be carried out by only part of the forces.

The army's main forces were to launch a frontal attack from the operational bridgehead in the general direction of Pecs.

The chosen form of action was conditioned by the nature of the terrain and the enemy's defense.

The territory between the Danube River and the Drava River possessed an exit to the northwest 35 kilometers wide. During extended fighting in this territory the enemy would have the necessary time to form a front along a favorable line: Mohacs—Beremend with the forces of his operational reserves.

The decision to renounce complex maneuvering by forces along the salient explains the desire to reach more quickly the operational depth. At the same time, the possibility was taken into account that the enemy would not leave his forces in defensive positions along the banks of the Danube and Drava while our breakthrough was being developed, but would attempt to pull them back to a new defensive line.

According to the army commander's decision, the 64th Rifle Corps (19th, 73rd Guards, 233rd and 119th rifle divisions), which was operating along the axis of the main attack along a 5.5-kilometer front, was to be reinforced by the following: the 1891st and 1202nd self-propelled artillery regiments, the 506th Cannon-Artillery Regiment and the 274th and 152nd howitzer regiments, the 528th, 563rd and 523rd mortar regiments, the 45th and 58th guards mortar regiments, the 23rd Mortar Brigade, the 49th Anti-Tank Artillery Brigade, and a battalion from the 160th Cannon-Artillery Brigade.

The corps had the task, while improving its positions, to broaden the bridgehead west of Batina with the 233rd and 73rd Guards rifle divisions, and on the morning of 18 November, upon the commitment of the 19th Rifle Division into the front line, to launch a decisive attack along the right flank in the direction of Gaic and Knezevi with the immediate task of capturing the line Gaic—Zmaevac and by the close of the day reaching the line Topola—Knezevi Vinogradi.

A supporting attack would be launched by one division through Zmaevac and Knezevi Vinogradi to bypass height heights 243 and 241 from the south and southwest.

The offensive would subsequently be continued toward Popovac, Knezevo and Majs.

The 75th Rifle Corps, which was operating along the secondary axis along a 6.8-kilometer front, was reinforced with two anti-tank artillery regiments (521st and 1312th), the 140th Mortar Regiment, the 252nd Guards Mortar Regiment, and the 10th Mortar Brigade.

On the morning of 18 November the corps was to launch an attack along its right flank in the direction of Kozarac, with the immediate task of capturing the line Sebeser—Mirkovac—Koejak and by the close of the day reach the line one kilometer south of Knezevi Vinogradi—Darda.

As it advanced, the left-flank 74th Rifle Division was to be employed for reliably covering the army's left flank along the northern bank of the Drava River.

The corps had the task of developing the offensive on Zeleno Polje from the morning of 19 November.

The army artillery group consisted of the 9th Artillery Division and the 160th Cannon-Artillery Brigade and a regiment from the 28th Guards Mortar Brigade.

The 42nd Anti-Tank Artillery Brigade was allotted to the army anti-tank artillery reserve.

The army's operational organization was in two echelons, with the 64th and 75th rifle corps in the first, and in the second the 6th Guards Rifle Corps and the 32nd Mechanized Brigade as the army's mobile group.

Upon the arrival of the first-echelon corps at the line Majs—Bezedek—Branin Vrkh—Beli Monastir, the 41st and 23rd howitzer brigades, a regiment from the 160th Cannon-Artillery Brigade, the 45th Guards Mortar Regiment, 26th Light Artillery Brigade, two regiments from the 10th Mortar Brigade, 230th Howitzer Regiment, and a regiment from the 28th Guards Mortar Brigade were to be subordinated to the 6th Guards Rifle Corps. Besides this, upon the commitment of the 6th Guards Rifle Corps into the battle, it was to be supported by all of the army artillery group's artillery.

As its units concentrated in the Sombor area, the corps was to concentrate by 21 November two rifle divisions in the Knezevo—Branin Vrkh—Beli Monastir area, ready to launch a decisive offensive on the morning of 22 November in the direction of Beli Monastir, Viragos and Pecs, while it was planned to have the third division in the second echelon and to cross it over the Danube during the night of 21-22 November.

The 32nd Mechanized Brigade, with the 53rd Motorcycle Regiment and the 252nd Special Designation Battalion (amphibious), comprising the army's mobile group, was to be committed into the breakthrough through the 6th Guards Rifle Corps' combat formations, with the task of developing the attack toward Pecs, and by the close of 23 November to seize the line Pecsvarad—Pecs—Szentlorinc and hold it until the arrival of the army's main forces.

The artillery had the following task:

- to suppress the enemy in the areas of Draz, Gajic, the western slopes of height 205, Zmaevac, Sebeser, Bokrasat, and Aleksandrov Dvorac;
- to prevent the arrival of enemy reserves and supplies along the roads in the 64th and 75th rifle corps' operating ares;
- with the arrival of the infantry at the Topola—Knezevi Vinogradi—Darda line, the 42nd Anti-Tank Artillery Regiment was to create an anti-tank defense along the line Gajic—Kotlina—Suza—Knezevi Vinogradi, with an artillery density of 64.35 guns and mortars per kilometer of front, not counting 45mm and 76mm guns. There was to be a density of 6.45 rocket-propelled artillery vehicles per kilometer of front.

Anti-aircraft artillery received orders to cover the crossing near Batina with two anti-aircraft regiments, and with one regiment near Apatin. Two anti-aircraft regiments were to accompany the 64th and 75th rifle corps' forces. The limited number of positional areas forced us to station a significant part of the artillery weapons along terrain under the enemy's aimed fire. The enemy occupied the commanding heights 205, 206 and 136, from which he could view the entire depth of our combat formations. In turn, possessing a covered rear, he could freely maneuver his tactical reserves and regroup men and weapons, etc.

Having up to 72 guns of various calibers and more than 64 mortars along this sector, the enemy could fire to a significant degree on the entire depth of our combat formations, particularly in the areas of our observation posts and firing positions.

The 17th Air Army had the task of continuing to cover the troops' regrouping and crossing from the air and supporting the 57th Army's operations along the western bank of the Danube River.

The engineer troops were given the following assignment:

- to secure the troops' crossing to the Batina bridgehead and northwest of Apatin with ferry crossings and laying down bridges on 18 November near Batina and on 20-21 November northwest of Apatin;
- to continue the cross-country routes of march and to repair them before nighttime along the crossing sectors for the uninterrupted movement of artillery and combat equipment;
- to support the troops' movement and the consolidation of lines reached through reconnaissance and the clearing of mines.

This was, in general form, the decision by the commander of the 57th Army for the expansion of the bridgehead.

During 14-17 November, in order to disorient the enemy and to distract his attention from the 64th Rifle Corps' crossings, operational masking measures were carried out. In the Mohacs and Felse Kertik area an officers' reconnaissance was carried out, two moorings were established and the impression of concentrating infantry was created through by movement of allotted commands. The movement of transport with boats and the movement of artillery were organized along the entire sector, and 16 firing positions were outfitted. Roving artillery batteries carried out registration fire on reference points. A demonstration attack by a reinforced rifle company trying to force the Danube was carried out in the Felse Kertik area.

These measures achieved a certain effect: the enemy conducted a ceaseless artillery and mortar fire against the areas of the false sectors, expending up to 1,500 shells and mortar rounds.

Prisoner testimony established that the enemy had moved up to a battalion and a half of infantry from the Batina area to the Mohacs area and had strengthened his engineer work there.

Bulgarian forces, having captured Kumanovo and Bujanovice on 11 November, continued to attack toward Skopje.

The Bulgarian command's plan of 15 November called for the 1st Army (2nd Cavalry Division and the 11th Infantry Division) during the first stage to capture Kosovo, and with the 2nd Army's forces: a northern group (6th and 4th infantry divisions) to attack in the direction of Mitrovica, and a southern group (9th and 12th infantry divisions) toward Pristina from the east and northeast.

The Bulgarians were to capture the Raska—Novi Pazar area during the second stage by no later than 21 November.

The 15-18 November fighting along both bridgeheads was prolonged and without result. The enemy put up fierce resisting while holding his positions. During this period he carried out up to 19 counterattacks from a company to a battalion in strength, supported by three to 25 tanks and self-propelled guns. During this period the enemy air force carried out more than 150 sorties for bombing our forces along the bridgeheads and crossings.

By the close of 18 November the 64th Rifle Corps had finished regrouping its forces. The 19th Rifle Division was crossed over to the bridgehead and on the night of 17-18 November one of the division's regiments took over a combat sector from the 233rd Rifle Division northeast of Draz, while two regiments concentrated in the area of the western outskirts of Batina. The 113th Rifle Division was in the Bezdan area, ready to cross for developing the first echelon of the 64th Rifle Corps' success.

Almost all of the divisional artillery, two self-propelled artillery regiments and all of the reinforcement artillery, except for the army artillery group, had completed the crossing and was along the right bank of the Danube.

The 75th Rifle Corps had not completed regrouping its units. Two regiments of the 236th Rifle Division had been crossed on the bridgehead and were occupying positions near the dike two kilometers northwest of Kozjak and then to the south along the dike. The third regiment was at the crossing. The 74th Rifle Division was occupying a line with three regiments along the dike and along the Old Danube River.

The 6th Guards Rifle Corps: the 10th Guards Rifle Division passed through Sombor, the 20th Guards Rifle Division through Sivac, and the 61st Guards Rifle Division through Pasicevo.

The 4th Guards Army was completing its concentration in the Timisoara area, while a part of its formations were on the march.

The 31st Rifle Corps (34th, 40th Guards and 320th rifle divisions) became part of the *front* and was subordinated to the 4th Guards Army. A new boundary line was established: Timisoara—Szeged—Dunapentele—Szekesfehervar, with all locales, except for Szeged, for the Third Ukrainian Front.

The 31st Rifle Corps was occupying defensive positions along the following boundaries: from the right, Fulopszallas—Dunapentele; from the left, Backa Topola—excluding Baja.

The forward edge was 95 kilometers long and ran along the eastern bank of the Danube River. The enemy, occupying the western commanding bank of the Danube, could see the corps' entire defense. The 31st Guards Rifle Corps had two rifle divisions in the first echelon; in the divisions there were two regiments each in the first and one each in the second echelons.

With the exception of individual foxholes in the corps' sector, there were no other engineer structures or obstacles. The corps was inadequately supplied with elementary equipment. The corps had no artillery reinforcements. The divisions' artillery regiments had been stationed by battery along the likely axes of the enemy's attacks.

Thus the 57th Army's forces failed to carry out the first stage's combat assignment of expanding the bridgehead and reaching the line Gajic—Zmaevac—Sebeser—Kozjak.

The chief reasons for failing to carry out the assignment on time were as follows:

The accumulation of men and materiel along the right bank of the Danube River, which had been called for by the plan for employing them in the fighting to expand the bridgeheads was carried out with insufficient speed, along with the weak artillery support for the units operating on the bridgehead (too little artillery, the occupation of firing positions without preliminary reconnaissance, inadequate communications with the combined-arms commanders, firing according to inaccurately prepared data, etc.).

Complete initiative was accorded to the commanders of the formations and units in the forcing. It was necessary for the *front* and army command to concentrate in its hands the preparation of the troops and crossing equipment for the forcing and to accumulate the necessary men and materiel and then to launch a powerful attack.

The premature forcing without the prospect of developing the attack for the purpose of expanding the bridgehead only attracted the enemy's attention to the forcing areas and led to difficult and extended fighting. Both the condition and capacity of the crossings failed to secure the necessary pace in accumulating men and materiel on the bridgeheads.

The placing of artillery and all of the heavy combat equipment on the bridgeheads had been made very difficult by the fall rains, the absence or roads and the unfavorable terrain (the steep grades and difficult relief along the Batina bridgehead and the swampy low-lying ground along the Apatin bridgehead.

The attempts by forces of individual rifle divisions to break the enemy defense, which was being reinforced by his arriving units, through local battles were unsuccessful. This resulted in the decision by the commander to carry out the preparation for and the breakthrough of the enemy's defense as an army operation, involving the additional reinforcement of the active units with artillery, engineer troops and flamethrower battalions and to support their combat activities with aviation.

Before 18 November the 17th Air Army had been covering the regrouping of the *front's* forces, supporting the *front's* forces in seizing bridgeheads along the western bank of the Danube River and supporting the Bulgarian and Yugoslav forces (the aviation operational group consisted of the 10th Assault Air and 236th Fighter divisions) and had rebased to airfields northwest of Belgrade, and only from 19 November could it switch over to supporting the 57th Army's combat operations with all its forces, carrying out up to 550 sorties. As far as the enemy's air force was concerned, an average of about 20 sorties per day was noted.

It was first planned to break through the enemy's defense on 18 November, but this was shifted to 19 November in accordance with an order by the commander of the Third Ukrainian Front.

At 1000 on 19 November, following a 45-minute artillery preparation and with the support of the 17th Air Army, which carried out 450 sorties that day, units of the 64th and 75th rifle corps attacked, but were not successful. Counterattacked by the enemy, the 64th and 75th rifle corps' units fell back to their jumping-off positions.

The reason for the unsuccessful attack was the indecisiveness and lack of initiative of the units, especially of the 74th and 233rd rifle divisions. The artillery and mortars did not carry out aimed fire and failed to adequately support the infantry's advance. The battery and battalion commanders fell behind the infantry commanders of those subunits and units they were supporting. Guns firing over open sights and mortars also fell behind the infantry, as a result of which they were unable to render support to the infantry in destroying the firing points that were hindering its advance. The infantry's cooperation with the artillery, tanks and self-propelled guns was not organized with precision.

Alongside this, the Danube's autumn flooding made low-lying areas impassable. On the first day of the fighting the flooding river broke through the dike in several places and flooded the passages to the enemy's defensive positions.

Our forces had to attack under enemy fire, up to their chests in cold water, while carrying heavy infantry weapons and ammunition a distance of 2-3 kilometers. It is necessary to add to this that the artillery preparation for the attack was insufficiently effective. This caused the failure and significant losses in the first day's fighting.

According to the *front's* intelligence section, the enemy's dispositions by 24 November were as follows:

16 enemy formations were noted in the front line opposite the forces of the Third Ukrainian Front and the Bulgarian troops and units of the Yugoslav People's Liberation Army.

Units of the 31st SS Infantry Division, 44th Infantry Division, the 1st Mountain Infantry Division's 1st Mountain Infantry Regiment, 13th SS Muslim Infantry Division, individual regiments from the 118th and 117th light infantry divisions, 92nd Motorized Brigade, Hungarian composite and security regiments, and the SS "Brandenburg" Division were in the area of the bridgeheads along the western bank of the Danube River. Police battalions and a regiment from the 264th Infantry Division were further along the Drava River and the as far as Ilok.

Units of the composite "Bettcher" Division and 118th Light Infantry Division were along the front Ilok—Sremska-Mitrovica—Sabac.

The remnants of the 7th SS Mountain Infantry Division "Prince Eugen," Muller's corps group and a regiment from the 104th Light Infantry Division were along the line Cacak—Kraljevo.

Elements of the 22nd Motorized Division, the 7th SS Mountain Division "Prince Eugen," an infantry regiment from the "Skanderbeg" Division, the 104th Light Infantry Division, and the "Schultz" combat group were in the Mitrovica area facing the Bulgarian forces.

The 11th *Luftwaffe* Field Division, 22nd Motorized Division and units of the 21st SS "Skanderbeg" Infantry Division were falling back to the north, covered by rearguards from the Skopje—Veles—Stip area.

Thus all the German formations formerly located in Greece and Albania by 20 November were already either completely or partially operating in the first line or were being transferred north.

Before their arrival at the first line, the majority of the enemy's formations had been engaged in occupation duties in Greece, Yugoslavia and Albania. Some units had taken part in the fighting against the Yugoslav People's Liberation Army.

Thus by the time of our forces' offensive, the enemy in Yugoslavia and Hungary had begun to commit into the fighting well-equipped cadre units, the rank and file of which had received some training in combat operations in mountainous conditions. Some divisions had up to 18,000 men.

Our forces made a repeat attack, following an artillery preparation and a massed bombing strike by our air force.

A breakthrough of the enemy's defense also took shape on the Apatin bridgehead, but the units of the 75th Rifle Corps did not advance significantly.

According to the decision by the commander of the 57th Army, the 113th Rifle Division was subordinated to the 64th Rifle Corps, while the 233rd Rifle Division, having turned over its combat sector, went into the army commander's reserve. The enemy's resistance was crushed and by the close of 22 November units (19th Rifle Division) of the 64th Rifle Corps captured Gajic and had advanced along the crest of the heights in the direction of Podolje to a depth of five kilometers (113th Rifle Division) and captured the eastern part of Zmaevac (73rd Guards Rifle Division).

On the Apatin bridgehead, the 75th Rifle Corps (236th Rifle Division) expanded the breakthrough of the enemy's defense up to five kilometers toward the flanks and captured the Monorosz—Csiprasat area and, upon overcoming the last line of the enemy's defense along the second dike, advanced three kilometers in the direction of Mirkovac.

In his order, the army commander directed the attention of the combined-arms commanders to the poor employment of artillery fire and the bad organization of cooperation between the infantry and the artillery, as well as the absence of infantry maneuver on the battlefield so as to outflank the enemy from the rear and flank, the slow pace of the infantry advance, and its falling behind the artillery fire. Somewhat later the *front* commander demanded that the corps be given deeper assignments; while at the same time taking into account the seizure of favorable lines from which they could successfully develop their further offensive the following day. Simultaneously, the *front* commander pointed out that when breaking through intermediate lines for the purpose of achieving surprise, the artillery preparation should be conducted in minimal time (40-50 minutes and more was allotted earlier).

Throughout 23 November the breakthrough's success was developed by the forces of the corps reserves, while units of the 64th and 75th rifle corps, having linked up both bridgeheads, advanced 8-10 kilometers and reached the line Dubosevica—Branina—east of Knezevi Vinogradi—east of Brestovac.

During 22-26 November the 17th Air Army carried out 1,933 sorties, while actively supporting the 57th Army's forces by bombing and dive bombing strikes against the enemy's counterattacking forces and against railroads junctions in order to disrupt the delivery of reserves. The operational air group carried out 235 sorties in the interests of the Yugoslav forces.

Thus the mission of the operation's second stage—the breakthrough of the enemy's defense—was accomplished only after five days of intense fighting.

As a result of heavy losses in men and materiel, the enemy (the 44th Infantry Division's 131st Infantry Regiment, and from 22 November the 132nd and 134th infantry regiments, the 31st SS Infantry Regiment, the 117th Light Infantry Division's 750th Infantry Regiment, 92nd Motorized Brigade, and two regiments from the "Brandenburg" Division, as well as a number of independent subunits) had been significantly weakened, thrown out of his favorable positions (heights 205, 206 and the dikes along the Apatin bridgehead) and had been forced to fall back under pressure from our forces.

During his withdrawal, the enemy, taking advantage of the broken terrain, employed engineer obstacles, while blowing up bridges and the roadbed, in places. He also employed innovations, such as mines with a glass fuse, planting buried shells along individual sectors of the paved roads, enclosed false minefields and mined approaches to them, and others.

Besides this, the presence of a large number of cellars and wine cellars enabled the enemy to preserve his personnel and equipment during artillery and air strikes.

In the conditions of fighting to expand the bridgehead, the motivated actions of units and subunits played an enormous role. However, the poor organization of the combined-arms battle on the part of the corps commanders and a number of division commanders (which was often noted in the orders of the *front* and army commander) led to a situation in which the 57th Army's forces carried out a task in five days that was supposed to have taken 24 hours, along with excessive losses in men and a large expenditure of ammunition.

One of the reasons for the slow advance by the 64th Rifle Corps on the bridgehead up to 22 November was the fact that the enemy, not feeling any pressure along the other sectors, had the opportunity to bring up sufficient forces against the attacking troops and to stubbornly defend the bridgehead.

Upon capturing the dikes, the decisive role was played by assault groups, organized into groups of 15-20 soldiers under the command of a single officer, which had, besides rifles and automatic rifles, several anti-tank guns, light machine guns and hand grenades. The assault groups operated with particular success in those cases when they were supported by fire from artillery and mortars. For example, a single battery was allotted for supporting the assault groups' attack and consolidation. A gun crew, following behind the infantry, wheeled its gun onto the dike and opened fire along the dike. Then all the battery's remaining guns were placed on the dike. This decided the successful outcome of the entire rifle regiment's fight for the dike. Before the gun appeared on the dike, the enemy easily shifted his mobile reserve to any threatened axis, covered by the dike. The enemy's maneuver here was confined by the presence of guns firing over open sights. Two enemy tanks were knocked out as soon as they appeared.

The course of the fighting to break through the enemy's defense and the delay in carrying out the offensive's second-stage task brought about corresponding changes in the accomplishment of the third stage.

The arrival of the 4th Guards Army's units to the 57th Army's breakthrough sector and the uncovering of the enemy's withdrawal along the entire front of the army demanded that the commitment of the 4th Guards Army from the 57th Army's bridgehead be sped up, although for this it was necessary to speed up the crossing and commitment into the fighting of the 57th Army's second echelon for the purpose of forming an operational bridgehead of sufficient volume.

Because of this, on 22 November the *front* commander ordered the commander of the 57th Army:

- to more decisively and persistently develop the emerging success. To prevent the enemy from forming a new defensive front and to concentrate the army's and air force's main efforts along the Batina bridgehead;
- to set about the movement of the 6th Guards Rifle Corps to the right bank of the Danube on the night of 22-23 November, with the subsequent development of its attack along the army's right flank and to carry out the previously assigned task;
- to cross the 32nd Mechanized Brigade to the right bank of the Danube, employing it either to the northwest or west, depending on the situation.

A boundary line was established with the 4th Guards Army at 2400 on 23 November: Vrsac—Novi Becej—Mohacs, with all locales, except for Mohacs, for the 57th Army.

During the night of 22-23 November the 4th Guards Army's 41st Guards Rifle Division took over the combat sector of the 57th Army's 233rd Rifle Division and took up defensive positions along the line Baja—Mohacs, while preparing to force the Danube River.

Having occupied this sector, the division carried out a reconnaissance of the right bank of the Danube River, which was being defended by the Hungarian 11th Reserve Regiment, a composite regiment and the 39th Security Regiment. In order to free up the forces of the 31st Guards Rifle Corps and the 41st Guards Rifle Division, the commander of the 57th Army was ordered to relieve these formations with units of the 252nd Rifle Division along the sector Ordas (south of Dunapataj)—Mohacs no later than 28 November.

From this moment the staff of the 4th Guards Army set about drawing up an operational plan for forcing the Danube River and seizing a bridgehead along its western bank. Reconnaissance was carried out, crossings sectors were noted and local materials for the crossing were procured.

It was planned to main the main crossing in the Madocsa area.

In order to carry out tactical landings and to support them with fire, the *front* commander issued orders to the commander of the Danube Military Flotilla, who in his turn, issued a combat order to the flotilla's formations. The order instructed them to support the 57th Army's units in making tactical landings along the western bank of the Danube north and south of Batina and to support the activities of the army's units with artillery fire from combat vessels in this area. Subsequently, as the bridgehead along the right bank of the Danube was broadened, the armored cutters' main forces were to operate jointly with units of the 4th Guards Army upstream along the Danube.

In order to resolve the assigned tasks, it was ordered that by the close of 27 November 20 armored cutters were to be concentrated to the Bezdan area. The movement of the armored cutters was to be carried out along the Tisza River and the King Peter I Canal. From 26 November the brigade's headquarters was to be in Bezdan.

The commander of the river cutter brigade was to support the units of the 57th Army and the 68th Rifle Corps with the forces of a battalion of armored cutters and an escort battalion, with tactical landings and artillery fire, in the direction of Novi Sad upstream along the Danube River as far as the mouth of the Drava River, in order to secure the army's river flank.

In order to resolve these tasks, landing armored cutters and six small cutters were being concentrated to the Novi Sad area by the close of 24 November.

The staff of the 2nd Sulina Brigade of river cutters was to be rebased to Novi Sad from 27 November.

The commander of the 83rd Naval Infantry Brigade was ordered to complete the brigade's concentration to the Kolut—Becki Breg area and be ready to make a landing from the armored cutters of the 1st Kerch' Brigade of river cutters on the right bank of the Danube along the sector north and south of Batina. The brigade's headquarters was in Kolut as of 25 November. It was simultaneously ordered to send communications officers to the headquarters of the 57th and 4th Guards armies. As a result of the difficult mine situation in the Danube, the Danube Military Flotilla's cutters were not able to arrive by the beginning of the 57th Army's operation to force the Danube and arrived in the Bezdan area by 29 November.

On 24 November units of the 64th and 75th rifle corps, having begun an attack, by the close of the day had advanced 1-4 kilometers and were fighting for Knezevi Vinogradi and Lug. The 6th Guards Rifle Corps had completed crossing one division, which by the close of the day had concentrated in the Topola area. The remaining divisions and the 32nd Mechanized Brigade were on the march.

The enemy, having committed an additional two battalions from the 44th Training Regiment into the fighting along the flank and units of the 117th Light Infantry Division in the Beli Monastir area, were stubbornly holding the Udvar—Knezevo road and the commanding heights east of Popovac, Grabovac and Lug.

Due to the forthcoming commitment of the 4th Guards Army from the 57th Army's bridgehead on 26 November, there was the possibility of employing all of the 6th Guards Rifle Corps' efforts to develop the success, without distracting them for securing the right flank, as had been planned earlier.

By the close of 24 November the situation of the *front's* forces was as follows:

The 4th Guards Army and the 31st Guards Rifle Corps (4th, 34th and 40th guards rifle divisions), along with the 466th Mortar Regiment and 51st Guards Mortar Regiment, were occupying defensive positions within the following boundaries: from the right, Subotica—Dunapentele, and from the left, excluding Baja along a 95-kilometer front. The 34th and 40th guards rifle divisions were in the first echelon, with the 4th Guards Rifle Division in the second echelon in the Czinget—Akaszto area.

The 21st Guards Rifle Corps (41st, 62nd and 69th rifle divisions), with the 456th Light Artillery Regiment, 212th Howitzer Regiment, 123rd Cannon-Artillery Brigade, was to occupy defensive positions along the left bank of the Danube with the 41st Guards Rifle Division along the sector Baja—Mohacs and was preparing to force the river. Two divisions (62nd and 69th guards rifle divisions) had concentrated in the Gara—Ridica—Bacsbokod area.

The 20th Guards Rifle Corps (5th and 7th guards airborne, 80th Rifle and 84th Guards Rifle divisions), with the 188th and 200th mortar regiments and the 115th Cannon-Artillery Brigade had concentrated in the area Svetozar Miletic—Sombor area and east of Novi Savac.

The commander had in reserve the following: the 252nd Rifle Division on the march from the Subotica area, the 22nd Anti-Aircraft Artillery Division (1347th, 1337th, 1353rd, 1341st, 4257th, and 271st anti-aircraft artillery regiments), 56th Engineer-Sapper Brigade, 83rd Naval Infantry Brigade, and the Danube Flotilla's 1st Brigade.

The numerical strength of the 4th Guards Army's divisions was as follows: one division of up to 6,000 men, two divisions of up to 7,000 men, and eight divisions of up to 7,000-7,5000 men.

The 57th Army was fighting along the following line:

64th Rifle Corps (19th, 113th and 73rd Guards rifle divisions), east of Udvar—Branina—east of Kamenac—north of Knezevi Vinogradi, with three divisions in the first echelon.

75th Rifle Corps (74th, 236th and then the 233rd rifle divisions), east of Knezevi Vinogradi—east of Grabovac—northern outskirts of Lug.

The 6th Guards Rifle Corps (10th Guards Airborne Division, 20th and 61st guards rifle divisions) was completing its concentration with the 10th Guards Airborne and 20th Guards Rifle divisions in the Topola area and to the east; one division was at the crossing near Batina. The 233rd Rifle Division was in the army commander's reserve.

The 32nd Mechanized Brigade was completing the crossing of its motorized infantry in the Batina area.

The 18th Tank Corps had concentrated in the Bajmok—Stara Moravica—Backa Topola area.

The Danube Military Flotilla was arriving in the Batina area with part of its armored cutters along the King Peter I Canal. It was securing the troops' crossing by minesweeping the channel of the Danube River.

The 9th Artillery Division was completing its movement by rail and had unloaded 18 of 22 trains.

The situation of the 37th Army, 68th Rifle Corps and the 1st Guards Fortified Area was essentially unchanged. The 17th Air Army was supporting the 57th and 4th Guards armies' forces on the bridgeheads, while carrying out an average of 550 sorties per day. The army's airfield basing remained without particular changes.

The situation of the Bulgarian and Yugoslav forces was as follows:

a) The Bulgarian forces were regrouping and moving their troops to a different axis.
   2nd Army: the 6th Infantry Division was northeast of Mitrovica, along the front Vucitrn—Kurilovo, moving on Podujevo; the 4th Infantry and an armored brigade were in Mitrovica; the 9th Infantry Division was moving on Mitrovica, with its lead elements near Vucitrn; the 12th Infantry Division was moving from Pristina to the northeast, and; the 4th Army's 2nd Cavalry Division was moving on Novo Selo.
   1st Army: the 11th Infantry Division was moving from Urosevac to Pozeranje; the 1st and 2nd infantry divisions were moving on Petrovo Selo (east of Skopje) and Kumanovo.

b) The forces of the Yugoslav People's Liberation Army: the 2nd Brigade was in Petrovgrad; the 14th Brigade was east of Novi Sad; the 16th Infantry Division was on the move from Novi Sad to Petrovgrad; the 13th Brigade was in Srbobran; the 11th Infantry Division was in Sremska Mitrovica; the 1st and 5th infantry divisions were in Belgrade; the 45th Infantry Division was in Valjevo; the 23rd Infantry Division was in Pranjani; the 17th Infantry Division was along the line Western Morava River—Jajcana; further along part of the subunits of the 57th Army's 233rd Rifle Division were along the sector Targoviste—Vrbas; the 37th Infantry Division was in the Uzice area; the 47th Infantry Division was in the Majdevo area; the 22nd Infantry Division was in Mitrovica; the 46th Infantry Division was along the front Gusterice—south of Pristina, and; the remaining units and formations were mainly in their previous areas.

The enemy was withdrawing his forces facing the Bulgarian and Yugoslav troops, waging holding actions along some axes.

The enemy front was not continuous and mainly consisted of centers of resistance and strong points along the main road junctions and in major inhabited locales, and ran along the line Kraljevo—along the Western Morava River—then toward Cacak—two kilometers north and northwest of Morava—excluding Tabanovici—Poret—Uton.

The strength of the Third Ukrainian Front (minus the 37th Army) as of 24 November was as follows:

4th Guards Army:

rifle corps—20th, 21st and 31st guards rifle corps;

rifle divisions—5th and 7th guards airborne, 80th and 84th guards rifle divisions; 41st, 62nd and 69th guards rifle divisions; 252nd Rifle Division; 4th, 34th and 40th guards rifle divisions.

Artillery: an army cannon-artillery brigade—one anti-tank artillery regiment, two guards mortar regiments, and five anti-aircraft regiments.

Engineer Troops: one engineer-sapper brigade.

57th Army:

rifle corps—6th Guards, 64th and 75th rifle corps;

rifle divisions—10th Guards Airborne, 20th and 61st guards rifle divisions; 19th 74th 113th, and 233rd rifle divisions; 73rd, 236th and 299th rifle divisions.

Artillery: an army cannon-artillery brigade of cannon regiments; howitzer regiments, light artillery regiments; anti-tank artillery regiments; mortar regiments; guards mortar regiments; independent guards mortar battalions, and; anti-aircraft regiments.

Armored and mechanized forces: one mechanized brigade, one independent motorcycle regiment, one special designation battalion (252nd), and four self-propelled artillery regiments.

Engineer Troops: 11th Engineer-Sapper Brigade, 5th Pontoon-Bridge Brigade.

Chemical Troops: one independent chemical defense battalion, two flamethrower battalions.

Units subordinated to the *front*:

68th Rifle Corps—52nd, 93rd and 223rd rifle divisions.

83rd and 255th naval infantry brigades.

1st Guards Fortified Area.

Artillery: four anti-tank artillery regiments, one mortar regiment, two guards mortar regiments, 14 anti-aircraft regiments, two independent anti-aircraft divisions, and independent anti-aircraft artillery battalions.

Armored and mechanized forces—18th Tank Corps.

Engineer forces—one assault engineer-sapper brigade, one motorized engineer-sapper brigade and two pontoon regiments.

Chemical troops—three independent chemical defense battalions.

On 25-26 November the enemy continued to throw in fresh units (486th Reserve Regiment, the 118th Light Infantry Division's 755th Infantry Regiment, von Rudnow's assault brigade, and others) reinforced his counterattacks (on 25 November there were nine counterattacks, up to a battalion each in strength, and on 26 November up to 15 counterattacks, some of which were launched in strength of up to a regiment of infantry, with tanks and self-propelled guns).

The successful advance of the 57th Army's units forced the enemy to throw all of his reserves against them, including from other sectors of the front, which sharply reduced the enemy's firmness along neighboring sectors.

This created favorable opportunities for forcing the Danube River with the forces of the 4th Guards Army. The army's forward units (41st Guards Rifle Division), having begun the forcing of the Danube in the Mohacs area on the night of 23-24 November, had by the close of 25 November advanced beyond the shore dike and had begun fighting for Kelked, having expanded the captured bridgehead to two kilometers along the front and up to 1.5 kilometers in depth.

Part of the 45mm guns and 82mm mortars were crossed in the first echelon. Also crossed were the battalion and battery officers of divisional artillery, to whom was entrusted the task of supporting the first echelon's actions with fire from firing positions along the eastern bank. Horse-drawn regimental and divisional artillery was crossed with the second echelon. By the close of 25 November there were four guns of divisional artillery, seven guns of regimental artillery, 19 45mm guns, five 120mm mortars and 50 82mm mortars, for a total of 85 tubes.

The remaining artillery was located along the eastern bank of the Danube and fired across the river.

In capturing the town of Mohacs a major role was played by guns located with the infantry. These guns, firing over open sights, destroyed the enemy's firing points in buildings configured for defense, thus securing the rapid capture of this powerfully fortified strong point.

The crossing of the 4th Guards Army's units (41st Guards Rifle Division) unfolded slowly due to the absence of authorized crossing equipment (the crossing was carried out using materials at hand and on landing and fishing craft). However, as early as 29 November two ferries from a 120-A-3 park, with a capacity of six tons, was working, as well as landing and fishing craft.

On 26 November the *front* commander order the commander of the 4th Guards Army to do the following:

To continue to force the river, with the immediate objective of capturing the following line with the forces of the 21st Guards Rifle Corps no later than November 28: Dunaszeksco—Somberek—Liptod. The army was to then reach the line Bataszek—Bataapati—Ofalu—Pecsvarad—Szomod.

At the same time, it was pointed out that two of the 20th Guards Rifle Corps' rifle divisions were to be crossed in the Batina area and the 20th Guards Rifle Corps' remaining units in the Kozac area, behind the 21st Guards Rifle Corps' units.

The commander of the 57th Army was instructed to resubordinate one anti-tank artillery regiment, one mortar regiment and one howitzer regiment to the 20th Guards Rifle Corps along the western bank of the Danube.

Simultaneously, the commander of the 17th Air Army was ordered to support the 21st Rifle Corps' activities with one assault air and one fighter divisions.

The commander of the 4th Guards Army adopted measures to consolidate the bridgehead captured along the western bank of the Danube and ordered the commander of the 21st Guards Rifle Corps, as an immediate task, to link up with the 57th Army's units operating in the Udvar area and to capture Mohacs.

On 25 November the 57th Army continued to advance in heavy fighting. The 6th Guards Rifle Corps' 10th Guards Airborne Division, which had been committed into the battle, was fighting along the line Borza—east of Majs. Having outflanked Udvar from the north, the 6th Guards Rifle Corps' division, along with units of the 64th Rifle Corps, captured Udvar.

The 64th Rifle Corps (19th and 113th rifle divisions and 73rd Guards Rifle Division) cut the paved road south of Udvar, captured Branina, the eastern outskirts of Popovac, height 241, and the northern outskirts of Knezevi Vinogradi.

The 75th Rifle Corps (236th, 74th and 299th rifle divisions) was fighting for Knezevi Vinogradi with one rifle division, while the remaining units did not advance, due to the enemy's powerful fire resistance.

The cavalry-mechanized group completed its concentration in the Kiskoros—Kecel—Kiskunhalas area, where it was putting its equipment, personnel, horses, and weapons in order and was bringing its units up to strength.

On 26 November the 57th Army made its combat formations denser southwest of Mohacs by committing into the fighting the second echelon's main forces, the 6th Guards Rifle Corps, into the fighting. Because the corps' rifle divisions were committed into the fighting sequentially, but without adequate artillery and air support, the expected development of the success did not take place. By the close of the day the corps' formations were fighting along the line north of Nagynyarad—in front of Hercegtettes—Bezedek.

The 64th Rifle Corps advanced only 3-4 kilometers, capturing Knezevo, Popovac and Karanac. The army's remaining formations advanced little.

During the second half of the day the commander of the 57th Army committed the 32nd Guards Mechanized Brigade into the fighting with the immediate task of developing the 6th Guards and 64th rifle corps' success and capturing Nemetboly and Szederkeny and to subsequently be ready for operations on Pecs. While being committed into the fighting, the 32nd Mechanized Brigade was reinforced with an anti-tank artillery regiment and mortar, guards mortar and howitzer regiments.

Upon passing through the rifle troops' combat formations in the Nagynyarad area, the 32nd Mechanized Brigade captured Nemetboly from the march and by the close of the day had cleared the enemy out of Szederkeny and Szajk, thus expanding the captured bridgehead to 62 kilometers along the front and up to 15-20 kilometers in depth. Along the 4th Guards Army's front, units of the 21st Guards Rifle Corps (41st Guards Rifle Division), having reached by the close of 26 November a line north and northwest of Mohacs—south of Lanycsok—east of Bacsfapuszta, guaranteed the opportunity of laying down bridge crossings in the Mohacs area.

In the Fekete Kapu area the forces of the 4th Guards Army linked up with the 57th Army's right-flank units.

The seizure of prisoners in the Kelked area established that the 31st SS Infantry Division's 78th and 79th infantry regiments were defending along the Mohacs—Batina sector. The prisoners testified that these regiments consisted of two battalions, with each battalion consisting of five companies, with 120-130 soldiers in officers in each company, along with two heavy and four light machine guns and two mortars. The regiments did not have their own artillery.

The 32nd Guards Mechanized Brigade, while advancing in the direction of Pecs and encountering the opposition of only scattered groups of the enemy, began fighting for Pecs by the close of 27 November. The forward detachments of the 6th Guards Rifle Corps were rapidly moving up behind the brigade.

The 32nd Guards Mechanized Brigade's success was most apparent in the advance of the 6th Guards Rifle Corps, as well as of the 64th Rifle Corps.

By the close of 28 November the 19th Rifle Division made a combat forcing of the Karasica Canal; the 113th Rifle Division captured Ida and forced the Karasica Canal with its left flank in the Illocska area; the 73rd Guards Rifle Division was fighting for Sirine and the Sudraz farm.

The 75th Rifle Corps completely captured the enemy's powerful strong point of Knezevi Vinogradi. While continuing to clear the enemy out of the zone adjacent to the Danube River, the corps' units reached the line east of Zeleno Polje—Bolman—Darda—Bilje.

From 26 November all of the 20th and 21st Guards rifle corps' divisions, except for the 252nd Rifle Division, which had occupied the 31st Guards Rifle Corps's defensive sector, were moved up to support the further broadening of the bridgehead toward the crossings in the Mohacs and Batina area in the 57th Army's sector.

Units of the 4th Guards Army, while successfully widening the bridgehead, on 28 November captured Bataszek, Kevesd and Vemend.

Thus on 27 November the *front's* forces advanced 3-19 kilometers and the mechanized brigade up to 24 kilometers, and widened the bridgehead up to 87 kilometers along the front and up to 20-30 kilometers in depth.

As was shown earlier, on 27 November the cavalry-mechanized group arrived to reinforce the *front* and had concentrated in the area Kiskoros—Kecel—Kiskunhalas—Soltvadkert.

Simultaneously, as the operation progressed the 18th Tank Corps was being reinforced and put in order, for which purpose four trains with 50 tanks and 42 self-propelled guns arrived on 28 November.

The commander of the 18th Tank Corps had instructions from the *front* commander, without waiting to be fully brought up to strength, to begin crossing the Danube River, but due to the fact that the *front* had not organized by 29 November the crossing of mobile forces and self-propelled artillery, the crossings proved to be so overcrowded with a large amount of self-propelled artillery that the tank units were unable to approach the crossings. Besides this, the promised ferries for the crossing had not arrived by the indicated date.

In order to more securely support the *front's* right wing, the *front* commander resubordinated from 28 November the 83rd Naval Infantry Brigade to the commander of the 4th Guards Army and instructed the commander of the Danube Military Flotilla to complete the concentration of 25 cutters to the Bezdan area, to establish close communications with the headquarters of the 4th Guards Army, with the task of facilitating the army's forces in advancing along the right bank of the Danube River by putting ashore tactical landings and with artillery fire from armored cutters.

The enemy, striving to disrupt the advance by the 32nd Guards Mechanized Brigade and units of the 6th Guards Rifle Corps on Pecs, undertook powerful counterattacks toward Mariakemend, but these counterattacks were successfully repulsed.

On 29 November the enemy's resistance had basically been crushed and he began to fall back along some sectors. By this time the 62nd and 80th guards rifle divisions had been crossed to the right bank of the Danube and had been committed into the fighting, and on 30 November the 4th Guards Army's 69th Rifle Division and 7th Guards Airborne Division were fully ready to enter the fighting.

During 25-29 November the 4th Guards Army's forces advanced 53 kilometers with an average daily rate of advance of ten kilometers.

By the close of 29 November the *front's* forces occupied the following position:

4th Guards Army (41st and 62nd guards rifle divisions) had reached the line of the southern outskirts of Decs—Ebesicsard—southern outskirts of Bonyhad—northern outskirts of Pecsvarad—Hosszuheteny.

The 57th Army captured the city of Pecs with the forces of the 6th Guards Rifle Division and the 32nd Mechanized Brigade. The army's forces, while pushing aside the enemy striving to consolidate along intermediate lines, were fighting along the following lines by the close of 29 November: the 6th Guards Rifle Corps along the southern outskirts of Mecseszka Boles—Mecsekalya—Malom—Pogany; the 32nd Mechanized Brigade began to move out of Pecs during the second half of the day toward Szentlorinc and dispatched a forward detachment to seize the bridge near Marko (eight kilometers west of Mecsekalya).

The 64th Rifle Corps was fighting along the line Ata—Kistotfalu—eastern outskirts of Siklos; the 73rd Guards Rifle Division was in the corps' second echelon.

The 76th Rifle Corps reached the line of the eastern outskirts of Egyhazasharaszti—Torjanci—south of Bolman—Darda—Bilje.

The 68th Rifle Corps, which was subordinated to the *front*, captured Kraljevo with units of the 223rd Rifle Division, along with the Yugoslav People's Liberation Army's 2nd Proletarian Division. The position of the corps' remaining formations was unchanged.

The 1st Guards Fortified Area relieved units of the 299th Rifle Division.

The 37th Army remained in its previous area.

The Bulgarian 1st Army was concentrating its forces west of Belgrade, while 25 trains were dispatched.

By this time the Bulgarian 1st Army had the following strength: 83,649 soldiers and officers, 23,829 horses, 1,338 motor vehicles, 264 tows, 50,546 rifles, 639 heavy machine guns, 1,698 light machine guns, 2,218 automatic rifles, 200-285 guns of various calibers, 87 anti-aircraft guns, and 420 mortars.

The headquarters of the Bulgarian 1st Army was in Stara Pazova.

The Danube Military Flotilla was moving 25 combat vessels to the Batina—Baja area and was supporting the troops' transport and crossing, was sweeping the Danube for mines and carrying out mine reconnaissance.

During 9-29 November the enemy, trying to eliminate the bridgehead, threw the following units against this sector from southern Serbia: two regiments from the "Brandenburg" Division, the 1st Mountain Division's 99th Mountain Regiment, the 117th Light Infantry Division's 749th Infantry Regiment, the 118th Light Infantry Division's 750th Infantry Regiment, the 13th SS Muslim Infantry Division's 28th Infantry Regiment, an assault battalion from the Second Panzer Army, the 1022nd Anti-Tank Battalion, and the 105th and 668th artillery battalions from the high command reserve; from northern Italy: the 44th Infantry Division and the 71st Infantry Division's 194th Infantry Regiment; from Hungary: the 31st SS Division and the Hungarian 4th Reserve Division's 8th Infantry Regiment, for a total of up to five infantry divisions, with reinforcements.

From captured documents seized by our troops it is clear that the Hitlerite command had not counted on the rapid forcing of the Danube River and the possibility of our forces arriving at the approaches to the Nagykanizsa oil-producing area and to Budapest from the southwest. Because of this, it was only at the last moment that it made the decision to throw significant forces into the defense of the western bank of the Danube River and the so-called "Margarita Line." On 27 November an order was issued to throw the LVII Panzer Corps to the Dunafoldvar area. Here the corps was supposed, along with the forces of the 23rd Panzer Division and units from the high command reserve and the Hungarian Third Army, which had been placed at the disposal of the German Sixth Army (headquarters in Lovasbereny), to block our forces' offensive through the defile between Lake Balaton and the Danube. The Sixth Army was to allot the following formations and units for employment in the area to the west of the Danube: LVII Panzer Corps and corps units, the 325th Assault Gun Brigade, 809th Heavy Artillery Battalion, 2nd Heavy Artillery Battalion, 736th Mortar Battalion, 662nd Assault Gun Battalion, 503rd Heavy Panzer Battalion, and the 1335th Assault Gun Battalion. The order of subordination was as follows: the LVII Panzer Corps, consisting of the 23rd Panzer and 20th Infantry divisions, was to be subordinated to group Fretter-Pico[1], which was being formed and which later became the Balck[2] group. The command of the Hungarian Third Army was to be in charge of the front along the Danube until the completion of group Fretter-Pico. An anti-aircraft division, in conjunction with the remnants of the 31st SS Infantry Division, was to support the screen in the Dombovar area. The 23rd Panzer Division was to fight in front of the "Margarita Line." The Hungarian 20th Infantry Division was to secure the cover of the 23rd Panzer Division's attack from the east along the line

1 Editor's note. Maximilian Ludwig Julius Franz Fretter-Pico (1892-1984) joined the army in 1910 and fought in the First World War. During the Second World War he commanded a division, corps and an army.

2 Editor's note. Hermann Balck (1897-1982) joined the army in 1913 and fought in the First World War in France, Russia, Italy, and the Balkans. During World War II he commanded a tank regiment, division, corps, and army in the East and later commanded an army group in the West. He was convicted of war crimes, but released in 1950.

Kety—Kolesd. During this same period the 23rd Panzer Division was to be placed at the disposal of the LVII Panzer Corps. According to the original plan, the Hungarian Third Army was to be responsible for the defense of the western bank of the Danube, including the Budapest area as far as Vajcen.

Thus as a result of 20 days of fighting, the *front's* forces had won an operational bridgehead along the western bank of the Danube, while at the same time defeating an infantry division and had inflicted heavy losses on another three infantry divisions and a motorized brigade.

With the seizure of an operational bridgehead along the western bank, the opportunity had been created for an offensive along the western bank of the Danube toward Budapest from the south and southwest, as well as for developing the attack on Nagykanizsa.

Due to the threat of our forces arriving at his communications, the enemy began to pull back his forces to the area between the Danube and Sava rivers to the west and northwest, covering his retreat with a Croatian brigade.

Thus the Third Ukrainian Front's forces, upon assuming the offensive, had forced the Danube north of the Drava River, broken through the enemy's defense along the western bank of the Danube and, having advanced up to 40 kilometers in depth, had broadened the breakthrough up to 150 kilometers along the front. During the offensive the *front's* forces captured the towns and major communications centers of Pecs, Bataszek and Mohacs on Hungarian territory and had taken more than 330 other inhabited locales in fighting.

The *front's* forces completely or partially routed the 44th Infantry Division, the 31st SS Muslim Infantry Division, several independent regiments and battalions, the 92nd Mechanized Brigade, the 1222nd Anti-Tank Battalion, and several artillery battalions.

The following had been defeated, although they retained partial combat effectiveness: the 117th Light Infantry Division's 749th Infantry Regiment, the 118th Light Infantry Division's 668th Artillery Regiment, the 1st Mountain Division, the 39th Security Regiment, the "Brandenburg" SS Division, and von Rudnow's assault brigade.

During this period up to 30,000 soldiers and officers were killed, 75 tanks, self-propelled guns and armored transports were destroyed, as well as 290 guns, 170 mortars, 1,300 heavy and light machine guns, 56 planes, 27 locomotives, 252 train cars, 60 various depots, and 1,500 horses.

In all, more than 2,000 enemy soldiers and officers were taken prisoner. Captured were 20 tanks, self-propelled guns and armored transports, 20 guns, 150 mortars, more than 200 machine guns, 100 motor vehicles, 50 different depots, and 750 horses, etc.

The *front's* forces achieved these results, while operating in the complex conditions of the autumn rains. During November there were 16 days with precipitation and 12 days with fog. Travel over the dirt roads had been made difficult as early as 3 November, and during the final ten days the dirt roads became impassable for auto transport. During the month there were only six flying days, ten for limited flying, and the remainder not for flying. From 9 November the water in the rivers began to rise, which seriously hindered the crossing of troops and combat equipment.

The *front's* forces, while operating in these conditions, nevertheless broadly employed outflanking and enveloping maneuver and they encircled and destroyed some enemy garrisons in Podolje, Suza, Knezevi Vinogradi, and Petlovac.

The forcing of the Danube River and the seizure of an operational bridgehead became possible thanks to the organized work of the *Stavka* of the Supreme High Command, which not only indicated the axes of the attacks, but uninterruptedly reinforced the Third Ukrainian Front, which led to a material change in its combat strength and capabilities and also allowed the *front* command to employ the forces of the Bulgarian army in the offensive on Hungarian territory.

A unique feature of the river forcing was that it took place consecutively: first by the forces of the 57th Army, and then of the 4th Guards Army. During the seizure of an operational bridgehead, the creation of shock groups took place during regroupings for the forcing.

The planning for the forcing took place during the forcing itself, on the basis of instructions from the *Stavka* and the *front*, directly in the armies. The main planning documents were a graphic plan, a textual plan, an order and local combat orders that fine-tuned individual tenets of the orders or directives.

Intelligence gathering was carried out through the activities of forward detachments and by observation. Aerial reconnaissance was carried out insufficiently early and deeply. Nevertheless, by the start of the forcing the *front's* forces basically disposed of correct information regarding the nature of the river and the enemy's defense along its western bank.

A major role in the success of the forcing was played by operational masking: the secrecy in preparing the crossings, the organization of demonstration and false crossings, and the broad employment of smoke.

The forcing was carried out along narrow sectors, as a rule, at night or before dawn, without an artillery preparation.

This, to a certain degree, ensured surprise for our forces, although on the other hand the enemy had the opportunity to broadly maneuver his men and materiel at the expense of sectors of the front not being attacked.

Characteristic of the 4th Guards Army's artillery activities while forcing the Danube was the crossing of quite a significant part of the artillery weapons directly in the infantry's first echelon.

A feature of our forces' activities was the conduct of major regroupings and the creation of reserves during both the forcing period and during combat operations along the right bank, as well as the development of the success in the planned direction.

As a rule, the organization of the corps' and divisions' combat formations while seizing the operational bridgehead was in two echelons. The army commanders had combined-arms and artillery-anti-tank reserves at their disposal. The forward detachments were the first to force the river on materials at hand, followed by the main forces of the first-echelon regiments and divisions.

The enemy organized his defense of the river along a broad front. One should note the following in the enemy's organization and conduct of the defense:

- as a rule, the forward edge of the defense ran immediately along the bank and was stubbornly defended;
- in a number of cases, circular fire was organized, both from light and heavy guns, in both day and night. Fire was waged automatically in fog, with the employment of special orientation markers;
- control posts were scrupulously masked. All means of communications were employed, including sound and light signals for shifting continuous artillery-mortar and infantry fire;
- heavy and light infantry weapons were stationed at firing positions, from which the surface of the water was easily visible, and from which each weapon could wage flanking fire;
- it is necessary to note the stubbornness and persistence in the waging of the defensive battle: some inhabited locales changed hands. Counterattacks by subunits from a company to a battalion in strength were carried out several times during the course of a day along some sectors.

Troop control was exercised from command posts at the corps-regiment level: up to four kilometers for a corps commander; up to two kilometers for a division commander and; up to 1.5 kilometers for a regimental commander. As a rule observation posts were located along the bank.

The chief shortcomings while forcing the Danube were:

- the weak composition of the forward detachments and the insufficient support by artillery-mortar fire and aviation;
- the slow augmentation of force because of the shortage of crossing equipment;

- the poor organization of the combined-arms battle while seizing a bridgehead on the part of the commanders of the armies, corps and some division commanders and their staffs.

The Development of the Offensive and the Arrival at the "Margarita Line"

Upon the seizure of an operational bridgehead, the *front* commander made the decision to further develop the offensive for the purpose of destroying the enemy's Danube group of forces and capturing the important locales and road junctions of Szekesfehervar and Nagykanizsa.

The plan called for a decisive offensive by the *front's* main forces along the Szekesfehervar axis and by part of the *front's* forces along the Nagykanizsa axis to destroy the enemy's opposing units, preventing their withdrawal and consolidation along the previously-prepared defensive line along the line Erd—Baracska—Kapolnasnyek—Lake Velence—Balatonakarttya—Lake Balaton—Balatonkeresztur—Marcali—Nagybajom—Nagyatad—Barcs and capture this line from the march. While subsequently developing the attack, it was to take Szekesfehervar and Nagykanizsa and encircle the enemy's Budapest group of forces from the west.

The commander of the 4th Guards Army, in full accordance with the *front* commander's mission and plan, decided, while having his army's main forces along the right flank and in the center, to no later than 10 December capture the line excluding Lake Velence—Szekesfehervar—Moha—Varpalota—Vorosbereny.

At the same time, it was taken into account that the army's formations would have to force (cross) the Danube, deploy and while breaking and rolling up the enemy's defense from the march, decisively advance to the north and northwest.

The rapid advance of the formations operating in the first echelon and the difficulties connected with forcing and crossing the Danube River due to a shortage of crossing equipment, must inevitably have led to a significant overextension of the army's forces, artillery and rear establishments. Taking this into account, the commander of the 4th Guards Army requested that the *front* commander speed up the construction of bridges in the Mohacs—Baja area and to reinforce the army with crossing equipment and mobile forces (a mechanized corps or 2-3 mechanized brigades, an anti-tank brigade, howitzer regiments, and an artillery regiment for operational purposes, as well as a second organic automobile battalion).

The commander of the 57th Army decided on the following: to hold the army's main forces in the center and along the right flank and reach the line indicted by the *front* commander on 5 December.

While developing the offensive, the *front's* forces advanced 4-28 kilometers on 30 November. The enemy fell back, putting up his most powerful resistance west of Pecs.

The 4th Guards Army's forces advanced 16 kilometers and were fighting along the line Tolna—Harc—north of Bonyhad—Tofu—Karasz—Szalatnak—Kisvaszar.

In accordance with the previously drawn-up plan, the 31st Guards Rifle Corps was to force the Danube, with its main forces in the Madocsa area. For this reason, the commander of the 4th Guards Army assigned the following missions:

The 31st Rifle Corps' 40th Guards Rifle Division was to begin forcing the Danube River in the Madocsa area on 30 November, with artillery support. By 0800 on 1 December the division was to be entirely crossed and the Bolcske—Madocsa—Dunakemled area captured. By the close of the day it was to take the area Bikacs—Nagydorog—Gyorkony and cross the second rifle division's (4th Guards Rifle Division) forces and take Dunafoldvar by the morning of 2 December.

The Danube Military Flotilla's 1st Brigade of armored cutters and the 83rd Naval Infantry Brigade were to capture a bridgehead through joint action on the night of 30 November-1 December along the western bank of the Danube River in the Gerjen—Dunaszentgyorgy—Fadd area and to hold this area until the arrival of the 41st Guards Rifle Division's infantry operating in the Szekszard area.

It was further planned to carry out landing operations in conjunction with the forces of the 4th Guards Army in the Dunafoldvar—Dunapentele area.

In carrying out its task, the 31st Guards Rifle Corps set out at 2200 on 30 November to force the Danube River in the area three kilometers west of Solt and the pier west of Harta.

The corps was faced in the crossing areas by General Kiss's group in the Dunafoldvar area and to the north, and the Danube Flotilla's 1st Brigade by the 16th Border Battalion along the sector from Dunafoldvar to Madocsa, numbering up to 2,500 soldiers and officers, with ten tanks and self-propelled guns overall. According to the Soviet army's intelligence directorate, the 20th and the remnants of the 24th Hungarian infantry divisions, numbering up to 7,000 soldiers and officers, were in reserve facing the *front*.

The forcing of the Danube by the 31st Guards Rifle Corps was a surprise for the enemy, which enabled our forces, upon capturing Madocsa and Bolcske on the first day of the fighting, to expand the bridgehead up to six kilometers along the front and up to five kilometers in depth, and to organize the crossing of the army's forces along this sector.

Simultaneously, a battalion from the 83rd Naval Infantry Brigade and a regiment from the 252nd Rifle Division successfully forced the Danube in the Gerjen area and captured Gerjen by 0600 on 1 December and, upon reaching the Dunaszentgyorgy, linked up with units of the 41st Guards Rifle Division.

This sped up the rolling up of the enemy's defense and made the advance by the 41st Guards Rifle Division easier.

During 1 December the *front's* forces advanced 2-26 kilometers and had gotten involved in street fighting for the town of Donbovar, simultaneously outflanking it from the west and east.

In order to increase the offensive pace, the *front* commander subordinated the 12th Assault Engineer-Sapper Brigade (minus two battalions left behind until 4 December to finish the construction of a bridge near Mohacs) to the commander of the 4th Guards Army.

The 18th Tank Corps was ordered, without waiting to be fully brought up to authorized equipment strength, to move, consecutively by formations, to the area Tamasi—the woods west of Szaraszd—Pincehely by no later than 6 December, where it was to be at the disposal of the commander of the 4th Guards Army.

The commander of the 4th Guards Army was ordered to develop the offensive to the north and northwest, with the immediate task of reaching the area northwest and west of Szekesfehervar. The following units were to be resubordinated from the 4th Guards Army to the 18th Tank Corps by the start of the latter's commitment into the fighting: 230th Howitzer Regiment, 42nd Anti-Tank Artillery Brigade, the 10th Mortar Brigade's 200th Mortar Regiment, 58th Guards Mortar Regiment, 22nd Anti-Aircraft Artillery Division (minus the 1353rd Artillery Regiment), and a battalion from the 44th Motorized Engineer-Sapper Brigade. The commander of the 5th Guards Cavalry Corps was ordered to move to the Kaposvar area and to subordinate himself to the commander of the 57th Army by no later than 1 December. The crossing of the 5th Guards Cavalry Corps was to take place near Mohacs, and for this purpose a 16-ton pontoon bridge and two 30-ton ferries was to be placed at its disposal from 1800 on 6 December.

Further on, the commander of the 5th Guards Cavalry Corps was instructed to take decisive measures to flesh out his mounted squadrons by transferring everyone fit for service from the supporting rear establishments.

The enemy took emergency measures to cover Budapest from the south and southwest. For this purpose, he undertook counterattacks along the 4th Guards Amy's sector with recently-arrived units of the 23rd Panzer Division.

Along the 57th Army's front the enemy, by covering himself with powerful rearguards, mining roads, blowing up bridges and organizing other obstacles, continued his forced withdrawal.

Through the capture of prisoners and documents, the appearance of the enemy's 23rd Panzer and 20th Infantry divisions, which had been moved from the north from Budapest, was confirmed; the Hungarian 23rd Infantry Division was west of the Sarviz Canal and the Hungarian 8th Grenadier Reserve Division northwest of Kaposvar. During 30 November-3 December the enemy committed the following units into the front line: one panzer and four infantry divisions and two independent infantry regiments, while the appearance of the 15th Anti-Aircraft Artillery Division was noted in the Szekesfehervar area.

This gave the enemy the opportunity to somewhat alter the correlation of forces, which by the close of 3 December was as follows:

Along the 4th Guards Army's front it was 1:0.8 in men, 1:0.4 in mortars, 1:0.2 in anti-tank guns, 1:0.8 in field artillery, and 1:0.5 in tanks and self-propelled guns.

Along the 57th Army's front it was 1:0.6 in men, 1:0.4 in mortars, 1:0.3 in anti-tank weapons, 1:0.5 in field artillery, and 1:0.8 in tanks and self-propelled guns in our favor.

During 3-4 December the *front's* forces continued to develop the offensive and advanced 25-40 kilometers along some axes and, having captured at the same time the major inhabited locales of Dunafoldvar and Tamasi, had gotten into fighting for Szigetvar and forced the Kapos and Jelusa canals.

The enemy was pulling back his forces along a number of sectors. His aviation launched strikes in groups of 5-15 planes against our forces' combat formations and columns.

The 17th Air Army, limited in its operations because of the unfavorable weather and while supporting the troops' offensive, carried out more than 50 sorties per day, generally against the enemy's retreating forces north and south of the Drava River.

The commander of the 57th Army, despite the *front* commander's plan and demand that he have his main forces closer to the center and right flank, shifted them somewhat to his left flank during the course of the offensive, which was forced to a certain degree by the nature of the terrain, as well as a possible counterblow by the enemy from the southern bank of the Drava River. The *front* comamnder demanded that the 6th Rifle Corps' main forces be shifted to the north of Nagybajom, while the main forces of the 64th Rifle Corps were to be directed to bypass Szigetvar to Nagyatad, Labod and Samogyszob (30 kilometers southeast of Nagybajom), in order to reach the paved road to Szigetvar with one division and then to bypass it from the north.

The 75th Rifle Corps was to expand its border to the north and no less than two roads to it. Through these measures, the *front* commander sought to concentrate the 57th Army's main forces along the main Nagykanizsa axis, with the immediate task of destroying the enemy in the Marcali—Nagybajom area and to capture Nagykanizsa.

On 5-6 December the *front's* forces continued to attack and advanced 5-25 kilometers. The enemy reinforced his group of forces opposite the 4th Guards Army by committing additional forces into the fighting and attempted to delay the advance by the 4th Guards Army's forces through infantry counterattacks with 20-30 tanks and self-propelled guns.

The following units were identified facing the army: a Hungarian composite regiment, the German 271st Infantry Division's 979th Infantry Regiment, the Hungarian 2nd Panzer Division, the Hungarian 23rd Infantry Division, the 1st Brigade of the Danube Flotilla, the 153rd Infantry Division's 717th Infantry Regiment, the 46th Infantry Division, the Hungarian 20th Infantry Division, the 23rd Panzer Division, and the 44th Training Regiment. The commander of the 46th Army was ordered to secure the boundary with the Second Ukrainian Front's 46th Army along the Danube River with the forces of the 83rd Naval Infantry Brigade and a brigade of armored cutters from the Danube Military Flotilla.

As the offensive progressed, two of the 31st Guards Rifle Corps' rifle divisions were to be moved to the right flank. This decision by the *front* commander was conditioned by the necessity of establishing at this stage of the operation closer cooperation with the Second Ukrainian Front's left wing.

The commander of the 4th Guards Army made the decision to use the forces of the 31st Guards Rifle Corps to link up with the 46th Army's forces in the Ercsi area, 22 kilometers north of Nagyperkata.

On 6 December the *Stavka* of the Supreme High Command ordered the commander of the Third Ukrainian Front to temporarily halt the offensive and go over to the defensive upon the 57th Army's arrival at the line of the southeastern shore of Lake Balaton—Nagykanizsa—mouth of the Mura River, 18 kilometers southwest of Nagykanizsa.

Thus the *Stavka* of the VGK, in evaluating the overall correlation of forces and taking into account the fact that an offensive by all of the *front's* forces along two independent operational directions would only lead to a dispersal of force, made the correct decision to direct the *front's* main forces for the defeat, in cooperation with the Second Ukrainian Front, of the enemy's Budapest group of forces.

For this reason, the *front* commander altered his decision as regards the employment of the 5th Guards Cavalry Corps. The latter was resubordinated to the commander of the 4th Guards Army from 1800 on 7 December and was to concentrate by the morning of 10 December in the Sagvar—Koroshegy—Tenged—Som area.

The 57th Army was encountering increasing resistance by the enemy, who was taking all measures to hinder the advance of our forces toward Nagykanizsa and to hold the oil-producing area in its hands.

On 7 December the enemy's resistance increased significantly, particularly along the 57th Army's front, where the enemy reinforced his left flank with the 3rd Cavalry Brigade and throughout the day launched more than 20 counterattacks. The *front's* forces advanced 4-18 kilometers.

The 4th Guards Army's forces advanced 6-15 kilometers and were fighting along the following lines: the 31st Guards Rifle Corps, in conjunction with the 89th Naval Infantry Brigade, occupied Adony and, having linked up with units of the Second Ukrainian Front's 46th Army in the area north of Ivancsa, reached the front north of Ivancsa—west of Adony station—Szabolcs—eastern outskirts of Sarosd—Jakabszallas—south of Sarkeresztur; the 34th Guards Rifle Division concentrated in Nagyperkata, comprising the corps' second echelon. The 21st Guards Rifle Corps was fighting along the line southern outskirts of Kalov—southern outskirts of Polgardi—Mezoszentgyorgy.

The 20th Guards Rifle Corps reached the line northern outskirts of Lepseny—Balatonaliga; the 5th Guards Airborne Division had concentrated in the Balatonkiliti—Sagvar area, constituting the corps' second echelon. The 84th Guards Rifle Division was in the army's second echelon and had concentrated in the Ozora area.

The 57th Army's forces in the center and along the left flank advanced up to ten kilometers. The enemy's resistance continued to increase.

On 8 December the enemy facing the 4th Guards Army was falling back on a previously prepared line between Lake Velence and Lake Balaton and had increased his resistance.

In the second half of the day, following numerous attacks involving up to 110 tanks, self-propelled guns and aviation (up to 220 sorties), the enemy managed to restore the situation in the Polgardi area.

Up to 20 enemy artillery and nine mortar batteries had been identified opposite the army.

The attempts to break through the previously prepared "Margarita" defensive line from the march and to capture Szekesfehervar were not crowned with success and on orders from the *front* commander the 4th Guards Army's forces halted their offensive and shifted to assiduously preparing a breakthrough.

By the close of 8 December the *front's* forces occupied the following position:

4th Guards Army. The 31st Guards Rifle Corps was fighting along the line Dinies—Szerecen—north of Seregelyes—eastern outskirts of Belsobarand—Kulsekajtor—Guija; the 34th Guards Rifle Division comprised the corps' second echelon and was located in the Nagyperkata area.

The 21st Guards Rifle Corps was along the line south of Tac—Kisscseri station—Tekeres—Besnye. The 20th Guards Rifle Corps was along the line Balatonfokajar—southern part of Balatonakarttya; the 5th Guards Airborne Division was in its previous concentration area, comprising the second echelon; the 84th Guards Rifle Division was in the army commander's reserve in its previous location. The 3rd Anti-Aircraft Division, consisting of three regiments, arrived at the 4th Guards Army from the High Command Reserve.

57th Army. The army's forces along the right flank and in the center were subjected to powerful enemy fire from all types of guns and to bombing raids by the enemy air force, which bombed our troops in the Horvatkut—Nikla area.

Having repulsed 23 enemy counterattacks, the army's forces were engaged in heavy defensive fighting with enemy infantry and tanks along the following line: 6th Guards Rifle Corps, Keresztur—excluding Horvatkut—southern outskirts of Gomba—east of Marcali—Bize—Betyar—Nagyszakacsi; the 20th Guards Rifle Division, which had been subordinated to the commander of the 6th Guards Rifle Corps, was on the march in the Mastegne area.

The 64th Rifle Corps, having repelled with units of the 73rd and 19th rifle divisions five counterattacks by up to a battalion each, was fighting along the eastern outskirts of Labod; the 113th Rifle Division had concentrated in the Mike area.

The 75th Rifle Corps was fighting for Somogyvisonta, Erdecsokonya, Somogytarnoca, and Barcs; two battalions of the 233rd Rifle Division had crossed over to the southern bank of the Drava River in order to capture Virovitica.

The 32nd Mechanized Brigade in the Kapsmere area, was ready for action in the direction of Nagybajom and Bohonye.

The 68th Rifle Corps had set about carrying out a landing operation in Vukovar. Its 52nd Rifle Division was along its previous line, the 93rd Rifle Division had concentrated south of Belgrade, and the head of the 223rd Rifle Division's column had passed through Ilaca.

The 18th Tank Corps had concentrated southeast of Eling—Lajoskomarom—Deg.

The 7th Mechanized Corps was in its previous location; the 5th Guards Cavalry Corps was on the march, with its lead column near Szakaly.

The Danube Military Flotilla was carrying out a landing northwest of Vukovar.

The 17th Air Army carried out 265 sorties that day, supporting the 4th Guards and 57th armies' forces.

An operational group from the 17th Air Army was located with the 4th Guards Army's headquarters, but it did not command any planes and only transmitted requests, which often led to a disruption of cooperation with the ground forces.

The 37th Army was in its previous position. The *Stavka* continued to reinforce the Third Ukrainian Front, transferring the 1st Guards Mechanized Corps and three self-propelled artillery regiments to it.

By the close of 8 December the neighbor to the right, the Second Ukrainian Front's 46th Army, had reached the front southern outskirts of Erd—two kilometers northwest of Benta—0.5 kilometers south of Elvira—0.5 kilometers southeast of the bend in the railroad—two kilometers east of Martonvasar—one kilometer south of Baracska—0.5 kilometers southeast of Kapolnasnyek.

It was along this line that the army's units came up against the enemy's previously prepared "Margarita" defensive line, which covered the approaches to Budapest from the south and along the right bank of the Danube River.

Thus by 9 December the Third Ukrainian Front's forces and those of the Second Ukrainian Front's left wing had reached the enemy's previously prepared defensive line along the front Erd—Baracska—Kapolnasnyek—Lake Velence—Polgardi—Balatonakarttya—Balatonkeresztur—Mesztegnyo—Nagybajom—Nagyatad—Barcs and had seized a bridgehead along the right bank of the Drava River in the Virovitica area, south of Barcs.

As a result of the Third Ukrainian Front's offensive during 1-9 December, the enemy group of forces located between Lake Balaton and the Danube was defeated. However, the enemy, having hurriedly thrown in fresh forces, managed to occupy and organize a defensive position along with the remnants of his defeated forces.

Attempts to capture the enemy's prepared defensive line from the march were unsuccessful. The chief reason was the inadequate massing of men and materiel along the decisive axes on the part of the army commanders and the overextension of the troops and the rear organs.

In nine days of attacking the forces of the 4th Guards Army covered up to 100 kilometers, while the 57th Army's forces covered up to 60 kilometers in six days, with an average daily rate of advance of up to ten kilometers.

As a result of our arrival at the prepared defensive lines and the enemy's growing resistance, the *front's* forces consolidated along the new line, carried out a reconnaissance in force, and in the 57th Army's offensive sector regrouped their forces and strengthened their combat formations along the right flank.

On 12 December the *front's* forces were only attacking along some axes, while along the remainder of the front they were consolidating along their new lines, regrouping and repulsing the enemy's counterattacks.

Units of General Kiss's group (a composite regiment, the 153rd Reserve Infantry and 23rd Panzer divisions) facing the 4th Guards Army carried out seven counterattacks ranging from a company to a battalion in strength, with 5-18 tanks and 13 armored transports (in all, about six battalions, 39 tanks and 23 armored transports).

In the 57th Army's sector units of the "Saint Laszlo" Division, 3rd Cavalry Brigade, SS "Brandenburg" Division, 13th SS Muslim Infantry Division, 54th Border Detachment, an assault battalion from the Second Panzer Army, and the 92nd Motorized Brigade, were putting up powerful fire resistance to the army's attacking forces along all sectors of the front.

The enemy's air force, in groups of 6-12 planes, bombed the army's units and carried out reconnaissance flights with single aircraft.

The army's forces continued to wage offensive battles, during the course of which they advanced 3-6 kilometers along some sectors in the center and along the left flank.

The army commander, noting its shortcomings, established the reasons for the slow pace of the troops' offensive. Among these were the rifle companies' weak strength (15-20 men per company) and the broad offensive front (0.5-1 kilometer per rifle division). As a result of this, gaps developed between the regiments and divisions, which were poorly covered by fire and which offered the enemy the opportunity of getting into the flanks and rear of the attacking forces; the infantry's poor supply of artillery and mortars; for example, the 1292nd Rifle Regiment had only three 45mm guns and one 76mm gun, without shells. There were only 8-12 shells for the 122mm guns and there was no divisional or attached artillery.

For the purpose of unifying those forces operating to the west of the Danube River in the hands of a single commander, and for conducting an operation to break through the "Margarita Line" and to encircle and destroy the enemy's Budapest group of forces, on 12 December the *Stavka* of the VGK ordered that between 2400 on 12 December and 2400 on 15 December the 46th Army, with all of its reinforcements, be transferred to the Third Ukrainian Front.

By this time the 46th Army was occupying the front south of Erd—east of Elvira—eastern outskirts of Martonvasar—eastern outskirts of Baracska—Kapolnasnyek. The boundary line with the Second Ukrainian Front ran along the line Dunapentele—Szekesfehervar—Papa, with all locales for the Third Ukrainian Front. The 2nd Guards Mechanized Corps and the 7th Breakthrough Artillery Division were to be transferred at 2400 on 13 December. The rifle divisions located along the eastern bank of the Danube were to be relieved and transferred by 2400 on 15 December. The 46th Army was to be transferred, along with all of its rear units and establishments, with 1.5 combat loads (one combat load for 122mm howitzers), three refills of fuel and lubricants and 15 days' worth of forage.

Within the confines of the new boundary line, the 46th Army's forces were relieved by 2400 on 15 December by units of the 7th Guards Army and the 18th Guards Rifle Corps, the latter with the newly-subordinated 68th Guards Rifle Division, got an independent sector directly subordinated to the *front.*

Throughout 13 December the *front's* forces consolidated along their new lines and regrouped. The 4th Guards Army Kisvelence and was fighting to improve its jumping-off position in the Tac area. The 34th Guards Rifle Division was preparing to capture Kapolnasnyek, for the purpose of securing the boundary with the 46th Army and to improve its jumping-off position.

On 14 December the 83rd Naval Infantry Brigade was operationally subordinated to the 46th Army.

Along the 57th Army's front the 6th Guards Rifle Corps was consolidating its lines and the 64th and 75th rifle corps were attacking and advanced slightly along the army's left flank.

In accordance with the *Stavka* of the VGK's order, the 37th Army, consisting of the 34th, 66th and 82nd rifle corps (nine rifle divisions) was pulled into the *Stavka* reserve, along with its rear units and supplies.

On 14 December the 7th Mechanized Corps reached the Hercegfalva—Eloszallas area. The *front* commander ordered the commander of the 68th Rifle Corps to pull the 93rd Rifle Division into reserve to the Paks area.

On 16 December the 18th Tank Corps reached its new area of Nagyperkata—Belse.

The *front* commander, in order to secure his troops' regrouping, assigned the commander of the 17th Air Army the following tasks:

During 17-19 December to securely cover the *front's* main group of forces from the air, and the 18th Tank, 7th Mechanized and 5th Guards Cavalry corps' movement to their new areas. The air army was to cover the 46th Army's main body in the Rackeresztur—Kisvelence—Danube River area and the 4th Guards Army in the Seregelyes—Csosz—Sarkeresztur area.

During the 10-19 December preparatory period, the air armies' main efforts were directed at covering the *front's* forces and against the enemy's arriving reserves, especially against the roads leading to Budapest, and in conducting aerial reconnaissance for the purpose of uncovering the nature of the enemy's defense and the disposition of his forces and aviation.

In order to strengthen the shock group, the 68th Rifle Corps (52nd and 233rd rifle divisions) was to be pulled into the reserve on 17-18 December and which was to turn over its combat sector to units of the Bulgarian 1st Army and concentrate by 24 December in the Bonyhad—Szalka area.

Simultaneously, the 1st Guards Fortified Area was to concentrate west of Mohacs by the close of 22 December. For this reason, by decision of the *front* commander the Bulgarian 1st Army relieved by the morning of 18 December units of the 68th Rifle Corps east and south of Sotin and Opatovac with units of a single infantry division. The army reached the Faksic—Sidski—Banovaca—Tovarnik area with a second division, ready to relieve the Yugoslav People's Liberation Army's 1st Army Corps during 19-20 December. A third division concentrated in the army reserve in the area Sidski—Banovci—Lovas—Ilaca. A fourth division was unloading and concentrating in its designated area.

The commander of the 1st Bulgarian Army decided to begin his attack without waiting for the army's complete concentration, launching the main attack on Vinkovici and capturing the line Brsadin—Vinkovici.

Thus with their arrival at Budapest from the southwest, the Third Ukrainian Front had created the direct possibility for joint operations with the Second Ukrainian Front for the encirclement and defeat of the Budapest group of German-Fascist forces.

The presence of the Third Ukrainian Front's major forces along the right bank of the Danube threatened the most important areas of Hungary, Austria and Germany. The western part of Hungary had enormous political and military-economic significance for the German-Fascist command (oil in Nagykanizsa, bauxite in the Lake Balaton area, industry in Budapest, and Budapest as the capital of fascist Germany's last satellite).

Having lost the defensive line along the Danube River in the Third Ukrainian Front's sector, the enemy was counting on holding our troops' further advance along a previously prepared line, the so-called "Margarita Line," which ran along the line south of Budapest—Lake Velence—Lake Balaton—east of Nagykanizsa. This defense line had been prepared for 3-4 months.

It was planned to achieve the following basic tasks through the enemy's defense along the "Margarita Line":

- to prevent the further advance by the Third Ukrainian Front's main forces, to hold Budapest as a strategically important defensive locale along the road to Vienna;
- to gain time for the preparation of a secure defensive line along the approaches to Austria along the line Bratislava—the Neusiedler See—Szombathely—Kormend—Zagreb and for conducting another "super total" mobilization of human contingents and materiel means;
- to hold on to the Nagykanizsa oil-producing area;
- to secure Croatia and freedom of action for Field Marshal Weichs'[3] group of forces there.

The German-Fascist command, in evaluating the developing situation, believed that the Soviet army would not halt for long on its new line, but would try to develop the offensive further on Vienna, and thus undertook an entire series of measures for holding the "Margarita" defensive line. The forces designated for defending this line were hurriedly reinforced with men and materiel, the system of defensive structures was intensively improved and ammunition was accumulated. During November 10-December 10 alone the German-Fascist command threw in 19 formations from other sectors of the front, from the reserve and from Italy into the Third Ukrainian Front's offensive sector.

From the testimony of an entire series of prisoners, it was known that the German command was not limiting itself to defensive considerations, but was preparing a counterblow from the area southwest of Budapest to the south, for the purpose of foiling our forces' offensive preparations and eliminating the Third Ukrainian Front's bridgehead along the western bank of the Danube. For this purpose, it was planned to additionally employ the 3rd and 6th panzer divisions, which had been hurriedly transferred to this area from the central part of the front, and the *Feldherrnhalle* Motorized Division opposite the Second Ukrainian Front, above those already located southwest of Budapest. It was planned to begin the offensive on 21 December. But our troops' offensive, which began on 20 December, foiled the enemy's plans. The enemy was forced to commit all of his forces, which had been designated for the offensive, into the defensive fighting, while the 3rd and 6th panzer divisions, as we will see below, were thrown into the fighting in packets.

3 Editor's note. Maximillian von Weichs (1881-1954) joined the army in 1900 and fought in the First World War. During the Second World War he commanded a corps and an army, as well as army groups on the Eastern Front. Following the war, Weichs was arrested for war crimes but was not convicted.

A part of the German Sixth Army and Second Panzer Army, the Hungarian Third Army, and German Army "E" continued to operate opposite the Third Ukrainian Front.[4]

In all, this group included 17 infantry, five panzer, one motorized, and two cavalry divisions, and one cavalry brigade.

On 20 December the enemy had ten divisions, of which four were panzer, directly along the "Margarita Line" between Lake Balaton and the Danube against the 46th and 4th Guards armies.

In the middle of December the headquarters of the IX SS Army Corps arrived in Budapest from Croatia, and included the 22nd SS Cavalry Division, along with the attached Hungarian 10th Panzer Division; the 8th SS Cavalry Division and the 13th Panzer Division, with the attached Hungarian 10th and 12th infantry divisions; the *Feldherrnhalle* Motorized Division (without a headquarters, but under the command of the 13th Panzer Division); at first three, but then one battalion from the 959th Artillery Brigade from the high command reserve; two independent sapper battalions, and; a combat group from the 271st Infantry Division.

According to captured documents, this group's overall strength was 42-50,000 soldiers and officers, of which 9,000 were Hungarians.

According to the headquarters of the Hungarian I Corps, the overall strength of Hungarian forces in Budapest before the start of the encirclement was about 120,000 men, while there were also a large number of Hungarian deserters in Budapest, who were hiding in the cellars. It was impossible to accurately calculate their number.

During the third ten-day period of December General Woehler[5] was relieved of command of Army Group South and General Balck of command of the Sixth Army.

The relief of both commanders is explained by the fact that both of them, in the opinion of the supreme Hitlerite command, had incorrectly evaluated the situation and had not taken timely measures against the Soviet forces forcing the Danube River and creating a direct threat to Budapest.

By the start of the encirclement of Budapest, the 8th Cavalry Division was almost at full strength, while the 22nd Cavalry Division was short a cavalry regiment, a battery and a sapper battalion. The 13th Panzer Division and the *Feldherrnhalle* Motorized Division had been badly used in the fighting in the Vac area and together accounted for 60-70 tanks, self-propelled guns and armored transports.

The remnants of three Hungarian divisions were well supplied only with artillery. General Billnitzer's 14 assault guns were particularly combat worthy.

The IX SS Army Corps continued to be subordinated to the Sixth Army, commanded by General Balck.

By this time Army Group Weichs along the southern wing of the Third Ukrainian Front continued to move with its main forces from the Sarajevo area to Brod and Zagreb, fighting with the Yugoslav People's Liberation Army.

During 12-20 December preparations were underway to break through the fortified sector, the so-called "Margarita Line," which took place in conditions of the heavy fall rains and a lack of roads.

4 The Germans' Army "E" was formed in the beginning of December from Army Group E and was subordinated to Army Group F.

5 Editor's note. Otto Woehler (1894-1987) fought in the First World War. During the Second World War he served as chief of staff of an army and an army group and later commanded a corps, army and army group. Woehler was convicted of war crimes in 1948, but released in 1951.

Conclusions on the defeat of the enemy's Danube group of forces

The *Stavka* of the Supreme High Command carried out in a timely manner measures to strengthen the *front's* forces operating along the western bank of the Danube and brought up to strength formations designated for the decisive attack against the enemy's Budapest group of forces. The *Stavka* correctly directed the *front's* main forces along the Szekesfehervar axis, assigning the task of capturing the previously prepared defensive zone from the march.

The slow pace of the *front's* advance was conditioned by the absence during this period of combat-capable mobile formations (aside from the 32nd Mechanized Brigade) at the disposal of the *front*, as well as the heavy autumn rains, the great overextension of the rear and the inadequate capacity of the crossings over the Danube, which had a negative effect on the maneuverability of the *front's* forces and rear. All this, in turn, enabled the enemy forces to occupy in a timely manner the prepared defensive line and to delay our troops' advance. In turn, we do not find instructions on encircling and routing this or that enemy group of forces in the decisions of the *front* and army commanders. The offensive was conducted frontally. The enemy was pushed out and fell back from one intermediate line to another. Only individual subunits and units fell into encirclement.

In committing the 57th Army's second echelon and the 4th Guards army into the battle, the *front* commander and the commander of the 57th Army carried out in a timely manner measures to reinforce them with artillery and engineer equipment, which to a significant degree helped them achieve their assigned tasks (the 4th Guards Army received as reinforcements an anti-aircraft division, an artillery brigade, a mortar brigade, a light artillery brigade, a howitzer brigade, an anti-aircraft regiment, an assault engineer-sapper brigade, and a flamethrower battalion).

The operations of the Danube Flotilla during this period were many-sided: carrying out tactical landings, supporting boundaries and flanks with artillery fire and crossing troops and supplies. In conditions of heavy ice on the Danube and the insufficient number of crossings, the Danube Flotilla played an enormous role in crossing the troops and delivering freight to the western bank of the Danube.

Cooperation with the air force (17th Air Army) was not fully resolved. There were operational groups from the 17th Air Army with the armies' headquarters, but they only relayed requests, which in a number of cases led to a disruption of cooperation with the ground forces.

The air force dispersed its efforts among many targets and failed to ensure the launching of massive strikes against the most important targets and the enemy's groups of forces.

16

The Third Ukrainian Front's Preparations for Breaking Through the Fortified Defensive Zone, the so-called "Margarita Line," and the Defeat of the Enemy's Budapest Group of Forces

The *Stavka* of the Supreme High Command's Plan

As was mentioned above, on 12 December the *Stavka* of the VGK assigned the Third Ukrainian Front the task of preparing for and conducting an offensive operation for the purpose of, in conjunction with the Second Ukrainian Front, routing the Budapest group of forces and capturing the city of Budapest. In this regard, the Third Ukrainian Front's forces were ordered to break through the "Margarita Line" by launching an attack with the forces of the 46th and 4th Guards armies, along with the 18th Guards Tank, 2nd and 7th mechanized and 5th Guards Cavalry corps, from the area of Lake Velence in the general direction of Bicske, with the task of reaching the southern bank of the Danube along the Esztergom—Neszmely sector and to cut off the Budapest group of forces' path of retreat to the west. Part of these forces would attack Budapest from the west and, in conjunction with the Second Ukrainian Front's left wing, capture it.

The depth of the *front's* task was up to 75 kilometers for the 46th Army and up to 95 kilometers from the troops' jumping-off position before the offensive.

For the purpose of massing forces along the main axis, the *Stavka* of the VGK instructed the commander of the Third Ukrainian Front to employ his mobile forces along the Bicske—Zsambek axis.

At 2400 on 13 December a new boundary line was established between the Second and Third Ukrainian fronts, running along the line Timisoara—Mindszent—Kecskemet—Sari—Taksony—the Csepeli Dunaag River and then along the Danube River, with all locales reserved for the Third Ukrainian Front.

Responsibility for securing the boundary was entrusted to the commander of the Third Ukrainian Front.

The beginning of the offensive, both by the Second Ukrainian Front from the Sahy area and the Third Ukrainian Front from the area of Lake Velence, was set by the *Stavka* for 19-20 December 1944.

Facing the *front's* right flank the enemy was defending with formations from the German Sixth Army and the Hungarian Third Army, consisting of two infantry, one panzer and one cavalry division, one brigade of assault guns, three infantry regiments from various divisions, and seven battalions, as well as reinforcements. The German-Hungarian forces' front line ran along a line north of Szigetszentmiklos—Erd—Baracska—Lake Velence.

The *front's* left wing was faced by an enemy group of forces numbering up to six infantry divisions, two panzer divisions and reinforcements. The forward edge of the enemy's defense ran along the line Pakozd—east of Borgond—Kulsobarand—Tac—Besnye—north of Balatonfokajar—Balatonakarttya.

The Third Ukrainian Front Commander's Plan

1. Through two attacks by the *front's* concentrated forces, the first from the area northeast of Lake Velence in the general direction of Etyek, and a second from the area southwest of Lake Velence in the general direction of Bicske, to break through the enemy's defense and, in conjunction with the Second Ukrainian Front, to defeat the enemy's Budapest group of forces in detail and to capture the city of Budapest, while preventing the enemy's retreat to the west.

2. In order to achieve this goal, a northern group was to be formed, consisting of the 46th Army, and a southern, consisting of the 4th Guards Army.

The *front's* main forces were to be concentrated along the axis of the 4th Guards Army's operation.

To commit the *front's* mobile formations (18th Guards Tank and 5th Guards Cavalry corps) into the breakthrough and through their rapid movement in the general direction of Bicske and Bajna, split the German Sixth Army's main forces and reach the Danube River in the area west of Esztergom, having cut the enemy's entire Budapest group of forces' communications.

With the movement of the 46th and 4th Guards armies' rifle formations into the operational depth of the enemy's defense, part of their forces were to be deployed along the line Etyek—Zsambek—Szomor—Csolnok, facing east, in order to create an internal encirclement front around the enemy's Budapest group of forces and for attacking Budapest from the west.

In order to secure the attacking forces of the *front's* left wing, the forces of the 5th Guards Cavalry Corps, and then the 4th Guards Army, would form the external encirclement front.

3. The 46th Army's forces were to break through the enemy front along the 12-kilometer sector west of Baracska—Kapolnasnyek station.

The main attack was to be on Etyek and Bicske. The enemy was to be routed between the Vali River and Lake Velence and the capture of part of the city of Budapest as far as the Danube River.

A breakthrough of the enemy defense was to be carried out with the forces of a single rifle corps by an attack north of Lake Velence toward Lovasbereny, in order to assist the 4th Guards Army in capturing the city of Szekesfehervar.

The 4th Guards Army's forces were to break through the enemy's defense along a 10-kilometer sector excluding height 130—three kilometers south of Dinnyes—marker 124—two kilometers northeast of Potolle.

The main attack was to be launched in the direction of Szekesfehervar. The enemy group of forces was to be defeated between Lake Velence and the Sarviz Canal and the city of Szekesfehervar captured. Developing the attack on Csakvar and Szar and then to the front Esztergom—Neszmely—Tata, part of the forces would create an external encirclement front and secure, with the *front's* main forces, the encirclement and destruction of the enemy's Budapest group of forces and the capture of the city of Budapest from the west and southwest.

The *front's* immediate task, in conjunction with the Second Ukrainian Front, was to defeat the defending enemy and reach the southern bank of the Danube along the Esztergom—Neszmely sector and to simultaneously create an internal and external encirclement front.

The *front's* subsequent task, in conjunction with the Second Ukrainian Front's left flank, was to destroy the main body of the enemy's Budapest group of forces.

The *front* commander's plan for the Budapest operation is an example of when a *front* launches two concentrated attacks to carry out an operational breakthrough and, in conjunction with a neighboring *front*, encircles and destroys an enemy group of forces along one of its flanks and simultaneously carries out with a single combined-arms army a defensive operation along an independent operational direction for the purpose of securing the offensive by the *front's* main forces.

The breakthrough front along the two sectors was 22 kilometers, against an overall frontage of 80 kilometers.

The Third Ukrainian Front Commander's Decision

In accordance with the plan by the commander of the Third Ukrainian Front, as outlined above, the troops received the following assignments:

46th Army (23rd Rifle Corps, a naval infantry brigade, 37th Rifle Corps, 10th Guards Rifle Corps, and the 2nd Guards Mechanized Corps).

The army would launch an attack with the forces of two corps (seven divisions: 320th, 108th Guards, 59th Guards, 49th Guards, 180th, 109th Guards, and 86th rifle divisions) and reinforcements along a front west of Baracska and Kapolnasnyek station in the general direction of Etyek and defeat the enemy group of forces between the Vali River and Lake Velence. Developing the attack, it was to cut off the path of the retreat of the enemy's Budapest group of forces to the west, destroy or capture it and capture the western part of the city of Budapest as far as the Danube River.

The army's immediate task was to launch its main attack on Etyek and Bicske, and a supporting attack with one division from the Baracska area toward Tordas and to break through the enemy's defense northeast of Lake Velence along the sector west of Baracska and Kapolnasnyek, to defeat the enemy defending between the Vali River and Lake Velence and to capture the line Tordas—Lovasbereny.

Four rifle divisions (320th, 108th Guards, 49th Guards, and 180th rifle divisions) were to be in the first echelon.

With the capture of the line Tordas—two kilometers north of Pazmand—south of Lovasbereny, the 2nd Guards Mechanized Corps was to be committed with the immediate task of reaching the area Etyek—Zsambek—Bicske and then to hold itself in readiness to capture, along with the infantry, the western part of the city of Budapest.

While developing the attack to the northeast, the army was to roll up the enemy's defense opposite its right flank and, in conjunction with the 18th Guards Tank Corps, cut off the path of retreat for the enemy's Budapest group of forces and, in conjunction with the Second Ukrainian Front's left wing, destroy it and reach the Danube River.

The army was to capture the line Anasztazia—Ofalu—Lovasbereny no later than the second day of the offensive.

By the close of the fourth or fifth day, while developing the attack to the northeast, the army was to roll up the enemy's front along the Danube River and reach the line Danube River—Erd—Soskut—Etyek—Zsambek, with no less than one rifle corps (three divisions) along the front Etyek—Zsambek, ready to attack together with the 2nd Guards Mechanized Corps.

By the close of the eighth or ninth day the army, in conjunction with part of the forces of the 4th Guards Army and the 18th Guards Tank Corps, was to completely defeat the encircled enemy and capture the western part of the city of Budapest, having arrived at the Danube River along the army's entire front.

Simultaneously, the *front* commander instructed that in the event of the 4th Guards Army's offensive being delayed, the 18th Guards Tank Corps would be committed in the 46th Army's sector, behind the 2nd Guards Mechanized Corps, in the direction of Lovasbereny, Vertesacsa and Bicske, in order to reach the Dorog—Nyergesujfalu—Bajna—Dorog area (all locales southwest of Esztergom), for the purpose of cutting the path of retreat of the enemy in Budapest.

In order to organize cooperation with the 4th Guards Army, it was ordered that upon the breakthrough of the defense by a single rifle corps through an attack north of Lake Velence toward Lovasbereny, it was to assist the 4th Guards Army in taking Szekesfehervar.

The boundary line on the left was Adony—Adonyszabolcs—Kapolnasnyek—Sukoro—Lovasbereny—Vertesacsa—Felcsut.

The tasks of the 4th Guards Army (31st Guards Rifle Corps, 20th Guards Rifle Corps, 135th Rifle Corps, 21st Guards Rifle Corps, and the 7th Guards Mechanized Corps) were as follows:

To break through the enemy's defense with the forces of three rifle corps (eight rifle divisions: 4th, 40th Guards, 5th Guards Airborne, 80th Guards, 252nd, 7th Guards Airborne, and 84th Rifle) southwest of Lake Velence along the front excluding marker 130 (three kilometers south of Dinnyes station)—height 124 (2.5 kilometers northeast of Potolle), with the main attack in the direction of Szekesfehervar and a supporting one with a single division in the direction of Falubattyan.

There would be five divisions (4th, 40th Guards, 5th Guards Airborne, 80th Guards, and 252nd) in the first echelon.

The army's immediate task was to defeat the enemy group of forces between Lake Velence and the Sarviz Canal and to capture the city of Szekesfehervar. The army was to subsequently develop the attack with two rifle corps toward Csakvar and Szar and then to the front Esztergom—Neszmely—Tata—Kornye, while another corps (two rifle divisions) and the 7th Mechanized Corps moved on Mor and Varpalota.

The army was to capture Szekesfehervar by no later than the close of the first or second day and reach the line Patka—Sarszentmihaly—Nadasdladany—Polgardi.

By the close of the third or fourth day, while developing the attack behind the mobile formations with two rifle corps (six rifle divisions) on Csakvar and Szar and then to the front Esztergom—Neszmely—Tata, and with one rifle corps (two rifle divisions) and the 7th Mechanized Corps on Mor and Varpalota, the army was to reach the line Szar—Verteskozma. And create an external encirclement front along the line Almasfuzito—Tata—Banhida—Kecsked—Pusztavam—Mor—Isztimer—Varpalota—Osku—Balatonfuzto—northeastern shore of Lake Balaton.

One rifle division was to be held in reserve in the Szekesfehervar area.

By the close of the fifth or sixth day, one rifle corps (three rifle divisions) was to be pulled into the Bajna—Tarjan—Gyermely area and to be ready, along with the 18th Guards Tank Corps, to attack toward Budapest.

Units of the 5th Guards Cavalry Corps were to be relieved along the line Almasfuzito—Tata—Banhida—Kecsked—Pusztavam. The 80th Rifle Division was to be in reserve in the Alsogalla—Tatabanya area.

With the capture of Szekesfehervar, the 7th Guards Rifle Corps was to be committed, with the task of capturing the Mor area and, together with the army's rifle formations, to take Varpalota, for the purpose of encircling and destroying the enemy's group of forces southwest of Szekesfehervar. Subsequently, with the infantry's arrival along this line, the corps was to be pulled into the army's reserve in the Csokako—Bodajk—Fehervarcsurgo—Csakbereny area.

The boundary line on the left with the 57th Army was Tamasi—Zamardi.

The *Front's* Mobile Forces

On 20 December the 18th Guards Tank Corps was located in the Nagyperkata area and consisted of 186 tanks and 41 self-propelled guns.

By decision of the *front* commander, the corps was to be employed to develop the success in the direction of Bicske and Bajna, for the purpose of splitting the enemy Sixth Army's forces and arriving at the Danube River on the second day in the Esztergom—Tata—Bajna area.

The corps was assigned the following task: upon the capture of the city of Szekesfehervar by the 4th Guards Army's infantry on the night of the first day, to be ready to enter the breakthrough from the line Tordas—Tatka and to develop a vigorous offensive toward Csakvar, Many and Esztergom.

By the close of the second day the corps was to reach the area Takof—Nyergesujfalu—Bajna—Dag—Dorog and cut the path of retreat of the enemy's Budapest group of forces to the northwest and west along the Danube River.

By the close of the third day part of the corps' forces was to capture the pass west of Pilisvorosvar.

Subsequently, with the arrival of the 46th and 4th Guards armies' infantry at the line Etyek—Zsambek—Szomor—Csolnok, the corps was to develop the offensive, together with the infantry, on Budapest for the purpose of destroying the encircled enemy.

At the same time, it was pointed out that in case of a delay in taking Szekesfehervar and a success to the east of Lake Velence, the corps was to enter the breach in the 46th Army's sector, with its subsequent arrival at its main axis.

Along with this, the *front* commander instructed the commander of the 18th Guards Tank Corps to have by the morning of 20 December no less than three refills of fuels and lubricants, 2-3 combat loads of ammunition per tank and 0.5 combat loads apiece in the remaining units.

Cover from the air was to be exercised by a fighter division from the 17th Air Army in the jumping-off position, and from the time of the commitment into the breakthrough a fighter division and an assault air division would be allotted to support and cover the 18th Guards Tank Corps.

The *front* commander decided to entrust the support for the corps' commitment into the breach to the commander of the 4th Guards Army, and correspondingly to the commander of the 46th Army.

With the advance of the 46th and 4th Guards armies' rifle formations, it was planned to employ the 18th Guards Tank Corps to create an internal encirclement front around the enemy's Budapest group of forces from the Esztergom—Szomor line west to Budapest. Simultaneously, the operations of the Second Ukrainian Front's 6th Guards Tank Army from the Levice area to the south, also in the direction of Esztergom, were to lead to the complete encirclement of the enemy's Budapest group of forces.

The 5th Guards Cavalry Corps (11th, 12th Guards and 63rd cavalry divisions) was assigned the task to be ready, upon the capture of the city of Szekesfehervar by the 4th Guards Army's infantry on the second day, to enter the breakthrough behind the 18th Guards Tank Corps and the 7th Guards Mechanized Corps and to develop the breakthrough toward Csakvar and Tata.

By the close of the second day the corps was to cut all of the paths for the possible arrival of the enemy's reserves from the west and southwest to the line Almasfuzito—Tata—Bahnida—Kornye—Kecsked—Pusztavam and to reconnoiter to the west as far as the line Acs—Kisber—Sur.

By securely holding the indicated line and preventing the enemy from breaking through to link up with his encircled Budapest group of forces, the corps was to support the *front's* main forces in the destruction and to capture the city of Budapest.

Subsequently, with the arrival of the 4th Guards Army's infantry, the corps would turn over its sector to it and concentrate in the area northeast and east of Tata, in readiness to operate toward Komarom.

The jumping-off area for the commitment into the breach was Patka—Baklas—Sarkeresztes—excluding Szekesfehervar.

The corps in the depth, along with the 18th Guards Tank Corps, was to be supported by a fighter division and an assault air division from the 17th Air Army.

The artillery support for the commitment of the 18th Guards Tank Corps and the 5th Guards Cavalry Corps into the breach had been entrusted to the commanders of the 46th and 4th Guards armies.

Thus the 5th Guards Cavalry Corps was to secure the creation, along with the 7th Mechanized Corps and the 4th Guards Army, of the external encirclement front along the line Almasfuzito—Banhida.

Thus in accordance with the overall operational plan, the employment of the mobile forces was seen in the following manner: upon entering the breakthrough, the 2nd Guards Mechanized Corps would be directed to the north to a depth of 25-30 kilometers, after which it would turn sharply to the east, toward Budapest; the 7th Mechanized Corps was to develop the success to the northwest to a depth of 25-30 kilometers, after which it was to deploy with its front facing to the west; the 18th Guards Tank Corps was to enter the breach along the mechanized corps' adjoining flanks (it was actually committed behind the 2nd Guards Mechanized Corps) and, while developing the attack to the north to a depth of 60-70 kilometers, was to come out in the Esztergom area.

Aviation. During the operation's preparatory period, the 17th Air Army was to do the following:

- secure the regrouping and concentration of the *front's* main forces against enemy air strikes and aerial reconnaissance; particularly attention was to be devoted to the mobile forces: 18th Tank Corps, 5th Cavalry Corps and the 2nd and 7th mechanized corps;
- to support on the eve of the offensive, if summoned, the activities of the reconnaissance and reinforced rifle battalions.

During the breakthrough of the enemy's defense, the 17th Air Army received the following orders:

- to gain air superiority and to cover friendly forces, particularly mobile units;
- to support the breakthrough of the main defensive zone and the entire tactical depth of the enemy's defense by: a) carrying out a direct aviation preparation along the 46th and 4th Guards armies' breakthrough sectors; b) organizing the air force's direct escort of the 46th and 4th Guards armies' infantry and tanks;
- to support the commitment of the mobile forces into the breach and to cooperate with them in the operational depth, while from the moment of their commitment into the breach the 17th Air Army's main efforts were to be switched to cooperating with the mobile forces;
- to combat the enemy's operational reserves and to, first of all, cut them off from the routes to the breakthrough sectors of the enemy's defense;
- to reconnoiter the enemy throughout the entire depth of the operation in the sector to the west of the Danube River and to the east of the Drava River, Nadka and Nagykanizsa.

In resolving these tasks, the *front* commander demanded that the 17th Air Army's main efforts be concentrated along the Szekesfehervar, Bicske and Esztergom axes in the 4th Guards Army's sector. The remaining forces were to support the 46th Army's operations, while the commander of the 17th Air Army was to have a reserve of assault aircraft and fighters, with a reserve of assault aircraft and anti-tank planes for fighting the enemy's tanks.

The troops were to be ready by 1800 on 19 December. The hour for the attack was set for December 20 by an additional order. The length of the artillery preparation was set at 40 minutes, while the infantry attack was set for 1145.

The Army Commander's Decision

The Decision by the Commander of the 46th Army

The commander of the 46th Army decided to launch the main attack along the army's left flank with the forces of the 37th and 10th Guards rifle corps; the 23rd Rifle Corps was on the right flank along a supporting axis.

The corps were assigned the following combat tasks:

The 37th Rifle Corps (320th Rifle and 108th and 59th Guards Rifle divisions, with the 87th Guards Mortar Regiment, 1505th Self-Propelled Artillery Regiment, supported by the 25th Howitzer Brigade, 11th Light Artillery Brigade, and the 9th and 17th cannon-artillery brigades, was to break through the enemy's defense along the front excluding Baracska—marker 127 and by the close of the first day of the offensive reach the line Tordas—Enye. Upon breaking through the forward edge of the enemy's defense, forces numbering no less than a rifle regiment were to attack toward Martonvasar from the southwest and, in conjunction with the 23rd Rifle Corps' left-flank units, capture this locale.

The 37th Rifle Corps had two rifle divisions in the first echelon (320th and 108th Guards rifle divisions). It was planned to commit the second-echelon 59th Guards Rifle Division in the rifle corps' center, following the capture of the Tordas—Enye line by the first-echelon units, along the boundary between the 320th and 108th Guards rifle divisions, for the purpose of augmenting the attack in the direction of Kajaszoszentpeter and height 180 and to attack along the front Ufalu—Val.

The boundary line on the right ran along height 141 northern part of Martonvasar—Pusztazamor, with all locales for the 37th Rifle Corps.

The boundary line on the left ran along Gebeljaras—Janos—marker 127—Pettend—Val—Enye, with all locales, except for Gebeljaras, Janos, marker 127 for the 37th Rifle Corps.

Simultaneously, the army commander instructed the commander of the 37th Rifle Corps that upon the infantry's arrival at the line Tordas—Enye that he was to be ready to let the 2nd Guards Mechanized Corps pass through the infantry's combat formations.

During the 2nd Guards Mechanized Corps' arrival at the breach, he was to foresee the artillery support for the corps, according to the plan of the army artillery commander, as well as the engineer support (the construction of passages in the obstacles and clearing the roads of mines) for the corps in the 37th Rifle Corps' sector.

The 10th Guards Rifle Corps (49th, 109th Guards and 180th rifle divisions, with the 462nd Mortar Regiment, 437th Anti-Tank Artillery Regiment, 47th Guards Mortar Regiment and the 991st Self-Propelled Artillery Regiment, supported by the 3rd Mortar Brigade and the 46th Cannon-Artillery Brigade), was to break through the enemy's defense along the front marker 127—Kapolnasnyek station and by the close of the first day reach the line excluding Enye—Pazmand—Velence. It was to subsequently plan to attack toward the front Lovasbereny—Sukoro.

Two divisions (49th Guards and 180th rifle divisions) were to attack in the first echelon. It was planned to commit the second-echelon division (109th Guards Rifle Division) along the corps' right flank following the arrival of the first-echelon divisions at the line Pazmand—Velence for developing the success in the direction of Pazmand, Vereb and height 195.

With the corps' arrival at the line Lovasbereny—Sukoro, it was planned to establish communications with the neighbor to the left (the 4th Guards Army's right-flank units) and be ready to operate to the north and northeast.

The boundary line on the left (with the 4th Guards Army) ran along the line Adonyszabolcs station—Kapolnasnyek—northeastern shore of Lake Velence—Sukoro—Lovasbereny—Vertesacsa—Felcsut, with all locales for the 10th Guards Rifle Corps.

The commander of the 10th Guards Rifle Corps was also instructed that upon the infantry's arrival at the line two kilometers north of Pazmand—south of Lovasbereny, to be ready to let the 2nd Guards Mechanized Corps pass through the infantry's combat formations and to plan for the artillery and air support for the commitment of the 2nd Guards Mechanized Corps into the breakthrough.

The army's combined-arms reserve was the 86th Guards Rifle Division, with the 1897th Self-Propelled Artillery Regiment constituting the army's anti-tank reserve.

Along the secondary axis the 23rd Rifle Corps (99th and 316th rifle divisions and the 83rd Naval Infantry Brigade, with the 12th Anti-Tank Artillery Brigade) had the task of securely supporting the army's right flank and, with part of forces break through the enemy's defense along the left flank along the line Kismarton—the boundary of the railroad one kilometer east of Martonvasar and by the close of the day the 99th Rifle Division was to capture the line Kismarton—Erdohat. It was to subsequently attack along the front Elvira—excluding Erd.

In the 316th Rifle Division's offensive sector along the right flank, it was planned to employ artillery fire from units of the Danube Military Flotilla.

The boundary line on the right (the army boundary) was Sari—Taksony—the Csepeli Dunaag River—Danube River.

The boundary on the left was with the 37th Rifle Corps.

The 2nd Guards Mechanized Corps was to be committed into the breakthrough along the line Tordas—two kilometers north of Pazmand—south of Lovasbereny, with the task of reaching the Etyek—Zsambek—Bicske area.

Upon the start of combat operations the army was to be supported by one assault air division and one fighter division from the 17th Air Army.

The army's operational organization was in one echelon, with a mobile group (2nd Guards Mechanized Corps) and reserves, both combined-arms and artillery-anti-tank. The rifle corps' combat formation along the main attack axis was in two echelons, with all the regiments of the first-echelon divisions in a single line.

There was a combined-arms reserve in each division for augmenting the attack in the depth of the enemy's defense.

The commander of the 4th Guards Army decided to launch his main attack with the forces of three rifle corps (eight divisions: 31st Guards Rifle Corps—4th, 40th and 34th guards rifle divisions, with the 26th Light Artillery Brigade, 466th Mortar Regiment, 230th Howitzer Regiment, and the 58th and 247th engineer-sapper battalions) along the sector indicated by the *front* commander;

20th Guards Rifle Corps (5th and 7th guards airborne divisions and the 80th Rifle Division, with the 521st Anti-Tank Battalion, 10th Mortar Brigade, 529th Mortar Regiment, 152nd Howitzer Regiment, 23rd Howitzer Brigade, minus the 230th Howitzer Regiment, the 56th and 59th assault engineer-sapper battalions, and the 366th Heavy Self-Propelled Artillery Regiment);

135th Rifle Corps (252nd and 84th rifle divisions, with the 45th Guards Mortar Regiment, 9th Anti-Tank Artillery Brigade and the 140th Mortar Regiment) was to break through the enemy's defense and develop the offensive in the general direction of Szekesfehervar.

A supporting attack would be launched by part of the 21st Guards Rifle Corps' forces from the area of the fork in the railroad south of Szabadbattyan. On the remainder of its front, the 21st Guards Rifle Corps was to defend along the front Sarviz Canal—Balatonakarttya—the south-eastern and southern bank of Lake Balaton as far as Balatonszemes

The boundary line on the right (with the 252nd Rifle Division) was the Sarviz Canal, and to the left (with the 57th Army) was Balatonszemes—Liget, with both locales for the 21st Guards Rifle Corps.

It was ordered to have the greatest density of our combat formations in the sector of the right-flank 41st Guards Rifle Division (six kilometers).

In accordance with the decision, the army's main forces were to capture the city of Szekesfehervar by the close of the second day and reach the line Patka—Feher.

Subsequently, the task set by the *front* was to be carried out.

The army's operational organization was single echelon, with the army's mobile group—the 7th Guards Mechanized Corps—and an army anti-tank reserve. The rifle corps' combat organization was in two echelons; it was to be in a single echelon along the 21st Guards Rifle Corps' secondary axis. The rifle divisions' combat organization was in a single echelon, with the exception of the 4th Guards Rifle and 5th Guards Airborne divisions.

Thus the decisions by the commanders of the 46th and 4th Guards armies completely corresponded were to the *front* commander's decision and guaranteed the successful breakthrough of the entire tactical depth of the enemy's defense and the development of the offensive in the operational depth by the army's and *front's* mobile formations to encircle the enemy's Budapest group of forces.

The Planning and Preparation for the Operation

The Third Ukrainian Front's operation was planned during the 13-19 December time period on the basis of the commander's decision and in strict accordance with the 12 December 1944 directive from the *Stavka* of the Supreme High Command for the operation, which demanded the defeat of the Budapest group of forces, in conjunction with the Second Ukrainian Front, and the capture of Budapest.

The operational plan called for the arrival of the mobile forces (18th Guards Tank and 5th Guards Cavalry corps) at the southern bank of the Danube River on the second or third day of the operation along the Esztergom—Neszmely sector and the creation of an external encirclement front on the fifth or sixth day along the line Almaszfuzito—Tata—Banhida—Mor—Varpalota—Balatonfuzto; the arrival of the *front's* main forces on the third or fourth day at the line Tordas—Etyek—Zsambek—Uny—Esztergom for launching an attack against the enemy's encircled Budapest group of forces from the west. To capture the Buda area on the eighth day.

The actions of the *front's* forces within the confines of the operation were planned to a depth of 65-70 kilometers for the 46th Army and up to 85 kilometers for the 4th Guards Army.

The length of the operation to complete the encirclement of the enemy's Budapest group of forces was determined to be 4-6 days, and 8-9 days counting the capture of Buda.

The average daily pace of advance was determined at 8-13 kilometers for the infantry and 16-20 kilometers for the mobile forces.

The *front's* forces were assigned an immediate task in strict accordance with the demands of the directive by the *Stavka* of the Supreme High Command and consisted of defeating the opposing enemy by breaking through his entire defensive tactical depth and completing the encirclement of the enemy's Budapest group of forces on the second or third day.

The main planning document of the *front* headquarters was a graphic plan of the operation, which had been drawn up on a 1:200,000 scale map. A feature of the plan was the planning of the *front's* efforts by days of the operation throughout the entire depth, beginning on D+1 and ending on D+8-9.

According to the essence of the tasks being resolved, the first 2-3 days of the operation may be grouped under the heading of the first stage of the operation, during the course of which the *front* resolved its immediate task; that is, the defeat of the opposing enemy throughout the entire tactical depth of his defense and the creation of an internal encirclement front for the Budapest group of forces, with the simultaneous arrival of part of the mobile forces' body at the external encirclement front.

The second stage of the operation was the development of the offensive along the external encirclement front and the defeat, in conjunction with the Second Ukrainian Front, of the enemy's Budapest group of forces and the capture of the city of Budapest (Buda for the Third Ukrainian Front).

In time, the second stage of the operation could be planned from the fourth day through the eighth day.

The first three days of the operation, or its first stage, were planned in detail, according to lines for each day, indicating the men and materiel attached to the armies, their subordination and their cooperation with each other and with the air force.

For the remaining days, or the second stage, only the overall direction of the offensive was indicated to the armies, as well as their main groups of forces and the timetable for arriving at the line of the internal and external encirclement fronts and the capture of the city of Budapest.

The encirclement and destruction of the enemy's Budapest group of forces was planned in close cooperation with the Second Ukrainian Front, which was to launch the main attack from the Sahy area in the general direction of Kebelkut.

The 7th Guards Army, 6th Guards Tank Army and Pliev's cavalry-mechanized group were allotted for resolving this task, the main forces of which were to attack along toward the front Neszmely—Esztergom and, upon linking up on the third or fourth day with the Third Ukrainian Front's forces along the line indicated above, were to thus complete the encirclement and then the destruction of the enemy's Budapest group of forces.

The cooperation between the forces of the Second and Third Ukrainian fronts was closely linked by the operational plan according to lines for each day. Cooperation with the Second Ukrainian Front's left-wing forces, which were to attack Budapest from the east, was planned by launching an attack by part of the Third Ukrainian Front's forces on Budapest from the west.

In accordance with the directive by the *Stavka* of the Supreme High Command and the *front* commander's decision, the operational plan called for the concentration of the efforts of the Third Ukrainian Front's forces for breaking through the enemy's defense in two groups northwest of Lake Velence (the 46th Army, reinforced by the 2nd Guards Mechanized Corps, and the 4th Guards Army, reinforced by the 7th Guards Mechanized Corps and the *front's* mobile forces—the 18th Guards Tank and 5th Guards Cavalry corps).

The overall breakthrough front for the Third Ukrainian Front's forces was defined by the plan at 22 kilometers.

It was planned to employ the greatest percent of reinforcements for the Supreme High Command Reserve and aviation with the southern group of forces (4th Guards Army), as shown in the table below.

The two combined-arms armies comprised one of the *front's* operational echelons and were to break through the enemy's defense and secure the commitment of the *front's* mobile forces into the breach. One combined-arms army was to remain along its defense line along the Nagykanizsa operational direction (57th Army) and secure the Third Ukrainian Front's southern wing against possible enemy counterblows.

A feature of the planning for the operation in the 4th Guards and 46th armies was that the depth of the stages, as well as the pace of the offensive, were insignificant. For example, the 46th Army's operation was planned in four stages. The first stage's content was the carrying out of the immediate task to a depth of 8-13 kilometers, with an average daily rate of advance of 4-6 kilometers.

The second stage was the development and carrying out of the following task, although the depth was equal to 16-20 kilometers, with an average daily pace of 8-10 kilometers, and it was only during the third stage—the completion of the encirclement of the Budapest group of forces that an increase in the average daily rate of advance to 18-20 kilometers was foreseen.

The *front's* mobile force (tanks, cavalry) were to be employed following the breakthrough of the enemy's defense by the combined-arms armies and, as the *Stavka* of the Supreme High Command demanded, were to launch an attack in the general direction of Szekesfehervar and Bicske.

The plan called for the 18th Guards Tank Corps to be employed according to one of two variants: in the 4th Guards Army's sector according to the first variant, and in the 46th Army's sector according to the second. At the same time, one should note that the variant for committing the 18th Guards Tank Corps in the 46th Army's sector was conditioned by the enemy's powerful anti-tank defense along the Szekesfehervar axis and a possible delay in the development of the offensive by the 4th Guards Army (the city of Szekesfehervar was a powerful enemy center of defense). As we shall see later, such foresight in the employment of the 18th Guards Tank Corps completely justified itself.

The securing of the commitment of the *front's* mobile forces into the breach was entrusted to the commanders of the 46th and 4th Guards armies.

The operational plan called for the creation of the following troop densities along the breakthrough sectors:

The northern group of forces, consisting of the 46th Army and reinforcements, along with the 2nd Guards Mechanized Corps.

The overall width of the breakthrough front in the army's sector south of Baracska—Kapolnasnyek was 12 kilometers.

The operational density was more than one division per kilometer of breakthrough front.

Tactical Densities Along the Breakthrough Sector. In the 46th Army one rifle division was to break through the enemy's defense along a 2-3 kilometer front and a 2-2.5 kilometer front along the 4th Guards Army's sector and, according to the *front's* operational plan, including guns and mortars of 76mm and more, the 46th Army was to have 152 tubes per kilometer of breakthrough front and the 4th Guards Army 168 tubes. This came to an average of 160 guns and mortars per kilometer of breakthrough front.

In calculating the indicated densities of troops and combat equipment along the breakthrough sectors, the size of each army's breakthrough sector, according to the armies' account maps of 20 December 1944 were as follows:

12 kilometers for the 46th Army;

Ten kilometers for the 4th Guards Army.

Table 8 Armies' Combat Composition for Breaking through the "Margarita Line," 20 December 1944

	46th Army	4th Gds Army	18th Gds Tank Corps	5th Gds Cavalry Corps	7th Gds Mechanized Corps	2nd Gds Mechanized Corps	Total
Rifle Divisions	9	11	–	–	–	–	20
Cavalry Divisions	–	–	–	3	–	–	3
Mechanized/Motorized Rifle Brigades	–	–	1	–	3	3	7
Tank Brigades	–	–	3	–	1	1	5
Self-Propelled Artillery Regiments	3	2	2	1	2	2	12
Independent Heavy Tank Regiments	–	–	–	–	1	1	2
Breakthrough Artillery Divisions	1	1	–	–	–	–	2

	46th Army	4th Gds Army	18th Gds Tank Corps	5th Gds Cavalry Corps	7th Gds Mechanized Corps	2nd Gds Mechanized Corps	Total
Cannon-Artillery Brigades	1	1	–	–	–	–	2
Howitzer Artillery Brigades	1	2	–	–	–	–	3
Anti-Tank Artillery Brigades	1	1	–	–	–	–	2
Anti-Tank Artillery Regiments	1	3	3	1	1	–	9
Anti-Tank Artillery Battalions	–	1	–	–	–	–	1
Guards Mortar Regiments	1	–	1	1	1	–	4
Guards Mortar Battalions	–	–	1	1	1	1	4
Anti-Aircraft Divisions	1	2	–	–	–	–	3
Independent Anti-Aircraft Regiments	1	–	3	1	1	1	7
Engineer-Sapper Brigades	1	1	-	–	–	1	3
Engineer-Sapper Battalions	–	–	2	–	–	–	2
Motorcycle Regiment/ Battalion	–	–	1	–	–	1	2
Independent Howitzer Regiment	2	1	–	–	–	–	3
Independent Mortar Regiment	1	2	1	–	–	1	5
Corps Artillery Regiment	1	1	–	–	–	–	2
Operational Density Along the Breakthrough Sector							

Rifle and cavalry divisions from the 46th Army—9
Rifle and cavalry divisions from the 4th Guards Army—11
Rifle and cavalry divisions from the 5th Guards Cavalry Corps—3
Total—23 divisions

As a result of concentrating and regrouping, by 20 December the Third Ukrainian Front's forces had achieved the following correlation of forces: 1:3.3 in men, 1:4.8 in tanks and self-propelled guns, and; 1:1.25 in planes.

On 20 December the enemy disposed of the following opposite the 46th and 4th Guards armies' front.

Facing the 46th Army: a Hungarian screening security detachment and parachute battalions; Hungarian 271st Infantry Division and the 20th Infantry Division's 24th Infantry Regiment; the Hungarian 64th Infantry Battalion and a machine gun battalion, German 8th Panzer Division and the Hungarian 8th Infantry Division's 17th Infantry Regiment; 8th Police Regiment, 802nd Sapper Company, 159th Battalion of six-barreled mortars, and the Hungarian 23rd Infantry Division and the "Saint Laszlo" Infantry Division.

Facing the 4th Guards Army: General Kiss's Hungarian group, 131st Composite Infantry Regiment, 3rd Cavalry Regiment, a composite regiment, 152nd Artillery Battalion, a tank group; elements of the Hungarian 2nd Infantry Regiment, 23rd Panzer Division and units of the 1st Panzer Division, 44th Training Regiment, 31st SS Infantry Regiment, units of the Hungarian 20th and 24th infantry regiments, and nine battalions of specialized units.

The work of the *front* headquarters and the command of the *front's* combat arms in planning and preparing for the operation unfolded in the following sequence.

Before 16 December the *front* commander had heard sufficient reports from the combat arms and the conclusions of the *front* chief of staff on the plan for the forthcoming operation and, after going out in the field to the armies, heard the latters' opinions, after which he issued his basic instructions on planning the *front* and army operation.

All orders connected to the elaboration of the decision and the planning of the operation were personally issued to the executors and only orally, or by laying out the tasks on their personal maps. Written orders were not issued during this time.

On 16 December the *front* commander played out the operation with the corps and division commanders.

During 16-19 December the *front* directives were issued in code to the commanders of the 46th and 4th Guards armies, as well as to the commanders of the 18th Guards Tank and 5th Guards Cavalry corps (local operational orders).

During this period the *front* commander heard the army commanders, who were summoned in turn, and their decisions, which were confirmed on the spot along with the necessary amendments and additions. At the same time, the army headquarters worked to prepare the operation in the short time available (16-19 December).

This method of planning and preparing the operation in a limited time period best secured both the hands-on leadership on the part of the *front*, but also the operation's secrecy.

Thus the *front* had no more than ten days to prepare for the operation, while the preparation for the operation got fully under way only on 12 December; that is, from the moment the directive from the *Stavka* of the Supreme High Command was received.

The control and checking of the operation's preparation was organized by going out among the troops and the subordinate headquarters, both by the general and officers of the *front's* field directorate and by the *front* commander and members of the military council. Defensive work was widely carried out and obstacles erected along the designated breakthrough sector between Lake Velence and Lake Balaton during 10-18 December in the 4th Guards Army's sector.

By 18 December the following had been dug: 63.5 kilometers of trenches and communications trenches, 1,089 trenches for heavy and light machine guns, 548 trenches for anti-tank rifles, 665 trenches for guns, 76 observation posts, and 287 overhead covers. Aside from this, 6,323 anti-tank and 1,117 anti-personnel mines had been laid in from of the forward edge along this sector.

During the preparation for the operation the engineer troops checked 687 kilometers of roads for mines and repaired 102 kilometers of roads.

A density of eight sapper companies in the 4th Guards Army and four sapper companies in the 46th Army per kilometer of breakthrough front was created for supporting the armies' breakthrough along the main attack axes.

The Organisation of Control and Communications

The working out of the *front* commander's decision, the planning of the operation and the organization of the troops' cooperation were carried out by the *front* under the leadership of the representative of the *Stavka* of the Supreme High Command, Marshal Timoshenko. This work was carried out at the Third Ukrainian Front's main command posts, which on 12 December was located in the Dunafoldvar area.

The planning for the operation in a limited time frame and the transmission of the *front* commander's decision to the troops was carried out by means of personal interaction between commanders and subordinates and the issuing of all orders for preparing the operation orally or by noting the tasks on personal maps. A limited number of persons were initiated into the problems of planning and preparation.

The operational cooperation of the *front's* forces and the air force was organized in accordance with the plan for the *front* offensive operation.

The organization of the troops' tactical cooperation along the breakthrough sector and the refinement of the *front* operational plan took place in the armies under the leadership and control of the *front* commander's visits to headquarters and the field.

During this same time the commanders of the 2nd and 7th guards mechanized corps and the 17th Air Army's air formations were summoned to the headquarters of the 46th and 4th Guards armies, and with their participation questions of cooperation of the given army's forces with these formations were worked out throughout the entire depth of the army operation.

The working out of problems of tactical cooperation during the breakthrough of the enemy's defense by the army commanders was conducted by the method of war games on maps with the corps and division commanders, and with the commanders of supporting unit and formation commanders and aviation.

The army commanders were obliged to go out into the field, where they checked the organization of the troops' cooperation and their readiness for the offensive on the spot.

In organizing tactical cooperation on the spot, particular attention was paid to the precise knowledge of combat assignments, the definition of the troops' jumping-off places and the objects of their attack, refining the artillery's aviation's and engineering troops' tasks (the activities of obstacle clearing groups and mobile forces of the 2nd and 7th guards mechanized corps), their combat formations, and refining the line where they would bypass the infantry and their support during the commitment into the breach. Common reference points and cooperation signals were established.

An officer from the army's operational sector was dispatched with a radio set to improve cooperation communications between the combined-arms armies and the mechanized corps.

Operational Support

A. Intelligence

Intelligence was conducted without a halt together with combat activities to improve the troops' jumping-off position for the breakthrough.

Immediately on the eve of the breakthrough, on 18 and 19 December a reconnaissance in force was carried out by reinforced rifle battalions from each first-echelon rifle division, with the support of all the division's artillery.

The purpose of combat reconnaissance was to determine the forward edge of the main defensive zone and the destruction of the enemy's combat security.

A very important task was to uncover the enemy's disposition and his defensive system in the zones of the forthcoming breakthrough.

The procuring of this intelligence data was to be completed by the close of 19 December 1944.

On the basis of this intelligence data, detailed maps and diagrams of the enemy's dispositions and his fire and obstacle system along the sectors of the forthcoming breakthrough were compiled, in the armies under the leadership of the *front* headquarters.

B. Measures for Ensuring Surprise

Preparations for the operation were carried out by observing secrecy measures for concentrating and moving our forces to the jumping-off position. At the same time, large-scale measures for fooling the enemy were not carried out.

One may explain this situation by the following. First of all, a very limited amount of time was allotted for preparing the operation (no more than eight days). Secondly, the 46th and 4th Guards armies' narrow attack zone (60 kilometers) and the creation of shock groups in two areas between lakes (Lake Balaton and Lake Velence) did not allow us to fool the enemy by means of revealing false troop concentrations of operational significance, as in this situation the true concentration of forces might be revealed in another area next to the fake area. Operational masking for the purpose of distracting the enemy's attention to a secondary axis was carried out in the armies. Defensive work was conducted along the entire front occupied by the 46th and 4th Guards armies to a great depth and the preparation of a jumping-off position for the troops' offensive was carried out under their cover. Trenches were dug, wire obstacles were put up (stakes driven in and *cheval de frises* planted), and false mining carried out, etc. 2-3 battalions were engaged in this work in each division's sector. All of this work was carried out for the purpose of creating the impression among the enemy that our troops were going over to the defensive.

Aside from this, the construction of false firing positions was carried out. In the area south of Tac and the grove south of Kelestelek, 50 false guns had been built and emplaced. "Wandering" guns fired in order to liven up the firing positions along the 4th Guards Army's left flank. The impression of the movement of supplies, tanks and motorcycles to the front was created along the sector south of Lake Balaton, along the roads running along the shore. Further, 65 dummy tanks were prepared along the 4th Guards Army's left flank in order to create the impression of our tank group's concentration, which were emplaced in groups of 5-10 in the areas of Enying, Siofok, Balatonkiliti, and Balatonszabadi. At the same time, activity in this area was demonstrated by the nighttime movement of 2-3 T-34 tanks and two self-propelled guns where the dummy tanks were stationed.

An attack with part of our forces was carried out along secondary axes in order to distract the enemy's attention from the main axes. For this purpose, roads were built at an increased pace along the secondary axes during 16-20 December. Road construction was carried out with the maximum involvement of the local population and horse transportation.

Particular attention was given to the masking of troops and combat equipment. The troops were not stationed closely together and mainly outside of inhabited locales, while each subunit and unit was obliged to carefully mask its location and observe the rules of masking discipline. All troop movements were carried out exclusively at night, with switched-off headlights, and during the day by special passes.

The masking measures were checked by specially assigned officers.

Throughout the entire preparatory period and the offensive operation, the enemy continued to strengthen those sectors where our troops' offensive was not planned and conducted intensified aerial reconnaissance of the false tank and artillery concentration areas. Throughout 18 December he carried out intensive artillery and mortar fire, including fire from long-range artillery, against the areas of our false artillery positions.

The German-Fascist command nevertheless failed to uncover the concentration of powerful groups of forces northeast and southeast of Lake Velence and had no idea of the scale of the operation under preparation.

C. The Aviation Offensive

The commander of the 17th Air Army, proceeding from the *front* commander's plan and decision, decided to detail the 186th Assault Air Division from the 10th Assault Air Corps and the 295th Fighter Division to support the 46th Army and the 10th Assault Air Corps' 306th Assault Air Division, and the 189th Assault Air Division and the 288th Fighter Division to support the 4th Guards Army. The bomber air divisions were to remain in the reserve and be directed for operations in the interests of both armies. With the commitment of the mobile formations into the breakthrough, the assault air and fighter air divisions would be redirected to support them.

Thus the air army commander's decision corresponded to the idea of the operation and called for the concentration of all aviation forces along the axis of the *front's* main attack axis. The 4th Guards Army, which was making the main attack, was assigned the greater number of air units.

Proceeding from the air army commander's decision, a cooperation plan of the army's units with the *front's* forces was drawn up. Besides this, plans for the aviation's cooperation with the 18th Guards Tank, 7th Mechanized and 5th Guards Cavalry corps were drawn up and a special directive was issued with specific instructions on the organization of air combat activities and the methods of attacking targets.

The plan for the combat employment of the 17th Air Army foresaw the troops' and aviation's tasks before the start of the operation and during the first day of the offensive. Before the start of the offensive, it was mainly planned to carry out aerial reconnaissance and covering the concentration of the shock groups.

A direct aviation preparation was planned for the first day of the offensive simultaneously with the artillery preparation, which was expressed in strikes against the enemy's headquarters and communications centers.

It was planned to uninterruptedly support the attack throughout two hours by echeloned strikes by groups of assault aircraft against the enemy's artillery, personnel and equipment. Following this, the air forces would begin operating on call, chiefly against the enemy's reserves. Simultaneous with this, the activities of hunters in the depth of the enemy's defense was planned.

A great deal of attention was devoted to the planning of fighter aviation's activities to cover the shock groups by means of uninterruptedly patrolling by groups of fighters beyond the front line over the enemy's territory in order to intercept his planes before they could reach the front line. Besides this, it was planned to allot hunters 20-40 kilometers into the depth of the enemy's territory to intercept his planes and to report by radio the approach of the enemy's aviation.

The plan called for the air army commander's reserve, consisting of bomber divisions, two groups of assault aircraft and one group of fighters.

The control and cooperation with the ground forces was organized by moving up the command posts of the air formation commanders to the front line and emplacing radio guidance stations with the attacking forces. Command posts with communications equipment, along with the commanders of air formations and units, were also organized in the mobile formations.

Thus planning called for active air operations on the first day of the operation and approximately during the succeeding days, while command posts, which had been moved forward to the troops, guaranteed centralized control and precise tactical interaction with the ground forces.

Anti-Aircraft Defense

Fighter Aviation Cover. By the start of the Third Ukrainian Front's operation the 17th Air Army included the following fighter units and formations:

- 295th Fighter Division (31st, 116th and 164th fighter regiments);
- 288th Fighter Division (611th, 866th, 659th, and 897th fighter regiments);

- 194th Fighter Division (56th, 530th and 848th fighter regiments).

In accordance with the decision by the commander of the Third Ukrainian Front for the operation and the decision by the commander of the 17th Air Army for the combat employment of the 17th Air Army, the air cover of the troops and rear area targets was chiefly planned for the *front's* shock groups during their regroupings and in their concentration areas. The chief means of covering was to be by fighter patrols over the enemy's territory and over the concentration areas of the front's chief groups of forces and rear targets.

It was planned to move the patrol zones beyond the front line for the purpose of intercepting the enemy's planes before their arrival at the front line and along the far approaches to the targets being covered.

It was planned to secure cooperation with the ground forces by sending representatives from the fighter divisions to the troop headquarters. For example, the 288th Fighter Division had its representatives in the headquarters of the 4th Guards Army and 7th Mechanized Corps and the 295th Fighter Division in the headquarters of the 46th Army and the 18th Guards Tank Corps.

It was planned to direct the fighters mainly from the 17th Air Army commander's command post and auxiliary command post.

Anti-Aircraft Artillery Cover. By the start of the operation, the Third Ukrainian Front disposed of the following anti-aircraft artillery mean:

- 9th Anti-Aircraft Artillery Division (800th, 974th, 981st, and 993rd anti-aircraft artillery regiments);
- 22nd Anti-Aircraft Artillery Division (1335th, 1341st, 1347th, and 1358th anti-aircraft artillery regiments);
- 3rd Anti-Aircraft Artillery Division (772nd, 1390th, 1396th, and 1398th anti-aircraft artillery regiments
- 159th, 1384th, 271st, 1713th, 585th, and 1694th independent anti-aircraft regiments, for a total of 20 anti-aircraft regiments (12 anti-aircraft regiments were with the 57th and 37th armies).

There were four army anti-aircraft regiments and two independent anti-aircraft battalions.

The above-listed weapons were employed for organizing the anti-aircraft cover of the troops and targets in the *front's* and armies' rear in close cooperation with the 17th Air Army's fighter aviation.

In accordance with the *front* commander's decision, all three anti-aircraft artillery divisions and independent anti-aircraft artillery regiments were allotted for covering the *front's* forces and the *front's* two shock groups, both during their concentration and regrouping and during the offensive. The main part of the anti-aircraft artillery equipment was allotted to the 4th Guards Army.

By decision of the 46th and 4th Guards armies' commanders, the army anti-aircraft artillery regiments were to be employed for covering army rear targets and the army headquarters.

Fighter aviation, based on their own airfields, were designated for cooperation with the anti-aircraft units at a distance of 20-25 kilometers from the forward edge.

D. Securing Boundaries

The right flank of the 46th Army was secured by the Danube Military Flotilla and the 83rd Naval Infantry Brigade. The security of the left flank was entrusted to the commander of the 4th Guards Army, who had prepared counterattacks by the forces of the 34th Guards Rifle Division along the following axes: a) Adonyszabolcs—Katalin station, and b) Adonyszabolcs—Kisvelence. Besides this, fire had been planned by two artillery regiments against the area of the boundary with the 46th Army.

On the basis of instructions by the *front* commander, in order to secure the left flank of the *front's* shock groups, on 15 December the commander of the 4th Guards Army ordered the 21st Guards Rifle Corps to go over to the offensive along the front Sarviz Canal—Balatonakarttya—southeastern and southern shore of Lake Balaton as far as Balatonszemes.

At the same time, it was ordered to have powerful reserves and the following engineer outfitting of the defensive zone: two fully-outfitted continuous trenches along the forward edge, communications trenches and developed centers of resistance in areas for second echelons and reserves.

Anti-tank areas were to be created in Tac, the Polgardi passing track, the northern outskirts of Lepseny, Balatonfenarvar, the southern outskirts of Balatonakarttya (there was no depth along the forward edge).

5,000 anti-tank and 25,000 anti-personnel mines were to be laid along axes vulnerable to tanks (Polgardi station and Lake Balaton).

Aside from this, it was ordered to create a detachment, consisting of the 252nd Special Designation Battalion, an army reconnaissance detachment and the 3rd Motorcycle Regiment, for reliably securing the southeastern and southern shore of Lake Balaton, which was assigned the task of preventing the forcing of Lake Balaton and the landing of enemy forces in the areas of Siofok, Zamardi, Felder, and Balatonszarszo.

17

Activities of the *Front's* Left Wing. The 57th Army's Assumption of the Defensive, 20 December 1944

The Instructions by the *Stavka* of the Supreme High Command to the Commander of the Third Ukrainian Front

The *Stavka* of the VGK, in its directive of 6 December, ordered the commander of the Third Ukrainian Front, upon the 57th Army's arrival at the line of the southwestern shore of Lake Balaton—Nagykanizsa—mouth of the Mura River (18 kilometers southwest of Nagykanizsa), to temporarily halt the offensive and go over to the defensive.

With its arrival along the line indicated by the *Stavka*, the 57th Army's forces would occupy a favorable operational situation in regard to the enemy and favorable conditions would have been created for the organization of a defense and to secure the southern wing of the Third Ukrainian Front.

Besides this, the seizure of the Nagykanizsa oil-producing area would put the Hitlerite command in a catastrophic situation as regards its forces' supply of fuel.

The 57th Army, having by 5 December 1944 arrived at the line Lake Balaton—Marcali—Nagybajom—Nagyatad—Babocsa—Barcs, was engaged throughout the following ten days, until 19 December, in unsuccessful fighting and did not advance.

The 21 December decision by the commander of the Third Ukrainian Front came down to the following: the forces of the 57th Army were ordered to go over to the defensive along the line of the southeastern shore of Lake Balaton—Balatonkeresztur—Marcali—Mesztegnyo—Nagybajom—Kisbajom—Babocsa—Prinke—Barcs, in order to cover the flank and rear of the *front's* shock group attacking to the north and northwest with the task of encircling the Budapest group of German-Fascist forces from the west.

The 57th Army Commander's Decision to Defend

The following group of enemy forces was unearthed by fighting and all forms of intelligence:

- units of the "Saint Laszlo" Division, three reserve squadrons from the Hungarian Cavalry Division, of the Hungarian 3rd Cavalry Brigade, from the 1st Mountain Division, an assault battalion from the Second Panzer Army, units of the "Brandenburg" Division, the Hungarian 11th Reserve Regiment, 92nd Motorized Brigade, units of the Hungarian 71st Infantry Division, and the 1222nd Anti-Tank Battalion were along the sector Lake Balaton—Balatonkeresztur—Nagyatad;
- units of the 44th Infantry Division, the 117th Light Infantry Division's 749th Infantry Regiment, a reconnaissance detachment, the 188th Light Infantry Division's 750th Infantry Regiment, the 13th SS Muslim Infantry Division, and the Hungarian 54th Border Detachment were defending along the sector Nagyatad—Vizvar.

In all, this amounted to 8-9 divisions.

Table 9 Correlation of Forces in the Sector of 57th Army, Late December 1944

Soviet Forces	Axis Forces	Correlation
10 rifle divisions	9 infantry divisions	1:1
871 guns and mortars	850	1:1
128 tanks	132	1:1

Thus the enemy had managed to create a significant density in men and materiel, which enabled him to equalize his forces.

In carrying out the *front* commander's order, the commander of the 57th Army assigned his forces the following tasks:

The 6th Rifle Corps, consisting of the 61st, 113th, 19th, and 20th guards rifle divisions, and reinforced with the 47th Cannon-Artillery Regiment, 528th and 563rd mortar regiments, a battalion from the 25th Guards Mortar Regiment, 249th Tank Regiment, 1008th and 184th anti-tank artillery regiments, and the 53rd Motorcycle Regiment, was to go over to the defense along the line Fonyed—Balatonkeresztur—Marcali—Mesztegnyo—Saponyapuszta, with the task of preventing the enemy from breaking through along the Balatonkeresztur—Fonyed, Marcali—Nikla and Mesztegnyo—Somogyfajsz axes.

The corps' combat formation was in two echelons: three divisions (61st, 113th and 20th rifle divisions) in the first echelon and one division (19th Rifle Division) in the second, which was to move to the Nikla—Somogyfajsz—Pusztakovacsi area and prepare counterattacks along the following axes: a) Nikla—Marcali; b) Pusztakovacsi—Mesztegnyo, and; c) Somogyfajsz—Nagybajom.

The first-echelon division's combat organization, except for the 20th Rifle Division, was also in two echelons.

It was ordered to complete the troops' regrouping by 23 December.

The 53rd Motorcycle Regiment was defending the southeastern shore of Lake Balaton.

The boundary line on the left was Somogysard—Soponya—Szenyer—Nemesvid.

The 64th Rifle Corps, consisting of the 10th, 73rd Guards and 299th rifle divisions, and reinforced by the 1st and 2nd regiments of the 160th Cannon-Artillery Brigade, 1172nd and 1249th anti-tank artillery regiments, 274th Howitzer Regiment, 523rd Mortar Regiment, 1084th Anti-Aircraft Artillery Regiment, and the 5th Flamethrower Battalion was to go over to the defense along the line excluding Soponya—Nagybajom—Kutas—Beleg, with the task of preventing the enemy's breakthrough along the following axes: Nagybajom—Szamajom; Nagybajom—Jako; Kutas—Jako, and; Mesztegnyo—Soponya.

The corps was to mainly pay attention to the creation of the most durable defense possible east of Nagybajom and southeast of Kutas,

The corps was to be organized into two echelons: two rifle divisions (299th and 10th) were in the first echelon and one division (73rd Rifle) in the second echelon in the Szamajon—Kaposfo area and to prepare counterattacks along the following axes: Kiskorpad—Somogysard—Koroknya—Futora—Al Sokak; Kiskorpad—Nagybajom, and; Kiskorpad—Jako—Kisbajom.

The corps was to have its artillery-anti-tank reserve in the Kiskorpad area, in readiness to repel enemy tank attacks along the following axes: Mesztegnyo—Soponya; Nagybajom—Szamajon, and; Nagybajom—Kutas.

The corps was to complete the relief and regrouping of its forces by the morning of 23 December 1944 and be ready to defend by 24 December.

The 75th Rifle Corps, consisting of the 74th, 236th and 233rd rifle divisions, reinforced by the 160th Cannon-Artillery Brigade's 3rd Artillery Regiment and the 23rd Flamethrower Battalion, was to go over to the defense along the line Beleg—Babocsa—Prinke—Barcs, with the task of preventing an enemy breakthrough along the following axes: Beleg—Babocsa—Nagykorpad; Nagyatad—Nagykorpad; Nagyatad—Labod, and; Vizvar—Babocsa.

The corps was to mainly pay attention to the creation of the most secure defense possible along the corps' right flank, east of Nagyatad along the line marker 125.8—Heresznye—along the Drava River as far as Barcs.

Units of the 233rd Rifle Division were to continue to reliably hold the bridgehead along the right bank of the Drava River in the Barcs area.

The corps was to be organized into a single echelon, having a single rifle regiment from the 233rd Rifle Division in reserve and to station it in the Csokonyavisonta area.

Two regiments from the 233rd Rifle Division, along with the 23rd Flamethrower Battalion, were to be left in their previous defensive positions, with the task of preventing an enemy breakthrough along the Gorne—Baze axis, along the southern bank of the Drava River toward the crossings in the Barcs area.

The corps was to have an artillery-anti-tank reserve in the Somogvisonta—Ranyaujlak—Csokonyavisonta area.

The regrouping and relief of forces was to be completed by the morning of 23 December.

The corps was to be ready to defend by 24 December.

The 32nd Mechanized Brigade, following the movement of the 19th Guards Rifle Division into the second echelon of the 6th Guards Rifle Corps and the consolidation of the defensive zones by the first-echelon divisions, was to concentrate in the Samogyag area in the army reserve.

The 864th Self-Propelled Artillery Regiment was to be held in the army reserve and by 0900 on 22 December be concentrated in the Kaposmero area, ready to launch counterattacks together with the 73rd Guards Rifle Division along the following axes: Szamajom—Nagybajom and Szmajom—Kiskorpad—Kutas.

The designated counterattack axes were to be studied beforehand, communications established with the commander of the 73rd Guards Rifle Division and cooperation organized.

The army's anti-tank artillery reserve, the 374th Anti-Tank Artillery Regiment, was to be stationed in the Szamajom area, in readiness for operations along the following axes: Szamajom; Nagybajom; Szamajom—Kutas, and; Szamajom—Babocsa.

2-3 deployment lines were being prepared along each of these axes.

The Organization of Anti-Tank Defense

Seven anti-tank areas were being prepared in the 6th Guards Rifle Corps' defensive zone, with areas nos. 1, 2, 5, and the Mestegne area particularly heavily fortified; six anti-tank areas were being prepared in the 64th Rifle Corps' defensive zone, with areas nos. 2, 3, 4, and 5 particularly securely fortified and, in which aside from anti-tank artillery, there were 122mm howitzers and 152mm guns firing over open sights for fighting the enemy's heavy tanks.

Thus the anti-tank defense in the army's zone was organized into 13 anti-tank areas to a depth of 1-3 kilometers.

140 anti-tank guns were brought in to create the 13 anti-tank areas, which resulted in an overall anti-tank density of about two guns per kilometer, while this figure reached 6-7 guns per kilometer of front along the axis of the enemy's main attack.

The commander of the 57th Army recognized this depth of anti-tank defense as insufficient and adopted the following measures for increasing the depth of the anti-tank defense for the purpose of securing the army's defensive strength:

- to create engineer obstacles along the main axes of tank danger to a depth of 8-10 kilometers;
- to create nine anti-tank areas in the defensive depth along the main axes of tank danger, at the expense of artillery located in covered positions, in which there were to be 80 76mm guns, 30 122mm howitzers, and eight 152mm gun-howitzers, for a total of 118 guns.

As a result of creating the anti-tank areas in the defensive depth and reinforced by engineer obstacles, the army's anti-tank defense along the main axes of tank danger reached a depth of ten kilometers along the Nagykanizsa—Kaposvar axis; six kilometers along the Marcali—Nikla axis, and; six kilometers along the Nagybajom—Somogysard axis, with the following amount of artillery: (see table).

The remaining artillery was either located among the reserves, or in covered firing positions outside the axes of tank danger.

Table 10 Concentration of Artillery in the 57th Army's Sector, Late December 1944

Caliber	Total Guns in the Army	Of these, the following were located in the anti-tank areas					
		In the Main Defensive Zone		In the Depth of the Army's Defense		Total	
		Tubes	Percentage	Tubes	Percentage	Tubes	Percentage
45mm Guns	83	52	62.6	–	–	52	62.6
76mm Regimental Guns	55	41	78.8	–	–	41	78.8
76mm Divisional Guns	162	64	40.0	80	49.4	144	89.4
122mm Howitzers	77	16	20.7	30	39.0	56	59.7
122mm Cannon/ Howitzers	42	12	28.7	8	19.1	20	47.3
Total	419	185	44.1	118	28.2	303	72.3

Almost all of the army's artillery disposed of reserve firing positions for firing over open sights against enemy tanks. Batteries, located in closed positions and forming part of the anti-tank areas in the defensive depth, had been placed along axes of tank danger, so as to cover these axes in the army's tactical defensive depth, so that each gun could fire over open sights up to a distance of two kilometers.

The system of anti-tank fire was organized by taking into account natural and artificial anti-tank barriers.

Minefields were laid in front of the anti-tank areas and individual guns. Wooden obstacles were created along forested sectors.

Command and control was exercised through the chiefs of the anti-tank areas, who were appointed by orders of the corps commanders. In the anti-tank areas in the main defensive zone these were from the combined-arms subunits' senior officers and from among the artillery commanders in the anti-tank areas in the defensive depth. Each chief of an anti-tank area new the maneuver plan for the anti-tank artillery and reserves and who was to reinforce him in case of necessity.

Engineer Outfitting

The army commander's decision called for the creation of a deeply echeloned defense with a depth of up to 60 kilometers, with a main defensive zone of 5-6 kilometers, a second defensive zone of 3-4 kilometers, and three army defensive lines.

The density of anti-tank mining along the main axes of tank danger was to be increased to 3,000 mines per kilometer of front.

25 main centers of resistance were to be created in the main defensive zone and 11 main centers of resistance in the second zone. They were to be outfitted with 2-3 lines of trenches and communications trenches.

It was planned to outfit the defensive zones with fully-developed trenches and have two trenches each in the centers of resistance.

Alluvial trenches were dug in areas with a high level of ground water. Special shelters were built for covering the rank and file and equipment. Inhabited locales were configured for perimeter defense. Axes of tank danger were mined, with a total of 30,531 ant-tank mines and 58,793 anti-personnel mines laid.

56 kilometers of wire obstacles were laid in front of the forward edge of the defense.

56 kilometers of new roads were built to support the maneuver by second echelons and reserves.

An order by the army commander called for completing the outfitting of the main defensive zone by December 25 and the second zone by 30 December 1944.

The army's engineer troops (65th Engineer-Sapper Brigade, 11th Independent Engineer Brigade and the 892nd Independent Sapper Battalion) were employed in a centralized fashion, under the leadership of the chief of engineer troops.

Thus the decision by the commander of the 57th Army, taking into account the enemy's presumed actions, as well as our forces and their capabilities, called for the organization of the army's forces in a single echelon, with reserves (113th Rifle Division and 32nd Mechanized Brigade). The army was defending along a 113-kilometer front. The corps was defending along the following fronts: 6th Guards Rifle Corps along a 33-kilometer front, the 64th Rifle Corps along a 30-kilometer front, the 75th Rifle Corps along a 50-kilometer front, while the first-echelon divisions along the enemy's likely attack axes were defending along a 12-kilometer front; the divisions along the secondary axis were defending along an 18-28-kilometer front.

The army's main forces and materiel were to concentrate along the axes of the enemy's probable attacks along the Marcali—Kutas setor, along a 35-kilometer front. The army's reserves were located along the axes of the enemy's likely attacks: the 32nd Mechanized Brigade in the area Osztopan—excluding Bodrog—Somogyjad, and the 113th Rifle Division in the area Szamajom area, with the reserves 6-8 kilometers from the forward edge.

The 57th Army had the following average densities along its 160-kilometer defensive front, taking into account the defensive sector along the southern shore of Lake Balaton: 16-18 kilometers per division; 3-4 guns and mortars and 2-3 machine guns per kilometer of front.

Given an average divisional strength of 4-5,000 men, the personnel density must be viewed as insignificant.

This density was significantly greater along the axes of the enemy's likely attacks and reached the following:

- 11-18 guns and mortars per kilometer of front;
- 10-11 anti-tank guns and mortars per kilometer of front;
- 1-2 tanks and self-propelled guns per kilometer of front.

Anti-aircraft defense was organized by the forces and weapons of the corps and the first-echelon divisions. A corps defending along the axis of the likely enemy attack, was to be reinforced with one anti-aircraft artillery regiment.

Planning the Defensive Operation

The plan for the defensive operation called for the organization of a deeply-echeloned and multi-zone defense capable of repelling the enemy's massed tank attacks.

The defense was built to be anti-tank, employing broad maneuver using anti-tank artillery and mobile obstacle detachments, as well as maneuvering all of the army's artillery from the defensive sectors not under attack to the sector of the enemy's attack. Tasks were assigned to formations and combat arms by individual combat orders and combat orders to the commanders.

As is known, the army's operational organization was in a single echelon, with all three corps in a single line. The corps' combat formation was in two echelons, with the exception of the 75th Rifle Corps, which was defending along a secondary axis and had a single-echelon formation, with a single rifle regiment in reserve.

The 57th Army commander's reserve consisted of the 32nd Mechanized Brigade, 113th Rifle Division and the 864th Self-Propelled Artillery Regiment, which were located along the axis of the enemy's expected main attack.

Reinforcement artillery was basically concentrated along the axis of the enemy's likely attack and was attached to the corps.

The army commander disposed only of the 377th Anti-Tank Artillery Regiment as the army anti-tank reserve.

The plan for the defensive operation called for preventing the enemy from arriving at, deploying from and occupying a jumping-off position by hitting him with concentrated artillery fire against the areas of the enemy's troop concentrations and deployment. For this purpose, long-range artillery attacks were prepared beforehand against road junctions, communications centers, locations of headquarters, and depots with munitions and fuel. Sectors of concentrated fire against concentration areas of the enemy's infantry and tanks were prepared.

Mobile barrage fire sectors were prepared along sectors of tank danger. Immobile barrage fire sectors were prepared in front of the forward edge along the axis of the enemy's expected main attack. All of the fire sectors were registered and the data noted in the batteries. In all, up to 83 sectors for long-range attack and concentrated fire were prepared, as well as eight mobile barrage fire sectors and ten immobile barrage fire sectors were prepared.

It was planned to carry out a counterpreparation, which was to begin on orders from the army commander, against concentration areas of the enemy's infantry and tanks.

Besides this, the staff of the 57th Army's artillery drew up a system of massed fire, called "Storm," in accordance with which the chief targets of massed artillery fire were established beforehand in the interests of the army. This fire system was then supplemented by fire plans from the rifle corps, divisions and regiments, which comprised a unified plan for massing the army's artillery fire. Each participant in the massed fire was assigned an army number, after which a schedule for bringing in artillery for concentrated fire against each sector was compiled.

This plan was transmitted to all of the combined-arms commanders and gave the rifle corps commander the right to call up the fire of all the artillery which had been subordinated to him and upon approval from the senior commander of the artillery that had not been subordinated to him, but which could fire on the necessary target.

Air support, in accordance with the 17th Air Army's plan, called for employing the forces of the 189th Assault Air Division (126 Il-2s) and the 184th Fighter Division (117 La-5s) and one night light-bomber air regiment (32 Po-2s),[1] for which airfields west of the Danube River were being prepared. Besides this, it was planned to bring in the 244th Bomber Division (115 planes) for operations against the enemy's forces facing the 57th Army, depending on the situation.

In accordance with the army's operational defense plan, plans for the defensive engagement were drawn up in the corps, divisions and regiments, which reflected the idea of the army commander's decision. The corps' and divisions' second echelons and the army reserves were located in areas convenient for launching counterattacks.

A great deal of attention was devoted to the question of securing boundaries and flanks. Senior combined-arms and artillery commanders reconnoitered the areas of the boundaries and flanks.

The following were detached for securing the 57th Army's flank with the Bulgarian 1st Army: 43 guns and mortars from the 57th Army and 18 guns and mortars from the Bulgarian 1st Army.

In all, 61 guns and mortars were detached from both armies. Nineteen general sectors for concentrated fire were designated for securing the flank, against which data was compiled and gun registration carried out.

In order to secure observation along the flanks and cooperation, a general artillery observation post was outfitted in the Kiserda area, which had direct communications with the 299th Rifle Division's and the Bulgarian 10th Infantry Division's observation posts, as well as with the artillery subunits securing the flank.

The 20th and 10th Guards rifle divisions were to secure the boundary between the 6th and 64th rifle corps, for which 30 guns were detached and 19 sectors for concentrated fire were prepared.

Cooperation was organized personally by the army commander on site, where the following were worked out: the cooperation of the first echelons and of the corps in the fighting for the main defensive zone; the cooperation of the rifle corps' second echelons in launching their counterattacks; the cooperation of the army reserves with the first-echelon corps in launching their counterattacks; the cooperation of the artillery with the army reserves for supporting the counterblows, and; the order and sequence of artillery maneuver through trajectory and movement.

The defensive plan called for the employment of each combat arm in the fight for the main defensive sector. Aside from this, the chiefs of the combat arms drew up plans for employing their combat arm in the operation, based upon the army commander's decision.

Troop command and control in the defensive operation was planned by outfitting main and reserve command posts for the corps and first-echelon divisions, as well as by outfitting a broad network of observation posts (the rifle division commanders had two observation posts each at a distance of 1.5-2 kilometers from the forward edge of the defense). Besides this, in the event of an enemy breakthrough of the main defensive zone, observation posts had been outfitted in the second defensive zone.

The corps commanders disposed of observation posts in their own sectors at a distance of 2-3 kilometers from the forward edge.

The army commander had two observation posts in the main defensive zone at a distance of 3-4 kilometers from the forward edge of the main defensive zone.

Besides this, observation posts were outfitted along each army line along the axis of the enemy's likely attacks.

All of the observation posts were outfitted with communications equipment, both along the front and in the depth.

Such a stationing of observation posts enabled us to uninterruptedly control the troops, both during the defensive preparation period and also during the conduct of the defensive battle.

1 Editor's note. The Po-2 (also known as the U-2) was a general purpose Soviet biplane that first appeard in 1929. One model had a crew of one and a maximum speed of 152 kilometers per hour. It was armed with one 7.62mm machine gun and could carry six 50-kilogram bombs.

The command posts of the first-echelon corps and divisions were located at the following distances from the forward edge of the main defensive zone: 6-8 kilometers for rifle divisions, 12-16 kilometers for the corps, with the army's command post at a distance of 30 kilometers.

Conclusions

1. The following are characteristic features of the 57th Army's assumption of the defensive during the *front's* offensive operation:

a) the shift to the defensive was carried out in conditions of direct contact with the enemy and subject to his fire and powerful counterattacks, and in the absence of a prepared line;
b) the troops had extended communications and rear establishments;
c) the time for assuming the defensive was limited and the army command demanded speed in the adoption of a decision and transmitting it to the troops, both as concerns the regrouping of men and materiel, as well as concerns the organization of a defense.

2. The principle of massing men and materiel along the decisive axes was adhered to; the defensive battle was planned according to variations (the likely axes of the enemy's main attacks).

3. The plan for the defensive operation included the conduct of an artillery counterpreparation, the conduct of counterattacks in the event of the enemy's breaking through into the defensive depth, the massing of artillery fire along the decisive axes, and also problems of operational security and the engineer outfitting of the terrain.

4. The firmness of the defense was to be achieved through the deep echeloning of the defense (its overall depth was up to 60 kilometers); through the creation of a main defensive zone up to 5-6 kilometers deep; the creation of a second defensive zone up to 3-4 kilometers deep; the creation of an army defensive line 50 kilometers from the forward edge of the main defensive zone, and; two switch lines.

5. The anti-tank defense was organized throughout the entire tactical depth of the defense and was most dense along the first position of the main defensive zone. A large part of the anti-tank weapons was employed for fighting for the main defensive zone.

The basis for the 57th Army's anti-tank defense was the anti-tank areas at a depth of 6-10 kilometers, which included 72 percent of all the artillery.

In the event of a massed attack by a large enemy tank group, this depth would not have guaranteed the defeat of the main body of enemy tanks. The modern theory of operational art requires in these cases the organization of an anti-tank defense to a depth of 30-50 kilometers.

6. The plan, drawn up by the army staff along with the artillery commander, called for the massing of fire along the most threatened sectors, which guaranteed the successful conduct of the defensive operation.

The 57th Army's experience in massing fire and maneuvering artillery from passive sectors to the sector of the enemy's attack during the defensive battle exerted its influence on the modern theory of employing artillery in the army defensive operation.

7. The problems of securing boundaries and flanks sufficiently fully resolved.

18

The Breakthrough of the "Margarita Line" by the Forces of the 46th and 4th Guards Armies

The directive from the headquarters of the Third Ukrainian Front of 19 December indicated that the offensive was to begin on 20 December, with the artillery preparation scheduled for 1015 and the infantry attack for 1115.

At 1115 on 20 December the forces of the 46th Army, following an artillery preparation, attacked to the north and northwest. While overcoming the enemy's fire resistance and beating off his infantry and tank counterattacks along individual axes, the army's forces broke through the enemy's defense along the Baracska front.

By the close of the day the army's forces had reached the line of the northwestern outskirts of Baracska—height 133—one kilometer east of Kenesseytanya—one kilometer southeast of Pazmand—northwest of Velence.

The corps' second echelons reached the following areas: the 59th Guards Rifle Division height 145—Pettend—height 127; the 109th Guards Rifle Division northeast of Kapolnasnyek.

Our aviation rendered significant support to the army's attacking troops, uninterruptedly strafing the enemy's combat formations and bombing the concentration areas of his tanks and reserves. Fighter aviation covered the troops from the air, while carrying out a significant number of successful air battles with the enemy's air force.

The *front* commander ordered the commander of the 46th Army to continue to more decisively develop the offensive along the previous axes from the morning of 21 December. The 2nd Guards Mechanized Corps was to be committed upon the capture of Pazmand and by the close of 21 December the corps was to capture the Bicske area, while the infantry was to reach the line Elvira—Erd—Vertesacsa—Lovasbereny.

The troops of the 4th Guards Army attacked with the forces of three corps (five rifle divisions) and, while overcoming the enemy's stubborn resistance, penetrated into the fortified zone of his defense between Lake Velence and the Sarviz Canal along a front 15 kilometers wide and up to nine kilometers deep.

Units of the 31st Guards Rifle Corps, while bypassing Lake Velence from the west, forced the Csaszar Viz River and, while beating off numerous attacks, each in strength up to an company, with 4-6 tanks, by 1900 on 12 December were fighting along the line northern outskirts of Pakozd—northwestern slopes of height 242—south of Kisfalud—0.5 kilometers east of Kisfalud—1.5 kilometers west of Borgond. The 34th Rifle Division, the corps' second echelon, had passed through Kisfalud at 1800 and was on the move toward Kisfalud.

Units of the 20th Guards Rifle Corps captured the enemy's powerful strong points of Kulsobarand and Belsobarand, fighting against the enemy's tanks and armored transports, and by 1800 reached the line 300 meters south of the intersection of the railroad with the paved road—two kilometers west of Borgond—Janosfutas—500 meters north of the intersection of the railroad and the paved road. The 7th Guards Airborne Division, which comprised the corps' second echelon, was in Seregelyes.

The 21st Guards Rifle Corps gave fire support to the 252nd Rifle Division's attack with the forces of its right-flank 41st Guards Rifle Division. At 1330 the 41st Guards Rifle Division itself attacked and, having repulsed two enemy counterattacks in up to a battalion in strength, supported by 10-12 tanks and self-propelled guns and 15 armored transports, captured Tac by the close of the day.

The enemy put up particularly powerful resistance during the first day of the offensive along the line Kisfalud—Menes—marker 114—the bridge over the Sarviz Canal—west of Pezs. The enemy counterattacked the army's attacking units five times from this line, committing up to a regiment of infantry into the fighting, supported by 30-35 tanks and 13-15 armored transports.

The *front* commander ordered the commander of the 4th Guards Army to break through the enemy's defense during the night along the town's outer ring. Part of the 31st Guards Rifle Corps' forces were to capture the crossings over the canal along the sector Kerenas—Csala—the eastern suburbs of Szekesfehervar, thus securing the commitment of the 7th Guards Mechanized Corps.

Simultaneously, the army was to move up its artillery, particularly anti-tank, during the night.

The offensive by the *front's* forces continued from the morning of 21 December.

The enemy's resistance noticeably stiffened during the second part of the day along the 46th Army's front. The army's forces fought off numerous counterattacks in up to a company or battalion in strength and supported by 7-10 tanks and self-propelled guns.

The rifle corps' second echelons were committed into the fighting during the second half of the day in order to augment the strength of the attack: the 37th Rifle Corps' 59th Guards Rifle Division along the boundary between the 320th Rifle Division and the 108th Guards Rifle Division in the direction of Kajaszoszentpeter; the 10th Guards Rifle Corps' 109th Guards Rifle Division along the corps' right flank along the axis east of Pazmand.

The commitment of the corps' second echelons facilitated the increase in the offensive pace of the army's forces. The 86th Guards Rifle Division, located in the army commander's reserve, was concentrated in the Pettend area.

The army's main forces, while continuing the offensive and overcoming the enemy's stubborn resistance, by the close of the day broke through the enemy's defense along a 12-kilometer front to a depth of 8-10 kilometers and reached the following line: east of Elvira—northeast of Kismarton—0.5 kilometers east of Martonvasar—the southwestern outskirts of Martonvasar—southern outskirts of Kajaszoszentpeter—height 151.1—one kilometer east and south of Vereb—Nadap—Sukoro.

In accordance with the task set by the *front* commander, on the night of 20-21 December the commander of the 46th Army moved the 2nd Guards Mechanized Corps to the jumping-off point.

The commander of the 2nd Guards Mechanized Corps decided to commit the corps from the line Tordas—two kilometers north of Pazmand—Lovasbereny.

The commitment zone was as follows: from the right, Martonvasar—Pusztazamor—excluding Bija; from the left, Kapolnasnyek—Pazmand—Vertesacsa—excluding Obarok.

The 2nd Guards Mechanized Corps' immediate objective was to reach the area Zsambek—Bicske—Etyek.

The corps' actions were made difficult by the washed-out roads. The movement of vehicles, particularly wheeled ones, was possible only along paved roads.

By the morning of 21 December the dismounted mechanized brigades occupied their jumping-off positions behind the rifle units: one kilometer north of Ada and two kilometers southwest of Ada, with the task of attacking in the direction of Pazmand and Vereb. The tank brigade received orders to attack from behind the right flank of the left-flank mechanized brigade in the direction of marker 184.

Thus the 2nd Guards Mechanized Corps was committed into the fighting for the purpose of completing the breakthrough of the tactical depth of the defense along with the rifle formations.

This led to a situation in which the mechanized brigades, having deployed in the spaces between the infantry's combat formations, came into immediate contact with the enemy and made little progress. Following extended fighting, the 2nd Guards Mechanized Corps was only able to break contact with its infantry by the close of the day and reach the line south of Buvari—Vereb.

The 4th Guards Army's forces, while continuing the offensive, advanced up to three kilometers during the night of 20-21 December and captured the enemy's powerful strong points along the approaches to Szekesfehervar and Kisfalud and heights 134 and 122.

Powerful enemy counterattacks were renewed at dawn on 21 December in the 31st Guards Rifle Corps' sector. The corps' second echelon (34th Guards Rifle Division), which had been committed into the fighting along the boundary between the 4th and 40th Guards rifle divisions, with the task of forcing the Csaszar Viz Canal and capturing height 183 and Csala, did not carry out its assignment due to powerful enemy resistance.

Throughout the day the 31st Guards Rifle Corps fought off nine enemy counterattacks, in strength from a company to a battalion, supported by 5-10 tanks and 10-15 armored transports.

The 20th Guards Rifle Corps, while also encountering powerful enemy resistance and having beaten off nine counterattacks in strength from a battalion to a regiment, and supported by 8-12 tanks and self-propelled guns each, from the southern and southeastern outskirts of Szekesfehervar, was slowly advancing. As a result of skillful maneuver, individual units of the corps managed to break into the southern outskirts of the Szekesfehervar suburbs.

The 135th Rifle Corps' 252nd Rifle Division, having beaten off a number of enemy infantry counterattacks, supported by tanks and self-propelled guns, got into a fight for the southern outskirts north of Techen.

The enemy, taking into account the threat which the units of the 252nd Rifle Division had created for the city of Szekesfehervar, undertook a powerful counterattack at 1630 on 21 December along the western bank of Lake Sosto, which was supported by 40 bombers. This counterattack, as before, was successfully repulsed by units of the 252nd Rifle Division.

Due to the fact that during 20-21 December an obvious success was evident in the 4th Guards Army's sector, the 7th Guards Mechanized Corps was committed on orders from the *front* commander.

Thus the 7th Guards Mechanized Corps, just as the 2nd Guards Mechanized Corps, was committed when then the breakthrough of the entire tactical depth of the enemy's defense had not yet been completed, while the very powerful resistance center of Szekesfehervar still had to be taken.

At 1330 the corps began to move up to the jumping-off area of Dinnyes—Borgond station—Seregelyes, with the task of attacking in the direction of Kisfalud and Csala and reaching the line height 183—height 165 (north of Szekesfehervar), while part of its forces would launch an attack on Szekesfehervar from the northeast.

The enemy's powerful fire resistance and the limited opportunities for maneuver in the bottleneck between Lake Velence and the city of Szekesfehervar, as well as the insufficiently decisive actions of the corps, led to a situation in which it failed to carry out its task and units of the corps were fighting among the infantry.

It was only after cooperation had been more precisely organized with the rifle formations, artillery and aviation that the corps' units managed to advance and capture Csala, height 159 and the northeastern part of Szekesfehervar's suburbs.

Thus by the close of December the 4th Guards Army's forces, having broken through the enemy's main defensive zone enveloped in a half ring from the east, southeast and south the enemy's very important center of resistance, Szekesfehervar.

By the close of 22 December the *front* commander ordered the 46th Army to capture the following: a) the 2nd Guards Mechanized Corps the area Etyek—Herceghalom station—Bicske; b) the infantry the line Elvira—Pusztazamor—Alcsut—Lovasbereny.

During the night reinforced detachments were to capture Val and Vereb and to free the road from Nadap to Lovasbereny. At the same time, the *front* commander demanded more decisive actions than on 21 December.

This related in particularly to the commanders of the mobile formations. For example, the *front* commander instructed the commander of the 7th Guards Mechanized Corps to "immediately change your command post and be there, from where you can see the fighting and control it." The command post of the commander of the 7th Guards Mechanized Corps was located in Seregelyes, 15 kilometers from the corps' forward units.

The enemy opposite the 46th Army, with units of the Hungarian 20th Infantry Division, German 271st Infantry Division, Hungarian 1st and 8th panzer divisions, and an SS police regiment, along with recently committed units of the Hungarian 29th Infantry Division, the German 6th Infantry Division and the 68th Machine Gun Battalion, was engaged in stubborn defensive fighting, while attempting through fire and counterattacks to delay the army's further advance to the north.

Due to the fact that throughout 21 December the greatest success had been achieved in the 46th Army's sector, where the entire tactical depth of the enemy's defense had been broken through, while at the same time the enemy continued to hold the powerful center of resistance of Szekesfehervar, the 18th Guards Tank Corps, on orders from the *front* commander, was to be committed into the breach in the 46th Army's sector, behind the 2nd Guards Mechanized Corps on December 22, according to the second of the variations foreseen by the plan.

For this purpose, at 1600 on 21 December the 18th Guards Tank Corps left its intermediate area and by 0500 on 22 December had occupied the jump-off line height 151—Pozmand—Janos.

At 1000 on 22 December the corps was committed into the breach in the general direction of Pazmand, Vereb, Bicske, Many, and Esztergom.

Due to the commitment of the 18th Guards Tank Corps in the 46th Army's sector, the 2nd Guards Mechanized Corps was turned from the Vereb area to the east, in the direction of Val. Subsequently, while carrying out is previous task, the corps was to reach the area Etyek—Zsambek.

At 0900 on 22 December units of the 2nd Guards Mechanized Corps, having bypassed the 10th Guards and 37th rifle corps' infantry, attacked toward Val. A tank regiment from the 4th Guards Mechanized Brigade managed to break into Val from the march, followed by the mechanized brigades. The 2nd Guards Mechanized Corps, while developing the offensive, was fighting by 2000 along the line the eastern outskirts of Gyuro—height 211—Farkasnya.

The 18th Guards Tank Corps, having passed through the 10th Guards Rifle Corps' infantry formations with part of its forces, was immediately forced to wage difficult tank battles with the enemy.

The German-Fascist command, as was mentioned above, was determined to launch on 21 December a powerful counterblow against the forces of the Third Ukrainian Front operating along the right bank of the Danube. For this purpose, tank regiments from the 3rd and 6th panzer divisions, which had been transferred from the central sector of the Soviet-German front, were additionally concentrated in the Szekesfehervar area. Our forces' offensive, which began on 20 December, foiled the enemy's planned counterblow, while the 46th Army's successful offensive forced the enemy to employ his tank regiments in order to eliminate the breakthrough.

On the morning of 22 December the enemy undertook a counterblow from the Lovasbereny area and to the south, throwing in his tank regiments into the fighting in order to eliminate the breakthrough.

On the morning of 22 December the enemy undertook a counterblow from the Lovasbereny area and to the south, throwing tank regiments from the 3rd, 6th and 23rd panzer divisions. Up to 300 enemy tanks and self-propelled gun took part in the fighting of 22 December, along with infantry. The enemy air force became significantly more active.

Having captured Velence, more than 60 enemy tanks and self-propelled guns broke through toward Kapolnasnyek. Up to 20 tanks from the Velence area repeatedly counterattacked to the northeast, trying to cut the Kapolnasnyek—Pazmand paved road to get into the rear of our attacking units. Up to 40 tanks were operating from the Vereb area to the east and southeast. 30 tanks and self-propelled guns counterattacked the 10th Guards Rifle Corps' units from the Belse area. Simultaneously, the enemy undertook several powerful counterattacks against units of the 37th Rifle Corps.

The 18th Guards Tank Corps, along with the 10th Guards Rifle Corps' recently arrived infantry, was successfully repelling the enemy's counterattacks. The Kapolnasnyek—Pazmand highway was cleared of the enemy by an attack by the 181st Tank Brigade from the Pazmand area to the south. By 1700 the 18th Guards Tank Corps threw the enemy out of Vereb and Belse. A regiment from the 180th Rifle Division's second echelon cut the road from Nadap to Velence with an attack to the south from the area of height 268 and forced the enemy to fall back on Velence.

The 37th and 10th Guards rifle corps' artillery, which was rapidly maneuvering and boldly blocking the road against the enemy tanks and inflicting heavy losses on them, played a big role in repulsing the enemy's tank counterattacks.

The 18th Guards Tank Corps attacked the southeastern outskirts of Vereb from an area one kilometer north of Pazmand, following a preliminary short fire onslaught from the tanks and anti-tank artillery weapons.

Due to the fact that the terrain conditions limited the conditions for maneuver from the flanks, the attack had to be carried out along a comparatively narrow front in the zone of the roads.

The enemy, in turn, taking advantage of the favorable terrain conditions, with his tanks, of which a large number were heavy, operating from ambushes, and artillery from previously prepared positions, put up extremely powerful fire resistance, as a result of which, despite the vigorous pace of the attack, the 110th Tank Brigade lost in this engagement 16 tanks and had no success in the first attack. The tanks were once again pulled back to their jumping-off positions.

After this, having brought up the corps artillery from the 31st Guards Rifle Corps and the 18th Guards Tank Corps and carrying out a powerful bombardment of Vereb, two of the tank corps' brigades attacked Vereb a second time and captured it at 1700.

The 181st Tank Brigade, operating in the corps' second echelon, fought off enemy tank counterattacks throughout 22 December along the line western outskirts of Kapolnasnyek—height 120, which were directed at Nadap and Velence. Having beaten off the enemy's tank counterattacks with the assistance of the 31st Guards Rifle Corps' artillery, by the close of the day the brigade reached the northwestern outskirts of Pazmand, in readiness to develop the first echelon's success from the morning of 23 December.

By the close of 22 December the situation along the 46th Army's left flank had been restored. The army's main forces did not halt their attack during the repulse of the enemy's counterblow and continued to advance in stubborn fighting, and advanced 4-8 kilometers during 22 December and by the close of the day were fighting along the line Elvira—south of Erd—southern outskirts of Tordas—southwest of Ufalu—northeast and northwest of Val—height 230—Lovasbereny station—height 281, having linked up along its left flank with units of the 4th Guards Army's 4th Guards Rifle Division, which was attacking north of Lake Velence. As a result of this linkup, individual enemy groups in the Nadap area and the Lovasbereny woods were cut off from their units and were destroyed during the night of 27-28 December by units of the 180th Rifle Division.

The 86th Guards Rifle Division, comprising the army commander's reserve, was located in the Pettend area, while one of its regiments was fighting in the woods southeast of Lovasbereny.

While repelling the enemy's numerous counterattacks from a company to a battalion in strength, supported by tanks and self-propelled guns and aviation, by the close of 22 December the army's forces reached the following line: its right flank linked up with the 46th Army's forces in the areas of Sukoro and the northwestern outskirts of Lovasbereny. The remaining forces had reached the line Patka—Mariamajor—due south along the eastern outskirts of Szekesfehervar—southern and southwestern outskirts of Szekesfehervar—excluding Imre—Sarszentmihaly—Urhida—eastern outskirts of Polgardi.

The 7th Guards Mechanized Corps, while continuing the offensive, was to bypass Szekesfehervar from the north. However, the corps failed to carry out this assignment and operated in the 31st and 20th guards rifle corps' combat formations along the line west and northwest of Csala—eastern outskirts of Szekesfehervar.

The city of Szekesfehervar had been outflanked by the 4th Guards Army's forces from three sides and the army commander assigned the mission of encircling and taking the city by storm during 23 December.

Thus during the course of three days the *front's* forces carried out a breakthrough of the enemy's prepared defense along the so-called "Margarita Line" along a 75-kilometer front to a depth of up to 15-20 kilometers, thus completing the breakthrough of the entire tactical depth of the enemy's defense. The resistance of the German-Fascist troops had basically been crushed. On 23 December they were still trying to put up fierce resistance along a number of sectors along the front, particularly in the city of Szekesfehervar. However, his reserves had been spent and there were no prepared lines in the operational depth, so that the enemy was forced to fall back under the blows of our troops to the north and northwest.

On 23 December the *front* commander assigned the following missions to the *front's* forces: the 46th Army was to continue its further offensive no later than 23 December and by the close of the day capture the following: a) the 2nd Guards Mechanized Corps the area Bicske—Herceghalom station—Bicske; b) the infantry the line Erd—Seregbalit—Bija—Herceghalom station—Alcsut—Vertesacsa.

The 4th Guards Army was to continue the offensive, with the chief task of launching an attack with the forces of the 20th Guards and 135th rifle corps and the 7th Guards Mechanized Corps in the general direction of Sarkeresztes and to encircle and destroy the enemy group of forces in the Szekesfehervar area and to reach the line Zamoly—Csor.

The army was to launch a decisive offensive no later than 0900 on 23 December with the forces of the 31st Guards Rifle Corps, behind the 18th Guards Tank Corps, which had reached the Vertesacsa area, and with units of the 46th Army reach the line Vertesboglar—Csakvar—Forna.

Simultaneously with this, the *front* commander ordered his forces not to get bogged down in extended fighting for inhabited locales (the 18th Guards Tank Corps' attack on Vereb), to bypass them, while leaving behind an organized part of their forces for destroying the enemy garrisons in them.

In order to more successfully combat the enemy's tanks, the *front* commander ordered an increase in the number of guns firing over open sights, particularly at the expense of the heavy calibers, such as 122mm and 152mm guns (directive no. 00979 of 22 December from the Third Ukrainian Front's headquarters).

The *front's* forces, while carrying out the tasks assigned by the *front* commander, continued to develop the offensive on 23 December.

The enemy was trying with all his might to hold the line Etyek—Gebeljuras—Tabajd, launching numerous counterattacks up to a battalion in strength, each supported by 8-11 tanks. He was organizing a defense In the area of the vineyards east of Gebeljuras—Zatvany, with 20-25 tanks and up to three battalions of artillery. His air force was operating against our forces in groups of 5-12 planes and carried out a total of up to 160 sorties.

The 2nd Guards Mechanized Corps beat off a number of enemy counterattacks from the area of height 277, tied down the enemy in the area of the height with small forces, while it launched an attack with its main forces west of height 277 in the direction of Bot and outflanked Etyek from the west. By 1400 on 23 December Bot had been seized by the corps' units. The enemy continued to put up stubborn resistance in the Gebeljuras area. The corps commander, having left a screen against Gebeljuras, pulled the corps' main forces back to the area of height 214, crossed them over the Laszlo Canal and began to move them on Bot, behind the 6th Guards Mechanized Brigade.

At 1615 on 23 December the corps' units captured Herceghalom station, cutting the railroad from Budapest to Bicske. The enemy was forced to hurriedly fall back from the line Etyek—Gebeljuras, abandoning a significant amount of heavy and anti-aircraft artillery.

Thus the 2nd Guards Mechanized Corps carried out its task of reaching the area Etyek—Zsambek, for further operations against Budapest from the west.

The corps commander received the thanks of the *front* and army commanders for his bold and skillfully executed maneuver.

The 18th Guards Tank Corps, while developing the offensive in the operational depth of the enemy's defense, by the morning of 23 December captured Vertesacsa, forced the canal in the Alcsut area and by 1700 had captured Alcsut.

The enemy, while striving to secure the communications of his Budapest group of forces, carried out several tank counterattacks from the areas of Felcsut and Vertesboglar and from the direction of Csakvar. All the counterattacks were repulsed with heavy losses for the enemy. By the close of the day the 18th Guards Tank Corps reached the line 500 meters southeast of Felcsut—west of Vertesboglar station—Vitezitelep.

The 46th Army's rifle formations, while taking advantage of the mobile formations' success, also successfully advanced 6-12 kilometers and by the close of the day were fighting along the following line: the 23rd Rifle Corps, Benty—Tarnok—excluding Soskut; the 37th Rifle Corps, Pusztazamor—southeastern outskirts of Eden—Etyek—Bot—south of Gebeljuras, and; the 10th Guards Rifle Corps, southwest of Gebeljuras—southeastern outskirts of Tabajd—the northern edge of the woods east of Vertesboglar station.

The 18th Rifle Division was in the 10th Guards Rifle Corps' second echelon in the Vertesacsa area.

The 86th Guards Rifle Division was in the army commander's reserve in the Pettend—Baracska area.

The 4th Guards Army's forces continued to develop the offensive. On the morning of 23 December the army's forces broke into the city of Szekesfehervar: the 80th Guards Rifle Division from the northeast, the 7th Guards Airborne Division from the south and, simultaneously, the 84th Guards Rifle Division from the west. The enemy put up particularly stubborn resistance in the city of Szekesfehervar and along the line of the Szekesfehervar—Imre paved road. In all, the enemy launched up to 23 counterattacks in strength up to a battalion, supported by up to 100 tanks and self-propelled guns. At 1100 on 23 December the army's forces captured the city of Szekesfehervar and advanced up to 15 kilometers and were fighting along the line west of Vertesboglar station—Vitezitelep—Forna—height 136—Baklas—Gyulamajor—excluding Sarkeresztes—Imre—Feherzkhvalcsa—Urhida—Polgardi.

The 7th Guards Airborne Division was moving to the Zamoly area. The 80th Guards Rifle Division was in the army commander's reserve and was consolidating the line Csala—northwestern outskirts of Szekesfehervar.

The 7th Guards Mechanized Corps captured Borbalamajor and Gyulamajor and was fighting for Sarkeresztes. Its 16th Mechanized Brigade was in the corps' second echelon. From 1830 on

23 December the 5th Guards Cavalry Corps was on the march toward its jumping-off area of Lovasbereny and the woods to the southeast.

On 24 December the enemy's IX SS Corps received orders that in the event of Budapest's encirclement, that it should defend until the arrival of reinforcements, which, according to the Hitlerite command's assumption, were supposed to restore the situation and relieve the encircled troops. At the same time, it was pointed out that the 4th SS Panzer Division, under the command of General Gille, and which consisted of the *Totenkopf* and *Wiking* panzer divisions, was already approaching Budapest.

Due to this, the commander of the IX SS Corps shifted the 3rd Panzer Division and a reconnaissance detachment from the 8th Cavalry Division to the Budapest area and south of the city to cover the approaches to Budapest from the south. The 8th Cavalry Division was removed from the eastern bridgehead fortifications and thrown into the fighting north of Budafok and east of Budaors and along the heights northeast of Obuda.

The 22nd Cavalry Division was defending along the eastern bridgehead fortifications along the line Dunaharaszti—the Budapest—Nagykata road, and the 13th Panzer Division west of Ala.

Reconnaissance and observation on 23 December noted the intensive evacuation of rear establishments and industrial enterprises from the city of Budapest and the movement of a number of major headquarters to the west and northwest.

For this reason, the *front* commander ordered the following: on the morning of 24 December the 46th Army was to continue vigorously attacking to the northeast and east and to deny the enemy the opportunity to occupy a defense along the internal ring of Budapest, west of the Danube River, and to cut off his path of retreat to the west and northwest.

Simultaneously, the *front* commander ordered the commander of the 18th Guards Tank Corps to continue vigorously developing the offensive from the morning of 24 December, with the task, in cooperation with the 10th and 31st guards rifle corps, of defeating the enemy group of forces in the Bicske area and by the close of 24 December to take the area Tinnye station—Dag—Szomor—Perbal, and with part of its forces capture the road junction near Tag, cutting off the enemy's escape route from Budapest to the northwest.

On the morning of 24 December units of the 18th Guards Tank Corps began their attack on Bicske, an important enemy strong point, lying along the main communications from Budapest to the west. The corps, having seized Ujbarok and Obarok with part of its forces following a short fight, the corps attacked Bicske with a flanking maneuver from the northwest and by 1500 had completely captured this locale. Without delaying in this area, the corps' units continued to vigorously advance to the north and by 1830 captured Perbal, Many and Tinnye station, cutting the last artery leading out of Budapest to the northwest. Having securely cut the roads, the corps' units destroyed the enemy troops and rear establishments retreating from Budapest.

While carrying out its task, the 2nd Guards Mechanized Corps occupied the following jumping-off position by the morning of 24 December: the 4th Guards Mechanized Brigade in the area of height 185, with the immediate task of capturing the southern part of Budapest, followed by Zugliget; the 6th Guards Mechanized Brigade in the Juresitarienya area, with the immediate task of capturing the northern part of Budakeszi, followed by Pitomeze, and; the 37th Guards Tank Brigade, in the second echelon north of David, had the task of developing the mechanized brigades' success.

Following a 15-minute artillery preparation, the corps' units resumed the offensive at 0800 on 24 December. In the Paty area the enemy attempted to offer resistance with a force of up to two battalions of infantry and 15 tanks and self-propelled guns, but was thrown out of Paty.

While developing the offensive, the corps' units were fighting by the close of the day in the suburbs of Budapest, Pitomeze and Zigliget.

The 37th Guards Tank Brigade was shifted from the Budakeszi area to the south through height 218 and, following a short fight, threw back the enemy's infantry and tanks, which were trying to break through from the Torokbalint area to the north. Part of the 37th Tank Brigade's forces were dispatched to the Budaors area to destroy the enemy groups active there and to assist the advance of the 46th Army's right flank.

The 46th Army's rifle formations behind the mobile formations and, encountering resistance only from scattered enemy units, had already reached the Bicske area in the first half of the day.

The following elements and units were noted facing the army: Hungarian 20th Infantry Division, German 271st Infantry Division, the German 8th, 6th and 23rd panzer divisions, the 1st Panzer Division's 130th Panzer Regiment, and the *Feldherrnhalle* Motorized Division, which had been recommitted into the fighting. The enemy attempted to halt the army's advance with this division's counterattacks, but the division's resistance was quickly crushed. The enemy was thrown from the line of the Torokbalint—Bicske railroad.

The army's main forces turned from the Bicske area to the east and northeast. Having prevented the enemy from consolidating along the outer ring of Budapest and rolling up his defense opposite its right flank, the army's forces reached the following line by the close of 24 December: the northern outskirts of Erd—height 219—western outskirts of Torokbalint—east of height 344—height 353—east and north of Paty—Zsambek—northwestern outskirts of Bicske.

The 180th Rifle Division was on the march in the Bicske area; the 80th Guards Rifle Division was in the Ufalu—Gyuro area.

The *front* commander, taking account of the developing situation along the 46th Army's front, ordered the following: the 46th Army, along with the 2nd Guards Mechanized Corps and the 12th Assault Engineer-Sapper Brigade, while taking advantage of the 2nd Guards Mechanized Corps' success and the absence of organized enemy resistance, splitting the city by no later than 26 December, was to defeat the enemy in detail, capture the western part of Budapest and the crossings and reach the Danube River. The 18th Guards Tank Corps was to reach the following area by the close of 25 December: Tat—Bajna—Dag—Talaje station—Dorog, and with part of its forces capture the tunnel and pass two kilometers west of Pilisvorosvar, so as to prevent the enemy from retreating to the west and northwest, and to seize Esztergom and the crossing over the Danube River.

Combat operations were not to halt at night and the infantry's movement would be sped up in order to link up with the 2nd Guards Mechanized Corps in the city of Budapest.

During the course of 25 December the 10th Guards Rifle Corps was to capture Pilisvorosvar and prevent the enemy's retreat to the northwest.

The boundary line on the left was extended from 2400 on 24 December as far as Pilisvorosvar (inclusive for the 46th Army). Simultaneously, the *front* commander demanded that the 46th Army commander take all measures to bring up his heavy artillery of 152mm and 122mm guns to the infantry's combat formations for firing over open sights, and to also bring up all the sappers for street fighting.

In order to cut down on personnel losses during the street fighting, the density of the combat formations was to be reduced by removing a rifle division apiece in each rifle corps and a rifle regiment apiece in each rifle division into second echelons. At the same time, the *front* commander instructed that the rifle corps' second echelons were not to be moved east of the line Budaors—Pitomeze without necessity; the 180th Rifle Division was to have two regiments in the Bicske area and one in Zsambek.

The commander's order had great significance for the forthcoming storming of the city of Budapest. Not only were the tasks tightened up, but specific measures were taken for splitting up the encircled group of forces in the city of Budapest and, in particular, for organizing street fighting.

The *front* commander demanded that the commander of the 4th Guards Army, in conjunction with the 5th Guards Cavalry Corps, continue decisive operations from 0930 on 25 December along the previous axes:

a) the 31st Guards Rifle Corps was to commit the 80th Guards Rifle Division along the boundary between the 4th and 34th Guards rifle divisions toward Tarjan and by the close of 25 December reach the line Tinnye—Szomor—Gyermely—height 269—Szar station;
b) the forces of the 20th Guards Rifle Corps were to capture Csakvar and Zamoly, with the latter to be captured in cooperation with the 5th Guards Cavalry Corps, which by the close of 24 December was located in the following areas: 12th Guards Cavalry Division in Bodmer, the 11th Guards Cavalry Division in Alcsut, and the 63rd Cavalry Division behind the 11th Guards Cavalry Division.
c) the 21st Guards Rifle Corps was to free up the 69th Guards Rifle Division and by the morning of 26 December was to move it into the Szekesfehervar area.

At the same time, the *front* commander pointed out that throughout the entire night of 24-25 December our aviation would launch bombing strikes against the Csakvar area.

During the day of 25 December the *front's* forces, while carrying out their assigned tasks, completed the encirclement of the enemy's Budapest group of forces.

The 18th Guards Tank Corps, while holding the road junction with part of its forces along the enemy's path of retreat from Budapest, captured Pilisvorosvar and the mountain passes and tunnel by 0900. By the close of the day the corps captured Tat, thus cutting the last communications link from Budapest along the Danube River. This essentially completed the operational encirclement of the enemy's Budapest group of forces.

The 46th Army's rifle formations arrived at the second ring around Budapest, which ran along the outskirts of the city, thus completing the formation of the internal encirclement front.

The army's forces, having broken through the second ring, captured Budateteny, Budafok, Budakeszi, Nagykovacsi and Pilisvorosvar and advanced 8-12 kilometers, having gotten into fierce street fighting in the western part of Budapest.

In the Pilisvorosvar area prisoners were taken belonging to the 8th SS Infantry Division and the 22nd SS Cavalry Division, which earlier had been defending in the eastern part of Budapest.

Having repulsed several enemy counterattacks from the Budaors area, in strength up to a battalion, with 3-5 tanks and self-propelled guns, and along other axes, by the close of the day the army's forces were fighting along the following line: northern outskirts of Budateteny—southwestern outskirts of Budaors—western outskirts of Zugliget—Pitomeze—Solymar—Pilisvorosvar.

In order to close the exit to the north to the enemy, the *front* commander ordered the commander of the 46th Army to remove the 180th Rifle Division from the defense of the inhabited locales of Bicske and Zsambek, and by forced march move it to the left of the boundary line with the 10th Guards Rifle Corps to Pilisvorosvar, from where the division would develop the attack toward Pomaz.

The 86th Rifle Division, along with an anti-tank artillery regiment, was to be moved from the reserve to replace the 180th Rifle Division, with the task of preparing Bicske and Zsambek for defense from the north, northwest and west.

The 4th Guards Army's forces achieved the greatest results along the right flank (taking advantage of the success of the 46th Army's and *front's* mobile formations), where they advanced up to 20 kilometers. The 5th Guards Cavalry Corps, which had been committed into the breach on 25 December in the 20th Guards Rifle Corps' sector from the line Szar—Marics, was advancing in stubborn fighting to the northwest, repulsing the enemy's numerous counterattacks, supporting by air attacks.

The army's forces had the following task: the 31st Guards Rifle Corps was to attack behind the 18th Guards Tank Corps with one division and reach the front Esztergom camp—Kesztolc—Csev on 26 December, with its front facing east, while the remaining two divisions, taking advantage of the 5th Guards Cavalry Corps' advance, was to reach the area Bajna—Hereg—Tarjan—Felsogala.

The 20th Guards Rifle and 5th Guards Cavalry corps were to capture Csakvar and Zamoly and by the close of the day reach the line Csakbereny—Ujgut.

The 21st Guards Rifle Corps, supported by the 252nd Rifle Division from the north, was to crush the enemy's resistance with a decisive attack on the morning of 26 December and reach the line Osi—Kungos—Csajag. The 5th Guards Cavalry Corps was assigned the task of capturing Csakvar, after which it was to operate toward Gant and Csakbereny, to roll up the enemy's front from the rear and, in conjunction with the 20th Guards Rifle Corps, capture Csakbereny and Granasy. It was to subsequently reach the Banhida area, cut the paved road northwest of Tolna and capture the Kornye—Oroszlany area.

A new boundary line was established on the right as far as Bicske, and then Tinnye—Csev, exclusively for the 4th Guards Army.

This order correctly dispatched the 4th Guards Army's forces to carry out their assignment.

In accordance with the *front* commander's decision, part of the 1st Guards Fortified Area's forces took over during the night of 24-25 December the 62nd Guards Rifle Division's defensive zone along the line one kilometer south of Fule—Balatonfokajar—south of Balatonakarttya—marker 167, in order to free up the 4th Guards Army's forces for employment along the main axis. For this purpose, the 68th Rifle Corps was to be shifted to the Lovasbereny area, with the task of organizing the defense of the area with its forward edge along the line of height 269—height 153—Forna and to prevent the enemy's breakthrough from the west and northwest to the east.

The corps was to be moved by a combined march (by railroad and auto transport as far as Lovasbereny, and then by auto transport and by foot to Vertesacsa). Three hundred motor vehicles were detached from the *front's* stocks.

The Danube Military Flotilla, while securing the 46th Army's flank with fire and a landing by the 83rd Naval Infantry Brigade, captured Nagyteteny.

On 26 December the *front's* forces, while carrying out the tasks assigned by the *front* commander, completed the encirclement of the enemy's Budapest group of forces and formed dense internal and external encirclement fronts.

The linkup between the Third and Second Ukrainian fronts occurred with the arrival of the 46th Army's units (10th Guards Rifle Corps) at the Danube River in the Budakalasz area. Nine enemy divisions, with an overall strength of up to 100,000 men, were thus encircled in the Budapest area. Simultaneously, enemy units located in the woods northwest of Budapest were isolated from the city and encircled. Units of the 13th Panzer Division, the *Feldherrnhalle* Motorized Division, the Hungarian 1st Panzer Division and the rear establishments of the Hungarian 10th and 8th infantry divisions, numbering more than 6,000 soldiers and officers were encircled and individual detachments of these forces made attempts to break out to the west, but were destroyed by our forces. On orders of the commander of the 46th Army, detachments allotted by the rifle divisions set out to eliminate the encircled group of forces from the morning of 26 December and, operating in the difficult conditions of mountainous and wooded terrain, were successfully carrying out their assigned task.

The 46th Army's forces, taking advantage of the 18th Guards Tank Corps' success, advanced 10-15 kilometers by the close of the day and were fighting along the line south of Budaors and had captured a number of blocks along the western outskirts of Buda, as well as Pilisborosjeno, Csobanka, Pomaz, and Szentendre. Two of the 180th Rifle Division's regiments were in the Pilisvorosvar—Nagykovacsi area, while one regiment occupied Piliscsaba. The 86th Guards Rifle Division was covering the army's left flank along the line Zsambek—Bicske.

The 2nd Guards Mechanized Corps was fighting along the western outskirts of Buda.

The 4th Guards Army's right flank advanced up to 16 kilometers, as before encountering the most powerful enemy resistance along its left flank. The enemy along the front Csakvar—Balatonfokajar was putting out intense machine gun and artillery-mortar fire, counterattacking along individual sectors in strength of up to an infantry company, each supported by 3-6 tanks and self-propelled guns. In all, up to 150 tanks and self-propelled guns were noted along the army's front, of which 11 were heavy "Tiger" tanks, and 50 armored transports.

By the close of the day the army's forces reached the front Csev—Kesztolc—Esztergom camp—Nagysap—Domonkas—west of Tarjan—Tatabanya—Ielsogala—height 426—two kilometers northwest of Csakvar—east of Gant, and then along their previous lines.

The 93rd Rifle Division, the army's reserve, was in its previous position.

The 5th Guards Cavalry Corps captured Banhida, Csen and Kehacsjas and was fighting for Kornye, two kilometers west of Oroszlany and north of Csakbereny.

The 18th Guards Tank Corps captured Esztergom and Nyergesujfalu.

The *front* commander, in order to strengthen the external encirclement front, ordered the commander of the 18th Guards Tank Corps to leave one tank brigade behind to defend Esztergom and with its main forces attack from the morning of 27 December along the Danube River to the west and by the close of the day reach the line Dunaalmas—Tavaros—Tata—Vertemszteles.

The commander of the 5th Guards Cavalry Corps was ordered, following the capture of Csakbereny, to launch a surprise attack with part of its forces, in conjunction with the 4th Guards Army's 20th Guards Rifle Corps, no later than the morning of 28 December from the northeast and capture the town of Mor. The corps' remaining forces were to continue to energetically carry out their assigned task and reach the line Vertemszteles—Banhida—Kornye—Pusztavam.

Simultaneously, the *front* commander issued instructions to the commander of the 46th Army to cover with sufficient artillery density all of the roads leading from Budapest to the west and northwest. A sufficient reserve of anti-tank mines should be maintained along these axes.

Besides this, he ordered part of the 31st Guards Rifle Corps' forces to move up behind the 18th Guards Tank Corps to the Dunaalmas front.

The army was to launch a decisive offensive with its main forces and by the close of 28 December complete the cleansing of the western part of the Budapest and reach the Danube River. Foreseeing the difficulties of fighting in a city, the *front* commander reinforced the 46th Army with the 11th Independent Assault Engineer-Sapper Brigade, which was to arrive from the 57th Army to the Erd area by the morning of 28 December.

The army was ordered to leave individual garrisons in Esztergom, Dorog and Tat and to secure the Esztergom—Pilisszentkeraszt—Budapest road with the remaining forces of the 86th Guards and 180th rifle divisions, upon clearing the enemy out of the woods as far as the line Pilisszentkeraszt—Damos.

In order to avoid excessive losses on our side and to speed up the enemy's capitulation, the *Stavka* of the VGK ordered the employment of artillery of all calibers, including the largest ones, as well as aviation and sapper demolition commands, to destroy the enemy holed up in large buildings in Budapest as well as in the city's fortress along the western bank of the Danube.

Artillery of all calibers, including the largest, was to be employed for destroying the enemy's defense nests with guns firing over open sights for urban fighting and accompanying the infantry.

The 68th Rifle Corps was regrouping its forces in the Lovasbereny area and, on orders of the *front* commander, was to be subordinated to the 4th Guards Army from 1800 on 27 December, with the task of organizing a defense along the line Szar station—Csalaskut—Szentamas—excluding Vertesboglar—Kehacsjas—Gant—Vaskap, and then to operate toward Kornye and Oroszlany, while part of its forces were to attack along the front Bokod—Mor.

The timely adopted decision to regroup the 68th Rifle Corps and to move it to the axis of the *front's* main attack, as we shall see below, had enormous significance for the subsequent repulse of three counterblows by the German-Fascist troops in January by the forces of the Third Ukrainian Front.

The commander of the 4th Guards Army was assigned the task of continuing the offensive on 28 December and, by taking advantage of the 18th Guards Tank Corps' success along his left flank, to capture the line Almasfuzito—Naszaly—Tata—Kornye—Rigo (south of Banhida). The 34th Guards Rifle Corps' forces were to relieve units of the 5th Guards Cavalry Corps operating in the Banhida area.

In the center, the corps was to occupy the line Mor—Isztimer—Csir.

The 5th Guards Cavalry Corps had the task of attacking with its main forces, in conjunction with the 20th Guards Rifle Corps, to the southwest, clearing the woods east of Mor, and by the close of 28 December reaching the line height 137—Pusztavam—Mor.

The 57th Army, while continuing to wage defensive fighting, was to basically remain in its previous position.

The Bulgarian 1st Army (3rd, 8th, 11th, and 12th infantry divisions) was occupying the line Szabados—Cakovici—the Baksic siding—east of Orolik—Atovci—Vinkovacki—Banovci—Sidski with two divisions and with two others was continuing to concentrate closer to this line.

The Bulgarian 1st Army's attempts to carry out offensive fighting for the purpose of improving its operational position and distracting the enemy's forces from the *front's* main axis and tying down his reserves were not successful.

The *front* commander was forced to direct the attention of the Bulgarian 1st Army's commander to the following shortcomings:

- the enemy's defense and the disposition of his guns and forces had been poorly studied;
- the army's forces were evenly spread along the front, including along the axis of the main attack;
- the artillery offensive had not been planned with precision;
- cooperation between the artillery and the infantry had been poorly organized;
- observation of the battlefield was not carried out systematically and with purposefulness;
- combat tasks were assigned without precision, etc.

For this reason, the *front* commander suggested the following:

- organizing a breakthrough along a narrow front (3-4 kilometers) and develop it into the depth in the direction of the flanks with the forces of the divisions' and armies' second echelons. The infantry's and artillery's main forces should be along the axis of the main attack.

An artillery density of up to 100-120 guns and mortars per kilometer of front should be created at the expense of the second-echelon divisions. The enemy's defense should be studied. Fire should be planned and no less than 20 percent of the artillery in the infantry's combat formations should be for firing over open sights. Specific combat tasks should be assigned and cooperation should be more precisely organized.

On the basis of these instructions, the commander of the Bulgarian 1st Army and his staff prepared for the offensive operation.

The *front's* forces, while continuing the offensive, encountered throughout 28-30 December the enemy's growing resistance.

The 46th Army was engaged in offensive fighting to capture the western part of the city of Budapest and to clear the woods southeast of Esztergom and was encountering insignificant resistance.

The enemy, by taking advantage of the stone structures in the city and widely mining the terrain, was trying to hold up the advance by our forces. In the woods southeast of Esztergom he undertook a number of attempts to break through in the direction of Esztergom and Dorog, while trying to bring out along this sector his encircled troops, numbering up to 5-6,000 soldiers and officers.

In connection with the issuance on 29 December of an ultimatum to the encircled Budapest group of forces, the *front* commander ordered the commander of the 46th Army that in the event the offer was accepted by the enemy, negotiations with parliamentarians on the conditions and order for halting military activities and the capitulation and drawing up an agreement would be entrusted to the commander of the 46th Army.

It was proposed that negotiations be carried out in Budaors

The parliamentarians, following negotiations, would be delivered to the front line, with our side responsible for their safety. Combat operations would not halt and the assigned task of reaching the Danube River would be carried out.

Upon the acceptance by the enemy of the conditions for capitulation, our forces were to cease firing and not conduct offensive operations, but at the same time be in full combat readiness to once again attack and repulse a possible enemy trick by agreeing to the ultimatum for the purpose of breaking out of the encirclement.

In the event the enemy rejected the ultimatum, it was ordered that a 15-minute fire onslaught be prepared and carried out at 1230 on 29 December, bringing in all calibers of artillery, rocket-propelled mortars and the *front's* aviation, after which the forces of the 46th Army were to launch an attack to capture the city of Budapest.

The 4th Guards Army's formations, having exhausted their offensive possibilities to a significant extent, were stretched out up to 160 kilometers from the Danube to the southern shore of Lake Balaton and, encountering powerful enemy resistance, advanced little.

The *front* commander described the actions of the 4th Guards Army as insufficiently decisive. Instead of powerful attacks by concentrated forces, the army's forces were carrying out scattered and weak attacks, which were also insufficiently supported by artillery fire and air strikes, which enabled the enemy to easily repulse such attacks.

On 28 December a difficult ice situation arose along the Danube River. A bridge in the Dunapentele area was swept away by floating ice, which threatened the timely concentration of the 1st Guards Mechanized Corps, which was moving up to join the *front*.

For this reason, the *front* commander ordered the commander of the Danube Military Flotilla to remove the 1st Kerch' Brigade of armored cutters from the 46th Army's control at 1500 on 29 December and to concentrate it in Dunapentele and be ready to transport troops across the Danube.

As a result of the arrival of cold weather, many rivers, swamps and lakes began to freeze and thus lose their significance as natural barriers. This brought about additional difficulties for the Third Ukrainian Front's forces operating along their extended front. Because of this, the securing of boundaries and flanks acquired particular importance.

Taking into account the fact that along the majority of sectors opposite the 4th Guards Army the enemy employed tanks and self-propelled guns with a small amount of infantry, the 4th Guards Army's formations began to more widely carry out nighttime activities with reinforced detachments and regiments for the purpose of destroying his tanks and self-propelled guns. At the same time, the allotted subunits and units slated for nighttime fighting were not committed into the fighting during the day, but instead prepared for nighttime operations.

During the last days of December it became known from intelligence data that the German-Fascist command was concentrating fresh forces for the purpose of relieving his encircled Budapest group of forces.

From the experience of the Great Patriotic War, the Soviet command was aware that in all cases of encirclement of major enemy groups of forces by our troops the German-Fascist command undertook all possible measures to relieve the encircled group of forces, launching attacks for this purpose by the encircled group of forces themselves and by a newly-created group of forces from the external encirclement front.

A similar plan of likely enemy actions was considered in the situation that was arising in the Budapest area. However, the *front* command believed that it was unlikely that the enemy could mount a major offensive for the purpose of breaking through to Budapest with the forces available to him opposite the 4th Guards and 46th armies. The enemy needed fresh reserves in order to carry out this plan.

According to prisoner testimony and radio intelligence data, the *front* command learned on 29 December of the German-Fascist command's preparations for attacking from the area southeast of Komarom for the purpose of relieving the encircled group of forces. There was also information regarding the transfer to this area of the 5th SS Panzer Division *Wiking* and the 3rd SS Panzer Division *Totenkopf* from Poland. It was also known that the enemy group of forces encircled in Budapest was preparing a simultaneous attack from the Buda area to the northwest. However, until the very last day the axis of the enemy's main attacks remained unknown.

In evaluating the enemy's group of forces, the terrain and road network, one could assume that the enemy would launch his counterblow from the area west of Szekesfehervar. One could broadly employ major tank and mechanized formations in this area. Besides this, the distance between the external and internal encirclement fronts was the shortest along the Szekesfehervar—Budapest axis.

Aside from this, the enemy group of forces that had been uncovered in this area was the most combat capable and stable and possessed the greatest striking power.

On 30 December the enemy's concentration of crossing equipment and the construction of crossings in the Moca area, 20 kilometers east of Komarom, was established. Simultaneously, previously existing data about the concentration in the Komarom area of a major tank group in the form of the IV SS Panzer Corps, consisting of the *Totenkopf* and *Wiking* panzer divisions, was being confirmed.

The staff and army commander did not have precise data about the concentration of the enemy's shock group and his intentions and therefore the command post and all the reserves were not located along the axis of the enemy's forthcoming main attack, but in the Szekesfehervar area, at a distance of more than 50 kilometers from the breakthrough sector.

Of course, without disposing of precise intelligence data, the army commander could not adopt in a timely manner the necessary measures for concentrating reserves to the army's right flank.

The enemy opposite the 4th Guards Army, in order to distract our attention from the counterblow being prepared from the northwest, undertook a powerful counterattack, following a powerful artillery preparation, along the army's left flank, supported by tanks and up to four battalions of artillery.

The counterattack was beaten off and by the close of the day the 4th Guards Army's forces occupied the following position:

The 31st Guards Rifle Corps (4th, 80th and 34th guards rifle divisions), in conjunction with the 18th Guards Tank Corps, were engaged in intensive fighting in the northern part of the Vertes Hegyseg Mountains and clearing the enemy from the southern bank of the Danube.

Units of four enemy divisions and four battalions were operating opposite the corps' front.

The corps' operations were complicated by the presence of a large number of small and scattered enemy groups, which were falling back from the woods northwest of Budapest in the direction of Komarom.

Besides this, the entire left bank of the Danube west of Esztergom had been occupied by the enemy and the corps' right flank was constantly under the threat of an enemy attack from the north. All of this distracted significant numbers of men and materiel to secure the flank, guarding the rear establishments and headquarters and eliminating small groups of the enemy.

By the close of the day the corps was consolidating the line Neszmely—Adas—Szomod—Banhida—Rigo.

The corps was covering the southern bank of the Danube with individual garrisons (4th Guards Rifle Division) along the line Nyergesujfalu—Kirp—east of Neszmely, as well as the front Bajna—Nagysap—Tat, facing east.

The 68th Rifle Corps (223rd, 52nd and 93rd rifle divisions), in conjunction with the 20th Guards Rifle Corps' right-flank units, had cleared the enemy out of the southern part of the Vertes Hegyseg Mountains and had arrived at their western slopes along the line south of Rigo—east of Kornye—two kilometers north of Oroszlany—Pusztavam. Its 93rd Rifle Division was on the march and had passed through Kapolnapuszta.

The corps' progress had been halted along this line. Numerous attempts by the corps' formations to capture the Kornye—Bokod—Mor area were unsuccessful.

The 20th Guards Rifle Corps (7th and 5th guards airborne divisions and the 40th Guards Rifle Division), as well as the 135th Rifle Corps (84th and 252nd rifle divisions) were engaged in unsuccessful fighting to push the enemy back to the west and northwest from the city of Szekesfehervar and to occupy more favorable positions. The firmest and most combat capable units of the enemy's 23rd and 1st panzer divisions, the 6th Panzer Regiment and the 3rd Panzer Division, the 8th Police Regiment, and 8th and 88th artillery regiments from the high command reserve were defending along this sector. The enemy often launched counterattacks in order to create a constant threat to the city of Szekesfehervar.

By the close of the day the 20th Guards and 135th rifle corps were fighting along the line south of Pusztavam—west of Rudnid—Vajal—the Csokako church—west of Alsopuszta—Margit—Sarkeresztes—Moha—Csor siding—Nadasdladany.

The 21st Guards Rifle Corps (69th and 62nd guards rifle divisions and the 1st Guards Fortified Area) was securing the army's left wing and repelling enemy counterattacks in the direction of Birkas and Osi. A composite detachment (a motorcycle company, an amphibious company and a screening detachment) was covering the southern bank of Lake Balaton. The 21st Guards Rifle Corps was occupying the line northern bank of the Sed Canal—south of Szeged—western outskirts of Osi—east of Denes—one kilometer east of Fodor—the western edge of the Oregardo woods—south of Oregard—south of Balatonakarttya.

The Hungarian 25th Infantry Division and the 44th Training Regiment and 85th Landing Battalion were defending along this sector.

The 41st Guards Rifle Division, having turned over its combat sector to the 252nd Rifle Division, was in the army reserve in the Szekesfehervar area, having taken over the 93rd Rifle Division's sector along the line Csala—northern outskirts of Szekesfehervar—Kallom—Lake Sosto.

The *Front's* Mobile Formations

At 1700 on 31 December the 18th Guards Tank Corps departed for the Bicske—Zsambek area.

The 5th Guards Cavalry Corps continued to concentrate in the area northeast of Mor for carrying out its assigned task.

The Bulgarian 1st Army began crossing its forces near Ilok and Backa Palanka on two tows, four barges and six armored cutters.

The 57th Army was occupying its previous defensive line.

On 31 December the *Stavka* of the VGK issued instructions to the Third Ukrainian Front's forces to continue squeezing the encirclement ring with the 46th Army's forces and, in conjunction with the Second Ukrainian Front's forces, destroy the enemy's Budapest group of forces.

The 4th Guards Army's forces were to go over to the defensive and strongly cover the Budapest axis from the west; it was to simultaneously carry out local operations in the center and along the army's left flank for the purpose of capturing Mor and the northern shore of Lake Balaton.

While the Third Ukrainian Front had broken through the enemy's prepared defensive line along the line Budapest—Lake Balaton, the German-Fascist command was counting on not only delaying along the second the further advance by the Soviet forces surrounding Budapest, but also to launch an offensive from it to the south for the purpose of reaching the Danube, although this further complicated the German forces' situation along the Vienna strategic direction.

While admitting to all the consequences of the developing situation, the German command decided to launch a powerful counterblow from the area southeast of Komarom, the preparations for which had begun as early as 26-27 December. The concentration of enemy forces in the area southeast of Komarom was carried out by adopting all security and masking measures.

Conclusions on Breaking Through the "Margarita Line"

The breakthrough of the "Margarita" defensive line was to be achieved by the creation of high densities of men and materiel along the breakthrough sectors and by the echeloned organization of the *front's* mobile forces.

A rifle division along the main axis was to break through the enemy's front along a 2-2.5-kilometer sector. The artillery density in the 46th Army was to reach 150 tubes per kilometer of breakthrough front and 168 tubes in the 4th Guards Army.

Mobile groups were to be created: the 2nd Guards Mechanized Corps in the 46th Army and the 7th Guards Mechanized Corps in the 4th Guards Army. It was planned to commit them into the breach following the breakthrough of the tactical depth of the enemy's defense.

It was planned to commit the *front's* mobile group (18th Guards Tank Corps and the 5th Guards Cavalry Corps) into the breach in the 4th Guards Army's sector. At the same time, the 5th Guards Cavalry Corps was to be committed into the breach for developing the 18th Guards Tank Corps' success and the 7th Guards Mechanized Corps in the direction of Csakbereny.

The *front's* and the armies' operational organization was in two echelon, with a mobile group.

The rifle corps' and divisions' combat formation was organized in two echelons—2/3 of the forces were allotted to the first echelon and 1/3 to the second.

The depth of the operation was 65-80 kilometers.

The planned pace of the operation was 8-13 kilometers per day while breaking through the tactical depth of the defense and 16-20 kilometers per day while developing the breakthrough.

Thus the *front* commander's decision and the planning for the operation were conducted in complete accordance with the *Stavka's* instructions on massing men and materiel along the decisive axes. Internal and external encirclement fronts were to be created simultaneously (26 December 1944). At the same time, the allocation of men and materiel for splitting up the encircled group of forces and capturing Budapest was called for beforehand, which was the result of the distribution of forces while planning the operation.

The *front's* main forces were allocated to the external encirclement front: the 4th Guards and 57th armies, 18th Guards Tank, 7th Guards Mechanized and 5th Guards Cavalry corps. During the operation the 18th Guards Tank Corps was directed to the internal encirclement front.

A large number of mobile forces were allotted for the formation of the external front. The distance of the external front from the internal one reached more than 50 kilometers to the west of Budapest, which enabled us to split and destroy the enemy's encircled group of forces.

The troops' shift to the defensive at the end of December along the external encirclement front, in accordance with instructions from the *Stavka* of the VGK, had decisive significance for the successful conclusion of the defeat of the encircled group of forces.

Having gone over to a temporary defensive, the *front's* forces were able to consolidate their lines, carry out a regrouping of forces, bring up the rear, and reconstitute their reserves. All of this determined the failure of all of the enemy's attempts, as we shall see below, to render assistance to its encircled group of forces.

In four days of the offensive the *front's* forces occupied 140 inhabited locales, 12 railroad stations and the major strong point and road junction of Szekesfehervar, which covered the approaches to Budapest from the southwest. The breakthrough was widened to 95 kilometers along the front and up to 50 kilometers in depth, while territory up to 1,000 square kilometers was occupied.

As a result of the 20-31 December fighting the German 1st and 23rd panzer divisions, the panzer regiments of the 3rd and 6th panzer divisions, part of the 8th Panzer Division, 8th Police Regiment, 44th Training Regiment, and the 239th Assault Gun Brigade, and the Hungarian 1st Cavalry Division, 25th Infantry Division and 1st Security Regiment, and an entire series of specialized units were defeated and suffered heavy losses.

The enemy suffered the following losses: 24,000 soldiers and officers were killed, 340 tanks and self-propelled guns were destroyed (burned or knocked out), 180 guns, 78 mortars, 430 machine guns, 9,300 rifles and automatic rifles, 89 armored transports, and 87 planes, while 17,200 soldiers and officers were captured, as were 126 tanks and self-propelled guns, 177 guns of various calibers, 47 mortars, 290 machine guns, 770 motor vehicles, and many other kinds of equipment and munitions, food, and other property from depots.

19

The Repulse of the Enemy's Counterblows

The Repulse of the First Counterblow (1-7 January 1945)

According to observation data and prisoner testimony the enemy's forced concentration continued on 1 January in the northwestern part of Budapest, as well as the preparation of a major counterblow from the Komarom area. By this time the enemy had managed to reinforce the III and LVII panzer corps, so that he was able to make his defense denser opposite the 4th Guards Army. The enemy had the following per kilometer of defensive front: 198 riflemen, 18 light machine guns, 7.5 guns and mortars, and 1-2 tanks and assault guns. Such a defensive density made it possible to successfully oppose the offensive by the 4th Guards Army's forces, which had been weakened in the previous fighting.

Thus our troops attacking in the areas north of Mor and south of Osi were met with the enemy's powerful organized fire. The fighting continued several hours, but we were not able to crush the enemy's resistance. A heavy snowfall began during the second part of the day. Visibility sharply worsened and the artillery was not able to carry out aimed fire. The offensive was halted along these sectors.

By the close of 31 December the enemy had completed the concentration of a powerful shock group in the Komarom area, which consisted of the IV SS Panzer Corps, which included the following:

- the SS *Totenkopf* and *Wiking* panzer divisions, which had been transferred from the Warsaw area to the Komarom area at the end of December 1944;
- the 3rd and 6th panzer divisions, which had earlier been operating opposite the Second Ukrainian Front;
- a regiment from the 23rd Panzer Division and units which had earlier been operating in this area (3rd Cavalry Brigade)[1]. Besides this, more than 200 guns from the high command artillery reserve, ranging from 105mm to 150mm, had been concentrated in this area.

The German-Fascist forces continued to be supported by the Fourth Air Fleet, which numbered up to 775 planes by the beginning of January. The enemy's aviation was most active along the external encirclement front, while transport aviation chiefly operated in the Budapest area. Our aviation was chiefly opposed by the enemy's anti-aircraft artillery, which numbered more than 20 batteries of medium and heavy caliber alone.

The German-Fascist group of forces, which was designated for the counterblow, had the task of defeating the 4th Guards Army's right-flank units, breaking through to Budapest and linking up with the forces encircled there. Simultaneously, the troops encircled in Budapest were to break out to the northwest to meet them. In the event of success, the Hitlerite command counted on reconstituting the front along the line Budapest—Lake Velence—Lake Balaton. The main attack

1 The 3rd Cavalry Brigade had been moved up to the breakthrough sector and was committed into the fighting on 7 January.

was to be launched by the *Totenkopf* and *Wiking* SS panzer divisions and the 6th Panzer Division from the front north of Tavaros—Banhida in the direction of Bicske and Buda.

Simultaneously with the concentration of the tank group, the 96th Infantry Division, which had previously been operating against the Fourth Ukrainian Front in the Sutto area, had been concentrated along the northern bank of the Danube in the Karva—Muzla—Buc area, and was to support the main group's offensive by launching a supporting attack along the southern bank toward Esztergom. In order to reinforce the shock group, the transfer of the 711th Infantry Division from the Netherlands was being completed, and by the start of the offensive the division was approaching Komarom and did not take part in the fighting during the initial period.

With the development of the offensive by the enemy's main forces, the III Panzer Corps (1st and 23rd panzer divisions and the 4th Cavalry Brigade), was to begin an attack to the east, capture Szekesfehervar and, in conjunction with the IV SS Panzer Corps, continue the offensive in the direction of Budapest.

The enemy also considered the Third Ukrainian Front's extended front (480 kilometers) from the Danube River to the Sava River, the absence of the latter's reserves and time for organizing a defense, the absence of prepared lines, the fact that the 46th Army was tied down around Budapest, as well as the great gap between the *front* and its supply bases and the presence of the Danube River in the rear, with its weak and temporary crossings that made communications with the rear and maneuver from the depth of operational and strategic reserves difficult.

In all, the enemy's shock group disposed of 3,630 machine guns, 661 mortars, 716 guns, and 528 tanks.

In turn, the 4th Guards Army, which was operating along a 160-kilometer external encirclement front, disposed of 2,827 machine guns, 2,166 guns and mortars, including 280 anti-tank guns, and 104 tanks and self-propelled guns.

The Third Ukrainian Front's operational situation was extremely unfavorable for defense. Along the *front's* right wing, the lagging behind of the Second Ukrainian Front, the forward edge of which ran along the Hron River, led to a situation in which the Third Ukrainian Front's right flank was open from the mouth of the Hron River to Dunaalmas. In the shallow rear (40-50 kilometers from the forward edge) ran the Danube, which made it difficult to carry out maneuver, deliver supplies and evacuate wounded. By 1 January the *front's* forces had just completed 11 days of offensive fighting and had begun regrouping to organize a defense. Our offensive was still continuing in the Mor area and the western part of Budapest, while our units were repulsing powerful enemy counterattacks in the Osi area. The *front* had no available reserves that could be employed for repelling a powerful enemy counterblow. The 46th Army was completely tied down in storming the western part of Budapest, while in the corps' second echelons and in the army reserve there was only a rifle regiment from the 99th Rifle Division and the 40th Rifle Division, which had been pulled back to the line Harsakalja—Marijke, due to the expected enemy attempt to break out of Buda to the northwest. The army's 86th Rifle Division, which was not tied down in the storming of Buda, was completing the elimination of enemy groups with part of its forces in the woods northwest of Budapest, while one regiment was covering the bank of the Danube River along the Esztergom—Tat sector. The 4th Guards Army's reserve consisted only of the 41st Guards Rifle Division in the Szekesfehervar area, due to the enemy's unremitting counterattacks on Osi. Along the army's right flank, a regiment from the 4th Guards Rifle Division was deployed along the front Nyergesujfalu—Sutto, securing the open right flank, while another regiment was along the line Bajna—Nagysap—Mogyorosbanya, with its front facing east and constituting a screen in the event of an attempt by enemy groups to break out from the woods northeast of Budapest. One regiment from the 223rd Rifle Division was in the second echelon in the Majk—Orozslany area. All of the army's remaining forces were in the first echelon, while the 21st Guards Rifle Corps was repulsing enemy counterattacks in the Osi area and three divisions from the 68th and 20th Guards rifle corps continued to attack along the front Mor—Pusztavam.

The mobile formations:

The 5th Guards Cavalry Corps was attacking toward Mor with two cavalry divisions, while another cavalry division was in the corps' second echelon in the Vergesztes—Mindszentpuszta area.

Two of the 7th Mechanized Corps' brigades, together with the 7th Guards Airborne Division, were defending in the Csakbereny area, while another brigade was with the 5th Guards Airborne Division in the Sarkeresztes area, and the 16th Mechanized Brigade was in the corps commander's reserve in the Tallian—Marija area. The 18th Guards Tank Corps (minus the 170th Guards Tank Brigade) had just finished concentrating to the Csabdi—Bicske—Zsambek area. Since 30 December the 2nd Guards Mechanized Corps had been putting itself in order in the Pilisszentkeraszt—Piliscsaba—Pilisvorosvar area. Thus the following could be used as reserves for repulsing a possible enemy counterblow: one rifle division and three rifle regiments in the 46th Army, two rifle regiments in the 4th Guards Army, one cavalry division, the 2nd Guards Mechanized Corps and part of the 18th Guards Tank Corps. Besides this, the 1st Guards Mechanized Corps was concentrating in the Seregelyes—Aba area, to which it had arrived at the *front* by rail on orders from the *Stavka* of the VGK, although by the start of the enemy offensive the corps' concentration had not been completed and some of its units were still en route. The creation of new reserves had also been made more difficult. The formations in the defense, despite their weak strength, occupied a broad front, as a rule (31st Guards Rifle Corps—48 kilometers; 68th Rifle Corps—18 kilometers; 20th Guards Rifle Corps—16 kilometers; 21st Guards Rifle Corps—20 kilometers and about 35 kilometers along the southern shore of Lake Balaton, while individual divisions had the following frontages—14 kilometers for the 80th Guards Rifle Division and 12 kilometers for the 34th Guards Rifle Division, etc.

The following units of the 4th Guards Army were defending immediately along the sector of the forthcoming enemy counterblow: one of the 4th Guards Rifle Division's regiments was covering the southern bank of the Danube along a 15-kilometer front; the 18th Guards Tank Corps' 170th Guards Tank Brigade was in the Dunaalmas area; the 80th Guards Rifle Division was along the 14-kilometer front Dunaalmas—Baj, with all three of its regiments in line; the 34th Guards Rifle Division was along the 12-kilometer front excluding Baj—Rigo, also with three regiments in line. There was only one regiment from the 4th Guards Rifle Division in the depth along this axis, in the area of heights 259 and 321. Despite the measures adopted the defense along this sector at the beginning of the enemy's attack; that is, by the close of 1 January, had not been completely prepared. For example, in the sector of the 80th Guards Rifle Division, which had taken up the defense only from 2000 on 30 December, in view of the rocky soil only 2,016 linear meters of trenches, 880 paired foxholes and 143 machine gun trenches had been dug along a 13-kilometer front, and a single trench outfitted for each gun and mortar. Only five anti-tank minefields had been created, with a total of 513 mines. It is necessary to add that by this time the average density of men and materiel was also not very high. There were 275 riflemen, ten light machine guns, five heavy machine guns, seven anti-tank rifles, and 13 guns and mortars per kilometer of front, of which only nine guns could be used for anti-tank defense. The division commander's reserve consisted of a training battalion. The regimental commanders had no reserves. A large part of the divisions' men and materiel were located near the forward edge of the defense. There were no prepared anti-tank areas and line in the defensive depth.

The following were also shortcomings in the organization of the defense: anti-tank areas had been created without taking into account the waging of effective fire against enemy tanks. The fire of one anti-tank area was not linked to another. The Tavaros—Agostyan paved road was listed as having been mined, although it was not, while the mines lay unburied by the sides of the road.

Uninterrupted reconnaissance and officer observation had not been organized. Nor was cooperation between the artillery and the infantry organized. All of the divisional rears and command posts were located immediately adjacent to the forward edge. The divisions had lost a significant part of their hauled and carried entrenching tools. Commanders at all levels had divorced themselves from directing the engineer outfitting of the defense. Open trenches were not sufficiently configured to the terrain and in many cases did not support the waging of fire at the effective range of infantry weapons.

The 17th Air Army continued to render support to the troops. Our aviation enjoyed a qualitative and quantitative superiority in force and retained air superiority, as before. Our aviation's activities were limited by difficult winter meteorological conditions (low cloud cover, fog). In all, from 1 January through 16 February there were only seven flying days and 18 limited flying days.

Thus as a result of the group of forces created by the enemy, he achieved an enormous superiority of force along his offensive sector: along the Dunaalmas—Banhida sector the correlation of forces by 2 January was 4.5:1 in men, 7.5:1 in machine guns, 5:1 in mortars, 4:1 in guns, and 17:1 in tanks in favor of the enemy. At the same time, the enemy's main forces were operating along the 14-kilometer sector Dunaalmas—east of Tavaros, where his superiority was even greater. This was true even along the enemy's secondary attack sector. Even along his secondary attack sector (along the Danube along the 10-kilometer Nyergesujfalu—Sutto front), the enemy had nearly a 3:1 superiority in men and more than 2:1 in machine guns, artillery and mortars.

On 1 January; that is, a day before the beginning of the enemy counterblow, the capture of prisoners established the completion of the concentration of the SS *Wiking* Panzer Division, the last trains of which had unloaded at Komarom on 31 December. This data enabled us to reach a conclusion about the enemy's intention to begin a counterblow in the immediate future.

Due to this, emergency measures were adopted to strengthen the defense northwest of Budapest: the 12th Anti-Tank Artillery Brigade (55 guns) was removed from the 46th Army and two regiments from the 86th Rifle Division, with the task of organizing a screen along the line one kilometer east of Nyergesujfalu—Bajot and then along the eastern bank of the unnamed stream.

The 5th Guards Cavalry Corps, which was to leave by the morning of 3 January from the first line to the area Kehanjas—Gant—Morics, received orders to be ready to operate with one division in the direction of Tatabanya.

At 0230 on 2 January the enemy, following a 10-minute powerful fire onslaught (up to 40 artillery and 12 mortar batteries took part), the enemy began his attack with the forces of the IV SS Panzer Corps (3rd SS *Totenkopf* Panzer Division, 5th SS *Wiking* Panzer Division, 6th Panzer Division, part of the 3rd and 23rd panzer divisions) from the Tata area to the east. Along the Dunaalmas—Banhida front he committed more than 340 tanks and self-propelled guns into the fighting. Simultaneously, the 96th Infantry Division began to force the Danube in the areas of Nyergesujfalu, Piszke and Sutto. In order to achieve surprise, the attack was begun at night. As a result of his enormous superiority in men and the unready state of our defense, the enemy managed to break through the first line of our defense and push back our units, capture Labatlan and Piszke and link up with the 96th Infantry Division's landing in the Nyergesujfalu area. The fiercest fighting took place near the Agosztiani Gorba mountain and along the right bank of the Danube along the Sutto—Nyergesujfalu line. East of Agostyan the enemy was striving to capture the pass and break into the valley. However, the reserve of the commander of the 31st Guards Rifle Corps (a rifle battalion and the 407th Light Artillery Regiment, which was later reinforced by engineer and artillery units from the army commander's reserve), which had been moved up to the area of the pass, having repulsed the attacks, continued to hold the pass on 2 January.

On the morning of 2 January the enemy committed his main forces into the fighting. On this day the Germans, having concentrated a powerful shock group, consisting of the 13th Panzer, 8th

Cavalry and the *Feldherrnhalle* Motorized Division, along the northwestern outskirts of Budapest in the Obuda area, launched an offensive to the northwest.

However, along this sector the Germans, having only pushed back units of the 180th Rifle Division (46th Army) a little bit and having suffered heavy losses, were halted and did not advance further. His air force appeared and uninterruptedly bombed and strafed our troops' combat formations in groups of 10-15 planes. The enemy air forces carried out 491 sorties in the 31st Guards Rifle Corps' sector on 2 January.

Along the remaining sectors of the 4th Guards Army's front, the enemy carried out unsuccessful attacks with small groups of infantry and tanks.

Summing up the results of the first day of the attack, the enemy managed to achieve only insignificant tactical successes—to break through the 80th Guards Rifle Division's defensive front and advance 4-6 kilometers into the depth of our defense along a 12-15 kilometer front along the right bank of the Danube.

The enemy tank divisions along the axis of the main attack had to operate in conditions of mountains and woods difficult of passage and the natural passage through the mountains near Agosztiani Gorba mountain had been securely shut by the rifle battalion and several artillery batteries.

However, although the enemy was unable to carry out the breakthrough of the entire depth of the defense on the first day, it was clear that the weak forces of the 4th Guards Army's right flank would not be able to halt the further attack by the enemy's large tank forces.

This forced our command to take emergency measures to strengthen the 4th Guards Army's right flank. On the morning of 2 January the army anti-tank artillery reserve from the Szekesfehervar area, consisting of the 438th Anti-Tank Artillery Regiment and an engineer-sapper battalion, was subordinated to the commander of the 31st Guards Rifle Corps. This was followed later by two cannon and one howitzer and one mortar regiments from the 20th Guards Rifle Corps. At the same time, three sapper battalions from the army mobile obstacle detachments (from Szekesfehervar) were subordinated to the commander of the 31st Guards Rifle Corps. The concentration of the rifle troops was difficult because they were tied down in fighting enemy units in the first echelon of the operational formation, while the army commander's reserve—the 41st Guards Rifle Division—was located more than 60 kilometers from the breakthrough sector. Because of this, the army commander removed the 93rd Rifle Division from the 68th Rifle Corps and ordered that it be concentrated by the close of 2 January in the Tarjan area. The division was to carry out a 45-kilometer march, while the corps was ordered to take up a static defense.

The *front* commander, in turn, also adopted a series of measures to reinforce the 4th Guards Army. Five anti-tank artillery regiments were placed at the disposal of the army commander, four of which occupied positions in the Csabdi area and one concentrated in the Felcsut area in the army commander's reserve. The *front*, in order to rapidly create obstacles along the axis of the enemy's counterblow, moved up its own mobile obstacle detachment, consisting of the 44th Mortar Brigade, to the 4th Guards Army's right flank and subordinated it to the commander of the 4th Guards Army.

With the start of the enemy's counterblow, the 4th Guards Army's troop and army mobile obstacle detachments, in conjunction with the fighting troops, hurriedly created obstacles.

The 18th Guards Tank Corps responded to the alarm and by the morning of 3 January was to move to the Dag—Sarisap—Bajna area for the purpose of creating a new defensive front in the depth (15-20 kilometers) along the line Tat—Sarisap—Dag—Bajna. Subordinated to it was the 12th Anti-Tank Artillery Brigade, which was deployed along the line east of Nyergesujfalu—Bajot, as well as two anti-aircraft regiments from the 3rd Anti-Aircraft Artillery Division and the 45th Guards Mortar Regiment. The corps' task was to secure the units' deployment along this line and, given favorable conditions, launch a counterblow and restore the situation along with other formations.

The Agostyan—Tolna and Banhida—Szar axes were to be reinforced with artillery. Most importantly, it was planned to fully employ the 31st Guards Rifle Corps' artillery weapons and the 18th Guards Tank Corps' artillery weapons (58th Guards Mortar Regiment, 200th Mortar Regiment, 42nd Anti-Tank Artillery Regiment, and the 23rd Anti-Aircraft Artillery Division) for the task of preventing an enemy breakthrough through the pass east of Agostyan. It was also planned to employ the 170th Guards Tank Brigade, which was fighting in Dunaalmas with part of its forces to clear the enemy out of the Sutto area, to operate with the infantry against Agostyan. This brigade, upon getting into a fight with major enemy tank and infantry forces, beat off all the attacks. The brigade was subsequently cut off from our forces and fought in encirclement. Simultaneously, due to the threat of an enemy attack from the Banhida area on Szar, the commander of the 5th Guards Cavalry Corps was ordered to immediately concentrate his attached reinforcement artillery (7th Anti-Tank Artillery Brigade, 140th Mortar Regiment and two anti-aircraft regiments from the 3rd Anti-Aircraft Artillery Division) in the Szar—Bodmer—Vertesboglar area, in the reserve, and be ready to operate toward Banhida together with the 18th Guards Tank Corps. The 11th Guards Cavalry Division received orders to move up to the line Nagy—Kemele—Felse—Gala by the morning of 3 January, for the purpose of covering the Szar—Bicske axis.

A guards mortar regiment, an anti-tank artillery brigade and an anti-aircraft artillery division were removed from the 18th Guards Tank Corps and dispatched to the area of the pass at Agosztiani Gorba mountain; an anti-tank artillery regiment was sent to the Tardos area; a self-propelled artillery (122mm) regiment was sent to the Tona area; tank screens, a tank platoon each in strength, were set up in the areas of Tarjan and Bajna. Two rifle regiments from the 46th Army's 86th Rifle Division and the 2nd Engineer-Sapper Brigade were moved to the line of the eastern outskirts of Nyergesujfalu—Mogyorosbanya.

Thus on the first day of the enemy offensive, *front* and army men and material, mostly artillery, were concentrated to the breakthrough sector. However, on the first day of fighting of these men and materiel ten rifle battalions, seven sapper battalions, 36 152mm guns, 19 122mm howitzers, 22 120mm mortars, and 24 76mm cannons were committed into the fighting along the enemy's breakthrough sector. Our forces laid 11,275 mines during the course of the day.

Due to the sharply worsening situation and the necessity of creating new and powerful reserves, it was decided to halt the 46th Army's offensive activities in Budapest as of 3 January and to go over to a static defense and create powerful reserves in each division.

Simultaneously, measures were taken to create new reserves. As has already been shown, in the 4th Guards Army the 93rd Rifle Division was to be pulled from the front line, and then the 40th Guards Rifle Division to the area Kotlo—the vineyard north of Csakvar to the army reserve. The 62nd Guards Rifle Division was to be moved up to the Szekesfehervar area at the expense of widening the 69th Guards Rifle Division's front. A new defensive front, created according to the *front* commander's decision, was to be occupied by both available and by newly created reserves. In order to create more rapidly a defense along a new line, artillery and tank units and formations were to be moved up to this line, without awaiting the arrival of the rifle units there. By the morning of 3 January the 2nd Guards Mechanized Corps was moving into the Dag—Kriva—Uny area. The 49th Guards Rifle Division, with the 45th Howitzer Artillery Brigade and mobile mortars from guards mortar units were moving to the Szomor—Zsambek—Palinkahaz area, with the task of preventing an enemy breakthrough toward Perbal, Zsambek and Bicske. The 46th Army's tank and artillery reserves—the 1st Light Artillery Brigade, a self-propelled artillery regiment, an anti-tank artillery regiment, and two engineer battalions—were deployed by 1600 along the line Szomor—Gyermely—Polinkahaz and were subordinated to the commander of the 49th Guards Rifle Division. Thus as early as the middle of the day on 3 January a new defensive position was being created along the line Sarisap—Kriva—Sandor—Szomor—Gyermely—Palinkahaz. To the north, the defensive positions occupied by the 86th Rifle Division and the 12th Anti-Tank Artillery Brigade, and to the west of Polinkahaz by the 93rd Rifle Division and the 11th Guards Cavalry Division, was a continuation of this line.

During the night of 2-3 January the enemy, while striving to develop the tactical success achieved on 2 January, committed all of the IV SS Panzer Corps' forces into the fighting, launching the main attack along the Neszmely—Dunaszentmiklos—Agostyan sector to the east and southeast in the direction of Dorog and Bicske. The enemy's tank columns (up to 300 tanks and self-propelled guns), with infantry on armored transports, while bypassing the stubbornly resisting units of the 80th Guards Rifle and the 170th Guards Tank Brigade from the north and south, streamed into the breach and, while operating with part of their forces in the direction of Bajna, with their main forces on Bicske, reached in the first half of the day the line Nyergesujfalu—Bajot—Nagydap—Bajna—Tarjan—Vertesszollos.

However, as early as the middle of the day the enemy once again encountered our fierce resistance. Units of the 86th Guards Rifle Division and the 12th Anti-Tank Artillery Brigade, which had been moved up as an anti-tank screen east of Nyergesujfalu, were heroically fighting along the line Kirp—Kelsoszentkerest. Units of the 18th Guards Tank Corps, which were moving to the Sarisap—Bajna area, got into a fight on the march and, together with the 4th Guards Rifle Division's withdrawing units, stoutly repulsed the enemy's tank attacks along the Sarisap—Bajna line. The 93rd Rifle Division, which had moved into the Tarjan area, was involved in intense fighting in this area. However, the poor management of the fighting on the part of the division's and regiments' headquarters, the absence of communications (the regiments' headquarters were located five kilometers behind the division's headquarters in Csabdi), the absence of organized cooperation with the artillery, and a shortage of ammunition, the division fell back, abandoning Tukros. On the breakthrough's left flank the 34th Guards Rifle Division, having bent its right flank, continued to put up resistance along the line Peszke River—the firing range.

The enemy's fierce attacks during the second half of the day did not yield him any kind of material results. At the cost of heavy losses, he managed to push our units back insignificantly along individual sectors and by the close of the day the fighting continued along the line Kirp (east of Nyergesujfalu)—the center of Bajna—south of Tarjan—the firing range. Thus the main task of the 86th Guards Rifle Division, the 18th Guards Tank Corps and the 93rd Rifle Division—to hold the enemy and win time for creating the planned new defensive line—had been fulfilled.

The enemy's advance throughout 3 January is explained by his great superiority of force along the breakthrough sector. The army and *front* reserves were mainly still on the march and had not yet arrived at the line indicated by the *front* commander. The presence of our weak infantry forces in the area of Agosztiani Gorba mountain enabled the enemy to infiltrate automatic riflemen into Tardos and Tolna and thus clear the path for his tanks, while the somewhat delayed movement of the 18th Guards Tank Corps' forces into the Dag—Sarisap—Bajna area (by the morning of 3 January) gave the enemy tanks the opportunity to capture Nagysap and reach Bajna.

Throughout the day the 4th Guards Rifle Division, while fighting the enemy's superior forces and suffering losses and not receiving reinforcements, was unable to withstand for long the enemy's massed tank and infantry attacks.

During the second day of the offensive the enemy managed to overcome the northern part of the Vertes Hegyseg Mountains and penetrate our defense to a depth of 12-16 kilometers. The enemy's units reached the roads leading to Bicske and Budapest. Throughout 3 January our attacks by individual reinforced battalions continued along the center and left flank of the 4th Guards Army. Before 3 January the 17th and 5th air armies' main forces had been operating against the enemy's encircled group of forces. Only one assault air division and a fighter division were operating along the external front. From 3 January the 17th Air Army was completely switched to operations against the enemy's troops, which were launching the counterblow, carrying out an average of about 600 sorties per day, of which 150 were at night. In order to reinforce it, the 5th Assault Air Corps was brought in, which carried out no less than 100 sorties per day. The strikes by both air armies were concentrated against the combat formations of the enemy's tank groups. Strikes were carried out at night against tank concentration areas and against their march routes to the front.

The 4th Guards Army's commander, fearing an enemy breakthrough along the Szekesfehervar axis along the 20th Guards Rifle Corps' sector, continued to hold his reserve, the 7th Guards Mechanized Corps and the 41st Guards Rifle Division, here. However, the serious threat of a breakthrough by the enemy's tank formations to Bicske and then to Budapest forced him to make a decision that fully corresponded to the developing situation, namely:

- to concentrate part of the 7th Guards Mechanized Corps' forces (16th Mechanized Brigade, 78th Heavy Tank Regiment and the 1289th Self-Propelled Artillery Regiment) to the Bicske—Csabdi area to be employed in the capacity of the 4th Guards Army's mobile anti-tank reserve. Three self-propelled artillery regiments (382nd Guards, 1821st and 1453rd) from the 1st Guards Mechanized Corps and the 7th Anti-Tank Artillery Brigade, which had arrived from the *front* reserve, were to move to this area and be subordinated to the commander of the 31st Guards Rifle Corps;
- the 41st Guards Rifle Division, along with one artillery regiment and one mortar regiment was to be moved by forced march to the area northwest of Bicske, from where it was to move to the new defensive line by 0600 on 4 January, with the task of preventing an enemy breakthrough in the direction of Bicske, and to delay him in the narrow mountainous area and to destroy him with fire. The 62nd Guards Rifle Division was to be removed from the 21st Guards Rifle Corps and sent to the Szekesfehervar area;
- the 40th Guards Rifle Division, following its relief by units of the 7th Guards Airborne Division, was to be concentrated in the Csakvar area, while the remnants of the 4th Guards Rifle Division were to be gathered and put in order and moved to the line of the southern outskirts of Bajna—excluding height 335, and elements of the 80th Guards Rifle Division were to be taken out of the fighting and put in order.

By this time the 80th Guards Rifle Division and the 170th Guards Tank Brigade, which had been left in the enemy rear, in spite of their heavy losses, broke out to the southeast and linked up with friendly forces, having maintained their cohesion and withdrawing all of their surviving equipment.

Measures were being adopted simultaneously for strengthening the new defensive front. By 0600 on 3 January an anti-aircraft division and a guards mortar regiment had been removed from the 5th Guards Cavalry Corps and dispatched to the 18th Guards Tank corps in the Dag—Uny area, and a self-propelled artillery regiment (100mm guns) from the 1st Guards Mechanized Corps. The commander of the 18th Guards Tank Corps organized close communications and cooperation with assault aviation. The commander of the 306th Assault Air Division was located uninterruptedly at the headquarters of the 18th Guards Tank Corps.

By the morning of 4 January the 86th Guards Rifle Division, along with reinforcement units, was occupying defensive positions with two regiments along the line Tat—Sarisap—along the eastern bank of an unnamed stream.

By the close of 3 January the 2nd Guards Mechanized Corps had occupied defensive positions in the Dag—Kriva—Uny area; one of its brigades was to be moved to the Sarisap by the morning of 4 January. By the close of 3 January the 46th Army's 49th Guards Rifle Division had taken up defensive positions with two regiments in the area one kilometer north of Kriva—height 255—Gyermely—Szomor; the third regiment was moving to the Zsambek area. the 41st Guards Rifle

Division, along with the 115th Cannon-Artillery Brigade, the 152nd Howitzer Regiment and the 205th Mortar Regiment occupied the Polinkahaz line on 4 January.

In order to strengthen the axis from Bajna to Budapest, the 18th Guards Tank Corps' 181st Tank Brigade, which had been in the corps' second echelon in the Sarisap area, was shifted to the Szomor area.

Simultaneously, a defensive depth was being created along the most important axes by the forces of the 5th Guards Cavalry Corps and the 46th Army's 99th Rifle Division.

The newly created front was suffused with artillery and engineer anti-tank weapons and anti-tank areas were being created.

Thus during the course of two days the *front's* forces, which holding the enemy's large tank forces, which had broken through our first defensive line, had created a new defensive front, 40 kilometers long, having increased the depth of the defense along the most important axes to 7-12 kilometers. At the same time, three defensive lines had been created along the most threatened axis (Bicske), and were occupied by the troops ahead of time. The operational density of the defense along the main line was as much as eight kilometers per division and, if one takes into account the 18th Guards Tank Corps, the 93rd and 4th Guards rifle divisions operating ahead of this line and the three cavalry divisions and the 99th Rifle Division located in the depth, then the density reached as much as 3.5 kilometers per division. The artillery density reached 20 tubes, and along the Bicske axis up to 32 tubes per kilometer of front. A powerful mobile anti-tank reserve (one light artillery brigade, one tank regiment and four self-propelled artillery regiments), the 78th Heavy Tank Regiment, 1289th, 1821st, 1453rd, and 382nd Guards self-propelled regiments (a number of artillery units) was created in the Bicske area. Insofar as the further removal of formations from the first line of defense was fraught with great risk and could lead to a sharp weakening of the defense along the remaining external encirclement front, it was necessary to create new reserves from sectors of the front not under attack. The 57th Army's 19th Guards Rifle Division was pulled into the reserve and transferred over a distance of more than 170 kilometers was carried out in 1½ days from the moment the order was issued.

Throughout 3 January the 5th and 17th air armies' formations operated against the enemy's tanks and artillery, carrying out 984 sorties.

During the night of 3-4 January the enemy's tanks and infantry, having overcome our troops' resistance, streamed in the direction of Tukros in one group, a second broke into Gyermely and a third was developing the offensive on Nemelyeghasa.

The 4th Guards Army's commander's reserve (16th Mechanized Brigade, 78th Heavy Tank Regiment, 1289th Self-Propelled Artillery Regiment, and 117th Anti-Tank Artillery Regiment, which included sixteen T-34s, twelve IS-122s[2], four SU-85s[3], seven SU-76s[4], eight armored transports, and 20 85mm guns), which had been moved up in a timely manner, engaged the enemy from the march and halted him along the line height 224—Tukros, destroying at the same time 17 tanks and 16 armored transports.

The 16th Mechanized Brigade's subunits and units fought especially stoutly and skillfully. The commander of the Third Ukrainian Front noted this in his order, where it was noted that "the 16th Mechanized Brigade is carrying out its combat assignments exceptionally. I express my thanks to the entire rank and file. Those who distinguished themselves in the fighting are to be decorated.

2 Editor's note. The IS-122 was a Soviet heavy tank that appeared in 1944. It weighed 46 tons and carried a crew of four. It was armed with a 122mm gun and three 12.7mm machine guns.

3 Editor's note. The SU-85 was a Soviet self-propelled gun which first appeared in 1943. One model weighed 29.6 tons and carried a crew of four. It was armed with an 85mm gun.

4 Editor's note. The SU-76 was a self-propelled gun produced in the Soviet Union during 1942-45. Mounted on a T-70 tank chassis, it had a crew of four and was armed with a 76mm gun.

I decorate the commander of the 16th Mechanized Brigade, Guards Colonel M.F. Marshev, with the Order of the Red Banner. I'm sure that the 16th Mechanized Brigade will not let the enemy reach Bicske."

The tank troops carried out this order. The enemy did not pass through Bicske.

On the morning of 4 January the enemy resumed his offensive, committing all of his forces (3rd SS Panzer Division *Totenkopf*, 5th SS Panzer Division *Wiking*, 23rd Panzer Division, the 3rd Panzer Division's 6th Panzer Regiment, 130th Panzer Regiment, high command artillery, part of the 8th Panzer Division, 96th Infantry Division, the 271st Infantry Division's 279th Infantry Regiment, and the Hungarian 20th Light Infantry Division) into the fighting, with the exception of the 711th Infantry Division and, taking no notice of losses, sought to break through to Budapest. He directed his main forces toward the Tat—Bajna sector and in the direction of Bicske. The offensive was supported from the air by the enemy's massive air strikes (more than 900 sorties were carried out that day).

Simultaneously, the enemy prepared and launched a flank attack, forcing the Danube River from Tatan Island. As a result, he managed to capture Tat and Tokod station. This attack had no further success. Along the Dag axis the enemy managed only to push back units of the 18th Guards Tank Corps from the Bajna area to the new defense line organized by the *front*. The enemy's success was insignificant along the breakthrough's left flank as well, where he pushed back units of the 35th Guards Rifle Division. The enemy penetrated 6-8 kilometers along the Bicske axis, pushing back units of the 41st Guards Rifle Division and the 12th Cavalry Division to the Vasztol—Nemelyeghása area.

On this day our forces, in order to delay the enemy advance on Bicske, were forced to carry out numerous counterattacks, as a result of which the enemy advance in the direction from Tarjan to Bicske was halted.

However, the threat of a breakthrough along the Bicske axis made it necessary to adopt new emergency measures to strengthen this axis. The 18th Guards Tank Corps, which was carrying out its mission of holding the enemy in order to win time and which had fallen back to a defensive line occupied by infantry, had been pulled back to the Zsambek—Felsersmanj area by the morning of 5 January, in readiness to launch a counterblow in the direction of: 1) Many, 2) Szomor and 3) Perbal and Tinnye station. While repulsing the counterblow, many of the 18th Guards Tank Corps' crews displayed exceptional determination and heroism. For example, the crew of tank No. 662 (mechanic-driver Sinyavskii, gun commander Senior Sergeant Bezenko and gunner radio operator Kurilov), which had been acquired at their own expense, destroyed two "Panthers",[5] one "Tiger" and two enemy guns in this fighting. In the fighting for Esztergom the crew of Lieutenant Trikin, the commander of the 2nd Tank Company, especially distinguished itself, destroying two "Tigers", two "Panthers," three anti-tank guns, and 50 German soldiers and officers. The commander of the 41st Guards Tank Brigade's 3rd Battalion, Senior Lieutenant Novoselov, while beating off an attack by 60 German tanks and two battalions of infantry, set fire to 18 tanks and killed up to 150 German soldiers and officers.

The 1st Guards Mechanized Corps, which consisted of three mechanized brigades, a tank brigade, three self-propelled artillery regiments, one mortar regiment, one anti-aircraft artillery regiment, a battalion of guards mortar platforms, six special designation battalions, and several companies, had concentrated in the Nagyperkata area. The corps was fully supplied with ammunition, fuel and food, although a significant part of the supplies were located on the left bank of the Danube. The corps was to make a forced march to the Bicske—Felcsut—Etyek—Herceghalom

5 Editor's note. The Panzer V ("Panther") was a German medium tank which first appeared in 1943. One model weighed 44.8 tons and carried a crew of five. It was armed with a 75mm gun and two 7.92mm machine guns.

station area by the morning of 5 January, in readiness to attack in the direction of Bajna, Tat and Bicske, and Tarjan. The 24th Anti-Tank Artillery Regiment was attached to the corps.

The 40th Guards Rifle Division, while moving north from Szar, deployed from the march and was committed into the fighting in conjunction with the 16th Mechanized Brigade, while the 63rd Cavalry Division remained in the Vertesacsa—Csakvar area.

The commander of the 4th Guards Army made the decision to concentrate the army's main forces along the sector of the enemy's main attack and to halt his advance to the northwest of Bicske. For this purpose, the 31st Guards Rifle Corps, consisting of the 40th and 11th guards rifle and 93rd Rifle divisions, 16th Mechanized Brigade, a tank regiment, a self-propelled artillery regiment, the 7th Anti-Tank Artillery Brigade, two mortar regiments, and reinforcement engineer units, was ordered to securely defend the sector Many—Gyermely (west)—Szar station—Szar. A corps artillery group, consisting of two cannon and one howitzer regiments from the High Command Reserve, was created to support the corps. Part of the 31st Guards Rifle Corps' sector from Szar station and to the west was transferred to the commander of the 68th Rifle Corps, which was entrusted with the defense of the line excluding Szar station—Tatabanya—Banhida. A powerful anti-tank reserve, consisting of three self-propelled artillery and two anti-tank artillery regiments, was created in the Bicske area. In the depth along the Bicske axis a new defensive line was being created by the forces of the 62nd Guards Rifle Division and the 80th and 4th guards rifle divisions, which had been hurriedly put into order, along the line Gebeljuras—Hatvan—Alcsutdoboz. This new line was to be reinforced by the 49th Anti-Tank Artillery Regiment.

As a result of these measures, three rifle divisions, one mechanized brigade, a heavy tank regiment, four self-propelled artillery regiments, and six engineer-sapper battalions had been concentrated along the axis of the enemy's main attack, by the close of 4 January. In the 31st Guards Rifle Corps' defensive sector a powerful artillery group of forces had been created, consisting of 464 guns and mortars, which yielded a density of up to 40 tubes per kilometer of front. The artillery density was even higher along the main axes of the enemy's offensive. Aside from the anti-tank artillery, 50 percent of the divisional artillery, 30-40 percent of the howitzers and 20 percent of the artillery regiments from the High Command Reserve were allotted to fight against the enemy's tanks and for firing over open sights.

The developing situation demanded that part of the 4th Guards Army's sector from Gyermely and to the north be turned over to the 18th Guards Tank Corps. Simultaneously, a new defensive position along the line Telki—Paty—Bija—Etyek—Alcsutdoboz—Veresboglar—Morics was to be prepared by 6 January and which was to be occupied by the forces of the 46th and 4th Guards armies. The 17th Air Army carried out 773 sorties on this day.

Keeping in mind that the enemy could launch an attack with the forces of the III Panzer Corps from the Szekesfehervar area, it was decided to pull back the 7th Mechanized Corps into the reserve in the Zamoly area. All of these measures determined the results of the subsequent fighting.

Fierce fighting continued during 5-6 January. The enemy threw all of his forces into the fighting and made continuous attacks. The fighting continued day and night, however, he was unable to break through the 31st Guards Rifle Corps' defense.

5 January was the turning point in the fighting. Heavy fighting, involving a large number of tanks from both sides, took place throughout the day. The enemy's tanks suffered colossal losses during the fighting and achieved only insignificant territorial successes, which were not justified by the losses incurred. The enemy managed to penetrate our defense along some axes, but the breakthrough elements were thrown back or destroyed by our counterattacks. It was only along the Zsambek axis that the enemy managed to push back units of the 40th Guards Rifle Division and capture Gyermely (east) and Szomor. A counterattack by the hurriedly moved-up 5th Guards Mechanized Brigade (2nd Guards Mechanized Corps) and part of the 18th Guards Tank Corps'

forces halted the enemy's advance along this axis as well. The enemy enjoyed no success on this day along the 4th Guards Army's front.

Measures continued for strengthening our defense. In order to more securely defend the axis to the northwest of Budapest, the 19th Rifle Division was transferred from the reserve and subordinated to the commander of the 46th Army for employment on the defensive along the line Telki—Paty—Biatorbagy.

Thus the line, which had been created in the depth of the defense by the 4th Guards Army along the line Gebeljuras—Alcsutdoboz—Morics was continued in the 46th Army's sector along the line Csev—Tinnye—Telki—Paty—Bija. An anti-tank artillery line had been created between this line and the main defensive line along the line of the grove two kilometers southeast of Kirva—Anyacsa—Zsambek by the forces of two self-propelled artillery regiments (SU-100[6]) and three artillery regiments.

The 93rd Guards Rifle Division, which had been pushed back to the 40th Guards Rifle Division's defensive line and which had suffered heavy losses, was pulled back into the reserve in the Alcsutdoboz area, thus strengthening the rear line's defense. A powerful anti-tank center was created in the Bicske area.

On 5 January a new boundary line between the 46th and 4th Guards armies was established: two kilometers south of Bajot—Gyermely (west)—Many—Etyek—Ufalu (all locales, except for Etyek and Ufalu were exclusively for the 46th Army).

On 6 January the enemy strained all his efforts in order to capture Bicske. For this purpose, he threw large tank forces into the fighting along narrow sectors. However, these attempts were eliminated by our forces with heavy losses for the German-Fascist troops. It was only along the northern sector of the front that the enemy, having committed the 711th Infantry Division into the fighting along with the 96th Infantry Division and part of the 3rd SS *Totenkopf* Panzer Division into the fighting, managed to push back the 86th Rifle Division's right flank somewhat and seize Esztergom and Esztergom camp.

By the close of 6 January the 4th Guards Army occupied the follow lines:

The 31st Guards Rifle Corps was holding the line of the northwestern and western outskirts of Many—the grove west of Many—Csabdi and to the east—Szar station. The 93rd Guards Rifle Division in the second echelon was preparing a defense along the line Etyek—Gebeljuras.

The 68th Rifle Corps, with units of the 34th Guards Rifle Division, was holding its former line, while the 52nd Rifle Division captured Pusztavam.

The 20th Guards Rifle Corps (7th and 5th guards airborne divisions, 84th Guards Rifle Division) occupied its previous position and the 84th Guards Rifle Division, together with its defensive sector, was subordinated to the corps.

The 135th Rifle Corps, which was reinforced by the 69th Guards Rifle Division and the 1st Guards Fortified Area, along with their combat sectors, occupied its previous position. The 21st Guards Rifle Corps (4th, 80th and 62nd guards rifle divisions) was preparing a defense along the line Gebeljuras—Hatvan—one kilometer northeast of Vitezi—Marija.

The responsibility for the boundary with the 46th Army was entrusted to the commander of the 4th Guards Army.

The mobile formations occupied the following position:

2nd Guards Mechanized Corps: the 37th Tank Brigade, in conjunction with units of the 86th Guards Rifle Division, was fighting along the western outskirts of Dorog; the 6th Mechanized

6 Editor's note. The SU-100 was a Soviet self-propelled tank destroyer that saw action during the latter part of the Second World War. Mounted on a T-34 chassis, the SU-100 weighed 31.6 tons, carried a crew of four and was armed with a 100mm gun.

Brigade was along the northern and western outskirts of Sarisap; the 4th Guards Mechanized Brigade was 1.5 kilometers west of Dag, and; the 5th Mechanized Brigade was in Tinnye.

18th Guards Tank Corps: one brigade (170th) was in Felsvers; the 32nd Motorized Rifle Brigade and the 181st Tank Brigade were in Many, and the 110th Tank Brigade was in the Tok area.

1st Guards Mechanized Corps: deployed with part of its forces, plus two self-propelled artillery regiments and a regiment from the 24th Anti-Tank Artillery Brigade, in the area northwest and west of Perbal. The remaining forces were in their previous location.

7th Guards Mechanized Corps: one brigade (16th), along with units of the 41st Guards Rifle Division, repelled enemy attacks throughout the day along the line 1.5 kilometers northwest of Csabdi. The remaining forces (41st Guards Tank Brigade and the 63rd and 64th mechanized brigades) reached the area Laja—southern outskirts of Zamoly—Borbalamajor—Gyulamajor.

Thus as early as the close of 6 January the failure of the enemy's offensive had been clearly traced. All of his forces, including the 711th Infantry Division, had been completely expended and the attacking units already bled white, although he had not managed to achieve even a local operational success along a single sector. By the close of 6 January our defense had become significantly stronger than at the beginning of the enemy's offensive. The echeloning of the defense in depth reached 12-14 kilometers, while the defense had been organized into 2-3 echelons along the main axes.

The defense's operational density reached 3.8 kilometers per division, and along the Bicske axis two kilometers per division. The artillery density reached 24 tubes per kilometer of front and 33 tubes along the Bicske axis. There were powerful tank and anti-tank reserves in the Zsambek and Bicske areas.

Heavy fighting continued over the course of six days. Paying no attention to casualties, the enemy stubbornly sought to relieve his encircled Budapest group of forces. During this time the German-Fascist forces' panzer divisions, which were part of the shock group, as well as the 96th Infantry Division, lost up to 80 percent of their equipment. The enemy advanced at most 30 kilometers in six days along the axis of his main attack, with an average daily rate of up to five kilometers.

Taking into account the enormous superiority of force that the enemy had along the axis of his main attack, this rate of advance should be considered miniscule. During the entire period when we were repelling the enemy's first counterblow, there was a difficult ice situation on the Danube, which made the feeding of the front with munitions, fuel, combat equipment, and arriving reinforcements very difficult, as well as carrying out maneuver.

Conclusions on Repelling the Enemy's First Counterblow

As a result of the six days of intense combat, the enemy was nevertheless unable to resolve his assigned operational mission—to relieve his encircled Budapest group of forces, and this was in conditions when he possessed a decisive superiority in men and materiel; he launched a surprise attack against our forces' poorly prepared defense, who did not possess sufficient reserves; he held the initiative in his hands during the attack, as well as a superiority of forces along the main axis.

The decisiveness of goals called for by the counterblow, which was directed at liberating the encircled group of forces and the participation of the maximum amount of men and materiel, particularly mobile, in the counterblow, brought about frequent changes in the situation and demanded from the troops extreme exertion, steadfastness, a high degree of maneuverability, heightened intelligence gathering activity, and constant readiness to repel attacks.

Combat activities were conducted around the clock and were especially intense at night. The enemy showed a preference for nighttime activities in order to achieve surprise, as well as to reduce losses from our anti-tank artillery and aviation.

The stability and activity of our troops' defense foiled the enemy's plans. During the fighting our forces manifested extreme heroism, which was more than once noted in the command's orders (18th Guards Tank Corps, the 7th Guards Mechanized Corps' 16th Mechanized Brigade, the 86th Guards Rifle Division, the 12th Anti-Tank Brigade, and others).

The repulse of the German-Fascist forces' first counterblow took place by our forces going over to a temporary defense. An active static defense pursued the aims of exhausting and halting the enemy forces, inflicting a defeat on them and creating conditions for subsequent offensive operations. Such goals, tasks and methods of the troops' activities were determined by specific conditions, the chief of which was the circumstance that the Third Ukrainian Front's troops disposed of limited forces and thus the method of operations employed by them in the given specific conditions was the single correct and expedient one.

The experience of repelling the first counterblow by the German-Fascist forces around Budapest confirmed the correctness of the theoretical tenets that the defeat of a counterblow is secured by the following:

- good intelligence, the troops' constant readiness, decisiveness of actions, and the correct employment of all men and materiel for the purpose of inflicting a defeat on the enemy's main group of forces.

The repulse of the first counterblow was mainly carried out by the forces of the 4th Guards Army, which occupied a front up to 160 kilometers and which was 50-60 kilometers from the internal encirclement front, as well as by part of the 46th Army. One may consider the following densities established during the repulse of the counterblow—24 guns, as well as 33 guns along the Bicske axis, and up to 10-15 tanks and self-propelled guns—to be sufficient, and if one takes into account that the defensive depth reached 12-14 kilometers and had been organized into 2-3 echelons with an operational density of 3.8 kilometers per division, then such a defense was unassailable for the enemy. In turn, the 50-60 kilometer distance of the external encirclement front enabled our forces to carry out maneuver from the internal front to the external one and to create a deeply echeloned defense.

Upon the start of the counterblow, the *front* commander adopted the necessary measures, namely: he directed the air force's activities against the tank concentration areas; thickened the 4th Guards Army's combat formations (particularly along the axis of the enemy's main attack); created a defensive depth by creating a new defensive front and moving up *front* reserves; reinforced measures for securing the troops and consolidating the breakthrough's flanks, and; clarified the troops' tasks. In order not to scatter our forces, all of our attention was concentrated on repelling the counterblow along the external encirclement front, as a result of which the 46th Army was ordered to halt its offensive activities in Budapest and go over to the defensive; the commander organized the regrouping of forces from the internal to the external encirclement front from the sectors of the front not under attack. While repelling the counterblow during 2-6 January, the transfer of rifle and cavalry divisions was carried out 31 times from one sector to another, and eight times for mechanized and tank corps. Aside from this, numerous transfers of individual regiments from divisions and individual brigades from the mechanized and tank corps were carried out. At the same time, individual transfers were carried out with great rapidity over great distances; the commander issued instructions for organizing cooperation between formations and combat arms designated for repelling the enemy's counterblow and his destruction, all of which facilitated the creation of a stable, active and deeply echeloned defense in short order in conditions when the troops were forced to wage a defensive battle in semi-encirclement, having only a narrow bottleneck between the Danube River and Lake Velence for maneuver and supply. A breakthrough by the enemy along any axis would have led him into the flank and rear of our neighboring groups of forces.

The artillery in general and anti-tank artillery in particular, played an extremely important role in repelling the first counterblow, as it did in succeeding ones. The artillery maneuvered broadly through target and movement. During 2-6 January 29 artillery reinforcement regiments were thrown against the breakthrough sector, including an anti-tank artillery brigade from the 37th Army (from Bulgaria), and three anti-tank artillery regiments from the left bank of the Danube River. The artillery units exhibited extreme steadfastness In repelling the enemy's tank attacks. In many cases, the rank and file of the artillery units independently repulsed the enemy's attacks, without the infantry. In conditions of a shortage of infantry, the artillery was fully the basis for the defense.

The *front* and army commander exhibited skill in creating reserves in a complex situation (mostly at the expense of men and materiel from sectors not under attack).

The precise coordination of our aviation with the ground troops, especially with the mobile formations (18th Guards Tank Corps and 2nd Guards Mechanized Corps) facilitated our success in repelling the enemy's tank attacks and which was supported by centralized control from the commander of the 17th Air Army's command post, and the presence among the ground troops of the air formation commanders' command posts and guidance stations. Our air force's successful operations were also guaranteed by the *front's* air superiority in the air, which forced the enemy air force to reduce its activity to 100-200 sorties per day as early as the second day, and also to lose up to 20 planes a day in aerial combat. During 1-6 January the 17th Air Army carried out 3,961 sorties, of which 917 were at night. Of this number, 2,737 (69 percent) were for operations against enemy troops, 935 (24 percent) against his aviation, and 289 (7 percent) for reconnaissance. Only 1,287 enemy sorties were noted, of which 1,042 were by fighters, which lost 82 planes in 96 air battles.

It's necessary to note shortcomings in the troops' activities while repelling the counterblow:

- the absence of operational intelligence and air operations against the concentration of the enemy's reserves enabled the latter to secretly concentrate a large group of forces and to launch a surprise attack against the weakest place in our forces' defense along the external front;
- the excessive centralization of command and control. The *front* commander assigned tasks to repel the counterblow not to the armies, but to individual formations and units;
- the absence of reserves along the axis of the main attack, as a result of the mistaken planning of the *front's* offensive operation, which resulted in men and materiel being scattered along a 160-kilometer front and the weakening of the 4th Guards Army's left flank;
- the exaggeration of the enemy's forces and the power of his equipment and the underestimation of our anti-tank weapons (anti-tank rifles and small-caliber artillery).

It was discovered that all combat arms were poorly trained for fighting at night. In a number of cases, the echeloning of anti-tank artillery weapons was missing and maneuver by anti-tank artillery reserves was not foreseen. Cooperation with tanks was organized insufficiently precisely, as a result of which there were cases when our artillery knocked out our own tanks and our tanks crushed our own guns (1st Guards Mechanized Corps).

There were instances of troop control being lost in some formations (the 31st Guards Rifle Corps on 2 January), and in a number of cases command was exercised not from an observation post, but from a command post, or that observation posts were chosen far from the battlefield and in buildings, from which it was impossible to observe the course of the fighting.

The Repulse of the Enemy's Second Counterblow

Seeing the hopelessness of its offensive along the main axis and calculating on weakening our defense north of Szekesfehervar, the enemy shifted the 23rd Panzer Division to the area northwest of Szekesfehervar and on 7 January began an offensive along this sector with the forces of the III Panzer Corps (1st, 3rd and 23rd panzer divisions, and the 4th Cavalry Brigade).

The goal of his offensive was to break through our defense north of Szekesfehervar and to encircle our group of forces operating against Bicske, to capture Szekesfehervar and to subsequently develop the offensive on Budapest.

Thus the German-Fascist command had not renounced its initial plan of relieving its encircled group of forces at any cost and by any means.

By the close of 6 January the 4th Guards Army's main forces and equipment and the *front's* reserves were concentrated along the axis of the enemy's main attack—north and northwest of Bicske. A large part of the remaining forces and equipment, including the 7th Guards Mechanized Corps, had been concentrated in the center of the army's zone—north of Szekesfehervar. The remaining sectors of the army's zone were being defended by minimal forces and equipment.

The 31st Guards Rifle Corps (4th, 41st and 40th guards rifle divisions and the 16th Mechanized Brigade) was defending along the axis of the enemy's main attack from Many to Szar station. The 68th Rifle Corps (223rd and 52nd rifle divisions) was operating along the sector from Szar station to Pusztavam. The 20th Guards Rifle Corps (7th and 5th guards airborne divisions and the 84th Rifle Division) was fighting along the line from Pusztavam to Moha. The 135th Rifle Corps (252nd and 69th Guards rifle divisions and the 1st Guards Fortified Area) was defending along the left flank. The 21st Guards Rifle Corps (93rd Rifle and 80th and 62nd guards rifle divisions) was preparing a defensive position south of Bicske. The 7th Guards Mechanized Corps (minus the 16th Mechanized Brigade, 78th Heavy Tank Regiment and the 1438th Self-Propelled Artillery Regiment) was in the area east and south of Zamoly in the army's commander's reserve. An anti-tank artillery reserve (two anti-tank artillery regiments and two self-propelled artillery regiments) was in the area Bicske—Felcsut.

Our command correctly evaluated the situation and assumed that the enemy would continue attacking toward Bicske, while it was simultaneously necessary to expect an attack on Zamoly, because the enemy's fully combat-capable III Panzer Corps continued to remain along this axis. For this reason, the commander of the 4th Guards Army adopted a number of measures to strengthen the defense (the creation of second echelons in the divisions and the engineer reinforcement of the defensive zone) northwest of Szekesfehervar and placed his reserve—the 7th Guards Mechanized Corps—along the axis of the enemy's likely counterblow.

The enemy launched his main attack along the sector of the 20th Guards Rifle Corps, which was defending along a 28-kilometer front. All three divisions were located in the first echelon. Two of the rifle divisions (5th Guards Airborne and 84th Rifle divisions) had a two-echelon combat formation and one division (7th Guards Airborne) was in a single-echelon formation. The corps commander had one anti-tank artillery regiment in his anti-tank reserve. The corps had been reinforced with an army artillery sub-group, consisting of the 123rd Cannon-Artillery Brigade (thirty four 152mm howitzers) and the 188th Howitzer Regiment (twelve 122mm guns).

There were 1.2 rifle battalions, 18 guns and mortars (of these, eight were anti-tank guns) and two tanks a self-propelled guns per kilometer of front in the corps' defensive sector.

The greatest density of men and materiel had been created along the 5th Guards Airborne Division's 9-kilometer defensive zone, in the sector of which the enemy's main attack was expected. The 7th Guards Mechanized Corps, the anti-tank reserve of the commander of the 20th Guards Rifle Corps, was concentrated in this zone, and the army artillery group was located in its firing positions.

Taking into account these forces and equipment, there were 1.7 rifle battalions, 28 guns and mortars (of these, 13 were anti-tank guns) and 5.5 tanks and self-propelled guns per kilometer of front in the 5th Guards Airborne Division's sector. This density was already sufficient to withstand attacks by major enemy forces.

The correlation of forces in the 20th Guards Rifle Corps' sector by the morning of 7 January is as follows:

Table 11 Correlation of Forces in the Sector of the 20th Guards Rifle Division, 7 January 1945

	Enemy	Our Forces	Correlation
Personnel	16,400	5,468	3.0:1
Machine Guns	750	172	4.4:1
Guns and Mortars	907	252	3.6:1
Tanks and Self-Propelled Guns	300	50	6:1

It is clear from the table that in the 20th Guards Rifle Corps' sector the enemy had created a significant superiority in men and materiel.

At 0920 on 7 January the enemy, following an artillery preparation, resumed his attacks along the entire front with the forces of six panzer and three infantry divisions. Up to 280 tanks and assault guns participated simultaneously in the attack. In view of the poor meteorological conditions, his aviation did not support his troops.

The enemy had concentrated his main forces along the Csolnok—Sarisap sector, while trying particularly to break through via Bicske. Simultaneously, the enemy attacked along the Csakbereny—Sarkeresztes sector with units of three panzer divisions and one infantry division in the direction of Zamoly and Bicske. The enemy somewhat pushed back units of the 20th Guards Rifle Corps with an attack by more than 120 tanks and self-propelled guns along a narrow sector.

It was once again necessary to rapidly maneuver reserves and, in particular, artillery for the purpose of countering the enemy attack.

On orders from the army commander, one howitzer regiment, one anti-tank artillery regiment and one artillery regiment, and the 20th Guards Rifle Corps commander's reserve—a rifle regiment with an anti-tank artillery regiment—were immediately moved up to the most threatened axis to the line Lajamajor—Borbalamajor. Besides this, the 20th Guards Rifle Corps was reinforced, according to the decision of the army commander, during the second half of the day by two anti-tank artillery regiments, three howitzer regiments, one artillery and one mortar regiments from the 68th and 135th rifle corps' army reserve. In all, the following arrived to reinforce the corps during the first day of the enemy offensive: 43 76mm guns, 63 122mm howitzers, ten 152mm guns, and 16 mortars, for a total of 132 tubes. The rapid and skillful maneuver of artillery units along the axis of the enemy's main attack enabled us to create a powerful artillery group, which played a decisive role in repelling the enemy's counterblow along the Zamoly axis. Besides this, the 7th Guards Mechanized Corps entered the fighting in the first hours of the enemy's offensive, operating among the rifle formations.

The engineer troops, which had laid about 5,000 anti-tank mines in the two days preceding the enemy offensive, played a significant role in repelling the enemy attack.

The 17th Air Army, despite the poor meteorological conditions, carried out 102 sorties against the enemy's forces. All of these measures enabled us to hold the enemy's advance (he advanced along some axes from one to four kilometers) as early as the first day and to destroy 43 tanks and self-propelled guns. Attacks were also beaten off in the 31st Guards Rifle Corps' sector.

The commander of the 4th Guards Army correctly concluded that the lack of success during the 7 January fighting along both axes would not force the enemy to call off new attempts to continue the offensive, which had as its immediate goal the splitting of the army's defense and the subsequent relief of the encircled group of forces. Thus the most urgent tasks were to reinforce the 20th Guards Rifle Corps, particularly with infantry, and to create reserves in the center of the army's zone. The 5th Guards Cavalry Corps was operationally subordinated to the commander of the 4th Guards Army by order of the *front* commander.

The 93rd Rifle Division was moved up from the 4th Guards Army's second defensive line and the 63rd Cavalry Division from the Kesanjan—Csakvar—Verteskozma area and five artillery regiments to the axis of the enemy attack.

In the conditions that had arisen by the close of 7 January, the army commander decided on the following: the 62nd Guards Rifle Division, as the most combat-capable one, was to remain in his reserve along the Bicske axis; the 93rd Rifle Division was to occupy the line Miklos—Patka; the 63rd Cavalry Division was to be moved to up to the line toward Zamoly and be subordinated to the commander of the 20th Guards Rifle Corps; the 69th Guards Rifle Division was to be relieved during the night of 7-8 January by units of the 252nd Rifle Division and the 1st Guards Fortified Area and be pulled into the army reserve to the Szekesfehervar area for organizing the city's defense from the north.

At the same time, he detached the 1st Guards Mechanized Brigade and one self-propelled artillery regiment from the 1st Guards Mechanized Corps and ordered them to occupy the line Forna—Miklos—Antal by the morning of 8 January.

On the morning of 8 January the enemy renewed the offensive along both breakthrough sectors, concentrating, as before, his main efforts along the army's right flank in the direction of Bicske in the 41st Guards Rifle Division's and the 16th Mechanized Brigade's defensive sector. All of the enemy's attacks were beaten off here. In view of the 41st Guards Rifle Division's heavy losses, by the close of the day the army commander relieved units of the 41st Guards Rifle Division in the Bicske area with his reserve (62nd Guards Rifle Division) and thus reinforced this axis.

Following its relief, the 41st Guards Rifle Division was pulled into the second echelon to the Alcsut—Vertesboglar—Morics area. The enemy managed to capture Sarkeresztes and Moha in the center of the army's zone and up to 30 tanks broke into Gyulamajor. The enemy's further advance was halted by the forces of the 82nd Rifle Division, the 64th Mechanized Brigade, a regiment from the 5th Guards Airborne Division, and one anti-tank artillery regiment and one cannon-artillery regiment, which had been transferred here on the army commander's orders.

The 17th Air Army, despite the unfavorable meteorological conditions, supported the 4th Guards Army's combat activities and carried out 326 sorties.

Simultaneously with the repulse of the enemy's counterblow, on orders from the *front* commander, the commander of the 4th Guards Army was to prepare a retaliatory counterblow against the enemy's group of forces west of Zamoly with the forces of the 20th Guards Rifle Corps (a regiment from the 7th Guards Airborne Division, 63rd Cavalry Division, 5th Guards Airborne Division, two brigades from the 7th Guards Mechanized Corps, and two brigades from the 1st Guards Mechanized Corps) in the direction of Magyaralmas for the purpose of defeating the enemy's shock group operating here, restoring the situation and reaching the front Csokako—Sored—Igar—Moha.

The attack by two brigades from the 1st Guards Mechanized Corps ended in complete failure because of the snowfall and the absence of an artillery preparation. 70 percent of the tanks had not been under fire and were in a battle for the first time. Due to a lack of time, the commanders and their staffs organized the engagement poorly, particularly reconnaissance. Insofar as the counterblow on January 9 was launched by units that had suffered significant losses and lacked sufficient strength, the territorial result was small, although the enemy, having suffered enormous losses as a result of our counterblow, was forced to halt his further offensive.

With the onset of darkness, the 1st Guards Mechanized Corps was withdrawn to the line height 203—height 214, with the task of taking up a static defense and to prevent the enemy from breaking through in the direction of Csakvar and Lovasbereny. It was ordered to have one brigade along the northern outskirts of Szekesfehervar's suburbs, in Csala, in readiness to repulse the enemy's attacks.

The enemy set about shifting tank units from the Bicske area to the northwest.

Throughout 10 January the enemy continued attacking from the line Bicske—Mor—Gyulamajor in up to an infantry battalion in strength, with 11-17 tanks, and supported by 1-2 artillery battalions. He was not active along the other sectors. The enemy committed up to 70 tanks and self-propelled guns into the fighting along the sector Csokako—southwest of Zamoly—Sarkeresztes, but all of his attacks were beaten off with heavy losses for him.

The commander of the 4th Guards Army made the decision to take up a static defense, for which he ordered the following: the 20th Guards Rifle Corps (5th and 7th guards airborne divisions, the 93rd Rifle Division and the 63rd Cavalry Division, and the 762nd and 1963rd anti-tank artillery regiments, 188th and 200th howitzer regiments, and the 366th Self-Propelled Artillery Regiment) was to securely hold the sector Csokako—Csala station—Forna.

The 7th Guards Mechanized Corps and the 84th Rifle Division (with the 521st and 338th anti-tank artillery regiments, 212th Howitzer Regiment, the 1st and 2nd batteries of the 221st Howitzer Regiment, the 251st Independent Anti-Tank Battalion, and the 217th Engineer Battalion) were to take over the 20th Guards Rifle Corps' defensive sector by 1800 on 10 January.

The chief of the army's engineer troops ordered that an additional 6,000 anti-tank mines be laid on the night of 10-11 January in the 7th Guards Mechanized Corps' sector, of which 4,000 would be along the most threatened sector height 264—height 153.

The commander of the 1st Guards Mechanized Corps, according to the *front* commander's orders, was supposed to station the 1st Mechanized Brigade's and the 9th Tank Brigade's tanks for defending the Zamoly—Tallian area and in the rear along the line Miklos—Patka, and to entrench them in readiness to repulse possible enemy attacks in the direction of Csakvar and Lovasbereny. At 0900 on 11 January the enemy north of Szekesfehervar, following a short but powerful artillery onslaught, attacked the 4th Guards Army's positions in the Zamoly area with up to 100 tanks and self-propelled guns belonging to the 1st and 23rd panzer divisions. The attack was launched *en masse* along a narrow 3-3.5-kilometer sector of the front. The enemy concentrated his main efforts in the direction of Zamoly and Miklos. The shock group included a large number of heavy tanks and self-propelled guns. The enemy air forces bombed and strafed our troops in groups of 5-8 planes in the Zamoly area, carrying out more than 100 sorties.

The fighting here became extremely bitter. Our artillery troops fought in a particularly heroic manner. Hundreds of artillery troops accomplished heroic feats on this day. One battery from the 1963rd Anti-Tank Artillery Regiment was in its firing positions west of Zamoly. The artillery troops from this battery set five tanks on fire and knocked our four more in 40 minutes of fighting. More than 20 enemy tanks rode right up to the battery. Hundreds of shells exploded around our guns. Seven tanks broke through to the firing positions of Junior Lieutenant S.I. Yermolaev's platoon. The platoon knocked out another three "Tigers." However, enemy fire put all of the gun crews out of action. All of the ammunition had been expended. Only Komosmol[7] member Yermolaev remained against four "Tigers." He grabbed a bundle of anti-tank grenades, threw himself under a tank and blew it up. Within a few days, by decree of the Presidium of the Supreme Soviet of the USSR, Junior Lieutenant S.I. Yermolaev was posthumously awarded the title of Hero of the Soviet Union. 38 enemy tanks were destroyed this day along this sector.

The 4th Guards Army's forces, while waging bitter battles with the attacking enemy, were forced to abandon Zamoly and fall back 1-2.5 kilometers. The 4th Guards Army command highly rated

7 Editor's note. The Komsomol (*Kommunisticheskii Soyuz Molodezhi*) was the youth auxiliary of the Soviet Communist Party.

the air force's actions, issuing a special order. In supporting the troops, the 17th Air Army's formations carried out more than 600 sorties this day.

In order to strengthen the defense, the commander of the 4th Guards Army regrouped his forces during the night of 11-12 January. He subordinated the garrison of Szekesfehervar to the commander of the 21st Guards Rifle Corps. He transferred the 84th Rifle Division and the 251st Independent Anti-Tank Battalion, the 2nd Battery of the 221st Howitzer Regiment, and the 338th Anti-Tank Artillery Regiment from the 7th Guards Mechanized Corps to the commander of the 21st Guards Rifle Corps. At the same time, he concentrated two cavalry divisions from the 5th Guards Cavalry Corps to the area Alcsut—excluding Vertesacsa to be ready to launch powerful counterattacks in the directions of Zsambek, Bicske, Ujbarok, Szar station, Csakvar, Zamoly, Lovasbereny, and Csala.

By the close of 11 January the front line in the 4th Guards Army's sector ran as follows: western outskirts of Many—Csabdi (northern)—Szar station—Nagy Mountain—Kesele—Stajn Mountain—Banhida—Pusztavam—Keves—Felse—Miklos—Baklas—southern outskirts of Moha—Osi—Lake Balaton.

On 12 January the enemy had basically halted his offensive in the Zamoly area and in the Bicske area, limiting himself to an attack by small forces in the Dorog—Pilisszentelek area and from the line Csokako—northwest of Zamoly—Gyulamajor.

Two of the 5th Guards Cavalry Corps' divisions (11th and 12th guards cavalry divisions) were operationally subordinated to the commander of the 46th Army and were concentrating in the Pomaz—Piliscsaba—Csobanka area. The 63rd Cavalry Division remained operationally subordinated to the 4th Guards Army, because it could not be immediately pulled out of the fighting.

Conclusions on Repelling the Enemy's Second Counterblow

It follows that the enemy's second counterblow, launched by him along two axes with the forces of six tank (3rd SS Panzer Division, 5th SS Panzer Division, 3rd, 6th, 23rd and 1st panzer divisions), two infantry divisions (96th and 711th) and two cavalry brigades (3rd and 4th) ended for this the same way as the first—in complete failure.

Our defense was capable of withstanding the enemy offensive, having an operational density of 4.8 kilometers per division and an artillery density of 34 tubes per kilometer of front, and 54 tubes per kilometer along the Bicske axis.

Nor did the enemy manage to break through to Budapest during his second counterblow and link up with his encircled group of forces. The outcome of the fighting in our favor was decided, first of all, by the skillful maneuver of men and materiel and the high degree of combat skill and steadfastness of the Soviet troops. Despite the fact that a significant part of our forces were tied down by the operations of the enemy's IV SS Panzer Corps, the *front* and army commanders skillfully regrouped their reserves and artillery units and created a defense impregnable for the enemy. This was facilitated by the fact that, as opposed to the first counterblow, our forces had five days to organize a defense.

An anti-tank defense 4-6 kilometers deep was created at the expense of artillery weapons taken from sectors not under attack, and with the arrival of artillery from the 68th and 135th rifle corps, and then from the 57th Army, this was increased to eight kilometers. The defense was active. The enemy's penetrating subunits and units were subjected to unrelenting counterattacks.

The retaliatory counterblow by the forces of the 20th Guards Rifle Corps and part of the forces of the 7th Guards Mechanized Corps, the 1st Guards Mechanized Corps, and the 5th Guards Cavalry Corps played a decisive role in repulsing the enemy's second counterblow. This counterblow by our forces, while it did not result in the complete defeat of the main forces of the enemy's shock group in the Zamoly area, the German-Fascist forces nevertheless suffered enormous losses, which sharply reduced the offensive drive and shock force.

The anti-tank obstacles that had been laid beforehand by the engineer troops along the chief axes of the enemy's offensive tied down the maneuver by his tank forces to a significant degree. For example, in repelling the first and second counterblows, the engineer troops laid 31,071 anti-tank and 13,000 anti-personnel mines during 2-13 January 1945 in the 46th Army's sector and 31,966 anti-tank and 14,012 anti-personnel mines along the internal encirclement front of the Budapest group of forces. 39 tanks and ten armored transports were blown up on obstacles while repelling the counterblows.

Despite the unfavorable meteorological conditions, the 17th Air Army was able to operate quite effectively, launching massive strikes against the enemy's main group of forces and carrying out 3,200 sorties (of these, about 70 percent against the enemy's forces and 19 percent for battling his air force).

The Repulse of the Third Counterblow

Thanks to the testimony of defectors and prisoners, it was known that the enemy had transferred the 1st Panzer Division to the Osi area, while the active movement of auto transport was noted in the Varpalota area. All of this data indicated the enemy's possible attack along the 4th Guards Army's left flank.

Prisoner testimony confirmed the enemy's preparation of an offensive from the Balatonakarttya area to the east.

The commander of the 4th Guards Army adopted a number of additional measures to strengthen the defense of the army's center and left flank. The 7th Mechanized Corps was relieved by units of the 41st Guards Rifle Division, which was in the army commander's reserve, as was pulled back to Szekesfehervar into the army commander's reserve. The corps commander was ordered to put his units in order and prepare counterattacks in the direction of Imre and Csor; Fejer station, Zihfalva and Osi; Szekesfehervar and Nadasdladany, Szekesfehervar and Falubattyan, and; Szekesfehervar, Polgardi and Lepseny. Simultaneously, the corps commander was instructed not to remove tanks and self-propelled guns when relieving units, without special orders. The artillery (21st Howitzer Regiment, the 221st Howitzer Regiment's 2nd Battalion and the 521st Anti-Tank Artillery Regiment) was subordinated to the commander of the 21st Guards Rifle Corps, while remaining in their firing positions. The 16th Mechanized Brigade, 78th Tank and the 1289th Self-Propelled Artillery regiments were subordinated to the corps.

The defense of the city of Szekesfehervar and the approaches to it from the west were entrusted to the 21st Guards Rifle Corps, which included the 41st Guards and 84th rifle divisions, which comprised the corps' first echelon, and the 69th Guards Rifle Division, which comprised its second echelon. By this time the most combat-capable 80th Guards Rifle Division had been committed to strengthen the defense, while the 93rd Rifle Division was in the second echelon.

All of the army's center and left-flank units were working to strengthen the defense. The following engineer work had been completed as of 14 January: 12,647 linear meters of fully-outfitted trenches had been dug, 1,602 foxholes for light and heavy machine guns, 528 foxholes for anti-tank lines, 799 for guns, and 828 for mortars, and 1,019 covers and light shelters. 25,315 anti-tank mines and 6,367 anti-personnel mines and 354 controlled explosives had been laid, and 16,000 linear meters of wire obstacles and 6,000 meters of electrical obstructions erected.

In order to create reserves, the *front* commander concentrated the 10th Anti-Tank Artillery Brigade in Baracska, as an anti-tank reserve.

Throughout 14 January the enemy continued to regroup his forces. Aerial reconnaissance, which was operating on orders from the 4th Guards Army's headquarters, was unable to discover the concentration areas of the enemy's shock group, due to the careful masking adopted by the enemy, as well as due to the poor meteorological conditions: complete cloud cover and frequent snowfalls and rain. The enemy's vigilance along the forward edge increased sharply. Our reconnaissance subunits encountered powerful fire resistance everywhere.

At the same time, in Budapest the enemy was carrying out all sorts of measures to strengthen his defense and to put things in order. On 14 January the commander of the IX SS Mountain Corps received a telegram from Hitler to occupy the second belt of the Budapest defenses and "to hold out until relieved." In order to eliminate, or rather to lessen, friction between the German and Hungarian soldiers, the German-Fascist command issued orders regarding the conduct of German soldiers and their relations with the Hungarian soldiers and the civilian population. However, this had little effect. Friction continued to increase and desertion particularly grew. For example, order no. 1091 by the commander of the Hungarian I Corps of 15 January, dealing with "reprisals against violators of order," wrote:

"Having come out of the fighting, individuals and entire groups roam around the city, stirring up panic, drinking and robbing. In this they are not only demoralizing the civilian population, but also destroying their faith in the troops of both nations defending them,"

For the most part, the so-called Hungarian "volunteers" were still roaming along the road to the front, or ran away following a few days at the front line.

On the night of 15-16 January the 1st Guards Mechanized Corps was supposed to relieve the 18th Guards Tank Corps along its line. The 1st Guards Mechanized Corps' was to prevent a breakthrough by a stubborn defense and to plan an attack from the Zsambek area toward Szomor, Bajna and Hereg.

Following its relief, the 18th Guards Tank Corps was to concentrate in the Paty—Zsambekir—Herceghalom station area and, while constituting the *front's* reserve, be ready for operations along the following axes: Paty—Tinnye—Dorog station; Etyek—Vertesacsa—Zamoly, or Szekesfehervar; in the event of an enemy offensive from Zsambek toward Paty, prevent his breakthrough to Budapest.

There was a great shortage of weapons among the 4th Guards Army's forces as of 15 January. In order to completely arm 14 rifle divisions, calculating 7,000 men per division, the following was required: 24,487 rifles and carbines, 4,342 pistols and revolvers, 7,854 automatic rifles, 1,952 light machine guns, 536 heavy machine guns, 18 DShK[8] machine guns, 1,138 anti-tank rifles, 78 82mm mortars, 75 76mm regimental guns, 191 76mm divisional guns, 36 1938-model 122mm howitzers, 2,947 binoculars, 171 battery commander's telescopes, and 205 compass azimuths.

The following were needed for the anti-tank units: the 49th, 42nd and 7th anti-tank artillery brigades, 521st and 131st anti-tank artillery regiments, and the 251st Independent Anti-Tank Artillery Battalion lacked 41 57mm guns, three 75mm guns, 53 76mm guns, and nine 88mm guns, for a total of 106 guns. The 9th Artillery Division from the High Command Artillery Reserve was short 16 76mm guns, 31 120mm mortars, 33 122mm howitzers, and six 152mm howitzers, for a total of 86 guns.

On 15 January a large concentration of enemy motor vehicles was established in the Csor—Varpalota area. Simultaneously, the activities of the German 3rd Cavalry Brigade, which had earlier been noted in the Mestegne area, were established in the area north of Many. Hungarian soldiers who had defected to our side along the army's right flank testified to the movement of a large amount of motorized infantry, armored transports and tanks from the *Wiking* SS Panzer Division from 1300 on 15 January. This served as the basis for the chief of the army's intelligence

8 Editor's note. The DShK was a 12.7mm machine gun capable of firing up to 600 rounds per minute.

section to draw a conclusion and report to the army commander that according to defector and aerial reconnaissance data the enemy was pulling his forces back to Komarom, although hard data from aerial reconnaissance regarding the transfer of the IV SS Panzer Corps to the northwest had not been received. There were only reports that the enemy's motorized infantry and tanks were moving to the Komarom area; no intelligence means were able to establish where they subsequently moved.

Rumors to the effect that the enemy was preparing to attack from the Osi—Balatonakarttya area began to spread from the first days of the transfer of troops to this sector.

Prisoners and defectors from the Hungarian 20th Infantry Division, who had been captured or who had crossed the front line during 13-14 January in the Balatonakarttya area, testified that rumors were circulating among the soldiers as to the Germans' intentions to attack, together with Hungarian units, from the Balatonakarttya area.

Particular attention was paid to the Osi—Balatonakarttya area by the heavy movement of auto transport to the southeast along the roads from Lazi and Kisber to the southeast, through Veszprem and Varpalota, which had been noted by our aerial reconnaissance during the night of 14-15 January.

In order to fool our intelligence, the enemy carried out a regrouping of his forces from the Esztergom—Bicske area not along the nearest roads along the front, but by first pulling them back to the west to the Gyor area. It was namely this movement of the enemy's *Wiking* and *Totenkopf* panzer divisions from Esztergom to Gyor that the Hungarian soldiers who defected reported on 16 January. Our aerial reconnaissance carried out special observation of the enemy's movements on 16-17 January in the Varpalota area and did not discover any signs of him concentrating his forces in this area. The enemy carried out his regrouping in secret and took advantage of the night for this, with the employment of all necessary masking measures. Testimony from defectors, which was compared with the negative data from aerial reconnaissance and other information, led to the false conclusion that the enemy was pulling back his tank units to the west. Insofar as the enemy's maneuver toward the 4th Guards Army's left flank was not detected, then naturally the *front* commander did not exhibit particular concern. Quite the opposite; in order to strengthen the 46th Army's right flank, the 113th Rifle Division, which by the close of 16 January was concentrating in the Erd—Tolnok station area, was subordinated to this army. The headquarters of the 75th Rifle Corps was being shifted to this area at the disposal of the commander of the 46th Army, while the 991st Self-Propelled Artillery Regiment and the 523rd Anti-Tank Artillery Regiment were to be transferred as well. The 366th Self-Propelled Artillery Regiment was also transferred from the 4th Guards Army. All of these measures to reinforce the 46th Army were linked to the possibility of the encircled enemy group of force's breakthrough out of Budapest, which, according to prisoner testimony, had been set for 0900 on 17 January. For this reason, the *front* commander ordered that an artillery onslaught be conducted from 0845 to 0900 on 17 January against the enemy's jumping-off positions.

Thus the preparation by the German-Fascist command of a new counterblow was carried out with extreme secrecy. The IV SS Panzer Corps had been removed from the front north of Bicske and transferred to the Komarom area, where the soldiers were told that the corps was being pulled back in order to be reinforced and shifted to the central sector of the Eastern Front. The false movement of the IV SS Panzer Corps' radio stations to the north was carried out; strict radio silence was maintained for the actual regrouping. During the regrouping the enemy did not cease his demonstration activities northwest of Budapest.

The 18th Guards Tank Corps was to be in readiness for a counterattack in the direction of Budapest and Pilisvorosvar (there were only 49 combat vehicles ready). Quantitatively, matters were somewhat better in the 1st Guards Mechanized Corps, which had 133 tanks

(American M-4s[9] and M-2s[10]) and 37 100-mm self-propelled guns, for a total of 170 combat vehicles.

The poor flying weather aided the secrecy of the regrouping. By taking advantage of this, the German-Fascist command loaded up the corps' formations in Komarom into rail cars and shifted them first to Gyor, and them to Veszprem, where they were unloaded and quartered. Here the *Totenkopf* and *Wiking* panzer divisions had been brought up to strength in men, weapons and equipment and, according to prisoner testimony, brought up to authorized strength. The 1st and 3rd panzer divisions, which up until 11 January had been attacking in the Zamoly area, had been pulled back into the rear, reinforced with men, weapons and equipment and brought up to the breakthrough sector. All the movements and measures were carried out in the strictest secrecy. The rank and file had been forbidden to speak about where and why there units were moving. The panzer divisions began their movement to their jumping-off positions only during the second half of the night of 17-18 January, and the formation commanders issued combat assignments to their units for the offensive after 2000 on 17 January.

Thus by the close of January the enemy was ready to carry out a major counterblow for the purpose of relieving his encircled Budapest group of forces and destroying the main forces of the 4th Guards and 46th armies. In the event of this counterblow's success, the Hitlerite command hoped to distract the Soviet command's attention from East Prussia and Poland to the south and to secure the southern wing of its front.

The sector between Lake Velence and Lake Balaton had been chosen for launching the third counterblow. The Hitlerite command was pursuing far-reaching goals with the launching of this counterblow: to break through our defense by an attack between Lake Velence and Lake Balaton and reach the Danube north of Dunafoldvar, thus cutting the Third Ukrainian Front's forces in two. Covering itself from the south, it was to develop the main forces' attack around Lake Velence, and, upon arriving at Budapest from the south, relieve his encircled group of forces in conjunction with a supporting attack launched in the direction of Bicske. Along with this, the enemy would launch an attack into the rear of the 46th and 4th Guards armies and defeat and destroy the forces along the Third Ukrainian Front's right wing. The IX SS Corps was to prepared and launch a meeting attack from the Budapest area toward Budaors with the forces of the 13th Panzer Division and the *Feldherrnhalle* Division (as we shall see below, this attack was not carried out, due to the failure of the main forces' counterblow toward Budapest). It was planned to subsequently turn the main forces' attack to the south along the Danube and to simultaneously launch an attack with the forces of the Second Panzer Army from the area east of Nagykanizsa to the east and with the forces of Army Group Weichs from the southern bank of the Drava River along the Danube to the north. By a concentric attack from three directions, the offensive was to defeat or at least throw us back to the Danube River and deprive the Third Ukrainian Front's forces of the capability to launch major offensive operations for a long time; to seize major operational bridgeheads along the left bank of the Danube.

By 17 January the enemy had completed concentrating (the regrouping continued during 13-17 January) to the area southwest of Szekesfehervar the IV SS Panzer Corps (3rd SS *Totenkopf* Panzer Division, 5th SS *Wiking* Panzer Division and the 3rd Panzer Division), having left behind the 6th Panzer Division, the 3rd Cavalry Brigade and various Hungarian elements in the area north and northwest of Bicske. Thus along with the troops located southwest of Szekesfehervar, the enemy

9 Editor's note. The M-4 "Sherman" was a US-made medium tank which first appeared in 1942. One model weighed 30.3 tons and carried a crew of five. It was armed with a 75mm gun, a 50 caliber machine gun and two 30.06 machine guns. The tanks referred to here were probably obtained by the Red Army through Lend-Lease.

10 Editor's note. The M-2 was an American light tank that saw limited action during the Second World War. One model weighed 11.6 tons and carried a crew of four. It was armed with a 37mm gun.

disposed of the following: five panzer divisions (3rd SS *Totenkopf* Panzer Division, 5th SS *Wiking* Panzer Division, 1st and 3rd panzer divisions, and part of the 23rd Panzer Division's forces); one infantry division (Hungarian 25th Infantry Division); four independent brigades (303rd Assault Artillery Brigade, 17th Mortar Brigade, 19th Mortar Brigade, and the 4th Cavalry Brigade); three panzer battalions (a panzer battalion, two battalions of "Tiger" tanks); one artillery corps (403rd Artillery Corps), and; three reinforcement units; the combat strength of these forces was defined at 2,780 machine guns, 560 mortars, 535 guns, and 644 tanks a self-propelled guns.

Thus the new enemy group of forces had been reinforced by a number of independent tank units and artillery units from the high command reserve; the divisions had been reinforced with equipment, so that the group of forces was more powerful, according to the number of tanks and artillery tubes, than the enemy forces that had conducted the two previous counterblows. However, despite the significant forces that it managed to concentrate for the third counterblow, the Hitlerite command's plans were hopelessly adventurist and based completely on surprise and the force of the first attack and excluded a possible change in the correlation of forces during the operation in our favor. The German-Fascist command essentially committed an operational miscalculation: having suffered a failure in its offensive northwest of Budapest and along the Bicske axis, it decided to launch an attack with almost the same forces on Budapest along a lengthier route. The main attack was to be launched by the forces of the IV SS Panzer Corps from the line Csor—Lake Balaton, with a supporting attack by the forces of the III Panzer Corps along the front Sarkeresztes—Csor. The IV SS Panzer Corps' combat formation was in a single echelon. The IV Panzer Corps was to launch its main attack in the center along a 6-7 kilometer front with the forces of the *Totenkopf* and *Wiking* panzer divisions. The beginning of the offensive was set for 0500 on 18 January. The panzer divisions had the task of breaking through our defense, launching an attack as far as the line of the Kapos Csatorna Canal and the Sarviz Canal and to seize bridgeheads and develop the offensive to the northeast. The 3rd Panzer Division, reinforced by detachments from the 1st and 23rd panzer divisions and assault gun divisions, had the task, while attacking to the south and southeast, of securing the shock group's right flank. The 1st Panzer Division's attack on Szekesfehervar was to secure the shock group's left flank. The enemy plan called for a short artillery preparation and the accompaniment of the infantry and tank attack by concentrated fire.

The engineer troops were to secure passages in the obstacles for the infantry, tanks and artillery. The sapper units' main forces were to be concentrated in the zones of the SS panzer divisions launching the main attack. The task of covering and securing the panzer divisions' operations from the air was entrusted to the Fourth Air Fleet.

By this time the Third Ukrainian Front's operational situation was very unfavorable. Most of all, there was an absence of reserves, and the *front's* main forces were concentrated northwest of Budapest at a great distance from the axis of the enemy's main attack. The following formations and units were in the depth along the axis between Lake Velence and Lake Balaton: 7th Mechanized Corps (16th and 64th mechanized brigades, 41st Guards Tank Brigade) and the 69th Guards Rifle Division in the 4th Guards Army commander's reserve in the area of Szekesfehervar; the 18th Tank Corps had just finished concentrating to the *front* reserve in the area Paty—Zsambekir—Herceghalom station. Only the 113th Rifle Division was located in the 46th Army's reserve in the Erd area.

The following were in the armies' second echelon: in the 46th Army, one mechanized brigade from the 1st Guards Mechanized Corps in the Paty—Inje area and one mechanized brigade from the same corps in the Bicske area. In the 4th Guards Army the 63rd Cavalry Division was along the line height 313—the passing track north of Zamoly, and the 93rd Guards Rifle Division along the line height 176 (north of Patka)—Jeraksany. These second echelons were tied down by enemy actions along the Bicske and Zamoly axes.

The 74th Rifle Division was to be transferred to the 46th Army from the 57th Army, but it was supposed to concentrate in the Sarasd area only by the close of 23 January and was still on the march.

The *Stavka* of the VGK transferred to the *front* the 133rd Rifle Corps, which was supposed to concentrate in the area Seregelyes—Hor—Nagyperkata—Kitperkata area. By 18 January this corps had not completed its concentration: part of the artillery and the rear establishments were still *en route*. The 133rd Rifle Corps was poorly outfitted. The outfitting of the 46th and 4th Guards armies' forces was low. The average strength of the rifle divisions in the 46th Army did not exceed 4,200 men, and 4,800 men in the 4th Guards Army.

The operational density of our defense between Sarkeresztes and Lake Balaton was (counting the 7th Guards Mechanized Corps and the 1st Guards Fortified Area as a division) 12.6 kilometers per division, and with the reserves (7th Guards Mechanized Corps and the 69th Guards Rifle Division) 7.6 kilometers per division, and counting the 133rd Rifle Corps, 4.5 kilometers per division. Along the sector Csor—Lake Balaton, where the enemy was to launch his main attack, the operational density was 15 kilometers per division, and ten kilometers per division, including reserves.

It was planned to launch the IV Panzer Corps' attack along a 15-kilometer front along the sector of a single regiment from the 252nd Rifle Division and throughout the entire sector of the 1st Guards Fortified Area. The enemy had 560 tanks here, which amounted to an average of about 40 tanks per kilometer of front. In the center of the breakthrough sector the tank density was two times higher and reached 80-90 tanks and assault guns per kilometer of front. Against this enemy group of forces the 1st Guards Fortified Area had the following per kilometer of front: four heavy machine guns, four anti-tank rifles, 1.1 45mm guns, 1.6 76mm guns, and 1.4 mortars. On the average, there were 20-30 enemy tanks per gun for the 1st Guards Fortified Area. The 1st Guards Fortified Area's defense was shallow and, together with the anti-tank guns' firing positions did not exceed 1.5-2 kilometers. No anti-tank areas and positions had been created in the defensive depth. The reserve of the fortified area's commander consisted of one company from a motorcycle regiment and seven T-34 tanks. It should be noted that the German command disposed of outdated data on our forces along the breakthrough sector, determining them to be three rifle divisions and one fortified area. Actually, from 8 January there remained only one division and a single guards fortified area along the 15-kilometer front (the sector from Lake Halasto to Lake Balaton). Along the fortified area's entire nearly 13-kilometer front a total of 7,000 linear meters of trenches and 1,500 meters of communications trenches had been dug, and 3,000 anti-tank and 4,500 anti-personnel mines laid. Electrical obstacles had been erected in front of the front line along the sector from height 176 to Lake Balaton. The defense along the sector of the 252nd Rifle Division's 928th Rifle Regiment was better prepared. Three anti-tank areas, with 8-10 guns in each, were created along this regiment's 5-kilometer sector. There were 11 self-propelled guns in firing positions 4-5 kilometers from the forward edge. The combat formation was in two echelons. The defense along the Nadasdladany axis was echeloned up to five kilometers in depth. There were no men and equipment at the disposal of the commander of the 135th Rifle Corps, with which he could decisively influence the course of the fighting. He distributed his reserve—the 63rd Mechanized Brigade and a self-propelled artillery regiment—along the corps' entire front.

The level terrain eased the attack by the enemy's tank formations and, just the opposite, made the organization of a stable defense more difficult. The reclamation canals, the majority of which were not serious anti-tank obstacles along this sector, were the only natural lines, although the Sarviz Canal could be could have been an anti-tank obstacle, but it was a switch line. Along the southern sector the Kapos and Jelusa canals, which ran from east to west, could have been employed as natural anti-tank lines.

The bridgehead was limited by the Danube to a depth of 45-50 kilometers from the forward edge. The 17-kilometer wide bottleneck between the Danube and Lake Velence remained for operational maneuver. It was not possible to employ the 10-kilometer deep sector between Lake Velence and the forward edge for operational maneuver.

By the beginning of the enemy's third counterblow the correlation of forces was as follows (in favor of the enemy):

Table 12 Correlation of Forces for the Third German Counterblow, January 1945

	Enemy	Our Forces	Correlation
A. Along the Front Szarkeresztes—Lake Balaton			
Men	49,850	13,931	3.8:1
Machine Guns	2,644	723	3.9:1
Mortars	543	194	2.9:1
Guns	521	275	2.1:1
Tanks and Self-Propelled Guns	644	–	Absolute
B. Along the Sector Osi—Balatonakarttya			
Men	48,850	4,817	10.2:1
Machine Guns	2,391	329	7.3:1
Mortars	413	97	4.3:1
Guns	473	120	3.9:1
Tanks and Self-Propelled Guns	526	–	Absolute

Such an enemy superiority in men and materiel along the axis of his main attack should have unconditionally guaranteed him initial success in breaking through the defense along the 4th Guards Army's left flank.

Simultaneously, while preparing a meeting attack from Budapest, the commander of the IX SS Mountain Corps ordered his forces at 2300 on 17 January to abandon the Pest bridgehead and pull back the troops (22nd SS Cavalry Division and the 1st Motorized Division) by 0700 to the western bank of the Danube River and to blow up the bridges.

At 0630 on 18 January the enemy, following an hour-long artillery preparation, attacked from the line west of Osi and Csajag and from the Sarkeresztes area with the forces of the III and IV SS panzer corps. The offensive was supported by the enemy's artillery and mortar fire. Units and subunits of the 1st Guards Fortified Area and the 252nd Rifle Division's 928th Rifle Regiment opened fire from all types of guns. Fierce fighting unfolded along the entire front from Osi to Lake Balaton.

The first enemy attacks were beaten back. His aviation repeatedly bombed our forces southwest of Szekesfehervar (more than 300 sorties were noted) opposite the 9th and 2nd machine gun-artillery battalions' defense.

The 17th Air Army concentrated all of its efforts on repelling the counterblow, carrying out 718 sorties on 18 January and shooting down 37 enemy planes in 43 air battles. The 5th Air Army, which was limited in its operations by the poor weather, was unable to take part in repelling the counterblow until 20 January and operated only in the interests of the Second Ukrainian Front.

A feature of the 17th Air Army's operations was that, without ceasing its combat activities in support of the troops, it had to rebase a number of divisions (189th Assault Air, 288th Fighter and 262nd Night Bomber divisions) from airfields located in the area Szekesfehervar—Borgond—Nagyperkata area to airfields east of the Danube River. The air army thus concentrated its main efforts against the enemy's tank groups, mainly using assault aircraft, operating in groups of 20-30 planes, and 4-6 planes in poor weather.

Uninterrupted aerial reconnaissance helped the *front* command understand a rapidly changing situation, while the centralized control of the 17th and 5th air armies from the command post of the 17th Air Army commander enabled us to direct our aviation's efforts against the enemy's most vulnerable areas.

The III Panzer Corps' fierce attacks along the Sarkeresztes—Csor sector, each of which was supported by 30-40 tanks and self-propelled guns, were successfully repulsed by our forces. The enemy launched his main attack along the IV SS Panzer Corps' sector along the sector southwest of Osi and Csajag, committing 150 tanks and self-propelled guns and up to 60 armored transports into the fighting simultaneously.

The army commander adopted a number of emergency measures. Within two hours of the start of the offensive by the enemy's main forces (at 0830), the following army reserves were dispatched to the breakthrough sector: one anti-tank artillery regiment and one self-propelled artillery regiment (from the army mobile anti-tank reserve and the 7th Guards Mechanized Corps) were placed at the disposal of the fortified area's commandant. Simultaneously, he resubordinated his anti-tank artillery reserve (two anti-tank artillery regiments) to the commander of the 135th Rifle Corps, while he shifted the army mobile obstacle detachment (one engineer-sapper battalion) to Szabadbattyan. The army commander ordered the commander of the 7th Guards Mechanized Corps to immediately leave for the Falubattyan—Urhida area and be ready to counterattack the enemy's breakthrough units. The 93rd Rifle Division was moved from the area northeast of Szekesfehervar to the line Fejer station—Zihfalva—Tac. Somewhat later, two of the 133rd Rifle Corps' divisions (21st and 122nd), on orders from the *front* commander, were to be moved to the line excluding Tac—Kirp (two kilometers south of Nagylang. The 133rd Rifle Corps' third division was also aroused and moved to the area Sashalom—Petele—excluding Seregelyes.

The commitment of the army and *front* reserves in detail was a forced measure and, it did not promise great success, then it might have halted the enemy's offensive.

The German tanks, having an overwhelming superiority in forces, broke through the fortified area's shallow defense and reached the rear, capturing Osi and Sandorka.

The 9th Independent Machine Gun-Artillery Battalion beat off seven enemy attacks until 1500. The battalion's soldiers, sergeants and officers fought heroically. Guards Sergeant Fesenko, having been seriously wounded, did not leave the battlefield and continued to fight the enemy. Guards Sergeant Kursak knocked out an enemy tank with a 45mm gun and, when he ran out of shells, killed seven Germans with a carbine. The entire crew of a 45mm gun was put out of action by enemy fire. The battery commander, Guards Senior Lieutenant Skvirtsov, manned the gun himself and knocked out two tanks. Guards Sergeant Debel'skii, who was wounded, crawled up to an enemy tank and blew it up with grenades.

It was only by 1600, when the 9th Independent Machine Gun-Artillery Battalion had lost all of its weapons, that the enemy managed to capture the battalion's positions and break into Balatonfokajar, where fierce fighting broke out.

The fortified area's subunits were fighting in scattered groups, without artillery support from the depth. By 1300 the enemy's tanks and armored transports had attacked Urhida. By this time units of the 7th Mechanized Corps reached the Urhida—Falubattyan area and joined in the fighting against the enemy's tanks from the march and by the onset of darkness were holding them along the approaches to the Sarviz Canal. The corps' units destroyed up to 40 enemy tanks and self-propelled guns in this fighting.

The army commander shifted two anti-tank artillery regiments, one light artillery regiment, one howitzer regiment, one anti-aircraft artillery regiment, and two engineer-sapper battalions to the eastern bank of the Sarviz Canal. The artillery took up firing positions for firing over open sights, while the engineer subunits blew up six bridges over the canal and laid about 5,000 anti-tank mines.

In turn, the *front* commander undertook further measures to repel the enemy's counterblow, rousting the 18th Tank Corps, which was moving to the Aba—Sertesz—Sarkeresztur area from 1800, with one brigade moving to the Injefalva—Bebic area.

The enemy was attempting to take advantage of his success as quickly as possible. By the close of 18 January his units reached the Sarszentmihaly—Falubattyan—Polgardi—Lepseny area and continued to spread to the northeast.

As a result of the day's fighting, the enemy managed to break through our defense along the army's left flank and advance 16-30 kilometers into the depth.

The enemy's losses amounted to more than 120 tanks and assault guns, 60 armored transports and a large number of personnel.

Our units hurriedly occupied defensive lines along the Sarviz Canal. The 93rd Rifle Division, which had been transferred from the army commander's reserve, occupied defense positions along the eastern bank of the canal from Urhida to Szabadbattyan. The 9th Tank Brigade, from the 20th Guards Rifle Corps, was attached to strengthen the division. The 252nd Rifle Division, which had suffered heavy losses, fell back and was putting up resistance along the line two kilometers west of Imr—east of Sarszentmihaly. The 69th Guards Rifle Division occupied defensive positions along the western and southern outskirts of Szekesfehervar. By the close of the day, the 8th Mechanized Corps, part of whose forces had reached the western bank of the Sarviz Canal, was, together with other units, repelling the enemy's attempts to force the canal along the line east of Urhida. Its 63rd Mechanized Brigade was making a fighting movement from the Urhida area to the Polgardi area. The *front* commander entrusted the battle with the enemy who had broken through south of Falubattyan to the 18th Tank and 135th Rifle corps.

In order to cover the line five kilometers northwest of Cece—Saregres—Simontornya, a composite group from training subunits and units was formed. However, by the close of 18 January the defense in the Sertesz area along the eastern bank of the Sarviz Canal had still not been occupied by our forces. The enemy in this area forced the Sarviz Canal at night and captured Simontornya. While continuing to develop the offensive during the night, by the morning of 19 January he captured Saregres and a bridgehead on the eastern bank of the Sarviz Canal and was able to lay down crossings in the areas of Urhida, Szabadbattyan and Tac.

The *front* commander, taking into account the possibility of active enemy operations along the *front's* southern wing, and in connection with the commitment of the Bulgarian 1st Army to the front line and a certain weakening of the 57th Army's strength, issued an order to reinforce the 57th Army's defense. It was ordered to have five rifle divisions in the first echelon and two rifle divisions and the 32nd Mechanized Brigade in the second. The army was assigned the basic task of preventing an enemy breakthrough along the army's defensive front into the rear of the *front's* main group of forces.

The *front* commander demanded the further development of engineering defense and its echeloning in the depth (the creation of a second zone, switch positions, anti-tank strong points, etc.).

The commander of the 4th Guards Army adopted a series of measures to strengthen the defense. Units of the 93rd Guards and 252nd rifle divisions were subordinated to the 21st Guards Rifle Corps, which also contained the 41st Guards and 84th rifle divisions defending along the front line and the 69th Guards Rifle Corps, assigned to defend the town. Bridges were blown up all along the canal under the leadership of the chief of the army's engineer troops. By 0100 on 19 January all the bridges in Tac, Falubattyan, Sarszentmihaly, and Feven had been blown up. Our artillery was intensively firing against crossing areas.

Throughout the night and under the cover of fire, the enemy had been hurriedly constructing crossings along a sector of the Sarviz Canal between Szabadbattyan and Tac and by morning had begun to force the canal. The weather was suitable for flying and only the enemy's air force was operating during the first half of the day (carrying out up to 350 sorties), without encountering any resistance from ours, and it was only during the second half of the day that our aviation began to operate actively, launching mass strikes against the enemy's personnel and combat equipment, while carrying out 745 sorties.

When the threat of the enemy outflanking Lake Velence from the south and penetrating into the area between Lake Velence and the Danube River became clear, the commander of the 4th Guards Army adopted emergency measures to organize a defensive line between Lake Velence and the Danube River. The 63rd Cavalry Division received orders to organize a defense along the line Kapolnasnyek—Kapolnasnyek station, with the task of preventing the enemy's breakthrough to the north. Anti-tank batteries and a battalion of rocket-powered mortars were moved up to this line.

At dawn on 19 January the main forces of the IV SS Panzer Corps (the *Wiking* and *Totenkopf* panzer divisions), having forced the Sarviz Canal, continued to develop the offensive to the east, striving to reach the Danube and thus split the Third Ukrainian Front's forces into two parts. The enemy was making his main attack south of Lake Velence. Simultaneously, he was attacking with part of his forces in the direction of the western and southwestern outskirts of Szekesfehervar. He halted the III Panzer Corps' unsuccessful attacks along the Sarkeresztur—Csor sector and committed the latter's main forces into the already-accomplished breakthrough.

In these conditions, the *front* commander made the decision to reinforce the southern approaches to Budapest, and for this purpose ordered the 5th Guards Cavalry Corps (11th and 12th guards cavalry divisions), along with reinforcements, to be detached from the 46th Army and concentrated in the Nagyperkata—Adony station—Szabolcs—Gyorg—Fedescikola area, where it was to be operationally subordinated to the commander of the 4th Guards Army. Simultaneously, the 63rd Cavalry Division was to be detached from the 20th Guards Rifle Corps and returned to its own corps.

The 18th Guards Tank Corps, which was arriving in the Aba—Sarkeresztur area, entered the fighting from the march, holding the enemy's advance. However, the enemy's units, while outflanking the 18th Guards Tank Corps from the south, vigorously advanced to the east. During the middle of the day on 19 January up to 25 enemy tanks and a battalion of motorized infantry reached the Danube River and captured Dunapentele. Somewhat later, the enemy, having moved through Nagyperkata, captured Adony, and continued to spread to the south along the Sarviz Canal with part of his forces. Southeast of Lake Balaton, the enemy's 3rd Panzer Division, having overcome resistance by units of the 1st Guards Fortified Area in the Lepseny area, captured Mezokomarom. The Hungarian 25th Infantry Division was advancing behind the 3rd Panzer Division.

By the close of the day the forces of the 4th Guards Army remained along their previously occupied lines with the forces of the 31st, 68th and 20th guards rifle corps. The forces of the 21st Guards Rifle Corps, along with units of the 7th Mechanized Corps (the 7th Mechanized Corps, having suffered heavy losses in the preceding fighting, had only nine T-34 tanks and up to 500 motor vehicles in its ranks), were engaged in intensive defensive battles with the attacking enemy along the line Sarpentele—Szentvencel—west of Feven—Dambi. The 1st Guards Mechanized Corps occupied its previous position with three mechanized brigades (1st, 2nd and 3rd guards). Its 9th Guards Tank Brigade, together with the 93rd Guards Rifle Division, was engaged in heavy defensive fighting south of the city of Szekesfehervar along the line Sarpentele—Szentandel.

The 133rd Rifle Corps, which was arriving from the *Stavka* reserve, was to be subordinated to the 4th Guards Army at 0600 on 20 January.

It's necessary to note that from the start of the German-Fascist forces' first counterblow and throughout the following second and third counterblows, the formations' organizational structure had been disrupted. In a number of instances, individual brigades and divisions were removed from one or another formation, which weakened their shock force and, on the whole, lowered the combat possibilities of the given formation, which often led to dispersing their men and materiel.

Thus by the close of 19 January an extremely difficult situation had developed along the Third Ukrainian Front's center. The enemy's shock tank group, not meeting any serious resistance, developed the offensive to the east and southeast. Simultaneously, the encircled enemy group of forces in Budapest (IX SS Army Corps) had completed by the close of 19 January all of its preparatory measures for launching a meeting attack. The enemy was threatening the crossings over the Danube River and was trying to capture the road junction of Szekesfehervar. South of Szekesfehervar were our weak forces, which were unable to put up serious resistance to the enemy's tank divisions.

The enemy tanks, having arrived in the operational depth of our troops' defense, encircled the 18th Tank and 135th Rifle corps' formations that had been moving up to the front line. The *front's* forces had been cut in two. All the communications and communications lines along the right bank of the Danube River had been cut. There were no operational reserves, from which we could have constructed a new defensive front. In these conditions, our command carried out a maneuver of men and materiel from the quiet sectors and adopted emergency measures to create defensive lines in the depth and, particularly, along the breakthrough's flanks. The 5th Guards Cavalry Corps, which had been operationally subordinated to the 4th Guards Army, left for its zone by forced march and at 2300 on 19 January set about organizing a defense between Lake Velence and the Danube River along the line Kisvelence—Groftanya—Gyorg—Katalin—Eregmajor. The corps was reinforced with three anti-tank regiments, two howitzer regiments, one mortar regiment, a battalion from the 123rd Cannon-Artillery Brigade, a regiment of 100mm self-propelled guns, and a guards mortar regiment. The corps' task was to prevent the enemy from breaking through to the encircled group of forces in Budapest. The width of the corps' defensive zone did not exceed 20 kilometers. The corps was organized into a single echelon. The divisions were organized into two echelons. By the morning of 20 January a density of up to 18 guns and mortars and five tanks and self-propelled guns had been created in the corps' defensive zone per kilometer of front.

Thus as early as daybreak on 20 January a stable defensive front had been created along the line Sarszentmihaly—Szentfendel, Borgond, Lake Velence—Kisvelence—Felsobesnyo—Szinatelep.

The 17th Air Army, while maintaining air superiority and carrying out up to 450 sorties every day, continued to launch mass strikes against the enemy's tank groups. Night bomber aviation, while launching 220-230 strikes every night against the concentration areas of the enemy's tanks and against his arriving tank columns, exhausted and wore them out before they even entered the fighting.

In order to concentrate all of Marshal of the Soviet Union Tolbukhin's efforts toward defeating the enemy group of forces along the external encirclement front, the destruction of the enemy's group of forces encircled in Budapest was entrusted to the forces of Marshal of the Soviet Union Malinovskii at 1000 on 20 January. This enabled us to carry out a reorganization of troop control along the Third Ukrainian Front's right wing and to create more flexible control.

Following the reorganization of the control of the 4th Guards Army, which was repelling the enemy's counterblows, also disposed of the newly-subordinated 5th Guards Cavalry Corps.

In order to relieve the burden on the army and to concentrate its efforts on repelling the enemy's counterblow, the *front* commander, on the basis of the *Stavka's* instructions of 19 January, transferred the 31st and 68th rifle corps, along with their combat sectors, to the 46th Army and established a new boundary line between the armies of Mor—Csokako—Csakvar—Vertesacsa—Val—Baracska, with all locales, except for Csokako and Csakvar for the 46th Army. Somewhat later the 135th Rifle Corps was also transferred from the 4th Guards Army to the 46th Army and thus the size of the 4th Guards Army was made easier to control. In this matter, as in others, one could feel the guiding role of the *Stavka* of the VGK.

According to captured operational documents from the Sixth Army, which was part of Army Group South, the German-Fascist command's plan for 20 January was as follows. The IV SS Panzer Corps' shock group was to continue to break through to the northeast for the purpose of seizing the passage between the Danube and Lake Velence and creating bridgehead fortifications along the Sarviz Canal. Along the cavalry corps' sector (6th Panzer Division and the 3rd Cavalry Brigade), the main efforts were to be concentrated north of the Bicske—Many line for a further offensive to the south or east.

The LVII Panzer Corps was to hold its front line.

It was planned to shift the Hungarian 25th Infantry Division around the northern extremity of Lake Balaton to the Sio sector. The division was to be attached to the IV SS Panzer Corps. An armored battalion from the *Feldherrnhalle* Division was to operate along with the Hungarian 25th Infantry Division.

Due to the beginning of the First Ukrainian Front's offensive, the German-Fascist command of Army Group South set about transferring two infantry divisions and the headquarters of the LVII Panzer Corps to eastern Silesia from the area west of the Hron River.

On the morning of 20 January the enemy continued to attack to the east and northeast, striving to capture Szekesfehervar and break through to his group of forces encircled in Budapest, covering himself from the southwest along the line of the Jelusa Canal and the Kapos Canal, and from the south and southeast along the line Sarszentmiklos—Dunapentele. During the second half of the day his tanks and motorized infantry reached the Adony—Gardony area and came into contact with units of the 5th Guards Cavalry Corps.

The *front* commander and the commander of the 4th Guards Army continued to take measures to strengthen the defense. The 7th Guards Mechanized Corps, which had suffered heavy losses in equipment, was pulled back to the left bank of the Danube for refitting and organizing a defense. All of its equipment was concentrated in a single brigade (16th Mechanized), which remained subordinated to the commander of the 4th Guards Army. The 233rd and 236th rifle divisions were to be pulled out of the 57th Army's front line in order to create new reserves and for employing them to defend the southern sector of the newly-created defensive front. Along the 4th Guards Army's right flank, the army's forces were pulled back to the line three kilometers northwest of Szekesfehervar—the fork in the roads west of Lake Sosto—Techen—north of Kisfalud (south)—the western shore of Lake Velence, in order to eliminate the dangerous salient west of Szekesfehervar, which was unsecured from the south. This achieved not only an improvement in the tactical position of the defense in the Szekesfehervar area, but also freed up two rifle divisions (93rd and 252nd) from the front line. A number of artillery units were also freed up from the front.

In order to reinforce the Third Ukrainian Front, the *Stavka* of the VGK in turn transferred to it the 30th Rifle Corps (69th and 36th guards and 155th rifle divisions) from the Second Ukrainian Front. However, this corps could not be employed immediately, because it was far from the area of combat operations and by the close of 20 January was concentrating in the Domsod—Szalkszentmarton—Kunszentmiklos area. Besides this, the corps' strength was low.

In order to strengthen the 4th Guards Army's left flank, the *front* commander resubordinated the 113th Rifle Division and the 1st Guards Mechanized Corps, consisting of two brigades and three self-propelled artillery regiments, to the commander of the 4th Guards Army, while the latter, in turn, transferred the 113th Rifle Division to the commander of the cavalry corps, who stationed it in the corps' second echelon, employing the anti-tank line of the Vali River and covering the main paved road to Budapest. The mechanized corps was stationed in the second echelon, behind the cavalry corps.

The new defensive line was reinforced by a number of artillery units that had been moved up to it. Thus by the close of 20 January a sufficiently strong anti-tank defense had already been created to a depth of 7-8 kilometers between Lake Velence and the Danube River, with an operational density of four kilometers per division, (counting two mechanized brigades as one division) and with an artillery density of 26 tubes per kilometer of front.

During this period the enemy, who had broken through to the Danube River and the Jelusa Canal, was forced to reduce the pace of his advance. The reason for this is that our troops were continuing to hold Szekesfehervar, through which the main communications feeding the German-Fascist forces' shock tank group of forces had to run. Also, the presence of the IV SS Panzer Corps in the rear of our forces (18th Guards Tank and 135th Rifle corps) tied down the maneuver possibilities of the enemy's shock group to a significant degree. Besides this, it was necessary for the enemy to concentrate his forces, which had been scattered in the breakthrough zone, to the sector between Lake Velence and the Danube River, to bring up his lagging infantry, to organize the cover of his right flank, and to bring up his rear organs (fuel and munitions). Due to the above-listed reasons, the enemy's actions on 20 January were of a limited character.

Having regrouped his *Wiking* and *Totenkopf* panzer divisions during 20 January, the enemy carried out a nighttime reconnaissance in force between the Danube and Lake Velence. The enemy's attacks were beaten off along the cavalry corps' entire front. Only in the 12th Cavalry Division's sector did a group of tanks and armored transports manage to break through to the Aggszentpeter area. There it was encircled by subunits of the 43rd Cavalry Regiment. At 0500 on 21 January, following a brief but powerful artillery preparation, the enemy attacked the cavalry corps' units, launching his main attacks as follows: part of the 5th SS *Wiking* Panzer Division's forces along Lake Velence from Gardony and Hajdu on Kisvelence and Kapolnasnyek, and with the forces of the 3rd SS *Totenkopf* Panzer Division from the area north of Adonyszabolcs station and toward Aggszentpeter. In all, about 150 enemy tanks attacked simultaneously in the corps' sector. Simultaneously, the enemy attacked in up to a battalion in strength, with 17 tanks, the 61st Guards Rifle Division in the direction of Sarviz, for the purpose of tying down the 57th Army's main forces and to prevent their being shifted to the Budapest axis, and broke into the first trench line. Besides this, individual subunits crossed the Danube River on 40 pontoons and occupied the unnamed island northwest of Vukovar. The enemy along the main axis, at the cost of heavy losses, managed to capture Kisvelence and Kapolnasnyek, but a counterattack by units of the 5th Guards Cavalry Corps threw the enemy out of the northern part of Kapolnasnyek. The enemy only managed to penetrate slightly into our defense along the rest of his attack front.

Thus as early as 21 January our defense between Lake Velence and the Danube River was already so strong that it was able to withstand the fierce pressure of two of the IV SS Panzer Corps' two panzer divisions, which had been concentrated along a 9-kilometer front.

At the same time, the 133rd Rifle and 18th Tank corps, which were fighting in encirclement, received orders to break out to the southwest and reach the line Alap—Eloszallas. At 1200 on 20 January these corps made an attempt to break out, but were unsuccessful. The attack was repeated on the night of 20-21 January. The corps broke through in two columns through the enemy's forces and in the middle of the day on 21 January reached the area Eloszallas—Alap, occupying defensive positions in this area. The 18th Tank Corps' 110th Tank Brigade, captured Hercegfalva while breaking out of the encirclement and, having only ten combat-ready tanks, held this locale until 24 January, repelling the enemy's numerous attacks and only on 24 January was it forced to abandon Hercegfalva and consolidate 1.5 kilometers to the south.

As a shortcoming, one must make note that in order to destroy the enemy group of tanks that had broken through to the Aggszentpeter area, the cavalry corps commander detailed insufficient forces (three squadrons and six tanks), which enabled the enemy to beat off the counterattacking subunits in detail and to subsequently accumulate forces in this tactically important area.

Alongside the repulse of the enemy attacks, measures for strengthening the defense continued. At 0400 on 21 January the commander of the 5th Guards Cavalry Corps was given operational control over the 1st Guards Mechanized Corps, units of which came into contact with the enemy at 1100, with the task of eliminating, along with units of the 5th Guards Cavalry Corps, the enemy groups that had broken into the Kapolnasnyek and Aggszentpeter areas. Then, in order to prevent the enemy's arrival from Kapolnasnyek to Baracska, the 93rd Rifle Division (which had been removed from a quiet sector) was moved to the line Sukoro—northern outskirts of Kapolnasnyek, for the purpose of occupying defensive positions facing southeast. Simultaneously, the 252nd Rifle Division moved to the line Pettend—Annamajor—Kishalom, with its front facing south, where it was subordinated to the commander of the 5th Guards Cavalry Corps, forming its second echelon. The 122nd Rifle Division (133rd Rifle Corps), which had become separated from the corps while leaving the encirclement, broke through to the north and joined the 5th Guards Cavalry Corps, strengthening its defense. The 68th Rifle Division (30th Rifle Corps) crossing over to the right bank of the Danube, occupied defensive positions along the line Nagykaracsony—Cece, while the 74th Rifle Division, which had completely concentrated to the Dunafoldvar area, moved up to the line Kisapostag—Nagykaracsony—Robertvolgy. The 36th Rifle Division concentrated in the Dunafoldvar area.

Thus a continuous front had been organized along the sector between the Danube River and the Sarviz Canal by the forces of two of the 30th Rifle Corps' divisions, two of the 133rd Rifle Corps' divisions, the 57th Army's 74th Rifle Division, and the 18th Tank Corps and individual artillery reinforcement units.

The 57th Army's 233rd Rifle Division, which was moving up on auto transport and by rail, was concentrating in the Pincehely area. The 133rd Rifle Corps, along with the 18th Tank Corps, made a fighting advance to the area south of Hercegfalva—Dunafoldvar—Alsosismanto—height 164—Eloszallas—Alap—Cece. The 18th Tank Corps contained 29 tanks and 12 self-propelled guns.

Simultaneously, measures were adopted to strengthen the 5th Guards Cavalry Corps' anti-tank defense. The corps was reinforced with three sapper companies, which had been supplied with anti-tank mines.

The 113th Rifle Division was preparing a defense along the line Kis—Ranszentpeter—Simon—marker 125.

Attaching great significance to Szekesfehervar, upon the capture of which the shock group would dispose of good communications, the German-Fascist command was making great efforts to capture the city.

The enemy plan for 22 January called for destroying our forces in the Hercegfalva—Sarbogard area with the forces of the IV SS Panzer Corps' 3rd Panzer Division. The forces of the *Wiking* Panzer Division would continue to develop the attack in the direction of Budapest, while the forces of the *Totenkopf* Panzer Division would attack in the direction of Etyek. At the same time, the main forces of the 1st Panzer Division were to be brought up to secure the left flank.

Following a short artillery preparation, which began at 0530 on 22 January, the enemy's tanks and infantry attacked. The 3rd SS *Totenkopf* Panzer Division attacked in the direction of Aggszentpeter. Part of the 5th SS *Wiking* Panzer Division attacked in the direction of the eastern suburbs of Szekesfehervar, while the 1st Panzer Division attacked the western outskirts of Szekesfehervar.

At dawn units of the enemy's 23rd Panzer Division attacked from the area east of Sarkeresztes in the direction of Szekesfehervar.

As is known, the threatening situation that had arisen by 22 January along the line between Lake Velence and the Danube River forced us to transfer from the center of the front units of the 252nd and 93rd rifle divisions and a significant part of the reinforcement artillery to this sector.

The Szekesfehervar defensive front, which was occupied by units of the 21st Guards Rifle Corps (41st Guards, 84th and 69th Guards rifle divisions), had been heavily weakened. At the same time, the enemy, having outflanked Szekesfehervar from the northwest, west and south as a result of the January fighting, occupied a very favorable operational situation in relation to it. The enemy had concentrated more than 150 tanks and self-propelled guns along the main attack sectors. As a result of repeated fierce attacks, the enemy managed to push back the 21st Guards Rifle Corps' defending units and capture the city and suburbs of Szekesfehervar by 1800. Simultaneously, up to 30 enemy tanks and a regiment of infantry attacked our units north of Szekesfehervar from the Szarkeresztes area and captured Gyulamajor, thus freeing up the lateral road from Szekesfehervar to Zamoly.

Southeast of Lake Velence, the enemy continued his unbroken attacks along the entire front of the 5th Guards Cavalry Corps, directing his main efforts in the area of the Felsobesnyo. In an attack involving up to 100 tanks and armored transports, with a significant amount of infantry (5-6 battalions), he managed to break through the 12th Guards Cavalry Division's defense in the Aggszentpeter area and thus form a narrow "sack" up to three kilometers wide and to a depth of 4-5 kilometers. His further advance was delayed by the forces of the 1st Guards Mechanized Brigade and part of the 5th Guards Cavalry Corps' forces. During the day the enemy lost up to 70 tanks and 23 armored transports. The enemy's offensive was supported by large aviation forces. However, the actions of the enemy's aviation were relatively effective only during the first 2-3 hours of the offensive.

The actions by Marshal of the Soviet Union Tolbukhin's forces during this period were supported by two air armies. They carried out 1,034 sorties during the day's fighting. Our aviation's air superiority in the middle and second half of the day determined the subsequent course of the fighting. 36 enemy planes were shot down in air battles. Massed strikes were carried out against concentration areas of the enemy's tanks and infantry, particularly against the Szekesfehervar area. By 1900 the enemy's offensive had been halted by air strikes and fire from three artillery regiments that had been moved up to the Szekesfehervar. Units of three divisions (41st and 69th guards and 84th rifle divisions) consolidated along the line Tallian—west of Csala—Kisfalud station—Pakozd. On orders from the *front* commander, the 223rd Rifle Division was transferred from the 46th Army to the 4th Guards Army for employment in organizing a defense along this line. At 2400 the division was operationally subordinated to the commander of the 21st Guards Rifle Corps.

In order to distract the enemy from the axis of his main attack, active operations were begun by two of the 30th Rifle Corps' rifle divisions, which were defending along the southern sector adjacent to the Danube River. These divisions, while pushing back the enemy's covering units, began to slowly advance and by the close of 22 January they reached the line four kilometers south of Dunapentele—south of Krisztina—northern edge of the Kokasd woods—Erde—Baracsmeted station—Andgyorg—Nagybartal.

In order to eliminate the salient south of Tatabanya, the 68th Rifle Corps was pulled back during the night of 22-23 January to the line Szar station—Kertveles—Verteskozma—Gant and occupied this line with a single rifle division. The corps' second division occupied the line Vertesboglar—Vertesacsa and further along the canal.

The German-Fascist command's plan for 23 January called for the forces of the III Panzer Corps to continue attacking along the right flank through Pakozd to Vertesacsa. The forces of the 6th and 3rd panzer divisions would attack through the Bicske—Zsambek line in the direction of Etyek and capture the latter. On the morning of 23 January the IV SS Panzer Corps was to break through the 5th Guards Cavalry Corps' line, having concentrated for this purpose all three panzer divisions and all available artillery. Their missions were, following a powerful artillery preparation and by means of densely concentrating in one place, to first break through and then widen and breach and break through to Budapest. On 23 January Hitler ordered the encircled group of forces in Budapest to continue "to hold Budapest until the hour of liberation tolls." The Hungarian Third Army took command of the 3rd Panzer Division, the 25th Infantry Division and the 23rd Reconnaissance Battalion, with the mission of holding the Sio Canal. The 3rd Panzer Division, having concentrated its forces in the area between the Sarviz Canal and Dunafoldvar, was to clear this area of the enemy and, in particular, to destroy the 18th Tank Corps' units there. The mission of the Hungarian II Army Corps was, as before, to guard the northern shore of Lake Balaton. A boundary was established between group "Pape" (25th Infantry Division) and the II Army Corps along the line Varpalota—Balatonakarttya and the southern shore of Lake Balaton.

The Second Panzer Army's task was to break through the 57th Army's front north and south of Nagybajom with the forces of the LXVIII Army Corps' 1st Mountain and 71st Infantry divisions. The XXII Mountain Corps, together with the newly-arrived units of the 118th Light Infantry Division, was to tie down the 57th Army's main forces (2½ rifle divisions and one tank brigade) from the front and, following the breakthrough to Nagybajom, link up with the LXVIII Army Corps' offensive. On 23 January the enemy, without halting his fierce attacks along the axis of his main attack, attempted, as had been expected, to launch simultaneous diversionary attacks along the Bicske axis and north of Szekesfehervar, calculating that our forces had weakened these axes, and trying to disperse our forces. Along the Bicske axis the enemy, following a powerful artillery preparation, launched an attack with the forces of the 6th Panzer Division and 3rd Cavalry Brigade from the line Szomor—Csabdi. He managed to capture Many and advance beyond the Bicske—Zsambek road. However, the enemy was halted by counterattacks by units of the 59th Guards Rifle Division and the 2nd Guards Mechanized Corps' 5th Guards Mechanized Brigade and 37th Guards Tank Brigade and was again thrown back beyond the road. Having suffered heavy casualties, he was forced to halt his attacks. North of Szekesfehervar, the enemy attacked in the direction of Patka with up to 50 tanks and armored transports and infantry. All of his attacks along this axis were beaten back. Along the southern sector of the breakthrough front the enemy, while opposing our forces' attack, launched a series of attacks with up to 30 tanks and self-propelled guns. The enemy was trying along the axis of his main attack to develop the success achieved in the Aggszentpeter area and reach the rear of the 11th Guards Cavalry Division with an attack from this area. However, he had little success during the day.

A significant role was played along this sector by the 252nd and 113th rifle divisions, which had been moved up in time to this line and which repulsed the enemy tank attacks by fire from all kinds of weapons.

During the day's fighting the enemy carried out 536 sorties along the 4th Guards Army's sector, of which 178 were transport flights, while our aviation carried out 723 sorties.

At this time the headquarters of the 133rd Rifle Corps was attached to the 57th Army and had the 233rd and 236th rifle divisions subordinated to it. The 57th Army's right-flank boundary line with the 133rd Rifle Corps was established along the Sarviz Canal. The commander of the 133rd Rifle Corps was responsible for the boundary.

The enemy's enormous losses in anti-tank artillery from our artillery and mortar fire, as well as from air strikes, forced the German-Fascist command to issue an order "on preserving captured Russian anti-tank guns and forming anti-tank defense subunits, armed with Russian equipment." Information was received from the forces of the IV SS Panzer Corps that there would be fuel only for 23-24 January. Due to this, measures were taken to reduce fuel expenditure norms and reinforce the IV SS Panzer Corps with anti-tank artillery from Hungarian formations.

A new boundary line between Army Group Balck (a cavalry corps) and the Eighth Army along the junction of the borders of three countries to the bend in the Danube near Vaicen and Gyongyos.

During the night of 23-24 January the enemy, having partially regrouped his forces and following a powerful hour-long artillery preparation and, having concentrated more than 100 tanks and 70 self-propelled guns, launched an attack in the direction of Kapolnasnyek and Pettend. He managed to break through the 5th Guards Cavalry Corps' defense, crush part of its forces and force the corps to fall back to the second prepared defensive line along the line of the center and northern part of Velence—northern outskirts of Kapolnasnyek—Pettend—Anna—Kollegium—Kis—Racszentpeter—Ismon, which were occupied by the 252nd and 93rd rifle divisions and units of the 1st Guards Mechanized Corps.

An instructive moment in this period was the employment of night bombers for a strike against the enemy's artillery and mortar firing positions during the artillery preparation. The 17th Air Army carried out 413 sorties and sharply reduced the intensity of the enemy's artillery and mortar fire during the second period of the artillery preparation, which lasted two hours and ten minutes.

The 5th SS *Wiking* Panzer Division, 1st Panzer Division, 3rd SS *Totenkopf* Panzer Division, part of the 3rd Panzer Division's forces, and independent subunits and units of heavy tanks and self-propelled guns attacked opposite the front of the 5th Guards Cavalry Corps. All of the German Sixth Army's artillery was concentrated to this area for supporting the attack by the panzer divisions.

At dawn the enemy reinforced his attacking units with fresh reserves and continued to attack in the direction of Baracska. A group of enemy tanks managed to break through to Baracska; however, this group was destroyed by our forces' counterattack.

In daylight conditions our artillery could already employ aimed fire, which decided the outcome of the subsequent fighting. While attacking throughout the day, the enemy penetrated only 1-2.5 kilometers into the 252nd Rifle Division's defense.

Due to the threat of an enemy breakthrough in the direction of Pettend and Baracska, the *front* command adopted the following measures:

The 34th Guards Rifle Division was pulled back from the 46th Army's front and transferred to the 4th Guards Army and stationed along the line Kajaszoszentpeter—Martonvasar; the 4th Guards Army's 41st Guards Rifle Division was pulled back from the front line to the Lovasbereny area, where it took up a perimeter defense.

Our active operations to distract the enemy's forces continued along the southern sector. The 30th Rifle Corps' 36th Rifle Division was committed to the front line and the 57th Army's 236th Rifle Division relieved the 32nd Mechanized Brigade, which was pulled into the army commander's reserve in the Tamasin area. Our forces along this sector continued to advance and by the close of 24 January reached the line 1.5 kilometers south of Dunapentele—Nagyvenyim—southeast of Hercegfalva—Kiskaraceny—the center of Sarszent—Miklos—Narmedsy—Saregres—height 108.

Our units' advance forced the enemy to reinforce his southern and southeastern sector with infantry, artillery and tanks from the Szekesfehervar and Sarosd, thus weakening the axis of his main attack.

In order to more effectively employ the heavy gun brigades and regiments along the Lake Velence—Danube River sector of the front, a long-range army artillery group was created, consisting of the 15th, 123rd and 17th cannon-artillery brigades.

Simultaneous with the repulse of the enemy's counterblow, the *front* command, in carrying out the *Stavka* of the VGK directive of 22 January, which assigned the following task: "the command is to eliminate the breakthrough by a counteroffensive and destroy the enemy forces that have broken through to the Danube" and prepare a retaliatory counterblow with its own forces and those attached from the reserve (the 104th Rifle and 23rd Tank Corps from the First Ukrainian Front).

It should be noted that the strength of the formations transferred by the *Stavka* to the Third Ukrainian Front was not high. The 104th Rifle Corps' divisions had a strength of 4,800-4,900 men and the 23rd Tank Corps had only 67 operating tanks and self-propelled guns and 2,600 men in the motorized rifle brigade. These formations were designated to launch a counterblow from the north, in the 4th Guards Army's sector. Before the start of the offensive, the 104th Rifle Corps occupied the following defensive positions along the right bank of the Danube as it arrived: Anasztazia—Elvira—Szazhalombata; the 151st Rifle Division was along the line Ufalu—Erdomajor—Tarnok; the 3rd Guards Airborne Division was concentrating in the Terenbalas area, and; the 23rd Tank Corps was concentrating in the Etyek—Bija—Tabajd—Paty area.

In order to create a group of forces for a counterblow along the southern sector, the 133rd Rifle Corps' 22nd Rifle Division and the 30th Rifle Corps' 155th Rifle Division were to be relieved from defending the left bank of the Danube and concentrated in the Dunafoldvar area. An operational group from the *front* headquarters was temporarily created to control the 30th Guards Corps, 133rd Rifle Corps and the 18th Guards Tank Corps. The headquarters of the 135th Rifle Corps was transferred to the 57th Army, with the 233rd and 236th rifle divisions subordinated to it. A temporary command post was created in Dunaharaszti to control the counterblow to be launched from the north.

On the morning of 25 January the enemy made yet one more attempt to distract our forces from the axis of his main attack. Following a 40-minute artillery preparation, at 0920 he once again began an attack from the Zamoly area to the east, with the forces of up to 30 tanks and up to a regiment of infantry, but upon losing 12 tanks, was unsuccessful. Within two hours of the beginning of the enemy's operations in the Zamoly area, up to 60 tanks and infantry attacked in the direction of Pettend and Baracska. This attack was beaten back. Subsequently, the enemy sought to renew his attacks throughout the entire day. He only managed to penetrate a little in the Pettend—Baracska area.

Units of the 1st Guards Mechanized Corps, which were defending Pettend (seven tanks from the 19th Tank Regiment, a battery from the 1453rd Self-Propelled Artillery Regiment, a company of automatic riflemen, and a headquarters company from the 1st Guards Mechanized Brigade), fought most successfully on this day. Over the course of five hours they repelled uninterrupted attacks by enemy tanks and infantry and burned 12 tanks and armored transports, at the same time destroying a large number of enemy personnel. In all, our forces burnt and knocked out 48 enemy tanks on this day.

Having failed to achieve success with his attacks to the northeast and north, the enemy carried out a partial regrouping and on the night of 25-26 January began an offensive from the northwest along the Vali River. The enemy evidently intended through this offensive to reach Budapest by a roundabout way north of Val and, by possibly launching an attack from the area north of Bicske, to encircle our units operating west of Val and create a broad breakthrough toward Budapest.

The enemy's plan of operations for 26 January was as follows:

> Through an offensive by the forces of the IV SS Panzer Corps from the Pettend area in the direction of Acsa, and by concentrating the main forces of tanks, infantry and artillery, to destroy, in conjunction with the III Panzer Corps, the enemy forces located north of Lake Velence. The forces of the III Panzer Corps are to widen the breakthrough sector northeast and north of Zamoly, in order to develop the offensive from there, following the arrival of the artillery and 6th Panzer Division, to Csakvar.

Somewhat later there followed a refinement of the III Panzer Corps' task, where it was stated that "The III Panzer Corps is to launch an attack from the Zamoly area to the east, in order to establish, first of all, contact with the IV SS Panzer Corps, which has broken through between Vertesacsa and Lovasbereny, and then to destroy the enemy in the area of both shock groups." The 403rd *Volkssturm* Artillery Corps was to depart to the position along the line Nagyhalom—Pettend in order to encircle the enemy in Baracska and to the east.

It was planned to employ along this axis the 356th Infantry Division, which was arriving in the Veszprem area. Simultaneously, an order was issued to employ the 15th Anti-Aircraft Division for anti-aircraft purposes. For this purpose, the 15th Anti-Aircraft Division was to station mixed anti-aircraft battalions before noon on 26 January along the sector between the Sarviz Canal and the Danube along the line Ienefalva—Nagyhantos—Racalmas for defending against tanks. A battalion apiece would be employed for defending the Sarszentmiklos—Szekesfehervar and Dunafoldvar—Adony roads.

The German-Fascist troops' offensive, which was launched on the night of 25-26 January, was also adventurist. The offensive's success was based on happenstance and the surprise of a nighttime attack. Even in the evaluation by the commander of Army Group "Balck," the combat capability of the German-Fascist forces and their strength was rated as quite low. In his evaluation, he noted:

> The enemy's passive actions in the West (the US and British armies, S. Tarasov) have had a favorable effect on the troops' mood; however, the external situation in the East is very depressing, particularly the arriving reinforcements. Major difficulties: the uninterrupted employment of the panzer divisions has severely worn out not only the tanks and armored transports, but the remainder of the vehicles as well. The situation with fuel, tires and spare parts is dire. The shortage of infantry divisions and the related losses in men and materiel have led to a situation in which the panzer divisions, being employed along a broad front, have lost a significant share of their combat capability, which could not be rectified by the arrival of reinforcements from the reserve. Both infantry divisions (271st and 357th), which had excessive demands placed upon them, were routed in difficult fighting north and northwest of Budapest. Due to the loss of territory north of the Danube, the army was deprived of bread and forage (25 percent of supplies). The bases are far away. Auto transport is not coping with its tasks. The high level of ammunition expenditure has caused serious problems, particularly in the provisioning of anti-tank artillery shells. The fuel situation is even worse.

Such was the conclusion as to the army's combat capability and materiel-technical provisioning, made by the commander of Army Group "Balck" himself, before the offensive on the night of 25-26 January.

Particularly heavy fighting unfolded in the Pettend—Baracska area; elements of the 1st Guards Mechanized Corps, a cavalry regiment from the 63rd Cavalry Division, and elements of the 252nd Rifle Division, which were defending here, had suffered significant losses in the preceding fighting. The enemy had created a several-fold superiority in men and materiel along these elements' defensive sector. At 0130 up to 50 tanks and more than 100 motor vehicles with infantry and towed artillery, having crushed two battalions from the 1st Guards Mechanized Corps and an artillery regiment's firing positions, broke through from the Pettend area to the north and occupied Kenesseytanya and Felsopettend. Uninterruptedly attacking our units, the enemy spread in the direction of Vereb, Pazmand and Kajaszoszentpeter.

More than 100 enemy tanks and armored transports were already operating in this area in the second half of the day. Our insignificantly deep defense along the Ada sector was broken through. Despite the heroic resistance by elements of the 1st Guards Mechanized Corps, the 252nd Rifle Division and the 34th Guards Rifle Division, the enemy managed to capture Pettend, Pazmand, Vereb and the western part of Kajaszoszentpeter, while we had no more forces in the depth. As a result of the nighttime breakthrough, the enemy penetrated up to ten kilometers into our defense and broadened the breakthrough to five kilometers. The 3rd SS *Totenkopf* and 1st panzer divisions, the 303rd Assault Brigade from the high command reserve ("Ferdinands" and "Panthers"), the 50th Panzer Battalion's "King Tigers," the 24th Panzer Regiment, and a large number of the enemy's artillery and mortar weapons were operating in this narrow corridor.

As a result of the breakthrough by major enemy forces, the 4th Guards Army was in a difficult situation. The army commander did not dispose of sufficient numbers of men and materiel to halt the enemy's offensive. Thus our command was forced at 1000 to roust the 23rd Tank Corps and move it in the direction of Vereb. Although this corps previously had another task: to concentrate in the Etyek—Bija—Tarbajd—Paty area and be ready, in conjunction with the 104th Rifle Corps, to attack in the direction of Martonvasar and Sarosd on the morning of 27 January.

The measures adopted by the commander of the 4th Guards Army boiled down to the following: two of the 93rd Rifle Division's rifle regiments were taken from the northern shore of Lake Velence and deployed facing east along the line of the eastern outskirts of Kapolnasnyek—Bagryom—Janos—Gyula; one of the 69th Guards Rifle Division's regiments was shifted to the area south of Vereb and occupied defensive positions along the Gyula sector. To the left, one of the 41st Guards Rifle Division's rifle regiments, which had been moved from Lovasbereny, occupied defensive positions. All of the regiments were reinforced with artillery and a small number of tanks and self-propelled guns. The anti-tank reserve of the commander of the 20th Guards Rifle Corps occupied firing positions north of Vereb and delayed the advance by the enemy's tanks in the direction of Bicske.

The army reserve (a rifle regiment from the 80th Guards Rifle Division, an anti-tank artillery regiment, a mortar regiment, two battalions from an artillery brigade, and two battalions of rocket-powered mortars) occupied defensive positions along the western and southern outskirts of Val and halted the enemy's advance to the north and east. The 34th Guards Rifle Division, which had been returned to the 46th Army and one anti-tank artillery regiment occupied defensive positions along the eastern bank of the Vali River from Kajaszoszentpeter to Baracska.

In accordance with the decision, the 23rd Tank Corps was operationally subordinated to the commander of the 4th Guards Army, with the task of cutting off and destroying the enemy group of forces that had broken through to Vereb and by 1400 capture the line Pazmand—Kajaszoszentpeter. Units of the 23rd Tank Corps, upon entering the fighting, deployed in unfavorable conditions from the march under heavy enemy fire, particularly from his anti-tank artillery and fire from tanks and self-propelled guns in ambush.

The corps was reinforced with one anti-tank artillery regiment and a battalion of rocket-powered mortars. Part of the army long-range artillery group, consisting of one brigade and two artillery regiments (54 152mm cannon-howitzers), supported the corps.

The correlation of forces along the sector for launching the counterblow was in favor of the enemy. The enemy in the Kajaszoszentpeter—Val—Vereb—Pazmand area had more than 220 tanks and assault guns and about 350 guns and mortars. Our forces numbered 165 tanks and self-propelled guns and 264 guns and mortars. The overall correlation of tanks and self-propelled guns was 1:1.3 in favor of the enemy. Moreover, the enemy had a significant number of heavy tanks and self-propelled guns.

Among the main shortcomings in the corps' combat operations were the following: poor knowledge of the enemy; cooperation with the artillery had been insufficiently worked out; a shortage of ammunition and; the absence of air support.

However, this attack, in conjunction with offensive operations along the front's southern sector, was so sensitive for the enemy that as early as 27 January he was forced to switch from the offensive to the defensive. As a result of the 23rd Tank Corps' attack, the enemy's breakthrough sector was narrowed in the north to 1.5-2 kilometers and 3-4 kilometers in the south. The arrival of the 135th Tank Brigade in the Veg area created the threat of encirclement for the enemy's breakthrough group.

During 18-27 January the 17th Air Army carried out 6,234 sorties, of which 2,018 were at night. Of this number, 4,450 (72 percent) were carried out against the enemy's troops and 1,206

(19 percent) in combating his aviation. The enemy air force was able to carry out only 1,706 sorties, of which 1,229 were by fighters, and losing 113 planes in 152 air battles.

While combating the enemy air force, the 17th Air Army forced it to sharply reduce its activity by 27 January to 40-50 sorties per day, thus creating a favorable air situation for launching the *front* counterblow.

The decision to launch the counterblow was as follows: to launch an attack from the area northeast of Lake Velence with the forces of the 104th Rifle Corps and 23rd Tank Corps in the direction of Adony—Sarosd, toward the attack by the *front's* two rifle and one tank corps operating from the south toward Sarosd.

For the offensive, it was necessary to bring in the 1st Guards Mechanized Corps, 2-3 rifle divisions and a large part of the army. It was then planned to throw in all the army's forces to restore the situation.

The 104th Rifle Corps and the 23rd Tank Corps were supposed to occupy their jumping-off positions during the night of 27-28 January, and with part of their forces on the night of 26-27 January.

The beginning of the offensive was set for the morning of 28 January.

With the beginning of the 23rd Tank and 104th Rifle corps' offensive, the 5th Guards Cavalry Corps was to be pulled into the reserve along the line Kisvelence—Felsobesnyo—Szinatelep, where it was to put itself in order.

The corps launching the counterblow were reinforced with the following: 23rd Tank Corps with a long range artillery group, consisting of three artillery regiments, one artillery brigade, a battalion of rocket-powered mortars, and a sapper battalion; the 104th Rifle Corps with a howitzer regiment, an artillery regiment, and a sapper battalion.

The plan called for the 23rd Tank and 104th Rifle corps' actions to be supported from the air by the forces of no less than one fighter division and two assault air divisions. At the same time as the offensive along the main axis, it was planned to wage active operations with part of the 21st Guards Rifle Corps' forces to capture heights 204, 183 and the town of Csala.

It was planned to begin the offensive with a 10-minute fire onslaught at 1310.

During the night of 26-27 January our combat formations were further strengthened along the entire front between Lake Velence and the Danube River. The commander of the 21st Guards Rifle Division was to secure the sector Velence—northern outskirts of Kapolnasnyek—Janos—Gyula—excluding Vereb—Lovasbereny and Vereb—Vertesacsa with the forces of the 93rd and 69th Guards rifle divisions. The 23rd Tank Corps organized a screen, facing south, along the sector height 216—Felso (north of Vereb)—height 230—Val—excluding Kajaszoszentpeter.

The advance by our units from the northeast on Kajaszoszentpeter and the simultaneous pressure along the entire front of the enemy's penetration created an encirclement threat against the enemy's breakthrough group and he was forced to begin falling back from the "sack"; at the same time, our formations' active operations along the southern sector of the front forced the enemy to reinforce this sector. By 27-28 January, besides the 8th Panzer and 25th Infantry divisions, which were already defending along this sector, there was also the 23rd Panzer Division, which had been transferred from the Szekesfehervar area. All of our forces' active operations demanded that the enemy create reserves, which could be formed at the expense of the shock group.

The heart of the enemy's shock group—the SS *Wiking* and *Totenkopf* panzer divisions—suffered heavy losses and were worn out, while their offensive capabilities were sharply reduced. As a result of these circumstances, the German-Fascist command was forced to review its plan for further operations.

The German-Fascist command's plan for 27-28 January called for the following:

The forces of the Hungarian Third Army (3rd Panzer and 25th Infantry divisions) were to delay our advance east of the Sarviz Canal with the aid of a counterattack and the IV SS Panzer Corps' offensive was to be halted and it was to go over to the defensive between the Danube and Baracska and north of the Baracska—Kapolnasnyek road. The 1st Panzer Division was to be pulled into the reserve in the Adony area; the III Panzer Corps' 23rd Panzer Division was to be pulled into the reserve to the Aba—Szekesfehervar area, and the offensive was to be halted in the Vertes mountainous area and the sector turned over the IV SS Panzer Corps' units.

The 1st Panzer Division was to be transferred to the III Panzer Corps, which was subordinated to the Hungarian Third Army, and it was to launch an attack with the forces of the 1st, 3rd and 23rd panzer divisions to the south. A new boundary line was established between the IV SS Panzer Corps and the cavalry corps: Sur—three kilometers south of Mor—Gant—Vertesacsa. The newly-arrived 356th Infantry Division was to concentrate in individual combat groups in Szekesfehervar. This division was to be subordinated to the IV SS Panzer Corps and to occupy the front between Lake Velence and Zamoly as it arrived.

As a result of these regroupings, the enemy's shock group was dispersed and weakened.

In accordance to the order by General Balck, the IV SS Panzer Corps was ordered to go over to the defensive along the front Vali Viz Canal from the Danube to Baracska—eastern extremities of Lake Velence. The 5th SS *Wiking* Panzer Division was to defend the sector Danube River—Vali River between Adony and Baracska and to restore the front to the east of Aggszentpeter.

The 3rd SS *Totenkopf* Panzer Division was ordered to fall back to the line Baracska—Lake Velence, where it was to occupy defensive positions and secure the withdrawal of the heavy tanks and self-propelled guns. This division was to subsequently be pulled into the reserve of the commander of the IV SS Panzer Corps to the Szabolcs area during the night of 27-28 January.

However, the German-Fascist command was not able to fully realize its operational plan. Our forces attacked the enemy without pause and forced him to fight in unfavorable conditions and operate in a way not foreseen by the plan. Our artillery, which was located in firing positions north of Lake Velence and north of Kapolnasnyek, kept the entire enemy position under fire and hammered his retreating units. It was only by the close of 28 January that the enemy managed to extricate himself from the "sack" northeast of Lake Velence, while suffering enormous losses.

Thus the enemy's offensive operation, which was launched by him on 2 January, suffered a complete failure.

By the time the German-Fascist forces were forced to go over to the defensive, without having carried out their mission, our defense was stronger than at the start of the enemy's offensive. By the close of 26 January we had 11 formations, echeloned up to 11-13 kilometers in depth, defending between Lake Velence and the Danube River. The operational density along this sector was two kilometer per division, and the artillery density was 41 tubes per kilometer of front.

By this time our forces had already shifted from the defensive to the offensive along the southern sector. The 18th Tank Corps, three of the 30th Rifle Corps' divisions and three of the 133rd Rifle Corps' divisions were operating along a 34-kilometer front between the Danube River and the Sarviz Canal, which yielded a density of 4.8 kilometers per division. The artillery density was insignificant and amounted to 22 tubes per kilometer of front.

The sector along the Jelusa Canal, 50 kilometers in length, was covered by two of the 135th Rifle Corps' divisions, with an artillery density of five tubes per kilometer of front. The 32nd Guards Mortar Brigade was in the corps' reserve.

As a result of nine days of intensive fighting, the following correlation of forces had developed by the close of 27 January:

Table 13 Correlation of Forces, 27 January 1945

	The Enemy	Soviet Forces	Correlation
A. Between Lake Velence and the Danube River			
Men	19,230	67,110	1:3.5
Machine Guns	1,115	1,606	1:1.4
Mortars	184	501	1:3.0
Guns	238	517	1:2.2
Tanks and Self-Propelled Guns	284	129	1:0.4
B. Between the Danube River and Lake Balaton			
Men	17,020	46,877	1:2.7
Machine Guns	934	1,203	1:1.3
Mortars	224	469	1:2.1
Guns	189	523	1:2.7
Tanks and Self-Propelled Guns	130	112	1:0.8

Thus a situation was created during our defensive battles for our troops launch a retaliatory counterblow, while the *front's* forces received only the 23rd Tank and 104th Rifle corps, both of which were under strength.

Aside from foiling the enemy's offensive between Lake Velence and Lake Balaton and creating conditions for our counterblow, our forces simultaneously foiled the offensive by the German Second Panzer Army, the planning for which was underway, from the area east of Nagykanizsa and by the forces of Army Group "Weichs" from the southern bank of the Drava River.

The German command considered the withdrawal of our forces from the area south of Lake Balaton a mandatory condition for beginning this offensive. However, as is clear from the conversations between the commander of the German Sixth Army, General Balck, and the commander of the IV SS Panzer Corps, Lieutenant General Gille, on 26 January even Hitler considered that we had not yet withdrawn sufficient forces from this area and did not authorized the beginning of the offensive by the Second Panzer Army and Group "Weichs."

Proceeding from the necessity to first exhaust the enemy's forces in defensive fighting, as well as proceeding from the deadlines for concentrating the 23rd Tank and 104th Rifle corps, it was decided to begin offensive operations on 27-28 January 1945.

The immediate objective was to launch meeting attacks from the north from the area between Lake Velence and the Danube River to the south, and from the south between the Danube River and the Sarviz Canal, to the north, for the purpose of clearing the enemy from the right bank of the Danube River and restore the *front's* communications and the opportunity for maneuver along the right bank of the Danube River. The offensive was to then be developed to the west to completely restore the situation.

Thus our forces' counterblow was limited in character. This is explained by the fact that we did not have the necessary superiority in force along the main attack axes (the overall correlation of forces along the breakthrough sector to the north, including the 23rd Tank and 104th Rifle corps, was 1:3.25 in men, 1:2.4 in artillery and 1:0.45 in tanks), aside from the fact that our forces had been significantly weakened by many days of defensive fighting, during the course of which they had suffered heavy losses, both in men and particularly in equipment, while the *front* did not dispose of sufficiently powerful reserves.

The troops were given the following assignments:

The 4th Guards Army was to launch an attack with the forces of the 104th Rifle and 23rd Tank corps from the area northeast of Lake Velence in the direction of Adony, Szabolcs and Sarosd, toward the attack being launched from the south.

The 1st Guards Rifle Corps, 2-3 rifle divisions and a small part of the army's artillery were to be thrown in additionally.

It was planned to begin this group's offensive on the morning of 28 January.

The 30th and 133rd rifle corps and the 18th Tank Corps were to launch an attack from the south toward the 4th Guards Army's attack. For this purpose, the 30th Guards Rifle Corps, in conjunction with the 18th Guards Tank Corps, was to attack in the general direction of Nagyperkata and then reach the line Ivancsa—Adony station—Szabolcs—Sarosd. At the same time, upon the approach of our units from the north, it was planned to turn the front to the west in the direction of Seregelyes.

The 133rd Rifle Corps, which had been reinforced with the 10th Anti-Tank Artillery Brigade, 407th Light Artillery Regiment and the 200th and 529th mortar regiments, was also to attack on 27 January, in conjunction with the 18th Guards Tank Corps, in the general direction of Sarkeresztur and consolidate the front with two divisions along the Sarviz Canal as far as Aba. It was then be in readiness to force the Sarviz Canal and attack in the direction of Lepseny.

The 18th Guards Tank Corps, with the 274th Howitzer Regiment, 1658th and 1089th anti-tank artillery regiments, 3rd Anti-Aircraft Artillery Division, and a battalion of M-31[11] rocket-powered mortars, was given the assignment of attacking in the general direction of Hercegfalva and Nagyperkata in close coordination with the 30th and 133rd rifle corps. The corps was to capture Nagyperkata on the first day and Adonyszabolcs station and Sarosd on the second. It was then to be ready to turn its offensive front toward Seregelyes.

In order to distract the enemy's forces from the main attack axis, the beginning of the offensive along the southern sector was set for two days earlier than in the north; that is, on the morning of 26 January.

On 28 January the 30th Guards Rifle, 133rd Rifle and 18th Tank corps were united under the 26th Army's field headquarters.

The 57th Army was given the task (bearing in mind that a wedge dangerous for the enemy had formed between the Sarviz and Jelusa canals in the Saregres area) of attacking with one rifle division, in conjunction with the 133rd Rifle Corps, and capturing Saregres and Igar on the first day of the offensive. It was later to reach the line Ers—Szilas-Balhas—Kula.

On the offensive's second day, taking advantage of our troops' success, it was planned to begin an offensive with the 135th Rifle Corps' remaining forces in the direction of Enying and Lepseny, with the task of encircling and destroying the Hungarian 25th Infantry Division.

Thus the overall idea of our counterblow was to disperse the enemy's attacking group, cut it into two parts and to throw back the more powerful tank group and destroy his weaker infantry group of forces; to render the enemy incapable of resuming the offensive for the near future.

At 1000 on 27 January the 4th Guards Army (23rd Guards Tank Corps, 5th Guards Cavalry Corps, the 252nd and 93rd rifle divisions, and two rifle regiments) attacked northeast and east of Lake Velence, with the task of eliminating the enemy breakthrough in the direction of Val and restoring the previous situation.

Simultaneously, the Third Ukrainian Front's formations continued to attack along the southern sector of the enemy breakthrough west of Dunafoldvar (18th Guards Tank and

11 Editor's note. The M-31 was a heavy (300 caliber) version of the Red Army's rocket-launched artillery vehicle, which was widely employed during the Second World War.

133rd Rifle corps). On 26 January a brief preparation for the general offensive was carried out and on the morning of 27 January the 30th and 133rd rifle and 18th Guards Tank corps began their offensive from the line south of Dunapentele—height 173—Bernatkut—Melykut—Kezen—Kishantos—Nagy—Felso—Keresztures—Bebic.

While overcoming the enemy's stubborn resistance and repelling his counterattacks, our forces, which were attacking from the south, slowly advanced, throwing the enemy out of a number of strong points.

These attacks forced the German-Fascist command to make significant changes to its initial plan. The commander of the IV SS Panzer Corps decided to pull the panzer divisions out of the sack that had formed northeast of Lake Velence. In accordance with the decision by the commander of the IV SS Panzer Corps, the corps' formations received the following tasks: the 5th SS *Wiking* Panzer Division was to defend the sector Danube River—Vali River between Adony and Baracska and restore the front to the east of Aggszentpeter; the 3rd SS *Totenkopf* Panzer Division, in conjunction with the 1st Panzer Division, was to fall back to the line Baracska—Lake Velence, where it was to take up defensive positions and to secure the arrival of the heavy tanks and self-propelled artillery regiments.

Simultaneously, while attempting to delay the advance by the 30th and 133rd rifle and 18th Guards Tank corps, the enemy sped up the transfer of the remaining units of the 23rd Panzer Division from the Szekesfehervar area to the sector between the Danube and the Sarviz Canal, and transferred on 28-29 January part of the 5th SS *Wiking* Panzer Division to this sector from the area east of Lake Velence.

The enemy foresaw his next plan of action for 29 January. The forces of the Hungarian Third Army were to prevent our forces from expanding the penetration area north of Simontornya. For this purpose, it was also planned to direct all available air assets to this area.

The forces of the III Panzer Corps were to continue the offensive for the purpose of destroying our forces east of the Sarviz Canal. The main attack was to be made toward Nagyperkata and to the west (3rd Panzer Division). All of the attacking formations (3rd, 1st and 23rd panzer divisions) were to be unified in the Hercegfalva area.

In the IV SS Panzer Corps, it was decided to create reserves in the Szekesfehervar area, consisting of a sapper battalion with tanks and an armored group from the 6th Panzer Division.

The 23rd Tank Corps, with one rifle division, an artillery regiment, a mortar battalion and a guards mortar battalion, had the task of developing the attack in the direction of Baracska, Janos and Gyorg, and to capture Sarosd by the close of 29 January. The tank corps' combat formation was in two echelons. Three brigades (3rd Tank, 56th Motorized Rifle and 39th Tank) and one rifle division were in the first echelon. The breakthrough front was three kilometers wide. The second echelon included one tank brigade (135th), with two self-propelled artillery regiments and two battalions of rocket-powered mortars in the reserve. The 23rd Tank and 104th Rifle corps' formations attacked and by 1500 they had advanced 1-2 kilometers. By the close of the day the second echelon (135th Tank Brigade), which had been committed into the fighting to develop the success, in conjunction with the 39th Tank Brigade, captured Aggszentpeter, although the infantry (151st Rifle Division) attacking behind it was unable to take advantage of the tanks' success, fell behind them and fell under fire from the enemy's surviving groups and was delayed northeast of Anna.

The fighting was also fierce in the 104th Rifle Corps' sector. The corps' forces, while overcoming the enemy's stubborn resistance, were only able to advance 3-4 kilometers.

The 104th Rifle Corps' insignificant success can be explained not only by the enemy's stubborn resistance, but also by the fact that the corps commander dispersed his forces along a significant front. Each division attacked independently, without coordination with its neighbors. A powerful shock group was not created in the corps. The artillery density was very low (up to 30 tubes per kilometer of front) and did not guarantee the suppression of the enemy's guns.

Our troops' advance in the south was slowed even further because the enemy, as is known, significantly reinforced his group of forces operating there.

The German-Fascist command assigned its forces the following tasks for 30 January:

The Hungarian Third Army, employing the 6th Panzer Division's armored group, was to prevent the further widening of the breakthrough in the Enying area. The forces of the III Panzer Corps were to continue the offensive along their previous axis. The IV SS Panzer Corps was to localize our forces' penetration in the Aggszentpeter area. The 356th Infantry Division was to defend the sector between the IV and III panzer corps (along the line of the four farms—Kisfalud—Zamoly.

The absence of enemy reserves forced the German-Fascist command to try and create shock anti-tank groups during the fighting, which it employed for launching brief attacks against our most threatening attacking groups. For example, the 6th Panzer Division's armored group, a panzer regiment, a reconnaissance detachment, a battalion on armored transports, and a battalion of self-propelled artillery were attached to the Hungarian Third Army with the task of launching an attack against our units that had penetrated in the Enying area. Then this group, upon completing its assignment in one place, was to be shifted to another threatened sector. The course of combat operations showed that in the specific conditions of the situation the creation of such groups justified itself.

On the morning of 30 January the 23rd Tank and 104th Rifle corps' formations resumed the offensive. The heaviest fighting unfolded in the Aggszentpeter area. In the Anna and Janos area elements of the 3rd SS *Totenkopf* Panzer Division were encircled and were destroyed by the close of the day. On this day the 23rd Tank Corps advanced up to six kilometers, while the 66th Guards and 113th rifle divisions, taking advantage of the tanks' success, widened the breakthrough to eight kilometers along the front.

The 3rd Guards Airborne Division forced the canal and advanced three kilometers. The 93rd Rifle Division cleared the enemy out of Kapolnasnyek.

By the close of 30 January our forces were fighting along the following lines:

a) along the northern sector: southern outskirts of Kapolnasnyek—Pers—north of Janos—two kilometers west of Nagyhalom—north of Gyorg—northern outskirts of Felsobesnyo—south of Szinatelep;
b) along the southern sector: south and west of Dunapentele—Galambas—southern outskirts of Nagyperkata—south of Nagyhantos—Nagy—Felse Kertevedes—Lake Sosto—Domokosmajor.
   At 2000 on 28 January the 30th and 133rd rifle corps and 18th Guards Tank Corps, which were operating along this sector, were subordinated to the 26th Army, which had arrived and become part of the *front*;
c) along the sector between the Sarviz Canal and Lake Balaton (57th Army), two kilometers southwest of Harsan)—Huszara—west of Igar—east of Val—then along the Jelusa Canal to Csiksat-Patak—Mihalfa—Felsekustjap—height 157—Iormeny—height 115—Iomaros, then further along the Jelusa Canal to Lake Balaton.

Our command in this situation correctly determined that the forces attacking from the north and south were still insufficient for completely restoring the situation. The enemy, hanging on to each inhabited locale, was seeking with all his forces to hold the captured bridgehead in order to renew the offensive from it in the immediate future. Additional measures were necessary, which could sharply change the situation in favor of our forces.

At the same time, the enemy's transfer of the 23rd Panzer Division from the Szekesfehervar area to the southern sector and its replacement in the Szekesfehervar with the less combat-capable 356th Infantry Division, which had arrived from Italy, weakened the enemy's defense in the Szekesfehervar area and created favorable conditions for launching our attack. For this reason, in order to achieve a sharp change in the situation and the creation of more favorable conditions for defeating the enemy group of forces that had broken through to the Danube River, the *front* commander decided to regroup part of his forces and launch an attack on Szekesfehervar from the area north of Lake Velence. Szekesfehervar was a very important communications junction for the entire enemy group of forces and its loss would place this entire group of forces in a very difficult situation. The development of our offensive from Szekesfehervar to the southwest, toward the 133rd Rifle Corps' attack, would threaten the IV SS Panzer Corps' main forces with complete encirclement. Taking into account the very important operational significance of Szekesfehervar, it behooved us to expect that the enemy would be forced to pull back part of his forces from the Danube to repel the attack, which would ease the offensive by our forces located there.

Proceeding from these considerations, the *front* commander decided on the following:

To regroup the 1st Guards Mechanized Corps to the Baklas area on the night of 29-30 January, and the 5th Guards Cavalry Corps to the Lovasbereny area; on the morning of 31 January, the forces of three divisions from the 21st and 20th guards rifle corps, along with a sufficient amount of artillery, were to launch an attack along a narrow front in the direction of Baklas and Sarkeresztes, with the task of cutting the enemy's communications from Szekesfehervar to Mor, and upon completion of this task to cover oneself from the north and capture the city of Szekesfehervar through the main forces' rapid actions to the south.

The Hitlerite command, taking into account the real possibility of our forces' attack north of Szekesfehervar and, having established the regrouping to this axis of an entire series of the Third Ukrainian Front's formations through all intelligence means, adopted a number of measures, in particular: to group the 15th Mortar Brigade and a battalion of 12.2 centimeter guns from an artillery corps to the 356th Infantry Division's area; detached regimental groups, reinforced with tanks, from the *Wiking* and *Totenkopf* panzer divisions and subordinated them to the corps command in the Szekesfehervar area; put the 356th Infantry Division's arriving 2nd Regimental Group into a state of combat readiness and dispatching it to the Szekesfehervar—Sarkeresztes area; concentrated artillery and mortar fire against our likely troop concentration areas—Pakozd, Patka, Lovasbereny, and Csakvar; established a new boundary line between the Hungarian Third Army (III Panzer Corps)and the IV SS Panzer Corps: Sarszentmihaly—Seregelyes—the rail junction 4.5 kilometers south of Adony and Kunszentmiklos (all locales, except for Seregelyes, were for the Hungarian Third Army).

The Third Ukrainian Front's forces launched their attack in the middle of the day on 31 January along the front northwest of Zamoly and Kisfalud and by the close of the day, as a result of stubborn fighting, advanced up to four kilometers and captured the following: the 1st Guards Mechanized Corps Barbala, three kilometers northwest of Sarkeresztur, the 21st and 20th guards rifle corps' divisions the Csala line, while part of their forces reached the eastern outskirts of Szekesfehervar. The 4th Guards Army's offensive along the entire front, and particularly the attack by the 20th and 21st guards rifle corps along the Zamoly—Szekesfehervar sector, placed the enemy's forces in a difficult situation.

Along the 57th Army's front, the enemy launched a powerful counterattack along the 236th Rifle Division's sector in up to a regiment in strength and supported by 80 armored vehicles and 35 tanks. The division's subunits, while fighting in encirclement and semi-encirclement, inflicted a defeat on the counterattacking enemy. They destroyed up to 15 armored vehicles and captured 700 prisoners, six guns, 30 machine guns, and more than 100 motor vehicles and military hardware.

On the morning of 1 February, following a brief artillery preparation, the 4th Guards Army's forces (20th and 21st guards rifle corps and the 1st Guards Mechanized Corps) resumed the attack, launching their main attack on Szekesfehervar.

Units of the 21st Guards Rifle and 1st Guards Mechanized corps broke into the eastern suburbs of Szekesfehervar and by the close of the day cleared it of the enemy. Szekesfehervar's eastern suburbs, which are located on heights that tower over the surrounding terrain and the city itself, had great importance in the enemy's defensive system. The loss of the suburbs was the same as losing the city itself, because all the roads running through Szekesfehervar were under the observation and fire of our artillery and mortars. Our forces' capture of Szekesfehervar and the breakthrough by our tanks into the city immediately and sharply changed the entire situation. Because of this, the Hitlerite command took emergency measures to hold its positions and to eliminate the 4th Guards Army's penetration in the Szekesfehervar area. The Hungarian Third Army was ordered to restore the situation along the 25th Infantry Division's left flank along the line Mezokomarom—Deg—six kilometers south of Kalozd. The III Panzer Corps was to occupy Sarosd and height 130 (eight kilometers east of Seregelyes) and the freed-up 1st Panzer Division was to be subordinated to the IV SS Panzer Corps, which was to restore the situation along the line height 130—Gardon. The forces of the freed-up *Totenkopf* SS Panzer Division and the attached 1st Panzer Division were to destroy our forces in the area east of the eastern suburbs of Szekesfehervar. Simultaneously, an order was issued to pull back the main forces on the night of 1-2 February, approximately to the line Goboljaras—Basene—Gyorg—northeast extremity of Lake Velence.

In a night attack by the adjacent flanks of two corps, we managed to capture Adonyszabolcs station, Ivancsa and Adony, where the 4th Guards Army's forces linked up with units of the 26th Army's 18th Guards Tank Corps. As a result of this attack, the enemy was thrown back from the Danube. Fearing encirclement, he began to pull back his forces. By this time, the 1st Guards Mechanized Corps' tanks and motorized infantry broke into Szekesfehervar and became involved in street fighting there. The enemy, at the cost of heavy losses, launched powerful counterattacks and threw our forces out of the city, although he was unable to restore the previous situation. Our forces were holding the line Zamoly—Vorosivizmuvek—the Szekesfehervar suburbs—Kisfalud—excluding Nadas, creating a constant threat to the enemy's most important communications center.

Having mainly freed his communications through Szekesfehervar, the enemy once again applied all his efforts to hold at least some part of the territory captured by him southeast and southwest of Lake Velence, as a bridgehead for a repeat offensive. His resistance increased once again. While repelling numerous counterattacks and overcoming the enemy's stubborn resistance, the 4th Guards Army's forces had by 6 February made a fighting advance to the line eastern outskirts of Dinnyes—Borgond—Borgond station—Kulsobarand—excluding Sejmes, and by this time the 26th Army had reached the line Sejmes—Kulse Kantor—Aba—Soponya. Our advance was halted along this line by the enemy, who had consolidated along the forward positions of the "Margarita Line."

Units of the 26th Army continued offensive battles between the Malomcsu Canal and Lake Balaton up to 10 February and by the close of the day also reached the "Margarita Line."

From 13 February our front on this sector stabilized along the line Soponya—Nagylang—south of Jaslang—Agatok—Bal—Bozsok—Gamasa.

Thus as a result of our counterblow, the enemy along this sector lost everything that he had achieved as a result of his month-long offensive. The position occupied by our forces between Lake Velence and Lake Balaton by the start of the Budapest operation had been almost completely restored.

Overall Conclusions on Repulsing Counterblows

Our command understood that the relief of the enemy's encircled group of forces in Budapest had not only operational-strategic significance for the Hitlerite command, but enormous political significance as well. In the event of success, the German-Fascist command would keep Hungary as an ally and would maintain the solidity of the entire southern wing of the strategic front, thus covering the Vienna strategic direction.

The repulse of the counterblows took place in a very diverse situation, and it follows that the means of repulsing the counterblows were not patented. At their heart lay the striving not only to repulse the enemy's counterblow, but to defeat the forces forming the enemy's shock groups of forces.

The extended character of the struggle with the enemy's counterblow groups was conditioned by other fundamental reasons: first of all, by the enemy's insistent and stubborn desire to break through, despite his losses, to the encircled Budapest group of forces and, secondly, by the absence of sufficient reserves.

During the course of repelling the enemy's third counterblow, the Third Ukrainian Front's forces did not limit themselves to only defense, but prepared and carried out a retaliatory counterblow, as a result of which we inflicted a defeat on the enemy group of forces and almost completely restored the previous situation along the external front, and along the internal front completed the destruction of the enemy's encircled group of forces in Budapest in conjunction with the forces of the Second Ukrainian Front.

It was only the absence of a superiority in men and materiel during our forces' launching of a counterblow that enabled the enemy to avoid encirclement and a complete rout. This circumstance did not enable us to launch an attack to a great depth and thus achieve greater operational-strategic results.

Taking into account the unfavorable correlation of forces along the external encirclement front, our forces took up the defensive along favorable lines, with the task of wearing out and bleeding the enemy forces and to then commit fresh forces from the reserve and from other axes and by a decisive attack, in conjunction with the forces of the Second Ukrainian Front, rout the enemy's shock group.

The sufficient distance of the external encirclement front (when the enemy launched his first and second counterblows, the distance from the encircled group of forces was 50-60 kilometers, and up to 90 kilometers during the third counterblow) had positive significance for repelling the enemy's counterblows.

This enabled us to prevent the rapid breakthrough of the front and the striking of the internal front's forces by artillery fire from the area of the external front, and also guaranteed conditions for the maneuver of reserves between both fronts and the reliability of command and control.

The German-Fascist command was unable to destroy or inflict a material defeat on the forces of the Third Ukrainian Front's main forces by means of the counterblows carried out during 2-27 January. Having failed to achieve its goals along one axis, it shifted its counterblow to another axis, striking at random, while the absence of sufficient reserves for developing the initial success doomed the counterblow to failure. In the final analysis, having exhausted and bled his groups, the enemy halted active operations and moved from counterblows to the defensive.

The maneuver of men and material (the armies', *front's* and the *Stavka's* reserves) had decisive significance in repelling the counterblows.

The augmentation of forces and the strengthening of reserves took place during the course of the operation, which not only guaranteed the repulse of the counterblows, but also the defeat of the enemy's counterblow groups of forces.

During the conduct of the defense, a stubborn defensive battle was waged to wear out the enemy through the uninterrupted reinforcement of the defense and the increase of its depth during the course of the operation.

However, the subsequent arrival of reserves, although comparatively small, enabled us to assign an active mission to the defense and wear out the enemy's attacking forces, so that we could subsequently ourselves go over to a counteroffensive in order to restore the situation. To assign our counteroffensive a more decisive task—to destroy the enemy's forces and decisively develop the offensive—was impossible due to our forces' insufficient superiority (2.3 in artillery and 1.4 in machine guns, while the enemy continued to enjoy an almost twofold superiority of tanks) even at the close of the operation's defensive stage.

Due to the operationally active tasks assigned to our defense, defensive tactics were correspondingly directed at creating favorable conditions for our going over to a counteroffensive. The wearing out of the enemy was to be achieved through numerous counterattacks and a stubborn defense by our entrenched troops. In order to economize our forces for a counterblow, local counterattacks to restore the situation were almost never launched during the course of the operation. The retention of this or that sector of territory not having operational significance, was viewed as a means of exhausting the enemy's attacking forces, and if territory should be lost our forces were not expended on its return. The nature of such activities was conditioned by the following situation:

- the defensive depth was insignificant along the breakthrough sector (135th Rifle Corps) and the enemy broke through it in five hours. By the middle of the day (18 January) the enemy had penetrated up to 15 kilometers into the defensive depth and had split the 135th Rifle Corps' combat formations and disrupted command and control;
- the second echelons and the reserves arriving at the breakthrough area encountered the enemy's superior forces, which were developing the attack into the depth. In this situation, one could only halt the enemy, first of all, through the method of stubborn defense.

Counterattacks during the defensive operation were employed only when this was the result of actual necessity (the enemy's penetration in the Aggszentpeter area, which threatened to collapse the entire first defensive zone; the enemy's breakthrough in the direction of Val; the enemy's forcing of the Jelusa Canal). The offensive activities of our units along the sector between the Danube River and the Sarviz Canal before the launching of the general counteroffensive played a significant role in the preparation of conditions for out counteroffensive. These activities led to the dispersal of the enemy's forces and made the task of exhausting him easier.

In both the defensive fighting of 2-13 January and during the repulse of the enemy's offensive of 13-26 January, the correctness of our evaluation of the situation was fully manifested, as well as the bold creation of new reserves by means of weakening secondary sectors and the timely reinforcement of even those secondary sectors, where by means of a deep analysis of the situation, one could expect the enemy's supporting attacks (the Zamoly and Bicske axes).

The offensive undertaken by us along the Danube scattered the enemy' s main forces, tied them down and even forced him to weaken his most dangerous Szekesfehervar axis. Our subsequent attack on Szekesfehervar forced the enemy to quickly remove significant forces from his defense along the Danube, which sharply weakened his defense and secured the success of our counterblow as a whole.

In conditions of the absence of a sufficient number of fresh reserves, one should view the result of the counterblow as being quite satisfactory: the situation was restored to such a degree that the *front's* operational situation that existed before the enemy offensive did not suffer; as a result of our counterblow, the enemy lost all the operational advantages achieved by him in the offensive.

The rapid maneuver of our units along the Szekesfehervar axis and the surprise of the attack played a very large role in the success of our attack on Szekesfehervar.

In repelling the enemy's second counterblow, our forces exhibited a high degree of heroism and resilience in the defense. Yet another quality of our troops manifested itself in this operation and showed that it had fully matured—the absence of the fear of encirclement (the example of the 133rd Rifle and 18th Tank corps).

In repelling the enemy's offensive during 18 January-2 February the entire rich experience acquired by us in the defensive operation in the first half of January, was fully employed. This is why victory was achieved in this operation, despite the fact that with the enemy's 18 January breakthrough of our defense and his arrival at the Danube River, the *front's* situation was much more serious than had been the case in the first half of January and despite the fact that the enemy's forces, particularly in tanks, were greater than in the first offensive, and, it is necessary to emphasize, that our losses at the same time were less than in the first half of January.

At the same time, it should be noted that many shortcomings which revealed themselves in the first half of January were not eliminated in this operation:

- our forces adapted insufficiently to repel nighttime actions, which the enemy employed more broadly in the second half of January than in the first half;
- the situation with the defensive capability of the rear units was clearly unsatisfactory. During the enemy's breakthrough into our depth, the rear units proved to be uncontrollable and they ran away in disorder, overburdening the roads and disorganizing the maneuver of combat units which were moving up to oppose the breakthrough;
- as before, observation and reconnaissance suffered. The regrouping of the IV SS Panzer Corps was not discovered in time, while the enemy's forces were often overestimated during the offensive, the enemy fooled our intelligence, sending out motor vehicles with switched-on headlights at night, instead of tanks;
- there were instances of the incorrect employment of tanks in the defense. Instead of operating from ambush and firing in place, the tank formations in some situations got into tank battles with the enemy's superior forces.

The repulse of the German-Fascist forces' counterblow was carried out through the combined efforts of all the combat arms and aviation, as well as the Danube Military Flotilla. Aviation, armored and mechanized forces, engineer and chemical troops played a major role in repelling and defeating the enemy's counterblow groups. The artillery played the main role in fighting the enemy's tanks. In repelling the enemy's counterblows, great significance was attached to anti-tank artillery and cannon and anti-aircraft artillery. This is explained by the fact that the main core of the enemy's forces launching the counterblows consisted of tanks, the density of which reached 15-30 per kilometer of front in each echelon. During the repulse of the counterblows, the 4th Guards Army received considerable reinforcements at the expense of the *front's* other armies and from the High Command Artillery Reserve (15 artillery regiments and two artillery brigades, for a total of 480 guns). In all, at the time of the repulse of the third counterblow, the 4th Guards Army had 2,166 guns and mortars. During the repulse of the counterblows, the artillery density per kilometer of defensive front rose from 12-20 guns to 40-60 guns per kilometer of front, due to maneuver.

An anti-tank defense was created along the axis of the enemy's tank group attacks, which was built according to the principle of creating anti-tank strong points and anti-tank areas. 39 anti-tank strong points had been created within the 4th Guards Army as early as 1 January 1945, numbering 523 guns. At the same time, there were five to 30 guns in each anti-tank strong point. In conditions of repelling massed enemy tank attacks, the artillery, all the way up to heavy caliber guns, was moved up to the troops' combat formations and fired on the enemy's tanks and self-propelled guns from open positions. For example, along the sector of the 4th Guards Army's 31st Guards Rifle Corps, aside from battalion and regimental artillery, up to 50 percent of the divisional artillery, 30-40 percent of the howitzer regiments and up to 20 cannon-artillery regiments from the High Command Artillery Reserve was moved up for firing over open sights. 100mm and 122mm guns and 152mm gun-howitzers were broadly employed against heavy tanks. The army's and *front's* anti-tank artillery reserves played a major role in repelling the enemy's counterblows. Also of great significance in repelling the enemy's counterblow was artillery maneuver carried out chiefly through the High Command Artillery Reserve's units and formations. In order to repel the first counterblow, in the course of two days 28 artillery regiments were concentrated to the 4th Guards Army's right flank by order of the senior commander, which included up to 670 guns and mortars, which enabled us to successfully repel the enemy's tanks and infantry, while inflicting significant losses on them.

Aside from army artillery units and formations, 53 anti-tank artillery units from the High Command Reserve took part in maneuver in January 1945. At the same time, the High Command Reserve's 12th Anti-Tank Artillery Brigade travelled 220 kilometers in a day from the 57th Army, while the 10th Anti-Tank Brigade carried out a march of more than 1,300 kilometers under its own power from the Plovdiv area in Bulgaria over the course of four days, overcoming three snowed-in passes and crossing the Danube River twice.

The repulse of the counterblows required a significant expenditure of munitions; for example, in the 4th Guards Army the munitions expenditure during 1-31 January amounted to 1.5-2 combat loads for each gun and mortar. The overall expenditure of munitions was more than 7,600 tons; that is, more than 618 train cars.

Mine obstacles were widely employed in repelling the enemy's counterblows. Mobile obstacle detachments and engineer units, which had been brought in for mining, rapidly created and ceaselessly augmented obstacles along the most important axes during the course of repelling the counterblows. In all, 117,932 anti-tank and 60,560 anti-personnel mines were laid. These obstacles, which were protected by fire, constrained the enemy's maneuver to a significant degree and inflicted serious losses on him. 87 enemy tanks and 12 armored transports were knocked out in our minefields.

The operation had a number of features: the limited bridgehead in our rear formed by the Danube River (with a difficult ice situation), the necessity for the 4th Guards Army to wage the battle along its left flank with an inverted front, and the very broad and rapid maneuver, led to peculiarities and difficulty in organizing troop command and control.

The enemy's breakthrough along the 4th Guards Army's right flank and the movement of the 46th Army's units to create a new defensive front required the radical alteration of the boundary lines between the 4th Guards and 46th armies.

Before the enemy's offensive, the boundary line ran along the line Sukoro—Vertesacsa—Bicske station—Tat (all locales, except from Sukoro and Vertesacsa for the 46th Army), then beginning on 5 January it ran along the line Nika—Gyermely—Many—height 195 and then further to the southeast along the Ufalu Canal—Baracska (all locales, except for Many and Ufalu for the 46th Army).

The absence of reserves and their creation by removing formations from other sectors of the front and shifting them from sector to sector brought about the frequent resubordination of divisions. During the operation there were 22 instances of resubordinating divisions from corps to corps and one instance of the operational subordination of one corps to another (the 5th Guards Cavalry and 20th Guards Rifle corps).

The rapidly changing situation and the necessity of the broadest maneuver—not only within the army, but between armies in conditions of an insufficient amount of forces—required the concentration of the entire control of the regroupings in the command's hands. For this reason, the creation of all lines and almost all movements of formations and units were carried out according to the combat orders of the higher headquarters.

The rapid communications of headquarters with reserves and mobile forces acquired special significance in troop command and control. Thus aside from radio communications, the headquarters had wire communications with the mechanized, tank and cavalry corps. In some cases there was even direct communications with divisions (12th Cavalry Division). Radio communications played an extremely important role. The frequent shifting of mobile formations did not always allow us to maintain direct wire communications with them. The presence of our formations that were fighting in encirclement enabled us to communicate with them only by radio.

The impossibility of any kind of break in command and control during the most intensive moments of the fighting and the necessity of bringing the headquarters close to the troops in order to exercise direct communications, as well as the necessity inculcating among the troops confidence in the strength and stability of the situation often led to a situation in which the headquarters were so close to the troops in the defense that it was risky (the 4th Guards Army's headquarters was eight kilometers distant, the headquarters of the 20th Guards Rifle Corps was five kilometers distant, the headquarters of the 18th Guards Tank Corps was two kilometers distant, and the command post of the commander of the 31st Guards Rifle Corps was 500-600 meters from the forward edge).

The splitting of the *front's* forces by the enemy's arrival at the Danube River required the special breaking up of the operational apparatus of the *front's* field headquarters in order to move it closer to the troops: upon the beginning of the enemy's offensive the *front's* main command post was shifted from Paksi to Felepszalas, while an operational group was left behind in Paksi and an auxiliary command post was moved to Dunaharaszti.

The lack of clarity, and often the confusing nature of the situation, frequent overestimations of the enemy's strength and the necessity of control over the troops' actions on the ground required the broad employment of staff officers dispatched to the front. A large part of the officers were almost constantly with the troops and mobile communications (planes, for the *front* headquarters) were the chief methods. The most significant shortcoming in troop command and control was the fact that in a number of cases the headquarters of formations and armies sought to operationally subordinate the reserves allotted to them to lower headquarters.

Very rarely did the headquarters actually get involved in organizing cooperation among the combat arms. The cooperation of the ground forces with the air forces for an attack against the enemy's main tank group was coordinated with insufficient precision.

Operational intelligence at the *front* level was poorly organized, which enabled the enemy to launch surprise counterblows and achieve certain tactical successes, while our forces were placed in a difficult situation and the opportunity for fully preparing the headquarters and troops for repelling the counterblows was excluded.

It was not planned to repel the counterblow beforehand throughout the entire depth of the operation and, as a result, the army's and *front's* operational formation at the moment the enemy launched his counterblows was unable to quickly secure their successful repulse (the second echelons and combined-arms and other reserves were not located, as a rule, along the axis of the enemy offensive or were absent).

It is necessary to take into account that the repulse of the enemy's counterblow, which was launched for the purpose of relieving his encircled group of forces, is an inseparable part of the overall plan for a *front* offensive operation.

The *front* commander and the commander of the 4th Guards Army, failed to do the following in organizing the offensive operation:

- they did not foresee the most likely axes of the enemy's counterblows;
- they did not indicate the men and materiel necessary for repelling the counterblow and the form of the allotted forces' actions;
- failed to assign a task to the air army for routing arriving reserves (IV SS Panzer Corps and three enemy infantry divisions);
- did not specify the maneuver of men and materiel from the depth and from quiet sectors, or the procedure for securing boundaries and flanks, and;

- did not determine the bases for the cooperation of the internal and external troops' fronts, particularly that of the mobile forces with the combined-arms armies and the air army in repelling a possible counterblow.

While developing the success on the opposite bank of the Danube River and in encircling the enemy's main Budapest group of forces, the *front* failed to carry out in a timely manner engineer measures to consolidate the operational bridgehead and favorable lines in the depth of the enemy's defense, which made significantly more difficult conditions for the *front's* forces to repel the enemy's powerful counterblows.

The decision to construct *front* defensive lines, for the purpose of consolidating the operational bridgehead along the Danube River, was adopted only on 31 January 1945; that is, following the repulse of the enemy's third counterblow.

The experience of the Budapest operation once again confirms the necessity of the timely consolidation of bridgeheads while forcing rivers.

All of these questions had to be resolved during the course of repelling the counterblows, which led to the commitment of units in detail and the lack of a previously thought-through plan (the assigning of tasks to aviation, the strengthening of the troops along the axis of the main enemy attack at the expense of reserves from quiet sectors), the consolidation of occupied lines and large inhabited locales, the creation of new defensive lines and operational obstacles, the strengthening of measures for supporting the troops (anti-tank and anti-air defense), and the movement of army and *front* reserves, etc.

The German command committed a number of major mistakes during the course of the operations, which once again demonstrated the fallaciousness of German operational art. The chief of these are: the failure of the just-completed offensive northwest of Budapest did not force the German command to review its calculations regarding the success of a surprise attack by large tank forces backed up by sufficient reserves and a sufficient number of infantry. Nor did this failure teach the German command to correctly evaluate our troops' strength, the capability of our command and the high level of our operational art. This once again demonstrated the routine nature and stereotypical character of German operational art.

The offensive was launched by the enemy with the complete absence of operational reserves; thus it was completely based not upon the real correlation of forces, but exclusively on a surprise attack and the rapidity of its development in the depth.

A major mistake was not only the insufficient securing of the wedge's base in the Szekesfehervar area, but also its weakening during the operation (the removal of the 23rd Panzer Division). This mistake significantly eased the success of our counterblow and, given our large forces, threatened the enemy with catastrophe.

Thus in January the forces of Marshal Tolbukhin won a major victory in the defensive fighting with the enemy's superior tank forces, thus foiling the enemy's long-range plans for defeating our forces along the right bank of the Danube and thus guaranteeing the elimination of the enemy's Budapest group of forces and the capture of Budapest.

In the 2 January-10 Febuary fighting the enemy suffered heavy losses:

Table 14 Enemy Losses, 2 January-10 February 1945

	Killed or Destroyed	Captured	Total
Men	53,750	21,170	74,920
Guns	333	68	401
Tanks, Self-Propelled Guns and armored transports	789	87	876
Planes	287	5	292

Aside from this, in the fighting to eliminate the enemy group of forces that had broken out of Budapest, 12,800 enemy soldiers and officers were killed and 18,700 captured.

One may point to the overall conclusion that the Third Ukrainian Front's experience in repelling the counterblows in a *front* operation has not lost its significance for modern conditions.

20

Conclusions on Military Art from the Experience of the Third Ukrainian Front's Operation

Strategy

As a result of the coordinated activities of the Second, Third and Fourth Ukrainian fronts' forces during the period from 29 October 1944 through 16 February 1945, the enemy's strategic group of forces along the southern wing of the Soviet-German front was defeated.

The main political goal was achieved: under the blows of the Soviet army, the bloody regime, which had been established by the Germans in Hungary, collapsed and the Hungarian people, who created a provisional national government in Debrecen on 24 December, were liberated. This government announced Hungary's withdrawal from the war on Germany's side and declared war on her, which led to the complete political isolation of the latter.

Simultaneous with the defeat of the German-Fascist forces in Hungary, Soviet forces inflicted a defeat on the German-Fascist group of forces in the Carpathians, liberated trans-Carpathian Ukraine and, upon entering Czechoslovak territory, rendered assistance to the Czechoslovak people in its struggle for liberation from the German-Fascist aggressors.

The Soviet army liberated a large part of Hungary and Yugoslavia. Having forced the enemy to evacuate his forces from Greece and Albania, the Soviet army thus facilitated the activization of the national-liberation movement among the peoples oppressed by fascist Germany and foiled the plans of the Anglo-American imperialists to use the countries of southeastern Europe as a springboard for an attack on the USSR.

Due to the expulsion of the German-Fascist occupiers from the Balkan countries, Hitlerite Germany's military-economic situation worsened considerably: it was deprived of Hungary's and the other Balkan countries' most important industrial and agricultural areas and, which supported the German-Fascist army to a significant degree with food, raw materials, fuels and lubricants, weapons, and ammunition.

The Soviet army's forces had the opportunity to prepare an attack along the Vienna strategic direction, as well as to develop the offensive along the territory of Czechoslovakia for the purpose of completely liberating it from the German-Fascist occupiers.

An important circumstance was the fact that the enemy was forced to weaken his tank shock groups; of the 24 panzer divisions operating along the Soviet-German front, 11 had been transferred by the end of 1944 to the Budapest direction. The remaining panzer divisions were forced to battle Soviet forces in East Prussia and the Baltic, while only four enemy panzer divisions remained along the central sector of the Soviet-German front.

Besides panzer divisions, the Hitlerite command transferred 30 divisions and brigades from other sectors of the front to delay the Soviet forces' offensive.

Therefore, by the end of 1944 the plan of the Supreme Command of the Soviet army, which was based upon distracting the enemy's forces from the Berlin strategic direction and weakening the latter, had been completely fulfilled, which enabled us in January 1945 to unleash a powerful offensive by a group of *fronts* in the center of the Soviet-German front, which predetermined the complete defeat of the German-Fascist forces and facilitated the final rout of the enemy's Budapest group of forces.

In the Budapest operation the Soviet forces' offensive was primarily carried out by the forces of the Second and Third Ukrainian fronts. The coordination of these *fronts* was achieved thanks to direct control by the *Stavka* of the Supreme High Command.

As early as 18 October, the *Stavka* of the Supreme High Command, foreseeing the necessity of joint efforts by the Second and Third Ukrainian fronts along the Budapest direction, ordered the commander of the Third Ukrainian Front to regroup his main forces to the left wing of the Second Ukrainian Front.

Subsequently, on 12 December the *Stavka* of the VGK assigned the troops of both *fronts* the mission of organizing a simultaneous and coordinated attack for the purpose of encircling the major Hitlerite group of forces in Budapest.

Further on, on 18 January 1945 the *Stavka* of the VGK entrusted the elimination of the enemy's encircled group of forces in Budapest to the Second Ukrainian Front. This enabled the commander of the Third Ukrainian Front to concentrate all of his efforts on defeating the enemy's tank group along the external encirclement front, and the commander of the Second Ukrainian Front on defeating the enemy in Budapest.

During the operation the regrouping of forces from the Second Ukrainian Front to the Third Ukrainian Front played a decisive role, as well as the timely allocation of forces from the reserve of the *Stavka* of the High Command.

In the *Stavka* directives issued during the course of the Budapest operation, decisive significance was allotted to problems of the *front's* cooperation. The *Stavka* uninterruptedly controlled through its representative—Marshal of the Soviet Union Timoshenko—the operations of the *fronts*, determined their tasks, issued instructions on regrouping forces and on shifting the *fronts'* attacks, corrected individual mistakes by the *front* and army commanders, supported the troops with long-range aviation, reinforced with men and materiel in a timely manner, and supplied the *front's* forces with all necessary equipment.

Our troops' offensive developed in conditions of a favorable air situation. The enemy did not have air superiority along one of his attack axes. Air superiority was securely held by our aviation. The concentration of the efforts of three air armies and long-range aviation's formations on carrying out the most important tasks along the decisive axis was one of the main elements securing the successful actions of the Soviet forces.

Operational Art

The planning of the *front* operation, as well as the preparation of the *front's* forces for activities along new operational directions began while still completing the Belgrade operation. At the same time, the *front* began preparing for an offensive (the regrouping and crossing over the Danube and Tisza rivers) upon receiving the *Stavka* of the Supreme High Command's directive of 18 October; that is, 19-20 days before they began crossing the Danube River in the areas of Batina and Apatin.

Thus the *Stavka* of the Supreme High Command was planning an offensive operation by a group of *fronts*, directed at achieving a major strategic goal—the encirclement and destruction of the enemy's Budapest group of forces. The *Stavka* not only defined the goal and plan, but also specifically controlled the preparation and organization of the operation, operational support, the inter*front* relief of forces, regrouping, and the creation of reserves, etc. The *Stavka* demanded that the regrouping be carried out in secret, in order to subsequently achieve surprise. The regrouping of the Third Ukrainian Front's main forces was to be carried out along a new axis, beyond the *front's* sector, in another *front's* sector, which undoubtedly made the preparation for and conduct of the Third Ukrainian Front's operation for forcing the Danube and defeating the enemy's Danubian group of forces more difficult. In these conditions, the *front* had to distribute the railroads and dirt roads, build crossings over the Danube and Tisza rivers, carry out special measures for operational masking, and establish the sequence and relief of forces, etc. The organization and conduct of intelligence along a new axis and in another *front's* sector was made particularly difficult, because the arrival of our forces at the Danube was carried out several days before the start of the operation.

The operation's preparation was conducted in conditions when the enemy's defense was insufficiently developed and occupied by limited forces.

A feature of the operation was that the *front* headquarters set about directly planning the operation as early as the forcing of the Danube River and during the fighting for the creation of an operational bridgehead.

The *front* was to launch a single frontal attack, having a single-echelon operational formation. Such an operational formation was correct in this specific situation and corresponded to the *front's* goals and tasks, as well as the enemy's group of forces and defense, who had concentrated his main efforts on holding the first position.

As a rule, the rifle corps' operational formation was in two echelons.

The skillful conduct of the *front's* regrouping of forces and the rapid creation of powerful groups of forces along the decisive axes facilitated the achievement of operational surprise. For example, the seizure of bridgeheads along the Danube River in November by the Third Ukrainian Front's forces was, according to the testimony of captured German-Fascist generals, a complete surprise and caught the Hitlerite command off guard. Also unexpected was the coordinated attack by the concentrated forces of two *fronts* in the general direction of Esztergom for the purpose of encircling the enemy's Budapest group of forces.

Throughout the entire operation, the types of the troops' actions were distinguished by a variety of forms and methods, upon which the provisioning and training of the troops and headquarters, difficult meteorological conditions and the fall rains, the nature of the terrain, and the difficult ice situation on the Danube, as well as the enemy's resistance had a direct influence. To a significant degree, these conditions determined the pace of the *front's* advance.

The Third Ukrainian Front's battle to create a bridgehead was distinguished by unusual intensity and developed slowly. The forcing of the Danube was begun by the forward units of the 75th Rifle Corps during the night of 6-7 November; while the creation of an operational bridgehead stretched all the way to 30 November (it was actually created in nine days—22-30 November). The absence of mobile formations (except for one brigade), the poor infusion of the rifle troops with direct infantry-support tanks and the insignificant activity of our aviation as the result of inclement weather negatively told on the offensive's pace (5.5 kilometers per day from 22 November).

During 1-8 December the *front's* forces, while developing the offensive for the purpose of defeating the Danube group of German-Fascist forces, advanced up to 80 kilometers in depth with an average daily rate of advance of ten kilometers. While withdrawing, the enemy put up stubborn resistance, while simultaneously preparing the "Margarita" defensive line. The low rate of advance is explained not only by the enemy's resistance, but also because of the absence of mobile groups in the 57th and 4th Guards armies during the first period and the fact that the heavy-caliber artillery failed to completely cross the Danube and air activity was limited by inclement weather.

The *front's* forces along the main axis employed the 10-19 December time period to prepare an operation to break through the so-called "Margarita Line."

On 20 December, having broken through this defensive zone, the *front's* forces advanced 70 kilometers in seven days of offensive fighting, with average daily rates of advance of ten kilometers. Such a pace, in conditions of the fall rains, the enemy's stubborn resistance and the uninterrupted augmentation of his forces, should be seen as normal. The entire depth of the enemy defense was broken through by the *front's* forces over the course of four days (20-23 December) to a depth of 20 kilometers and with an average daily rate of advance of five kilometers. Following the breakthrough of the defense and the commitment of the mobile formations into the breach, the speed of the advance rose to 16 kilometers (50 kilometers were overcome in three days).

During 1 January-13 February combat operations of decisive significance took place simultaneously along the external and internal encirclement fronts, while the most intense and important fighting, according to their scale, took place along the external encirclement front. Typical of the *front's* actions during this period was the conduct of broad-ranging maneuver by men and artillery weapons, particularly anti-tank. The reserves, which were transferred in a timely manner by the *Stavka*, and the massed air strikes by the Second and Third Ukrainian fronts' aviation, played a decisive role.

During the fighting during this period along the external encirclement front, the situation in a number of cases became extremely unfavorable for the *front's* forces. For example, the Germans' breakthrough to the Danube on 19 January and the attack from the captured area to relieve the enemy's encircled group of forces in Budapest. However, the Third Ukrainian Front command found in all cases the most expedient decisions, which corresponded to the developing situation.

The Budapest operation confirmed the correctness of the theoretical tenets on creating internal and external encirclement fronts. The encirclement and destruction of the enemy group of forces formed a single and indivisible process. The splitting up and destruction was conducted simultaneously from the moment the encirclement was completed. A continuous internal encirclement front would be created along with the simultaneous formation of an actively operating external front, while blockading the encircled enemy from the air. The *front's* main forces were directed against the encircled enemy in order to rapidly encircle and destroy the enemy and to correspondingly free up rapidly forces from the internal to the external front for the purpose of developing the operation into the depth.

The troops' most important task was the encirclement and destruction of the enemy's Budapest group of forces. The main task of the troops, which had been detailed for combat operations along the external front, was the repulse of a possible counterblow from the depth of the enemy's reserves, directed at linking up with the encircled group of forces. The external front's forces were supposed to increase as forces were freed up along the internal front, where the operation was supposed to develop at a rapid pace. For example, approximately 1.5 times as many forces were allotted to the internal encirclement front than were in the enemy's encircled group of forces. The troops along the external front had the task of capturing an operational line which would secure the destruction of the enemy's encircled group of forces, as well as the subsequent development of the offensive for the achievement of the operation's goals, while at the same time the commander of the Third Ukrainian Front sought to push back the external encirclement front as far as possible from the internal one.

Operational support for the encircled enemy's defeat was realized in conditions of adopting a static defense, and not by attacking along the external front, as had been the case in the majority of similar operations. This was chiefly brought about due to the shortage of forces for continuing the offensive along the external front in their previous disposition and in the developing situation.

The successful repulse of the counterblows by the enemy's large tank groups was possible thanks to the maneuver of men and materiel and their massing along the axis of the enemy's main attack, as well as the preparation of new defensive lines and their stout maintenance in conjunction with the launching of a retaliatory counterblow.

New defensive lines were built at a distance of 25-50 kilometers from the main one. In the beginning they were occupied by artillery and tanks, and later by combined-arms formations. The anti-tank defense, which was built according to an anti-tank defense system, constituted the heart of the defense of all the lines. All of the regimental and anti-tank artillery, 50 percent of divisional artillery, 30 percent of the howitzers, and 25 percent of the High Command's gun reserve were put forward for firing over open sights against enemy tanks. In those same interests, there was a constant anti-tank reserve, consisting of tanks, self-propelled artillery and anti-tank artillery units and formations in the armies and *fronts*. Mobile obstacle detachments were widely employed in organizing anti-tank defense. 37mm, 45mm and 75mm guns, firing over distances of 400-800 meters, fully justified themselves in fighting massed enemy tank attacks. 57mm, 82mm, 122mm, and 100mm guns, both field type and self-propelled, which fired at an average distance of 1,200 meters, as well as divisional guns, were especially effective against "Panther," "Tiger" and "King Tiger" heavy tanks.

The operational maneuver (within the *front*) of men and materiel was broadly employed. It was carried out rapidly and embraced not only the second echelons and reserves, but troops from quiet sectors. During the fighting to repel the enemy's first counterblow, the following were regrouped to the breakthrough sector from the internal encirclement front and quiet sectors of the external front over the course of 2-3 days: 18th Guards Tank Corps, the 7th and 1st mechanized corps, 78th Tank Regiment, five rifle divisions, two cavalry divisions, and 28 artillery and mortar regiments. The following took part in maneuver to repel the third counterblow: 20 rifle and three cavalry divisions, one tank and two mechanized corps and 53 artillery units. The depth and density of the defense along the axes of the enemy's attacks continually increased as a result of employing maneuver. For example, while repelling the first attack, the operational density of the defense on the second day was: one division per eight kilometers and 20 artillery tubes per kilometer of front, while on the fourth day this was 3.8 kilometers per division and 33 artillery tubes per kilometer of front. During the repulse of the third counterblow, the defense's artillery density on the fifth day reached 19 tubes along the sector of the enemy's attack, while on the eighth day it reached 41 tubes per kilometer of front. On the eighth day the defense along the enemy's main attack sector already disposed of 11 formations, echeloned to a depth of 13 kilometers. All of this testifies to the high degree of activity, flexibility of maneuver and the invincibility of the Third Ukrainian Front's defense.

However, at the same time it is necessary to note that if the *front* command had foreseen the possibility of the enemy launching counterblows along the external front, then their repulse would not have required the expenditure of such an enormous amount of men and materiel, as well as time. In reality, neither the *front* commander nor the commander of the 4th Guards Army foresaw the possibility of the enemy's counterblows and thus failed to define the axes, lines and possible timetables for the enemy to launch counterblows. For this reason, the means for repulsing the counterblows (an offensive along some axes and the defensive along others) were not precisely defined and the maneuver of men and materiel for reinforcing the troops along the external front, for the purpose of not only repulsing, but destroying the enemy launching the counterblow. All of these questions, as well as the planning of air strikes and maneuvering anti-tank weapons, were resolved directly during the course of repelling the counterblows.

Nor were the problems of command and control foreseen during the preparation period and during the repulse of the enemy's counterblows.

In turn, the plan by the *front's* intelligence section did not call for continuous and deep reconnaissance for unearthing in a timely manner the enemy's reserves, which were being directed at relieving Budapest and the unceasing observation of these reserves (along the *front's* sector and also along the flanks).

Due to the surprise of the first and third counterblows, the *front's* reserves were not located along the axes of the enemy's forthcoming offensive. This led to a situation in which the density of the anti-tank artillery along the axis of the enemy's main attack was no more than 3-7 guns and it was only while repelling the attack that it reached 25-30 guns and higher per kilometer of front.

During the defensive battle, the forces of the Third Ukrainian Front organized and launched a counterblow against the attacking enemy, and by means of decisively concentrating men and materiel along those axes chosen for launching the attack a two to one advantage in infantry and artillery in our favor (with our air superiority) was created.

The decisive concentration of forces and the skillful selection of the axes of the attacks enabled us to rapidly defeat the attacking enemy and to restore the situation.

Tactics

The *front's* combat activities were conducted with the close cooperation of all the combat arms. The commanders and their staffs learned how to precisely resolve the chief problems of cooperation by the combat arms on site. However, during the fighting's crisis periods cooperation was often disrupted, which resulted in failure. A great deal of attention was devoted to the organization of cooperation at the level of the battalion, artillery battalion and tank company. Cooperation of the combat arms during the breakthrough was directed at supporting the infantry and tanks during their vigorous and uninterrupted attack of the first position and their subsequent non-stop advance throughout the entire depth of the main defensive zone. During this period, in order to maintain uninterrupted cooperation, forward observers, equipped with radios, moved up to the tanks' and infantry's combat formations and, for the same reason, in order to maintain communications with the air units supporting the combined-arms formation, aviation representatives with radios were assigned to the combined-arms commander's observation or command post. Cooperation was not yet planned throughout the entire tactical depth, but only for the breakthrough of the main defensive zone and in the greatest detail for the breakthrough of the first position of the main defensive zone.

The concentration of the main mass of men and materiel in the attacking troops' first echelons fully corresponded to the nature of the enemy's defense, which was distinguished by the great saturation of only the main defensive zone with men and materiel, the poor organization of the defense in the depth and the presence of insignificant reserves.

The deeply echeloned organization of the combat formation was called for in the breakthrough. For example, a rifle corps organized its combat formation, as a rule, in two echelons, having two divisions in the first echelon and one in the second; a rifle division organized its combat formation in one or two echelons. The depth of the combat formation in the division's single-echelon organization was achieved by organizing the regiments' combat formations in two echelons. Such an organization of the combat formation helped to maintain a more stable cooperation with supporting and attached reinforcement means, while fighting in the defensive depth and made the timely and rapid commitment of the second echelons' subunits into the fighting easier and made command and control more secure. From one to (more rarely) two rifle battalions were allotted to the division's combined-arms reserve (given a single-echelon organization).

The width of the breakthrough sectors of the enemy's defense along the axis of the main attack was defined at 3-5 kilometers for a rifle corps and 1-2 kilometers for a rifle division.

The pace of the rifle forces' attack was expressed as from four to 8-10 kilometers per day, and sometimes more.

Immediate objectives were assigned to the rifle corps to a depth of 4-6 kilometers; that is, to the depth of the enemy's main defensive zone, and 2-3 kilometers for the rifle divisions; that is, to the depth of the first (main) position. It should be noted that the assignment of task in depth to the rifle corps was insufficient, but in these conditions the breakthrough of the main zone was not always successfully accomplished by the first-echelon troops. Thus the second echelons and mobile troops were more often committed to complete the breakthrough. Given a shallower echeloning of the enemy's defense and given its insufficient saturation with firepower, immediate tasks were assigned to a greater depth; the seizure of the first position (1.5-2 kilometers) for a rifle regiment, the seizure of the second position (3-4 kilometers) for a rifle division and the capture of the main zone (up to six kilometers) for a rifle corps.

Rifle divisions operating along the axis of the main attack were given reinforcements which supported their carrying out their assignments. On the average, a rifle division was assigned up to two artillery regiments, a self-propelled artillery regiment and a mortar regiment. A rifle corps was reinforced, on the average, with a mortar brigade, a howitzer brigade, an anti-tank artillery brigade, 1-2 mortar regiments, 1-2 howitzer regiments, 1-2 self-propelled artillery regiments, and 2-3 assault engineer-sapper battalions. This kind of reinforcement enabled us to create a density of guns and mortars of 80-150 tubes per kilometer of front.

The troops got a lot of experience in waging combat operations in a large town. The attack in a town was not conducted along a continuous front, but for the capture of the enemy's individual centers of defense and strong points. The immediate task was as follows: a rifle corps was to capture several of the town's areas; a rifle division was to capture a single area, and; a rifle regiment was to capture several strong points. The rifle corps' and rifle division's subsequent task foresaw the capture of new sites in the defensive depth.

On the average, the overall depth of the day's task was as follows:

- 2-3 kilometers for a rifle corps;
- 1.5-2 kilometers for a rifle division.

For example, the 37th Rifle Corps' divisions received a task for the day to a depth of 1.3-2 kilometers.

The width of the attack zone gradually shrank as the troops approached the town center and was 3-4 or six kilometers for a rifle corps. On the average, one may consider this to be 3-4 kilometers for a rifle corps, 1-2 kilometers for a division, and 500-700 meters (1-2 streets) for a rifle regiment.

Boundary lines ran along streets.

The combat formation of a rifle corps and a rifle division was organized into two echelons. A rifle division's combat formations consisted of the combat formations of rifle regiments, the divisional artillery group and a reserve, which also included a sapper company. The rifle regiments had, as a rule, a single-echelon organization for their combat formations. The regimental commander had in his reserve a company of automatic riflemen and a reconnaissance and sapper platoons. A rifle company's combat formation consisted of an artillery group for firing over open sights and a reserve, which up to a platoon of automatic riflemen was assigned to. Rifle companies were deployed in a line. The assault group was the basis of the company's combat formation.

The assault group's composition was determined by the nature of the assigned task and the availability of men and materiel.

The typical strength was 15-20 riflemen and automatic riflemen, up to a section of sappers, 2-4 men with flamethrowers, 1-2 heavy machine guns, anti-tank rifles and individual guns. An assault group was supported by 1-2 tanks and self-propelled guns and a heavy-caliber machine gun. Each solider in the assault group had several hand grenades, anti-tank grenades and bottles of flammable liquid. The sappers were supplied with explosive charges and accessories for blowing up and removing mines. Assault groups were supported by a large amount of ammunition, which enabled them to fight while encircled.

The assault group was divided into two subgroups: a subgroup for seizure, consisting of riflemen, automatic riflemen, sappers, and flame thrower operators; a support subgroup, which consisted of machine gun operators, artillery, tanks, and self-propelled guns. The consolidation of captured targets was often accomplished by the forces of the regiments' and divisions' rear elements.

3-4 groups were created in a rifle battalion. The assault group's attack was conducted in cooperation with neighboring groups. Reconnaissance, training and sometimes an air strike preceded the attack. As experience showed, nighttime activities, without an artillery preparation, were more successful.

Insofar as our forces, as a rule, did not lose contact with the enemy, then the offensive usually began in contact with him. This circumstance forced us to begin an offensive would begin with an attack against the enemy's defensive zone. The launching of the infantry and tank attack was conducted simultaneously along the corps' (division's) entire breakthrough sector from a jumping-off position outfitted by engineers (from the first trench or individual foxholes 150-200 meters from the enemy trench). The *front's* forces acquired a great amount of experience in the rapid outfitting of the jumping-off position for the offensive.

The troops also acquired experience in organizing a defense and repelling the enemy's counter-blows (see the conclusions on defending and repelling counterblows in the text). A feature of this was the fact that all the efforts of the defending troops were directed at preserving their forces and winning time necessary for the maneuver of formations and units from quiet sectors of the front to the axes of the enemy's attacks. This is most evident in the repulse of the first and third enemy counterblows, when the defending forces directed all their efforts at creating conditions for exhausting the attacking enemy.

The chief backbone of the defense was the artillery.

The experience of the artillery's activities showed the necessity of the preliminary training of the artillery located at closed firing points and for repelling enemy tanks; the selection of closed positions so that they can fight off the enemy tanks by firing over open sights along the likely axes of their movement into the depth of our defense and the assignment of each gun at a close firing point of a sector for firing over open sights, regardless of its caliber.

The extremely rapid maneuver of artillery enabled the *front's* forces in the January fighting to create a powerful anti-tank defense along just those axes where the enemy happened to be attacking.

The value of rapid artillery maneuver was particularly great due to the fact that the enemy's tank forces in these battles also displayed a high degree of maneuverability and rapidly shifted their attack to another sector in the event of its failure on one sector.

Mobile mine obstacle detachments completely justified themselves. During the January-February fighting 79 enemy tanks and 12 armored transports were blown up on minefields laid down by these detachments.

Troop command and control was firm in all events. Throughout the entire operation there was not a single case of the *front* headquarters losing communications with the armies' headquarters or of the latter with the corps. Wire and radio communications means enabled the army commanders to carry on direct talks with division commanders and, in a number of cases, with regimental commanders.

As a rule, command posts were located along the axis of the main attack and at a distance ensuring secure and uninterrupted command and control of the troops.

During the fighting's crisis periods representatives from the command and the army commanders and members of the military councils personally traveled directly to the troops and saw to the fulfillment of the *front* and army commanders' instructions in person. They periodically traveled to divisions and regiments and checked on the execution of orders, helped the staffs in organizing the engagement and systematically reported to the army commander and chief of staff the latest data on the situation.

The chief slogans that formed the heart of all of the party-political work among the troops were the instructions of the Communist Party Central Committee that the forces of the Soviet army, in carrying out their historic liberation mission, must rapidly defeat the German-Fascist forces on the territory of fascist Germany's last satellite—Hungary, remove the latter from the war on the side of fascist Germany and render assistance to the peoples of the Balkan states in their struggle against the German-Fascist enslavers.

Senior instructor in the department of the K.Ye. Voroshilov Higher Military Academy, Major General S. Tarasov.

10 September 1955. Moscow.

Index

INDEX OF PEOPLE

INDEX OF PLACES

INDEX OF AXIS MILITARY FORMATIONS & UNITS

INDEX OF SOVIET AND ALLIED MILITARY FORMATIONS & UNITS

INDEX OF MISCELLANEOUS & GENERAL TERMS